Sylvia Pankhurst's famous wo... biography. It chronicles how the ... and tells of her personal experiences of ... thirst and sleep strikes, and forcible feeding. It reveals how the advocates of women's suffrage became polarized into mutually antagonistic factions, holding very different attitudes both to the vote and the wider campaigns for women's rights at the beginning of the century.

Sylvia Pankhurst (1882–1960) was a central figure in these events. Working first with other members of her family in the Women's Social

and continued ... oks are to be returned on or before

Eas... the last date below.

THE SUFFRAGETTE MOVEMENT

AN INTIMATE ACCOUNT OF
PERSONS AND IDEALS

BY

E. SYLVIA PANKHURST

NEW INTRODUCTION BY
DR RICHARD PANKHURST

Published by VIRAGO PRESS Limited 1977
20-23 Mandela Street, London NW1 0HQ

Reprinted 1978, 1984, 1988
First published by the Longman Group Limited 1931
All rights reserved

Introduction copyright © Dr Richard Pankhurst

British Library Cataloguing in Publication Data

Pankhurst, Estelle Sylvia
  The suffragette movement.
  1. Women—Suffrage—Great Britain—History
  I. Title
  324′3′0941   JN379

  ISBN 0-86068-026-6

Printed in Great Britain by Cox and Wyman Ltd., Reading, Berks.

This book has been published
with financial assistance from
the Arts Council of Great Britain

D. Shaw 7709 /4.99.11.91

PREFACE

I GRATEFULLY render thanks to all who have assisted me in preparing this book, and especially to Mr. R. G. Longman for his sympathetic understanding of the author's aims and difficulties in a work at once so intimate and so composite.

I have essayed to describe events and experiences as one felt them; to estimate character and intention in the mellowing light of intervening years. My desire has been to introduce the actors in the drama as living beings; to show the striving, suffering, hugely hopeful human entity behind the pageantry, the rhetoric and the turbulence. In this effort I have often been thrown back upon my own experience. I have given it frankly, knowing that I could thus describe with greater poignancy and vigour the general experience of those who cherished and toiled for the same cause and encountered the same ordeals.

No history, whether of movements or of persons, can be truly expressed apart from the social and economic conditions and thought currents of its time. I have endeavoured to convey these not through the medium of statistics or argument, but by incidents in the moving course of life.

The book is largely made up of memories. In the earlier chapters, the key and the basis of those which follow, I have paid tribute to pioneers whose labours made later achievements possible. Their story is dear to me for its tender recollections and for the spirit of earnest public service which animated their work.

The many deeds of devotion and heroism chronicled in the later pages are greatly outnumbered by those I have been compelled, most reluctantly, to omit.

E. SYLVIA PANKHURST.

INTRODUCTION

My mother Sylvia Pankhurst, who dedicated this book to me close on half a century ago, wrote as an active participant in the events she describes. Her work is thus both history and autobiography. At one level it is a chronicle of " how the women of Britain won the vote "; at another it tells the story of her own imprisonment, hunger, thirst and sleep strikes—and the manner in which she, and so many other women militants, were forcibly fed by the Liberal Government of the day.

More fundamentally the book shows how the advocates of women's suffrage became increasingly polarized into two mutually antagonistic factions, the Women's Social and Political Union led by her mother Emmeline and her sister Christabel, which was essentially conservative, and Sylvia's East London Federation of the Suffragettes which stood on the far left of the political spectrum. For her part she followed the tradition, as she saw it, of her father Dr. Richard Marsden Pankhurst, a Manchester lawyer and disciple of John Stuart Mill, who had been an early member of the Independent Labour Party, and who, as she later wrote, was " earnestly immersed in all the advanced movements of his time ". Characteristic of her attitude to the vote are the final words of this book where, after relating how the government at last granted women's suffrage, she exclaims: " Great is the work which remains to be accomplished! "

The difference of approach within the suffragette ranks became even more marked during World War I when Emmeline and Christabel gave their full patriotic support to the war against the Kaiser, and in defence of " gallant little Belgium ", whereas Sylvia, then a pacifist and opponent of the war, devoted her energies to social work in the East End—and changed the name of the weekly newspaper she edited, significantly enough, from the *Woman's Dreadnought* to the *Workers' Dreadnought*.

During the first years of the war she established the Mothers' Arms, a maternity clinic and Montessori school, and four other clinics, two cost-price restaurants, and a co-operative toy factory designed to provide work for persons unemployed on account of the conflict. She also founded the League of Rights for Soldiers' and Sailors' Wives and Relatives, to work for better pensions and allowances, and became Honorary Secretary of the National

Labour Council for Adult Suffrage. In her subsequent record of those days, *The Home Front*, she tells of the suffering the war brought to the East End, and enquires:

> Must these things be? Can we not free humanity from the enslaving burden of war preparedness which leads to war? Must the see world yet another blood bath, yet more slaughter and sacrifice for vain, ignoble objects? Shall we not take the way of human solidarity and mutual aid at long last? I believe that humanity is advancing towards the establishment of the United States of the World, consolidated in a free Socialism,wherein all shall co-operate gladly, giving to the common stock according to their abilities and in receiving from its abundance according to their needs.
>
> To me it is as certain as the coming of day after night that humanity will rise above the present competitive struggle for existence, assuring the necessities of life to every one of its members as a matter of course, creating a world policy to cater for the needs of a world people. In that day the sad East End shall be joyous and beautiful as the Elysium of the Greeks and wars shall be no more.

The differences between the Pankhurst family, already vividly outlined in *The Suffragette*, were further sharpened by the 1917 revolution in Russia when Emmeline addressed meetings in support of intervention against the Bolsheviks, while Sylvia urged the workers of Britain to resist it, travelled (illegally) to Moscow to meet Lenin, as she related in *Soviet Russia As I Saw It*, and attended the second congress of the Third International. Though one of the first British socialists to welcome the Russian revolution —she founded a People's Russian Information Bureau—she refused to join the newly established Communist Party and was one of the main targets of Lenin's polemic *Left-Wing Communism: an Infantile Disorder*. In part because of the admiration she felt for Bukharin and other Bolsheviks she had met in Moscow she was later to deplore Stalin's purges with their supposed confessions of the prosecuted.

After the achievement of the vote, and the conclusion of her work in the East End, Sylvia's creativity found expression increasingly in the written word. She had originally trained as an artist—a number of her paintings, including a portrait of her friend Keir Hardie, the leader of the Independent Labour Party, are still extant—but had abandoned art for the suffragette movement, sadly, but with a feeling of duty. She now proved a prolific writer. One of my most lasting childhood memories—of a decade or so

INTRODUCTION

later—was on waking to go to my mother's room in the morning to find her still at her desk where she had been writing since dinner the previous night. This was by no means an infrequent occurrence.

She had already published a history of the women's movement, *The Suffragette*, in 1911, and a collection of poems produced in prison, *Writ on Cold Slate* in 1922. She now wrote on a wide range of subjects. Her first major work in this period was an analysis of Indian society, *India and the Earthly Paradise*, which was published in Bombay in 1926, and was followed in 1927 by *Delphos*, an enquiry into " the future of international language ". In 1930 she produced a verse translation of some of the poems of the great Romanian writer Mihail Eminescu, and *Save the Mothers*, " a Plea for measures to Prevent the Annual Loss of about 3,000 Childbearing Mothers and 20,000 Infant Lives in England and Wales and a Similar Grievous Wastage in other Countries ". A Japanese translation soon appeared. She was also to write a biography of her mother, *The Life of Emmeline Pankhurst*, published in 1936, and began work on an account of her experiences in the international socialist movement, entitled *In the Red Twilight*, but left it unfinished, as she found herself increasingly involved in more immediate matters. After her death I deposited the text in the Institute for Social History in Amsterdam.

Her most important literary achievement was, however, *The Suffragette Movement*, which appeared in 1931, a decade or so after the achievement of the vote, while her memory of the struggle for it was still alive. Though she was always happy to answer questions on the movement I recall her saying that she felt she had in fact put into this book everything she had to say on the subject. She was fully aware that though successive generations of historians would write and rewrite the story of the movement her book would, in the nature of things, always remain one of their major sources.

My mother, who before the suffragette movement had won a scholarship to study art in Italy, was from the outset a bitter opponent of Italian fascism which she saw both as the negation of everything for which she had ever worked, and a fundamental threat to world peace. One of the founders of the Society of Friends of Italian Freedom and of the Women's International Matteotti Committee—so named after the Italian socialist who was assassinated on Mussolini's orders—she was deeply moved by the Wal Wal incident of 1934 which the fascist dictator was soon to use as a pretext for his unprovoked invasion of Ethiopia, or Abyssinia as it was then better known in England. She wrote many letters to the press, urging her compatriots to back the League of

INTRODUCTION

Nations in defence of the far-off African country, addressed public meetings on the subject, helped to establish the Abyssinia Association, and in 1936 founded a weekly journal *New Times and Ethiopia News* which she was to publish in London for twenty years to keep interest in the Ethiopian cause alive. Throughout those years she published news of fascist oppression in Africa, and of the resistance of the Ethiopian patriots, and urged the British Government in and out of season to deal justly with the Ethiopians in their time of adversity.

Though an opponent of World War I she was from first to last fully convinced of the need to fight fascism by force of arms. She objected to the so-called Appeasement policies of the 1930s, was untiring in helping refugees from fascist Italy and its colonies, Nazi Germany, Falangist Spain—and on occasion totalitarian Russia—and gave full support to World War II. She was personally attacked by Mussolini in his writings, and was on the Nazi list of persons for arrest in the event of a German occupation of Britain.

My mother's involvement in Ethiopia, which began as an expression of her repugnance towards fascism, was to continue for the last quarter of her life when she became increasingly preoccupied with the African continent in general, and was known to Jomo Kenyatta, George Padmore and many other African nationalists and Pan-Africanists of the time. She was active during World War II in urging a reluctant British government to accord Ethiopia the status of an ally, and later to restore the country's full independence. She likewise espoused the cause of the people of the former Italian colonies to achieve what she considered their legitimate rights. She raised funds in Britain and elsewhere for a modern hospital in Addis Ababa to be named after Emperor Haile Selassie's daughter Princess Tsahai who had served as a nurse in England during the war, but who had died shortly after her return home. The former suffragette, by now a keen student of Ethiopian history, also wrote an extensive study, *Ethiopia, A Cultural History* in 1955, before going to live in the country in the following year. While in Addis Ababa she ran a monthly journal *Ethiopia Observer*, and was instrumental in founding a Social Service Society. She died in the Ethiopian capital in 1960 at the age of seventy-eight. Though a life-long atheist, she was buried beside the Ethiopian patriots of the struggle against the Italians at the Holy Trinity Cathedral where, Sylvia not being one of the names known to the Ethiopian church, she was given the name of Walata Krestos, or daughter of Christ. Emperor Haile Selassie was among the mourners.

My mother, for all her varied interests, was in no way a

INTRODUCTION

dilettante. She was, as her role in the suffragette movement suggests—and as I was myself to witness in the last decades of her life—essentially her father's child, " Life is nothing," he had told her " without enthusiasms." Everything she undertook she entered into with commitment, one could almost say without counting the cost. It was in that sense that the rest of her life was but a continuation of that which she depicts in the most harrowing passages in *The Suffragette Movement*, for it was in that great cause that she gained her political apprenticeship, and learnt the techniques of propaganda, public speaking, pamphleteering and lobbying which she was to employ for other causes. To each of these she gave of her utmost, for each, whether that of the un-enfranchised women of England, the poverty-stricken families of the East End, or the oppressed people of Ethiopia, seemed to her at the time of equal importance, and she never forgot another of her father's precepts to her, " If you do not work for others, you will not have been worth the upbringing."

RICHARD PANKHURST

CONTENTS

PART I

BOOK I

BOOK II

BOOK III

BOOK IV

CONTENTS

BOOK V

PART II

BOOK VI

BOOK VII

CONTENTS

BOOK VIII

BOOK IX

TO MY SON

RICHARD KEIR PETHICK PANKHURST

THIS RECORD OF STRUGGLE IS DEDICATED

IN THE CHERISHED HOPE THAT

HE MAY GIVE HIS SERVICE

TO THE COLLECTIVE WORK

OF HUMANITY

PART I

BOOK I

CHAPTER I

A S I leave the darkened bungalow where the tranquil child has dropped asleep, and gaze through the oak trees upon the setting sun and the flowers his father has planted mellowing in the soft glory of the departing light; when I muse alone under the old trees of Epping Forest, or watch my young hopeful playing in the short grass, finding the new-old treasures that we as children loved; as I pass through the sad, seer streets, the dreary wastes of crowded little houses, same in their ugliness, and among the pale and shabby throngs of the East End, and watch the drawn-faced mothers bargaining at the stalls; as I view the great shops and the flashing equipages of Piccadilly, or tread the stately, ordered precincts of Parliament Square, memories, vivid and turgid, crowd upon me, mingling with the events of the passing moment, imparting their influences to the experiences of to-day.

Earliest of my long memories is the faint vision of the house where I was born, 1 Drayton Terrace, Old Trafford, Manchester, called in our nursery parlance simply " Old Trafford."   I see of it only a soft, grey dimness; figures of people unrecognizable and flickering; the dazzling light of windows, filtering through the prevailing haze, and the deeper shade of some half-open door. This, overhung with a sense of vain and restless search to remember further, is all that I can discern.

That first home, in recollection long almost obliterated, yet cherished throughout our childhood as the mysterious shrine of our beginnings, was a centre of earnest and passionate striving. Our father, vilified and boycotted, yet beloved by a multitude of people in many walks of life, was a standard-bearer of every forlorn hope, every unpopular yet worthy cause then conceived for the uplifting of oppressed and suffering humanity.   Our mother, twenty years his junior, charged with the abounding ardour of impressionable youth, was the most zealous of his disciples, following his view of all public questions and having no dearer wish than to emulate him in the extremity of his ideas.

Without, he breasted the storm and stress of political turmoil;

at home he poured forth for us a wealth of enthusiastic affection, in the precious hours torn for us from the fabric of his vast activity, revealing to us in a fascinating and never-ending variety the brilliant facets of his thought and knowledge. His struggle was the background of our lives, and his influence, enduring long after his death, was their strongest determining factor. Past forty years before any of us were born, he had led already more than twenty years of strenuous public service. Our advent had entailed a certain lessening of his public activities, which he felt had laid upon us, his children, the obligation to be workers for social betterment—to be, as he often told us, " worth the upbringing." " If you do not work for other people, you will not have been worth the upbringing." Almost daily he exhorted us !

His sense of family was strong and tender. " My children are the four pillars of my house ! " he would say with joyous pride. Of his father, whom we children had never known, he spoke constantly, with a fervent affection and the thrill of a poignant loss ever new. Often as we clustered about the piano to hear her, he would ask our mother to sing his father's favourite song :

> " Jog on, jog on the footpath way,
>   And merrily hent the stile-a.
> A merry heart goes all the day,
>   Your sad tires in a mile-a."

Then he would call for his own favourite: " The Bailiff's Daughter of Islington," seeing in its gallant heroine a semblance of the young wife who had eagerly seized up many a gage of battle on his account. When she was away from home for a few hours, and the time had arrived for her return, he would rise from his work and pace to and fro, whistling always a single valse tune which had tender associations with his courtship, and from which, as his impatience grew, the melody would fade away.

On his father's side he was of old Kentish stock, tracing back to remote forebears of Lye and Penshurst before the coming of the Normans. His grandfather, for some reason outside my knowledge, altered the spelling of the name from Penkhurst to Pankhurst. Entering it thus in the family Bible where several generations of Penkhursts were recorded, he put a stroke under the *a* to emphasize the change. He it was who sold his land and moved to London, where he lost the proceeds of his inheritance by taking a share in one of the unlimited liability companies of the time. The directors of the company absconded, leaving him and others to meet the loss to the uttermost farthing of their possessions. Thus impoverished, he obtained the headmaster-ship of the Delves's School at Walgherton in Cheshire, where he remained for more than forty years, and so managed to earn a living for his family of thirteen children. He died in 1857 aged seventy-one—so long ago! I have the old memorial card in my hand, embossed in fine relief as though it were wrought but the other day.

His son Henry Francis, my grandfather, broke with the Conservative and Church upholding opinions of his family, and became a Liberal and a Baptist Dissenter. Settling in Manchester as an auctioneer, he married Margaret, daughter of Richard Marsden of Wigan, who bore him four children, John, Harriette, Richard and Elizabeth. Tall, blond, strikingly handsome and vivacious, the sight of him on his great black horse was an awe and a wonder to my father, Richard Marsden, his younger son, by whom he was ever greatly adored.

Ardent and eager in his affections, Henry Pankhurst was yet, on occasion, the stern, unbending parent of his day and generation. His elder son, John, as a mere lad, left the parental roof on account of some youthful peccadilloes and a marriage which aroused a father's displeasure, and sailed with his young bride for America never to return. There he encountered most terrible hardships. When I saw him, a tall, gaunt old man in Chicago, more than half a century later, John Pankhurst still spoke resentfully of those bitter days and of his little baby lying dead of privation on a bed of straw.

When Elizabeth, called Bess, went to her wedding, she walked out alone from her home, in face of her father's anger. Her bridegroom, young and impecunious, and noted for the beautiful white neck he displayed when appearing in women's parts at the Manchester Athenæum Dramatic Society, was regarded as an impossible match. Under the tender influence of her brother Richard, who had been a child, too young to interfere when his brother John left home, the breach was healed; and by Richard's aid and that of their father's sister, Mary, the impulsive Bess was saved from the pecuniary ills of an improvident marriage. Her husband was "stage struck," it is true. When Mary Pankhurst set him up in a hatter's shop he failed ignominiously; but eventually he became the manager of a theatre in Aberdeen. Thus reaching an assured position in a work he liked, he proved himself a patient and worthy paterfamilias, deferring in most things to his determined spouse.

The tragic fate of Harriette saddened the closing years of her father's life and cast upon her brother a deep sorrow, of which we, as little children, were aware, though she died in my first year, and only the silver mug she gave me remained to stir some vague elusive consciousness of a presence which had been. She had married a ne'er-do-well musician. Nominally he was editor of a musical magazine; actually it was she who edited the paper, and maintained their home, though afflicted by a slow cancer, caused, it was believed, by one of his blows.

It was on his younger son, Richard, that Henry Pankhurst's hopes mainly centred. Between that beloved son and his parents was never a jar. He lived with them until their death, when he had passed his fortieth year; and I have often heard him say that he never left their house for an hour without telling them where he was going and at what time he would return. Though his political views shot far ahead of his father's earlier type of Radicalism, the latter would only shake his head and warn him kindly: " You are making the steep road harder."

As a child Richard Pankhurst would creep under the table and read for long, delightful hours, hidden from all distractions by the drooping cloth. He early became a pupil of the Manchester Grammar School, the old school of Thomas de Quincey and Harrison Ainsworth, founded in 1519 by the enlightened Hugh Oldham, Bishop of Exeter: " to teach freely every child and scholar coming to the school," with the proviso, strange from a cleric, that no member of the religious orders should ever serve as headmaster. Reared in an atmosphere of sturdy public spirit, the lad grew up proud of the democratic traditions of his city. Manchester had then no university of its own; but, by the bequest of John Owens, a Manchester merchant, Owens College had been founded in 1851, to give an education equal to that of the universities, without religious tests, either for teachers or students. It was well for our young scholar that there existed such an institution to receive him; for, as a Dissenter, he was debarred from the older universities. Studying at Owens, he took his degrees at London University, instituted for just such Nonconformist youths as he, under the beneficent influence of Lord Brougham, the historian Grote, the elder Mill and other enlightened people. He graduated B.A. in the year 1858, LL.B. with honours in Principles of Legislation in 1859, and LL.D., with the gold medal of the University, in 1863. He became an Associate of Owens in 1859, and was later appointed a Governor of the college. After practising as a solicitor, he was called to the Bar at Lincoln's Inn in 1867, and joined the Northern Circuit and the Bar of the County Palatine of Lancaster Chancery Court.

Thus brilliantly equipped with academic distinction, he was to become, for forty years, the most outstanding public personality in his native city. His abilities never passed unperceived. Office was always refused him; honour never. At the great civic functions pertaining to art, education, science, his oratory and influence were always requisitioned. In the Press and generally he was commonly referred to as "the Doctor," and often, affectionately, as "our learned Doctor." His contemporaries caricatured, lampooned and abused him; they decried and discounted his policies, yet withal they loved him. His townsfolk were often most proud of him when they differed from him with loudest voice; and thousands of men and women regarded him as, before all others, the pattern of civic virtue.

In appearance he charmed and challenged. Younger in looks than his youthful years, graceful and vivacious in bearing, wearing his red beard pointed like a Frenchman, instead of the then meticulously observed legal clean shave, and occasionally other small departures from the then conventional dress of his profession. His voice, in platform speaking, higher pitched than that of most men, though it came appreciably down the scale as his years advanced, was often the subject of comment. I have seen it described as "weird and wonderful." I have heard admiring women tell him he would have made a glorious tenor singer, but, so far as I know, he never sang a note.

The community spirit was very strong in him; he took great joy in social and public life, regarding participation in civic functions and institutions as at once a duty and privilege of high worth. Lunch at the Club was, to him, no mere partaking of a meal in a crowded room, but a sacrament of fellowship and good will. A speech of his at some function of the old Manchester Brasenose Club is by chance preserved:

" Coming into this club we enter a new world, not dominated by the judgements of the vulgar world outside. . . . Here we ask one question : not what is a man worth, but what is the worth of the man? By slow degrees as the Club enters into our minds in association of feeling, one member after another, his tone of voice, his gesture, his phrase, his bearing, his character store up; and whether he be living, or whether he be dead, when we go about we see him and we hear him, as it were, just as we see dear Edwin Waugh[1] and hear him now."

When the set speeches were over, " the Doctor " was always a centre of animated argument, easily coping with a score of opponents, flinging about him bright sparkles of wit and eloquence; and Edwin Waugh, the poet of the Lancashire dialect, beloved of all the company for his power of humorous entertainment, would gaze with a warm affection on the younger man, and taking a pinch of snuff would chuckle in broad, soft Lancashire : " The doctor's gradely a-gate this evening : he is, by gum! "

[1] Edwin Waugh, b. 1817, d. 1890.

At the Arts Club Dr. Pankhurst might be heard addressing the company on Shakespeare and the Greek drama, or other congenial theme:

" In and through the individual, when he is in the hands of the poet, universal man speaks and thrills. . . . This is the real seat and fact of poetic truth—that in the individual there is translucent the universal. . . . The difference between Sophocles and Shakespeare is that the individual in each character in Shakespeare is richer, deeper, more abundant with the fullness of meaning, which the centuries had brought on from the calm Greek days. . . .

" Shakespeare had music in himself. His high heart, through all his works, beat ever in unison with that great music, the true sphere music, audible to the purgèd ear—the music which goes forth ceaselessly from the mighty harmonies of the universe, of nature, and of man."

Recorded, for the most part, only in the columns of the daily press, through the dulling medium of reporters' abbreviations, and the space-saving sub-editor's blue pencil, with few brief notes in hand, he poured forth his ardent thoughts in impromptu periods, glowing with an enthusiasm which cast its enchanting spell upon all around him. At such moments he appeared almost a meteoric figure among the " flat, unraised " influences of " cottonopolis." It was written of him that he had ceased to attend an old club when it deserted plain living and high thinking and grew opulent and conventional; I know that he left it when it black-balled an intending member because he was the son of a small butcher.

His reputation for solid legal knowledge was unchallenged. The journal of the Manchester Literary and Philosophic Association, of which he was a prominent member, wrote of him:

" As a jurist Dr. Pankhurst took a high place, and had not politics occupied his time to such a considerable extent, he would undoubtedly have achieved the highest distinction in the theoretical branches of legal science. As it was, he had a large share in the scheme for the reform of the Patent Laws in 1866, and published various addresses and essays of importance on questions of scientific jurisprudence and legal reform. . . . Dr. Pankhurst began his professional career during one of the transition periods of the English law when it is suddenly realized that the historical methods and ideas so long in vogue have ceased to be in agreement with the times. At such a time the danger is that a policy of compromise between the new and the old will end in confusion and complications. Dr. Pankhurst, who was ever among the extreme reformers, was sure to attract attention at such a time, and by the boldness of his ideas and the clearness of his views had a very great influence on current thought."

RICHARD MARSDEN PANKHURST

From its formation he was an active member of the Cou[
of the National Association for the Promotion of Social Scie[
which nourished in its day so many reform movements, a..d
was a factor of great worth in the emancipation of women.
In 1866 he was associated with Sir F. Bramwell, F.R.S.,
W. Newmarch, F.R.S., and T. Webster, Q.C., F.R.S., in preparing for the Association a report on the patent laws with a
view to agitation for their amendment. In the 'sixties and the
'seventies he was pleading for the education of the masses, and
the right of married women to their own property and earnings.
He was a member of the Royal Statistical Society and of the
Society for the Reform and Codification of the Law of Nations,
before which he laid a scheme of International Arbitration.
So early as 1862 he was a member of the Manchester Chamber
of Commerce, and in 1869, as a young man of thirty, he
received the thanks of that body for a digest of the then
Government's Bankruptcy Bill and for formulating proposals
for the amendment of the bankruptcy laws. He took a leading
part in securing better arrangements for litigation in Manchester,
especially in respect of commercial cases, wherein there was then
much inconvenience, delay and expense. He was the author of
many important legal papers, including *International Law, The
Law and the Nation, Local Courts and Tribunals, The Systematic
Study of the Law, The Study of Jurisprudence,* approaching the
subject from the historic, the logical and scientific and the
philosophical aspects; *Bankruptcy Reform,* urging control of the
bankrupt's estate by the creditors; the *Judicature Acts,* declaring
that to refer legal appeals to the House of Lords was a breach of
the Science of Judicature; *Reform and Codification of the Law
of Nations,* and *Pax Hominus in the Reign of Law,* a plea for
an international tribunal. As to the tangled skein of law in
this country he urged:

(1) A Code Commission to ascertain and express in abstract
terms the existing law.

(2) A Legislative Commission to preside over the enactment
of the work of the Code Commission, and superintend
the results, with a view to future amendment.

(3) An intermediate instrument of a consultative sort: a
Council of Judges reporting periodically.

He early contended for a Court of Criminal Appeal, and for
the view that the treatment of the law-breaker must be designed,
not to punish, but to reclaim. He was active in the movement
for the re-casting of the labour laws, then so iniquitous, advising
and aiding George Odger and others who were working to that
end. Many of his important papers were delivered before the

Law Students' and Law Clerks' Societies, and he was an ever-ready source of counsel and inspiration to his younger legal colleagues.

His vast legal and historical erudition, so much admired in purely professional dissertations, was always brought into service in the cause of popular reform. Far from influencing him in a conservative direction, his learning acted as a supporting buttress to his most advanced theories. " The history of England," he averred, " is the political Bible of the people of this country." For the cause of women's enfranchisement he laboured with tremendous devotion.

The textile districts of Lancashire and Yorkshire were then the political heart of England. " What Lancashire says to-day, England says to-morrow," was a common saying. The vast industrial population, with its claimant needs, was still voteless: the employers themselves had only secured the franchise in 1832; they still felt their interests sharply pitted against the landed gentry. Fortunes had been, and still were being made by men of all sorts and conditions, who were often rough, shrewd fellows, with little or no academic learning. Dissent, Free Trade, popular enfranchisement; all that was comprised in Radicalism and Chartism had their stronghold there. Yet Lancashire, and above all Manchester, had its own Conservatism; the conservatism of the large manufacturer, merchant, and employer of labour, an altogether harsher and more material product than appears in the great centres of art and learning. Well-to-do Manchester merchants heartily welcomed Dr. Pankhurst's efforts to simplify the course of justice, to remove its delays and inadequacies, and reduce its costs, in commercial matters of interest to themselves; but many of them entertained quite opposite feelings when they saw him applying the same drastic logic towards Parliamentary and economic institutions, on behalf of the labouring people they employed. The most extreme of Radicals in his opposition to all forms of privilege and exploitation, his piercing shafts of oratory were as bitterly resented in some quarters as they were received with ecstatic admiration in others.

" How silently the great Lords slumber on the body of the English nation, rolling in such infinite content, and ever wondering that everybody is not satisfied, since they themselves are! "

he cried, in the heat of the struggle for the abolition of the House which he impugned as:

" The most singular piece of mediæval mummery . . . without doubt the most preposterous institution in Europe."

" A public abattoir where the liberties and interests of the people have been butchered like cattle of the field, for the profit of the privileged few . . . no more a legislative assembly than was Procrustes with his den of blood and his bed of mutilation."

" Privilege," he declared, " is a creature that goes on two stilts; one of which is property, the other the Church of England." As to the Bishops:

" Let them be . . . sent about their spiritual business, and keep them there until the day of disestablishment and disendowment. . . . Let them be followers of the meek and lowly Jesus, and leave the gilded Chamber of the State."

The Clergy he referred to as " a portentous beadledum." The Manchester Cathedral, an insignificant edifice, which stands, as though forgotten by the growing city, amongst dingy warehouses and the smoke and noise of railway sidings, he dubbed " an obsolete mediæval residuum."

Always sparkling with epigram and allusion, his utterances became kindlier in later life, and I have heard him say that he had occasionally regretted some of the controversial acerbities of his youth.

For two older men, Ernest Jones the Chartist and John Stuart Mill, he conceived a profound admiration and love, which remained with him vividly till the end of his life. Long after they were dead he spoke of them frequently, with a high and tender regard. In the year he was called to the Bar he heard Ernest Jones making his memorable defence of the Fenians, for which he was complimented by Justice Blackburn, who nevertheless sentenced the prisoners to death. It was the last public execution in Manchester. When Ernest Jones died, three days after a test ballot in Manchester had indicated that his many efforts to enter Parliament were to be crowned with success, Dr. Pankhurst, hurrying up Market Street, heavy with the burden of his sorrow, saw a hawker in the gutter offering some of the dead Chartist's manuscripts for sale. He bought them and sent them to the young widow of his friend, a second wife, left with a baby in her arms. More than thirty years later that youngest daughter of Ernest Jones appealed for aid to the widow of Dr. Pankhurst, who had become a member of the Manchester Education Committee. The wife of an invalid, and mother of young children, Jones's daughter was earning a living for her family, as a teacher in a private school at Altrincham in Cheshire. She had been dismissed, because it had come to the knowledge of the owner of the school that she was a daughter of the long dead Chartist. So do political animosities endure.

It was characteristic of the Doctor that as soon as his University career was over, he bent his efforts to secure educational opportunities for others. He was to take an outstanding part in building the fabric of popular education, especially in Lancashire. Frederick Denison Maurice had started the Workmen's College in London in 1854. In 1858 Dr. Pankhurst was one of the small group of pioneers who initiated evening classes at Owens College, Manchester, for the benefit of working people. He was a member of the honorary teaching staff, taking classes at the College itself and in other parts of Lancashire. For thirteen years, dating from 1863, he was the honorary secretary of the important Lancashire and Cheshire Union of Institutes, retaining his active interest in its work to the end of his life. This organization had been formed in 1839 as part of the movement led by Lord Brougham and others to establish Mechanics' Institutes (the forerunners of the technical schools), to teach manual workers the principles of the arts they practised. It was in the same year that Melbourne's Government had established the Committee of Council on Education, and the £39,000 then voted was the largest grant to education yet given by any Government. At that time there were few elementary and no secondary schools for working-class children; indeed even twenty years later the Newcastle Commission reported that only one child in seven was attending an elementary school, and but one in twenty a school receiving a Government grant. Such schools as existed were for the most part unworthy to be so named, the teachers themselves being often almost illiterate.

Lacking thus the educational foundations on which to build, and wearied by the excessive hours of labour then exacted from them, the workers were unable to avail themselves of the scientific training offered by the Mechanics' Institutes. These hopeful institutions therefore largely fell into decay. Such of them as remained were centres mainly for amusement and recreation, and their attendances were small. They attracted clerks and shopkeepers rather than the labourers and artisans for whom they were intended, and little or no attempt was made to secure women students.

A fruitless effort was made by the Rev. S. A. Steinthal and others to re-establish the Lancashire and Cheshire Union; again it declined. Ardent for scientific education, Dr. Pankhurst yet saw the impossibility of establishing it, except upon a sound elementary basis. In 1862 he set himself to revise the constitution of the Lancashire and Cheshire Union to this end; and under his inspiration, it was reorganized in 1863, when he became its honorary secretary.

No one could have been better equipped for the hard task he had chosen, endowed, as he was, with abounding enthusiasm, for the people, for education, and for the intellectual and scientific achievements of his period. Darwin had but recently electrified the thinking world by his work on the origin of species. The theory of evolution had come as a magnetic stimulus to unprejudiced minds. Met in some quarters by an opposition so bitter as to be incomprehensible in these days, it received from its supporters a welcome even keener, and the eager zest only accorded to newly-acquired truths. Spencer, Huxley, Haeckel, Sir Thomas Maine, Joule, Kelvin, Faraday, and a host of others, each in his special field, were building a great edifice of knowledge of the origins and development of civilization and society, of marriage and law, of human nature and the principles governing natural phenomena. Physical science was making tremendous strides, the conception of energy took its place beside mass as a real quantity, chemistry and mechanical technique were advancing apace. The telegraph, the telephone and electric power were coming into practical use. An omnivorous reader, in 'buses and trains and wherever he might be, the Doctor kept abreast with all these developments, eager to open the minds of the people to the expanding treasury of knowledge, and to wed scientific training to the manual experience of the worker and the craftsman, in order that men and women might no longer be as mere automata in the industrial process, but intelligent and interested participators.

" Whoever it is that out of the smallest amount of raw material produces the highest amount of comfort and convenience to mankind is one of the true sons of the world—a trained and skilled artisan. He must be a thinker and an artist. . . . The artisan ought to know how far, and in what manner discovery, invention, thought, has penetrated the raw material. He ought to have a perfect mastery of the practical deductions from that theoretic knowledge, and finally, if he is not only to be a workman, but a leader in that trade—as many workmen are, and as many more will be—he will be in such a position from the action and reaction of the knowledge as to extend it. . . .

" Between the speculation of the philosopher and the work of the artisan there is a permanent connection. The thought of the philosopher passes down through successive stages until it arms the man at the loom, or the man at the bench, with that knowledge. . . . He who begins his education at the beginning in the first rudiments should be able—if he have devotion, if he have purpose, if he have energy—to rise, stage by stage, higher and higher, until he reaches those seats of learning, the universities, whose highest end and purpose is not to train men for callings and professions, but to keep alive speculation and thought; and he who takes advantage of these may go up from the beginning to the sublime. . . ." [1]

His views on pedagogy were then only shared by a few pioneer minds.   He urged that it was the duty of teachers

" not to impress themselves upon their pupils, but to place their pupils in possession of themselves.

" There ought to be a clear perception of the faculties of the mind in the mode and order of their development, involving a knowledge of their functions, relations and dependencies, so as to secure their gradual, harmonious, and progressive culture.

" Knowledge is a sort of mental food to be tendered to the growing mind for two reasons : either for information, or as gymnastics—to strengthen the faculties and power of the mind, the main object of education in its intellectual form being to develop and discipline the mental faculties, so that they may enter into the pursuit of truth. . . . The eye, the ear and all the senses should receive exact, clear and consistent training."

When, much later, as a great event in the educational history of the north of England, the new northern Victoria University, incorporating Owens College, was founded, we find him at the first convocation (November 2nd, 1880) moving the resolution of congratulation on behalf of the Associates of Owens, and expressing his hope that the University would be " a school of free inquiry," from which would go forth many who would devote themselves to the higher services of society, having in them " the old fire of devotion to city, to country and to mankind."

In the 'sixties and the 'seventies he was stimulating the minds of the worker students who flocked to hear him, with high appeals to their initiative and enterprise :

" . . . the man who is capable of sustaining protracted thought is, in the intellectual world, the monarch of men . . . he who has learned how to learn can soon learn anything." [2]

Under his leadership the reconstructed Union of Lancashire and Cheshire Institutes undertook to provide a connected system of classes and lecturers for its associated institutes, conducting a zealous intensive work within its own area, and adopting also a broad national policy, working to promote the cause of popular education, through the Mechanics' Institutes in all parts of the country, and the managers of public schools, and agitating for a State system of free elementary education.   Great efforts were made for the passage of the Education Act of 1870, " the Magna

[1] Annual Soirée of Mechanics' Institute, Accrington.   *Accrington Times*, October, 1867.

[2] Speech to Littlewood Mechanics' Institute, reported in *Glossop Chronicle*, 7th September, 1867.

Charta of Elementary Education," as Dr. Pankhurst called it, though he was far from failing to recognize its imperfections.

When the passage of this Act had placed the duty of providing elementary education on other shoulders, the Lancashire and Cheshire Union of Mechanics' Institutes returned to its original work of providing secondary and technical training, and an institution of great usefulness in this field was built up. By 1865 the Union had already 17,000 members. By 1875 it had established two scholarships at Owens College and provided several £10 exhibitions for the evening classes there; it had also a travelling library. Soon the City and Guilds of London subscribed to its work. In 1880 it took over the commercial examinations abandoned by the Society of Arts, and presently the Manchester City Council and the Lancashire and Cheshire County Councils made grants to its funds. In 1894 an agreement was reached by which all the educational institutions, aided by the Lancashire County Council, were admitted to the Union, which acted as their examining Board. In that year nearly 20,000 papers were examined.

In 1859 Fanny Hertz had pleaded before the Social Science Association for Mechanics' Institutes for working women. Dr. Pankhurst and others in the Lancashire and Cheshire Union of Institutes made efforts to attract women students; yet how slow was the progress made in securing a fair field for them may be gathered from an incident reported in the *Manchester Examiner and Times* in 1878. At the annual meeting of the Manchester Mechanics' Institute it appeared that a woman member, Miss L. E. Willis, had been nominated for election as a Director of the Union, but had been declared ineligible by the Board on the ground of her sex. Dr. Pankhurst promptly championed her claim and moved a resolution that her name be placed on the voting paper. Lydia Becker, the suffrage leader, supported the plea, which was carried by the meeting, though one of the members protested that to do so would lead to much confusion and would interrupt many of the proceedings. The resolution was carried, but unfortunately it must be recorded that Miss Willis was not elected, and that she received fewer votes than any of the men candidates.

In 1873, at the second election of the School Boards created by the Elementary Education Act of 1870, Dr. Pankhurst stood as candidate for the Manchester Board. He was necessarily an Independent, for none of the parties embraced the whole of his programme. Thus lacking the support of an organized party machine, he inevitably failed to secure election. He stood for universal, free, secular education, public control of all schools supported by public funds, the establishment of Board Schools in all localities.

Lydia Becker, who presently came to be regarded by the large public as the typical Women's Suffragist of her time, had already been elected to the first School Board. She avoided heroic courses, and stood as an Unsectarian candidate. Again securing election, her poll was 14,487, rather less than half that of the highest successful candidate, Canon Toole. Roman Catholics and Churchmen were at the head of the list, Unsectarians followed. Dr. Pankhurst and another Independent made up the rear. Vilified as an Atheist and a Communist, he obtained 10,535 votes, a substantial poll indeed, as compared with the four or five hundred votes, or even less, received by the candidates of the first Socialist organizations twenty years later. Free education was in 1870 regarded as an extreme proposal, not merely by the ignorant, but by those who had enjoyed the benefits of a liberal education, and were even regarded as politically advanced. Henry Fawcett, husband of the well-known suffragist Millicent Garrett Fawcett, and at that period referred to by *The Times* as " the most thorough Radical " in Parliament, was opposed to free schools, though an advocate of secular education.

The passionate acuteness of the then religious controversies is now difficult to realize. When education under national auspices was proposed in 1843 and 1847, the Nonconformists objected, in the interests of their own sects, and were but reluctantly brought round to it in 1870. The Church still opposed it, contending bitterly on behalf of its schools. Already in 1861 the Newcastle Commission had observed that the religious difficulty, and with it the obstacles to a national system of education, had originated, not with the parents, but with the organizers of the Voluntary Schools. It is curious to reflect what the course of educational history might have been if Gladstone had attempted to implement in legislation the view he was expressing privately,[1] that public funds should go only to secular education, and that the religious bodies ought to provide religious teaching at their own cost. To Lord Granville[2] he wrote that he had never made greater personal concessions of opinion than on the Education Bill " to the united representations of Ripon and Forster." John Morley attributes Gladstone's acquiesence to his preoccupation with the Irish Land Bill; but he admits, a fact which seems remarkable to-day, that the interest of the Liberal leader in education did not amount to zeal. Certainly Gladstone had no conception of a great national

---

[1] Letters to Lord de Grey (afterwards Lord Ripon) and John Bright. John Morley, *Life of Gladstone*, I, 704-708.

[2] June 14th, 1874. Morley, *Life of Gladstone*.

system of education; he preferred to proceed through the medium of the Church schools. In his mind the duty of the Government was merely to fill the gaps in the voluntary system. That this was no concession to the political exigencies urged upon him by his colleagues is clear from the fact that he opposed the setting up of a School Board at Hawarden. Thus great outsiders, Pankhurst, Mill, Huxley and others, were left to fight a forlorn hope for free secular education, to be provided for the whole country by the State. It could scarcely be otherwise: Gladstone had begun his political life with the view that it was a fundamental duty of the English State to give active and exclusive support to the Church of England; he had voted against the abolition of university tests for Dissenters, and had declared that the universities should be " seminaries for the Established Church." This view, from which Gladstone had broadened, was still tenaciously held by powerful contemporaries.

Pankhurst had no such prejudices to overcome. A sound education for every child stood out for him as the sole considera- tion. He smote vigorously at whatever appeared to him to bar the way. Convinced that the Church schools, organized primarily for religious instruction, were inimical to the provision of a first- class secular education, he set himself to prove that the contribu- tion to the total cost of education provided by the religious bodies was not large enough to justify the basing of the national system upon it. Since the passing of the Education Act the schools of the Established Church had received seventy-three per cent. of the total Government expenditure on education. The Government had granted £59,016 to the Church for the training of teachers, whilst the Church itself had raised only £10,064 for this purpose. He analysed the income of the Manchester Voluntary Schools, showing, for example, that of the £450 received by St. George's School, Hulme, in 1870, the voluntary donations amounted to only £1. In reply to his attack, the Churchmen hurled at him the then highly damaging charge of Atheism.

After ten or eleven years of his labours the Union of Mechanics' Institutes had become firmly established, and mean- while the cause of popular education itself had gained an assured status in popular favour. A cause which is won lacks neither advocates nor competitors for office; at the annual meeting of 1874 an attempt was made to oust him from the Hon. Secretaryship, a reverberation of the animosities raised in the '73 election, and a protest against his prominence in several as yet unpopular causes. Dr. Kerr, who belled the cat by suggesting Dr. Pankhurst's resignation, admitted that he had worked for the Union as no one else had done, but urged that subscribers were being alienated on account of his political views.   On inquiry it was revealed that a certain Mr. Hick of Bolton had actually refused a donation on this ground, but no other case could be cited; never before had the progress of the Union of Institutes been so great.   Dr. Pankhurst refused to resign, and his question : " Is Mr. Hick of Bolton to be the Commander-in-Chief of popular education in Lancashire? " was received with a general round of applause. The *Manchester Examiner and Times*, pointing out that he was, " as everyone admits, a very efficient " honorary secretary, commented, in the course of a witty leader :

"In point of fact, we cannot but think that these gentlemen owe Dr. Pankhurst some little apology.   Of course they felt for him nothing but friendship; of course they were the last men in the world to make his political opinions act as a disability in a matter with which politics have, or should have, nothing to do.   Still, though their motives were irreproachable, their conduct on this occasion was perhaps not equally so." [1]

The raging political controversies of his time forced him early to examine the foundations of religious belief.   As a youth he had been an earnest adherent of his father's faith, and had taught in the Baptist Sunday Schools.   In 1870 he addressed the Rochdale Sunday School Union, probably his last appearance on such a platform, describing religion as " a rule of conduct sanctioned by love," and love as " a kind of contagion that spreads all round." [2] He added : " The active faculties should be governed by the intellectual, and the latter by the feelings of the heart."   This, through all his intellectual striving, remained the guiding principle of his life, daily exemplified in a hundred ways.

In one of his old note-books he wrote :

"Mankind is beginning to find it must be its own providence. We are orphans, then.   We shall not be the less sober, thoughtful and mutually forgiving for thinking so, or for knowing the fact. Perhaps for the first time we may realize how important it is to love one another."

He had passed into a broad Agnosticism.   In his own words :

" Under the limitations of the human faculties, God, the infinite, the beginning and end of things, are each and all by the human intellect unknown and unknowable.   The mind of man does and can know the finite and the phenomenal.   The mind of man does not and cannot know the infinite and the noumenal.

" The origin of religion is, I hold, the sense of dependence in man, due to the consciousness of limitation before the universe.   It is the

---

[1] October 23rd, 1874. *Examiner and Times*.
[2] *Rochdale Observer*, October 22nd, 1870.

awe of the heart before the unknown. The origin of theology is the effort to express this sense of dependence, this awe of the heart, in intellectual forms and terms. . . .

"The intellect in offering its forms to the heart and employing the terms infinite, God, the soul, presents propositions without meaning to the mind, in order to render tentatively and provisionally the awe, the hopes and the aspirations of the heart." [1]

When questioned as to his religious opinions at political meetings held to promote secular causes, he always refused to answer, following in this respect the invariable practice of John Stuart Mill. His own platform reticence on religion sprang, in part, from his strongly held view that the affairs of a person's private life should not be dragged into controversy in relation to his or her public work and opinions; in part, it was grounded in his quick and gentle sympathy for the sorrows and aspirations of others. In private life he made no secret of his Agnosticism, and when the public occasions arose when he felt it incumbent upon him to explain them, he did so with frank simplicity.

In the early 'seventies a wave of Republicanism swept the country. Sympathy with the French Republicans in their struggle to overthrow the second Empire at the close of the Franco-German war, played its part in this manifestation. Moreover, rumour, since established as fact, by the publication of letters and memoirs of the period, declared that here in England the Queen was using her influence to oppose Reform, and striving to gain control of foreign policy. She had opposed the European movements of liberation which aroused popular sympathy here, and had striven to force the British Government into war on the side of Austria. The growing cost of the Royal family was a widespread source of grievance. The Queen was not prepared to maintain her children on the £385,000 granted to her by the nation, although since the Prince Consort's death the ceremonial functions of the Crown had almost disappeared. In 1871 Parliament voted £6,000 a year and a dowry of £30,000 to the Princess Louise, and a few months later £15,000 a year for the Prince Arthur. Republican clubs sprang up, and Republicanism of a vague sort became almost respectable. Joseph Chamberlain and Sir Charles Dilke were spoken of as Republicans.

Republicanism was an essential part of Pankhurst's equalitarian creed. Declaring it to be " a work of duty," he presided over the inauguration of the Manchester Republican Club on May 13th, 1873, and explained his view:

[1] Reply of R. M. Pankhurst to A. J. Balfour, M.P. *Manchester Examiner and Times*, June 21st, 1886.

" It is not so much the direct power of the Crown which is so injurious, as its indirect influence. It is the shelter of privilege, the centre of vested and sinister influences. It is the excuse for receiving large emoluments without rendering any service. . . .

" It was necessary in the days of the Commonwealth to get the liberties of the people by the people armed; it is now necessary to change an aristocratic into a democratic republic only by the people enfranchised. . . .

" We want, first of all, the complete enfranchisement of the people; having got that, the obvious and necessary consequence is the creation of a representative assembly—the organ of the national will. . . . This representative assembly will nominate the great chiefs of the Executive, and being nominated by the assembly, they will be the servants of the assembly."

" The Executive the lesser, the Parliament the greater; the Executive the learner, the Parliament the teacher; the Legislature supreme, the Executive subordinate."

Such were his slogans. In his Republican agitation he joined the demand for the abolition of the House of Lords with that for the repeal of the then most oppressive Labour laws:

" The lineal descendants of the despotic sovereign and the tyrannic nobility are the Crown, as held under the Act of Settlement, and the hereditary peerage sitting in the House of Lords. The lineal descendants of the serfs are the English working men and labourers, as their status is prescribed by the class legislation of the Master and Servant Act 1867, and the Criminal Law Amendment Act 1871."

With Jacob Bright he was long associated in terms of close friendship; but he fell foul of the more famous brother, John Bright, on account of the latter's opposition to Votes for Women, Republicanism, and other questions. John Bright, when asked by the Birmingham Republicans to speak under their auspices, emphatically refused:

" Our forefathers suffered from nearly a century of unsettled Government in consequence of the overthrow of the monarchy. . . . France has endured many calamities and much humiliation for nearly a hundred years past. . . . Spain is now in the same difficulty. . . . I have no sympathy with the object which gives its name to your club."

Pankhurst took up the cudgels for the Republican ideal:

" The blood and tears of France have purchased endless gain to Europe and to civilization. . . . The French Revolution initiated for Europe and for the world the great principles of political and social freedom upon which modern progress is based."

He complained that a " vile Carlist plot " was being nourished on English soil to attack the young republic of Spain, and that John Bright, from his seat in the Government, had made no protest:

" Eyeless quite as to his former aims, and captive to the Philistines of hereditary influence, he is now grinding in the Conservative mills."

Criticized thus from many quarters, and confronted with his own speeches in praise of American institutions, Bright defended himself. Pankhurst replied, and the Manchester Republicans placarded the walls of the city with copies of his letter. By all this the Doctor was raising a veritable hornet's nest of indignation and prejudice about his head. When he spoke at a public meeting to inaugurate a Liberal Club in Tyldesley, the Rev. Philip Haines left the meeting in a rage, and wrote to the Press complaining that he had found himself sharing the platform with a " Red Republican " and " Communist."

A Communist Pankhurst certainly was, in the broad sense which would cover William Morris, Peter Kropotkin and Keir Hardie; but not in the narrow meaning which has been given to the term since the Russian Revolution; he hated violence, and believed that by appeals to reason and the development of popular education, freedom would continue to broaden down from precedent to precedent, and the era of equality and fraternity be introduced by the votes of an enlightened people. He found historical precedent for his dauntless faith in democracy and progress:

" In land it must be remembered collective ownership is the old institution, individual ownership is the modern innovation." [1]

" The primitive law of the world is some form of ownership in common, by aggregates of men distributed over a local area. . . . Then succeeds the feudal system—a system of defence against enemies outside, and of mutual protection as regards those within . . . there is a supreme landlord and tenants under him. . . . The land stands under two conditions : first, that the revenue of the land received by the lord shall go to maintain the charges of the area, in war, justice and general government; secondly, that the land shall be cultivated on free terms by tenants who pay that rent." [2]

" In 1660, with the Restoration, the feudal lords got rid of their dues and services to their sovereign lord by imposing a tax upon beer and cider, a noble and disinterested way of getting rid of their burdens. Originally the feudal lord held his land on two great services—the peace service and the war service. As time grew on, money payments were made as substitutes; but in 1692 a land-tax was imposed at various sums, so as to meet existing emergencies from time to time. In 1798 a statute was passed fixing the land tax at 4s. in the £; but also fixing the amount which was to be raised. Thus these burdens, for the sake of which the landlord got these

[1] Election address as Parliamentary candidate for Manchester, 1883.
[2] Speech at Atherton.

immense possessions, were commuted for a fixed amount. Every
district in England now raises for that tax precisely the same money
as when the tax was originally levied in 1692. That amount has
never been changed. . . . The amount to be raised by Liverpool is
£168, and the value of the land in 1842 was £1,568,347. The land
tax, never changed all this time, has become but one-ninth of a
farthing. All the difference in the value which has come to that
land by increase of population and wealth goes into the pocket of
the landlord. . . . A more strange and terrible extension of the
feudal system is hardly conceivable. In respect of the land upon
which the Liverpool docks were built, formerly mere foreshore of
the Mersey, Lord Derby receives £40,000 a year."[1]

Passionate in desire that the great developments of his time
should be employed for the welfare and happiness of the entire
people, he saw, with intolerable distress, the hideous advance of
industrialism transforming broad acres of green country into
blighted wastes, and throwing up around the great docks and
factories the squalid dwellings of exploited operatives, dwarfed
and stunted by their privations. Appalled by the vast wealth
and the vast poverty born from the industrialized soil, as well
as by the piteous plight of the dwindling population of
agricultural workers he pleaded :

" What is the most forlorn object in the world? The dependent,
degraded agricultural labourer of England."

He agitated earnestly for the nationalization of the land.

" You know how much improvement might be effected by
chemical skill and scientific appliances, if this great body of land
existed for the public use. We might have the system of long leases,
peasant proprietors, co-operative farming; and great and wise
experiments might be instituted by public-spirited men and
agricultural labourers. . . ."[2]
" Let the land lie open, free to the public; then give the local
districts in which the land lies, power, by representative Councils, to
deal with it, so that they may offer to the inhabitants of that district
all kinds of tenure and tenancy . . . peasant proprietorship working
in one corner, large farming in another, long leases in a third, short
leases in a fourth. Try them, let them compete with each other,
and so find out the best way of dealing with the local land."[3]

Land nationalization was not to him a mere isolated reform,
but part of a comprehensive system, to be applied to Society as
a whole :

[1] *Rochdale Observer*, 10th December, 1873.
[2] Published address, " The Next Page in the History of Liberal Legislation,"
delivered at Leigh, June, 1878.
[3] Speech at Atherton. *The Leigh Journal*, October 9th, 1885.

" Suppose the mines were acquired by this district; then I should like to see opportunity offered to any body of men who desired to work mines to come to the land department of that elective body and make terms to work the mines and pay royalties to the elective Local Board."

An address to Co-operators, reported in the *Manchester and Salford Co-operative Herald,* of February, 1876, well expresses his ideals. (That his conception of a co-operative society was an institution owned by the workers therein, and that many co-operatives do not answer to this description, does not affect the argument):

" Very many times, in the conflict between capital and labour, production has been reduced, until the terms of difference have been settled. The result is a loss to the community, and to the wealth of the world. Now co-operation pursues a different plan and presents a higher ideal. There can be no loss or decrease in the quantity of production of industry when capital and labour are impelled by a common force. That common force is furnished by concentrating and combining in the same person the twofold interests both of capital and labour. This co-operation, which has been so successfully applied to distribution, must be applied to production with accelerated force. . . . Co-operation and self-government rest on the same foundation. . . . The strong sense and love of commonweal, dependent upon and calling forth individual and associated intelligence, virtue and activity, is essential to freedom, both in economics and in government. . . .

" The great natural agents of the land, such as coal, iron, and minerals, should no longer be the property of a class, to the detriment of the community, but should be brought under the control of the whole people in its corporate capacity, with a just regard to the rights of the individual on the one hand, and the rights of the nation on the other, in order that by co-operation there should be given to each and all a fair share of the products of joint exertion. Then the whole nation, in the individual and in the mass, being sustained by the justice of the laws, and the equity of the social system, and being animated and impelled by a strong sense of the commonweal, would steadily move forward in a constant course of prosperity and development." [1]

Though he had helped to reconstitute the National Reform Union and was a member of its executive, though he had been a founder of the Manchester Liberal Association and had drafted its constitution, he was never a Party man. Principles, to him, were always paramount; Party considerations he never permitted to affect them. A supporter of Negro Emancipation, he was as vigorous in denouncing an Admiralty circular issued under the Liberals, in 1871, to captains of war vessels, declaring that slave

[1] *Manchester and Salford Co-operative Herald*, February, 1876.

owners might seize their slaves upon British ships, as when the
same thing was done by the Tories, in 1876. Though he ever
desired to go faster and further, he rejoiced in the great Reform
measures of the Gladstone administrations: Elementary Education, the Ballot, and Irish Land Acts, the abolition of religious
tests for the Universities, the throwing open of the Civil Services
to competitive examination. The Liberal triumph at the polls,
which had followed the Tory gift of Household Suffrage, elated
him with high hope for the progress of democracy. The return
to office of the Conservatives in 1874, instead of the anticipated
further advance, came as a poignant grief and disappointment
to his ardent, ingenuous faith in democracy. He saw in the
imperialism of Disraeli, far-reaching possibilities of harm, and an
influence wholly destructive to the growth of international
fraternity, wholly opposed to his own cherished ambition that
Britain might be a disinterested mediator in the Council of the
nations, the friend and protector of weaker peoples. In opposing the Royal Titles Bill, to confer the title " Empress of India "
upon the Queen, the Doctor was in line with Gladstone and
Hartington; but the Tory *Manchester Courier* was not altogether
wrong in its observation that whilst the Liberal leaders opposed
the Bill " for purely Party purposes," Dr. Pankhurst was animated
by dislike of existing monarchical institutions. To him the
creation of this new title must be opposed as a flouting of the
movement towards an equalitarian social order, as a denial of the
right of India to become a self-governing entity, and as a symbol
of the aggressive Imperialism, of which Disraeli was the subtle
and tortuous protagonist. Those typical incidents of imperial
expansion, the annexation of the Transvaal and the Zulu and
Afghan wars, which occurred during that Parliament, he
regarded with pain as " an outrage on civilization and justice,"
deploring that a handful of men had been able to make such
wars, and declaring that " the nation ought not to answer " to
their call. He viewed with horror and foreboding Disraeli's
plans for imperial expansion in the East. He saw that they
involved commitments and projects of tremendous portent, which
in fact were not fully matured until the great European War of
1914-18. When the secret Anglo-Russian and Anglo-Turkish
conventions were brought to light, he recognized them as two
arms of the same policy of imperial expansion. The Anglo-
Turkish Convention, " a gigantic political combination to
guarantee the payment of a bad debt," as he termed it, had been
made to profit the holders of Turkish bonds. It had yet more
dangerous aspects. Under it England had undertaken, for all
time, to protect Asiatic Turkey against Russia, in return for which

Turkey assented to the British occupation of Cyprus. With horrified prescience, he declared his belief that the bargain had been struck with a view to the control and ultimate possession of Asia Minor by this country. As Cyprus was a State under the protection of Europe, it could not have been seized, he contended, without the assent of other Powers, above all of Russia. Undoubtedly, therefore, the English Government had entered into a pact with Russia to allow her all she demanded, on condition that she would not interfere with the British occupation of Cyprus. The World War, 1914-1918, has since justified these predictions: Asia Minor has been broken up into four separate dominions; the Turkish Republic, and the mandated territories of Syria, Palestine and Iraq, the first given to the control of France, the two latter to Britain. The abortive Treaty of Sèvres would have partitioned also the narrower area which still remains within Turkish frontiers. Save for the decisive victory of Turkey over Greece, in the war 1919-22, the area would by this time have been partitioned into Greek, French and Italian zones; Dr. Pankhurst's prediction of 1878 would thus have been fulfilled. Foreseeing the vast scope of these projects of annexation, he uttered most earnest warnings:

" We have no conception of what all this really involves, but we know that it can, and will, be made the excuse for an enormous increase in military and naval armaments. For the last thirty years the privileged classes have been manufacturing excuses for that increase. They know that if they can rouse in the people the war passion, they will be able to contract millions of obligations, and send up their bloated armaments to a position still more portentous. An excuse will also be furnished for an enormous increase of civil establishments, whose limit and purpose cannot be defined. . . .

" The people of this island, toiling for life, are to be taxed, their property is to be confiscated, they are to be disturbed in their interests and future, in order that an arrangement so criminal, so base, so fraudulent, shall take effect, to their ruin and degradation." [1]

Like many another honest man, he was both appalled and amazed by the chicanery of Disraeli's diplomacy. With his exalted views of international honour and responsibility, it was to him no less than monstrous that, at the Lord Mayor's banquet, the Prime Minister of England should have announced to the world that his Government sought no territory, but only the safety and happiness of the Christian subjects of Turkey; whilst actually an official document existed, stating that he required the cession of a portion of Bessarabia and of Batoum and the adjacent territory. To him it was a " dishonest act, justly a matter of

---

[1] Speech in support of a Resolution calling for the resignation of the Government at the General Council of the Manchester Liberal Federation, 23rd July, 1878.

reprobation by all Europe," that the emissaries of England should have gone into the Conference of Berlin, affirming that they had succeeded in inducing Russia to lay the whole Treaty of San Stefano before the Congress, whilst secretly they had entered into the Anglo-Russian agreement, which gave to Russia the very things for which the British Cabinet had pretended to assail her.

When the Anglo-Turkish convention threatened to involve this country in war with Russia, the Doctor, through Press and platform, was calling for a conference of the Powers to frame a pacific settlement of the war, on lines of freedom and self-government for the subject peoples over whose bodies the Powers were contending. As always, the large aspects of his social philosophy remained present to his mind, unobscured by the immediate issues. On the Executive of the National Reform Union, and the Council of the Manchester Liberal Federation, in Manchester Town's Meetings, in addresses delivered up and down the country and printed for broadcast circulation, he was, moreover, demanding that the decision of peace and war and the conclusion of Treaties must be made, not in secret, but openly and in good faith, not by the Cabinet, not by the Privy Council, but by Parliament itself. " Let Parliament work out the principles, and let a committee of skilled persons work out the details." He was advocating the creation of an international tribunal, to which international disputes and treaties should be submitted.

He saw in the Eastern crisis a serious phase in the struggle between personal and Parliamentary rule which had been continued behind the veil throughout the reign of Victoria; a struggle which had grown more pointed and systematic after her marriage to Prince Albert, of whom Disraeli, with his customary touch of bizarre exaggeration, observed : " If he had outlived some of our old stagers he would have given us the blessings of absolute Government." When in the development of the Eastern crisis Disraeli was created Lord Beaconsfield, the Doctor dubbed him " that old foe with a new face," protesting that it was " not sufficient for Lord Beaconsfield to go running like a lackey from Windsor to Downing Street; not enough for him to induce an aged and respected Lady to publish letters of her dear husband; he must act towards Parliament as a responsible Minister ! " He complained that " foreign affairs are for the Queen and me " represented the attitude of Lord Beaconsfield, whilst the Foreign Office had long been " the irresponsible despot of the British Empire." He called for the impeachment of Beaconsfield, and carried with him in this demand the National Reform Union and other organizations. It is interesting to recall that John Stuart

Mill's stepdaughter, that very drastic lady, Helen Taylor, spoke at the National Reform Union against the impeachment resolution, declaring the Liberal leader, Lord Hartington, as guilty as the Conservatives in the Eastern imbroglio, and blaming Gladstone for placing the direction of the Liberal Party in such hands. The Radicals, she said, were " like lions led by asses " since they followed such leaders.

Gladstone alone amongst Front Bench politicians was opposing the Beaconsfield policy of imperial expansion :

" If Cyprus and the Transvaal were as valuable as they are valueless I would repudiate them, because they are obtained by means dishonourable to the character of the country." [1]

Because of such utterances great unofficial public men, more advanced, more consistent in their internationalism than he, rallied about Gladstone in that dark hour. William Morris, Burne Jones, Carlyle, Froude, Ruskin and W. T. Stead were amongst the pacifists. When at the close of the session of 1876 Gladstone spoke in opposition to Beaconsfield's Eastern policy, he regarded it as " an opposition without hope." He had mentally postponed all further action till the opening of the new session, when he learnt that the country was stirred in the cause of peace. The unofficial public men had done the work. Yet war feeling was also rampant. The music-halls rang with : " We don't want to fight, but by jingo if we do ! " and " Hurrah for Beaconsfield, and God Defend the Right ! " For a copy of the latter effusion the Queen sent a letter of thanks to the author, which was published to show her support of the war party. Gladstone was mobbed. The men to whom he had resigned the leadership of his party gave him no support. Lord Hartington rebuked Sir Wilfred Lawson for voting against a Government war measure. Tory newspapers called Dr. Pankhurst " Pankurski " and denounced him and his pacifist friends as " the Anglo-Russians."

War seemed imminent; the Queen's speech suggested it; orders were issued for the Mediterranean Fleet to pass the Dardanelles, and for Indian troops to proceed to Malta; the Government demanded £6,000,000 for war preparedness; the Reserves were called up. The Liberal Front Bench supported the Tory Government in all these measures. A deputation representing most of the Liberal Associations of the country, including that of Manchester, waited on Granville and Hartington, vainly urging them to make a stand against the calling up of the Reserves. The *Manchester Guardian*, then, as now, the principal organ of Liberalism, defended the Conservative Government against the

[1] Midlothian campaign.

attacks of Gladstone and the Liberal and Radical pacifists. This was no new development in its history. It had opposed John Bright and his colleague, T. M. Gibson, for their hostility to the Crimean War and the little war with China, and had assisted in bringing about their defeat in the election of 1857. Rich Whiggism, then as always, was imperialist, and regarded altruistic internationalism with cold dislike.

Against such elements in the Liberal Association Dr. Pankhurst maintained a ceaseless contest, and succeeded by passionate energy and unresting vigilance in upholding his policy against theirs. He determined to secure a conference of North Country Liberal Associations, to adopt an address to Gladstone, calling on him to resume the leadership of the Party. Only with great difficulty was this purpose accomplished. He campaigned for it in public meetings, and won to it, first the Junior Reform Club, then the National Reform Union, and then fought for it in the Manchester Liberal Association, pleading for hours before he secured a tardy assent. As a result of his efforts 1,500 delegates assembled in the Manchester Free Trade Hall on April 31st, 1878, and John Bright presided at a great public meeting held in the same hall. The address calling on Gladstone to take the leadership was carried in a storm of enthusiasm. The *Darlington Herald* gave a graphic account of the proceedings :

" . . . Mr. Sedgwick . . . concluded with a vigorous and loudly cheered expression of regret that the Queen should have disgraced herself by going down among the jingoes to encourage the cads of the music-halls by her grateful appreciation of their brutal war songs. . . .

" Mr. Worthington of Wigan urged the drawing up of a monster petition. . . .

" Mr. Jacob Bright's personal appearance is singularly prepossessing. There is more of womanly tenderness in his face than in that of his illustrious brother. . . . His speech was a calm, clear survey. . . . Mr. Steinthal, in that ringing voice of his, read the address. . . . Dr. Pankhurst, who rose to move its adoption, was warmly greeted. The audience expected strong meat, and it was not disappointed, for Dr. Pankhurst served up strong meat, well peppered, hot enough for the most exacting palate. His appearance is as youthful as his voice is searching, and his words incisive. He declared that they were met in the midst of a grave and terrible crisis to oppose a guilty Government bent upon war. There was a stir in the assembly, and men pressed closer together as the winged words of the intrepid speaker were sent hissing through the hall. . . ."

Dr. Pankhurst insisted that Gladstone alone could save the peace of Europe and the liberties of the people, and on his motion it was resolved to send the address to Gladstone by a deputation of more than a hundred delegates from the Liberal Associations of the principal towns. The Doctor himself represented the Manchester Association.

So, before Midlothian, Manchester, and with it the entire industrial north of England, began to move in the great swing of the political pendulum which swept Gladstone back to power. If Pankhurst had been content henceforth to keep step with the Gladstonian Liberals, he would doubtless have been awarded a safe seat in Parliament, and, by easy stages, would have attained to legal preferment, a title of honour, and Cabinet rank; but he was of another calibre. When in November of the same year he spoke with Gladstone at a demonstration at Rhyl,[1] he urged, in face of the Liberal leader, universal equal suffrage for women as well as men, and other equalitarian proposals, and, worst of all, perhaps, to the ears of the Liberal leader, the democratic reorganization of the Liberal Party itself.

[1] *Rhyl Advertiser*, November 1st, 1878.

CHAPTER II

THE RISE OF THE WOMEN'S SUFFRAGE MOVEMENT

BEFORE the first Reform Act of 1832 representative Government in this country led but a shadowy existence. Mary Wollstonecraft, in her *Vindication of the Rights of Women*, justly described the situation in 1792:

" I may excite laughter by dropping a hint, which I mean to pursue some future time, for I really think that women ought to have representatives, instead of being arbitrarily governed, without having any direct share allowed them in the deliberations of Government.

" But, as the whole system of representation is now in this country only a convenient handle for despotism, they need not complain, for they are as well represented as a numerous class of hard-working mechanics, who pay for the support of royalty when they can scarcely stop their children's mouths with bread."

The Act of 1832, by employing the term " male person," for the first time in English history, expressly debarred women from exercising the franchise it created. Yet the women's claim to emancipation, launched by Mary Astell, in her *Serious Proposals to Ladies* in 1697, and wrought into comprehensive form by Mary Wollstonecraft in the eighteenth century, was steadily gathering support. It gained a remarkable impetus by the Parliamentary candidature of John Stuart Mill. Mill refused to permit canvassing on his behalf, and it was with difficulty he could be induced to address the electors; but at his first public meeting, in the St. James's Hall, he made a powerful appeal for the enfranchisement of women, and he included a like plea in his election address.

In October, 1865, a society for the promotion of Women's Suffrage was formed in Manchester.[1]   Mrs. Elmy always insisted that the society was formed in 1865, though other authorities say 1866. Her original minute book, handed to her successor, Lydia Becker, was perhaps lost, or destroyed. The original committee met in Upper Brook Street, at the house of the Rev. S. A.

[1] The committee seems to have been re-constituted, perhaps in a more formal manner, on January 11th, 1867, at the house of Dr. Louis Borchardt, according to Helen Blackburn's *Women's Suffrage* (Williams & Norgate, 1902), but I do not know if she had documentary evidence for this.

Steinthal, a great Manchester worthy, earnest in all good causes, and its members were Mr. and Mrs. Steinthal, Mr. and Mrs. Max Kyllmann, Jacob and Ursula Bright and Dr. Pankhurst. Alice Wilson was an early and active member. The honorary secretary was Elizabeth Wolstenholme, afterwards Mrs. Wolstenholme Elmy, a tiny Jenny-wren of a woman, with bright, bird-like eyes, and a little face, child-like in its merriment and its pathos, which even in extreme old age retained the winning graces of youth, and unbound hair falling in ringlets on her shoulders, which all her life she wore thus in the fashion of her girlhood. As a school-mistress, she had been working since 1861 for higher education and better opportunities of employment for women, and had been an initiator in the formation of the Manchester board of school-mistresses in 1865. Thereafter her labours were continuous; she toiled for fifteen years for the Married Women's Property Acts of 1870 and 1882. Then for three strenuous years to secure for married mothers the custody and guardianship of their children until the passing of the Custody of Infants Act in 1886. She worked with Josephine Butler for the Repeal of the C.D. Acts, which was secured in 1886. Inspired by the example and teaching of Mary Wollstonecraft, and in view of the legal disabilities then attaching to married women, she united herself to Ben Elmy without any legal ceremony. When it was obvious that she was pregnant, there was much fluttering in the suffrage dovecotes, and eventually Mrs. Jacob Bright induced the two to marry, on the plea that their continued refusal would be harmful to the suffrage cause.

I have heard my mother say that Elmy intensely resented and never forgave this interference. I remember him, many years later, as a stout, sallow man, whom my mother and her most intimate suffrage friends intensely disliked. Yet he was possessed of considerable ability and was an enthusiast for the advancement of women, and for the equal comradeship of the sexes, of which he had a genuinely exalted vision, as revealed in his long poem, "Woman Free," written under his habitual pseudonym, "Ellis Ethelmer." He co-operated with his wife in efforts to advance the study of sex and maternity, with a view to minimizing the physical afflictions of women and increasing marital happiness, in this, as in much else, anticipating the efforts of later students and propagandists. Together and severally they produced works on sex education for children, including Mrs. Elmy's little text-book, *The Human Flower*. It was alleged against Elmy that the high virtues he preached were grimly absent from his own marital life. He was perhaps no saint, but undoubtedly the prejudices against their original free union, and their temerity in writing on sex questions, then tabooed, above all to women, led to the manufacture of unpleasant stories about them. She was so obviously immersed in public work that to accuse her of frivolity would have been absurd, but it was whispered that he was violently cruel and unfaithful to her. It was said that she had boasted during her pregnancy that she would need no aid in delivering her child, for maternity was a natural function which need not be dreaded by any healthy woman who had lived normally. Then in her travail, finding the fact so painfully different from the theory, she had begged Elmy to go for a doctor, but he had jeered at her: " You said you would not have one ! " and only relented when she was in the final throes of the birth crisis. It was even asserted that whilst her child was an infant, Elmy gave him gin to torture his unhappy wife. It may be that poor human nature, wedded to poverty and excessive toil, in this case, as in many another, fell lower than its aspirations. Whatever may have been their relations in early days, whatever his faults, and his reputation with some of the suffrage ladies was as black as though he had been the Devil himself, his wife always spoke of him in their later years with reverent tenderness. At his death she mourned him as a great seer, taking his ashes in a boat to a point equi-distant from England, Scotland and Ireland, and scattering them to the winds, in company with three chosen suffrage friends, younger women, upon whose efforts in the common cause she set great store. As to the child, he grew up puny and frail and lacking in initiative. His want of vigour is not surprising. Always poor, always working for her living, and always giving to the Causes she had at heart a wealth of unpaid service, unable to employ household aid, or aid in attending to her child, could it be otherwise? Undoubtedly he was stunted from his birth, by solitude and by lack of material things, knowing only the care of that work-driven mother, who was here, there and everywhere upon her mission, and whose tiny hand daily covered a multitude of closely-written sheets on the all-important questions of women's emancipation. She was an instrument in the grasp of Progress; he was a victim of her time and work. For half a century no man or woman gained prominence in political and social work but was drawn into the enormous circle of her correspondence, receiving from her, if she could procure any hopeful response, a regular stream of information and exhortation. Having outlived most of her early contemporaries, she was one of the very few original suffrage pioneers to welcome and join the young militant movement which broke forth in 1905, forty-four years after she had first put her hand to the plough. A painstaking recorder of the long struggle, her store of facts was ever at the service of her younger colleagues.   On January 30th, 1910, she wrote to me:

"I am now in my seventy-seventh year and all work is a painful toil. This terrible and terribly increasing weakness will speedily make an end of life's work for me, unless I can have a long spell of complete rest."

On the following July 17th she wrote that she was steadily going through the thousands of letters she had preserved:

". . . for use in the book of recollections which I intend to finish before I die and to call, *Some Memories of a Happy Life*; for my life has been one of steadfast happiness, every day bringing something to work for, something to hope for and many to love."

Though a clear and voluminously informed speaker, Elizabeth Wolstenholme was never, I think, an orator, which partly explains the fact that her true worth has not always been recognized.   As a pioneer she ranks first amongst the women who took part in the birth of the Suffrage Movement.

Already before the formation of the Manchester National Society for Women's Suffrage there existed in London the Kensington Society, of which Emily Davies, the pioneer educationist, was honorary secretary, wherein though women's suffrage was not actually one of its objects, papers were read upon the question by Emily Davies and Elizabeth Wolstenholme.

Soon after his election to Parliament in 1865, John Stuart Mill had told his women's suffrage friends that he would present a petition for Votes for Women to Parliament of not less than a hundred names.   On April 27th an event occurred which seemed to Emily Davies and her co-workers to make a propitious opening for the presentation of the petition.   It was a pronouncement by Disraeli, speaking as leader of the Tory opposition against the then Liberal Reform Bill, an ill-starred measure which presently foundered in stormy waters:

"I have always been of opinion that, if there is to be universal suffrage, women have as much right to vote as men; and, more than that, a woman having property ought now to have a vote, in a country in which she may hold manorial courts, and sometimes acts as churchwarden."[1]

Emily Davies and her co-workers, Barbara Leigh Smith (Mrs. Bodichon) and Jessie Boucherett, came together next morning, drafted a petition, obtained Mill's approval to its terms, and with an informal committee, which met at the house of Elizabeth Garrett (afterwards Dr. Garrett Anderson), set to work to procure signatures, a total of 1,499 names being collected in little more

[1] Hansard's Parliamentary Debates.

than a fortnight. The Manchester Society joined in the work, and Elizabeth Wolstenholme personally collected three hundred of the signatures. The petition, based on the plea that since Parliament had made the holding of property the basis of enfranchisement women property owners should be entitled to vote, was other than it would have been if drafted in Manchester, where Liberty, Equality, Fraternity was the slogan which animated the suffrage workers.

During her secretaryship of the Manchester Society, Elizabeth Wolstenholme opened a long co-operation with two remarkable women, Josephine Butler and Lydia Becker, in both cases through Emily Davies. Lydia Becker had written a paper advocating Women's Suffrage, and had sent it to Emily Davies, asking her to use her influence to secure its publication in the *Contemporary Review*, then edited by Dean Alford, who in 1866 had become a member of the London Committee for Women's Suffrage. Davies had sent the paper to Wolstenholme to report upon, and so delighted with the manuscript was the latter that she induced the committee of the Manchester Society to print 10,000 copies of it, and to invite its author to become a member of the committee. Not long afterwards Becker succeeded Wolstenholme, who was removing to Congleton in Cheshire, as honorary secretary, afterwards becoming the paid secretary of the Manchester Society, which was already becoming a substantial body and for many years was the leading influence in the women's movement.

The name of Lydia Ernestine Becker was to become for twenty years synonymous in the public mind with the women's suffrage cause. Her paternal grandparents were natives of Thuringia, having settled in England before the birth of their children; her mother was of Lancashire stock, and she herself was born in Cooper Street, Manchester, on 24th February, 1827. Thus she was already what was in those days accounted an " old maid " when she joined the women's movement in 1867. She had written a little manual, *Botany for Novices*, and an unpublished companion volume, *Elementary Astronomy*, and had but recently initiated a Manchester Ladies' Literary Society, for which Charles Darwin had been induced to send a paper, to be read at the inaugural meeting on 30th January, 1867. She had previously written to that most accessible genius on the subject of primroses.

A woman of plain and solid exterior, her heavy features and severely dressed hair appealed to the popular mind as typical of the " strong-minded " woman who wanted to take part in politics. She had received a careful education, both at home and at her uncle's in Germany. Possessing no remarkable gifts of intellect or oratory, she was apt in making a clear, concise statement of her case. She had industry, and great capacity for making use of the services of others, an invaluable quality in an organizer, as well as that strong tenacity of her office and prerogatives, which are found in the successful political official. Her influence on the women's movement was on the whole a narrowing one. Her acceptance of a Suffrage Bill expressly excluding married women caused long-standing division. Entering political life as a Liberal, she became, like many of her successors, embittered against the Liberal Party because of its failure to apply its democratic professions to women. From detestation of reformers she found lacking in sincerity, she proceeded to detestation of reforms, desiring to postpone all legal changes, even those of most vital urgency to women, until after the vote should be won. In opposing all legislation intended for the protection of women in industry, and even with curious virulence, that very minor measure for the legalization of marriage with a deceased wife's sister, she expended the energies which Elizabeth Wolstenholme, Ursula Bright and Josephine Butler devoted to securing positive reforms. In women like these, on the one hand, and in Lydia Becker on the other, were embodied two main tendencies which strove to control the women's movement throughout its history.

When, as her first entry into political life, Lydia Becker joined the Manchester Committee for Women's Suffrage, her opinions were undoubtedly much impressed by the broad libertarian views of the advanced people who had started the women's movement in the industrial north. Especially was she influenced by Dr. Pankhurst. She appealed to him at every turn. His work, and his teaching, which she then followed energetically, speedily gained for the Manchester Society, and for herself as its secretary, the leadership of the Suffrage Movement. Her confident reliance upon his aid, which caused many observers to anticipate a romance which never materialized, is well displayed in the following characteristic letters. The first reveals the reflection of his influence, the second her own narrower view. They are interesting for the light cast on the early beginnings of the Suffrage Movement, and the general effort towards enlarged opportunities for women, as well as for the references to Josephine Butler.

> " MANCHESTER NATIONAL SOCIETY FOR
> WOMEN'S SUFFRAGE,
> " 85 Carter Street, Greenheys.
> " *May 24th.*

" MY DEAR DR. PANKHURST,—Thanks for your letter of this morning. I send you some copies of our paper, and shall be glad if you will distribute them where you think they will be useful, as I do not know what solicitors to send them to, but if you would rather I sent them, return them with a list of names and addresses. I am glad our deputation has had such an effect; it will have been an effective ' coup,' even if it fail in the immediate result we aimed at. This is owing, not only to the strength of our case, but to the skill of our advocate!

" I liked your addition to the report of your speech at our meeting.[1] It aims at the ultimate end to which all efforts at political enfranchisement are introductory—the full recognition of the principle that every human soul is an independent kingdom—nay, a *universe*, over which the individual is sole sovereign. The notion that anyone owes subjection or subordination to another is fatal to the higher life of both ruler and subject. Freedom and equality not only do not prevent self-devotion to the welfare of others, but seem essential to it, essential also to that enlightened and voluntary obedience, which is the only safeguard against anarchy, the only guarantee for the maintenance of peace and order in the Commonwealth.

" I am glad you will be with us on Friday. How about a reporter this time?

" Yours truly,
" L. E. BECKER."

" MANCHESTER NATIONAL SOCIETY FOR
WOMEN'S SUFFRAGE,
" 85 Carter Street, Greenheys.
" *July 17th.*

" MY DEAR DR. PANKHURST,—Please send me the extract from Disraeli's speech. I mean the newspaper cutting containing the debate.

" I should like to see the article in the *Solicitor's Journal.* Perhaps it would be worth while to buy a copy. I suppose it only costs sixpence. Can you procure one? I wonder if the writer who coolly analyses the question, as if it were one of abstract right, understands that women really feel it as a matter of political life or death. I believe men think women do not feel at all, at least that women do not feel as men would if they were similarly treated. Whenever men propose to women to pass their lives under conditions which men would not like for their own lives, they may be sure that women do not like it either and would not submit if they could help themselves.

" Miss Bancroft of St. Anne's Manor is intensely indignant at having no vote. Three of her employés—men who live in small cottages—have votes, and she who pays so large a rent and rates and keeps the three men at work cannot have one. ' It is infamous! ' she says.

---

[1] The meeting here mentioned was the first public meeting ever held for Women's Suffrage. It took place in the Manchester Free Trade Hall Assembly Rooms, April 14th, 1868.

" I shall be *very* glad if you can draft a feasible scheme for a co-operative store or warehouse. There is nothing like buying and selling for making money; and women can buy and sell very well. There is nothing either laborious or ' unfeminine ' in either process. Most of the plans for promoting ' employment for women ' seem to contemplate pursuits requiring bodily labour— handicrafts—the most irksome and least remunerative of all occupations.

" I sent you Mrs. Butler's pamphlet. Tell me what you think of it. The statistics are startling. Nearly 1,000,000 *wives* working for their bread! How many of their husbands live on their wives' earnings, I wonder! The census does not give *that*.

" I wonder whether you can trace in Mrs. Butler's page something of that vivid and far-reaching sympathy with all forms of human suffering which is the great secret of her influence. The circumstances of her life are such as would cause an ordinary woman to limit her *life* to her home. She is most happily married, has three children, and is in such weak health that if she were to make alleviation of her own bodily sufferings her chief care no one could wonder or blame her. But she maintains that it is not the disappointed and the personally unlucky women who feel most keenly the disadvantageous position of their sex; it is the happiest who are most induced to exert themselves for the benefit of others less fortunate, and she is an example of her own theory.

" Can you give the facts without the names of the cases illustrating the difficulties of the present marriage law, or is it a matter of professional confidence?

" I have procured the ' Official Manual.' . . . Miss Boucherett sent me £3 this morning, so I think we shall carry on till the end of the week. I went to collect a subscription promised me by Mr. Binney, solicitor and F.R.S. I was amused at his fright, for he had forgotten how much he had promised me—he is one of those rich people who look at both sides of a penny—and his suspense was something ludicrously touching. I told him I hoped he would give me more than he had promised; and when I revealed that his liability was only five shillings he cried, ' I'll give you ten ' with an alacrity which showed how his imagination had run on to alarming possibilities. I ought to have got at least £1 out of the situation, but am burdened with a conscience, an article a secretary ought to get rid of with all convenient speed.

" Yours truly,
" L.E.B."

In 1866 the destruction of the abortive Reform Bill caused the fall of the Liberal Government. To dish their discomforted rivals, the incoming Tories introduced the Reform Act of 1867, which established Household Suffrage. During the debates on this measure, John Stuart Mill made the first plea for Women's Suffrage ever heard in Parliament. His amendment, " to leave out the word *man*, in order to insert the word *person* instead thereof," was defeated by a majority of 123, but curiously enough an amendment to substitute the phrase *male person* for *man* was also defeated. This was the more remarkable because before the Bill went into Committee the Hon. John Denman, Q.C., had given notice to ask whether, having regard to Lord Romilly's Act, it was the intention of the Government to confer the franchise upon women, as well as men, by the use of the generic term *man*. Disraeli, then Chancellor of the Exchequer and leader of the House of Commons, replied that the matter was one for the lawyers, " the gentlemen of the long robe," a characteristic reply which would scarcely be accepted in these more democratic days. It was true that Lord Romilly's Act had laid down that words of the masculine gender should include women, unless the contrary were expressly provided. " But," he said, " that is, I believe, provided in this instance." Yet the Act contained no provision whatsoever suggesting the exclusion of women from the franchise. Denman again pressed his point in the discussion, declaring that if the Court of Queen's Bench had to decide to-morrow on the construction of the phrase, it would be constrained to hold that the Act had conferred the suffrage upon women. In the election for the City of Manchester on November 26th, 1867, Lily Maxwell, a small shopkeeper, whose name had been placed on the Parliamentary register, recorded her vote for Jacob Bright, no objection being raised by the Returning Officer, or indeed by any person. Her case was regarded as a valuable precedent, proving that if women were under any legal incapacity, it was not of voting, but of being registered as voters.

Dr. Pankhurst urged that the question whether women had been enfranchised by the use of the term " man " should be put to the test. The rest of the Manchester Suffrage Committee was brought to his view, and in the spring of 1868 letters were sent by the Committee to Boards of Overseers in all parts of the country, requesting them in accordance with the change in the law effected by the Act of 1867 to place upon the list of voters all persons, whether men or women, who had fulfilled the necessary qualifications. Deputations from the Committee waited upon the Overseers of the various townships within the Parliamentary Borough of Manchester. The case was argued by Dr. Pankhurst, who took, as he always did, the large and lofty view; in him were no hair-splitting reservations; no dallying with expedients to placate prejudice, by excluding this class of woman or that; none of that condescension as from man to woman, so general in the men of those days, even amongst those who were considered supporters of women's suffrage. He urged :

" We have no true conception of what political liberty means; we have no true idea of its real power in the world until we see that every sane human being . . . shall be enfranchised by the law of the land in which we live. . . . There is one way in which the liberty we have won shall never pass away from us, and it is this : Liberty will be everlasting when liberty is universal : then and then only. The granting of the present application will be a great step to the realization of that postulate."

In arguing that the Act of 1867 had enfranchised women by the use of the word *man*, he submitted that *man* was equivalent in good law with *homo*. In good Latin *homo* did not mean *man* as contradistinguished from *woman*, it meant *human being*. He could not cite a greater historical case, he said, than the one referred to by St. Augustine, *Homo sum : humani nihil a me alienum puto*. When that line from Terence's " Self-Tormentor " was spoken in the Roman theatre, the whole vast audience, composed of representatives from almost every nation in the world, rose with one consent and applauded, attesting thereby their acceptance of the doctrine that everything human had a distinct relation to every man. *Homo* was obviously intended there to mean *human being*. In Roman law the word *man* meant *human being*.

" Suppose you had before you instead of the expression *every man* the words of the Great Charter : ' No free man shall be taken, or imprisoned, or disseized of his freehold, or liberties, or free customs, nor will we pass upon him or condemn him, but by lawful judgement of his peers, or by the law of the land. We will sell to no man, we will not deny or defer to any man either justice or right.' Now suppose a woman came up before you and asked for the protection of the Great Charter, under the definition ' no free man,' would you there say : ' You are without the protection of the Great Charter; you are a woman, and you therefore are not within the definition, and are not within the intention of the Great Charter of our liberties.' If you would, then you would certainly depart from the known and acknowledged ruling of the judges and the law of England. . . . What greater instance, what more commanding precedent could any man cite before you than the Great Charter of our English liberties? " [1]

He pleaded further that though certain clauses in the Great Charter specifically referred to women, yet the phrase *no free man* had always been held to include women. He brought forth precedents for the broad use of the word *man* to include both man and woman, extending from ancient to modern times. By the statute 3 Henry VII, c. 1, it is stated that the heir of a murdered man has the right of appeal, and though only the

[1] Speech to the Cheetham Overseers.

masculine term is used, Lord Coke, in 4th Report, 46, stated that
the right of appeal extended also to the heir of a murdered
woman.   By 25 Edward III the killing of a master is made
treason, " and this extends by construction to a mistress "
(Poulter's case, 11 Rep. 34).   In " Rex v. Stubbs " (2 Term
Reports) it was decided that a woman was entitled to be an
Overseer, the qualification consisting in being a " substantial
householder."   In " Olive v. Ingram " (7 Modern Reports) it
was decided that a woman might fill the office of sexton, and that
women might vote in the election, for it was held that women
came within the definition of " persons paying scot and lot."
One of the judges in that case said :

> " In the election of Members of Parliament women are not now
> admitted, whatever they were formerly . . . as the choice requires
> an improved understanding, which women are not supposed to have."

If that judicial dictum were to be upheld, argued the Doctor, if
it were to be decided that women were by law disqualified on
account of an irremediable defect of mental power, they would
be as much disqualified by the use of the word *person* as by the
use of the word *man*.   To his hearers his contention perhaps
sounded exaggerated; but actually this was the ruling which
the Courts were presently to give; women were not to be
regarded as *persons* in respect of public rights and public functions.   It was bad law, but upheld by the prejudices of the time
and maintained for half a century.

He cited cases to prove that women had voted for Members
of Parliament in ancient times, and that no law or custom
to prevent them doing so existed prior to the use of the phrase
male persons in the Franchise Act of 1832.   In support of the
view that women had been previously disqualified, there was
only the unargued dictum of Lord Coke (4th Institute, p. 5) :

> " In many cases multitudes are bound by Acts of Parliament which
> are not parties to the election of knights, citizens and burgesses, as
> all they that have no freehold, and all women having freehold or no
> freehold, and men within the age of one-and-twenty years."

As to the intention of Parliament in using the term " man "
in the Act of 1867, the Under Secretary at the Home Office had
written on behalf of the Home Secretary, Mr. Gathorne Hardy,
to say that Parliament had no intention of granting votes to
women in the Act of 1867.   It was not, however, good law, to
pronounce upon the intention of Parliament except in view of
what Parliament itself had said.   In support of this assertion he
quoted a number of precedents, including : " The Queen v.
Capel," 12 A and E, 411, wherein Lord Denman declared :

" . . . we were pressed with the history of the introduction of this proviso into the Act in its passage through Parliament. Of such facts, if capable of being ascertained, we are not permitted judicially to take notice. The law must ever be interpreted by the general rules of construction, and we cannot travel out of its language in support of any supposed intention."

These deputations to the Overseers aroused great interest and discussion. When they were ended Lydia Becker wrote:

" 85 Carter Street, Greenheys.
" *June 29th.*

" MY DEAR DR. PANKHURST,—I will call on you early to-morrow for the papers we should have had to-day and to ask you about one or two things.

" I suppose our campaign among the Overseers is over, and I have had it on my mind to endeavour to express to you my sense of gratitude and obligation to you for consenting to act for us, and admiration of the great powers of reasoning and of oratory you have displayed. It has been a hard, uphill fight—against hopeless odds, but if any man could have won—you are he! Though defeated in the immediate objective your efforts will not have been thrown away —they will form the basis of more extended arguments, and will in the end prove to have been a powerful means of accelerating the success, which is, after all, only a question of time.

" You must have bestowed great labours and hard thoughts upon your speeches, and I beg you not to think that we are unconscious of the magnitude of the gift you have so freely and generously made us. It is no light thing that you have done and you must not think that we estimate lightly the cost at which you have done it.

" Your argument about the only legal ground for denying our claim being that of mental imbecility is one that has not been previously dwelt upon and will prove a powerful weapon. Of this I want to speak to you further, and as post time presses will only add another expression of gratitude.

" Yours truly,
" LYDIA E. BECKER."

As a result of the campaign, the Overseers of Salford and twenty-three other townships decided to place all duly qualified women upon the Parliamentary register, but the Manchester Overseers refused. It was therefore decided to canvass the 9,000 women householders in the townships of Manchester, Hulme and Chorlton-on-Medlock, advising them to claim registration. Shortage of time and means prevented a complete canvass, but 3,924 women out of a total of 4,215 (about ninety-two per cent.) sent in claims to be registered as voters in the township of Manchester, and in Chorlton-on-Medlock 1,106 claimed out of 1,850, whilst among the number who failed to claim were included those who had removed. The large proportion of women who claimed was a remarkable demonstration of desire for the vote amongst women at that period.

At the revision courts held in Manchester, on September 14th, 1868, Mr. Hosack, the revising barrister, struck off all the women's names, whereat a case for appeal was applied for, and granted, in which the claims of 5,346 women were consolidated (Chorlton *v*. Lings.) At Rusholme, on September 24th, 1868, Mrs. Max Kyllmann unsuccessfully claimed a vote under the statute 8 Henry VI, which enacts that elections of Knights of the Shire shall be made " in each county by people dwelling and resident therein, of whom each has freehold to the value of forty shillings a year." A case for the higher Court was granted (Chorlton *v*. Kessler). In the Salford court the revising barrister even struck out the names of the women whom the Overseers had placed on the register and to whom no objection had been taken, denying the claims of 1,341 women of Salford and 857 of Broughton and Pendleton. At Leeds the revising barrister went so far as to fine Mrs. Howell ten shillings for making what he termed a " frivolous claim " to be registered. The fine naturally deterred numbers of other women from claiming the vote. On the other hand, in at least twelve different townships the revising barristers decided to leave on the register all women's names not objected to, and in four revision courts it was decided that women were legally entitled to be registered and to vote. Mr. Chisholm Anstey published at this juncture some useful notes[1] on the ancient constitutional rights exercised by women. At Finsbury he decided to retain the name of Jane Allen on the register, basing his decision upon the cases of " Holt *v*. Lyle " and " Colt *v*. Lyle," tried in Westminster Hall in the reign of James I, in which it was decided that a *femme sole* had the right, if a freeholder, to vote for a " Parliament man." Similar decisions were given at Cockermouth, Lydiate, Scarisbrick in Lancashire, and Winterton in Lincolnshire. Whilst the Revision Courts were still in session, the question whether to take the case to the Courts for an authoritative declaration of the law was under discussion. Lydia Becker wrote to Dr. Pankhurst:

" . . . I wrote to Mr. Shaen as you directed. I asked him if he could be quite sure that opinions from Sir R. Palmer, Mr. Coleridge, or [illegible], or any other eminent counsel would be in our favour, to take steps to obtain one, but not to run the smallest risk or do it unless he were perfectly certain it would be right."

[1] *Some Supposed Constitutional Restraints on the Parliamentary Franchise. Notes on the Representation of the People Act* 1867.

When the Revision Courts had given their decisions, Miss Becker became nervous and confided to Dr. Pankhurst her fear of an adverse decision and reluctance to proceed. Ever a fighter, he replied with tactful expressions of respect for her alarms, but with evident intention that the case should go on:

> " St. James's Chambers,
> " Manchester.
> " 13th October, 1868.

" MY DEAR MISS BECKER,—The subject we discussed, and to which you refer in your note, exercises me very much. Certainly I feel keenly the critical character of the position. I saw Mr. Bright to-day and he spoke upon the question with that happy style of his which always converts even when it does not convince.

" For myself, I cannot help feeling that the stopping of proceedings at this point wounds the honour of the movement, and seems a breach of good faith with the public, to whose justice and sense of right we have appealed.

" On the other hand, nothing could be more disastrous than a false step at this moment.

" Still we must remember that if the judges decide that women have no part or place in the constitution, public opinion can create for them that position which judicial decision appears to deny.

" In sum, I will give the matter the best consideration I can, so that I may be able to vote in such a way that be the final issue of our policy what it may I have the satisfaction of knowing that that issue arose only after conscientious reflection.

" With regard to the annual meeting . . ."

His view prevailed; the case went forward. Four days before the hearing, *The Times,* in a leading article, observed that if the claim of the woman householder was refused:

" The nation will, no doubt, be formally and in the light of day committing itself, through its judicial tribunal, to the dangerous doctrine that representation need not go along with taxation."

The claim was heard by Lord Chief Justice Bovill and Justices Willes, Keating and Byles in the Court of Common Pleas on November 7th, 1869. Dr. Pankhurst had prepared the case with unsparing toil, Sir J. D. Coleridge, Q.C. (afterwards Lord Chief Justice) was retained to impress the Court by his eminence in the Manchester cases, and J. A. Russell, Q.C., for the women claimants of Salford, Broughton, and Pendleton. Only one case was heard, that of Mary Abbott, a householder of Manchester (Chorlton *v.* Lings). Lord Coleridge urged:

" Women have this right at the common law, they have in ancient times exercised it, and no statute has ever taken it away. . . .

" The great point which will doubtless be made on the other side is that for centuries no woman as a fact has voted. . . . But it is hardly necessary to maintain that if the right once existed non-user could not take it away."[1]

As to the Act of 1832, in which the phrase " male persons " had been introduced for the first time:

" If we compare the phraseology of the sections, I think we must conclude that where women already had votes, as freeholders or burgesses, they were meant to retain them; but that where fresh votes were conferred on copyholders, then women copyholders were not to acquire the right of voting, but men only were to do so. The late Reform Act (1867), I contend, leaves the rights of women as compared with those of men where it found it.

" As to . . . the interpretation of the word ' man ' as used in the Representation of the People Act, 1867, we must remember that Lord Romilly's Act was passed in 1850, some time after the Reform Act of 1832, and therefore at a time when the claims of women to vote had at least been heard of and discussed in modern times. Lord Romilly's Act may therefore have been passed with a consciousness that it might very probably be employed before long to the very purpose to which I seek to apply it to-day."

In support of these contentions ancient statutes were cited governing elections to Parliament. 7 Henry IV, c. 15, provided that knights should be elected to Parliament at the county court where the freeholders were judges, by " suitors duly summoned for the same cause as other." Women attended as suitors. The Statute of Marlbridge, 52 Henry III, c. 10, excused bishops, abbots, barons, and also nuns and others from attendance at the election of Members of Parliament in case of urgent necessity. 8 Henry IV, 6, c. 7, restricted the right to vote in counties to forty shilling freeholders, but in the Norman French the term *gens*, which could include women, was employed. 7 Henry VI, c. 15, provided that the names of the persons chosen for Parliament should " be written in an indenture under the names of all them that did choose them." Copies of such indentures were brought from the Record Office to which women were signatories dating from 13 Henry IV; 2 Henry V; 7 Edward VI; 1 and 2 Philip and Mary; 2 and 3 Philip and Mary. In the last case the only signatory was a woman. A copy was given from Heyward's treatise on County Elections of the return for a borough of Dame Dorothy Packington in 14 Elizabeth. A burgess and freemen's roll of 19 Elizabeth for the borough of Lyme Regis in which three women were named as burgesses and freemen was cited from Luders. In reply to the dictum of Coke that women were debarred from voting, Coleridge observed that all the other

[1] *Weekly Reporter*, 59 Carey Street, Lincoln's Inn, W.C.

instances of persons disabled from voting cited by Coke in the
same passage were in fact erroneous. Names of the clergy whom
he averred might not vote, were actually found amongst the
indentures of which copies had been brought into Court, the
clergy having surrendered the right to tax themselves before Coke
wrote. Said Coleridge:

" I have the most unfeigned respect for Lord Coke's learning,
but he had his weaknesses like other men, and one of them may
have been a dislike for the clergy. He had no special reason to
like women.

" All great constitutional writers make English freedom to
depend to a great extent on the connection between the right to vote
and the liability to taxation, why are women to form a striking
and unfair exception to this rule? "

These arguments failed to impress the Bench. Chief Justice
Bovill observed:

" A few instances have been brought before us where in ancient
times, namely, in the reigns of Henry IV, Henry V and Edward IV,
women appear to have been parties to the return of Members of
Parliament, and possibly other instances may be found in early times
not only of women having voted, but also of their having assisted
in the deliberations of the Legislature. Indeed it is mentioned by
Selden in his *England's Epinomis*, C. II, S. 19, that they did so. But
these instances are of comparatively little weight as opposed to
uninterrupted usage to the contrary for several centuries."

Justice Willes, the Master of the Rolls, added:

" In modern and more civilized times, out of respect for women,
and by way of decorum . . . they are excluded from taking any
part in popular assemblies, or in the election of Members of
Parliament."

The other judges concurred and the appeal was dismissed. When
the case of Chorlton *v.* Kessler came up, the Court refused to hear
it, on the ground that the issue had been decided in Chorlton *v.*
Lings. Dr. Pankhurst pleaded:

" It is so great a subject; there is so much to urge. It involves
so vast a mass of material . . ."

The Times reported that he was interrupted by laughter; the
judges would hear no more.

The attempt to win Votes for Women through the law courts
had failed. A General Election was now in progress. Next day
every candidate received a letter from Lydia Becker, on behalf of
the Manchester Society, stating that as the decision of the Courts
had been adverse, a Bill would now be introduced into Parliament establishing the right of women to vote on the same terms

as men. The letters had been separately copied by the ladies of the committee, and Becker had telegraphed, " Post your letters," as soon as she left the Court. So laborious was propaganda in those days; typewriting, shorthand, and duplicating machines were not yet regarded as the common necessity of every reform organization.

The Women's Disabilities' Removal Bill, drafted by Dr. Pankhurst, was now introduced, and so began the forty years' Parliamentary struggle.

" *A Bill to remove the electoral Disabilities of Women.*—Be it enacted by the Queen's most excellent Majesty, by and with the advice and consent of the Lords Spiritual and Temporal and Commons in the present Parliament assembled, and by the authority of the same as follows :—

" That in all Acts relating to the qualification and registration of voters, or persons entitled or claiming to be registered and to vote in the election of Members of Parliament, wherever words occur which import the masculine gender, the same shall be held to include females for all purposes connected with and having reference to the right to be registered as voters, and to vote in such election, any law or usage to the contrary notwithstanding."

John Stuart Mill having been defeated in the election of '68, Jacob Bright took charge of the Bill; but before it was introduced a remarkable triumph had been recorded. Prior to 1835 women had from time immemorial possessed and exercised the right to vote in local affairs; but in that year the Municipal Corporations Act had employed the phrase " male persons," in imitation of the Parliamentary Franchise Act of 1832. Even after the year 1835 women continued voting in the municipal elections of non-corporate towns, as they did throughout the country for Boards of Guardians and in vestry meetings. Mr. Lings, the Comptroller for the City of Manchester, declared that in proportion to their numbers they voted as freely as men. On the introduction of the Municipal Corporations Bill in 1869, Dr. Pankhurst drafted an amendment to include women, Jacob Bright moved it, and it was carried without a word of dissent. As Dr. Pankhurst said:

" There were high men in Parliament who would have scouted the notion of giving the Parliamentary franchise to women, but they did not take much part in Municipal affairs themselves, and, there-fore, they decided that it would not perhaps be too much to give the Municipal franchise to women."

Unfortunately thirty years were allowed to pass before any attempt was made to secure the election of women to municipal bodies. When the attempt was finally made, it was found that non-user had permitted another barrier of prejudice to grow up, barring the right naturally implied by enfranchisement. Appeal to the Courts resulted in defeat.

In 1870 the prospects of the franchise cause seemed wholly fair. The Manchester City Council had memorialized Parliament in support of the Suffrage Bill, and petitions with 134,561 signatures of private persons had been sent in by the Suffrage Societies which had now been formed in many principal towns. The Second Reading of the Bill was carried with cheers, by 124 votes to 91. The Cause seemed won. The Home Secretary had stated that the Government had not had time to consider the question and was therefore unable to guide the House; but now that a favourable vote thereon had been recorded the " high men in Parliament " intervened. When Jacob Bright moved for the Bill to go into Committee, the Cabinet had issued an urgent whip against it, and Gladstone himself was present to oppose it :

" I think I may say for most of my colleagues, as well as for myself, that we felt something more than surprise—that we felt disappointment—at the result arrived at on Wednesday last. We do not attempt to limit the freedom of anyone on such a subject, either within the official body or elsewhere; but undoubtedly it is an opinion prevailing among us—and one which I for one strongly entertain, in common with all those now sitting near me—that it would be a very great mistake to carry this Bill into law."

Jacob Bright again introduced the Women's Suffrage Bill in 1871; again Gladstone procured its defeat, protesting that the personal attendance and intervention of women in Parliamentary election proceedings would be " a practical evil of an intolerable character." Some day he might be prepared to permit them to vote by proxy, but not now. Disraeli spoke and voted for the Bill, but when he presently came to power, his Government also proved hostile. In 1872 the Bill was again out-voted.

So began half a century of Ministerial opposition, implacably maintained by the Governments of both political parties. Gladstone had expressly forbidden the members of his Government to vote for the Bill. His wry assumption of neutrality, in the phrase : " We do not attempt to limit the freedom of anyone," was to receive elaborate development in time to come. The Bill, so lately approved, was now defeated by 220 votes to 94. The potentialities of the Suffragette Anti-Government Policy were already born.

In spite of these repeated rebuffs in relation to the Parliamentary Franchise, the Education Act of 1870 had given to women the right of voting for the newly-created School Boards. They immediately offered themselves for election, and, as we have seen, Lydia Becker and others were returned.

More important still, in the year 1870 the first of the Married Women's Property Acts made the first breach in the iniquitous institution " coverture," the legal convention that a married woman, being assumed to be under the protection of her husband, was without legal existence, and could neither be sued nor sue, even under most flagrant injury. Having, by legal fiction, no existence as a separate entity, she was without redress against assault, libel, fraud, or other harm. She had no right in her children, her earnings or property by gift or inheritance. Foremost amongst the pioneers against this grievous condition was the long-suffering Caroline Norton, beautiful and talented, who in her own person, and through her children, suffered every iniquity of the law. The struggle commenced by her in 1855 gathered up most of such notable men and women of the time as were desirous of raising the depressed status of woman; for in the degradation of married women all womanhood was involved. Outstanding amongst the practical workers were Elizabeth Wolstenholme, Ursula Bright and Dr. Pankhurst, who from the first was active on the Council of the Social Science Association in preparing and working for the Bill which became the Act of 1870, and though grossly mutilated, gave women the right, hitherto denied, to possess their own earnings after marriage.

After the Act of 1870 had been won, came a period of great discouragement. Many who had worked for the principle now suspended all effort, content with this first imperfect instalment. Lydia Becker, at that time treasurer of the Married Women's Property Committee, was amongst the seceders. She wrote to Mrs. Elmy, its secretary, urging suspension of its activity.

" Manchester.

" *March 1st*, 1874.

" DEAREST,—I am sorry about the decision respecting M.W.P., chiefly because I think it has been adopted : (1) in disregard of the fact that Staveley Hill's Bill is not *imperfect*, but *retrograde*; (2) with reference to the prospect of introducing the Bill next year. Should Staveley Hill's or Morley's Bill pass I should be strongly averse to any attempt to re-open the question in the House of Commons *until women have votes. I am convinced that any such attempt would only retard the period of a settlement of the question on a just basis.* To my mind the question lies between seizing the opportunity of going in for a just Bill while Parliament is considering the question, or letting the whole matter lie over till the Suffrage Bill is passed. *If we look at the Parliamentary strength of the questions we see at once how far behind is M.W.P. You do not count more than 68 supporters—and every one of the Government who has voted at all is adverse, while on the suffrage question we have 217 supporters. We have two to one of the Members of the House of Commons who are in the Cabinet, and a clear majority of the subordinate Members of the Government.* It is a remarkable fact, brought out by your analysis, that *not one* member of the Government has given a vote on our side in any other women's question—and that a *majority* vote for the suffrage. That is *an unmistakable indication of which question is the right one to push while the present Government retain office.* I fear it will be very difficult to raise funds for M.W.P. with no Bill. I will try to get something from Mrs. Watts again and then I think the best plan would be to pay off our liabilities and rest on our oars. Of course we shall not have to spend so much with no Bill, but the other Bill will need to be carefully watched. Did you see a report of the case just decided that a married woman cannot be made a bankrupt! I will send the analysis back to-morrow. I have filled up the votes given in the late Parliament.

"Yours ever,
"L. E. BECKER.

"We are *very* glad Mr. Forsyth[1] has taken the Suffrage Bill."

Events completely falsified the predictions contained in this letter. Lydia Becker's colleagues on the Married Women's Property Committee were fully alive to the nature of Staveley Hill's measure. In spite of her defection they attacked, defeated it, and continued their work to complete legislative success. Dr. Pankhurst drafted a new Bill, which became the basis of the Act of 1882, acting as honorary counsel to the Committee, and active in platform and propaganda effort. Mrs. Elmy strove with the doubts and vacillations of legislators in the lobbies of Parliament. Ursula Bright, with her gracious charm, dined them and argued them into support. Eight years saw the legislative completion of their task, though more than half a century was to elapse before the franchise question was disposed of.

The Conservatives had taken power in 1874, Jacob Bright had lost his seat, and, as indicated in the postscript to her letter, Lydia Becker had passed the Suffrage Bill he had sponsored to a Conservative member, named Forsyth, who proposed to add to it a clause expressly excluding married women from the vote. Lydia Becker at first refused, but afterwards assented to the proposal, and fought for it against her earlier colleagues, Pankhurst, Wolstenholme, and Jacob Bright, who regarded the clause as a serious blow at their struggle against the enslavement of married women, and opposed it as a great wrong and a great folly. Despite all argument Becker carried the majority of the Suffrage Society executive with her, relying on the more retrograde elements in London. The result was a breach, which

---

[1] The Conservative Member of Parliament who insisted upon attaching to the Suffrage Bill a clause excluding married women from its provisions.

widened as the years went by; and in the long run, largely drove from co-operation with the original women's suffrage organization the most ardent and energetic of the early pioneers.

The Suffrage Movement was honeycombed with people—women as well as men—who themselves were prepared to go only a small part of the way towards complete social equality for women. Though thus half-hearted in their views, many of these persons came to occupy official positions in the movement, because they possessed means and leisure. Thus we find Helen Blackburn, in her *Record of Women's Suffrage*,[1] arguing that the eligibility of women to elective office

" forms no part of the women's suffrage question. The right to vote is the symbol of that freedom from which no human being should be debarred . . . eligibility for office is a question of individual adaptability for the performance of special duties."

The women's movement, in short, passed from timidity to timidity. Its opponents were prejudiced; many of its protagonists only less prejudiced. Obstruction from within the movement itself was a factor with which the broad-minded pioneer spirits had always to contend.

The moment was peculiarly inopportune for adopting the limiting clause. Though the Married Women's Property Act of 1870 had struck a strong blow at coverture in respect of property, the Courts still upheld it in respect of the franchise. Objection had been taken to the votes of two married women in a Sunderland municipal election. The case had been taken to Court (Regina *v.* Harrald). Sir John Cockburn had decided that a married woman was still " sui juris "; that is to say not a person in the eye of the law, notwithstanding the Act of 1870. It was hoped to reverse this decision by the passage of a new and wider Act, giving married women all the powers of which they were still deprived. At this moment, when the decision in Regina *v.* Harrald had made agitation for the married woman's status at once more hopeful and more imperative, came the demand of Lydia Becker to close down the Married Women's Property agitation, and the grafting of the Forsyth clause on the Bill drafted by Pankhurst and hitherto sponsored by Jacob Bright. Becker won the latter point with her executive, but the narrower Bill met no greater success than its predecessors. Hostile majorities were recorded against it in 1875 and 1876. Gladstone had now retired from the Liberal leadership, but John Bright rallied Liberal opponents to the Bill, declaiming against it, with the very arguments he had opposed in defending the

[1] P. 204 (Williams & Norgate).

enfranchisement of working men. The Tory opponents, whose party was now in office, needed no spur to vote it down.

Jacob Bright, returned at a by-election, again took charge of the Bill in 1877, dropping, of course, the obnoxious coverture clause. On the eve of the Second Reading, a deputation of suffrage women waited on Sir Stafford Northcote, Chancellor of the Exchequer, and leader of the House of Commons now that Disraeli had removed to the Lords. Northcote told them he did not consider the time opportune for re-opening the franchise question. The Bill was talked out amid the uproar of its opponents, who drowned the voice of Leonard Courtney, speaking in its support. In 1878 the Bill was again defeated. In 1879 it had no place; and a resolution drawn on similar lines was moved as the only thing left to do. Sir Stafford Northcote announced his intention to vote against the resolution, alleging that to support it would pledge the Government to bring in a measure to that effect. Yet he cast a sop to the women, which seemed important at the time, telling them that as they had shown themselves in the local elections " neither unworthy nor incapable," " at a fitting time " he would be prepared to assent to their Parliamentary enfranchisement. Suffragists hailed his statement as a pledge by the Conservative Government to include women in the next extension of the franchise. *The Times* said:

" This engagement is not definite, but it is no small triumph that it should have been obtained . . . when the claims of the agricultural labourers are to be satisfied, and when the time thus arrives for a great re-casting of the electoral scheme, the case of the women may be thrown into the crucible with the rest."

The Movement had now grown to substantial proportions. In the two previous years between 1,300 and 1,400 public indoor meetings had been held, 9,563 petitions for women's suffrage with 2,953,848 signatures had been presented to Parliament; no small effort for the women of those days, inured to retirement, and dreading the sound of their own voices on the platform. Lydia Becker herself deplored, in many a letter, her excessive nervousness, and thought she was making herself " ridiculous " by speaking in public. She hoped " Mr. Mill would be pleased."

From this time forward, however, year by year, the suffrage prospect worsened. When Gladstone returned to power in 1880, Jacob Bright had been obliged by ill-health to surrender the Bill. It passed to Leonard Courtney, who abandoned it when he became a Government Under Secretary in 1881, for Gladstone would by no means permit him to continue its sponsor. Another Liberal, Hugh Mason, then accepted the charge, but as he was already pledged to a Bill on some other question, he introduced for the women only a resolution; it was crowded out by Government business, doubtless with intent, and did not reach debate till 1883. Mason was but a halting believer in the Cause, and expressly excluded married women from his proposal, saying he had " not the slightest sympathy " with those who would enfranchise them. Gladstone and John Bright were present to vote the resolution down. It was defeated by a majority of sixteen. The Attorney-General, on the Government's behalf, declared that he would give a most earnest vote against the motion; the opinion of men was valuable in politics, because they were able " one and all to contribute something of a peculiar and particular knowledge," on law, trade and commerce, armies and war:

" To any one of these subjects can women contribute any experience? (Cries of ' No.') She can tell us no doubt of her great experience of domestic life, but unhappily for us that is not a subject with which we have to deal here."

He little knew that ere long women would be urging the enlarging scope of domestic legislation by Parliament as the strongest argument for their vote. How tremendously the field of Parliamentary activity has been extended since that time!

BOOK II

CHAPTER I

EMMELINE GOULDEN

AMONGST those who had rallied to the side of Dr. Pankhurst in the peace movement was Robert Goulden, a master cotton spinner and bleacher of Salford. Goulden was a " self-made " man. His mother, a notable character, had been a fustian cutter. She had sent her husband to the great franchise meeting on St. Peter's Fields, Manchester, in 1819, which became famous as the massacre of Peterloo. When the cavalry burst upon the people, striking them right and left with their swords, he fled with the multitude from the field. Chased by soldiers down a blind alley, he rushed into a cellar dwelling and took refuge in somebody's bed, pulling the blankets over him. Already as a youth old Goulden had been a victim of the " Press Gang," and had returned after many years to find no trace of family or friends.

Later, in " the hungry 'forties," when agitation arose against the Corn Laws and Cobden formed the Anti-Corn Law League, Mary Goulden became a member of the League, taking her husband with her. Their membership cards, with the inscription, " Give us this day our daily bread," have been preserved.

Robert, their only son, began work as errand boy in one of Manchester's largest manufacturing and merchant firms, reached a junior partnership therein, and afterwards branched forth as a manufacturer, first in partnership, and finally on his own account. Brilliant and impulsive, he was an enthusiastic amateur actor, much admired in Manchester's old Athenæum Society for his portrayal of great Shakespearian characters. In addition to his several business enterprises, he had opened the Prince of Wales's Theatre, Salford, rather from love of the drama than from pecuniary motives. He had married a Manxwoman, Jane Quine, and they had a family of five sons and five daughters. His eldest daughter, Emmeline, was the apple of his eye. Lively and precocious, tradition has it that she was able to read at three years of age, and her mother was fond of telling that at that tender age she had found her seated behind the window curtain reading *The*

Lamp of Love. Her father used to set her to read his morning
paper to him, and declared it a pity she was not a boy. She read
before she was twelve everything she could lay hands on, Bunyan's
Pilgrim's Progress and *Holy War* and Carlyle's *French Revolution*
making a lasting impression on her. Her father was a Liberal
and an ardent upholder of the North in the American Civil War.
He sat on the Committee appointed to welcome Henry Ward
Beecher when he came to lecture in Manchester, and the little
Emmeline was given a lucky bag to collect for the fund raised to
relieve the poverty of the emancipated slaves. Her mother was
thrilled by the romantic stories of the emancipation struggle then
current, and particularly by Harriet Beecher Stowe's novel, *Uncle
Tom's Cabin*. These were the talk of the home for many years
after the slaves were freed. Amid the discussions of Liberalism
and emancipation which whirled about her, the hero of her
childish heart was nevertheless Charles I.

Her first instruction was at a dame school. When she was
thirteen her father took her to Paris and placed her in the Ecole
Normale in the Avenue de Neuilly. Arriving during the
holidays she found in the school one solitary pupil, Noémie, the
beautiful daughter of Henri Rochefort, then exiled in New
Caledonia. The two girls became room companions, and what
the girls of their day called " bosom friends." Gone was the
vision of Charles I from the ardent mind of the young Emmeline;
in his place was set the Marquis de Rochefort-Lucay, who
refused to bear the title of his rank, the duellist and Communist,
who had narrowly escaped execution for his part in the Commune
the previous year. His subsequent escape in an open boat, and
the tales of his adventurous life she heard from his daughter,
stirred her to the core; adventure and excitement were ever the
lodestar of her being. It was the year after the Franco-German
war; she imbibed from the Parisians a hatred of Germany which
she never lost. Knowing on her arrival not a word of French,
she was unable to profit by the excellent curriculum of the school.
Moreover the change of climate caused some slight indisposition,
and the visiting physician, who perhaps set no great store by the
education of girls, advised that she should not be kept sitting in
class, but allowed to run about and amuse herself. With Noémie,
who seems to have enjoyed a like freedom, she took full advantage
of this permission. Paris was ever after the city of her desire.
To her, French dress, cooking, hotels and railways, French
women, the French language and literature, anything and everything French were the best in the world. She was soon able to
chatter with fluency and read an inordinate number of novels.

After her own Paris school days were over, she was permitted to return there with her younger sister, Mary. Noémie Rochefort was now married to a young Swiss artist named Dufaux, and she ardently desired that her friend Emmeline should marry and settle beside her in Paris. Emmeline was as eager as she, and Noémie, with this object, approached a man of letters, who declared himself exceedingly willing to marry the charming English Miss, provided she would bring him a suitable " dot." Anticipating no difficulty, the girls were now entirely confident that their wish was to be fulfilled, but when Robert Goulden was acquainted with the proposal, he flew into a passion and declared that he would not " sell " his daughter to any man. On learning that there was to be no " dot " the suitor promptly retired, protesting to the young lady that she had broken his heart and spoiled his life. She herself was indignant that her father had refused to provide her with a dowry. Her lively recollection of the breakfast-table scenes he was accustomed to make when her mother presented the household bills had given his daughter a strong desire to possess an income in her own right when she herself should enter the state of matrimony. She was disappointed that she had been deprived of the chance of a marriage which would have settled her in delightful Paris beside her friend. Yet she parted from her suitor without a shade of grief; her affections had not been engaged. She remained an advocate of the " dot " and the French system of marriage by arrangement. Indeed, she was altogether surprised when I, as a young girl, protested : " How horrible to marry without love, a person chosen by other people— for money ! " In spite of such theories, it was not long before she was going her own way to a marriage of love, with an impetuosity which would have brooked no restraint.

She was home again in Manchester; the city was in the throes of the peace agitation of 1878. Dr. Pankhurst was the name in every mouth about her. Her father admired him and followed him. " I was charmed with him; he was so eloquent ! " her mother said. As to herself—the first she saw of the Doctor was his hand, " a beautiful hand," opening the door of the cab in which he was arriving at some great meeting. When he appeared, rejoicing in his mission, and irradiating the fervour of his hopeful convictions, greeted with cheers and waving of hats and handkerchiefs by expectant thousands, her thoughts were set on fire.

She was astonished, as she told me long after, when he appeared to notice her. She had thought he would regard her only as an ignorant child; she, an ill-educated girl of twenty; he, twice her age, a distinguished scholar with a record of twenty years of public service. Yet with her svelte figure, her beautiful violet blue eyes, her clear olive skin with the warm flush in her cheeks, her jet black hair, and those perfectly arched, finely pencilled black eyebrows, that golden voice which lent a graciousness to her lightest word, and that indefinable and never failing charm she bore throughout her life; she was lovely enough to win the heart of any man.   What pretty clothes she wore, and how well she knew to wear them, so that they seemed wholly artless in their grace, although they were the subject of her endless interest and care!   The coquettish little bonnet, pretending to be staid and matronly, but making her look even younger than her years; the knot of scarlet ribbon in her hair, appearing to have been put there quite carelessly, and from pure enthusiasm for the Liberal Cause; how they became her!   The quick eagerness of her response to his enthusiasm would have touched a sterner heart than his.   Poetic, beauty loving and ardent as he was, he could not choose but come down from the cold, bright heights of his great endeavours to be her wooer.   Her mother accused her of " throwing herself at him," of failure to maintain a proper maidenly reserve, telling her of the firm rebuffs and persistent coldness with which she herself had received her prospective husband's attentions.   It mattered not: to her lover Emmeline was the very perfection of womankind.   His courtship was mingled with high discourse on important themes, in which a foremost place was accorded to the legal disabilities of women.   The agitation for the Married Women's Property Act was in full swing.   She proposed that they should manifest both their independence of spirit and their solidarity with the sufferings of unhappy wives, by dispensing with legal formalities in their own marriage.   He doubtless had spoken to her of Mary Wollstonecraft and of Shelley, and so, unconsciously, had led her to this thought.   He greeted her suggestion with ardent respect; but he shrank from exposing her, young as she was, to a position which might occasion her inconvenience or distress.   Like other early protagonists of women's emancipation, he had abundant reason to be alive to this; for however orthodox their conduct might be, the tongue of opposing slander had been ever ready to suggest that they might have some illicit sexual motive for espousing so queer a cause.   In that day, public sentiment was apt to be virulent against anyone who dared to question the virtue of the marriage laws.   I have often heard him say, in later years, that people who had displayed unconventionality in that direction, had usually been prevented from doing effective public work in any other.   Her parents naturally re-enforced his view.   The marriage took place in legal form.

His father had recently died; the death of his mother now

left him in a deserted home. He was bowed with grief, and seemed to be breaking down under the strain of his tremendous activities. The wedding was hastened on account of his loneliness. Few were informed, few invited. The bridal orange blossom was adjudged unsuitable. The brown velvet dress, which had been made for the young bride by Messrs. Kendal Milne, was delivered at the last moment. She wept to find it had been garnished by a row of brass buttons down the front, which made her look, she thought, " like a little page-boy." Her bridegroom was wholly oblivious of such mundane matters. Only the tender sorrow of his bereavement shadowed the perfection of his joy. She, too, was largely entranced, and when on the eve of her wedding her mother came to her room, saying : " I want to talk to you," she answered : " I do not want to listen." She did not wish the glamour he had cast upon their wooing to be intruded upon by one who had postponed the instruction she might have given until the eleventh hour.

After the wedding her husband's sister, Bess, solemnly warned her to keep him out of politics, and to concentrate on advancing him in his profession, so that he might become a judge. The advice fell on indignant ears, the young wife regarding it as the grossest treason.

Marriage with a scholar was to prove something of a trial to her in the early days, before she had gathered her own circle of companionships and interests. She confided to him her desire to repair the deficiencies of her education, and he, with care and zeal, prepared a course of reading for her instruction; but she was not a student. From her childhood she had read copiously, but mainly novels. Her attention would wander from the serious volumes he had chosen for her. She would go to him, as he pored over his books, wholly engrossed. Gently he would give her his unoccupied hand and proceed unpausing with his work. Perhaps with regret, certainly with finality, she early abandoned the quest of learning, and devoted herself to practical matters, winning from him a cordial, demonstrative appreciation in all her efforts. As a compliment to her husband, she was co-opted to the Married Women's Property Committee, finding herself the youngest and least informed of its members.

In 1880 her first child was born. She was eager to be a mother, and threw herself with characteristic energy into the labours of maternity. Subsequent children, when she was beginning to find a place in her husband's public work, were handed over to a nurse, but this first darling was her own charge. As it is reported of the infant that she was the only one of the five who slept much and cried little, we may take it that she was efficiently handled. The baby was called Christabel, the Doctor's choice, and by their joint agreement, Harriette, after his much loved sister. In May, 1882, came a second child, myself. Mrs. Pankhurst called her Estelle, the Doctor added Sylvia, and the minx at an early age would only respond to the latter name. Hitherto they had lived at Old Trafford; they now moved to the house of my maternal grandparents, Seedley Cottage, Pendleton, on the outskirts of Salford, where a third child, Henry Francis Robert, called Frank, was born in February, 1884. The girls had been named from the heroines of Coleridge and Shakespeare, the boy bore the names of his grandfathers.

Of Seedley, where we stayed till some time before the birth of my sister Adela Constantia Mary, in June, 1885, I have many clear recollections. There was the wonderful Christmas panto-mime produced by our four aunts and five uncles—how clever they were!—in which I, a flaxen-haired toddler, was given the part of Cinderella, and Christabel was the prince. My ball dress, of pink tulle, with a stiff little ballet skirt, came out of a monster cracker, and two of my uncles transformed themselves into an elephant to carry me to the ball. Everything was on a large scale at Seedley. Grandmother, brought up on a Manx farm, was the typical old-fashioned bustling housewife, working amongst her maids, in a household producing its own butter and bread, jams and pickles, where laundering was an art, and a sewing woman came in for weeks of garment-making at appropriate seasons. I have an odd recollection of grandmother coming into the nursery to take Christabel to the kitchen for the cake-making, I left behind on the knee of our nurse, Susannah Jones. I can dimly see my sister returning with a little piece of dough, made grey by grimy little fingers; of her sticking into it an orange pip, and putting it on the hob beside the fire; of her subsequent discovery that the dough had become a nice little apple tart, of her pleasure therein, and the thought: "How can she be deceived?" Susannah had spoken to us of the doll's-house of our young aunt, Ada, who was about twelve years old at the time, and of its wonderful dolls. I remember being taken to see them, their bodies of white calico, stuffed with sawdust, their heads and the lower part of their arms and legs of white pot, rudely daubed with paint. The Scotsman, Aunt Ada's favourite, which had been specially eulogized, was put into my hands, so limp and ugly, the calico half of his legs showing beneath his kilt. Christabel reached out to take him from me. I saw Aunt Ada fearful lest between us he should be injured. I handed him over with readiness, wondering how anyone could care for so poor an object, disappointed by his ugliness.

I remember the dreadful morning when I was running away from Christabel, we two alone in the breakfast-room, running away round the big dining-table, with its massive claw foot, as fast as my lesser legs would carry me; running, in a dizzy blindness, till I fell into the great fireplace, my head on a big, black block of coal, my hand and arm in the glowing fire. Only the lavishness of old-fashioned Lancashire fire-making had placed there that block which saved my life. Creeping quietly into the room, very late for breakfast, afraid of encountering a father who was a martinet in regard to punctuality, my Aunt Effie found, to her horror, one little niece sitting silent in dumb amazement, the other lying silent upon the fire. Hers was the first sharp cry of terror. She seized me in her arms, and there was hasty running through the grounds to my grandfather's bleachworks, for the first aid requisites always kept at hand there. I had to wear my arm in a sling, my nails came off, and my uncles called me " Little Briton," because I did not scream when the burns were dressed. They gave me a small black rabbit to console me; but to my grief, it soon died, making upon me an impression of awe and sorrow lasting through childhood. They buried it for me in the garden with a little headstone over its grave.

The accident was one of three, which perhaps accentuated in me a strong reluctance for active sports, inherited from both parents, and a tendency towards nervous despondency, perhaps implanted by their strenuous lives. It was after we had left Seedley, when our mother was in bed with the fourth little new-born baby, Adela, three years and a month younger than myself, that I cut my head open by striking it on a trestle table when I was running to fetch a sponge for Susannah. The doctor—I still remember his shepherd's plaid trousers—stitched up the wound, which left a life-long scar. Some months later I had a blow on the hip which caused a slight permanent crookedness. We were enjoined as children to make no fuss over our injuries. Having been exhorted to fortitude, I had schooled myself to practise it. I lay on the floor till I could control myself, and told no one of the blow. Only when Susannah bathed us that evening was a swelling discovered. My mother could not believe it possible that I had so hurt myself without complaining. She took me to the doctor, who assured her the swelling was caused by a blow.

CHAPTER II

THE Eastern crisis had left behind it many animosities. The Rev. Paxton Hood was ousted from the pulpit of Cavendish Street Chapel because he had preached three sermons against Imperialism and war. Dr. Pankhurst and his father-in-law, Robert Goulden, were amongst those who provided him with an extemporized congregation in the Hulme town hall, and arranged for him an honourable send-off when he accepted an appointment in the United States. The rich Imperialists of the Liberal Association, who had been vanquished by the Peace party during the crisis, now struggled to recover their ascendancy. Abel Heywood, one of the most popularly esteemed of Manchester worthies, a pacifist in the crisis, who had twice contested Manchester for Parliament in the Liberal interest, though almost unanimously adopted by the representative Council of the Liberal Association for the election of 1880, was thrust aside in favour of an Imperialist Whig, whose sponsor modestly described him as " a gentleman we have not seen here for some time." Dr. Pankhurst maintained the contest with the Imperialists in the Liberal Association till peace was assured and Gladstone returned to power; then, tired of the strife, he withdrew to advocate his own policy independently. In 1878 he had published an address on " The Future of Liberalism," giving his view of the reforms which should occupy " the next page in the history of Liberal legislation." In July, 1883, he resigned his membership of the Liberal Association, and announced that he would stand as an Independent candidate at the next General Election.

At that time Manchester was an undivided constituency represented by three Members. Since 1832 it had been contested unsuccessfully by William Cobbett, Gladstone and Ernest Jones, and though it had accepted John Bright, it had afterwards rejected him. It now returned two Liberals and a Conservative. The Liberals had no intention of running a third candidate : the Doctor would therefore have what was virtually a straight fight with the Tory. He published a characteristic programme : the removal from the constitution of all non-representative elements; adult suffrage for both sexes; payment, or rather indemnity of Members for loss of time and expense incurred in the public service, and indemnity on precisely the same terms and at the same rate for Ministers of State; Church disestablishment and disendowment; the cessation of religious privilege or disability in regard to public institutions and functions; and free, compulsory, elementary education; nationalization of the land; Home Rule for Ireland; transfer from the executive to the legislature of the power of peace and war and the making of Treaties, and an international tribunal, submission to which on the part of all nations would at first be voluntary. He forecasted " the United States of Europe " and thereafter " an International Commonwealth " of the world. He advocated an immediate saving of £30,000,000 in the cost of government, by an improved land system, drastic naval reductions and the reduction of the army to a small force only maintained for training a volunteer army.

Two months after the issue of this programme, an unexpected by-election occurred through the death of the Conservative Member for Manchester. Pankhurst immediately announced his intention to enter the contest. Surprise was expressed that he did not wait till he had created an organization to support him. He did not, however, rely on organization, but on the virtue of the principles he maintained. He elected to abide by the provisions of the new Corrupt Practices Act, which was not yet in force, and which precluded the hiring of vehicles to take voters to the poll, and the use of paid canvassers, and set a limit upon election expenses. Mill, in 1865, had rejected both cabs and canvassers, and, perhaps for this reason, had succeeded in only one election contest. The machinery of electioneering had been much developed since his day. The Liberal vote in the Manchester election of 1880 had cost officially 15s. per head, and extra expenses, not named in the return, had brought up the cost to £1 per vote. In the present contest Dr. Pankhurst's expenses were £541, those of his opponent £5,559.

It was at first thought that the Liberal Association would, as it was said, " leave the way clear for the stripling with the sling " to fight the Tory, but the Whigs who had opposed him in the Eastern crisis were determined to destroy any chance the Doctor might have of winning the seat. Now that he was no longer present to contend against them, they easily secured a decision of the Liberal Association directing that members should not give him their votes, on the ground that his Independent candidature was subversive of Liberal discipline. The several efforts of his friends to reverse the decision merely served to give publicity to the attacks upon him. Thomas Ashton, Sheriff of Lancashire, a masterful character, accustomed to rule the Association, said: " The larger the vote polled by Dr. Pankhurst, the greater will be the inducement to men like him to trouble us hereafter." The editors of the *Manchester Guardian* and the *Examiner and Times* were both members of the Liberal Association, and the former was on the General Purposes Committee, which had succeeded in carrying a vote of censure on the Doctor for requisitioning a meeting of the Council of the Association during the Eastern crisis. Their newspapers now led the attack on him, giving publicity only to the single point that the Doctor had flouted the Liberal Association, and that it was the duty of all loyal Liberals to obey the decision of their caucus. The Doctor retaliated by exposing the many failures of the Association and the record of the *Guardian* in its attacks upon Gladstone and Bright. He roundly declared that the conduct of the two editors could not have been more hostile towards him had their papers received a subsidy from the Liberal Association for the work. The *City Lantern*, a Manchester journal of the period, lampooned the Doctor in a parody of John Gilpin's ride to Ware:

> " ' He's off! He's off, the renegade! '
>   Boss Beith did wildly cry.
>   Th' High Sheriff rushed to bar the gate,
>   Sly Pankhurst had flown by."

Outside Manchester the Press took a broader view of the contest, devoting great space to it and discussing the new policies which the Doctor was urging upon the Liberal Party. The *Daily News*, though following in the main the hostile lead from Manchester, observed:

" Identified in the past with some of the highest efforts of the United Liberal Party in the city, especially with those that were made some eight or nine years ago to overthrow the Tory ascendancy, and distinguished long before that as a supporter of the American Union and the Emancipation cause, Dr. Pankhurst is not looked upon either as an untried man or as a presumptuous one by those Liberals—it remains to be seen how many—who prefer following a Liberal flag to holding back even at the recommendation of their local leaders."

The Tory *St. James's Gazette* saw in the contest a breach in the coalition of Whigs and Radicals which formed the Liberal Party. *The Spectator*, then an organ of moderate Liberalism, set itself to fight the Pankhurst doctrines:

" Dr. Pankhurst is substantially a French Red of the humane type, and not an English Radical at all.
" He is fighting for the seat as a fanatic, not as an adventurer. . . . His ideas are his ideas, not those of any section of the Liberal Party. The most determined Radicals are not unanimous for universal suffrage, and are distinctly hostile to the swamping of all

male votes in that of the large majority of women. They are opposed to all those projects, either for confiscation or for the foolish expenditure of public money, which are concealed under the phrase ' Nationalization of the land.' They desire to reform rather than to abolish the House of Lords. They are divided—probably about equally—on the disendowment of the Church, though more than half may be in favour of disestablishment. They are almost to a man against Home Rule for Ireland. . . .

" We admit that Dr. Pankhurst is honestly dreaming; and therefore we prefer, if we are forced to make the choice, a sensible Tory to Dr. Pankhurst."

The opinions on International affairs, which so long ago were championed by Dr. Pankhurst, in face of both ridicule and abuse, have gained a larger currency since the Great War, 1914-1918, revealed the result of opposite policies. Had his views triumphed in his day, the British Empire would not, perhaps, have attained to its present dimensions : some other nation might have pushed past Britain in the scramble for territory. On the other hand the general standard of world civilization might already have reached a higher plane whereon Imperialist ambitions would find no place.

Hugh Mason, the Member for Ashton, sent £100 to his election fund, hoping that he might win because he had " brains and pluck." Labouchere, the truculent old editor of *Truth*, who was later to become known as an inveterate anti-suffragist, but who began as a supporter of votes for women, wrote his support. So did the eldest son of John Bright, whose letter drew a statement from John Bright himself : " I have not said one word in favour of Dr. Pankhurst." Michael Davitt, an old friend, eulogized him as " a Radical of the right sort; an Englishman wise and just enough " to wish Ireland governed " according to Irish ideas." The Doctor was, in fact, the first English Parliamentary candidate to pledge himself to Irish self-government. When he declared also for the repeal of the Crimes Act, Parnell telegraphed that the Irish electors should vote for him. On the invitation of the local branch of the Irish Party Parnell arrived in Manchester to speak on the Doctor's behalf, but left without doing so, turning tail before the forces of the Roman Catholic Church, which he found arrayed against the candidate. The hostility of Canon Toole and his brethren, aroused by the Doctor's campaign for secular education in the 'seventies, had not been allayed. Whilst Parnell had retired, and the priests were doing all in their power to secure his defeat, the Press, Liberal and Tory alike, were attacking the Doctor's advocacy of the Irish cause as the strongest reason for rejecting him at the poll. Such is the fate of the pioneer !

In the School Board election ten years before the Doctor had gone into the contest in a gay spirit of knight-errantry, to which personal victory or defeat at the polls were alike victory, if principles had been sustained and advanced.   This spirit he maintained to the end, but to the ardent young wife now beside him such " moral " victories brought no satisfaction.   His actual presence in Parliament, to her, seemed vital to all good causes. She seethed with bitter resentment against his opponents, still more against those whom he had aided and who now refused to aid him in return.   She rushed impulsively to the Women's Suffrage Society, asking an official declaration in his favour and the active support of its members.   The stern, impassive Miss Becker received her with a cold refusal : the Society could not go out of its way to support Dr. Pankhurst : he was " a fire-brand," Becker declared.   Showing herself later a trifle more friendly than her words, she wrote some genial paragraphs in the *Women's Suffrage Journal,* but destroyed all their value to the eager heart of Mrs. Pankhurst by observing that as both Dr. Pankhurst and Mr. Houldsworth (the Conservative) had given their adherence to women's suffrage, the cause was assured of a supporter whichever candidate were returned.   The young Emmeline wept in her anger; the Doctor chided her, smiling : " You must not blame the slave for acting as a slave ! "   What could she know of the bitter dissensions of 1874 and the galling disappointment of Lydia Becker that the Doctor had stood with the Jacob Brights and Mrs. Elmy against her in the controversy over the married woman?   Moreover, who can say?   Becker had perhaps suffered another and a greater disappointment, as rumour persistently declared.   Did she not later exclaim in some argument with Mrs. Pankhurst : " Married women have all the plums of life ! "   Certainly in the popular estimate of that day the middle-aged spinster was inferior to the young wife already the mother of two children; yet the wife had still no legal existence.

It is not unlikely that the Doctor's support of the policy of the Women's Suffrage Societies cost him as many votes as his Irish sympathies.   Lydia Becker and her colleagues were insistent that no protective legislation, not extended also to men, should be applied to women workers, at least until women should be enfranchised.   As soon as the Doctor had pledged himself to adopt this demand of the suffragists, a statement, cunningly devised to arouse the prejudice of the male Trade Unionist dreading the competition of women's labour, was circulated against him.

Dr. Pankhurst received 6,216 votes, his opponent 18,188; but though defeated he was in good spirits, for his ideas had been sent flying round the country.   The natural outcome of the contest was the formation of the Manchester Radical Association, which took place immediately after the election.   Radical organizations were now springing up in all parts of the country, and Pankhurst was constantly sent for to address them.   The Radical movement represented, in part, the left wing of the Liberal Party; in part it was preparing the way for the coming Labour movement.   In its day it was the mainstay of the most advanced political causes.

The election had been a costly one to Dr. Pankhurst.   To the Independent candidate, elections are indeed always an expensive luxury; and even candidates running under the auspices of the political parties were, in those days, expected to find at least the greater share of the election expenses.   The acerbities of the contest had aroused against the Doctor a professional boycott, which made his legal work difficult and anxious.   Immediately after the election he won a case in the Chancery Court against the Manchester City Corporation, on behalf of the small market traders, upon whom an extra-legal tax was being levied in addition to the regular toll.   The case served to enhance the animosities cherished against him by some of the rich politicians of the city.

CHAPTER III

WITH the expectation of a fourth child, the Pankhursts moved from Seedley Cottage to Green Hayes. There were other reasons also for leaving the Goulden home.

A share of the boycott directed against Dr. Pankhurst was visited also upon his father-in-law, who had stood beside him in the Eastern crisis and throughout his election. Robert Goulden, a Liberal, pure and simple, had no liking for Socialism, which was the basis of the Doctor's philosophy. A lost election, with the enemy in full cry of contemptuous invective, is apt to lead men of more cautious mind to blame the candidate for rash impetuosity. In the discussions of Socialism, which became general when the Social Democratic Federation was formed in '83, the Doctor and his father-in-law were sharply opposed. Mrs. Pankhurst clove to her husband's view, and her sister Mary was so ardently of their opinion, that unable to hear them criticized, she left her father's house to make her home with them.

I have a glimpse of the journey from Seedley to Green Hayes: "Old Trafford!" cried Christabel, leaning from the cab window, "did you see it?" I looked out and saw only two big gate posts surmounted by balls of stone. I could not remember ever having seen them. I strove to picture the old home. . . . I could not see it clearly. . . .

Green Hayes; the very name seems caressing. In its garden were borders of London pride; the starry little pink flowerets wonderfully beautiful amid the black soot of Manchester; like fairy flowers I thought them.

Our nursery had two windows; one large, the other high and narrow. It was to the "little window" we always ran to wave good-bye to Father, our childish heads clustering at the pane to catch the last glimpse of him as he went out each morning, turning to smile and wave to us. Wonderful father, the lode-star of our lives, like a bright sunny morning, brimful of energy. His hair was always grey in my memory of him, but at first it was a dark iron grey, later a bright, clear silver, very soft and fine. His skin was clear and ruddy, his head beautifully shaped. His hands and feet were slender and sensitive; his nails, like no others I have seen. If he let them grow, as he was apt to do, they clove to the fingers, curling over the tips. " How splendid," we children said, " to have nails like father; they would never need brushing! " We were proud to see him in evening dress, and thought him the very perfection of manly beauty, gazing with admiration while Mother put in his father's diamond studs, preparing him lovingly for some function where he had to speak. For many years he brought a book home to us every night; history, travel, simple science, astronomy, botany, chemistry, engineering, fairy-tales, standard novels, reproductions of works of art, the best illustrations. He read aloud to us, told us stories, opened to us his beliefs and hopes. When we were still but toddlers he was for ever asking us: " What do you want to be when you grow up? " and urging: " Get something to earn your living by that you like and can do." " To do, to be, and to suffer! " was a favourite phrase of his. " Drudge and drill! drudge and drill! " he would exhort us.

Throughout our childhood we heard his beseeching adjuration: " If you do not grow up to help other people you will not have been worth the upbringing! " his proud joy: " My children are the four pillars of my house! " and his frequent appeal to us: " Love one another." There was bred in us thus a sense of destiny, and of duty to be servants to the commonweal.

For several years, from when we were tiny mites at Green Hayes, he maintained, as a humorous entertainment for us, two never ended extemporized stories, which lingered on for the younger children till I was probably ten or twelve years of age. One was about two boys, " Nobs " and " Dobs," who led a life of adventures startling and absurd; the other about " Miss Popinjay," whose fantastic dress and exaggerated vanity produced a wealth of ridiculous mishaps. As he recounted, he drew amazingly grotesque illustrations which delighted us immensely: yet in his serious moods we found him infinitely more enthralling. His rare eloquence, his love of knowledge for its own sake, his deep sincerity, his zest for life drew our young hearts to him. " I never met anyone one tithe part so clever," said Christabel to me many years later in the height of the suffragette turmoil, when we had both met all sorts and conditions of people. " Life is nothing without enthusiasms! " often, often he said it to us. I listened to him spell-bound, with tear-filled eyes, when he talked of Shelley, his idealism, and search after the perfection of human life, his poignant grief in the taking away of his children. I was elated when he read to us from Whitman: " Pioneers! O Pioneers! "

In his crowded life he found time to discourse to us on

literature, history and social questions, because he husbanded every moment of his day. He rose early, except on Sundays, and read aloud or recited poetry to himself in the bathroom during his very systematic ablutions. He read as he walked to the 'bus, and in the 'bus to his Chambers. He bought the smallest editions of his favourite books, in order that he might carry them in his pockets. Milton was his foremost love amongst the poets, constantly consulted as a refreshment to the spirit. I have his little red Milton; it is but three inches long, a complete edition set in the smallest type. He had numbers of little black note-books for his own jottings stowed away on his person. Mrs. Pankhurst, brushing his coat before he left home each morning, would complain of his bulging pockets, and many times I have heard her protest, with tears of exasperation in her voice: " Some surgeon will stop you in the street one of these days and ask you to leave him your body for dissection—you make such a sight of yourself! "

Political differences having embittered discussion, Mrs. Pankhurst quarrelled with her father on a matter which had no bearing on politics, though it affected her life-long desire for economic independence. She said he had promised her some property on her marriage. Her father said he had not. The breach remained unhealed. Mrs. Pankhurst never saw her father again, nor her mother till both were widows and sorrow had drawn the sting from their wrath.

She was now eager to get away from Manchester, and insistently urged the Doctor to the view that in London they would find more scope for achievement in the cause of progress.

CHAPTER IV

AFTER THE THIRD REFORM ACT. PANKHURST V. HAMILTON

THE Reformers of the eighteen eighties centred great hopes
upon the Third Reform Act. The serf-like state of the
agricultural labourer was to be transformed by his enfranchisement, the pace of Reform to be accelerated. In October, 1883,
a conference of 2,000 delegates from Liberal Associations and
the National Reform Union met at Leeds under the presidency
of John Morley, to voice the demand for a Franchise Bill. Dr.
Crosskey of Birmingham, Helen Bright Clarke and Jane Cobden,
daughters of John Bright and Richard Cobden, moved an amendment to include women. It was carried with less than thirty
dissentients. Resolutions to the same effect poured in upon the
Government from the Liberal Associations. Great meetings of
women were held, in size and enthusiasm greatly exceeding those
of the agricultural labourers, who cared little or nothing for
enfranchisement. As was soon to be proved, their condition
was too deeply depressed to admit of any interest in public
questions—even in those most nearly affecting them. The
enthusiasm of the women made no impression on the implacable
hostility of Gladstone. When introducing the desired Reform
Bill in February, 1884, he observed that it did not include
women. Lord John Manners vainly moved a funny little
amendment to enable a woman farmer to appoint a man-servant
to vote on her behalf. William Woodall, acting for the suffrage
societies, sponsored an amendment to give votes to women on
the same terms as men. There were said to be 249 " known
friends " of women's suffrage in the House, and 236 " known
opponents," giving a favourable majority of 13. Seventy-nine
Members of Parliament had memorialized the Government
asking that Members might be left to vote freely on the women's
amendment. Gladstone wrote refusing the request, and when
the amendment came on he chided Woodall for bringing it up
at all, complaining that he had given him written notice of his
objection :

" We will disclaim all responsibility for the measure if my
honourable friend carries the motion he has in view. . . . I offer it
the strongest opposition that is in my power."

In spite of this threat, some Liberal Suffragists remained

faithful to their pledges, amongst them the temperance advocate, Sir Wilfrid Lawson, and staunch James Stansfield, a devoted adherent of Josephine Butler, who refused for many years to take office until the C.D. Acts were repealed. John Morley and Hugh Mason, whom the Women's Suffrage Societies at one time called their "leader," were amongst the turncoats. Leonard Courtney, another lost leader, sat on the Front Bench and did not vote; and with him Henry Fawcett (Postmaster-General), the husband of Millicent Garrett Fawcett, who in later years came to be regarded as the leader of constitutional Suffragists. Mrs. Fawcett apparently regarded it as quite in the natural order of things that her husband should refrain from voting against the behest of his chief—herein was epitomized the world of difference between herself and Mrs. Pankhurst. Mrs. Fawcett, in her book *What I Remember,* has recorded that in spite of this subservience, Fawcett was rebuked by Gladstone, who wrote to him, saying that abstention from support of the Government in a critical division was equivalent to resignation. He enclosed, however, a memorandum, signed by himself, stating that in the approaching crisis of foreign affairs the resignation of a Cabinet Minister and two other gentlemen would be unfortunate. Therefore the President of the Local Government Board, Sir Charles Dilke, who had also failed to obey the Whip against votes for women, the Postmaster-General, and the Financial Secretary to the Treasury, Leonard Courtney, "will do us the favour to retain their respective offices." This piece of autocratic buffoonery gives rise to the reflection whether the tactful influence of a suffragist, Madame Novikoff, might not have converted the "Grand Old Man." Yet there were powerful anti-Suffragists behind the scenes, not least of them Queen Victoria, who had strongly expressed herself against the "mad folly of Women's Rights." Gladstone and Disraeli were both sedulously anxious to please the Queen.

When the Lords threw out the Franchise Bill, and great protest demonstrations were held, the Women's Suffrage Societies remained inactive, and on the re-introduction of the Bill no women's suffrage amendment was moved. Lydia Becker and the other suffrage officials acquiesced in this omission. They feared that by pressing their claim they might be charged with supporting the action of the House of Lords against the Commons. Moreover, the majority of them were Liberal women with family connections in the Liberal Party. Lord Denman had set down a votes for women amendment to be debated in the Upper House, but Mrs. Fawcett and the Suffrage Committee in London objected and induced him to withdraw it.

Doctor Pankhurst was working strenuously to build up the Radical movement. The rejection of the women's vote was by no means his only difference with official Liberalism, and he earnestly believed that the Radicals would be a force which would elevate politics to a higher plane. In 1885 he was invited by the Rotherhithe Liberal and Radical Association to stand for Parliament in its interest. He agreed to stand, " but only as a Radical." In this same election Helen Taylor was the Parliamentary candidate of the Camberwell Radical Association. She was early in the field, and though her nomination was eventually rejected, her campaign had already evoked a great discussion. Pankhurst went over to speak for her. The Women's Suffrage Societies held aloof; the attempt to put forward a woman candidate for Parliament was too daring for them; they considered it injurious to the suffrage cause. The fact that Helen Taylor cast off the trammels of skirts and wore trousers was an added and most egregious offence in their eyes. Even Mrs. Pankhurst was distressed that her husband should be seen walking with the lady in this garb, and feared that his gallantry in doing so, and in permitting her to appear thus in Rotherhithe, would cost him many votes.

The Doctor's election address emphasized his desire for economic changes :

" This is the hour of the people and of the poor. . . . This is a time of hope for the life of Labour. Old society was based on war, new society rests on work. There must be for every man a man's share in life, through education, free and universal, training for work through technical teaching; full citizenship. . . . Over the production of wealth preside the laws of nature, but over the distribution of wealth presides the heart of man."

Now that he was officially adopted by a Liberal organization, though maintaining the same programme as in 1883, the Liberal Press became cordial. The *Manchester Examiner* called him " a man of great parts, of much intellectual power, a sedulous student of political history." The *Pall Mall Gazette* : " A type rare amongst English politicians, at once a close student and an eloquent orator." As to the candidate, the grim, hopeless poverty of Rotherhithe, more terrible even than the squalor of factory-ridden Lancashire, stirred him to poignant sympathy, rousing to new fires his passionate desire to aid :

" We are men and women standing heart in heart . . . fighting in a hard world and fighting bravely . . . we want to know how the world is made, that in knowing how it is made we may have power over our lot and circumstances. . . .
" What I long and pine for is that our brethren shall have less

work to do. I want your life and my life raised to a higher point of power and happiness."

His Conservative opponent, Colonel Hamilton, called him a "slum politician," because he spoke to the people in the mean streets where they lived:

"I should be ashamed to exhibit myself at street corners like Dr. Pankhurst. Look at him in Salisbury Street—a place where I should be ashamed to be seen! The next time you bring out a candidate, bring a gentleman and not a slum politician!" [1]

To-day when every candidate speaks at the street corner, such observations read strangely indeed, but not more strangely than the Colonel's complaint that the Doctor's demand for free schools would raise the education rate from 9d. to 1s. The *Dundee Advertiser* said: "As a speaker he was no match for the Doctor, but in tactics the Doctor was no match for the Colonel." The Colonel's main weapon was the then most common one of slander. Hailing from Lancashire also, he declared that he would not like to tell the electors all he knew about Dr. Pankhurst, but that he knew him to be content, as a barrister, "to take up those cases left alone by everyone else."[2]

Manchester people were amazed when they read reports of the Colonel's speeches. "The great question is where Dr. Pankhurst has been all his life, for nobody knows him in Manchester." "Anybody who says he does not know Dr. Pankhurst does not know Manchester. . . ! His friends in Manchester may be counted by thousands who admire him for his lofty enthusiasm, and I will add his blameless life," replied Henry Dunckley, editor of the *Manchester Examiner and Times*, thus offering the *amende honorable* for the attacks of 1883.

The Colonel was not deterred from the path of slander. When Jacob Bright and Charles Russell (afterwards Lord Chief Justice) went down to Rotherhithe to defend the Doctor, the Colonel endeavoured to secure someone, if possible a workman, who would come down from Manchester to discredit him. Edward Ramsbottom[3] wrote from the Conservative Club, Higher Ardwick:

"I am afraid we cannot get any working man to come down. . . . Chesters Thompson would come down and speak against him, but I cannot spare him as he is the only reliable man I have."

The object was secured by a speech delivered in Manchester at a meeting addressed by A. J. Balfour (afterwards Lord Balfour),

---

[1] Evidence of several witnesses at the Court of Queen's Bench.
[2] *South London Press* and *Southwark Recorder*.
[3] Letter read in the Court of Queen's Bench.

who was then a candidate for East Manchester. Councillor Chesters Thompson, a brewer, declared that in the Manchester town hall, some six or nine months previously, Dr. Pankhurst had said:

"Let me tell you that I, to-night, am in a position, if there be a God—which I say there is not—to deny God; and let me tell you that if there is a devil, I am in a position to deny the devil."

The Tory *Manchester Courier* printed the statement, and on receiving a telegram that Chesters Thompson had uttered the slander, Colonel Hamilton proceeded to flood Rotherhithe with copies of it. The walls were placarded, handbills were delivered from door to door, thrust in the faces of people coming from church, and placed in the pews. Two printers had refused to reproduce the libel; but Colonel Hamilton had it done by his own firm of McCorquodale, with the false imprint: "J. Wighton & Co.," Wighton being works manager there at the time. To heighten the effect of the statement the word "defy" was substituted for "deny." At a meeting in the Surrey Light Horse Public House, Colonel Hamilton was brandishing a copy of the *Manchester Courier* in one hand, a handbill embodying the Chesters Thompson slander in the other, and was expatiating on the iniquitous character of his opponent, when he received a telegram from Dr. Pankhurst denying the libel. Nevertheless he persisted: "I am going to publish this. They cannot touch me, because these people in Manchester take all the responsibility." Some workmen asked him whether he had made inquiries into the truth of the report. His answer, according to several witnesses in the Court of Queen's Bench, was: "Certainly not! I do not care a snap of the fingers whether it is true or not: it will give me more votes than if I had all the Irish vote!"

The libel fell like a bombshell upon the constituency, obscuring the issues which had previously occupied popular interest. The Conservatives were jubilant; the Liberal Nonconformists taken aback. They had rejoiced to hear the Doctor advocating Church disestablishment, but it was a shock to them to appear in the eyes of their neighbours as supporters of publicly declared Atheism of the extremist type. Had the issue not been raised, the Doctor's opinions on religion might have been regarded as his own concern. Now that they had become the subject of public discussion, it seemed that to support him was to support his alleged religious views. He had denied the libel, but it was known that he was an Agnostic.

Darwinism and the spread of scientific thought in other

fields had aroused a great questioning of the basis of orthodox religion. Scepticism amongst savants had become so widespread as to compel toleration where men of education were gathered together; but any attempt to take free thought to the masses was met with an opposition so bitter as almost to exclude from other movements those who dared attempt it. Foote had been sentenced for blasphemy in 1883, Bradlaugh was at the height of his struggle against the Parliamentary oath. Pankhurst desired to enter into no discussion of men's religious beliefs. Education —free and universal—upon a basis which would stimulate the mind to the pursuit of truth for its own sake, and the abolition both of privilege and disability on religious grounds, together with juster and happier economic conditions, would, he believed, give the quietus to the fiercer aspects of the battle of the creeds. For these objectives he desired to work, unhindered by religious controversies. Yet no candidate who asked for religious freedom, Church disestablishment, and that affirmation should be made as valid as the oath, could escape denunciation as an Atheist. Even before the libel appeared, one clergyman had characterized Dr. Pankhurst's election address as "shocking and disgraceful."

The Radical election committee looked anxiously to the canvass; the canvassers reported that the bombshell was having an adverse effect. The noisiest and least intelligent sections of the community found the affair an occasion for stone-throwing and hustling. The Doctor was undismayed; he received such blows without flinching—even with gaiety. Young Mrs. Pankhurst seethed with indignant grief. Her heart set upon victory for her husband, she saw in the hue and cry raised over the libel the bitter augury of defeat. In Manchester she had never known the rude violence of these London crowds. Even by those who would not vote for him, the Doctor was loved and respected there: never as now had she seen him assaulted, his hat knocked off, blood on his face. She too was pelted with market refuse. She wept with rage when she and he were alone together that Saturday night. She besought him to do something to silence "these wretches," something to turn the tide. He tried to soothe her and console her, telling her personal victory was of no account; it was the cause of progress alone which mattered. But to her there was no one like him; for the cause itself his success was essential. "How could they dare to attribute anything like that to you who are incapable of using such vulgar language?" He had publicly denied the libel; his committee had stuck slips across the posters containing it: "Another Tory lie!" He must do more than that, she insisted; he must go to church with her: to prove that he would show no disrespect to religious views, even if he did not share them. He must indeed: she would take no denial: she knew it was the right thing to do: it would make her ill if he did not: "*I* understand these people, *I* know what to do; you have always got your head in the clouds!" So to church they go; but of what avail? The outcry was nowise stayed. The *South London Press* charged the local clergy and their helpers with having bribed their poorer parishioners with blankets to vote against the Doctor; such methods were common enough in those days. Yet probably in spite of all, for the Doctor's committee stood firm and his helpers were zealous, it was Parnell's command that the Irish electors must vote against all Liberal candidates, in order to bring pressure to bear on the Government, which did more than the famous libel to secure the return of Colonel Hamilton by 3,327 votes to 2,800. The storms of cheering and approbation, the illuminated address presented by the Doctor's supporters, did not assuage the grief of Mrs. Pankhurst. Against Parnell's decision she made bitter protest; the Doctor begged her not to take such things to heart, reminding her that the Irish were fighting against coercion.

It was now announced that he would bring an action for libel against the Colonel. The election had cost the Liberals £500, of which the candidate himself had paid the greater part; a heavy tax, the more so as it had followed so swiftly upon the Manchester contest. He was fully seized of the great cost entailed in the proposed action, and the exceedingly narrow chance of obtaining redress. Yet he was anxious to obtain a test decision under the then new law of libel which might check the flood of slander turned upon Radical candidatures. He therefore took action against Colonel Hamilton, J. Wighton, the ostensible printer of the libel, the *Manchester Courier* and Chesters Thompson. The action against Wighton came to nothing, for he died whilst it was pending, and though he was only the shield for the actual printer, Justice Grantham, Baron Pollock, and Justice Cave had decided that he could not be forced to disclose the name of the true printer. It is curious that the Court should thus have upheld the issue of literature with a bogus imprint—a breach of the law for which many people have suffered punishment before and since that date.

The case against Chesters Thompson was heard at the Manchester Assizes before Justice Grantham and a special jury, on May 12th, 1886. Dr. Pankhurst was put in the witness-box and submitted to a fire of cross-examination, not merely by the defending Counsel, but by the Judge himself, " who seemed," according to the *Manchester Examiner*, " to be doing his best to prove the defendant's case." Old jokes and controversies at the Club and in the houses of friends were raked up, political speeches of many years before were analysed and dissected. He was confronted with someone's recollections of a conversation he had had during a country walk, whilst visiting Carnarvon for an arbitration, when in a friendly contest with "witty and vivacious" professional colleagues, he had referred to the Holy Ghost as "the foggy member of the Trinity," and had said that he would like to have Him in the witness-box to examine His credentials. As to the Chesters Thompson slander, so far as it had any foundation, it seems to have been based on a talk with an employee at the Manchester town hall, who had been a member of the same chapel with him in their youth. He had told this man, Nixon, that he had shaken himself free from the trammels of creeds and had "derived considerable comfort" from the Agnostic view. Probed as to his opinions by Justice Grantham, he answered:

" I said my position was that I had found for myself that God, the soul and immortality . . . were things unknown and unknowable by the human intellect, quite apart from a region which is rarely the region of religion, the region of faith and hope, which region I have never entered in a discussion, because I think it is a sanctuary never to be entered."

In reply to further probing by the Judge he gave his opinion that the groundwork of the Christian faith was the historic personality of Christ, and that he lived with such an example as to be the social, moral and political reformer of the world. The Judge replied: " That is not the Christian faith and doctrine." Thereat the *Pall Mall Gazette* ironically observed: " The only thing that remains is to make Justice Grantham the Pontiff of universal Christendom." Having so delivered himself, the Judge proceeded to non-suit the Doctor, declaring that there was no case to go to the Jury, on the ground that the libel was not uttered with malice, and that the words attributed to Dr. Pankhurst were not injurious because, in the Judge's opinion (though some authorities thought otherwise), they would not have exposed him to conviction for blasphemy had he uttered them.

The action against the *Courier* was heard two days later. The defendant admitted that the libel was false and defamatory. Therefore Dr. Pankhurst did not go into the witness-box to deny it; but Justice Grantham declared that because he had not done so there was no evidence that the libel was false. He considered that the libel had actually been useful to Dr. Pankhurst, because it had given him an opportunity to explain his view. Newspaper proprietors, said the Judge, should be protected from charges of libel; they could not be responsible for what went into their papers, nor could reporters know if statements were true or false. Having heard Dr. Pankhurst give his views in the witness-box, in the previous case, he did not wonder that some people should feel strongly that such candidates ought not to be returned. If, however, the jury should find a verdict for Dr. Pankhurst, he should be " glad to know on what ground they had done so, as none had been suggested." After this summing up, the jury obediently gave a verdict for the defendant.

" Is it not a little hard," asked the *Pall Mall Gazette*, " that it should be the Tory candidate for Croydon at the last General Election, of all men in the world, to decide whether a lampoon by which the Tories defeated the Radical candidate at Rother- hithe was or was not within the limits of legitimate con- troversy?" The *Manchester Guardian* said: " We have read the case with an increasing sense of the difficulties of the English law."

Passionate loyalty was stirred within the breast of Mrs. Pankhurst; she wrote to Justice Grantham:

" MY LORD,—Your judgement of Wednesday, and your summing up to the jury to-day, are the concluding acts of a conspiracy to crush the public life of an honourable public man. It is to be regretted that there should be found on the English Bench a judge who will lend his aid to a disreputable section of the Tory Party in doing their dirty work; but for what other reason were you ever placed where you are?

" I have, my Lord, the honour to be

" Your obedient servant,

" EMMELINE PANKHURST.

" *May 14th*, 1886."

" Let him send me to prison! I want to go to prison for contempt of Court! " she cried. But her letter was ignored.

Dr. Pankhurst in the witness-box had described himself as one of those who are called Agnostics, like Professor Huxley and Mr. Balfour. This was by no means the first occasion on which his *Defence of Philosophic Doubt* had earned that title for A. J. Balfour, though he had several times repudiated it; indeed his election literature contained the phrase: " Vote for Balfour and Religion! " He at once issued denials of the Doctor's statement, and a Press controversy ensued. The Doctor declared that on final analysis Mr. Balfour's doctrine was Agnosticism. He cited amongst others the following passage from the *Defence of Philosophic Doubt*:

" The world, as represented by science, can no more be perceived or imagined than the Deity, as represented to us by theology; and in the first case, as in the second, we must content ourselves with symbolic images, of which the only thing we can most certainly say is that they are not only inadequate, but incorrect."

The Doctor insisted that Balfour was one of the family of Agnostics; but had a quarrel with Huxley, another member of the same family. Balfour, in the course of four letters, endeavoured to parry the charge, with as little reference as possible to his book which could hardly be acceptable to old-fashioned theologians. He avoided the question, which the Doctor pressed home in each rejoinder, whether he was prepared to disavow the speech of Chesters Thompson.

Meanwhile Pankhurst had appealed against the decisions of Justice Grantham. On December 11th Baron Huddleston and Justice Manisty, in the Court of Queen's Bench, granted his application for a new trial of his action against the *Manchester Courier*, observing that he had not had "that to which every subject is entitled, a fair trial," and rebuking the summing up of Justice Grantham in the strongest terms. Chesters Thompson now anticipated that the non-suit given in his favour was about to be reversed. Without waiting for the decision of the judges, which was still under consideration in his own case, he instructed his counsel to plead with Pankhurst to accept from him an apology and 40s. and costs, on the ground that he was in serious financial difficulties. As everyone knows, the taxed costs are considerably less than those who go to law must actually pay. Therefore it was an act of considerable generosity on the part of Dr. Pankhurst to accept this proposal. The arrangement was, moreover, a very unfortunate one, in view of the other actions pending, and the damages which might be awarded in these cases; for Chesters Thompson was the prime offender, and it could not be brought to the notice of judge and jury that the arrangement had been achieved by playing upon the plaintiff's tender heart. The Doctor's forbearance was ill repaid; as soon as the petitioner for mercy had secured the desired safeguard for his pocket, he wrote to the Press to indicate that his apology was not intended to be an apology, and when the Doctor's action against Colonel Hamilton was re-tried in 1887, Chesters Thompson went into the box to say that he had not withdrawn the original statement, and never would, but had merely expressed regret for giving utterance to it. Many years later this same Chesters Thompson came to the Doctor appealing for assistance to procure his discharge from bankruptcy; he did not appeal in vain. Truly indeed the man he had lent himself to injure was full of the milk of human kindness!

The new trial of the *Courier* case was re-heard on January
26th, 1887, before Justice Hawkins and a special jury. This
judge opposed Dr. Pankhurst's claim as strongly as Baron
Huddleston and Justice Manisty had supported it. He declared
that if the libel were true, it was for the public benefit that it
should be published, and that the newspaper was justified in
accepting it as correct, because it was uttered by a Councillor of
the city. All the jurymen could not be induced to accept this
view, and after being detained for deliberation from 3 to 9.15
p.m., they were still unable to agree upon a verdict, and were
discharged. Eventually it was decided that further proceedings
should be dropped, on condition that the *Courier* would publish
an admission that the libel was false, and an apology for its
publication.

In March the case against Colonel Hamilton was tried
in the Court of Queen's Bench before Justice Grove and a
special jury. Sir Charles Russell conducted the Doctor's case, and
the Solicitor-General defended Colonel Hamilton. When Sir
Charles Russell asked the defendant to name anyone who had
called Dr. Pankhurst an Atheist, Colonel Hamilton made the
astonishing reply: "You told me so yourself, Sir Charles."
Russell indignantly protested that he had never at any time said
or thought such a thing of his client, and asked the Judge's
permission to doff wig and gown and go into the box to deny
the statement. Eventually Colonel Hamilton returned to the box
to say that Sir Charles Russell had actually told him in the House
of Commons that Dr. Pankhurst was *not* an Atheist, and that the
conversation had not taken place until after the Rotherhithe
election and the publication of the libels had become things of the
past. When the trial was over, the gallant Colonel wrote to the
Press to say that though it had been made to appear that he had
retracted and apologized for his statement as to the conversation,
he had done nothing of the kind. The jury gave a verdict for
the Doctor, but asked to be directed as to damages, which
eventually were fixed at £60. "A small addition to the cost of
Colonel Hamilton's seat," observed the *Dundee Advertiser*.

These actions, whilst they showed clearly enough that British
justice in political cases depended to a truly amazing extent upon
who might happen to be the occupant of the Bench, threw some
measure of light upon the legal position created by the recently
passed Newspaper Libel and Registration Act. Unsatisfactory
though its ending was for the plaintiff, who was supposed to have
won the actions, it served in some measure to check the torrent of
libel and slander directed against candidates in those days. The
position of a sincere Parliamentary candidate, earnest for his

views, baited and harassed alike by his opponents and his friends, has always seemed to me a highly unenviable one.

Burdened with a heavy financial load in respect of the libel actions, the Doctor went forth boldly with faith undimmed, courageous as ever. Not for an instant did he flag in his public work. He was active in assisting W. T. Stead in his new campaign for the protection of young girls. At the thirteenth conference of the Association for the Reform and Codification of the Law of Nations, under the Presidency of Dr. Sieveking, President of the Hanseatic High Court of Appeal at Hamburg, he was reading a paper on the obligation of treaties in relation to the concert of nations. The casting of the Irish vote against him in Rotherhithe had in nowise retarded his zeal for Irish self-government, in support of which he delivered a number of addresses immediately after the election. He was zealous in championing the rights of public meeting and free speech, which were called into question during the unemployed demonstrations in the dark period of industrial depression of 1886-7, when John Burns, Hyndman, Champion, Williams and Cunningham Graham were prosecuted for sedition and incitement. Sir Charles Warren, the then Chief of Police, had prohibited all meetings in Trafalgar Square. Attempts to defy the prohibition were met with both police and military violence, in the course of which many were arrested, many injured, and one man, Albert Linnell, was killed.

In communications to the Press, and especially in the *Pall Mall Gazette*, which, under W. T. Stead's editorship, was the leading champion of oppressed causes in those days, Dr. Pankhurst insisted that there was a common law right of public meeting in the Square, and that the general proclamation prohibiting all meetings there was clearly illegal. In one of the cases arising out of the police and military charge on the so-called " Bloody Sunday," November 13th, 1887, Justice Stephen said:

" If a legal procession were stopped by the Authorities it was the duty of the people to go quietly away and take whatever remedy they had afterwards."

This dictum, the same that was later to be uttered towards the Suffragettes, the Doctor emphatically challenged, citing a wealth of precedent in support of his view that the right to repel by force unlawful violence is the absolute right of every citizen. He pointed out that Justice Stephen himself, in his works on the criminal law, had referred to this right of " private defence," as he had termed it, declaring that unlawful violence by a policeman may be resisted in the same way, and to the same extent, as that by any other wrong-doer, the citizen having the right of self-defence on the spot, and the policeman having no right to shelter himself behind the orders of his superior. " His duty does not and cannot extend to the unlawful." The Doctor's argument might have been accepted with respect had there been involved no political controversy, no deep-rooted social prejudice. In the then reactionary panic at the rise of a new Trade Unionism and of an infant Socialist movement, the lawyer who made himself the public exponent of such an opinion was regarded by the majority of legal luminaries as a traitor to his order. "The Law and Liberty League " was now formed to protect the right of public agitation against illegal action by the authorities. Dr. Pankhurst, W. T. Stead, Mrs. Besant, Herbert Burrows, Tims, Saunders and Frank Smith, then a Commissioner of the Salvation Army, formed its original committee.

In 1884, when the House of Lords had again challenged public opinion by blocking the County Franchise Bill, Pankhurst had published a scheme for the Constitutional abolition of the hereditary Chamber, which was embodied in the resolution passed by the great "Abolitionist" Hyde Park demonstration of that year. The scheme was simply that the House of Commons should resolve to terminate the existence of the House of Lords, and that the Crown, acting on the advice of Ministers, should issue no further writs of summons to that House. The scheme is extant, but the argument may be more pithily given in brief quotations from speeches by its author :

" Originally the House of Lords was no party to the legislation of this country. The laws were made upon petition of the House of Commons, and upon assent of the Crown. . . . The Lords were an advisory body, being, in fact, the royal council. . . . The petition and the assent were entered on the rolls of Parliament. The judges at the end of the Parliament drew up the law from the petition, and the law was entered on the Statute Roll. In so doing there was often put into the Statute what was not in the petition. Accordingly the Commons appealed that no petition which had been assented to by the Crown should afterwards be altered without their consent. A change therefore took place, and Statutes were drawn up from the petitions during the sittings of Parliament. Afterwards the process was introduced of passing each Statute by way of Bill. . . . Under the Constitution, the Crown takes no part in legislation until it is called upon to assent to the Bill, and until then the advice of the royal council was not, and could not constitutionally be appealed to. Therefore the claim of the House of Lords to equal part with the House of Commons in making laws is a distinct usurpation. . . .

" The Long Parliament passed this Resolution : ' The House of Peers in Parliament is useless, dangerous, and ought to be abolished.'

. . . We should follow partly the precedent of the Long Parliament, and partly the action of Mr. Gladstone in abolishing the Irish Church establishment. . . . Since the Revolution of 1688, by the theory of the Constitution, the House of Commons is not a mere estate, but is the representative of the whole people. It is not constitutional now for anybody to advise the Crown in legislation unless that person is answerable to the House of Commons."[1]

He argued further that the right of the Lords to sit in Parliament depends upon a writ of summons issued by the Crown to each Lord, a new writ being issued to each Lord for each Parliament.

" No man can have property in a Royal writ and no petition of right can lie against the Crown. . . . If the Crown, being well advised, did issue no more writs, then the only person responsible would be the Minister who gave that advice. Who could make Mr. Gladstone responsible for that? Only the House of Commons. Let Lord Salisbury present his petition at the Bar of that House, and what would the House of Commons say? ' You were lately a member of an assembly which always opposed this House of Commons and was always an enemy of the people.' "[2]

There was not the remotest chance of such a scheme as this of Dr. Pankhurst's becoming law in those days, for Gladstone, holding firmly the reins of government, was as determined as the Tories to avoid any serious menace to the stability and permanence of the Upper House.

Dr. Pankhurst was in earnest: Abolition was to him no mere question of platform fireworks. His scheme being given prominence in *The Radical*, edited by George Standring, in January, 1888, was attacked in the *National Reformer* by Charles Bradlaugh, who somewhat invalidated his arguments against the Doctor's method of abolishing the hereditary Chamber, by admitting that he stood not for Abolition, but for Reform.

[1] *Middleton Guardian*, 6th September, 1884.
[2] *Manchester Examiner*, 22nd September, 1884.

CHAPTER V

EMERSON AND COMPANY

AFTER the Rotherhithe election, we children were brought to London, and housed in cheerless lodgings whilst the new home was being prepared. We all felt ill, even Christabel, who usually escaped every ailment. Mrs. Pankhurst had never abandoned her desire for an income of her own, nor ceased to cherish resentment at the thought of being for ever dependent upon another person. She conceived the idea that if she were to open a shop she might support the family on its proceeds, and thus enable the Doctor to discard all legal work and concentrate completely on political efforts for the common-weal. Leaving him immersed in his labours, she took her project into her own hands, and presently rented a house and shop at 165 Hampstead Road, which she opened under the style of " Emerson and Company." The principal aim of the business was to be " artistic," and calculated to appeal to the supposed latent desire of the housewife to have beautiful things about her. The thought was prompted by the William Morris movement for improving the applied arts, Mrs. Pankhurst being one of the large number of people directly or indirectly influenced by that movement without knowing it. Her father, as a cotton printer, had been prejudiced against what he heard of Morris and his praise of handicrafts; and she, with characteristic loyalty, adopted the prejudice without examination. Actually it was ten years or more after the inception of Emerson's before she was able to appreciate the work of Morris and his colleagues. When she opened the shop in Hampstead Road she was groping mainly for more colour and brightness than was generally found in late Victorian house decoration. Handicapped by inadequate means, but well dowered with hope and courage, she purchased a stock of what are termed " fancy goods," including a liberal supply of milking stools, which she enamelled in pale colours and her sister Mary painted with flowers according to the fashion of the period. The estate agent had told Mrs. Pankhurst that the Hampstead Road was a rising neighbourhood; undoubtedly it was, but that part of it had not yet risen so far as to support the elegant establishment Mrs. Pankhurst intended. Oetzmann, the big house furnisher, was already there, but some distance nearer to Oxford Street than 165, in front of which squalid

83

market stalls were pitched in the gutter, butchers loudly shouted: " Buy! buy! buy! " on Saturday nights, whilst ill-dressed women, their baskets laden with vegetables, jostled each other upon the densely thronged pavements.

Financially the business proved a complete failure; customers were so few and far between that an enterprising vendor of fish-hooks easily secured a single purchase of his wares at Emerson's by sending thither in advance a couple of urchins inquiring for them. The bait was irresistible to the two shop-keepers, weary with hope deferred: perhaps there was a demand for fish-hooks! They grasped at the chance of supplying it, all thought of their mission to serve the housewife's desire for beauty cast to the winds.

A fair proportion of the unsaleable stock found its way into our nursery, including a cardboard model of the Tower Bridge, perforated with holes, intended for filling with cross-stitch, Mrs. Pankhurst's maternal interests having led her to purchase a stock of such commercialized kindergarten work. Waking early one Christmas morning, I examined eagerly the Christmas gifts laid out upon our beds. For Christabel was a square, for me an oblong box, both covered in red plush. My heart leapt. I was convinced that the box contained a violin. Having heard the instrument on some rare occasions, I yearned exceedingly to possess it and to master it—to be able myself to call forth at will, and for uncounted hours, that mysterious, heart-disturbing, heart-enchanting voice. My wish was known; I fancied it had been gratified. Already before it was light, I lay with the box in my hands, gently fingering its clasp, too stiff for me to open, in confident delight. I was unable to restrain my tears when the boxes proved empty, and we were told that they were merely a handkerchief and glove case; curious presents for little girls of five and seven years; but they had come from the stock of Emerson's. Though we children did not know it, politics and business were putting a serious strain on our parents' financial resources; our mother had not been able to bring herself to spend money on mere Christmas presents.

A Miss Pearson was now engaged as a daily governess for Christabel and me; but after a short time she habitually sent her sister, " Miss Annie," as a substitute. Coming in as a stop-gap, Miss Annie made little attempt at teaching, but read aloud to us the novels of Dickens, Thackeray, Scott, and George Eliot. The murder of Nancy by Bill Sikes made an indelible impression of horror upon me: for years I was haunted by visions of her beautiful face of agony and fear, confronting his brutal strength. The privations of Oliver Twist illuminated for me the public work we knew our father to be doing. Aunt Mary, our great coadjutor, helped us to dramatize the dialogue between Dick Swiveller and the Marchioness, as well as scenes from Thackeray's *The Rose and the Ring*, and *Harriet and the Matches* from Strewwel-peter, a book which was for years a favourite source of joke with us, so often quoted that we could recite the whole of it from memory. The fairy-tales of Grimm and Hans Andersen were now old companions, though the latter were almost too sad for me. I grieved for little Kay and little Gerda. The punishment of "The Girl who Trod on a Loaf" seemed to me diabolically cruel. Such stories dwelt in my mind; I could not eradicate the sense that they were really true, and tried to imagine they had ended in a happier way.

Aunt Mary's great friend at school in Paris had been an American girl, Alice Brisbane, who now often came to see us. She seemed the very embodiment of a fairy-tale princess, slender and lovely, with golden hair and charming eyes. We heard our mother and Aunt Mary talking of her expected marriage, and asked that we might make her a wedding present. The stock of Emerson's provided another example of commercialized kindergarten: a set of dressing-table mats, of pale yellow cloth, stamped with little holes, by the aid of which we worked a pattern in various shades of blue silk. Shortly before the wedding Miss Annie bought some new buttons for our high, black boots, and finding them too large, she took them back to the shop to be changed. Christabel told me that the large buttons were much nicer than the small ones we were wearing, and suggested that we should cut all the buttons off our boots and throw them away; because if Miss Annie were again to have the large buttons given her by mistake, she might not trouble to change them. I did not care at all whether the buttons were small or large, but out of loyalty to Christabel I joined her in the work of destruction. As a punishment, we were not allowed to go with mother to take our present to Alice Brisbane as we had been promised. Years afterwards Mrs. Pankhurst told us that she would have relented, but did not feel she could afford to buy us the new clothes she thought necessary for the occasion. On the day of the wedding we were permitted to go with Susannah to the church, where we sat in the dim light of a side pew, apart from the guests, unnoticed as we thought. I was surprised to see old Albert Brisbane's tall figure towering above us, his gentle and fine features shadowed against the white light of a lancet window. I put out my hand. He did not shake it, but patted it kindly. Susannah chided me for giving my left hand; but though somewhat depressed at having thus committed a breach of good manners, I was elated by the brief encounter with Brisbane, whose magnetic personality I realized with the instinct of childhood, which senses more than it can understand.

Described by Robert Owen as America's finest orator, he was the son of a mother who told him: " If I had followed a career of my own, I should have made millions." At fifteen years of age he asked : " What is the collective work of man on this earth? " and himself answered : " If the individual man does not know what the work of the collective man is he has no guide in his career. It is not right for the individual man to work for himself : he must keep on the great track which humanity is following." At twenty years of age, having means at his disposal, he set out for Europe to discover the destiny of man. He attended the lectures of the foremost philosophers and economists of France and Germany, and in his quest for the laws which govern mankind and the universe, he studied anatomy in a Berlin dissecting room, animal magnetism, music, astronomy, geology, the origin of life, and the laws of matter and force. He was on terms of friendship with his most famous compatriots, including Emerson, Wendell Phillips, Lloyd Garrison and Morse, and with the finest minds of Europe, the musicians Mendelssohn, Meyerbeer, and Liszt, the philosopher Hegel with Heine, Cousin, Froebel, Victor Hugo, Balzac, Eugène Sue for whom he arranged the American publication of the *Wandering Jew*, Augustine Thierry, Béranger, Savigny, Lamartine, Ledru-Rollin, Lagrange, Considér- ant, and many more, and with those three great figures in the development of Socialist thought : Fourier, Prudhon, and Karl Marx. Of Fourier he took a course of lessons, regarding him as the leader in creating the theory of Socialism, or the Science of Society, but holding, nevertheless, that his theories were imperfect and the science still to be created. Of Marx he wrote :

" Marx did not advocate any integral scientific organization of industry : he had not the genius to elaborate such an organization; but he saw the fundamental falseness of our whole economic system. . . . As I remember that young man uttering his first words of protest, I recollect how little it was imagined then that his theories would one day agitate the world."

With Prudhon, Brisbane became intimate when the former was editing *La Voix du Peuple* in the stormy days of 1848. Later he visited him in prison at Mazas; and observed that whilst in France the political prisoner received treatment differing greatly from that of the ordinary malefactor, in England no such distinction was made unless the political happened to be a person of wealth and influence. Prudhon, he said, was " a man who feared nothing, endowed with immense moral energy," and the initiator in France of "what may be called the political economy of Labour, or Modern Socialism."

Returning to America, Brisbane organized a Society to propagate the doctrine of "Association," based on the theory of Fourier. He published three books, *Brisbane on Association*, *The Destiny of Man*, which consisted in part of a translation from Fourier, and *The Theory of Universal Unity*, explaining Fourier's system of Labour Government and education. He left many unpublished works. In the heyday of his enthusiasm he published a weekly paper, *The Future*, and a small daily, *The Chronicle*, which had a circulation of 4,000; he occupied a daily page in Horace Greeley's *Tribune*, and wrote on the same question in *The Plebian*, *The Democrat*, and Emerson's *Dial*. His propaganda aroused so much interest that, in spite of his own protests that action was premature, a large number of mutual aid colonies on Fourier lines were started in various parts of America, the longest lived being the "North American Phalanx," which continued from 1843 to 1855. Brisbane believed that if mankind could apply to its own life the laws which govern the universe, human life would develop to a resplendent perfection. He conceived of our globe and its peoples in association with the other planets, the sun, and the cosmic whole to which they all belong. He declared that his work in this direction could not be rounded off unless he could live to a hundred years. Born in 1809, he died at the age of eighty-one. Whilst in Turkey he was shocked by the subjection of woman, and came to regard her complete emancipation as one of the most important social needs. As by-products of his researches, he made many inventions, including a system of transportation of hollow spheres in pneumatic tubes, a system of underground fertilization, a new form of steamship, a new propeller, an oven designed to cook in a vacuum. He spoke with pride of his son Arthur, now the well-known New York publicist. "Arthur," I remember him saying, "will do more than any of us; he will wait till he has an assured position and then he will come forward for Socialism." When the old man had gone home, my father reflected sadly: "Those who refrain from beginning until they are successful will never begin at all!" He turned to us then, as he often did, with anxious yearning, warning us that many who had struggled and made sacrifices for Freedom and Justice had been succeeded by children who had grown up to be supporters of reaction and privilege, and begging us that it might not be so in our case.

In September, 1888, we met our first great sorrow. Mrs. Pankhurst was in Manchester with the Doctor. We all went out that morning with Susannah. Adela was in the perambulator. Four-year-old Frank had been given a set of reins, and he wore them, pretending to be a little horse. I never forgot how merrily he ran. When we came home he began to have a cold; his face was flushed and he coughed hoarsely. There was a sense of terror in the nursery; the hours seemed endless. Mother came hurrying home. Doctors came. Little Frank was in a bath with a sheet over his head. At night, when Christabel and I had been in bed a long time, we heard a terrible cry from Mother: " My husband is a lawyer! " and a great sorrowful wailing for her little boy. Susannah whispered to us that little Frank was dead; that the doctors had treated him for croup and had discovered too late that he was suffering from diphtheria. It was found on examination that there was a serious defect in the drainage at the rear of the house.

Those were awful days; Mother seemed altogether distraught, and as though she could not look at us. " We must do what we can for the others," Susannah said, but Mother turned her head away with a gesture of impatient grief. Uncle Walter came from Manchester, tall and grave and very gentle. Mother had telegraphed for him. He returned at once to break the news to Father; Mother feared to shock him by sending a telegram. " He had much finer eyes than any of these children," I heard her say to Uncle Walter. The words fell like a stone upon my heart. I longed to have died instead of Frank. He was the only boy; there were three girls; one of us could better have been spared: I was considered not strong; I had weak eyes and headaches, and light hair Mother had called insipid; surely it would have been better for me to die instead of Frank! For years that thought would recur with a deep anguish.

Susannah asked me if I would go with her to see my little brother. I went, feeling stricken and stunned, so grieved that I could feel no more. I could not believe it was he, that beautiful little white figure, with dark, still hair and long black lashes. A lady came and painted two portraits of the little dead boy; but Mother could not bear to see them; she kept them in her bedroom cupboard, out of sight.

" We must not forget Frank," Father told us, but Mother could not hear him spoken of. I often cried for him, but always secretly. I tried to draw little Frank just as he was, but the figure I made on the paper was very ugly. Yet I gave it to Father. He encouraged me kindly, saying that he could see Frank in my drawing very clearly. I felt an inexpressible throb of gratitude and sympathy; his understanding tenderness seemed like sunshine on my grief-frozen spirit.

CHAPTER VI

THE WOMEN'S FRANCHISE LEAGUE

WE children were hurried away from Hampstead Road, Emerson's was closed, the premises were advertised to let. During the long lease they were frequently tenantless, and were another load on the already heavily burdened shoulders of the Doctor. Yet he was still at the height of his powers, and Mrs. Pankhurst was convinced that she would succeed in business, were she to re-start in an appropriate neighbourhood. She was determined also to take a more active part with him in the political life of the Metropolis. With the latter end in view, she rented a large house where meetings could be held—8 Russell Square, at the corner of Bernard Street; it has since been pulled down, a part of the Hôtel Russell being built on its site. Mrs. Pankhurst said at first that the house was so large and costly that she would let part of it to a doctor, but she liked it too well to surrender any of it. Moreover it was all needed for propaganda activities. She found a tremendous pleasure in furnishing it. The library, its walls almost entirely lined with the Doctor's books, had windows of frosted glass. She put up Japanese blinds of reeds and coloured beads, and covered the lamps with scarlet shades; their ruddy glow shone a cheerful welcome to us when we came home on dark winter afternoons. The first floor contained only two large communicating rooms; a double drawing-room, used for " At Homes " and conferences. It was decorated in yellow, Mrs. Pankhurst's favourite colour, and lit by tall standard oil lamps, with yellow shades; she hated gas, and this was before the era of domestic electric light.

Emerson's was re-opened in Berners Street, and seemed to be doing well; but owing to the demolition of the premises, it was moved to Regent Street, where the overhead charges were overwhelmingly high. Mrs. Pankhurst's ideas had developed considerably since her beginning in Hampstead Road. She now aimed at purveying artistic furniture and decorations, in the style of a miniature Liberty's, but more moderately priced, and bearing the impress of her own taste. She bought what she liked and believed the public would like it also. The white enamelled furniture, ornamented with fretwork, then fashionable, she got specially made to her own suggestions by an impecunious master cabinet-maker, to whom no idea was too fantastic or difficult, but who was for ever demanding loans and advance payments to enable him to complete the orders in hand. Mrs. Pankhurst was probably far from realizing how much she should add to the prices she paid for her wares, in order to cover the very high overhead charges. But in these days she was confident of success, and many beautiful things from the stock of Emerson's were bought for the furnishing of the house in Russell Square. Chinese tea-pots, old Persian plates, Japanese embroidery, Indian brasses, rugs from Turkey, silks from Wardle's of Leek, cretonnes by Morris and his imitators. She revelled in the gorgeous colours of the Orient and all that was brilliant and bizarre in old art and new. She expended a plenitude of ingenious effort to produce beautiful effects at moderate cost, and herself hung pictures, laid carpets, made curtains and upholstered furniture. The Doctor was apart from all this, engrossed in his work, and inapt for any sort of manual effort. " I am a helpless creature ! " he often said, handing over even the carving of the joint to his energetic spouse. On special occasions Mrs. Pankhurst always dressed the table for her guests, with elaborate arrangements of gauze and flowers. To a large extent she made her own and her children's clothes. Beauty and appropriateness in her dress and household appointments seemed to her at all times an indispensable setting to public work. She was a woman of her class and period, in this, as in much else.

The house was soon a centre for many gatherings, of Socialists, Fabians, Anarchists, Suffragists, Free Thinkers, Radicals and Humanitarians of all schools. Stepniak, Tchaykovsky, Malatesta, the Italian Anarchist refugee; William Lloyd Garrison, the apostle of negro freedom; Grant Allan, Dadabhai Naoroji, the first Indian Member of the British House of Commons; Morrison Davidson, William Morris, whom Mrs. Pankhurst declared to have been prejudiced against her because she was wearing a dress from Paris when they first met; Tom Mann, who became so hot and excited when making a speech that his clean white collar was a crumpled rag when he concluded; Herbert Burrows, with his red tie and bristling moustache, and the truculent manner which belied his kindly nature, dashed in and out in a state of perpetual excitement, red handed, as it were, from the strike of the match girls, or some other great adventure; Annie Besant, then active in the same causes, whose short skirts and short hair Mrs. Pankhurst thought hideous; Adolfe Smith, alias Headingly, stout, dark-eyed and vivacious, telling of his narrow escape from execution in the Paris Commune; Louise Michel, of the Commune, the " petroleuse," as her enemies called her, a tiny old woman in a brown cloak, intensely lean, with gleaming eyes and swarthy

skin, the most wrinkled you ever saw, which made me think of
the twisted seams in the bark of an ancient chestnut tree. She
had a beaming eye for children. I regarded her with admiration
as a tremendous heroine. She seemed to belong to the magical
world of imagination, not the commonplace life of every day.
Sometimes I fancied her wandering in strange old forests amid
the fantastic beings of fairy-tales; at others I saw her in the stress
of battle, her slight figure leaping forward in the darkness, lit by
the glare of conflagration, her bare arm uplifted with a torch, a
scarlet Phrygian cap upon her raven hair, wide-mouthed with a
shout of defiance, her lips drawn back from gleaming teeth, her
black eyes sparkling with fierce joy.

Henri Rochefort was a frequent visitor. In spite of the long
years of his exile in London he refused to learn English, declaring
that our barbarous tongue would spoil his French accent. Dr.
Pankhurst spoke French with punctilious exactitude, his love of
the precise word causing a frequent recourse to the dictionary.
Mrs. Pankhurst's passion for all things French was renewed with
its old fire. She declared the Doctor so utterly different from
the typical stolid Englishman that he must possess an admixture
of French blood. In the genealogical tree of his family she had
noticed that one of his forebears had married a woman named
Dore. The name, she declared, must certainly have been Doré.

A great event was the visit of Rochefort's daughter, her old
friend Noémie, and Noémie's daughter Lillie, solid and not very
pretty, and the two sons, Henri and Armand, tall, slight boys in
their early 'teens, the astonishment of our neighbourhood, on
account of their short socks and the round navy-blue capes they
wore in lieu of overcoats. They ran gaily about playing games
not known in England. A few years later these clever youths
had patented a small motor, which could be attached to any
bicycle, and had received an international gold medal for this
invention.

Discussions whirled about our young ears, mingling with our
childish interests; the New *versus* the Old Trade Unionism, the
Socialism of various schools; the delightful prophecies of Kropotkin, then at an early stage of his long exile here; the Socialist
magazine *To-day*, and the contributions therein of the much-
talked-of young man with sandy hair, the brilliant Bernard Shaw;
Annie Besant's *Link*, the Fabian Essays, Bellamy's *Looking
Backward* and later Blatchford's *Merrie England*; the decision of
Edith Lanchester to contract a free union, instead of a legal
marriage, a position in which the Doctor strongly championed
her; the Dilke Divorce Case. Dr. Pankhurst refused to judge, or
even to consider the charges against Sir Charles Dilke, insisting

that the man's public work should not be prejudiced by the case. He and Mrs. Pankhurst called on the Dilkes in the hour of their trouble.   Dilke, with head sunk in his hands, declared himself ruined; the Doctor answered cheerily: "No, you will live it down!" Theosophy was beginning to be talked of. It was said that its founder, Mme. Blavatsky, had been seen to extend her arm to abnormal length, in order to light a cigarette at the gas jet in the ceiling.   Mrs. Pankhurst and her sisters attended some of the séances, but nothing remarkable happened during their presence.   Mrs. Pankhurst was contemptuously sceptical and dismissed Blavatsky's occult phenomena as mere imposture.   The Doctor was an Agnostic; she, lacking his scientific, philosophical temperament and sustained mental training, was emphatically an Atheist.   Reform, to her, was the main business of life.

Prominent amongst the most cherished reform projects to both of them were women's enfranchisement and removal of the disabilities of married women.   The Suffrage Movement had dwindled since the exclusion of women from the Third Reform Act.   It had been sapped by the rise of the women's organizations formed by the political parties to do their election canvassing when the hiring of paid canvassers was made illegal.   The Primrose Dames (formed in 1883), the Women's Liberal Association (1886), the Women's Liberal Unionist Association (1888) absorbed many prominent Suffragists, and divided, where they did not monopolize their energies.

There was a yet more potent reason for the drift from the Suffrage Movement.   It had grown apace when a democratic franchise was the popular demand of the day, cheered by the masses, cherished by the most ardent reformers.   When the enactment of household suffrage for the men, both in town and country, had removed the crying scandal of a populace mainly disfranchised; when it was seen that the enfranchisement of the workmen had failed immediately to produce the great advance in their conditions which had been anticipated, and that the vote of the agricultural labourers was even proving a bulwark to Conservatism, the hopes of reformers were turned in other directions.   To secure enthusiasm for votes for women was therefore to work against the current of popular interest and desire, now flowing towards other objectives.   Moreover, the people who had gained control of the Suffrage Societies were not the dynamic natures who create new great currents in public life. Their policy was narrow and trivial.   Yet the leaven of women's desire for citizenship was still at work.

Dissension in Suffrage ranks on the question of the married women's vote was perennial.   Under the lead of Lydia Becker, the executive of the National Society for Women's Suffrage had again adopted a Bill expressly excluding married women in the following objectionable phrase:

" Provided that nothing in this Act contained shall enable women under coverture to be registered, or to vote at such elections."

Introduced in the Autumn Session of 1884, this Bill was not debated till 1886, when its passage of the Second Reading without a division raised a flicker of hope that it might become law. In the same year the Infants Act, which gave to widowed mothers the custody and guardianship of their children, reached the Statute Book, and two years later maintenance was secured for deserted wives. In securing these Acts the Manchester pioneers, and foremost of all Elizabeth Wolstenholme Elmy, toiled without ceasing, leaving Lydia Becker and her colleagues of the narrower policy dominant in the Suffrage field.

Under a new spurt of energy, five women stood as candidates for the County Councils created by the Local Government Act of 1888. Jane Cobden and Lady Sandhurst were elected to the London County Council in January, 1889, and Miss Cons was appointed an Alderman by the votes of 118 Councillors. Beresford Hope, who had been defeated by Lady Sandhurst, appealed against her election to the Court of Queen's Bench and won the action. Lady Sandhurst took her case to the House of Lords, where it was heard by six judges, including the Lord Chief Justice, the same Lord Coleridge who had been briefed by the Manchester Suffrage Society to appear with Dr. Pankhurst in the case of Chorlton *v*. Lings. Taking now an entirely opposite line he proved an enemy to the women's cause. Delivering judgement against Lady Sandhurst, he argued that the office of Councillor was a new office; consequently the right to exercise it must be found " within the four corners of the Act." The right expressly granted to women was the right to vote; more than had been expressly granted in terms they could not have. In the case of men the right of voting implied the right of election; not so with women. The Master of the Rolls, Lord Esher, capped these observations by a sweeping assertion:

" I take it that neither by the common law, nor the Constitution of the country until now, can a woman be entitled to exercise any public function."

" I venture to say," commented Dr. Pankhurst, " that even in the face of these decisions, the constitution of the country is this—that disability is not to be presumed—disability is not to be taken for granted—ability is to be presumed, and disability is only to be admitted if it is declared and expressed."

Not unnaturally Lord Coleridge was twitted on the incon-

sistency of his present judgement with his appearance for the
women in 1868.   His legal colleagues whispered that his late wife
was "not so much of a tartar" as the lady who occupied that
position when he tried Lady Sandhurst's case.

In 1888 a curious disturbance occurred in the Women's
Suffrage Society; there was still but one. The Central Committee,
despite the opposition of Lydia Becker and Mrs. Fawcett, decided
to accept the affiliation of women's organizations approved by the
executive, having other objects than Women's Suffrage. The
intention was to join up with the women's organizations attached
to the political parties, especially with the Women's Liberal
Federation. Members of the provincial organizations were not
permitted to attend the meeting called to adopt the new rules.
Miss Becker rushed for legal advice to her old friend, Dr. Pankhurst, whom she had so often opposed and flouted of late. Mrs.
Pankhurst, whose membership was in Manchester, hastily joined
up in London to cast a vote against the new proposal, despite a
letter of protest from Florence Balgarnie. The promoters of the
scheme had an empty victory; they carried their resolution, but
all the provincial organizations, and a large minority of the
central committee, retired next day to form a new organization.[1]

Both organizations continued to support the detested Woodall
coverture clause.   Three hundred and forty Members of
Parliament were now pledged to votes for women, an absolute
majority of the House.   Therefore when, at the opening of the
1889 Session, Woodall secured what appeared an excellent place
for his Bill, it was thought in Suffrage circles the disputed measure
might actually pass into law. The defenders of the married
woman aroused themselves to do battle; Mrs. Elmy at Congleton,
the Pankhursts in Russell Square, the Brights at St. James's Place
were the live wires of revolt against Coverture. At the annual
general meeting of the Central National Society for Women's
Suffrage, on March 21st, 1889, Mrs. Fenwick Miller, editor of the
old *Woman's Signal*, a pioneer among women journalists, Dr.
Kate Mitchell and Dr. Pankhurst appeared as insurgents, with a
resolution condemning the coverture clause, which they carried
against the platform by an overwhelming majority. The same
evening the Society held a public meeting in the Prince's Hall.
This time the anti-coverture amendment was moved by the
veteran Jacob Bright, who had secured the enactment of the Local
Government vote for women, and whose Parliamentary services
to women's enfranchisement were antedated only by those of
Mill. Woodall at first declared him out of order, but consented,
after a protest from Dr. Pankhurst, to put the amendment to the

---

[1] Eventually the two organizations re-united under the old constitution.

meeting. It was carried with acclamation. Florence Balgarnie, the secretary of the organization, then apologized for the coverture clause, saying it had been " slipped in, by whom no one seemed to know." Undeterred by this double, and most decisive condemnation from the members of the Society, the Executive Committee, elected by that very annual meeting to carry out its behests, yet decided to continue supporting the coverture clause. Such defiance by elected persons of the wishes of their constituents is even to-day so amazingly common that it is apt to occasion little surprise or resentment. In this case the result was the formation of a new organization—the Women's Franchise League.

It was early in July, 1889, that a little circle of ladies gathered in the bedroom of Mrs. Pankhurst, at Russell Square, to congratulate her on the birth of her youngest son. The treachery towards the married women of both the existing Suffrage Societies was hotly denounced, and the formation of the League decided on. William Lloyd Garrison, the apostle of negro emancipation, spoke at the inaugural meeting, on July 25th. Its Council included the Pankhursts, the Elmys, the Jacob Brights, Josephine Butler, Cunningham Graham, with Jane Cobden and Lady Sandhurst, then at the height of their struggle for membership of the L.C.C., and Mrs. P. A. Taylor,[1] the initiator, who in 1869 had called together the first women's suffrage society formed in London, who had taken the chair at the first public meeting ever held in London for that cause, and who had been a member of the London Committee which organized the first petition presented to Parliament by John Stuart Mill. Representing American Suffragists on the Council of the League was the aged Elizabeth Cady Stanton, foremost of all Suffrage pioneers, who did much to secure the American Married Women's Property Act of 1848, and in the same year joined with Lucretia Mott in organizing at Seneca Falls the first Women's Rights Convention ever held in the world. Thus nobly sponsored, the League came rapidly to the front as the most active force working for women's emancipation at the time. Its foremost plank remained defence of the married woman, and in a few years time it had succeeded in rousing a volume of opinion, which effectively put an end to the existence of disabilities founded on Coverture. The Jackson case of 1891, described by the *Law Times* as " the Married Woman's Charter of personal liberty," wherein it was decided that a husband might not imprison his wife to enforce his conjugal rights, was eagerly hailed, and was an evidence of the change which was coming over opinion in general. The case created a

[1] *Née* Clementia Doughty. Her husband, P. A. Taylor, was the Radical Member for Leicester.

furore far beyond Suffrage circles. I remember at that year's Christmas pantomime a little man wearing spats, who sang a song with the refrain: " The Jackson case! The Jackson case! "

The Franchise League adopted Dr. Pankhurst's original Women's Disabilities Removal Bill, first introduced by Jacob Bright in 1870, with a new clause, declaring that no person should be disqualified for election or appointment to any office or position by reason of sex or marriage. The League also worked to secure equality for women in divorce, inheritance and the custody and guardianship of their children. Its life was by no means tranquil. The cry: " Half a loaf is better than no bread! " was constantly raised against it. Many of its adherents became backsliders, unable to withstand the reproaches of those who were advocating the widow's and spinster's franchise, which, with the vehemence so often accorded to error, the leaders of the older suffrage societies insisted had the only chance of success.

Woodall's Bill, and its coverture clause, which had occasioned so much commotion, never came to the vote, for the Government again and again confiscated the day it should have had; but in 1892 Sir Albert Rollit secured a place for a similar measure, designed to enfranchise the widows and spinsters exercising the Local Government vote. Again the Franchise League demanded the inclusion of married women. Its adherents, led by Herbert Burrows, stormed the platform of a St. James's Hall meeting held in support of the Bill, and carried a resolution denouncing it— for those tranquil days indeed an adventure, and one of which its prime author was vastly proud. He was never tired of declaring in his vehement way that he had " kicked out the Ladies' Bill." On the other hand a Hyde Park Demonstration Committee created by the League was turned by its secretary into a weapon of support for the Rollit Bill. " I hope your difficulties with the Franchise League are smoothing over," wrote Lady Dilke, on August 22nd, 1890, in concluding a letter begun by her husband. The Overseers had put her on the list of County Council electors in respect of their country house, and Dilke was asking Dr. Pankhurst to prepare a statement to be read to the Revising Barrister in support of her claim to vote.

The difficulties of the Franchise League were indeed mani- fold. Mrs. Elmy withdrew to form the Women's Emancipation Union, objecting to the uncompromising attitude of the Franchise League and declaring herself willing to support a Widows' and Spinsters' Bill provided married women were not excluded in terms, a fine shade of distinction which made no appeal to the robust spirit of the Franchise League. R. B. Haldane (afterwards Lord Haldane), a frequent speaker at Russell Square, accepted the sponsorship of the Women's Disabilities Removal Bill, and Sir Edward Grey consented to back it; but unfortunately neither of these then young and rising politicians took a single step to advance the measure. When the Franchise League ladies interviewed Haldane in the Parliamentary Lobby, pressing for the Bill to be brought to a vote, he declared it was a declaration of principle, upon which legislative action could not be expected for fifty years. Thereby he lighted a smouldering fire of indignation in the breast of impatient Mrs. Pankhurst. She spoke of him ever after with intense dislike.

The Franchise League took advanced views on life in general. Co-education, Marriage Law Reform, Trade Unionism, Internationalism, the defence of oppressed races, and other causes found voice on its platform. It adopted Dr. Pankhurst's scheme for abolishing the House of Lords, printing it in leaflet form as one of its foremost planks. More impatient for the goal than any of its women members, the Doctor, an unwitting prophet of future militancy, would exclaim, more earnest than jesting: " Why are women so patient? Why don't you force us to give you the vote? " Then playfully clawing the air with his long fingers: " Why don't you scratch our eyes out? " Infinitely meek and cautious, infinitely resigned to wait, and wait indefinitely, was the Women's Movement of the period. Eager as through life she was, in all which captured her interest, Mrs. Pankhurst, the charming hostess of those days, had not yet become a public speaker. To her it was still an ordeal, evaded as far as possible, to introduce the lecturer in a brief sentence, to read out a list of announcements, or even to rise from her seat and pronounce the words: " I second the resolution." She regarded herself as the helper and understudy of her husband, and of that able woman, Ursula Bright, who was honorary secretary of the Franchise League during the greater part of its existence, and the staunchest of its members.

Mrs. Alice Cliff Scatcherd, the honorary treasurer of the League, was a highly sincere and genuine worker. A tall, bony Yorkshire woman of Morley, near Leeds, of substantial means and assured social position, she repudiated as badges of slavery, and refused to wear either a wedding ring or the veil with which every would-be well-dressed woman covered her face in those days. (Mrs. Pankhurst then never went out without her veil.) Because this middle-aged lady wore no ring, hotel proprietors many times refused to admit her, when she appeared with her husband, despite her appearance of indubitable respectability, and her staid, unfashionable dress, completed by large, low-heeled, elastic-sided boots. Such was the prudery of the nineteenth century.

CHAPTER VII

THE LITTLE GIRLS IN RUSSELL SQUARE

WE children took a lively interest in the political gatherings held in Russell Square, helping to arrange the chairs for the meetings, giving out leaflets, taking the collections in pretty little bags of brocaded stuff. I was proud to be given the task of printing the notices. "To the Tea Room" was invariably required: there were always refreshments, and frequently music and recitations, to draw an audience to Suffrage meetings in those days. Enormous quantities of strawberries had to be picked for some of these functions; there were masses of flowers, and especially heliotrope, Mrs. Pankhurst's favourite. I remember the deep contralto of Antoinette Sterling singing Elizabeth Barrett Browning's "Cry of the Children," and the frail accents of my mother's sister, Mary, reciting unhappy love stories. The Indian, Mr. Mulvi, whom the servants whispered with bated breath was teaching Hindustani to the Queen, a picturesque figure in a turban and flowing robes, was a frequent habitué of these gatherings.

Our nursery life was very simple. We breakfasted on oatmeal porridge, every day in the week save Sunday, when we were allowed bread and butter and milk, and occasionally, for a treat, an egg divided between us three girls. Our plain, two-course midday dinner on week-days always included milk pudding, but on Sunday we took a more elaborate meal with our parents. We wore outdoor coats of green "art" serge from Emerson's, and navy blue serge frocks, with knickers to match, because they were inexpensive and hard-wearing. Christabel resented the difference between our dress and that of the other little girls in the Square; above all she envied their dainty white petticoats. When Mme. Dufaux brought us white muslin pinafores from Paris, garnished with tucks and ribbons and laces, Christabel insisted that without letting any of the grown-ups know it, we should wear them under our frocks, letting the lace appear, in order that people might think we had white petticoats like the other girls. To such matters I was wholly indifferent, but as Christabel desired it, I agreed as a matter of course. She and I were throughout our childhood most constant companions. I remember only one quarrel between us. So brief was it, and for so slight a cause, that I have altogether forgotten what it was about. After the quarrel, I stood in the dusk of the landing outside the nursery door in a state of abject misery : then hearing her step I rushed towards her with outstretched arms, and realized in a glow of transcendent joy that she had reached out her arms to take me in.

She was our mother's favourite; we all knew it, and I, for one, never resented the fact. It was a matter of course; and I loved her too much to be jealous of her. It was a joy to me to walk beside her, half a step in arrear, gazing upon the delicate pink and white of her face and neck, contrasted against the young, green plants coming up in the Square garden in the spring. She was tenacious of her position as the eldest and the favourite, but she exercised it on the whole without offence. She generally saw to it that she should be the one to be taken about with our parents, and that the taking in turns which our father desired should be cast aside; but for my part I was always so busy with drawing, writing, copying the embroidery on a Japanese screen, watching insects and worms, or some other interest, that I was content to be left in my groove. Like Mrs. Pankhurst, Christabel began to read books at an incredibly early age. I had weak eyes in childhood, and therefore was not encouraged to read, and I cherished a lively sense of gratitude toward Christabel, who would read to me for many hours at a stretch. I was nearly eight years old when Susannah was reading to me the English translation of Jules Verne's *De la Terre à la Lune*. She stumbled so much over the task that I took the book from her hands and read aloud to her, and decided that I would read for myself henceforth.

In warm weather we were taken daily to the Square garden, and left there till it was time to come in for a meal. That garden held for us an endless store of fascinations. There was the circular path bordered by plane trees; hour upon hour we walked it, talking of what had happened and what might happen, looking up into the tracery of leaves and branches at the pendant balls of the fruit and the pale yellow patches left on the trunks by the scaling bark. At each of the four corners of the Square was a small circular enclosure, hedged round by bushes, wherein the gardeners piled the finely chopped grass from the lawn-mowers. Except the gardeners, grown-up people never entered here, nor, so far as I know, any other children; and we only when, as daily happened, our elders had left us alone in the Square. We had a name of our own for each of these sacred havens. Our favourite, called the " Swerdiggy," seemed a place of perfect beauty; it contained a few wild weeds, to us like fairy flowers, often more lovely in their delicate shapes than the showy garden blooms. " The Froggety " was so named because I had once discovered a toad there, a creature previously seen only in pictures, and recognized with excitement. Shakespeare's phrase:

> " . . . The toad, ugly and venomous,
>   Wears yet a precious jewel in his head "

came to my mind. Knowing there could be no jewel, I yet looked for it, and thought with pleasure that its eyes were more lovely than precious stones. As I took the toad in my hands, it seemed to me like a helpless baby with short, weak legs and tiny, clutching " fingers." I imagined it had become a little baby, and we were floating away together in the clouds. . . . I waked myself from the day-dream with a jerk to hear what my sisters were saying.

The lawns in the Square garden had each a peculiar excellence, one famous for white clover, one for its bordering laburnums, another for abundance of daisies; what happy hours we spent there making chains of that tiny blossom, before all others, the children's flower! Its slight, sweet fragrance still enthrals me. I used to think daisies were like little girls; the sort of good little girl I should like to be; a little girl who would never grow up.

I shrank with a fear I never analysed from the thought that I must leave my childhood behind. Stead's *Review of Reviews* was a great favourite with Christabel and me. When she was ten, and I a little more than eight, I read in it the statement that after ten years of age the brain can make no more cells, its formation is settled and completed. " How terrible," I thought, with acute anxiety, " that I have less than two years in which to develop my brain! How little I have learnt! How little I can do! " Many years later, I heard from Christabel that she too had read that passage; and had said to herself, in triumph: " My brain is fully formed! I have as much sense as anyone else! I will not be treated as a child any more! "

Seen through the intervening years, childhood presents itself as a period of great activity and keen interest, transfigured by high delights, guided by large enthusiasms; but torn at times by the anguish of ethical struggle, and depression descending into agony and despair for trivial failings, of longing for affection, and misery at being misunderstood. Anything ugly or sordid brought despondency, often recurrent and difficult to overcome, as though one's mind were a sensitive plate on which impressions bit deeply. Yet everywhere was beauty—light, colour, form, entrancing, even painful in the intensity of the pleasure they evoked. Blue skies with the larks soaring upward, the sun pouring down on the hay and its flowers were intoxicating, almost unbearable in their loveliness. There was magic delight in the breathing stillness of cool woods. Even the grey winter days in town had their charm, when one gazed from high windows on rain dashing itself on the pavements and rebounding in millions of little splashes like an army of knights in their mail. Yet when we returned from the country and the train steamed into the dingy purlieus of the terminus, I always wept.

From some petty cause: a scolding for dawdling behind when one's boots were tight and one's feet ached; for refusal to eat the every-morning porridge, often lumpy and cold, for only the children ate it: harsh words would fly, force would be attempted and frantically resisted. I remember, under the discipline of the servants, being tied to the bed all day as a punishment for refusal to take cod liver oil. For such rebellion against the orders of my mother, though others enforced them, I felt an almost unbearable remorse—and sense of degradation; yet from acute physical repulsion I offended in the same manner again and again over a period of years, and shaken by uncontrollable sobbing would end by imploring my mother on my knees: "Help me to be good!" Silent miseries of contrition, invariably mistaken for sulkiness, were accompanied by terrible headaches. In these dark hours it was generally Aunt Mary who brought comfort, and an understanding to which no words were needed. I never attempted to draw Christabel, my companion, from the sunny favour of the household into the drear wastes of misery, wherein the original cause of sorrow was submerged. Such troubles were all but unknown to her; her health was good, and she had no disposition towards distressful introspection. The others, I think, suffered in some measure as I did. I have often seen my brother Harry, with little white face, silently facing an accusation, as though turned to stone. Children to-day are freer and franker than they were in our generation; they meet their elders on a more genial plane, and are the happier for it. In my twenties I was surprised to hear my mother telling some friends that before I was three years of age, I had convinced her of the uselessness of beating her children, because when she had employed that means of bringing me to contrition, I had made her feel that she might kill me before I would give way. As was characteristic of the period, she remained throughout our childhood somewhat rigid in her discipline, which grew in severity by delegation to others. She demanded implicit obedience, and would tolerate "no likes and dislikes." "Young women are disciplinarians," I have heard her say, in recalling this fact in later years. Undoubtedly we children had all, in our different ways, an obstinacy inherited from both sides. We "could be appealed to," as Aunt Mary said, but to drive us was more troublesome than the attempt proved worth. "A want of conscience"; that was the terrible rebuke our father occasionally uttered, more painful than any punishment to me.

It was Father's rule—O splendid father!—that as soon as one said: "I am sorry," all punishment must end; benign forgiveness must erase all memory of offence. Was that clemency abused? Indeed no! To me at least, and I believe to all of us, there was a sacred character about that confession which precluded deception. It was preceded by a deep research to discover whether renunciation of that which had incurred reproof was in truth complete. Often I lingered, probing within me, longing to say that word, whilst the tears would stream from my eyes in such abandon that looking down from where I was crouching, with cheek leaning, perhaps, against the nursery sewing-machine, I have found a little puddle of tears upon the floor.

We seldom played games, but on rare occasions, at intervals of several months, we would have a wild romp, in which the servants would sometimes join—or perhaps it was they who began it. The house in Russell Square gave ample scope for a chase. There were two staircases leading to the basement, and there, and on other floors, were rows of large, unused communicating cupboards, large enough for several people to hide in. Twice a year, when our own summer and winter clothes were being made, by our mother and nurse, generally with a seamstress to help, we would bring out the dolls given to us by visitors— our parents invariably gave us books. Some days would be spent in imitating the dressmaking of our elders, with the dolls as our models; then the dolls would be put away for the rest of the year; none of us took any further interest in them.

Adela was a child apart. Her development had been retarded by a weakness of the legs, which, though happily overcome in time, necessitated the wearing of splints, and kept her from walking till three years of age. Petted and nursed by the grownups till she was four years old, she became rather a solitary little creature when a new baby was born. She spent much of her time improvising dramas she called "prince tales," and acted with much vigour, herself playing all the characters, and using everything she could lay hands on as stage properties. She was very small for her age, and a great favourite with visitors, whom she lay in wait to approach with the question: "Shall I tell you a tale?" As long as they could be induced to listen, she would pour her romances into their ears.

Our younger brother, Henry Francis, called Harry, was born on July 7th, 1889. To Mrs. Pankhurst, in her pregnancy, he had been "Frank coming again"; his birth was the subject of great rejoicing to us all. Mother and child were doing well; the Doctor set off to Manchester to attend a case. Some hours later the vigilant Susannah told the maternity nurse that Mrs. Pankhurst was "looking very white." The nurse declared nothing was wrong. Susannah wasted no words, but ran out in her cap and apron to summon help. That was before the days of telephones; the family doctor lived far away. Susannah ran to the nearest house displaying a doctor's plate. The occupant no longer took "maternity cases" and would not budge. Susannah ran on to the next plate. Rebuffed again and again, she ran on. The doctor she brought at last discovered Mrs. Pankhurst sinking under hæmorrhage. The Doctor was telegraphed for; he returned in an agony of distress, to find the danger at an end.

Harry, at birth, was the finest of Mrs. Pankhurst's children, but apparently his bottle did not agree with him; perhaps the nurse mismanaged him; he did not get his mother's personal care. His health at several stages gave occasion for anxiety. There was often a steam kettle puffing in the nursery on his account. The open-air life was not *de rigueur* for children, as it has since become, and in winter, for weeks at a time, we scarcely left the nursery. Yet he was a beautiful, sturdy-limbed child, and at three years spoke with remarkable fluency. Dr. Pankhurst's clerk, the dour Underwood, declared the boy would make a lawyer, because, when some assertion of his was questioned, the youngster replied: "It was words to that effect."

Our days alone in the Square garden were for a time quite cut off. Some big boys asked Adela strange questions. We confided them to Aunt Mary. Mother rebuked us for leaving Adela to play alone. She tried then, very haltingly, to talk to us about the mysteries of sex, which the modern mother imparts in systematic stages. "Father says I ought to talk to you," she began; but she did not get very much further, and never again reverted to the subject, leaving us as free from knowledge as before, on the question which disturbed her. Thereafter we were often in the little patch of ground behind the house, enclosed by a high wall. No flowers were there. Only a tall half-dead acacia tree and a lilac, which never flowered, and some weak and scanty grass. I used to sit there for hours imagining adventures. The wall would fade away, vistas of trees and flowers would take its place; a lake with swans and water-lilies; a river flowing through meadows, and fringed with yellow irises. Birds sang; lambs bounded upon the grass; a lovely woman in white robes came smiling towards me, surrounded by dancing children. I flew away on the back of a great bird, I soared above the clouds, I crossed the seas. I descended to yellow sands, where groves of palms and flowering trees came near to the water's edge, and barges lay moored, laden with bright fruits, gorgeous silks, wrought silver and gold and precious stones, and all the richest and loveliest things my child mind could conceive. Such splendid imaginings were the solace for all misunderstandings and sorrows. Only when the world of dream refused to open would the carping of a torturing conscience, or the too vivid realization of the griefs of unhappy people, whether of real life or of fiction, bring down upon my spirit a cloud of dark despond.

The thought of growth was magical. The seed bursting its sheath, and putting forth its first pale shoot, caused a thrill of rapture. The sight of the fallen leaves was always sad; yet as I stood with my eyes fixed upon them, would come the thought of life stirring under the leaves; and presently I would see trees arising from them; trees such as never were, for ever changing, growing from the dear, familiar trees one knew and loved, to marvellous creations, bearing wonderful, unknown fruits, with squirrels, lizards, birds of every hue, playing in their branches, which, reaching higher and higher into the skies, supported fair castles in the air. The goal of those dreams was always one cherished climax: a beautiful country house, which some day would be our home, surrounded by daisied lawns, with woods and fields beyond. Peacocks displayed their gorgeous tails upon the terraces, dappled fawns fed, confident, from the hand, pigeons cooed in the woods, little green love-birds perched in the creepers on the wall. Everything of beauty and desire I saw or read of found a place in that pleasant scheme. This house of blessing was soon surrounded by many others; for whoever desired would come to dwell in that place, and there the poor and sad would find plenty and joy. It was a childish fancy, gradually developing and extending to the hope of a commonwealth, where all should be "better than well." Somehow and somewhere I believed I should be associated with the realization of that vision.

It was early in our childhood that Father began to buy for us the toy books of Walter Crane, from whose delightful "Pan Pipes" we sang the Old English songs with our mother on Sunday afternoons. His Socialist cartoons, and especially his "Triumph of Labour," aroused in me the longing to be a painter and draughtsman in the service of the great movements for social betterment; and this remained the lasting and fervent hope of my youth.

At night when we went to bed it was a delightful game to tell each other what we could see in the dark with our faces on the pillow. Wonderful processions and pageants passed by, lovelier than one could tell. The shyness and restraint of the day would vanish, and one could speak with a freedom unknown at other times. That shyness: what a trouble it was! I was continually drawing—not things seen, always the things imagined. My sketch-books were carefully hidden, generally under the furniture. I was too keenly conscious of my failure to render adequately my precious visions, to endure without pain the inspection of my efforts by the relatively indifferent gaze of other eyes. Only when the original conceptions had been thrust, by a succession of others, into the background of my mind, and thus their sacredness was dimmed, would a drawing-book be carelessly left about, and so get picked up and examined by other people.

Harriot Stanton Blatch, daughter of the veteran Elizabeth Cady Stanton, had married an Englishman and lived at Basingstoke in Hampshire; she was one of the most active members of the Franchise League. She took great interest in the education of girls, and complained that even in the elementary schools where both boys and girls were taught in the same class, the cards used for arithmetic were marked: " For girls," with easier sums on one side, and " For boys," with more difficult sums on the other. I thought Mrs. Blatch immensely learned, and stood in great awe of her. When my mother first called me up to be introduced, Mrs. Blatch observed that I looked delicate. " She will not eat her porridge," my mother answered. To my astonishment, instead of joining in the reproach, Mrs. Blatch responded cheerfully, " Then why give her porridge? There are lots of other good things to eat for breakfast: eggs, fish, bacon, kidneys, fruit! " I regarded her in amazement; even to hear such words seemed treason to my mother. My loyalty rallied to her: was she not the most beautiful woman in the world? Not one of all the ladies who came to the house, distinguished as I thought them, could compare with her. How clear was her beautiful pallor, how finely arched her delicate black eyebrows, how soft and tender her large, violet eyes! She had the loveliness of the moon, and the grace of the slender silver birch. I gazed on her with adoration.

Mrs. Stanton Blatch was ever outspoken: Christabel, she told Mrs. Pankhurst, was " far too sentimental," she needed a stiff course of mathematics, instead of her perpetual novel reading. No doubt Mrs. Blatch was right: we both of us lacked any systematic education, and several years were still to elapse before we were sent to school.

Christabel and I decided to give lectures, she on coal, I on tea. We read up our subjects for several days; then committed the result of our studies to writing. Adela could not read; it did not occur to us that she would attempt to emulate our performance; but on the appointed day she announced that she would lecture on the cat, and shortly before the hour fixed, she seized our domestic puss, and lay down on the hearthrug to examine her. We were not pleased by such levity; we feared she would make our meeting ridiculous. We urged her not to attempt what was obviously beyond her powers, but our arguments entirely failed to dissuade her. Our parents, two aunts, a second cousin and a friend, all adults, assembled to hear our lectures. I trembled and wished myself a thousand miles away. Dr. Pankhurst called on Christabel to begin. Already quivering with apprehension, I was horrified to hear her stumbling, almost inaudible delivery. Her hastily written screed was difficult to decipher, but her nervousness precluded dispensing with the text. Dr. Pankhurst, desirous to aid her, made matters worse by interpolating: "Speak up." "Don't be self-conscious." Only the thought that it would be unutterably mean to desert her, spurred me to follow, grimly plodding on in what was undoubtedly a still more halting performance. Scarcely had I finished when Adela stepped gaily forward, unencumbered by notes, brisk and clear of voice; a single phrase sticks in my mind: "The cat has a nose and mouth joined together like a monkey or such-like." She was rewarded by rounds of applause.

Christabel was disgusted. Badly as we had delivered them, we had worked hard at our lectures. Many of our facts were new, she was sure, to some, if not to all our auditors. Adela, on the other hand, had taken no trouble at all. The great applause for her was a mockery of our serious efforts. I suspected it was simply an outburst of relief from our stumbling dullness, of which I was acutely conscious, but I would not add to Christabel's discomfort by saying so. Aunt Mary tried to console us; insisting that she had learnt much from our lectures. How little we, or she, in her unassuming gentleness, realized the measure of her great helpfulness to us.

I dreamt that a witch transformed us three sisters into three grey cats and transported us to a desert island. I wrote the story as a play; Aunt Mary agreed to act it with us. The

Fenwick Miller girls also took part in it. I was eager to paint the scenery. There were some large Japanese screens in the basement, discarded, I thought, as mere lumber. I persuaded my sisters to help me to paste sheets of notepaper all over them, in order that I might have a clean, white surface for the work. We had scarcely begun, when Susannah intervened, and Mrs. Pankhurst refused to permit us to " spoil " her screens. Aunt Mary urged that we should dispense with scenery, and put up a notice: " This is a wood," as they did in Shakespeare's time. I should have submitted, perforce, to Hobson's choice; but my mother's brother Bob, who was a scene painter by profession, came to spend Christmas with us; and with the aid of stout brown paper and paints and some pieces of wood he produced the requisite scenery—including the wings! His work was magnificently professional in my eyes, but I still had hankering thoughts of the beautiful scenes in my dreams, and the unsatisfied longing to cover those large white surfaces I had intended.

Already then, we children were publishing a manuscript newspaper for family circulation: *The Home News*, with the sub-title, chosen by Dr. Pankhurst, *And Universal Mirror*. This cherished organ appeared at first weekly, and as it grew larger, monthly. The Doctor contributed serious letters on important subjects, which Christabel copied in her sprawling hand. For the rest she usually confined herself to very brief reports of the Franchise League Meetings. Having early completed these, she would help me to copy out my own voluminous screeds, which included a series called " Walks in London," describing the House of Commons, the British Museum, National Gallery, Tower of London, and anything and everything we encountered. I also drew the illustrations for the paper. Adela, then about six years of age, clamoured to be allowed to put something in *The Home News*. She dictated to Christabel a long story about a poor widow woman with a large family of children, who were translated from destitution to comfort by a rich benefactor. One phrase from the story I still recall: " She said, ' I must have taken a sip from dreamland's lovely prime.' "

It was before this, in our earliest months at Russell Square, that Cecil Sowerby, an artist whom Aunt Mary had known in Paris, came to be our governess. She gave us no lessons, but read to us and took us to museums and places of interest. Much of our time was spent in the British Museum, where my greatest enthusiasm was for the Egyptian section; the massive shapes and gorgeous colours had a deep and permanent fascination, and the knowledge that those vivacious scenes and pigments were older than history lent an added thrill. The mummy cases, with their pictured life stories, woke in one's inmost thoughts the longing to solve the mysteries of life and death. I was eager to understand the construction of the human frame, and begged to be allowed to see a skeleton. Miss Sowerby would have taken us to a medical museum for this purpose, but as children we were refused admission. Father, however, brought home for us a cardboard anatomical man, whose muscular system, vital organs, and finally his skeleton were revealed by turning back successive layers of card.

Miss Sowerby had returned to her painting. We had been long without lessons. Father talked of sending us to school, but Mother objected; we were " too highly strung," and would "lose all originality " if put in a class with dozens of other children. We had heard our father say that all children ought to attend the public schools, as they do in the United States. We spoke of this to Susannah; but she told us that if we went to a Board School, we should catch " things in our heads," and all sorts of illnesses, the children would be " rough," and the teachers would use the cane. I believed her because the boys and girls in Marchmont Street, where she took us shopping, jeered at our brown stockings, then only beginning to be worn, and when Mrs. Pankhurst bought us some rather unusual hats from Liberty's, they shouted : " What are your hats made of : hay, straw, cane of a chair? "

I was relieved when Christabel agreed that instead of pressing to be sent to school we should give each other lessons. We began by setting each other addition and subtraction sums. The addition went well enough, but so hazy was our conception of arithmetic, which to us was only " sums," without any relation to actual things, that Christabel had set me to subtract the greater from the lesser, and we neither of us could understand why the sum would not come right. Mrs. Pankhurst came in while her daughters were puzzling over the problem. She explained the mistake in a few words, and rebuked our ignorance rather sharply. Our efforts at self-improvement in that form were thus abruptly checked.

Echoes of the Rotherhithe libel actions reached the nursery, and helped to accentuate the inner stirrings of the desire for knowledge. Susannah was always with us; the housemaids and cooks were a changing quantity. One of the succession of cooks, called Ellen, was a woman of dark, mysterious sayings, who dominated even Susannah. In the kitchen, where we went occasionally, we heard strange conversations. Ellen frequently spoke of " a certain party." It was some time before we knew she meant our mother. We heard the servants arguing as to whether our father was religious. Ellen declared that he was not. Susannah and Rose, the housemaid, insisted that he was a good man and could be heard saying his prayers in the bathroom every morning. He was reading from his favourite poets in actual fact. Ellen replied that we children were not taught to pray, and declared that we would all " burn in Hell fire." The talk distressed me exceedingly. I did not intervene, or pretend to understand; I would not even speak of it to Christabel; but I was constantly turning over the subject in my own mind, thinking of Frank and where he had gone, and whether we should ever see him again. The bare idea that our father could be considered other than perfect in those high ethical provinces, wherein he was the guiding inspiration to all of us, drew tears of agony. Especially when I was alone in the dark, the mystery of our apparent difference from other people thrust itself upon me. Ellen had said that evil luck would befall us in this world and the next because of our irreligious state. It was her habit at all times to weave a strange atmosphere of terror and mystery, compounded of robbery, murder and tragic catastrophe. At the end of a dark passage at the rear of the house was a little room with a glass-panelled wall looking on to the high-walled garden. At night it lent itself to memories of Ellen's fearful tales, and when sent to fetch anything from that room after dark, her grim prophecies assailed me. Then and whenever this portentous problem over-whelmed me, I would pray: " Oh God, if you are God, I know You will not hurt us. I know it is not wrong that Mother and Father have not told us about You, because I know they are good."

This worry about our religion seemed to continue for a long time. Suddenly Christabel and I spoke to each other of what the servants were saying. " I shall ask Father," Christabel said. We went to him together. He welcomed our questions, and answered them frankly, explaining that he had not spoken to us of this matter before, because he desired us to think and decide for ourselves. He gave us a brief outline of the Biblical version of the life of Christ, and of the Christian dogmas, expressing his own disbelief in the supernatural interpretation, and giving the two rival theories held by Agnostics, either that Christ was a persecuted reformer (as he himself thought), or merely a legendary figure, compounded from the stories of many martyrs.[1] He showed us books dealing with this and kindred subjects, which we might read when we chose, and urged us to use our intelligence to investigate for ourselves. He gave us,

[1] The theory elaborated by Brandes.

too, some brief account of the origin of species and the evolution of mankind.

Not then, but many a time as we grew older, he would say to us playfully, and yet in earnest: " If you ever go back into religion you will not have been worth the upbringing." Always he added, and more passionately: " If you do not work for others you will not have been worth the upbringing! "

My mind was henceforth completely at rest on the score of religion. Father had removed what previously had been made to appear a question of vice or virtue, luck and magic, to the realms of detached, scientific examination. A mistake in such matters would involve no guilt or moral failure; if failure there might be, it would be failure of knowledge or discernment, not of virtue. I saw my father as a lofty embodiment of the human mind, faring forth amid uncharted heights. The quest of knowledge was now a favourite subject of my drawings. Half-nude figures hewing roads in the rocky mountains, building with rude stone boulders, bearing lamps through the darkness, their unshod feet treading the rude and jagged stones; old scholars poring over great tomes and surrounded by scales and crucibles.

Some months at Clacton-on-Sea with Susannah and Ellen, our parents only visiting us there occasionally, opened vistas of squalid life hitherto only imagined from the romances of Dickens. Drunkenness was then far more common, far noisier in its excesses than to-day. There were frequent scenes of riotous intoxication amongst the people who came with cheap day tickets to Clacton, the " trippers " as they were called. I shall never forget the horrible sight of two drunkards, standing up wrestling with each other in a small rowing-boat, which lurched heavily from side to side, until one of them was thrown into the sea. Ellen, who derived the liveliest pleasure from such excitements, screeched out that he would be drowned; but he was rescued by another vessel, which put out from the shore. In the evening Ellen insisted upon taking us all to the railway station to see the " trip " trains start for London. She thought she might recognize someone she knew amongst the dockers. Men and women were running up and down the platform, shouting, cursing, fighting, to find a place in the crowded carriages. " Look! " cried Ellen, " he has gone in with the man who threw him into the water! He will be murdered before he gets to London! " I heard her with a pang of sickening fear, believing that she spoke what would really happen. Hours passed. Train after train went out, crowded with noisy, struggling people. Shivering with cold and horror, I clung to the perambulator of the younger children, and on reaching home at last, spent a night tortured by hideous visions of the incidents of the day, with Charles Dickens' murdered Nancy and the " Jack the Ripper " victims I had seen pictured in a Sunday paper.

I have vivid recollections of my first public meeting; a Socialist gathering addressed by H. M. Hyndman in a small and dingy hall in the year 1890.   The Socialist movement was then so impecunious that its meetings were generally held in the meanest of mean streets in miserable premises, and frequently over foul-smelling stables.   The chairman had scarcely finished speaking when Mrs. Pankhurst rose up and insisted on leaving the hall.   Outside she told us that she had found a bug on her glove, and therefore could not bear to remain any longer.

At a similar meeting I remember about that time the Doctor joining in the discussion from amongst the audience, asking in a suggestive way whether the old Radicals might not find a congenial home in the Social Democratic Federation.   Yet he did not join it.   He was not attracted by its raucous insistence upon economic interest as the all-embracing motive of sentient man.   Its internal squabbles and frequent expulsion of members, so often coupled with inactivity in large public issues, were irksome and distasteful to him.   Moreover Hyndman, Belfort Bax and others of its prominent committee men, were opposed to women's enfranchisement.   I remember, many years later, as a young girl, entering on Votes for Women propaganda in London, encountering Hyndman at the house of Dora Montefiore. " Women should learn to have influence as they have in France instead of trying to get votes," Hyndman shouted at me, in a fierce tirade, menacing me with his lion-like front.   He always seemed to me like an old-fashioned china mantelpiece ornament —the head and chest disproportionately large and prominent for the lower limbs, and everything from the back view small and unfinished.   Socialists in those days usually affected tweeds and a red tie, but Hyndman had always a dusty black frock-coat and a top hat.

Only once in our childhood was I parted from Christabel: Mrs. Stanton Blatch took her away to stay with her own little girl, Norah, at their home in Basingstoke.   I was delighted that Christabel should have this, to us, great adventure, but during her absence life seemed to have lost its savour.   Soon afterward we were invited to go to Basingstoke together.   What a joy that country was to me, a town-bred child who had rarely been beyond the suburbs !   The canal, with its water-lilies and irises, and the fields of scarlet poppies seemed like the realization of a dream. Norah Blatch, who later became a civil engineer, and specialized

in the designing of bridges, was then a slim little maid of remarkable daring and swiftness, with hair cut short like a boy's, a navy
blue sailor frock with a very short skirt and long, black-stockinged
legs.   As soon as we arrived she took us climbing up the wood-
pile, and initiated the sport of dropping fir cones on the heads of
people passing in the road below, whilst we crouched out of sight
to watch their wry faces.   I was more astonished than any of
those pedestrians would have been had they discovered us, to see
my sister zestfully entering into this prank.   In spite of our quiet
ways at home, she would not allow herself to be out-done by
Norah, who was a year or more younger than herself.   One
afternoon of general haymaking, whilst Mrs. Blatch was in
London, I learnt from the other two that when our bedtime came
we were to push the maidservants down in the hay, and then run
off across the fields, and not come back till late.   The project
succeeded; the maids fell down in the soft hay, laughing at the
joke, and off we ran.   Mr. Blatch brought us in at last and treated
our escapade as a piece of fun.   We were asleep before Mrs.
Blatch returned.   She came to our bedroom next morning and
scolded Christabel, saying that as the eldest she was to blame.   To
me she said not a single word.   At home I was never let off thus.
I longed to say: " Please do not blame Christabel only," but I
was too shy and unhappy to utter a word, and experienced an
agony of self-reproach, because I had not spoken up in my sister's
defence.   Whatever they really thought, Christabel and Norah
insisted amongst ourselves that we had done nothing wrong, but
I was oppressed by a dark sense that we had disgraced our parents.
Whatever Norah might do in her own home, I thought, we, as
guests, ought to have refused to defy the rules of our hostess.
Mrs. Blatch did not utter that reproach, but our parents would
certainly have done so.   Norah went back to school that day.   I
was sorry our visit must last still two days longer.

In the winter of 1892-3 the lease of the house in Russell Square
came to an end.   It was the tail end of a ninety-nine years lease,
and carried with it a heavy bill for the dilapidations which
had accrued during the whole period.   Already the sanitary
authorities had compelled Dr. Pankhurst to replace the old brick
drains by an approved modern system.   Now a bill was made
out for the entire house to be re-decorated, the balcony to be
strengthened; from sunk hearth-stone to missing keys, all wear
and tear had to be made good.   Mrs. Pankhurst had not realized
this point when she took the house, and the Doctor had not given
his attention to the matter.   When he had paid the bill for
dilapidations, he learnt that the repairs would never be executed,
as the house was to be demolished.

Burdened with liabilities which were to be as a mill-stone round his neck for many a year to come, his great energies had in the previous year begun to show signs of flagging under the strain of his unresting labours. A few weeks at Smedley's Hydro had dispelled the acute trouble, but he was often in pain thence-forward. Though he had chambers in London, the greater part of his legal work was still on the northern circuit, and his continual absences from home were a trial to him.

Mrs. Pankhurst was obliged to confess to herself that Emerson's was a costly burden, giving no hope of success. This realization, and the final winding-up of the business after a hard struggle against increasing difficulties, had made her ill. On her account, it was decided to move for a time to Southport, a Mersey watering-place, within easy reach of Manchester. This dull little town proved by no means congenial to Mrs. Pankhurst, to whom social interests and excitement were as the very breath of life. She grew so languid that by the following summer she felt herself scarcely able to take a short stroll down Lord Street to see the shops.

To us children the move to Southport brought a large emancipation. There was no nursery in the furnished "apart-ments," no special food for the children. We were more in touch with our mother than we had ever been before. Emanci-pated from the thraldom of the servants, we felt ourselves to be almost grown-up people. The morning after our arrival Christabel and I were up before anyone in the house and out on the deserted promenade for hours before breakfast. In Russell Square we had never so much as dreamt of opening the front door, and had never crossed the road to the Square garden unattended, but freedom seemed in the air. Mrs. Pankhurst protested against our escapade, and we never repeated it, but life was changed for us.

Our aunt, Mary Goulden, came to us at Southport for a holiday, but we had lost her as a permanent inmate of our home when we left Russell Square. Her younger sister, Ada, was a teacher of dress-cutting in the technical schools of Lancashire and Yorkshire, and at the winding-up of Emerson's, Mary Goulden had decided to qualify for the same work. Very soon she was married, unhappily, as it proved; a fact which, gradually coming to our knowledge, was a painful mentor of the legal and economic disabilities of women we heard so frequently discussed in abstract terms.

It was decided that Christabel and I should attend the South-port High School for girls. Adela insisted that she should go with us, in spite of her mother's opinion that she was too young.

Although we three sisters were immediately separated, in that pleasant atmosphere I was soon absolutely happy. The principal and his wife, Mr. and Mrs. Ross, shed about them the kindliest spirit, and I had the good fortune to have a charming teacher as my class mistress. I studied with a zest; every lesson gave new, keen interest. Father had stipulated that we should not take religious instruction, and I was given a history book to read while the other children were learning Scripture. Their lessons in the Old Testament, which I overheard, of necessity, were so interesting to me that I could easily have obtained full marks had I been examined thereon. In the history class we were occupied with the Roman invasion. Our teacher drew upon the blackboard the sort of hut in which the ancient Britons lived. "You can all try to draw that," she said, "but I don't think any of you could draw an ancient Briton." I answered that I thought I could, and she said that I might try. I went eagerly to the board, and rapidly sketched a figure, which was greeted by the warm praises of the teacher and the class. The teacher declared that the drawing should remain on the board for a week. Mr. and Mrs. Ross came in to see it and gave me kind words of encouragement. I felt myself surrounded by affectionate friends, ever ready to help me over the stiles in the path of learning: it was easy to obey Father's exhortation to make the most of our opportunities. Since I was so happy in my work, it was but natural that my report was endorsed: "A most promising pupil." I was sorry to leave the school, as we did at the end of the term. I saved up my pocket money to buy a little present for every girl in my class: I was friends with all. To Christabel, I know not why, the school did not make so happy an appeal. It was said of her that she could do better at her lessons if she tried, a reputation she carried with her throughout her school life.

From Southport we went to Disley, in Cheshire, a pretty rural spot in the hills, some sixteen miles from Manchester. We stayed in a farm-house, a great experience for us all. Mother was delighted to help with the haymaking, and rejoiced to think that her efforts had helped materially to save the crop from approaching rain. She seemed as young as ourselves. Certainly she was much keener in black-berrying, and would urge us on to gather the big berries almost out of reach, reckless of torn stockings and scratched arms. Sometimes she would hire a pony and trap and take us out for the day. Father had bought us a young donkey, named Jack, a most untamable and erratic steed. We rode astride him on a Spanish saddle, with a big pommel, to which one could cling when he kicked and reared. As the trap was too small to hold us all, somebody had to ride on Jack; this generally fell to my lot, for I alone was confident of not being thrown off. As long as he was in front of the trap Jack would run very well, but if, by cunning manœuvres, he could manage to fall behind, he would plant his four feet together, and refuse to budge till Mother at last dismounted from the trap, and drove him forward, threatening him with the pony's long whip. Before it came to this point, whoever was riding Jack was called upon many times to make an effort to get him to start, but coaxing, beating, dragging by the bridle, were all in vain. Such interludes detracted considerably from the speed of our excursions, but I loved Jack none the less for his tricks.

Christabel and I shared lessons with the governess of two little girls, Greta and Rotha Bell, who lived in the village. I liked nothing so well as the hours I spent in the fields, trying to paint the landscape, accompanied only by Vic, the little white fox-terrier dog the Southport landlady had given me.

It was a sorrow to leave those leafy slopes for smoky Manchester. We lost also our dear Susannah. She came with us to Manchester, but only to see us settled there, for she was to marry the keeper of the Disley Golf Links. One evening he had been with us through the fields and at parting kissed her over the gate. Pleased in the way of a child, to whom sex and marriage were beyond conception or speculation, to see that she had a friend, and surprised, for I had not known it, I said to her: " Mr. Hudson kissed you." " No, he did not," she contradicted, and I thought that I had imagined it; reality and imagination were not, to me, far removed. She was married from our house as a member of the family. There was champagne, but the bride-groom refused even to draw the cork for other people, so strict a teetotaller he was. The talk of it raised in my mind a long train of unsatisfied research into the merits of total abstinence.

One day, perhaps a year after her marriage, Susannah paid us an unexpected visit, and I at least was overjoyed. She missed the train home and stayed the night with us. Her baby was born before morning. " She did it on purpose," the servants said. I spoke up indignantly to defend her, but when her husband came next day, he told her their cow had calved the same night. " We said they would both come together," she laughed, with her tiny brown Gladys in her arms. " Never mind," said our mother, when she heard of it. " She saved my life when Harry was born, and now she has given me the opportunity to save hers." The poor little cottage in the midst of the Disley Golf Links was no place for a mother's travail.

BOOK III

CHAPTER I

WE were all pleased with our new home: 4 Buckingham Crescent, Daisy Bank Road, Victoria Park, a residential park of houses surrounded by substantial gardens with fine old trees. In those days a large field bounded the road opposite for some distance on either side of Buckingham Crescent, which consisted of only four houses, their small back gardens surrounded by walls, but the stretch of ground in front undivided. During the greater part of our time there the only other house occupied was number one, where lived Elias Bancroft, an artist, with his wife and only son. We children ranged at will through the gardens of the two empty houses lying between. The only flowers were irises which never bloomed and London pride; but the trees and shrubs bravely withstood the smoke. There was an abundance of white lilac, of lovely golden laburnum, and best of all, two beautiful red hawthorn trees, perfect cones; in springtime a mass of glowing blossom, from their apex almost to the ground. O the joy that those dear red may trees gave me!

" I hope you are not wearying yourself with all your work in the new house. In a few years time you will be stronger, if you can only spare yourself now," wrote Mrs. Jacob Bright to Mrs. Pankhurst on April 4th, 1894. Already whilst at Disley Mrs. Pankhurst had recovered her zest for politics. Settled again in Manchester, she was throwing herself with whole-hearted activity into public affairs.

The long struggle for the status of married women had now been carried an important stage further, by the inclusion in the Local Government Act of 1894 of clauses conferring upon married women the right to all local franchises, confirming their eligibility for election as Poor Law Guardians, and entitling them to election as Parish and District Councillors. This victory placed married women upon a footing of equality with widows and spinsters in relation to the franchise, and gave the death-blow to attempts to exclude married women from any political rights which might at any time be extended to widows and spinsters. The triumph must in large measure be ascribed to the unremitting toil of the Women's Franchise League, and above all to Mrs. Jacob Bright.

When the Pankhursts were in Southport, she wrote to them, much perturbed.   Walter McLaren had been given charge of an amendment designed to enfranchise all married women possessing the necessary qualifications.   In moving it, on November 21st, 1893, he said, to the consternation of the women who heard him from the Ladies' Gallery of the House, that his object was merely to prevent the disfranchisement by the new Act of such married women as were already voting for Vestries and Boards of Guardians but not to extend to them the other local franchises. Fowler, the President of the Local Government Board, who was piloting the Government Bill, paid but scant attention to this speech, which was causing so much consternation in the Ladies' Gallery.   He made the amazingly satisfactory promise that if the amendment were withdrawn he would introduce a new clause to remove altogether the disabilities suffered by married women; "in other words," as he said, "to repeal the decision of the Queen *v.* Harrald."   Mrs. Bright remained anxious; on November 25th, 1893, she unburdened herself to Mrs. Pankhurst:

"I am greatly troubled about the Local Government Bill.   I don't believe we shall get the married woman's vote after all. Fowler is being bullied.   And I am certain that, as Mrs. Stanton Blatch said, Parliament Street[1] and Great College Street[2] are simply mad at our success.   They never calculated upon such a decisive victory.   The Tories are trying to back out and Balfour is beginning to see that it will be impossible to carry a Parliamentary Spinsters' Bill if the married women are locally enfranchised.   Sir Charles Dilke says he will do his best for us, but he is not hopeful.   The only hope or chance for us is to convince the Government they will waste more time in dropping us than in maintaining our claim. Fowler promised, if necessary, to re-commit the Bill in order to secure the married women in towns.   Walter McLaren, by openly declaring that he never expected such an extension, has simply betrayed us. . . ."

On November 28th she wrote again:

" . . . When Fowler brings in his clause, if he ever does bring it in, but, as I tell you, he is being bullied to give up the whole thing, under the threat of Chamberlain to make the discussion last nine days. . . . I am anxious about this matter because I have really had the whole burden of it on my shoulders during the last six months. My illness was finally brought on by Fowler's statement to Mr. Bright that he would not touch the married women at all.   I *want* to throw the matter off my mind, but until we have that clause safe it will still burden me. . . . It would make so great a difference to my

---

[1] Office of the Central Committee of the National Society for Women's Suffrage.
[2] Office of the Central National Society for Women's Suffrage.

whole life if the clause were passed. Mrs. Stanton Blatch does not
believe in the other committees at all. She wanted to know *who*
was to give way and be amalgamated. . . . I told her when once we
could trust the other committees to fulfil their own programme we
should probably leave the Suffrage Cause in their hands and devote
ourselves to the other objects on our programme—and let them have
the glory of completing our work. What we want to secure ourselves from being made catspaws of is a *public* declaration that they
no longer intend to favour Spinsters' Bills.

" I send you Miss Blackburn's[1] reply. You will see that there is
no announcement of conversion. She waits for her Committee, and
her Committee is waiting to see how the cat jumps in the House . . ."

These forebodings happily laid to rest and the local franchises
with the clauses so important to married women safely on the
Statute Book, attention once more turned to the Parliamentary
suffrage. The efforts of all suffrage societies were directed
towards an amendment sponsored by Lord Wolmer to include
women in the then Liberal Government's Registration Bill. It
was an utterly forlorn hope. The suffrage societies had by no
means abandoned their mutual strife. Mrs. Scatcherd felt
" tired and cast down " after encountering " the set," as she
termed the dominant group in the older suffrage society. Yet
Mrs. Bright observed that Mrs. Scatcherd had " borne the brunt
of these widows and spinsters," and was " hardly aware that they
are really changing their feeling of animosity against her to one
of appreciation." In a voluminous correspondence Mrs. Bright
unburdened herself to Mrs. Pankhurst upon the woes of the
Parliamentary Lobbyist:

" The awful difficulty of getting all our friends up to the scratch
at the right moment is incredible to those who have not wearied
themselves to death with fruitless effort. First one, then the other
jibs, till I get so disgusted I only lose heart. Of course Walter
[McLaren] won't touch the lodgers. . . . The House of Commons
has an insane dread of women lodgers. It believes they are all
prostitutes."

Writing thus in April, and thereby inflaming a turbulent
ardour, which burned in her Manchester colleagues more fiercely
than she knew, she was expostulating in May against the
impatience she had helped to fan:

" Now you see, my dear friend, that it was not wise to adopt
the irreconcilable attitude of the Manchester Committee, urging
Liberal Members to vote against the Bill itself if the amendment is
not carried. I fear that will prevent many voting for our amendment even. . . . We must consider their Party sympathies. . . . Do
let us be reasonable and put ourselves in their place and remember

[1] Secretary of the Central Committee of the National Society for Women's Suffrage,
with which the names of Miss Becker and Mrs. Fawcett are associated.

they unfortunately lose nothing by voting against us (except their self-respect, which is only a trifle).   Mr. Bright will vote for the amendment, of course.   Dilke will not.   He has failed us utterly in this. . . .

" Think for me what can be done for this meeting.   If we could only get the working men to march in a body to the hall with banners and music ! "

Wistfully thus she wrote of those toiling masses, whom so many causemongers desired to enlist as an effective background to their own propaganda.   Yet already the elusive hordes were beginning to march away on a quest of their own, abandoning the politics controlled for them by others; and Mrs. Pankhurst, caught up in the enthusiasm of the vanguard, was marching away with them beyond her old friend's political horizon.

Keir Hardie had been elected for West Ham in 1892, and under his inspiration, and the great hopes aroused by his victory, the Independent Labour Party was founded at Bradford in the following January.   He was already known to the Pankhursts; they had seen him at the International Labour Conference in London in 1888, and the Paris International Socialist Congress of 1889.   They had rejoiced at his election to Parliament and ardently admired and supported his independent fight.   Already a warm friendship had grown up between the three, and their intimacy grew during the hard-fought Attercliffe by-election of July, 1894, when the Independent Labour Party fought its maiden Parliamentary contest with Frank Smith as its first candidate. On July 20th Mrs. Pankhurst was unanimously adopted as I.L.P. candidate for the Manchester School Board, though it was not until September that Dr. Pankhurst's letter declaring his decision to join the Independent Labour Party appeared in the Press, and Mrs. Pankhurst did not resign from the executive of the Lancashire and Cheshire Union of Women's Liberal Associations, on which she had been working to advance the suffrage cause, till September.   In announcing to her that she had been selected as an I.L.P. candidate, Mr. R. Anderson wrote :

" I took the liberty of reading the programme sent me by the Doctor, judging that you are in full sympathy with it, and to show the E.C. that you were far in advance of the programme adopted by the joint committee."

Mrs. Pankhurst told us in after years that Mrs. Jacob Bright had offered to join the I.L.P. with her, but that she herself had deterred Mrs. Bright, fearing the breach for the elder woman with old associations and old friends.   Yet the letters of Mrs. Jacob Bright show that she was by no means enthusiastic about the I.L.P.   She wrote to Mrs. Pankhurst on July 10th :

" You see how badly the Labour Party were beaten at Attercliffe. They have not the sympathy of their own class. There *must* be something wrong in their modes of working. They are *too* violent and contemptuous of other people's methods. . . ."

Yet the balance of £30 she had sent to finance a joint Suffrage meeting she asked Mrs. Pankhurst to apply " to help your work among poor women. Alas! it will take long to help them, they are able to do so little for themselves." Then she added ruefully, " Must you leave the L. and C. Union?[1] I am very sorry. These continued splits among women weaken us, and you all seemed to be working together so beautifully for the meeting "—the Free Trade Hall meeting she had thought so rash and so greatly feared would prove a failure, not realizing the popular support behind her colleagues. " It seems a pity," she sighed, " that we cannot all unite on some *one thing*. I have been doing my best to concentrate effort on the abolition of the House of Lords. That would suit all advanced parties." This was a vain hope indeed, though widely current then amongst Radicals of the old school, unable to adjust their ideas to the economic issues thrown up with the rise of the Labour Movement.

When the suffrage status of the married woman had been safely assured by the Local Government Act of 1894, Ursula Bright gradually drifted from political life. She became interested in securing the entry of women into Freemasonry, and thereafter joined the Theosophists; and, like many others taking the same course, lost interest in public questions. I saw her in after years—very gentle, very remote. We seemed to be conversing through a veil.

At the following annual conference of the I.L.P., Dr. Pankhurst was elected to its National Administrative Council. His connection with the Party of the much-abused Keir Hardie aroused against him in Manchester the fiercest of the old antagonisms and a host of new prejudices. Mrs. Pankhurst, always frankly explosive in her utterances, told an interviewer of the Manchester *Labour Prophet* that since allying themselves with the Independent Labour Party they had received none of the customary invitations to functions at the town hall. Many legal clients drew away from the Doctor, the Manchester City Council ceased to call for his services in legal matters. The Trade Unions and political organizations remained glad to receive from him the unpaid work he was ever ready to accord. His burden of liability was a heavy one. The digestive trouble for which he had been treated at Smedley's had increased; he was now chronically visited by acute attacks of pain. We children

[1] The Lancashire and Cheshire Union of Women's Liberal Associations.

scarcely perceived this, and much of his suffering was undoubtedly concealed from Mrs. Pankhurst.   To the outsider he appeared as vigorous as ever : he rose earlier and worked later.   He attended innumerable committees, and spoke constantly, never sparing himself the exhausting work of open-air meetings.

We girls were pupils now at the Manchester High School. Years later we were told by one of the teachers that the head mistress, Elizabeth Day, had unsuccessfully begged the Governors of the school not to admit us, on the ground that our father was a Republican and an Atheist; but if it were true, this was not known to us at the time.   With happy Southport memories, I went confidently to school.   Christabel was placed in a probationary class in the upper school, I in the lower school.

During the French lesson, that first morning, the teacher spoke to each scholar in French, and we, by word or action, must show that we understood.   " Chantez ! "   Not knowing the custom was to reply with a verbal phrase, I answered with a little song we had sung at the school assembly an hour before. The teacher praised me warmly; but when we were released for lunch, the girls rushed at me, gibing and mimicking.   One of them asked why I had not attended the Scripture lesson; the others took up the cry.   Was I a Jew?   The Jewish girls clamorously disowned me.   I turned away in disgust.   They followed with shrieks of laughter, thumping and pushing me, and pulling my hair, tore my hat and coat from the peg and trampled on them.   Thinking it beneath my dignity to fight or argue, I shook myself free and walked steadily toward the stairs, where my tormentors dropped behind, in fear of the teacher stationed there.   Next morning the head mistress, Elizabeth Day, dark browed and stern, stood by my desk.   The class teacher asked me to sing.   Not again would I do it in face of that jeering swarm.   I could answer nothing, but retired into the shy child's haven—silence.   The teacher endeavoured to coax me.   " I am sorry you have not more courage," the head mistress tartly said, and strode from the room.

The girls renewed their pranks against me whenever we left the class-room, until a few weeks later I was promoted to a higher class.   No longer baited, I still held aloof from the girls. I hated the school, though I enjoyed some of the lessons.   The art teacher asked that I might take modelling and drawing with the girls of the upper school, but Miss Day refused to allow it. The zest to master every subject I had felt at Southport no longer spurred me; I was bored by the excessive predominance in the time-table of arithmetic, French verbs, and the repetition of long lists of historical dates and geographical place-names.

There was far too much home-work, every teacher adding her quota. I seized upon any excuse to introduce a drawing into my lessons, and spending the greater part of the evening on this, was obliged to sit up late to finish the perpetual arithmetic. Most of the children detested the lessons, because they were dry and the home-work excessive, and found nothing to like in school except the playtime. The discipline seemed to me petty and ignoble. Instead of the assumption that we should naturally behave as reasonable beings, it seemed to be always anticipated that we should wilfully do wrong. "Conduct" marks were awarded for speaking at forbidden times, "fault" marks for inadvertently dropping one's ruler, or other such trivial matter; six "fault marks" made a "conduct mark." A list of pupils who had "conduct marks" was displayed for all the school to see. For mistakes in lessons, pupils were commonly kept in to write out a phrase a prescribed number of times. It once happened to me. I resented the punishment so much, that I defiantly wrote the phrase alternately very large and as small as I could. My teacher was astonished; she had considered me a particularly docile scholar. She asked me why I had done it. I answered: "Because it is a stupid waste of time!" I looked up at her fiercely, prepared to argue the case, come what might. She dropped her gaze, and told me I need not write any more, adding, in kind tones, that she was expecting me to do very well when I went to the upper school. This was my only act of rebellion. We were all three regarded as very quiet, well-behaved children, and great astonishment was expressed by the teachers who had known us when we broke forth in the Suffragette Movement.

At Southport Christabel and I had spent the playtime together; in Manchester I waited by the stairs till she came down from the upper school with her class-mates; but I soon saw that I was cold-shouldered by them as a little girl from the lower school. There was a rigid barrier between class and class. Therefore I ceased to wait for Christabel by the stairs. She accepted my withdrawal without comment. I contented myself by reading during the play hours, and was happy enough; but presently Miss Day made a rule that books must not be taken into the playroom or playground. Thereafter I sat apart, waiting impatiently the resumption of lessons. The macadamized playground was like a prison yard, surrounded by a high wall, with not a shrub or a blade of grass, the playroom the dingiest place imaginable. To-day the sight of the bare playgrounds of the elementary schools saddens me.

In my second year, two girls who had won scholarships at

the higher grade Board School came into my class. They were poorly dressed and the others were disposed to shun them. I had no special friends and did not want any, but I had a certain standing with the girls, largely because they admired my drawings. I made a special point of bringing these scholarship pupils into the circle and was able to break down the boycott against them. One of them confided to me that her father intended her to be a teacher, but she wished she need never work for her living. " I want to work; everyone ought to work," I expostulated. " Wouldn't you rather be a lady and ride on a pony? " she urged. Suddenly my old dream of a country house where everyone would be happy, rose up before me, confronted by the vision of smoke-belching factories and the grey little dwellings of Hulme and Ancoats; I felt almost guilty for having cherished it. " Why should I be allowed to ride on a pony when other people must work? " She looked at me with a puzzled stare. " It would be nice to be a lady," she said. " I should be, if I were you! "

As we were flocking out of school, I heard a great shouting. A girl with a yelling pack of youngsters about her, cried: " I am a Liberal! " It was Helen Byles, the younger daughter of the Member of Parliament of that name. " Shut up! We don't understand politics! " they shrieked at her. She was excitedly arguing. Of what use, I thought, to discuss any serious matter with these ignorant children? In reply to one of my essays in the composition class even one of the teachers had asked me: " If there were no poverty, what would become of all our charities? "

My sisters did not share my hatred of the school; Christabel entering the probationary class found herself amongst other newcomers, and at once struck up a friendship with a pretty girl, Edith G——. I was distressed to hear her presently praising Edith's home life at the expense of our own. At Edith's there appeared to be a constant round of visits and entertainments, whilst at home, according to Christabel's view, there was " nothing but politics and silly old women's suffrage." Christabel was from the first a favourite with her class teacher, and was at once appointed monitor of her class; but almost immediately she was punished with a " conduct mark " for speaking on the stairs as the girls filed down, unaware that it was forbidden. Her class mistress endeavoured to reprieve her, but Miss Day would take no excuse and insisted that Christabel's " conduct mark " and consequent forfeiture of the monitor's badge must be maintained. Molière's " Bourgeois Gentilhomme " was to be played by the pupils at Christmas. The

French mistress chose Christabel for the part of the dancing master. Mrs. Pankhurst was delighted. At one of the lessons Christabel had omitted to learn the last paragraph of her lines. As ill-luck would have it, Miss Day was present. She decreed that another girl must have the part. Mrs. Pankhurst was so much disappointed and distressed that the Doctor went to the school to plead with Miss Day. The principal refused to alter her decision, and the Doctor retired protesting: " There is no justice in this place! " Mrs. Pankhurst thereafter detested the school.

We learnt dancing from the Websters, an old dancing family in Manchester, and Christabel, who hitherto had never cared much or long for anything, roused herself to unexpected efforts to excel everyone in the class. Mrs. Pankhurst was delighted; no trouble was too great for her to take for the dancing outfits of her eldest daughter. Of all things, she now desired most that Christabel should become a professional devotee of Terpsichore, and that she, her mother, should travel with her to all the great cities where she would perform. With this much-cherished project in view, Mrs. Pankhurst regarded the teaching given at the High School with the utmost contempt, and kept us away on the slightest pretext. A week we spent with her helping at a bazaar she declared of greater educational value than school attendance.

One Sunday morning when Christabel was about sixteen, the Doctor spoke of her future. " Christabel has a good head," he ejaculated, " I'll have her coached; she shall matriculate! " Mrs. Pankhurst burst into tears, protesting that she would not have her daughters brought up to be High School teachers. The idea that Christabel was to be a dancer had continued for a number of years, when suddenly she tired of the project. She explained to me later that the thought came to her: " People will say my brains are in my feet! "

The lesser affairs of home and school life were always dwarfed for us by the great social and political struggles, in which our parents were active. Sometimes on Sundays we went to the Ancoats Brotherhood, organized by Charles Rowley, who brought to that factory-blighted district examples of the best things of the time, in music, art and science. By the pleasantly-framed reproductions of the great masters sold in his shops, and by his encouragement of the pre-Raphaelites, with whom he was on terms of friendship, he did much to influence the taste of his native city. His rotund little figure, with its bald head, long red beard, and shrewd, twinkling eyes, under most bushy and aggressive eyebrows, was pictured by Walter Crane in many a humorous guise as " Saint Rowley-Poly." In the winter of

1894 Dr. Pankhurst delivered under the auspices of the Ancoats Brotherhood, a series of lectures on the life and duties of citizenship, dealing with Society considered as an organism; primitive society; the development of law and ethics; and citizenship national and international. I well remember the rapt attention with which these lectures were received. The *Manchester Guardian* correspondent, William Haslam Mills, asked me with enthusiasm: " Are you not proud of your father? "

In July, 1893, 400,000 miners struck against a reduction in wages. The strike endured from July till November. Sir George Elliott spoke for a section of the employers in advocating a coal trust as a solution for the difficulties of the industry. Dr. Pankhurst, in a series of Press polemics, criticized the proposal, maintaining that this coal trust scheme was virtually a declaration on the part of its sponsors that the collective ownership of coal was expedient and right.[1] The Doctor proposed the acquisition of the mines by the County Councils; the terms of acquisition to be settled by the Commissioners, and the cost paid, half by Parliament, half by the County Council; the coal to be worked by concession under the County Council, which should prescribe the selling price of coal and the minimum wage of the miners, and should charge a royalty proportionate to the net profits. Concessions[2] to work the coal would be made to groups of miners. He preferred his scheme to the centralized plan embodied in the Mines Nationalization Bill at that time introduced by Keir Hardie, who had lately been elected to Parliament for West Ham. Thus in 1893 Dr. Pankhurst was making the demand for the management of industry by the workers in industry, which was to be raised by the miners and metal workers twenty years later.

Often I went on Sunday mornings with my father to the dingy streets of Ancoats, Gorton, Hulme and other working-class districts. Standing on a chair or a soap-box, pleading the Cause of the people with passionate earnestness, he stirred me, as perhaps he stirred no other auditor, though I saw tears on the faces of the people about him. Those endless rows of smoke-begrimed little houses, with never a tree or a flower in sight, how bitterly their ugliness smote me! Many a time in spring, as I gazed upon them, those two red may trees in our garden at home would rise up in my mind, almost menacing in their beauty; and I would

---

[1] *Manchester City News*, 22nd December, 1893.

[2] He quoted the survival of an ancient system in the Forest of Dean where the " free miners " (those born in the hundred who had worked for a year and a day in a mine) had a prior right to " gales," i.e. plots of land for mining, subject to the payment of a royalty.

ask myself whether it could be just that I should live in Victoria
Park, and go well fed and warmly clad, whilst the children of
these grey slums were lacking the very necessities of life.   The
misery of the poor, as I heard my father plead for it, and saw it
revealed in the pinched faces of his audiences, awoke in me a
maddening sense of impotence; and there were moments when I
had an impulse to dash my head against the dreary walls of those
squalid streets.

Keir Hardie's *Labour Leader* had made its appearance as a
weekly in the previous March, and was already a welcome
messenger to all of us at home.   The paper was strongly
expressive of its editor, who conversed in homely strain to his
readers.   " That poor devil, Bernard Shaw, is in trouble again:
he has fallen downstairs and broken his leg! " was a characteristic
utterance in the personal vein which relieved the tedium of
political pronouncements.   As familiar, though less popular with
us, were Robert Blatchford's *Clarion*, the Manchester *Labour
Prophet* and a host of smaller Socialist publications.   4 Buckingham Crescent now became a centre of Socialist agitations.   The
I.L.P. speakers who came to Manchester were housed there.   Keir
Hardie's first visit is vivid in my recollection.   To me he was a
tremendous hero, before all others the champion of the workers,
who had arisen from themselves to lead them to the promised
land when " Man to man, the warld o'er shall brothers be
for a' that."   I had seen the cartoon of him carrying the
unemployed on his back into the House of Commons.   I had
heard my father, with a tremble of enthusiasm in his voice,
praising the brave stand Keir Hardie had made in Parliament.   I
hurried home from school that day, knowing that he had already
arrived.   Seeing the library door ajar, I hastened upstairs to the
angle where one could see who was sitting in the big armchair by
the fire.   There he was; his majestic head surrounded by ample
curls going grey and shining with glints of silver and golden
brown; his great forehead deeply lined; his eyes, two deep wells
of kindness, like mountain pools with the sunlight shining
through them; sunshine distilled they always seemed to me.
Friendship radiated from him.   Kneeling on the stairs to watch
him I felt that I could have rushed into his arms; indeed it was
not long before the children in the houses where he stayed had
climbed to his knees.   He had at once the appearance of great
age and vigorous youth.   Like a sturdy oak, with its huge trunk
seamed and gnarled, and its garlands of summer leaves, he seemed
to carry with him the spirit of nature in the great open spaces.

In those days we met also Bruce Glasier, and his wife,
Katharine St. John Conway.   Of all the I.L.P. members Bruce

Glasier was next to Keir Hardie in the warm regard of our household. I loved to hear him speak of the beautiful life of Socialism, which was surely coming. For him, as for William Morris, from contact with whom his views on art and life were then profoundly coloured, the future of his ideal was grounded in the Middle Ages, which his mind invested with a golden radiance. The child of a love match, his father having eloped with his mother on horseback against her father's wish, his wage-earning life began as a Scots shepherd boy, and he later worked in an architect's office. He was something of a poet, and a draftsman of some ability. Kate Conway, as she was affectionately called by the I.L.P. members, was the daughter of the Rev. S. Conway, a Congregational minister in Walthamstow. She was one of the early students of Newnham College, and having passed the examination for the Cambridge B.A. she persisted in putting the letters after her name, though the University officially forbade their use to women, who were simply put off with a certificate. She was ardent for Socialism, much in love with Bruce. From enthusiastic loyalty to him, she adored everything Scotch, and interlarded her conversation with words from his native tongue, which assorted oddly with her London accent. She was also devoted to the Greek classics, and we were amused to hear her in eager discussion, referring to the " Greek lassies." For the sake of the Socialist cause they were happy to live sparely, and for many years denied themselves the joy of children. They gave their services for 2s. 6d. a lecture, or even less to impecunious branches, and accepted the poorest of hospitality in the best of humour. Katharine wore home-made dresses of art serge for economy. Their colour was sage green, as a tribute to her artistic ideas and the hope of Socialism; they were cut with aspirations towards Burne Jones.

The two other most prominent I.L.P. speakers of those days were Caroline Derecourt Martyn and Enid Stacey. The frail " Carrie," a woman of great sweetness and self-abnegation, was also an enthusiast for the Greeks. Tall and pale, she wore sandals and a long, whitish grey robe of would-be Grecian form. Mrs. Pankhurst, always much interested in dress, and by no means inclined to reflect her Socialism in her costume, declared when she saw these efforts of her colleagues, that if ever she wore a Greek costume, it would have to be " cut by a French dressmaker." Tirelessly writing and organizing, speaking in all weathers, Caroline Martyn literally worked herself to death. Enid Stacey, B.A.(Lond.), I remember as a big, handsome woman, with a very brilliant complexion. She was regarded as an exceptionally good speaker. She, too, undermined her originally fine physique by unresting labours, constant open-air speaking, constant journeying, poor food, uncomfortable quarters.   She died soon after her marriage to the Rev. Percy Widdrington. Tom Mann, at that time secretary of the I.L.P., was a favourite with all of us: Mrs. Pankhurst smiled at his exuberance, and we children, staid and quiet as we usually were, found it quite natural to romp with him.   On one occasion Christabel came silently behind him and slipped around his neck a harmless little snake we had bought in the market for a few pence.   So horrified was Tom Mann that he leapt out of the window.   Fortunately the room was on the ground floor, but he declared he would have taken the leap however deep the drop.

Wilhelm Leibknecht, the famous German Socialist leader, came to Manchester in those days.   He was then over seventy years of age; a strong, reserved man of powerful mind.   With him came Eleanor, daughter of the famous Karl Marx, an attractive personality, with dark brows and strong, vivid colouring.   Beside her was the repellent figure of Edward Aveling. Joseph Burgess, then editor of *The Miner*; James Sexton, whose face had been terribly crushed in an accident at the docks, and who complained that his employer had not even paid his cab fare home after the calamity; Pete Curran, liked by my father's old aunt, Mary, for the " naughty twinkle in his eye "; Ben Tillett, who roused her indignation by taking her favourite easy chair and pushing into the cab in front of her; Russell Smart, John Penny, T. D. Benson, the property broker who was treasurer of the I.L.P., and looked curiously out of place in his correct business dress amongst the many Bohemian-looking Socialists, are amongst the many figures which weave themselves into the memories of those days.

The central branch of the Manchester I.L.P. was in a poorly-lit, evil-smelling room over a stable, in a side street off Oxford Road.   Robert Blatchford had started a campaign for giving treats to the poor little girls of the slums, the " Cinderella children," as they came to be called.   The outcome of one of these treats was a " Cinderella " dancing class taught by Christabel.   By this time she was performing as a dancer at many I.L.P. functions, and she and I sometimes danced an Irish jig together.

In those early years of the I.L.P. in Manchester there was great enthusiasm, great activity, great willingness to work and to sacrifice, without recompense or reward.   Innumerable meetings were held, numbers of local elections contested.   On December 17th, 1894, Mrs. Pankhurst was elected to the Chorlton Board of Guardians, heading the poll in the Openshaw district.   Dr.

Martin was also elected to the Board. This remarkable man, a hard-worked medical practitioner in industrial Gorton, out-did the Fabians in his careful researches. His pamphlets were unique in their lucid simplification of difficult matter. He carried on an educational campaign against the domestic fly, as the cause of infantile diarrhœa, at a time when most Medical Officers of Health were scarcely alive to the dangers of this pest. Whilst advocating Socialism as a whole, he made special pleas for the immediate municipalization of milk and housing, non-contributory national sick pay, free convalescent homes and adequate provision for widows and orphans.

That winter was marked by its terribly high rate of unemployment. There was no State Insurance then; no Unemployed Workman Act; the Boards of Guardians gave no relief to the " able-bodied poor." Keir Hardie, for the third year in succession, had moved an Amendment to the Address, deploring that the Government had given no aid to the unemployed. The Government had appointed a select Committee, which presently issued an interim report, admitting the gravity of the distress, but offering no remedy.

In Manchester the situation was acute. Under the stirring energies of Dr. Pankhurst, a committee for the relief of the unemployed was formed, Dr. Pankhurst acting as honorary secretary, and Dr. Martin as honorary treasurer. Offices were opened in St. John's Parade, Deansgate. Collectors were sent into the streets, funds were advertised for, and subscriptions acknowledged in the *Manchester Guardian*. Food was distributed from 12 noon to 2 p.m. daily to all comers, no questions being asked. At first 1,000 people were fed each day, but soon the number was doubled. To supply so many people at short notice was indeed a large achievement. Mrs. Pankhurst went daily to Shudehill market to canvass the stallholders for gifts of food, and from thence to the city provision merchants. The doughty I.L.P. men and women organized the cooking and distribution, making soup at the two I.L.P. halls in great cans, and conveying it to the Square in pantechnicon vans with large quantities of half-pint mugs and loaves of bread. A van and a lorry drawn up together made an impromptu canteen, from which the food was given out to the masses of people filing up to receive it.

On Saturdays I went with my mother to help with the distribution, heartsick at the grim sight of those hungry thousands waiting in the bitter cold to receive that meagre aid; just the same sort of people who to-day draw unemployment insurance, supplemented from the local rates, on a scale undreamt of in those days. Similar distributions were made by the Committee in Ancoats,

Gorton and Openshaw, and a sub-committee endeavoured to cope with the urgent need of the wives and children.

These efforts to alleviate the immediate need were used as the basis for agitation. In this field none was more active than Leonard Hall, a doctor's son, who had thrown in his lot with the Socialist proletariat.[1] His tall, erect figure and handsome face, his ringing voice and odd, sardonic benevolence enlivened every procession and demonstration. Deputations led by Dr. Pankhurst and Leonard Hall marched to the City Council and the Boards of Guardians, and resolutions were sent to the Government demanding that Boards of Guardians and Town Councils should form joint committees to ensure the fullest use of existing powers; that local authorities should be empowered to find work for the unemployed at trade union rates and to acquire land to be used systematically for absorbing the unemployed; that Boards of Guardians should meanwhile be provided with powers and funds to afford adequate relief.

Mrs. Pankhurst, whose election to the Chorlton Board took place most appropriately in the height of the agitation, moved a Resolution there condemning the hampering conditions imposed upon Poor Law Guardians by the Local Government Board, and urging that decision of the powers of the Guardians in respect of relief be transferred to a special Committee of the House of Commons. She denounced the control of Guardians' activities by the permanent officials of the Local Government Board, as contrary to representative principles. Her resolution was scarcely defeated, when a procession, headed by Leonard Hall and the Doctor, was clamouring at the doors. The distracted Guardians received a deputation from the mob, but persisted that nothing could be done. A member of the Board referred to the "undeserving poor," a definition which Dr. Pankhurst hotly repudiated as "an insult to human nature." Mrs. Sale, a Roman Catholic, recently elected as a Guardian, asserted that the men outside had been compelled to join the procession by force and bribery. Leonard Hall cried out in a towering rage that he would attend no more deputations, and demanded the name of the lady, in order that he might " publish it to the admiration of the crowd." The deputation hastily ushered from the building, a storm of hooting against the Guardians met the graphic account of the interview given by Leonard Hall to the hungry mob outside. Agitated by this exhibition of popular excitement,

---

[1] He became an organizer of ship canal navvies, editor of the *Navvies' Guide* and member of the I.L.P. executive. Finally, after suffering great privations, he left the movement and devoted himself to commerce, with some success. During the War he was killed in a street accident. His daughters became Suffragettes.

unprecedented in their experience, the Guardians listened timidly to the din. Reversing their decision to take no action, they resolved to send a deputation to the City Council, urging it to find immediate work for the unemployed, and to take joint action with the Guardians in establishing permanent arrangements.

In the height of the distress, the employers declared a lock-out in the boot and shoe industry. Dr. and Mrs. Pankhurst immediately hastened to Leicester, the centre of the trouble. Whilst the Doctor pleaded the cause of the boot workers through the Press, Keir Hardie in the House of Commons demanded that the Government should open workshops for the locked-out men. Like the bit and brace, Keir Hardie and the Pankhursts seemed wrought to work in unison.

In September, 1895, Mrs. Pankhurst read a paper at the North Western Poor Law Conference at Ulverston on "the powers and duties of Poor Law Guardians in times of exceptional distress." This paper, which reviewed the historic and legal aspect of the question, as well as presenting a policy for the future, was actually prepared by the Doctor; its demands were substantially those of the previous winter's agitation. It was argued that Statutes of Elizabeth and of George III had empowered Boards of Guardians to employ workless people in all kinds of industry, and to acquire both land and material for the purpose. These powers had never been withdrawn, but had been put out of exercise by the restrictive actions of the Poor Law Commissioners, and their successors, the Local Government Board. The persuasive personality of Mrs. Pankhurst did much to obtain consideration for a view then widely regarded as extreme, and even fantastic in its benevolence. Sir Walter Foster, M.P., observed that he had never listened to a more able and lucid explanation of the problem, nor one more calculated to assist in its solution. Sir John Hibbert expressed agreement with the demand for wider powers for Boards of Guardians.

The stir created by this paper assisted Mrs. Pankhurst to establish a position of influence on the Chorlton Board. The clerk, David Bloomfield, gave her every assistance in his power. Mrs. Sale had become her devoted coadjutor. Together they discovered and secured amelioration for many great and small hardships suffered by the inmates and officials of the Workhouse, and unearthed many instances of official corruption. Mrs. Sale, on a surprise visit to the hospital, found the children who were patients there undressed and running about on a wet floor. At night a single probationer was often left in charge of three pavilions. The Workhouse children were miserably clad; the little girls had no night-dresses. Their cotton frocks were made with low necks and short sleeves. They shivered from lack of underclothing, because the matron and a couple of old lady guardians had been too modest to discuss with the Board the need of providing them with drawers. Thus poorly clad, these little ones were made to kneel scrubbing the long, draughty corridors. The diet was poor, bread forming too large a proportion of it, and was served to the inmates by weight, as in a prison, some going hungry, others unable to eat their ration. The old people sat on backless forms, and had nowhere to keep their letters and small possessions. All this was changed; but only after prolonged combat with the upholders of the old tradition. Foremost of the " die-hards " was the truculent Mainwaring, who presently realized that his outbursts of passionate rudeness were assisting the persuasive tactics of the charming Mrs. Pankhurst, and winning his supporters to her side. Thereafter, before attacking her proposals, he would write on the blotting-paper before him : " *Keep your temper!* "

Early in 1905 it was decided to remove the children from the Workhouse, and land was bought for cottage homes in the country. Mrs. Pankhurst was on the building committee and spared no pains to make the institution as perfect as possible. Her work on the Board now claimed her every waking thought and was the constant burden of her talk. Her hopes for the beneficent work of the cottage homes were far higher than could ever be realized. Having distressed herself acutely for the unhappy plight of the Workhouse children, she now sprang to the opposite extreme, declaring they would be better reared in the new institution than in the average working-class home. In this frame of mind, she collaborated with Mrs. Sale in a paper read at the Northern Poor Law Conference of 1897 entitled : " Increased powers of detention for children of degraded parents, or ' ins and outs.' " The clerk assisted in the preparation of this paper. Its argument was that Guardians should be entitled " to cancel parental power " and assume " direct guardianship," not merely where the parents had failed to secure the welfare of the child through " evil conduct," but also where the failure was due to " inability." A longer experience of institutional Guardianship under the best obtainable conditions would doubtless have corrected this impetuous view. Had her experience been that of Henry Neil, who, as a United States Judge, saw the sad results of the habitual use of the powers she advocated, Mrs. Pankhurst's conclusion might have been that the establishment of parents and home in a position of economic security and comfort is the ideal at which to aim; with Judge Neil her claim might have been for " Mothers' Pensions."

CHAPTER II

IN May, 1895, Dr. Pankhurst had accepted the invitation of the I.L.P. to be its Parliamentary candidate for Gorton, an industrial district on the outskirts of Manchester. The General Election took place in July. The I.L.P. ran twenty-nine candidates in various parts of the country and instructed its members to abstain from voting in constituencies where it had no nominee of its own. The Liberals, struggling against an obvious reaction of popular opinion towards the Tories, viewed the intervention of the I.L.P. with exceeding bitterness, and denounced its candidates as " Liberal smashers." Gorton had been a Liberal seat; but the sitting Member, Sir William Mather, had announced his decision to retire at the General Election. As soon as Dr. Pankhurst's candidature was announced, the Tory being already in the field, the Liberals declared they would enter a third candidate. Several others having refused, the President of the local Liberal Association agreed to contest the seat, but five days afterwards retired and joined the late Liberal Member in advising electors to vote for Dr. Pankhurst. Again, as in 1883, the Manchester Press opened its columns to the question whether the Doctor should receive Liberal support; and day by day, in all its stale monotony, the question of Party discipline was thrashed out anew. Efforts were made to induce the I.L.P. to withdraw its nominee in another constituency if the Liberals would vote for Dr. Pankhurst in Gorton. The I.L.P. refused the bargain, and the Gorton Liberal Association decided not to support Dr. Pankhurst. Mrs. Pankhurst went to Liverpool to plead with T. P. O'Connor for the Irish vote. He replied: " We have nothing but admiration for your husband, but we cannot support the people he is mixed up with." Thus, as in Rotherhithe ten years before, the Irish Party officially refused its support to the man who, of all candidates, had been first and most staunch in upholding their demands.

The view expressed by T. P. O'Connor was widely held in Manchester. Dr. Pankhurst's policies might be extreme, but he was a pillar of the city; Keir Hardie and his I.L.P. were an unknown bogey. His connection with this bogey the Doctor would do nothing to veil or minimize; on the contrary he was constantly dragging it to the fore, constantly attempting to clothe with the mantle of his familiar popularity, the hated figure of the man with the cap who had outraged every conventional standard by his conduct in the House of Commons. Had he not begun by getting himself escorted there in a brake with a brass band? Had he not baldly declared himself a Republican and attempted to couple with congratulations on the birth of a Royal infant, condolences in respect of a Welsh colliery disaster? Had he not even made references to the morganatic relationships of Royalty, which had caused certain passages of his speech to be expunged from the records of the House? Yet Dr. Pankhurst persisted in eulogizing him:

" When Keir Hardie stood up in the House of Commons for the people, with a faithful, earnest, manly appeal, he stood alone . . . are you not going to send other men to support him? "

Had Hardie not been a conspicuous favourite with Mrs. Pankhurst, she could not have endured this without protest. Even as it was she knit her brows fiercely when opponents described " the man with the cap " as her husband's " leader."

When the I.L.P. Election Committee appealed to the workmen: " Remember what Dr. Pankhurst has done for your children's education! " the unscrupulous vehemence of political controversy induced his Conservative opponents to deny that he had ever been connected with educational work. Thereupon numbers of people, who had attended the Mechanics' Institutes as students in their youth, sent up for publication examination certificates signed by his name.

Elections were not then held on one day; the towns polled first, the counties, the Tory strongholds followed. The towns had declared heavily against the Liberals; a great majority for their opponents was already assured. Most of the prominent members of the late Government had been defeated. Keir Hardie had lost his seat in West Ham before Gorton polled. Smarting from defeat, he hurled an oratorical bombshell at the Liberals, a prophecy thirty years later to be fulfilled, which doubtless cost his colleagues some votes at the time:

" The Labour and Socialist Parties will henceforth vote so as to sweep away the only obstacle in their path—the historic Liberal Party."[1]

The Conservative candidate placarded Gorton with this utterance to draw the Liberal voters into his net. Yet, though it seemed at the time to decide the issue against the Doctor,

[1] *Manchester Guardian*, June 15th, 1895.

Hardie's affront to the Liberals perhaps made no great difference; the public was not yet prepared to vote for Socialism; every Socialist candidate in that election was defeated.

When the I.L.P. had asked Dr. Pankhurst to contest the seat, he answered that he could not afford to bear the cost of the election: the I.L.P. replied that it was prepared to finance its own candidates. Dr. Pankhurst made this fact public, and the Tories found in it food for ridicule. The I.L.P., as a poor party of working people, conducted its propaganda by its own economical methods; methods which ten years later were to be the legacy received from the I.L.P. by the militant suffragette movement. Letters now appeared in the Press complaining of the "irregular manner" in which the Socialists were conducting the election:

"The meetings are called, not by circulars, but by announcements written in chalk on the footpaths."

Christabel and I went daily to Gorton with Mrs. Pankhurst, taking our meals in the homes of working-class comrades of the I.L.P. With a sense of impotent misery, I heard discussed over the tea-table the fate of a frail little girl about three years younger than myself, who sat there regarding us with large, sad eyes. The child of an unmarried mother, she had been placed in the care of two elderly workers. Her mother had disappeared; payments on her behalf had stopped; and now, under stress of poverty, the foster-parents were considering whether they should send her to the Workhouse. Yet apparently these old people loved her, and she called them "Mother" and "Dad."

I went canvassing with Mrs. Pankhurst; all the people had something kind to say about "the Doctor"; but many of them added they would not vote for him this time, as he had no chance now; but next time he would get in. They seemed to regard the election as a sort of game, in which it was important to vote on the winning side. Again and again people living in the greatest poverty told us of the courtship of the Conservative candidate, their faces brightening into benevolent smiles: "She won't have him unless he gets in this time. Poor fellow! We must let him have her!" "Poor people; you ought to choose someone who will help *you*!" I longed to say; but listened in anxious silence, believing that the arguments of a little girl would carry no weight. At an open-air meeting in Openshaw I stood at my mother's side as she spoke to the people from the soap-box: "You put me at the top of the poll; will you not vote for the man who has taught me all I know?"

Her voice broke; she was almost in tears, and so was I; yet I could not believe that Father, of whom everyone spoke with love; Father, so great and good, could be defeated by this unknown Mr. Hatch. On the evening of the poll I went with my mother through the dark streets to the public-houses, where she implored men with glistening eyes and thirsty lips to come out to vote. How terrible I thought it, this thought-destroying drink!

The result of the poll was: Hatch 5,865, Pankhurst 4,261; and the election expenses: Hatch £1,375, Pankhurst £342. At the I.L.P. meeting after the count, the Doctor was smiling and gay, and declared a great victory for progress had been won. I wept throughout his speech. He rallied me kindly: " There is life in the old bird yet! " When we got home Mrs. Pankhurst told me, though without anger, that I had " disgraced the family " by my tears.

Next day she hired a pony and trap, and drove off alone to the Colne Valley to help Tom Mann in his contest there. Returning through Gorton when all was over she was stoned by Tory roughs, who that Saturday night had celebrated their victory by revelry in the public-houses. Tired as she was, her nerve was unshaken. We children were awed by the thought that she had passed through great peril.

In May, 1906, a tremendous excitement arose in Manchester; members of the I.L.P. were being sent to prison for speaking in Boggart Hole Clough. The Clough, an open space of sixty-three acres, had been recently acquired by the City Council for public use. The I.L.P. had been holding meetings there for several years; but the Parks Committee, in the words of Needham, its chairman, had decided to put an end to the meetings of " a certain Party." John Harker, a member of the Trades Council, was summoned to appear before the Bench in Minshull Street for speaking in the Clough; it happened that he had been a candidate in opposition to Needham at the previous municipal election. Headlam, the stipendiary magistrate, observing that he would be lenient, imposed a fine of 10s. Dr. Pankhurst, defending Harker, protested that there was no by-law to limit the public right of meeting, and gave notice to appeal. In the meantime both meetings and prosecutions continued. Audiences grew from a few hundreds to 5,000, 10,000, 50,000. Fines were imposed on speakers, collectors, and literature sellers; the defendants in most cases refused to pay. Time being allowed for them to find the money, a wide public was waiting in excitement to know what would happen when the time had expired.

On June 7th Leonard Hall spoke in the Clough; Mrs. Pankhurst stuck the ferrule of her open umbrella in the ground, that it might serve as a receptacle for the pennies of the crowd. With Leonard Hall, John Harker, and six other persons thought to be associated with the meeting, she was summoned before the Bench. The Court was thrilled, the stipendiary taken aback; was she not the wife of one of the senior members of the Bar of the Northern Circuit?   She stood there, looking entirely well at ease and self-possessed, wearing an elegant little bonnet of pink straw, her slender, black-gloved hands lying quietly on the rail of the dock before her.   In opening her defence she announced her determination to pay no fine, and to return to the meetings in the Clough as long as she were permitted to be at large.   Yet the case against her was dismissed.   Leonard Hall, Harker, and Brocklehurst were soon in prison, but Mrs. Pankhurst remained free, and Sunday by Sunday took the chair in the Clough, gaining thereby an experience which stood her in good stead during the years to come.   In the enthusiasm of the struggle, her old platform nervousness disappeared.   The little pink bonnet she had worn in the dock was the rallying centre to which all eyes were turned.   So popular it grew, that again and again, as it faded, she made it anew with fresh straw.

In spite of protests in the City Council by its Labour Members, Jack Sutton (afterwards M.P.) and Jesse Butler, the prosecutions continued.   William Cobbett (son of the famous namesake), in prosecuting for the Corporation, complained that the meetings were attended by people in clogs, and known thieves from Angel Meadow.[1]   That gave the cue to Dr. Pankhurst; he advertised for witnesses to disprove Cobbett's aspersions; an endless stream of volunteers was forthcoming to testify to the respectability of the crowd, and subpœnas were issued for the unwilling.   Not expecting this move, the City's great ones had gone to the Clough to see the meetings; the stipendiary himself, his clerk and other magistrates.   The Town Clerk, the chairman of the Parks Committee and the Lord Mayor were caught in the net.

Mrs. Pankhurst was repeatedly summoned, but her case, with that of other I.L.P. women, was continually adjourned.   Keir Hardie and Bruce Glasier spoke and were summoned in their turn; the cases were blocked by the mass of evidence.   When Keir Hardie was in the dock he was able to announce that four hundred and thirty-one witnesses were waiting to be heard.

In August the City Council, knowing the weakness of its case, passed a new by-law prohibiting public meetings in the

[1] *Manchester Evening News*, June 19th, 1896.

parks, including Boggart Hole Clough, except under special authorization by the Parks Committee; it was made clear during the discussion that such permission would not be granted to the I.L.P. Since the adoption of a new by-law strongly implied that the previous prosecutions had been without legal warrant, the Council withdrew all the existing summonses. The I.L.P. continued its meetings. The Council issued new summonses. The Court cases were resumed. The excitement grew. To the dismay of the Council the Home Secretary refused to sanction the new by-law. Eventually, after a stiff tussle with the chairman of the Parks Committee, the City Council agreed to adopt another new by-law, framed under the advice of the Home Secretary, and accompanied by a letter promising him to refuse no reasonable request for the use of the parks for public meetings. Thus, with a signal victory for the I.L.P., ended the attempt to suppress its meetings.

Whilst the struggle was at its height, the Party had issued a manifesto urging electors to vote against the members of the Parks Committee. This method of attack was repeatedly adopted by the Manchester I.L.P. members in those active years. It was a weapon which ran counter to the so-called "Fourth Clause," one of the great bones of contention in the Socialist movement at the time. Robert Blatchford was one of the main advocates of the "Fourth Clause," the object of which was to exact a pledge from I.L.P. members to support and vote always and invariably for Socialist candidates only.

Leonard Hall's imprisonment had left his family destitute. His wife, Pattie, was again expecting a baby; but, proud and brave, she made no complaint. It was some time before her plight was discovered in the Party; and even then she received but meagre aid. Poor Leonard, the best of good fellows, suffered so much anxiety on behalf of his family, that his release was followed by his own serious illness. Fred Brocklehurst, a young unmarried man, declared that his health had been broken by his month's imprisonment; a large subscription was raised and he was sent abroad to recuperate. John Harker served his sentence and said little about it, continuing his work on release as though nothing had happened. As a result of the struggle Harker and Brocklehurst were elected to the City Council at the next election. Brocklehurst was afterwards run as I.L.P. Parliamentary candidate for North-West Manchester. He was defeated, and soon after left the I.L.P., resigned his seat on the City Council, was called to the Bar, and joined the Conservative Party and the Volunteers. His membership of the Council had given him a footing which secured him a legal connection. He died comparatively young; one of the men who had climbed up by the working-class movement and left it behind. Mrs. Pankhurst indignantly condemned him.

An amusing echo of the Boggart Hole Clough episode was provided by the Manchester Law Students' Society in their annual mock trial at the Assize Courts, when " Mrs. Chorlton Board," " Dr. Blank Burst," and the Chief Constable of " Smokeyopolis " figured in a claim by " Swear Hardie " for £100,000 damages for a torn shirt, and the pain and suffering caused him by an assault in " Winterhill Clough."

In July, 1896, Dr. Pankhurst, with the I.L.P. members of Bury in Lancashire, was urging upon the Council of that town that it should take steps to acquire the rights of the ground landlord within the area of the borough. Dr. Pankhurst prepared a paper showing that the land owned by the ground landlord was in origin a feudal estate as to grant and obligations. The ownership had subsisted for three hundred and fifty years. The feudal obligations had lapsed. The land which had passed from rural to urban conditions, was a source of increasing wealth to the ground landlord. The purchase of his rights would vitally contribute to the permanent prosperity of the town. The City fathers listened courteously to this reasoning, as though it had been a lecture upon the inhabitants of Mars, and so dismissed the discussion. Agitations followed swiftly to induce the Manchester City Council to purchase Trafford Park, a large estate on the outskirts of the town, also to induce the Council to build working-class dwellings to eradicate a state of overcrowding, which, in the Doctor's words, meant " the moral death of the masses."

Those were the high days of Robert Blatchford's *Clarion,* and the cycling clubs which helped to make its popularity. Christabel had already been demanding a bicycle at Southport in 1893, but the Doctor shrank from the thought of his young daughters riding among the traffic, and it was not until 1906 that she had her way. I had no desire to ride; but from the habit of loyalty to her, I stood by her side when she made her demands. Our parents took it as a matter of course that if Christabel rode I must go with her as a companion. We were now entered as members of the Clarion Cycling Club. Christabel and Mrs. Pankhurst scanned the catalogues of the principal cycle makers, and consulted the club to discover the best machine for speed. The first grade Rudge Whitworth was the final choice; it cost something over £30. I did not care what sort of bicycle I might get. Already, though our parents never discussed such matters in our presence, I had learnt from our aunts that they were not without financial worries. Therefore I was pleased when our teacher mentioned to Mrs. Pankhurst a cheap little machine, which a comrade had made at home out of gas piping. It was of curious design, low-geared and rather too small for me; but it did not occur, either to Mrs. Pankhurst or to me, that the machine was placing upon me a considerable handicap, when, in rather poor health, I attempted to keep pace with my elder and more athletic sister.

Thenceforward every available day was spent in cycling. Though the journeys were often too long for me, and I could scarcely pedal the last miles, the Sundays with the club were pleasant. It was delightful to be out in the country away from the grime of Manchester. There were usually some slow women riders amongst the company, and the men were kind in helping to push one up the steepest hills. It was when riding alone with Christabel that I endured a veritable torture. My crimson face and gasping breath were the wordless answer to her impatient: " Come on! " Afraid of being considered a nuisance, I would strain and strive till it seemed that my heart would burst. Finally she would disappear from me, climbing some hill, and arrive home sometimes an hour before me. I remember being thrown over the handle-bars and rising up so shaken that I had to walk for some distance before I could re-mount, while she rode on, not noticing that I had ceased to follow. She delighted in hill climbing, and was proud to be able to mount the noted steeps which some of the men in the club essayed in vain. Dr. Pankhurst accepted, but obviously regretted this craze for cycling, which took us away from home every Sunday and seemed to be drawing us away from the public interests so dear to him.

One summer holiday we all had rooms in a farm-house at Pickmere, close to a camp held there by the Clarion Club. Crowds of young men and women, generally rather ostentatious in their love-making, in what was then the Clarion way, came down there, and parties of " Cinderella " children were brought in relays for a week's holiday. Robert Blatchford spent a few days there with his daughter, keeping exclusively to his chosen circle of friends, as he always did. About that time the Clarion Clubs held their annual gathering in Chester. Christabel insisted that we should go, and I managed to accomplish the journey somehow. Mrs. Pankhurst joined us by train. Blatchford and his friends had booked the commercial room, the only comfortable room in the hotel, whereat there was much murmuring among the members. He came out to talk to Mrs. Pankhurst, and endeavoured to persuade her that Keir Hardie could not be " straight," because his paper, the *Labour Leader,* must be losing money every week. Christabel and I were both annoyed by this attack on our friend, and when Blatchford presently invited us into the commercial room, Christabel interposed: " Mother, do not go! " Blatchford's attacks on Hardie because of Hardie's work for peace and internationalism were a prominent and regrettable feature in the Socialist movement of those days.

A curious incident of 1906 was the imprisonment in Antwerp, and subsequent deportation by the Belgian Government, of Ben Tillett, who was endeavouring to enrol members of the International Federation of Ship, Dock, Wharf and Riverside Labourers. At the request of Tom Mann, Dr. and Mrs. Pankhurst and James Sexton went to Antwerp to hold a meeting of protest. Attempts to speak in the open were dispersed by the police; a meeting in a tavern had just concluded when the police arrived; at a second indoor meeting James Sexton was arrested. Dr. Pankhurst repaired to Brussels to lodge a protest, and returned to Antwerp to find that Sexton had been deported.

CHAPTER III

" THE ENEMY OF THE PEOPLE "

IN 1897 came the terrible Engineers' Lock-Out, which lasted for six months, and in which the heroic readiness of the men to starve, and their Union's large reserve fund of £300,000, proved unavailing. In that struggle for the eight-hour day, Dr. Pankhurst was active at innumerable street corner meetings with the rank and file, as well as at the great demonstrations with John Burns and George Barnes. When the employers applied to the City Council for assistance against the locked-out workers, a Councillor rose in his place to say that he had seen " a howling mob of women and children " outside an engineering works, and that " a dose of grapeshot would serve them right." A storm of protest was raised, and the offending Councillor compelled to apologize; yet I remember that when Dr. Pankhurst spoke to the engineers of their need of a Labour Party, the cry went up from many voices: " No politics! " It was a tragic struggle, in which homes were sold up, the health of adults was undermined, and infants died. It did much to advance the growth of the Labour Party idea.

One of our great events in those days was the opening of the Ship Canal. The Doctor had been a pioneer of this project; he was an active director of the Canal Company, and when at last all the great difficulties of finance and construction were overcome, it was he who made formal application to the Hundred of Salford for a certificate that the enterprise was complete and fit for the reception of vessels. " *Floreat flumen navigerum Mancuniense,*" he concluded. His speech was printed in several languages, and circulated in foreign ports, to encourage the use of the canal. Earlier in the winter we had gone with him to see that enormous work in process of construction, and on the opening day, January 1st, 1894, we all went with the directors in the first boat to travel the canal. What a sight it was: the gigantic locks working with perfect smoothness. To me the wonder of wonders was the great aqueduct, in which the Bridgewater Canal is carried on high across the Ship Canal. To make way for the funnels of our steamer, the aqueduct swung apart, its waters so wonderfully dammed that there fell from it only a trickle, so small that it appeared as though a teacup had been emptied from the great height.

The Manchester City Council having given financial aid to the building of the canal, it was therefore entitled to representation on the Directorate of the Canal Company. It was characteristic of Dr. Pankhurst that he urged the direct election of these representatives by the people. It was still more characteristic that he upheld the dockers when the Canal Company locked them out for wearing the Trade Union badge.

About this time, he entered, at first single-handed, upon a contest in relation to the disposal of the Manchester sewage, which resulted in one of the most notable achievements of his life. At great cost a sewage works had been established at Davyhulme, the effluent from which was discharged into the Ship Canal. Though the works included means for chemical precipitation, artificial filtration, and sludge disposal, untreated sewage, in respect of a population of 181,000, had been passed into the Ship Canal. As might have been expected, the Mersey and Irwell Joint Committee, which was responsible for the purity of the canal and the rivers, prosecuted the Corporation of Manchester for this gross offence. The Corporation was heavily fined because, in the words of the judge, it had not used "the best available means" of dealing with the sewage. It had been argued that the effluent, even when treated by chemical precipitation at Davyhulme, was not so good as it might be. This, however, was not by any means the reason the Corporation had been fined; the prosecution had been purely for discharging untreated sewage. Instead of seeking to improve the effluent, the Rivers Committee, and its expert, Sir Henry Roscoe, now proposed to abandon the sewage works, and build, at tremendous cost, a great culvert to carry the sewage of Manchester beyond the jurisdiction of the Mersey and Irwell Joint Committee, and to discharge it into the Mersey between Warrington and Liverpool, where the river might be fouled with impunity. The City Council approved the scheme. The Press unanimously supported it. Dr. Pankhurst alone opposed it, denouncing the culvert as costly and unnecessary, "a blind despair of the resources of science." A good effluent, he insisted, could be secured by chemical precipitation, whilst a needed manurial agent would be returned to the land by treating the sewage on scientific lines. The out-to-sea policy, he pointed out, would abstract from the Ship Canal from 40,000,000 to 70,000,000 gallons a day, thus reducing its flow, and holding in its bed whatever might descend from its upper reaches. To secure a good effluent the Mersey and Irwell Joint Committee, which had hitherto adopted no fixed standard, should establish a test acceptable to the general body of chemical experts, and then make the worst effluents in the watershed conform to the general average. He hammered home his points by constant letters to the Press. Gradually scientific men drew to his side. Norbury

Williams, the "Citizens' Auditor," directly elected by the rate-payers to guard their interests, a most zealous and able public servant, gave the Doctor his support, declaring that though the cost of the culvert was estimated at £280,000, it would probably amount to £500,000. The Council having formally adopted the culvert scheme, a Town's Meeting of ratepayers was requisitioned by Pankhurst and his supporters. To the public at large, the issue lay between the Doctor and the Council; the rival schemes involving technicalities outside their experience, it was a question of their trust in the wisdom and public spirit of the contestants. The Town's Meeting decided by an overwhelming majority against the culvert. A poll of the ratepayers was called by demand of the Lord Mayor. Before it took place the Rivers Committee published and distributed at the public expense, even pressing a sanitary inspector into the service as bill distributor, 100,000 handbills, declaring that the culvert would cost not more than one penny in the pound; whereas if the scheme were defeated, expenditure of more than threepence in the pound would have to be incurred. The Doctor led a deputation to deny the statements made in the handbill and to protest against the distribution of such one-sided propaganda at the public charge. The Lord Mayor refused to intervene. A few days later the poll was taken. Policemen brought round the voting papers for open signature by the ratepayers: we waited in great excitement for the result. The poll was declared: for the culvert 20,528; against the culvert 49,069; for the policy of the Doctor a triumph indeed, and a public vote of confidence of an important sort!

Pasted amongst the Press cuttings kept by Dr. Pankhurst at this period is this note from his hand:

"On entering Town Hall at 10.25 to attend to hear debate in Council on culvert scheme Alderman Joseph Thompson (Chairman Rivers Committee) stopped me and said:

"'A year ago when culvert just resolved on (I then being in London with Town Clerk and City Surveyor) we decided to instruct you to appear as Counsel on it for the Corporation. But immediately after we saw your letter in the *Guardian* against it and so all was stopped.'

"I replied that by opposition to the culvert I did the Rivers Committee, the Corporation, and the City a lasting service.

"I made mem. at 3.30 on the 15th September, 1897.
"R. M. PANKHURST.

"Councillor Bradley, member of Rivers Committee, some short time ago intimated to me that if I accepted the culvert as all right I should be instructed for the Corporation in it.
"15th September, 1897.
"R.M.P.

" Councillor Bradley again intimated to me that if I gave up opposition to culvert could and should be instructed by Corporation.

"24th September."[1]

"R.M.P.

My friend Edward Bell, of Messrs. Carter & Bell, tells me that Dr. Pankhurst might have looked to make upwards of £8,000 out of the culvert scheme had he been retained for it. Such a consideration weighed with him not a straw. He noted the incident as a piece of history, revealing the seamy side of civic politics. Talking of him years later, Keir Hardie said to me: "The greatest gift a hero leaves his race is to have been a hero." I always felt that deeply. Mrs. Pankhurst declared that Henry Irving, in his representation of Dr. Stockmar in Ibsen's *Enemy of the People*, had modelled himself on the Doctor. It might well be so; yet with the struggle against the culvert in her memory, it was but natural that she should discover a similarity.

Just then, at the annual meeting of the Lancashire and Cheshire Union of Mechanics' Institutes, T. R. Wilkinson, an old coadjutor in such labours, handed the Doctor a note, which later I found among his papers:

" Being deaf and hearing nothing, I can only think.
I only see you now and then,
But always in some fruitful cause,
Striving to make or mend our laws;
As fluent with your tongue as pen.
Go on, old friend, though hairs be white,
Still vigorous remain at heart
And ne'er shall from the true depart,
But struggle to the end for right."

Perhaps the majority of Manchester citizens would have echoed those words.

A happy incident of 1897 was the winning of a footpath over old Kinderscout for the use of the people for all time. This was the result of a three years' effort by the Peak and District Preservation Committee, of which the Doctor was honorary counsel. I remember crossing the Scout by the ancient right of way with parties of people from Manchester, and helping to remove obstructions placed across the path by the agents of the landlords, the Duke of Devonshire and others. I remember too that famous May 31st, when we celebrated the victory, placing the title deeds in the safe keeping of the Chairman of the Hayfield District Council.

[1] The date of the Town's Meeting.

CHAPTER IV

BEREAVEMENT

IN the spring of 1897 anxiety about the Doctor's health, of which his children were but dimly aware, caused Mrs. Pankhurst to search out a farm-house at Mobberley, in Cheshire, where we stayed until the autumn. Dr. Pankhurst went thence to his work in Manchester each day. Christabel accompanied him several times a week to take classes in French, logic and dressmaking, a curious combination, selected by herself with some prompting from her mother. The rest of us were away from school. The younger children were happy on the farm. I was supremely content, drawing and reading; Ruskin and Richard Jefferies then specially attracted me; I had no other desires.

Walking to the station with my father one morning, I was distressed to see him stop short, obviously in pain, and press his beautiful hands among the sharp thorns of the hedgerow. " Why are you hurting yourself, Father? " I exclaimed in alarm. He answered: " It is to counteract the other pain." When in a little while he had recovered himself, he was solicitous for my distress, assuring me, with gentle endearments, that it was only a passing attack of indigestion of no importance. After that he often paused a few moments when out walking, and though we understood he was in pain, he made light of it, and no thought of danger entered even the threshold of our minds.

We returned to Manchester for the winter, and in the early summer of the succeeding year I was allowed, to my great delight, to take lessons with Elias Bancroft, a well-known Manchester artist, who lived at the other end of Buckingham Crescent. Charcoal, Whatman's drawing-paper, stamps and rubbers of squeezed bread, came to my knowledge as a revelation. I felt a sense of power in seeing the rounded shapes stand forth from my blank paper, and the rich chiaroscuro which charcoal could produce. I revelled in still life groups, and at home, arranging jars, bowls and foliage to my own fancy, attempted to reproduce them in water-colours.

Harry had just been sent to school. There was a tender bond between the little brother and me. We were much together; for I had been a long time away from the High School, having become subject to fainting and headaches. The child poured out his eager thoughts to me: " Spring came and stretched out one gentle hand, but cruel Winter drove her back; and then she came again, and stretched out ten thousand lovely arms ! " His soft, sweet voice thrilled with emotion. A solitary child, the gulf made by four years between himself and Adela seldom bridged, he had been apt from a much earlier age to wander away alone. When the household sought him in alarm, probably he would be found watching a football or cricket match on some vacant lot, or talking to the workmen mending the road. When new houses were being erected he was sure to be among the builders, permitted to try his hand at something they were doing. When an excited searcher came to drag him home, the men would protest that the little chap was perfectly safe with them. The menservants at a neighbouring big house taught him to ride the pony kept for the little daughter of their employer, who would never be well enough to mount the saddle. To his father, Harry's wandering was incomprehensible. On the advice of Elias Bancroft, the boy was sent to a little school kept by an old man, named Lupton, who suffered from goitre, and taught all his pupils without assistance. He was a kind old fellow, and doubtless had a gift for teaching; but the single schoolroom was dull and ill-lit, and having an assortment of boys of different ages, he was unable to devote much attention to the newcomer, the youngest boy in the school.

Christabel was seventeen. I heard her telling some friends at the Clarion Cycling Club that she wanted to find an easy job which would occupy her from about ten a.m. to four in the afternoon. I listened in consternation, hoping she spoke in jest. I wanted life to be a great adventure, in which every shred of one's energy would be poured into some chosen work of beauty and value. Mrs. Pankhurst was anxious that Christabel should perfect her French; she arranged with Mme. Dufaux to exchange daughters for a year. Mrs. Pankhurst was to take Christabel to Geneva and bring Lillie back. She looked forward with pleasure and excitement to the visit to her old friend; dressmaking went on for weeks, in preparation.

At the last moment the Doctor could scarcely bear to let his wife go. He was always sad when she was away, as she often was in the evenings at meetings now; always restless if she were late in returning.

"Look after Father ! " my mother exhorted me as she left that day. I took the charge very seriously.

The Doctor was now again retained by the Manchester Corporation, but on a case which he intensely disliked: an inquiry held at the town hall into alleged financial irregularities by the indoor superintendent of the Corporation cleansing department.   Norbury Williams, the Citizen's Auditor, was instructing the Doctor in the case.   He came every night to discuss it after the Doctor came home from his chambers.

Father was worried and tired.   I knew he hated the search after the misdoings of the accused man.   The auditor followed the trail with a hunter's zest.   I heard the keen tones of his voice, piecing together the links in the chain of evidence.   I knew him to be actuated by zeal for the public interest; but, seeing my father's sad, strained face, I longed for the power to drive him from the house.   For hours I would hover about the closed door of the library, waiting the moment when I might venture to take in coffee, and so create a diversion which might perhaps bring the work to a close.

When the auditor had left us one Friday night, my father seemed forlorn and lonely; he took me on his knee and talked of life and its work.   " Life is valueless without enthusiasms "; as often, he emphasized that thought, which was the guiding mentor of his being.   Yet there was a note of sadness in his voice, a clinging affection in his clasp which caused me a strange uneasiness I could not overcome.

He left his Chambers on Saturdays at noon, and that day I went to meet him and bring him home.   It was his habit to grasp one's upper arm in his hand as he walked beside one; for in the days of his youth it was not good form to walk arm in arm. To be gripped thus held for me, as I often told him, a suggestion of being under compulsion, and I would draw his hand down to my wrist, so that our two arms were folded together.   Thus we came home that lovely summer day. . . .

He rose suddenly from the midday meal, taking a strawberry from the dish, perhaps to allay my anxiety.   " Serve the children," he said to me, and left the room.   I followed him presently, and found him, not in the library as I expected, but in my mother's yellow drawing-room, huddled uncomfortably in a small arm-chair, his every line denoting agony.

" You are not well, Father.   Shall I go for Doctor X? "

" No, leave me; it is nothing."

I went to the kitchen, grieved and anxious.   " Father is ill ! "

The two servants, occupied with some interest of their own, discounted my alarm.   " I suppose he thinks he's dying ! " the cook snapped curtly, resenting my intrusion during their meal.

Rebuffed, miserable, impotent, I stole back to him, and sat apart regarding his pain.   After a time he agreed to my plea for bed and a hot water bottle.   Mother was often ill—those were always her remedies.   Agonized by seeing him thus, I yet conceived no least inkling of danger.

Next morning the awful change in him shocked me. I ran immediately, without consulting him, to find our doctor. He was out and would not return until 2 p.m.

"Father, I have been to Dr. X. He is out. Tell me whom to bring to you?"

"I will wait for Dr. X."

With raging fear I could not name or analyse, I waited. What was this that was torturing Father? What had so changed him? . . .

Dr. X came at last. He sent me away during the examination. . . .

The two servants were all solicitude now. . . .

"What is the matter with Father?" I searched the ashen face of Dr. X to find an answer before his slow lips opened: "He will soon be better; do not worry."

Oxygen cylinders arrived; I stood by the bed holding out the india-rubber tube for my father to inhale from it. At times he had his usual lucidity; at times his mind wandered in delirium. He seemed helpless as a little child.

Dr. X had promised to return to him every two hours to administer restoratives. The doctor was always late; my father always impatient for his return. "When is Dr. X coming?" "What is the time?" He questioned me desperately, with rising excitement. "He is late! He has been detained, he will not come this time. . . . I am faint . . . if I faint they will have difficulty in bringing me round!" He held his palms upward, murmuring feverishly: "As they do in hot countries! As they do in hot countries!"

He was struggling for breath, but he waved aside the red tube of the oxygen I held towards him. "No, not that," and then: "I am sorry, I thought you were offering me a cherry."

What was the matter with Father? The maddening question seethed within me as I stood holding the tube, striving to soothe and comfort him, striving to allay the excitement which seemed to consume his waning strength, telling him the doctor was just coming; he was not late; he was not detained; he would come; he would come immediately; no, there was not long to wait. . . . Then suddenly he would turn to me in anxious solicitude, urging me almost in his old tones: "You must not stand; you are tired. Do not distress yourself; you must rest." The effort to restrain my grief seemed turning me to stone.

Sunday wore on. Sunday night passed. Still we fought the same desperate, agonizing fight. Mother must not see him like this! We must get him better before she comes. Mother could not bear it! This was my ever present thought. Sometimes I was alone, sometimes the two maids were beside me. Dr. X suggested a nurse; but Father, turning to them, answered: "No, they will help me," and they begged that they might.

On Monday morning he told Father to telegraph for Mother. The word was a knell of doom to me, but I knew not why. No conception of death crossed my mind; only the misery of witnessing his awful pain. He dictated to me: "I am not well. Please come home." I told Dr. X that the telegram had been sent and asked him: "Will he be better soon? I cannot bear my mother to see him like this!" He answered: "Yes, he will soon be better."

Some time during Monday night Father sent me away to rest; he would take no denial. I slept. It was morning when I woke. I hastened to his room. Adela and Harry had been brought to his side. I had kept them away and begged them to go to school as usual on Monday—"Like good little dears, to keep the house quite quiet for Father." They gazed with awe at his changed face. Ellen, the housemaid, took them silently away.

The time crept on, and as I stood holding the tube, which seemed a line of life to him, he turned away his head as though to gaze at something. The cook crossed herself, murmuring a prayer. I went to the other side of the bed to see his face. . . . The skies were crashing down, the world was reeling. . . .

Father was dead.

From the depths the tears were rising. Sobs and cries were rending me. . . . Not here; one must make no noise here; here must be quietness. I rushed away into the blazing sunshine of the garden. All went dark. I fell on the grass and knew no more. . . .

I rose with one thought: a doctor! No delay; no delay; his plea through those long, slow hours of agony. No delay! no delay! I ran to the gate. A man drove by in a trap; I cried to him: "Bring a doctor! Bring a doctor!" He whipped up his horse. A cab came towards me. "Bring a doctor!" Two men who heard me ran swiftly away. I turned to the house, but again I fell. . . .

Several conveyances were drawn up on the drive when I came to myself. I went up to Father's room. Dr. X was there and three other men, grave and sad. "I have known him ever since I came to Manchester," one of them said.

Suddenly a flood of joy burst over me. I thought that Father had moved. No: one of the doctors had touched him. I crept away, the sore refrain repeating itself in my mind: "You did not get a doctor immediately. You did not send for Mother. If she had been here he might not have died."

Dr. X came to me.

"Why did you not tell me to send for my mother?"

"I did not think he would last the night when I saw him on Sunday. I did not think she could arrive in time."

"You said he would soon be better."

"I could not tell you the truth. . . ."

"What was the matter with him?"

Dr. X explained that the stomach of the patient was ulcerated; the ulcer had perforated the stomach. He had known of this periodic condition for some time, but the patient had not taken sufficient care. "Those green vegetables he thought so much of."

"Did you tell him his stomach was ulcerated?"

"I did not want to worry him."

Rage and grief contended within me. I gazed at the white face before me; it seemed a sepulchre of unhappy impotence. Reproaches died unuttered. Against myself only knelled the thought: "You did not send for Mother."

But how could Mother bear it? What would she think of me that I had not sent for her? I longed for her coming, and yet dreaded it. Uncle Herbert came; Aunt Mary came. I had only one thing to say to them: "I did not send for Mother." I could remain nowhere. I went to Father. They had tied a white cloth around his head. The sight benumbed me. I wandered through the darkened bedrooms, up and down the stairs. When will she come? When will she come?

She came in the small hours of Wednesday morning. Dear, brave Mother; she held me in her arms. "Mother, I did not send for you; I did not get a doctor till Sunday." She uttered no complaint, she only tried to soothe me; but nothing could stem the agony of my self-reproach.

Returning in the belief that Harry was ill and that the Doctor had worded his telegram to minimize her anxiety, she had read the news in the black bordered evening paper in the train, and had cried out in the shock of her grief. People in the railway carriage had asked her: "Are you Mrs. Pankhurst?" and offered such poor comfort as they might.

Uncle Herbert tried to divert us. Little Harry told us pretty little jokes to make us smile. I scarcely knew what was happening around me. Through my mind passed the tragic procession of the events of those sad days, every incident clearer than in its happening; and the tears, pent at the time, would flow for days unquenchable. For years such attacks recurred, with gradually lessened intensity; but even now . . .

The following Saturday we went to Brooklands Cemetery with Father. They laid his coffin upon an open bier covered with wreaths. A great procession of the many Movements he had worked in, the thousands who loved him came with us. The streets were lined with people as we passed. I gazed at my mother, sitting opposite me in the carriage, beautiful and strangely young, as though the years since her marriage had fallen from her. "The widow and the fatherless" a voice seemed to be sounding in my ears. What poignant words!

Bruce Glasier, beside the grave, spoke tenderly. The sky was a glorious blaze of radiance; but our life was broken.

"Faithful and true and my loving comrade"—words of Walt Whitman Father had read to us Mother chose to be graven upon his headstone.

Mrs. Pankhurst was brave; she had work to do; we should have nothing to live on now. She could not bear to be alone; she must always have one of us beside her. Henceforth I slept with her. Sleepless nights we had; our sorrows and our worries we talked out together, often through half the night. The housekeeping became my charge: I could make the money go further than she. In those days I thought it would be my destiny to be her life's companion; that my brother and sisters might go away into the world, but I should always remain with her. Even when I left her I believed it was only for a short time. How strange is Fate!

BOOK IV

CHAPTER I

DR. PANKHURST had left no will; he had little to leave. Everything was to be sold to pay off the last of the old debts he had been toiling for years to liquidate. Mrs. Pankhurst was determined as to that; a proposal made by her solicitor, which would have improved her position at the expense of the creditors, she indignantly rejected. Even the books and furniture were to go; we should leave Victoria Park and move into a smaller house. Her brother, Herbert Goulden, came to share his expenses with her, and she took a house at 62 Nelson Street, off Upper Brook Street. Ellen, the housemaid, remained with us; a good friend she proved.

There was a widespread feeling that something should be done to aid Mrs. Pankhurst in her struggle; but she discountenanced the idea. To an appeal by Robert Blatchford in the *Clarion* she replied that she did not wish working people to subscribe for an education for her children which they could not provide for their own. She urged that the fund Blatchford proposed in memory of the Doctor should be used to build a Socialist hall. Into this channel subscriptions were thus diverted; but from other sources a testimonial was raised, which was a supplementary aid in the succeeding years.

Meanwhile she had at once decided to open another Emerson's, persuading herself that it would certainly be a success in Manchester. Eager to be at work, she purchased some yards of material, and aided by her sister Mary, now Mrs. Clarke, made them up into cushion covers, a few dozens of which were stowed away in a dress basket as completed. On August 30th, 1905, she resigned from the Chorlton Board of Guardians; she had no heart now for public work. The Guardians showed the utmost friendliness and sympathy. A registrarship of births and deaths at their disposal happened to fall vacant; they offered her the position, and she accepted it, but she was still determined to open the projected shop, though nothing was as yet provided for it, save the contents of the dress basket. This proved a great mistake; the business was always an anxious burden and eventually had to be given up.

Christabel was to remain in Geneva. She wrote when she heard from Mrs. Pankhurst that she was going to open a shop: " You are so clever; I think you could do something better than that! "

Work and sorrow were dominant: it was Ellen who remembered our physical needs. Kind Ellen, she loved those of us best whom she felt had most need of her. When she heard our knock at the door she ran to open it with a cup of tea in her hand. She made a very queen of our mother, tears coursing down her cheeks when she ministered to her in those periodical " sick headaches " from which Mrs. Pankhurst suffered all her life.

The mother attempting more than she could accomplish, and feeling her life's happiness destroyed, it was a home of distressful atmosphere, above all for little Harry. He had chicken-pox; no one had much time to attend to him. He had measles, which appeared to be the cause of his permanent and acute astigmatism. Mrs. Pankhurst had one of her strong, unreasoning prejudices against spectacles; he might not have them, though it was painful to him to read. It was borne in upon him that sorrow and stern necessity were ruling the spirit of his home, that his childhood had no rights. When he fell and broke his front tooth, the good Ellen enjoined him: " Do not let your mother see you till she has had her tea." Obediently he effaced himself, then came forward apologetic: " I'm sorry, Mother; I could not help it." Unhappy at Mr. Lupton's school, unable to read by the dim light shed on his desk, he strayed away to the railway stations to watch the trains. Uncle Herbert, suspecting his truancy, followed him. The boy was removed to another school. He immersed himself in solitary interests: dug clay from the garden, and, using his own mirrored reflection as a model, made busts and fired them in the kitchen stove; engaged in the usual abortive electrical and chemical experiments of small boys without means or guidance. Attending the Higher Grade Board School for a time, he learnt that his class mistress was a candidate for the Board of Guardians. He surprised us by announcing that he had been canvassing for her from door to door, and requested that Adela should accompany him that evening, because though most of the people had promised to vote for his teacher, a few had told him he was " too little to know anything about it."

Charles Rowley came to advise as to the value of the pictures which were to be sold; he saw some of my drawings, and said

I was more promising than the pictures. My still life groups were sent to the Municipal School of Art, and I received a free studentship. What joys that opened to me!

In spite of our grief and my nervous depression, when absorbed in the work I knew the greatest happiness. Students and teachers all were kind, especially that generous enthusiast, Henry Cadness, who presided over the Design School. Yet the first year I was so tortured by neuralgia in my head and arms that I was often obliged to stay at home. In my weak state, standing to draw and model led to a slight but obstinate internal weakness. I was tormented by chilblains, and often went out of the hot life-room to gain relief by pouring on my feet the methylated spirits we used in fixing our drawings.

During my time at the school, the Whitworth Institute, an extension of Owens College, was opened by King Edward VII, and an illuminated address of welcome to him was prepared. The teachers and some of the students were given each a page to design and illuminate. I had a page, and applied myself to make it as beautiful as I could, for Art's sake. Yet on the opening day I took part, none the less eagerly, in the Socialist Propaganda organized in connection with the affair by the I.L.P., which I had joined at sixteen years, as soon as I was old enough. It had been agreed that we should sell to the crowds of sightseers Keir Hardie's " Open Letter to the King," and his pamphlet on unemployment. The people were largely hostile, but I tramped about all day, and came home with a heavy bag of copper. I was surprised to find that most of the other sellers had given up at the start, and that I had broken the record by selling £2 worth of pamphlets.

Dr. Pankhurst had taken the part of the Boer republics in Gladstone's time. When the South African War broke out, the year after the Doctor's death, Mrs. Pankhurst held to the same tradition, and in 1900 resigned with sixteen others from the Fabian Society, on account of its refusal to oppose the War. Her youngest brother, Harold Goulden, who had been touring in South Africa with a theatrical company, came home during the fighting, ardent for peace, and decrying the new *Daily Mail* which came to the front with its war propaganda, as "the ignorant boy's own paper"! We of the younger generation, were also against the War, and believed that we arrived at our conclusion by independent thinking. Harry, who had spoken up for Peace to the boys at school, was assaulted by them in the street outside. Mr. Lupton found him unconscious in the road, and carried him home. Adela, at the High School, for the same cause, was struck in the face by a book thrown at her across the class-room in the presence of one of the teachers, who uttered no rebuke to the assailant. Walter Crane came to lecture at the School of Art on ornament and design. In illustrating his lecture he drew Britannia's trident, interpolating: " Let her be as careful to respect the liberties of others as she is in safeguarding her own! " This observation I quoted in reporting the lecture for the school manuscript magazine. Cicely Fox Smith, since known for her books on seafaring ways and London inns, was the jingo of the school. She dressed in khaki and looked as much like a soldier as a girl could. When she saw the Britannia trident sentence in the magazine, she rushed to the editor, demanding the excision of the entire report, and declaring that she would follow me home and break our windows. War madness gathered during the series of British defeats, which began the War, and burst forth, in unrestrained drunkenness and violence, when the news of victories came. Mafeking became a by-word, but the same hideous scenes were enacted on many such occasions. Hats were knocked off, women's clothes torn; even those who had gone out to rejoice with the rest being brutally assaulted. Peace meetings of course were broken up, speakers were ducked and beaten. The death of one whom we knew resulted from the rowdyism: Larna Sugden, the Socialist architect of Leek, a friend of William Morris. Though the European War of 1914-1918 brought its menace to our very homes, the passions it evoked were less ferocious than those displayed in the Boer War. Popular education and social reform had worked an appreciable improvement in the intervening years. Drunkenness itself has abated tremendously since I was a child.

Christabel had now returned from Geneva. Mrs. Pankhurst had assumed, as a matter of course, that her eldest daughter would be with her at Emerson's, in spite of her protest from Geneva. She had told the rest of us, indeed, that she was starting the business largely on Christabel's account; for since she had given up the idea of being a dancer she had " no particular bent." Christabel expressed no other desire for her future, but she detested Emerson's. She arrived there as late as she could each morning, took a couple of hours off for lunch and got away as early as possible in the afternoon, stifling her thoughts by a constant succession of novels. As the registrar-ship necessitated attendance only during a couple of hours in the morning and evening, Mrs. Pankhurst was able to give the greater part of the day to her shop. Whilst Christabel was still in Switzerland she had engaged assistants, and had arranged for her brother Walter to keep the books, which he did as a labour of love, having retired from business for ill-health. There was no obvious place for Christabel to fill, and Christabel had no desire to make one. Mrs. Pankhurst was satisfied to have her daughter beside her, and if she had any regret that Christabel sat in the dark little office all day with her head in a novel, she did not say so.

I had been so often away ill during my first year at the School of Art, that I became conscience-stricken at the thought of holding a free studentship. Moreover, I saw that Christabel was discontented, and I wanted to do my share of the disagreeable work. I persuaded Mrs. Pankhurst that we should pay the low fees for part-time attendance the second year, and that I should give half my time to Emerson's, but I found there absolutely nothing to do, save writing window tickets. At the close of that school year (1901) I obtained the Lady Whitworth scholarship of £30 and fees, awarded to the best woman student of the year, and had to revert to full-time attendances.

One afternoon during the General Election of 1900 I was at Emerson's. Mrs. Rose Hyland came in to make some purchase and said: "Keir Hardie is elected for Merthyr Tydfil." Mrs. Pankhurst threw her arms round the astonished old lady's neck and kissed her, a thing she had never done before, and cried in delight: "That is for bringing the news!" She added, by way of explanation: "He is a good man." Mrs. Hyland was obviously unconvinced. "Parliament will be more interesting to us now," wrote Mrs. Pankhurst to Keir Hardie. Her interest in public work had been re-activated by the agitation against the Boer War; her friendship with Keir Hardie and Bruce Glasier had always kept a spark of it alive. In November, 1900, she was elected as an I.L.P. candidate to the Manchester School Board, retaining her membership of that body till March 31st, 1903, when the School Boards were abolished by the Education Act of 1902. Women not being eligible for election to the City Council, which now took control of education under the Act, she was co-opted to the Education Committee on April 1st of the same year, and served thereon till October 31st, 1904. The fact that women could now only take part in educational administration by co-option was another argument for full enfranchisement.

At Easter, 1901, she and I went together to the I.L.P. Conference at Leicester. An elected Persons' Conference preceded the main function. At its close an old man stood up and invited the delegates to tea at his hotel. Almost everyone went. The old man introduced to the company his son, a shy young fellow, whom somebody said he was "trying to introduce to public life."

In later years I met that young man occupying a government under-secretaryship.

Old Mrs. Bridges Adams came to us afterwards in her knowing way: " I went for the experience, of course, but I was surprised at you taking your daughter ! "

" Oh, now I remember ! " exclaimed my mother. " I could not recall where I had heard his name."

The idea that I, as a young girl, could be in any way contaminated by what the old man had done once upon a time was a Victorian point of view we sisters at home could never comprehend.

During the I.L.P. Conference I was amazed and indignant to hear Philip Snowden opposing a resolution to abolish the half-time work system for children of school age in the cotton mills, on the ground that the I.L.P. would lose votes in Lancashire were it to press for this reform. The Conference voted him down. Christabel joined us two days later. The redoubtable Sam Hobson was engineering a little insurgent movement against the policy of the executive. He had already won the support of Mrs. Pankhurst, but Christabel, who detested Hobson, emphatically rebuked her, declaring that after two years' absence from the conferences it ill became her to oppose the N.A.C. Mrs. Pankhurst accepted this ruling, an early evidence of her daughter's ascendancy. Keir Hardie was anxious that Christabel should address the Conference, and arranged for her to take the place of a delegate leaving before the end. Christabel immediately used her opportunity to oppose a resolution of Mrs. J. R. Macdonald, advocating passive resistance to the Tory Government's education proposals by the withdrawal of teachers and children from the schools. Christabel took the part of obedience to law, and advocated ordered propaganda and submission to the arbitrament of the ballot box. Her position in relation to Law and Order and that of Mrs. Macdonald were speedily to be reversed.

In 1902 I won a National Silver Medal for designs for mosaic, a Primrose Medal, and the highest prize open to students of the Manchester school, the Proctor Travelling Studentship, a vacation scholarship to enable the holder to make a short visit abroad. In the fine, free spirit of the Manchester school, students might choose where they would go. From my desire to decorate the meeting-places of the workers' movement, I selected Venice to study mosaics, Florence for frescoes. Mrs. Pankhurst, triumphant at my success, decided to go with me as far as Geneva, where we should stay a month with Mme. Dufaux.

Travelling by Ostend and over the Belgian State Railways, our first halt was at Bruges, the charm of which wrought on me so much, that with the wonders of Italy lying on before, I was loath to leave it. We took our evening meal at the tables on the pavement outside the Hôtel Panier d'Or in the market square; the tuneful chiming of the old belfry sounded at the beginning and ending of our leisurely repast. Two little Italian boys sang to us " Santa Lucia," as though calling me not to be seduced from my goal by the beauties of this old-world town. The hotel was full, but Mrs. Pankhurst's accomplished pleading procured an impromptu lodging. We slept between lavender-scented sheets, under the heavily-timbered roof of an ancient attic granary of reposeful shade, and emerged with a great sense of renewed life to the early morning sunshine playing upon the pleasant waters of the northern city of bridges. We were so happy together. Mrs. Pankhurst was as eager and pleased as though she too were going abroad for the first time; delighted with everything, the coffee, the rolls, the pictures, the architecture. My wishes lingered in Bruges when she tore me away to Brussels, where she revelled in the shops and purchased hats for us all, and where I lost my heart to the ornate architectural riches of the Hôtel de Ville. The mellow glories of Belgian art, the tranquil radiance of Belgian scenes and the tuneful chiming of the old belfry hung round me still as our train sped on. Mrs. Pankhurst excited herself over the naughty behaviour of some little German boys, who disturbed the sleep of a young Swiss governess. She declared them typical specimens of their uncouth nation. With memories of her girlhood thick upon her, she commiserated the governess, and recounted the odious doings of the Germans in Paris after the Franco-German War.

Enthralled by my first sight of great mountains, the talk slipped away from me. At last, as we wearied to be at our journey's end, came a gap in the dark and jagged peaks, disclosing a far, ethereal blue, ineffably soft and clear. " Mother, the lake! " I knew it, though yet unseen; those mystic ranges were the mountains upon its further marge.

Soon we were on the breast of that fair Lake Leman, and now landing at the Quai de Corsier. Stout Mme. Dufaux, with her two tall sons and husband and her daughter Lillie were meeting us at the jetty. What a babble of vivacious French! I, understanding most of it, was too shy to utter a word. In the well-ordered ménage our hostess floated about in ample white wrappers; cooking with primus stoves, a novelty in those days; bustling in with her excellent dishes; pressing the daintiest morsels upon my mother and me; urging all of us to join in finishing the last crumb; consuming herself whatever she could not induce the rest of us to take, and before eating it deluging it with sugar,

whether it were savoury or sweet. Her sons laughed affectionately, reminding her that she desired to grow thin. She was
perpetually scolding; her cat, her servant, her husband and sons,
above all her daughter. Accidentally I trod on the plate she had
put down for the cat. I burst into tears from the memory of the
outcries she directed against others for such offences. " Ma petite
chatte! Mais non! Mais non!" I was taken into her ample
embrace.

Each morning M. Dufaux worked at a portrait of Mrs.
Pankhurst, in which she appeared round-faced and young, whilst
I made pencil drawings, making her older and very sad. "Elle
cherche bien les formes," Dufaux commented, and I was pleased
to receive his encouragement, but by no means pleased with
my drawings. Each afternoon I was on the lake with Lillie,
she rowing, I reclining at ease with hands in the water, supremely
content in that immensity of shining loveliness, wherein our
barque was a speck. As at Bruges, so on the lake, the beauty
about me seemed to draw my spirit within itself and whisper:
" Do not go."

Mme. Dufaux insisted that she and Mrs. Pankhurst should
come with me to Venice, and come they did, chattering as merrily
as though it had been thirty years before, their gaiety incessant,
their energy inexhaustible. I was almost stunned by the grandeur
of the great mountain pageant through which the train passed,
entranced by the picturesque glimpses of peasant life, the women
labouring in the fields, the cottages with the maize and the tunny
fish drying on the wall, the bare-footed children gambolling
among the domestic fowl. At last came the hour-long ride over
the great railway bridge to Venice, first seen in the soft, iridescent
gold of the sinking sun; a wondrous city of fairest carving,
reflected in gleaming waters swirled to new patterning by every
passing gondola. Venice in the brief, violet twilight; Venice in
the mournful loveliness of pale marble palaces, rising in the velvet
darkness of the night; the promised land of my sad young heart,
craving for beauty, fleeing from the sorrowful ugliness of factory-
ridden Lancashire, and the dull, aching poverty of its slums;
Venice, O city of dreaming magic!

Mme. Dufaux, our pilot in these new scenes, was no linguist.
She possessed but one oft-repeated English phrase : " Shudder-
door!" and one Italian word, "Avanti," which she told us meant
"Go away." Mrs. Pankhurst and she both urged me to
remember this useful word in case anyone should molest me, yet
its failure to achieve its alleged purpose was conspicuous. Our
stout friend shrieked it constantly to the crowds of persistent
urchins who flocked about us shouting: " Soldini Moossue!

Soldini Moossue!" but the more she cried "Avanti!" the closer they clung about her, till, tired of their importunity, she flung them a handful of small coin. My elders trotted over the many bridges from the Piazza San Marco to the Rialto, in and out of the curio shops and the confectioners, then over the water by gondola to Murano to visit the factory for Venetian glass and beads. They enjoyed themselves immensely in buying for Emerson's in Manchester, large quantities of glass, opalescent and flecked with gold, beaten copper and brass and wrought iron-work; delightful, but, as it proved, unsaleable. Her losses unforeseen, Mrs. Pankhurst felt she was acting the part of benefactor to her native city by importing thither the products of Venetian craftsmen. I toiled after their speeding steps like a tired dog; and when they paused to conduct shrill bargains in the dark little shops, I sank down on whatever would hold me, happy to gaze upon surroundings lovely as the fabric of a dream.

At the week's end, they left me to take up my residence with a middle-aged Manchester spinster, who had come with a research scholarship from Victoria University to study the Venetian sumptuary laws, and lived as the guest of a Polish Countess, Sophie Bertelli Algarotti, who had generously given the Englishwoman leave to take such paying guests as she chose into the house and make what she could out of them for herself.

Mme. Sophie, as we called the Countess, had married when only sixteen an Italian officer, and had early been left a widow. Afflicted with cardiac asthma, she could not endure a Venetian summer, and had fled to Poland during the hot season. Her apartment in the Calle dell'Arco, San Antonino, reflected the atmosphere of her youth, the salon upholstered in yellow satin, its walls draped with brocade, and lined with bric-à-brac and old-fashioned pictures. There I parted from my mother, my eyes streaming with tears; the anguish of the separation seemed greater than I could endure.

Work gave the only solace; and indeed the quiet life of study in surroundings of peace and beauty was what my young being most urgently needed, for the building of health, and the soothing of jaded nerves.

Eager to use every available moment, I rose each morning at five, and went into the streets to paint until eight. Then, having breakfasted, I changed my tackle and proceeded to St. Mark's to copy the mosaics, to San Georgio degli Schiavoni to copy the Carpaccio's, or to some other church or the Academia, on similar intent. In the afternoons I had another painting on hand: the Rialto and its moving crowds, the Cà d'Oro, some gaily furnished stall or shop, with its picturesque vendors. After these long hours of work, I even attempted to paint on the balcony by moonlight, but was obliged to desist, for my hand trembled.

When the people gathered to watch my work I would take out my sketch-book, and call on them in turn to stand for their portraits. They readily complied, and I worked in eager haste, to a generous chorus of "Brava! brava!" as the figure began to appear. On one early occasion, in a little-frequented calle, the children crowded so closely round that I felt faint from the heat. My easel swayed, my paint-box was in danger of being trampled under foot. "Avanti! Avanti!" I gasped, using Mme. Dufaux's talisman. The children but crowded closer, laughing and shouting more loudly. At last two men appeared through the press, scattered the urchins, strapped up my tackle, and told me to go home. Exhausted, I did so, only to learn that the famous word "avanti" simply meant "come forward!" That was my only unpleasant experience. As a rule some members of the crowd, which invariably collected, constituted themselves the custodians of order. Most of the group would discuss the sketch; the young girls usually discussed me, and pronounced me "Brutta."[1] The women would answer: "Si, si, ma simpatica."

When the cold weather came I attended the Academia delle Belle Arti, and worked in the life class under Tito. No other woman student was studying the human figure, and when I applied for admission, Tito sent me to the antique room, where I found not a solitary student at work. I guessed that I should never get into the life class if I waited to be sent there, and next day I simply walked in. "So you are here," said Tito when he saw me, and thereafter treated me like any other student. The young men of the class behaved with shy politeness. One of them said he could "masticate" a little French, but this proved to be so little that our conversation never passed beyond the briefest greeting. I let the young men believe I knew no Italian, though I soon understood all they were saying. I fancied that if they knew me to be an auditor, my presence might prove an irksome check to their conversation. Thus they spoke together as though I had not been present, and I knew them as they really were. Occasionally their talk was of sex. The majority said they thought celibacy best for their age and work. One vigorously proclaimed the opposite opinion, and several refused to commit themselves. Presently there came to us a new model; a Swiss, who possessed, so Tito pointed out to us, the beauty of the ancient Greeks. This model was himself an art student, walking to Rome to attend the school there. He entered vigorously into the discussions, warmly taking the part of the celibates. He was

[1] "Brutta": plain-looking or ugly.

a keen athlete, and some of the lads rose early to see him swimming at the Lido those cold December mornings. I was happy amongst them, a shy girl who did not speak, glad of their clean thoughts and enthusiasm for their art.

I attended also the landscape class, where there were several women students. Ciardi, our teacher, was warmly encouraging, and a diploma followed me to Manchester for the little work I had done under his guidance.

Mme. Sophie had returned to Venice, a beautiful woman of fifty, April-swift in her changes from grave to gay. I soon regarded her as my dearest friend. She encouraged me in my hopes and told me her own great sorrow: the devoted love of her maturity for a man who became insane on the eve of their marriage, and whom she had visited constantly in the asylum till his recent death. He had been a writer of brilliant talent, she told me. Her mother, an able woman, the friend of the foremost Polish poets and patriots of her time, had been ardent in the cause of her country's liberation, and therein had gradually sunk the whole of her fortune, even forging the signature of the infant Sophie, in order to use her inheritance also. Though she had not been a consenting party to the sacrifice thus thrust upon her, Mme. Sophie was proud that her mother had assisted the liberation movement. She spent the greater part of her days at the piano, whilst I, to please her, would sometimes sing the soprano arias to " La Traviata " and other operas she had sung in her youth. When I spoke of proceeding to Florence, as I had intended, she urged me to remain, and having fallen in love with Venice, and with her, I easily persuaded myself I should learn most by remaining to worship the " Bride of the Adriatic."

The months sped by. The spring had come. I spoke of returning to England. Mme. Sophie begged me to remain with her permanently, as friend and as daughter. I answered, not without grief, that my duty and my destiny were calling me back to Manchester. My decision was confirmed by a letter from Christabel, telling me that she intended to prepare herself for matriculation at Victoria University in order to become a barrister, and that I must return home to help at Emerson's. My mother wrote that she and Adela would meet me in Paris at Easter. " It would be better for you to remain. Stay with me here," Mme. Sophie urged, assuring me: " You will have no expenses," but I had no doubt of my duty, and prepared methodically to finish the works I had in hand by the appointed time.

CHAPTER II

MRS. PANKHURST had already hired the attic over Emerson's as a studio for me. I took up again my old tasks at home: housekeeping, darning, dusting; wrote window tickets for Emerson's, sold designs for cotton prints and the paintings I had made in Venice.

Christabel was being coached for matriculation. In 1901 she had come to know Esther Roper, the secretary of the North of England Women's Suffrage Society, and Eva Gore Booth, secretary of the Women's Trade Union Council of which Sir William Mather, a Liberal employer of labour, was the chairman. The Council itself was mainly composed of well-to-do people desirous of encouraging working women to join. Eva Gore Booth was a minor poet of some distinction and a pacifist-non-resistant. An elder sister of hers was Constance Markievicz, who at that time devoted herself to painting, but later played a prominent part in the Irish rebellion of 1916, was sentenced to death and reprieved, and subsequently was elected as the first woman Member of the British Parliament, though owing to her Sinn Fein pledge of abstention, she did not take her seat. Eva herself had left home, dying of consumption, as it was thought, to give the few months she was told she had to live to the service of working women. Her aim was culture as well as politics. She formed an enthusiastic class of working girls who studied Shakespeare under her guidance. Tall and excessively slender, intensely short-sighted, with a mass of golden hair, worn like a great ball at the nape of her long neck, bespectacled, bending forward, short of breath with high-pitched voice and gasping speech, she was nevertheless a personality of great charm. Christabel adored her, and when Eva suffered from neuralgia, as often happened, she would sit with her for hours, massaging her head. To all of us at home, this seemed remarkable indeed, for Christabel had never been willing to act the nurse to any other human being. She detested sickness, and had even left home when Adela had scarlet fever and Harry had chicken-pox, on the first occasion going into hired lodgings, on the second to stay with friends.

Mrs. Pankhurst was intensely jealous of her daughter's new

friendship. She complained to me bitterly that Christabel was never at home now; my words of comfort availed little. Yet through this friendship Christabel was finding the serious interests she had hitherto lacked. She was now an active member of the North of England Women's Suffrage Society Executive, and of the Women's Trade Union Council, and presently her two friends induced her to study law. Shortly after my return from Venice, Miss Roper and Miss Gore Booth decided to spend a holiday there, and Christabel went with them to see what I had seen.

That summer the building the I.L.P. had erected in memory of Dr. Pankhurst at Hightown in Salford was completed. I was invited to decorate the lecture hall, and gladly entered upon the task. None of us ever dreamt of asking that I should be paid for the work. It was a most insignificant edifice, but nevertheless greatly superior to anything the Party in Lancashire had hitherto possessed. Less than three months was allowed for the work of decoration. Having prepared the designs, I was aided in the heavier manual work by R. C. Wallhead, afterwards M.P. for Merthyr Tydfil, and then a working decorator near Manchester, and an evening student at the Municipal School of Art. The hall, when decorated, was opened by Walter Crane. I was asked to give a lecture there on the principles of ornament and to explain the decorations, and thus made my first platform appearance. I was so nervous that in demonstrating on the blackboard I forgot to remove my gloves.

Coursing through the Socialist movement to working-class circles beyond its confines was the confident, imminent hope of a Labour Party. The long, solitary struggle Keir Hardie had waged for it in contests of indescribable bitterness in the Trade Union Congress since first he appeared here in 1887 was at last to be crowned with success. Now would appear the harvest of his fight at Mid-Lanark in 1888, where without support from the official leaders of organized Labour, he put his faith to the test by opposing both Liberal and Tory as a Labour candidate, contemptuously spurning an offer of a safe Liberal seat, his election expenses and £300 a year, if he would only retire now and appear under Liberal colours next time. His brief Parliamentary experience as the Labour Member for West Ham had been but a meagre presage. The Labour Representation Committee, to the formation of which the Trade Union Congress had at last assented in 1899, was not, as yet, a Labour Party. The conference of Trade Union and Socialist bodies which had drawn up its constitution in 1900, had given it no power to promote candidatures, only to "keep in touch" with organizations running Labour candidates, and to secure the formation of a "Labour group" in Parliament, which, though it was to form its own policy and possess its own "whips," was to associate with "any party introducing legislation" in the direct interest of Labour. Yet the notorious Taff Vale Judgement of 1901,[1] by endangering the funds of Trade Unions, had spurred the movement towards Labour representation, and in 1903 the constitution of the L.R.C. was so far tightened up as to declare that its object was to secure the election of representatives of affiliated organizations, who must be run as "Labour" candidates only, and must pledge themselves to abide by the constitution of the L.R.C. and to abstain from promoting the interests of the Liberal and Conservative Parties. The phrase about co-operating with other Parties was now dropped. Even yet, this was not a Labour Party running its own candidates. Nevertheless a fund was established for the maintenance of Labour M.P.'s at the rate of £200 a year, and for the payment of twenty-five per cent. of the returning officers' expenses in respect of candidates run under L.R.C. auspices. That same year Will Crooks and Arthur Henderson were elected at by-elections to join Keir Hardie as Labour Members. The Party of one was already at an end.

The Socialist organizations, even the S.D.F., which at the Conference of 1900 had endeavoured to secure the formation of an avowedly Socialist Party, were elated at the prospect that the hitherto inert masses of Trade Unionists were to be swung into line in support of Socialist candidates. Observant people in all parties were looking with expectation to the new movement. In the election of 1900 fifteen candidates ran under L.R.C. auspices, and two were returned: Keir Hardie and Richard Bell. Bell was presently to declare against an independent party for Labour, and in three years' time had left the L.R.C. It is curious to recall now that Christabel, who was a stickler for the independence of Labour in those days, had warned Keir Hardie of Bell's tendency to be a backslider immediately after the election.

With the prospect of a Labour Party had arisen the thought —What would that Party do for women? This was the ruling idea behind the propaganda Esther Roper and Eve Gore Booth were conducting amongst the women textile workers. Leaving the North of England Suffrage Society and the Women's Trade

---

[1] In this case the Law Lords decided that a Trade Union could be sued for loss and damage alleged to be caused by its officers. The decision was not reversed till the Parliamentary advent of a substantial Labour group in 1906.

Union Council, they formed, with Miss Reddish and Mrs. Sara Dickinson, a rival organization, composed almost entirely of working women, called the Manchester and Salford Women's Trades Council, the foremost purpose of which was to do battle for the representation of women's labour. No one seized upon this idea, to which they had aroused her, more eagerly than Christabel Pankhurst. She made it her business to address Trades Councils and Trades Union branches in order to induce them to pass resolutions demanding votes for women.

Isabella Ford, of Leeds, a prosperous Quaker lady, a Suffragist of old standing, and an early member of the I.L.P., was elected to the Party executive in 1903, and reported to us that it was no more than lukewarm on the subject of votes for women. The I.L.P. speakers who came to stay with us in Manchester, now had to pass a searching examination by Christabel. Bruce Glasier, far from realizing the new spirit which had taken possession of our home, offended badly. It was not essential, he argued, that the whole people should be enfranchised. So long as the division were not upon class lines, those outside the suffrage would be represented by those within; their interests would be the same. There was no distinction of interest on sex, but only on class lines. It was not important that women should have the vote; for whilst some people would take an interest in politics, others would specialize in other directions. His opinion, common enough amongst Socialists at the time, was received with bitter resentment. Our friendship with the Glasiers, knit and cemented in the early days of bereavement, was strained to breaking.

Whilst I was working on the decorations at the Pankhurst Hall, a part of the building was already in use. I learnt, with astonishment, that women were not permitted to join that branch of the I.L.P. The reason given was that a social club, open to men who were not members of the I.L.P., but closed to all women, was attached to the branch. The excuses made for this state of affairs were worse than the fact itself, and aroused so much indignation in my family that they proved the last straw which caused Mrs. Pankhurst to decide on the formation of a new organization of women.

Isabella Ford reported, and his own declaration confirmed, that Philip Snowden, then a member of the I.L.P. executive, was not merely indifferent, but actively hostile to women's suffrage. Especially was he opposed to votes for women on the same terms as men, which, he declared, would assist the Conservative Party. When he came to lecture at the Pankhurst Hall, the day after the opening, Christabel refused to speak to him. Mrs. Pankhurst was now declaring that she had wasted her time in the I.L.P. She astonished, by an abrupt refusal to contribute, the good comrade who called for her small annual donation to the Keir Hardie wages fund, the modest £150 a year, voted by the I.L.P. Conference in 1901, to maintain him in Parliament. She declared that she would do no more for Labour representation till women's interests were considered.

She decided that the new organization, which she would form without delay, should be called the Women's Labour Representation Committee; but when Christabel returned from a meeting with Miss Roper and Miss Gore Booth and learnt the name her mother had chosen, she said it must be changed, for her friends had already adopted this title for the organization they were forming amongst the women textile workers. Christabel did not at that time attach any importance to her mother's project; her interest lay with that of her friends. Mrs. Pankhurst was disappointed and distressed that Christabel should insist upon their prior claim to the name she wanted, but she bowed to her decision and selected instead: "The Women's Social and Political Union." It was her intention to conduct social as well as political work; she envisaged the provision of maternity benefit, and other such amenities for the members of the new organization, which at that time she intended should be mainly composed of working women, and politically a women's parallel to the I.L.P., though with primary emphasis on the vote.

On October 10th, 1903, she called to her house at 62 Nelson Street a few of the women members of the I.L.P., and the Women's Social and Political Union was formed. Under its auspices a campaign of resolutions calling for action by the N.A.C. was immediately initiated amongst the I.L.P. branches. It must be admitted that a degree of impatience was evinced, which was somewhat precipitate, following, as it did, on a long period of inaction towards women's suffrage on Mrs. Pankhurst's own part. Christabel, young and impetuous, was scarcely two years old in active suffrage work; the rest of us younger still. As in a family quarrel, bitter reproaches were let fly too readily on both sides of opinion regarding the new activity.

Katharine Bruce Glasier was then editing the *Labour Leader* in Black Friars' Street, Manchester. I called at her office with a W.S.P.U. resolution for which publication was desired. She at once commenced to scold me for the aggressive attitude of our family, declaring that since her daughters had grown up, Mrs. Pankhurst was no longer "sweet and gentle" as of old. I burst into tears at thought of the breach growing up between

old friends, but my weeping only inflamed the annoyance of the
irate lady, who by no means realized that she had an advocate
for friendship and conciliation in my own breast. I was as
anxious as she for the growth of the Labour movement. I saw
very clearly that the bulk of the I.L.P. membership was ready
to support us, and that it was not in the I.L.P. that either the
power or the opposition lay.

Keir Hardie came presently to Manchester. The torrents of
W.S.P.U. frenzy were outpoured before him. A bevy of
angry women prepared to fight him on every point. He
raised no objection to the most impatient of zeal. On the
contrary he greeted all this with the keenest sympathy. Votes
for women? Of course! The Party must be brought into line,
and a big campaign set on foot. A separate women's organization? Excellent! The very thing to provide the necessary spur.
A simple one-clause measure to give votes on the same terms as
men? Certainly. Give him the necessary data; he would
prepare a pamphlet and get the I.L.P. to publish it. Christabel
wrote out the facts and arguments. With a few words of his
own to preface and conclude the manuscript, he signed it and
sent it for printing as it stood. On the N.A.C. he moved at
once; a request was sent out to I.L.P. branches to ascertain the
proportion which would be regarded as working class amongst
the women local Government voters in their area; working-class
women being defined as "those who work for wages, who are
domestically employed, or who are supported by the earnings of
wage-earning relatives." Upwards of forty branches undertook
this laborious task, and out of a total of 59,920 women local
Government electors canvassed, the working women voters were
found to number 82·45 per cent. Here was the evidence which
would enable the I.L.P. executive to convince its members that
they could press for the enfranchisement of women on the same
terms as men without handing an advantage to the propertied
classes. Mrs. Pankhurst toured the I.L.P. branches, calling for
the adoption of such a Bill; Keir Hardie, wherever he went,
urged the same plea. At its Cardiff Conference, Easter, 1904,
the I.L.P. elected Mrs. Pankhurst to its executive, which was
instructed to secure the introduction to Parliament of a Votes
for Women Bill. Keir Hardie arranged for this to be done by
Will Crooks. The nucleus of the Parliamentary Labour Party
was already in being; a long and stormy struggle to win for
Votes for Women a place in its active programme had begun.

Behind all this arose a poignant, human incident: the kind
Ellen had married; her husband was chronically unemployed.
She had taken to charring, then returned to be our housekeeper,

bringing him and their child along with her. She was in travail a second time. The others were going to a suffrage meeting. The sound of those piteous moans held me; abstract argument seemed hollow beside her pain. I lingered near the door, longing to be of service. Good Dr. Margaret Bell sent me to sterilize her instruments. The long labour was in vain; the child was still-born. I knelt beside poor Ellen. " After all this sad work ! " her plaintive cry breathed piteously in my ear. My heart yearned to her, her sorrow graven indelibly on my consciousness.

There was little need of me at Emerson's, in which the interest of Mrs. Pankhurst was waning fast. As soon as the Pankhurst Hall was open I began preparing for a National Scholarship to South Kensington, for which I had to sit for a large number of examinations. The first was geometry. Though every problem on the paper was familiar to me, I was so nervous that I did not complete one of them. My fingers shook, my ruler dropped, I rubbed the paper almost into holes. I dragged myself home in despair. The house was shut up; everyone had gone to the theatre. I crawled in through a window and went to bed with hopes utterly quenched. Thereafter, having lost the scholarship, as I thought, my nervousness altogether disappeared. I secured a first-class certificate in every other subject, and scored so many marks that I wiped out my first failure, and not only won a scholarship, but headed the list of competitors for the whole country. I was surprised, but not elated; the standard is not very high, I concluded.

BOOK V

CHAPTER I

I WAS lonely in the impersonal vastness of London, as I had never been in Venice. My first days at South Kensington were anxiously miserable. They began with a contest between myself and Spencer, the Principal, in which I was inevitably worsted. Under a rule introduced the previous year, all students at Kensington must spend their first six months of the day course in the architectural school, the evening only being given to life drawing. Most of the students objected to the new rule. I, too, deplored the fact that out of the precious two years of my scholarship a quarter should be given to a branch of study not in the direct line of my objective. I sought an interview with the Principal and endeavoured to discuss the question with him, requesting that I and all who wished it might be allowed to devote the evenings to architecture, and to reserve the day for the study of the human figure, which we regarded as more important to us. Had I been received with kind civility, as always at the Manchester school, it would not have been difficult to convince me that to a decorative painter some study of architecture was essential, or even that the college organization would not permit of the arrangement I proposed. I was not so received, but ordered furiously from the room. Thereafter, whenever I met the Principal in the corridor, we glared at each other, like two savage dogs. I was further informed by the students that there was great discrimination against women students in the award of prizes and scholarships obtainable at the college. In the scholarship examinations outside the college the identity of the students was unknown to the judges; in the college itself, whilst the judges recommended on viewing the works, the final decision lay with the Principal. Whilst many women entered the college with scholarships, few obtained scholarships there. At my request Keir Hardie asked a Parliamentary question on this point, and received the answer that the award of R.C.A. scholarships was in the proportion of one woman to thirteen men. All of us knew that this was not the proportion of merit amongst the students. As a matter of fact, it was an understood thing in the painting school that only one woman each year would get one of the college scholarships. The news that I was responsible for the question naturally reached the Principal.

Most of the first year students in my day suffered intense depression. Scathing criticism from the teachers replaced the genial encouragement of the Manchester school. We were made to suffer an abject feeling of incompetence. The scholarship of £50 a year (and travelling expenses from our home town), paid at the rate of £5 a month during the term, necessitated the strictest economy, particularly as we were obliged to find our own artists' materials during our first year. I was worried about the rent of that room over Emerson's, which my mother had taken for me, and also about the home finances generally. On Saturday mornings I used to go to the city to sell my designs for cotton prints, and as I was paid in guineas, I kept the shillings for my 'bus fares and sent the pounds home to my mother. My rent for a small, cheerless room in a tall house off the Fulham Road was 10s. a week. The students were mostly divided into little groups: almost every girl had her special girl friend with whom she shared her room, in order to economize rent, and almost every girl had also her special man friend. Thus a little group of four was created. In most cases the lads also joined two or three at a room. I was on terms of rather distant acquaintance with several groups and many individuals, but I made no special friends. My own two friends were outside the college: my brother Harry, at school in Hampstead, and Keir Hardie. I heard after I left the college that the young men regarded me as a " haughty female with her head in the air saying: ' Men are deceivers ever! ' " Yet it was not so: it did not occur to me that others desired to know me unless they made the first advances: the girls did so: the men left the initiative to me, and I, very much absorbed by many interests, made no move.

Austin O. Spare was a fellow student, a pale, flaxen-haired youth in a white shirt and scarlet sash: the weirdness of his work in those days caused the first year women students to regard him as a rather dangerous person, though he was younger than any of them. We heard that he was about to publish a book, and was asking advance subscriptions for it. I told the girls I meant to order a copy, and several who were too timid to approach him asked me to order for them. There was a college dance once in three weeks, and many students spent the spare time of several months preparing for the annual fancy-dress ball; yet on the whole they were a body of very anxious young people. They dreaded the day when their scholarships would come to an end, and leave them faced with the difficult task of earning a living in a precarious profession. The more ardent feared they would be driven to teaching instead of creative work; the more timid that they might fail to procure employment as teachers. The women, especially, knew they were handicapped in this field, for the best of the teaching posts would inevitably go to the men, even though less qualified than themselves. The atmosphere of disquiet, which became intense as the school year neared its close, heightened my Socialist opinions. Our anxiety was kept awake by news of the struggles through which the ex-students were passing. We saw their work deteriorating, their early promise fading under the destructive necessity of doing trade work merely for money, and for a pittance at that; from inability to pay for models, or devote time to study; from meagre living and lack of encouragement. A few were able finally to extricate themselves from penury, many were not. I knew of five cases of insanity amongst men students, during or near to the time I was at the college. One of these had been a married man trying to support his wife and children on his £50 a year scholarship when he went mad. I happened to meet him some years later; he told me he had suffered great privations, and had even worked as a potato picker. I went to but one of the college functions: a concert I never forgot, because Gilbert came; and Lanteri embraced his old pupil and wept on his neck.

Harry was free from his school on alternate Sundays, and those days we spent together. Keir Hardie gathered us both under his benevolent wing. I was often at his rooms at 14 Nevill's Court, an Elizabethan building, the oldest inhabited house in London. A dark winding stair led to his dwelling in that narrow alley off Fetter Lane. It had originally been one large room, but was divided, partly by partitions, partly by a curtain, into a living-room, a bedroom and a tiny box of a kitchen. The woodwork, which reached nearly to the ceiling, was painted a dark green. There was a window-seat, and a high, old-fashioned fireplace with hobs on either side. On the walls were engravings framed in polished rosewood: an excellent representation of one of the great franchise demonstrations of 1867, a charming portrait of Robert Owen in a circular frame, portraits of William Morris and Robert Burns, a bas-relief of Walt Whitman and some paintings by Socialist comrades. On the high, narrow mantelpiece were a bust of Emerson and a little iron figure of Dr. Johnson. A polished table by the door held a collection of curios, mostly old silver. Beside his big chair was a standard lamp draped with the Union Jack, a trophy captured from invading jingoes at one of his meetings against the South African War. The lamp was not used, for he preferred always to work by candlelight. To see him here came people of all sorts and stations: Socialists and social reformers, peoples from India and the small nations, Russian exiles, writers, painters, musicians, dreamers of dreams, to whom the legend of this man of the people was an inspiration and a light.

He lived with extreme frugality, cooking his food, doing his housework, blacking his boots, be it said with care, for he was a model of cleanly neatness. An old woman came to char for a few hours each week; for the rest he looked after himself. He had a marvellous way with him in lighting a fire. As a miner he had made a fine collection of the fossils he found in the workings, and he seemed to have a very affection for the coal itself. He liked " the grip of it," he told me; but he was always scrupulous in washing his hands immediately after touching it. I have seen him come home on a cold, dark evening after an arduous day, strip his overcoat, go to the fireplace, and light a fire on the top of the spent coals left in the grate. In a few moments there would be a cheerful blaze. Then he would bring forth bread, butter and Scotch scones, the main staples of his diet, and tea, which he would often cast into a saucepan of cold water, taking it off the fire as soon as it came to the boil. After this simple repast, he would light his pipe and seat himself for a chat; a brief one; for work was always clamant. Soon he would turn to his letters, or an article, giving me a book to read, and perhaps asking me to mark and annotate the salient passages, or it might be a printer's proof to correct. Books were his chief companions, and if work was not too pressing, he would lay it aside after a time and read aloud: Shelley, Byron, William Morris, Scott, Shakespeare, Walt Whitman—his taste was catholic. " Bobbie " Burns was probably nearest his heart; Keats was another special favourite. He was intensely interested in the modern writers who dealt with social questions: Ibsen, Anatole France, Galsworthy, Shaw. My first winter in London, Shaw's " John Bull's Other Island " was produced at the Court Theatre; we saw it together. Afterwards we took a meal at a nearby restaurant. When I asked for black coffee, which he had never tasted, he was as much astonished, he told me later, as though I had " called for a cigar." This was saying a good deal, for few women smoked in those days, and fewer still outside the privacy of their homes. Inspired by my example, he afterwards adopted black coffee as his favourite beverage; one of the very few indulgences he permitted himself.

Isabella Ford once aptly said of him that he seemed " as though he had been brought up in a glass case." Not until he had passed middle life did he ever enter a theatre. Reared in the

Calvinistic atmosphere of a Scotch village, he believed theatrical life to be sordid and debasing, and therefore would take no share in promoting it. During a conference in a provincial town, some I.L.P. friends suggested a visit to the local playhouse. Hardie refused, but relented when Mrs. Pankhurst, for whom he had a warm regard, urged him to see the thing for himself. The piece proved a crudely presented melodrama, but he was vastly amused, roaring with laughter in the sentimental passages and making great friends with a little boy who sat beside him and acted the part of showman. During a world tour, many years later, one of Keir Hardie's well-wishers advised him of the impending rubber boom and offered him facilities to acquire shares, but in his rigid adherence to principle he refused to accept any stake in the system it was his life's struggle to oppose.

He spoke to me often of his hard childhood, and striving youth, and of his mother, whom all her children held in singular reverence. "She was no ordinary woman," Hardie's stepsister said of her to me. I did not then know that Hardie was not his name. I first learnt it when, after his death, I read the fact in the proof of the first chapter of his autobiography, which was mislaid at the *Labour Leader* office. He had mentioned this projected work to me many times, saying that the lack of the first chapter had deterred him from continuing. He had not the patience to begin the book again. He often spoke, too, of his notion to write his life story in the form of a novel called : *Who Goes Home?*—the cry of the policemen within the precincts of the House when Parliament rises. Many of the tales he told me of his early life have since been published by others; many have not. In the days before the Truck Act his stepfather and his workmates handled not a penny of their wages; they lived in the mine-owner's house and procured the food of their households at the mine-owner's shop. When as a child he fell ill, and his mother's efforts failed to cure him, she begged the employer for half a crown of her husband's wage in cash, so that she might take her boy to the hospital. Her request curtly refused, she tramped the long journey to Glasgow with him on her back. He told me how, as a little lad, he stood with his mother and younger brothers and sisters in the road beside their poor household goods—evicted from their home. The employer rode by on his great horse, and in an impulse perhaps of pity, told his mother that she might return to the cottage if her husband would give up the Trade Union. "Nay, nay; he'll ne'er do that!" his mother cried.

Regarded as a youth of promise in his village, some men of means there proposed sending him to the university. He refused the offer, because the young men he knew who had returned from college seemed to him to have gained but little of real value by their studies, and to have lost touch with their own folk. At one time he went in the evenings to the village Roman Catholic priest to study French. This fact was used by his opponents in the Miners' Union to arouse against him the narrow prejudices of the men he was trying to help. At that time he had a shop, and put a girl in charge of it whilst he was in the pit. A strike came, his shop supplied goods on credit to his fellow workers to enable them to hold out. The wholesalers trusted him to repay; a considerable debt was incurred. After the strike was over the men were reluctant to pay their debts. The miners' agent, who was his principal antagonist, declared that the debt could be gradually made good by the men, but only if Hardie himself would leave the district. This incident deeply wounded him: he spoke of it, even so long after, with a stir of emotion in his voice.

In his young manhood pamphlets on hydropathy were circulated amongst the Dissenting Chapels in the Scotch villages. He read them with interest, the more poignant because he had but recently lost a little daughter. By the methods prescribed he relieved many suffering neighbours, giving his services without fee or reward, and became renowned in the neighbouring villages as a healer of great power. One of the founders of a hydro, afterwards widely known, invited him to enter into partnership. He refused, believing that his mission was to better the economic lot of the working class.

One afternoon that first summer, I met him on some business and went with him to a tea-shop. Over-worked and over-anxious, I fainted from the oppressive heat. Striving to recover myself, but relapsing again, I saw a glimpse of his agonized face. He told me after that he had never before seen anyone faint and believed me to be dying. I answered, laughing, that a spoonful of brandy would have revived me. That seemed to astonish him. Strongly confirmed in his teetotalism, the idea of administering a stimulant never occurred to him; indeed he would probably have considered it a sacrilege to offer brandy to a young girl.

When the I.L.P. executive met in London he would arrange for some little entertainment for its members and invite me and others to join them. When we went to see " Romeo and Juliet," I was surprised to hear Frank Smith asking him who was the author of the play. At one of the big Lyon's restaurants, then newly opened, the coming of Socialism was discussed, as it often was in those days, as something to be anticipated in the early future. " When Socialism comes I shall have a schooner of

lager," Keir Hardie said in joke. " No, no, don't break teetotal,
Hardie!" Snowden pleaded earnestly, dropping into broad
Yorkshire. " You don't realize what a great influence it has with
men to be able to say that *you* are a teetotaller."

Sometimes at rare intervals during the following years, I went
with Keir Hardie, or with him and others, for a day in the
country. He would pick up little stones and play with them as
children do, throwing them up and catching them in his hand,
and keeping five or six of them going dexterously. He insisted
that I should try, but I was quite incapable at the game. He was
astonished. " Did you not play it when you were a child? " he
asked me. " All the little girls do it! " I answered: " You
know I never played games! " " Ah! " he said with infinite
compassion and tenderness, " that is what is the matter with you!
You heard too much serious talk; children ought not to be
brought up like that." At such times he was merry, and liked
to talk of pleasant, childish remembrances. I told him I used to
think the daisies were like the faces of little girls; he said he had
thought them like his grandmother in her white cap. He had
plaintive recollections of the hard lot of the pit ponies he knew in
his boyhood. The dearest of them was Donald, whom he rescued
from the lads who were lighting a fire of straw under him because
he would not go, and who obeyed him at once, most willingly,
when he laid his hand gently on his soft nose. When the boy
Keir Hardie removed from that pit, poor Donald plunged into a
pond and drowned himself.

When striving to ward off recurrent illness, he stayed for some
months at the old Roebuck Hotel on Richmond Hill. I went
down many times to sit with him on the Terrace and walk under
the old trees in Richmond Park. With what pleasure he told me
that he had heard the nightingale singing in a copse close by!
Rarely had his strenuous years left time for the rural joys for
which his nature profoundly craved. Sometimes after I left the
college, when I had some business to take to him at the House,
he would declare for a breath of air in St. James's Park, and later,
when I lived near Kensington Gardens, he would walk even
thus far for a glimpse of Watt's " Physical Energy," the round
pond and its gulls, and the brilliant flowers of the Dutch garden.

During my first year in London I joined the Fulham branch
of the I.L.P., and was asked by the branch to debate on Votes for
Women with Margaret Bondfield, then an organizer for the Shop
Assistants' Union. Too modest to attempt to uphold our cause
against so practised a speaker, I asked Isabella Ford to act in my
stead. Miss Bondfield appeared in pink, dark and dark-eyed,
with a deep, throaty voice many found beautiful. She was very

charming and vivacious, and eager to score all the points that her youth and prettiness would win for her against the plain, middle-aged woman, with red face and turban hat crushed down upon her straight hair, whose nature yet seemed to me so much kindlier and more profound than that of her younger antagonist. Miss Bondfield deprecated votes for women as the hobby of disappointed old maids whom no one had wanted to marry. What women required, she said, was not votes, but industrial organization. If they were to vote at all, it must be on the basis of adult suffrage, but votes were of little importance to them. My indignation rose, I wished I had fought her myself instead of subjecting our old friend to her shafts. My heart was in adult suffrage, but this sort of argument was destructive of any sort of enfranchisement.

A few weeks later I made, unexpectedly, my first suffrage speech. Dora Montefiore, whom we had met in Manchester, had announced a Sunday open-air meeting in Ravenscourt Park, an unusual event for the suffragists of those quiet days. I went, intending to be a spectator, but found Mrs. Montefiore alone, a shower of rain having deterred the other speakers. She spoke of abandoning the meeting as she had never taken the chair in the open air, and did not think she could collect a crowd. My tenacity was aroused. " We can't give it up! " I said. She replied that in that case I must take the chair for her. There was not so much as a soap-box to take! How could I catch the ear of the Sunday strollers? My heart thumped terribly, but my voice sounded clear and steady. We were well received. The affair seemed tame enough when over; ground neither for nervousness nor elation.

I went sometimes to the crowded " At Homes " given by Margaret and Ramsay Macdonald at their flat in Lincoln's Inn Fields. Though her difficulties were eased by a substantial unearned income, Mrs. Macdonald was not exempt from the troubles encountered by mothers who busy themselves with activities outside their household affairs despite a growing family of small children. She had little time to attend to her dress, and it was no uncommon thing to see her with her blouse put on back to front, several of its buttons undone, and parting company with her skirt at the waist. On one occasion, when some of us were taking off our coats in a bedroom of the flat, we heard a slight cry from the bed, and found that the guests had been piling their coats on top of two little Macdonalds asleep. I met there Emily Hobhouse, newly returned from South Africa, telling of her work amongst the Boers left destitute after the war. She was asking me where she could obtain good designs for lace-making, when our hostess intervened to introduce her to someone else. Then Aylmer Maud began talking to me about Tolstoy, but almost immediately we were swept apart to be introduced to other people.

On Sunday I sometimes visited Aunt Mary (Mrs. Clarke) in a dreary south-east London suburb. I knew her to be unhappy, and though her husband received me with affability, I was oppressed by the thought that he was unkind to that gentle and timid being. He had adopted a child of alien parentage, a passionate little creature, who seemed like an infant wild cat confided to the cherishing of a doe. One Saturday I received a note from my aunt apprising me that she had left her home. I found her, with the child, in a little back room, devoid of all furniture, without so much as a bed to lie on, almost penniless, and in extreme distress. I pressed on her what money I had about me, and sent her a bed next day. She presently returned to her husband, but only for a time.

That year Christabel applied to the Benchers of Lincoln's Inn for admission as a student at the Inn with a view to being called to the Bar, but they refused either to admit her or even to allow her to appear in support of her application. Miss Cave had already unsuccessfully applied for admission a short time before. The result of Christabel's application was an invitation to plead for the admission of women to the Bar at the open night of the Union Society of London, where she gained the majority vote of those present.

One day in the Lobby, Keir Hardie called my attention to a grey-clad figure passing swiftly: Joseph Chamberlain. With neck curving high at the back, his head set forward, his pointed nose and small, keen eyes, he seemed to me extraordinarily like the wolf he appeared in some of F. C. Gould's *Westminster Gazette* cartoons. He was then in the thick of his struggle to force Tariff Reform upon the Conservative Government. A. J. Balfour, "Pretty Fanny," as his Liberal opponents dubbed him in those days, was vainly endeavouring to keep his Party and his Government together by evading the efforts, both of the Unionist Free Traders and of the Birmingham oracle to commit him to their policies. The life of the Conservative Government was ebbing fast; the aftermath of the South African War and its scandals, Chinese labour in South Africa, and unemployment at home, were raising a storm of opposition. Workless people were demonstrating in the industrial districts, and marching to Westminster from the East End. Keir Hardie was hammering away at their cause in Parliament, denouncing as "well-fed beasts" those who made light of the distress. When the House rose at midnight, he often went, as he had done winter after winter, to assist in relieving the destitute at a Salvation Army shelter, returning in the later small hours to attack his endless piles of correspondence; then with, or without, a more or less successful attempt at an hour's sleep, he would journey breakfast-less to the East End, and so march fasting to Trafalgar Square with the unemployed. He could not bear to go well fed, he told me, amongst the starving people.

Before the end of 1904 I had found a couple of rooms, one unfurnished and therefore happily free from bric-à-brac, at Park Cottage, Park Walk, Chelsea; a little square house in a short street running between the King's and Fulham roads. My landlady and her husband made riding breeches. They considered a Tory Government the best for their business, but Mrs. Roe, a typical warm-hearted Cockney, was prepared to embibe enthusiasm for Votes for Women, Labour and Socialism, and anything else with a strong, sentimental appeal. In these simple but congenial surroundings I began to feel myself at home. On Saturday afternoons I invited the women students of my year to paint with me, one of them taking turns to pose for the rest.

Mrs. Pankhurst came to London for the opening of the Parliamentary Session of 1905 and stayed with me at Park Walk. I absented myself from College to go Lobbying with her. Keir Hardie's lone fight for the unemployed received a measure of encouragement that session; the King's speech contained a promise of legislation. In earlier years this would have delighted Mrs. Pankhurst. She dismissed it now with the observation that when women had won the vote such matters would be dealt with as a matter of course. Keir Hardie would know then what it was to have genuine supporters; women would be true to him.

Eight days intervened before the ballot by which are allocated the Friday afternoons set apart for private Members' Bills. All the hours the House sat we spent in the Lobby, waiting for Members to come out to us, and when for a few moments they came, pleading with them to give a place in the ballot to Votes for Women. Expressions of sympathy were offered in plenty; but not one pledge did we get to add to that of Keir Hardie. By the time we were done each night, Mrs. Pankhurst was in a frenzy of suspense; all the woes of the world, and all the sorrows of women hung, one would say, in the balance. Her life's work, her husband's long struggle, the efforts of all who had striven for this old Cause would be thrown away, unless, this very year, Votes for Women were enacted. The Liberals were coming in; they would introduce manhood suffrage; the franchise question would then be closed for twenty years. She knew it would be so; that was the history of the franchise. Consider the periods which had elapsed between the Franchise Bills: 1832, 1867, 1884. Unless women got inside the Constitution before the introduction of manhood suffrage, they would never get in at all; never! If manhood suffrage came, men would never agree to bring the women in; they would be afraid of womanhood suffrage, because it would place women in a majority. Yes, women must get inside now! This year, this very year, was their only chance! So she insisted. Far into the night she railed against the treachery of men, and bemoaned the impotence of women! "Poor women!" The overburdened mothers, the sweated workers, the outcasts of the streets, the orphan children of the Workhouse mingled in the imagery of her discourse. She appeared so greatly to distress herself that I feared for her health and her reason. On some later occasion, when, after a night of these agonies, I was rising wearily one winter morning to be at College at half-past eight, she began again to declaim. I gazed at her in sorrowful concern, asking myself anxiously how I could leave her in such a state. Suddenly turning to me with a smile, she struck me lightly on the arm: "Don't look at me like that! Bless you, your old mother likes it. This is what I call life!" It was an awakening to me, and caused a revulsion of feeling. To her, too, it was perhaps an unusual self-revelation; nor was it entirely true, for she was as many mooded as the sea.

On that fateful Wednesday, February 21st, 1905, we waited the result of the ballot, Keir Hardie's welcome figure at last appeared. He had won no place. We were in blank despair. He reassured us; there was hope yet! The first fourteen places could be considered possible; we must get in touch with their holders, and induce one of them to take up our Bill. He hurried away to seek them out for us. One of them, Dr. Shipman, had promised his sponsorship to a Bill qualifying women for election to local governing bodies. The Parliamentary franchise was more important, Mrs. Pankhurst urged, insisting that he must give it preference. He referred us to Mrs. J. R. Macdonald; he had pledged himself to her. She was seen hastening through the Lobby. Mrs. Pankhurst confronted her; surely she would release Dr. Shipman. She hesitated. "You see, it's the others," she said in her amiable, babyish tones, showing her small, childish-looking white teeth, set wide, with a space between each one. Her words meant "no"; and "no" was the word of all the others, save one, who was not in the House that day: Bamford Slack, the holder of the fourteenth place. After urgent telephoning, he was finally caught at his home, Mrs. Pankhurst saw him, and he capitulated at the request of his wife. The

Bill was set down for the Second Order of the Day on Friday, May 12th.

The old National Union of Women's Suffrage Societies, with its Parliamentary secretary, and its offices in Westminster, had taken no part in the negotiations, its representatives were not in the Lobby during the disposal of private Members' places. Apparently, it left all this to its friends in Parliament, with the result that, session after session had been allowed to pass without the introduction of a Suffrage Bill. Yet it was on the private M.P. that the old N.U.W.S.S. relied; the necessity of a Government measure was first enunciated by the young W.S.P.U.

We now printed a petition for the Bill and worked to procure signatures. My own slender resources were strained to the uttermost by 'bus fares to meetings in all parts of London. In March the N.U.W.S.S. held a meeting in the Queen's Hall in support of the Bill. I went there alone. Fifty Members of Parliament, all in evening dress, were on the platform, and, one after one, they testified their approval in a few trite words. A trim, prim little figure, in a clear, pleasant voice, assured them that she regarded them merely as " ins and outs." It was Millicent Garrett Fawcett. Other ladies followed with brief utterances, in nervous, high-pitched voices; suffrage ladies were not accustomed to speaking at big meetings in those days. It was all very polite and very tame; different indeed from the rousing Socialist meetings of the North, to which I was accustomed.

The Easter Conference of the I.L.P. was held that year in Manchester. Our little W.S.P.U. group, our family and a few friends as it was then, Lobbied unceasingly to commit the Conference to support of Bamford Slack's Bill. A reception to the delegates at our home in Nelson Street, to make room for which the whole house was turned upside down, provided unrivalled opportunities of buttonholing each in turn. Mrs. Jennie Elcum Baker of Stockton was determined to circumvent us, and to secure a declaration for nothing short of adult suffrage. The struggle resolved itself into a debate between herself and Christabel, in which Christabel was an easy victor.

As Second Order of the Day, our Bill was hopelessly placed. Certainly the opponents would drag out discussion on the measure preceding it; probably it would not come on at all. Mrs. Pankhurst returned to London as the date approached, and with Keir Hardie vainly pulled every possible string to secure the withdrawal of the preceding Bill. From such orthodox negotiations Mrs. Pankhurst would pass, in the seclusion of Park Walk, to discussing such militant possibilities as tripping up old

Mr. Labouchere, who was expected to talk out the Bill. It might be done, she thought, with a fine wire held by herself and Mrs. Montefiore. I do not know whether the project ever advanced so far as to be broached to that lady.

In February my mother and I had been alone in Lobbying for Votes for Women; on May 12th so many women came to Parliament that they overflowed from the densely packed Lobby to the passages approaching it, and a large number were drafted on to the terrace. Suffragists of all grades were present, amongst them members from the twenty-eight branches of the Women's Co-operative Guild, brought thither by Nellie Alma Martel from Australia who had polled 20,000 votes for the Commonwealth Parliament. The new recruits were in high spirits, believing that they were to witness a brilliant victory, whilst inside the Chamber a little Bill to provide that vehicles on the public roads should carry a light behind as well as before was being spun out with jocular absurdities. Mrs. Pankhurst sent a written message to Balfour, telling him that unless he would give facilities for the further discussion of the Women's Bill, her Union would work against his Government at the General Election. The threat seemed empty, the Women's Social and Political Union was regarded as only a family party in those days; and in fact, for the moment, it was little more. Moreover, Mrs. Pankhurst, as he well knew, had been opposing the Conservatives as much as she could throughout her political life. The talk continued till but half an hour remained. Then our Bill came on amid roars of laughter from the opponents.

Suddenly a shout was raised; a man was dragged past by a dozen policemen and hurled into the street. Almost simultaneously we learnt that the Bill was talked out, and the House had risen. Someone said the man had been ejected for protesting on our behalf. The women rushed out, and crowded about him, thanking, congratulating, even kissing him. Only later we learnt that it was Councillor Gribble of Northampton, a member of Hyndman's Social Democratic Federation, who had marched with the unemployed from the Midlands and, so far from desiring to aid our Bill, had protested against Parliament wasting its time in talking about " votes for ladies " whilst men were unemployed.

The excited women were swarming about the Strangers' Entrance, loath to disperse. Mrs. Pankhurst suggested a meeting. The veteran Mrs. Wolstenholme Elmy, with grey curls falling to her shoulders, raised her tiny voice, inaudible except to the few beside her, and essayed to tell how the movement was started in 1865. Dozens of policemen began to push us away.

We moved to the statue of Richard Cœur de Lion before the House of Lords. Again the police hustled us, but Keir Hardie came out to stand by us, and after some argument the Inspector offered to take us to a place where a meeting might be held. So we were led off, Keir Hardie hand in hand with old Mrs. Elmy, to Broad Sanctuary by the Abbey Gates, where, as people with a grievance generally do, we passed a resolution of indignation against the Government.

The most important provision of the Unemployed Workman Bill promised by the King's speech was the employment of workless men on farm colonies, and the power to levy a penny-rate for the payment of their wages. Introduced in April, the Bill was hung up for two months, by opposition from the Government's own supporters. Impassioned protests by Keir Hardie, and unrestful manifestations by the unemployed, secured a second reading; but Government utterances then prepared the way for its withdrawal. Lansbury, Will Crooks, Dora Montefiore, and others at work amongst the East End unemployed, marched a thousand destitute women to Westminster, and led a deputation of the most wretched into the presence of Balfour, who protected himself with a scent spray from the smell of their poverty. Keir Hardie conceived the notion of placarding the walls with great coloured posters, demanding the passage of the Unemployed Bill. He came to me for a design, and gave me a week-end to produce it. I was delighted by his evident pleasure in the result, but owing to the mutilation of the Bill he abandoned the poster plan.

On July 24th the Government, to placate its supporters, issued amendments striking out rate aid for the payment of wages to the unemployed, thus leaving them only charity to depend on as before. Keir Hardie now denounced the Bill as useless; the Parliamentary Committee of the Trade Union Congress and the General Federation of Trade Unions decided to oppose it. Balfour replied by announcing the postponement of the measure and declared it " a travesty of the facts " to say that unemploy-ment absolutely required to be dealt with that session. On the same day a measure, only introduced in June, to settle a dispute between the Scottish Churches was passed into law. Reproached for thus advancing an absolutely new measure, whilst abandoning the unemployed, Balfour replied that in the case of the Scottish Churches a " crisis " had arisen. On July 31st came what Mem-bers of Parliament call " the massacre of the innocents "; the Unemployed Bill was placed amongst the measures the Govern-ment had relegated for sacrifice. Thereupon the Manchester unemployed decided to produce " a crisis " of their own. In defiance of the police, they held a meeting in front of the town hall and afterwards flocked into Market Street, deliberately holding up the traffic, and offering sufficient resistance to the police to procure the arrest of four men. Keir Hardie telegraphed congratulations, and moved the adjournment of the House, but in the meantime the arrested men had apologized to avoid imprisonment, and Hardie indignantly described them to me as " poltroons." The Government, anxious not to concede that it was acting in response to disturbance, declared that the progress of the Unemployed Bill would depend solely upon the views of the House of Commons; in ten days the Bill had become law. When rate aid was finally knocked out of the measure, Keir Hardie declared he would divide the House against it; but in response to the pleading of the I.L.P. executive, he agreed merely to abstain from voting for it.

The lesson of these two " crises " was not lost upon the W.S.P.U. It was only a question now as to how militant tactics would begin.

When I returned to Manchester for the summer holidays I found some new recruits at Nelson Street. The most active of these was Annie Kenney, a cotton operative, who had lived all her life at Lees, near Oldham, and had begun work as a half-timer at ten years of age. She was eager and impulsive in manner, with a thin, haggard face, and restless knotted hands, from one of which a finger had been torn by the machinery it was her work to attend. Her abundant, loosely-dressed golden hair was the most youthful looking thing about her. Her parents and all her family had worked in the mills, but her three younger sisters[1] had been pupils at the night school, and one of them had left the mill to become a shop assistant, one an elementary school teacher. The third, Jessie, then only sixteen, was studying to be a shorthand typist. Their youngest brother, Roland, some years later was for a short time the editor of Lansbury's *Daily Herald*. Annie Kenney had no aptitude for study; she did not go to classes like her sisters, but she had vague ambitions. She wanted what is called culture, and to get away from the mill. Upon those who saw her only on the platform or in the height of a propaganda discussion, she often made a distressful impression. " She seemed to be burning herself up! We thought it impossible that she could live long—yet now she has married and got fat," Beatrice Harraden said of her in after years. Actually she was always much sturdier than a superficial observer might judge; indeed she had a vigorous constitution, and possessed also a substantial dose of what the Scotch call

---

[1] All four sisters afterwards became organizers of the Women's Social and Political Union.

" canny." The wild, distraught expression, apt to occasion solicitude, was found on better acquaintance to be less common than a bubbling merriment, in which the crow's feet wrinkled quaintly about a pair of twinkling, bright blue eyes.

As a worker in the movement she had enthusiasm, and great self-confidence. Yet she was essentially a follower, and when she was organizing a district, it was necessary to bolster her up by an efficient secretary. She had the first essential of a speaker, a powerful carrying voice, though scarcely a melodious one; and at times a pithy, or pathetic vividness of expression gave colour to her speeches. On occasion her utterances could be bitterly cruel, as when during the European War she contemptuously referred, in a recruiting speech, to the physical infirmity of Philip Snowden, dismissing him as " only fit to be shelling peas." Her lack of perspective, her very intellectual limitations, lent her a certain directness of purpose when she became the instrument of a more powerful mind. Her obedience to instructions ignored all difficulties.

Like thousands of other Lancashire workers of their time, she and her brothers and sisters had come under the influence of the Independent Labour Party. She was singing in the choir of the Oldham I.L.P. when Mrs. Pankhurst came to speak for the branch. There she might have remained; but when Christabel followed soon after, she talked, not of women's woes and helplessness, but of the young working women who were to come forward and take their own part in politics. She spoke especially of the cotton operatives and of their strong trade unions, which, in common with the unions in other industries, were now determined to run their own candidates and secure direct Labour representation. The women members formed the great majority of the textile unions, yet they had no votes, and so were considered of no account. She urged them to rise up and fight for their rights. To Annie Kenney the words were a personal appeal. She went to Christabel and asked to join the movement, which was to open the doors of opportunity to girls like her. Immediately she was invited to Nelson Street. She was anxious to be a speaker, and took to the platform without a sign of hesitation. Impatient to begin, she urged us to set up our platform amongst the crowds gathered in each Lancashire village on the Sunday before its annual fair, or wakes, to see the outside of the monstrosity shows and merry-go-rounds already arranged for the coming revels, and to listen to the quack medicine vendors and revivalists who mounted the empty booths to tell their tale. To these motley throngs of sight-seers we girls, in the exuberance of our youth, made our appeal that summer's

Sundays, passing from wakes to wakes: Staly Bridge, Royton, Mosley, Oldham, Lees, Hyde, and so on. Generally I took the chair for the rest; a negro preacher, maybe, on one side of us, a long-haired medicine vendor on the other. " I have a young woman here to speak to you who has worked as a half-time hand in the cotton mill, and another young woman who wants to be a lawyer." Mrs. Pankhurst was meanwhile pursuing the crusade for the vote from town to town, on the platforms of the I.L.P., her presence always in demand.

About this time Annie Kenney announced her intention of standing for the local committee of the card and blowing-room operatives, to whom she belonged. As was usual then in the Textile Unions, no woman had stood for election in the memory of its membership. Many of her fellow-workers advised her against this step: " Don't go in for it, Miss Kenney! They are a drunken lot; they talk about nothing but whippet racing and hold their meetings in a public-house! " Nevertheless she stood her ground and was elected. She intended to devote the small sum paid for her attendance at committees to a Ruskin College correspondence course, but the project fell through; she was no student.

Another recruit was Theresa Billington (afterwards Mrs. Billington Greig), a teacher in a Manchester elementary school. Born in Blackburn in 1877, of Roman Catholic parents, she was by this time very aggressively a Socialist and an Agnostic. She had come into conflict with the education authorities, by refusal to give the prescribed religious instruction. She went with her difficulties to Mrs. Pankhurst, then a member of the Manchester Education Committee, who saved her from dismissal by arranging that she should be transferred to a Jewish school, where she would be exempted from religious teaching. " Tess," as she liked to be called, was a large, powerfully-built woman, with a round, pleasant face. Her lips curled perhaps rather too much, and, like many other bright young people, perhaps she pushed her arguments rather too crudely. She had far more capacity than little Annie Kenney, who flattered her immensely : " Oh, Tess, I think you're so splendid! Oh, Tess, I wish I could speak like you! " Tess was at that time honorary secretary both of the Manchester Teachers' Equal Pay League and of the Associates of the Ancoats University Settlement. She was not afraid to be considered unconventional; on the contrary, she sought to be so regarded. She had an adequate voice and was generally accounted a good speaker, but lacked the high emotional quality which belongs to oratory. Certainly she found a great zest and enjoyment in life and was vastly interested in herself and her doings. She was one of the " new " young women, who refused to make any pretence of subordinating themselves to others, in thought or deed. She had the impulse, usually ascribed to men, to return blow for blow, as was presently to appear. An honest fellow, the only working man on the Committee of the University Settlement, whom she treated with good-humoured superiority, bestowed on her a dog-like devotion. When at last she told him they were unsuited to each other, he blamed the Suffragette movement for taking her away from him. Doubtless the movement had caused her to be more exacting in her demands on life, and had roused her to insistence that marriage should provide a satisfying intellectual companionship and enable her not only to receive, but also to give an enthusiastic love. At the request of Mrs. Pankhurst, Theresa Billington was appointed a paid organizer for the I.L.P. in June, 1905. Hers was only the second such appointment. Hitherto the work of the I.L.P. had been done by unpaid volunteers, and by speakers who travelled as free-lances; getting their modest fees and expenses from the branches which chose to engage them for meetings.

CHAPTER II

MILITANT TACTICS BEGIN

EVERYONE knew that a Liberal Government would soon be in office. When Sir Edward Grey came to speak in the Manchester Free Trade Hall, on October 13th, 1905, it was as a Cabinet Minister of the immediate future. A letter was despatched to him from the infant W.S.P.U. in Nelson Street, asking him to receive a deputation. He did not reply. A favourable answer had neither been expected nor desired. At Nelson Street they had other plans. On the night of the meeting Christabel set out with Annie Kenney to heckle the coming Liberal Minister. " I shall sleep in prison to-night! " she gaily said; the lesson of Boggart Hole Clough had been well learnt.

Sir Edward Grey was making his appeal for the return of a Liberal Government when a little white " Votes for Women " banner shot up. " Labour Representation " was the cry of the hour. Christabel thrust Annie Kenney forward, as one of the organized textile workers, and a member of a trade union committee, to ask : " Will the Liberal Government give women the vote? " Other questions were answered; that question was ignored. When it was persisted in, Annie Kenney was dragged down by the men sitting near her, and one of the stewards put a hat over her face. Christabel repeated the question. The hall was filled with conflicting cries : " Be quiet! " " Let the lady speak." In the midst of the hubbub the Chief Constable of Manchester, William Peacock, came to the women and told them that if they would put the question in writing, he would take it himself to Sir Edward Grey; but it went the round of chairman and speakers, and none of them vouchsafed a reply. When Sir Edward Grey rose to acknowledge a vote of thanks, Annie stood on a chair to ask again, whilst Christabel strove to prevent her removal; but Liberal stewards and policemen in plain clothes soon dragged both from the hall. Determined to secure imprisonment, Christabel fought against ejection. When detectives thrust her into an ante-room she cried to her captors : " I shall assault you! "; she retorted, when they pinioned her : " I shall spit at you! " Her threat was not carried out in a very realistic manner, but she made as though to accomplish it, and also managed to get a blow at the inspector as she and Annie Kenney were flung out of the building. Yet still she was not arrested.   Outside in South Street she declared they must hold a meeting, and when they attempted to address the crowd now flocking out of the hall, her desire was attained: they were arrested and taken to the town hall.

Meanwhile in the Free Trade Hall cries of protest had been raised against the ejection of the two women.   Sir Edward Grey, feeling that some explanation was expected of him, expressed regret for what had happened:

" I am not sure that, unwittingly, and in innocence, I have not been a contributing cause.   As far as I can understand, the trouble arose from a desire to know my opinion on Women's Suffrage. That is a question which I would not deal with here to-night, because it is not, and I do not think it is likely to be, a party question."

Christabel was charged next day with spitting in the face of a police superintendent and an inspector.   Always slow to realize how a given action would present itself to the minds of others, she was surprised by the horrified astonishment expressed that a young lady could so behave.   " I was thinking of my law books," she told me, smiling a little ruefully.   " I knew that anything of that kind would be technically an assault, and I couldn't get at them in any other way."   One question to the police witnesses was the only explanation she vouchsafed to the Court: " Were not my arms held at the time? "   She was ordered to pay a fine of 10s. or go to prison for seven days, and Annie Kenney 5s. or three days.   They were placed in the Third Division, the lowest class, to which the majority of prisoners are sent; they wore the prison dress and ate the prison food.

The Press, almost without exception, adopted a hostile tone. The two following extracts are typical of the rest:

" If Miss Pankhurst desires to go to gaol rather than pay the money, let her go.   Our only regret is that the discipline will be identical with that experienced by mature and sensible women, and not that which falls to the lot of children in the nursery."—*Evening Standard.*

" If any argument were required against giving to ladies political status and power, it has been furnished in Manchester."—*Daily Mail.*

Keir Hardie at once telegraphed:

" The thing is a dastardly outrage, but do not worry, it will do immense good to the Cause.   Can I do anything? "

It was stated by those who ought to have known, that Lady Grey told her friends she considered the women were justified. " What else could they do? "   It was also said that Winston Churchill, who had been present in the Free Trade Hall, had considered it tactful, as prospective Liberal candidate for a

Manchester seat, to present himself at Strangeways Gaol to pay the women's fines; but the governor refused to accept the money.

A campaign of indignation meetings was organized. Pressed against the wheels of the lorry from which Mrs. Pankhurst was speaking was a little stout woman with rosy cheeks, and a most aggressive pug nose. This was Flora Drummond, a native of the Island of Arran, who had a standing grievance against the Government, because after she had qualified as a post mistress, she had been excluded by the raising of the height standard for such posts. A journeyman upholsterer coming to Arran on a holiday trip, fell off the steamer, and thus became the hero of the hour on that eventless isle. Florrie Gibson, as she was then, being a leader amongst the girls, needs must marry him. He was usually out of work, and after marriage she was obliged to continue a wage earner. She secured employment at the Oliver typewriting office in Manchester. It was her husband, she said, who had sent her to the protest meeting in Stevenson's Square, but she was nothing loath to join the Nelson Street band. Merry and energetic, brimful of self-assurance and audacity, she was always able to draw a laugh from her audiences by jocular stories, in which she never scrupled to draw the long bow. She was of the rough-and-tumble comedian type, good at organizing and directing, in a rough-and-ready way, and delighted to display herself in the attitude of command.

In spite of the Press, Manchester public feeling largely supported the two prisoners. A great crowd welcomed them at the gaol. Esther Roper and Eva Gore Booth presented them with flowers. Opinion as to their action was divided in suffrage ranks throughout the country. Some sympathized, but showed no sign; many preferred to wait and see. A crowded Free Trade Hall meeting on October 20th gave the prisoners an almost unanimous welcome. Christabel insisted that no reference should be made to their prison experiences, in order that attention might be fully concentrated on Votes for Women.

She was now threatened with expulsion from Owens College, and, as a condition of remaining to take her degree, was obliged to pledge herself to refrain from making any further disturbance. Meanwhile she devoted herself mainly to addressing Trade Union branches, and inducing them to send Votes for Women resolutions to the Government and the Labour Party. Annie Kenney did not return to the mill. She spent much of her time at Nelson Street, and was constantly speaking with the others of the group.

From the day of Christabel's imprisonment, Mrs. Pankhurst, to whom her first-born had ever been the dearest of her children, proudly and openly proclaimed her eldest daughter to be her leader. Christabel, she often told me, would never be deflected from her purpose in life by her affections, as most women were apt to be. "We are politicians, Christabel and I," she often said exultantly. "Christabel is a politician born! And I have had so much experience."

On December 4th Balfour's Government resigned, amid such public excitement as had not been witnessed in politics for many a day. There was a great cry that the long reign of reaction was at an end, that new ideals and new policies were to arrive. Every Reformer was alert with hope; above all the young Labour Representation movement was eager to try its strength. Sir Henry Campbell-Bannerman, who had held to the Liberal Leadership during his Party's long period of discouragement, was called to form an administration. John Burns was made President of the Local Government Board. "This is the most popular thing you have done, Bannerman," the one-time leader of the unemployed was alleged to have said. Probably that estimate was an accurate one, yet Burns had been steadily drawing aloof from the organized working-class movement since 1893, when he supported a Liberal to join him in the representation of Battersea on the L.C.C. against the nominee of the S.D.F., and, indeed, since his first election to Parliament in 1892. Keir Hardie, who had once waited for Burns to form a Labour Party, publicly expressing his willingness to serve under him, now wrote: [1]

"Morley is philosophic, timid and pedantic; Burns headstrong, impulsive and dashing, but they are one in their lack of faith in democracy."

A great meeting, at which the entire new Cabinet was to be present, was announced for the Albert Hall. Christabel wrote that I must get tickets for it. There was a tremendous rush for seats; I applied in vain at several offices. At last, on the promise of two tickets for the demonstration, I agreed to attend two rehearsals of Liberal campaign songs. In the meantime Annie Kenney came up to stay with me at Park Walk. Mrs. Montefiore took her to the East End, and introduced her to the women of the unemployed movement there. Several of these women agreed to help in the struggle for the vote, and went with Annie to create a disturbance at a Liberal meeting in the Queen's Hall a few days before the great Albert Hall demonstration. Annie Kenney had seated herself among the choir, singing as lustily as the rest till the speeches began. When I appeared at my second rehearsal a

[1] *Labour Leader.*

member of the choir denounced me as the woman who had made the disturbance in the Queen's Hall. I had not been there and I said so, but I did not get the ticket.

Keir Hardie, to whom I had confided our plans and difficulties, had meanwhile written to the Liberal Association for tickets for "friends from the country," and had received some tickets—two of them, as we discovered later, for the private box of John Burns. When the Prime Minister began to speak, Annie Kenney hung a banner over the edge of the box of John Burns, and raised her shout. Immediately afterwards Theresa Billington let down from the balcony near the platform a nine foot banner: "WILL THE LIBERAL GOVERNMENT GIVE JUSTICE TO WORKING WOMEN?" The vast audience was in uproar. While the disturbers were being thrown out, the organ was played to drown the noise.

Next day we returned to Manchester for Christmas. Christabel (though she could take no part) had decreed that we must oppose the Liberal Government in the person of Winston Churchill. Our method of opposition would mainly consist in disturbing his meetings. *Votes for Women* had to be written out hundreds of times on white calico in order that several examples might be held up at each meeting. They would certainly be snatched away as soon as they were displayed. As a matter of course, the job was mine—a tedious business, in which I continued early and late, with scarcely a pause, throughout the festive days!

I was at Churchill's first meeting in a schoolroom in Cheetham Hill. There was a running fire of questions of all sorts. Churchill answered them as they came. I put mine as soon as he gave me an appropriate cue. He attempted to ignore me, but my brother and some I.L.P. men at the back of the room led the audience in demanding that I should be answered. Such a clamour was raised that Churchill could not proceed. As soon as I stood up again there was complete silence, but when my question was put and again ignored the din began once more. This continued for some time. To end the deadlock the chairman asked me to put my question from the platform. I did so, and turned to go, but Churchill seized me roughly by the arm and pushed me into a chair at the back of the platform, saying: "No, you must wait here till you have heard what I have to say." Then, turning to the audience, he protested that I was "bringing disgrace upon an honoured name" by interrupting him, and added:

"Nothing would induce me to vote for giving women the franchise; I am not going to be henpecked into a question of such importance."

I would have gone then, but in a scuffle, during which all the men on the platform stood up to hide what was happening from the audience, I was pushed into a side room. I was left there, the door being locked on the outside, but not before I had opened the window and called to the people in the side street to witness the conduct of an enthusiastic Liberal, who was jumping about like a madman, and threatening to scratch my face. It appeared that I was a prisoner, for the windows were barred, but the people who had gathered outside called to me that a window at the other end of the room had a couple of bars missing. They helped me out, and called for a speech. Someone brought a chair, and I had a rousing time of it. Adela and Mrs. Drummond met Churchill at his second meeting. I joined Annie Kenney at his third. When the night's talking was done, I gave my story to the Press. It appeared with big headlines next day, producing innumerable jokes at the candidate's expense. There was no more kidnapping. Occasionally we were roughly handled, but as a rule the audiences in that Manchester election were so friendly to us, that if, as seldom happened, the stewards managed to eject us, the greater part of the meeting came out with us. More than once Churchill was left with only his bodyguard to listen to him. Indeed on several occasions Flora Drummond, in her stentorian tones, simply appeared at the door, and without putting any question to the candidate, called to the people to come out, and the people came.

I felt a contemptuous interest in seeing the desperate eagerness of the candidate to win the election, his uncontrolled exasperation at our interruptions and arrogant determination not to deal with us as he did with other questioners. There was a spice of poignant satisfaction in spoiling his meeting as a punishment for his insulting attitude towards women and women's claims. Then the whole thing would appear to me as a sordid business, and I would wish myself out of it for the rest of my life.

We had behind us the kind comradeship of the I.L.P., and the memory of Dr. Pankhurst, still green in the popular heart of his native city; but it is not solely at meetings that elections are fought and won. Moreover, a man might sympathize with Votes for Women, and yet not be willing to vote to put in a Tory Government. Churchill was elected, but by a smaller majority than the other Manchester Liberals.

Our intervention was more difficult in other constituencies; it often seemed like flinging oneself before the hounds in full cry after the fox. The hoardings were placarded with the big loaf of Free Trade, and the little loaf of Tariff Reform, with representations of the 45,000 Chinese coolies, the 21,000 African

Kafirs and the 4,000 white labourers at work in the mines of
South Africa under Tory rule.   These, and the war scandals, the
reversal of the Taff Vale judgement demanded by the Trade
Unionists, and the more or less vague promise of Social Reform,
were the issues the Parties were trumpeting for the election.   It
was of these the speakers desired to argue and the audiences to
hear, not this woman's question.   I went with Annie Kenney to
Asquith's meeting in the drill hall, Sheffield.   It was my first
experience outside Manchester.   Annie chose to come first.   She
held the seat of her chair firmly in both hands, and started off in
a sort of wail, which sounded more like a mechanical siren than
the human voice, repeating over and over again without a pause
the familiar words: " Will the Liberal Government give women
the vote? "

The people cannot understand a word she says; they will
think she is mad, I thought.   Then as the stewards rushed at
her, I reflected: " Poor girl!   She is no longer asking a question;
she is only giving the signal which will bring this violence upon
her! "   The men in the audience struck at her with fists and
umbrellas as she was carried past them.   Asquith stood silent
with contracted lips.   I tried to make my interruption comprehensible to the audience, but a rain of blows frustrated clarity.   I
was soon flung into the street, where Annie was waiting for me.
We held a meeting there, and received great sympathy from the
people, as was almost invariably the case.   Everywhere there was
a nucleus of the I.L.P. movement which rallied round us, and
everywhere the new militancy was arousing interest in the cause
of women, which had slumbered for so long.   The membership
of the W.S.P.U. was now growing.   Groups of women, and men
also, could be relied on for support in a number of towns.   Nine
women assisted in the heckling of Sir Henry Campbell-Bannerman at the Sun Hall, Liverpool; a larger number helped Mrs.
Drummond, who was sent up to confront him in Glasgow.   At
the first of these meetings the Prime Minister broke his silence on
this question to say he was " in favour of women's suffrage "; but
he gave no promise of action.   On January 25th Mr. Lloyd George
spoke at Altrincham in Cheshire.   The W.S.P.U. members
waited till question time to interrogate him.   His reply was:

" I was going to congratulate myself that I had escaped this:
however, at the last meeting of the campaign the spectre has
appeared."

The women were then hauled out.

Christabel had now lost all interest in the Lancashire and
Cheshire Textile and Other Workers' Representation Committee,

and the activities of Eva Gore Booth and Esther Roper, which had once been so important to her. The Women's Suffrage candidate of that organization, Thorley Smith, polled surprisingly well in Wigan, securing 2,205 votes, the successful Conservative getting 3,575 and the Liberal 1,900. During the following years there were several other Women's Suffrage candidatures, but with two exceptions, Thorley Smith and George Lansbury, both of whom were virtually Labour candidates, they all polled a miserably low vote.[1] During that 1906 General Election, Margaret Llewellyn Davies, of the Women's Co-operative Guild, herself stimulated by the new militancy, made an effort to bring forward the question of Votes for Women by publishing a manifesto on its behalf signed by the Guild and other organizations, including the Women's Liberal Federation, the North of England Weavers' Association, the British Women's Temperance Association, and the I.L.P. Such efforts were virtually unnoticed by any save the signatories.

Mrs. Pankhurst was meanwhile in Merthyr Tydfil, working for Keir Hardie. With characteristic self-abandon, he was anywhere and everywhere, save in his own constituency. The Labour Representation Committee had fifty candidates in the field, and wherever speakers were most needed he was to be found. Only on the last two days of the contest did he appear in Merthyr, wellnigh voiceless, to tell Mrs. Pankhurst, in his generous way, that he owed his return to her.

Under the fever of the General Election the lads at the Grammar School held a mock election. Their speeches at the hustings were reported at length in the Manchester Press. Harry, as earnest in the cause as any of us, stood as Women's Suffrage candidate. He won a middle place between the Liberal and Conservative candidates and the Socialists, one of whom, George Benson, the son of the treasurer of the I.L.P., was later elected as Labour Member of Parliament for Chesterfield. The boys assured us that Harry was by far the best speaker.

I was in London again before the election was over, and went down to Fleet Street, a solitary watcher, to see the results put up. The Labour Party—our Party, as it still was to me—with its twenty-nine Members of Parliament, was a reality at last! The

[1] The Hon. Bertrand Russell was put forward as Women's Suffrage candidate for Wimbledon in 1907. It was a Tory stronghold in which the Liberals had no chance, but Bertrand Russell ran as " a Liberal through and through." Nevertheless he did not get Liberal support and polled 4,000 votes less than the previous Liberal candidate. The N.U.W.S.S. promoted Women's Suffrage candidatures at Camlachie and East St. Pancras in the General Election of 1910, the candidates being at the bottom of the poll.

future seemed full of promise. I went about my work at the R.C.A. (where, so far as I knew, none of the students cared a straw for such matters) with a joyous exhilaration, as though I were the possessor of a precious secret.

Christabel, in Manchester, was already moving in the opposite direction. She had taken a W.S.P.U. deputation to interview Balfour, then a candidate in East Manchester, and had been sympathetically received. It is easy, of course, to be sympathetic when one has no longer the power to assist. She had interviewed Winston Churchill's opponent, " young Mr. Joynson Hicks," and had found him even more pleasant: he had told her it was his great ambition to win the seat because Churchill had been so " disloyal " to Mr. Balfour. He wrote subsequently, however, in curt and peremptory style, complaining that the W.S.P.U. was still interrupting Churchill's meetings, a practice which he feared would rebound against himself.

A few days after the election Annie Kenney was again in London with me. Mrs. Pankhurst had advanced £2 to send her up, and she told me she had come to " rouse London." There were no more Saturday painting parties at Park Walk after that. My life was changed. It became a matter of course to write Annie's letters and convey her hither and thither, introducing her as the mill girl who had gone to prison for a vote. I had been so horribly nervous when I went to sell my designs, but as soon as it was a question of agitating for a cause, my nervousness was gone. When all the letters were done, and I took up a book for a brief half-hour's delight before going to bed, she would sit at my feet and demand to be read to, and particularly that I should pick out favourite little snatches of verse for her to learn; from Tennyson: " A flock of sheep that leisurely pass by . . ."; from Shelley: " Rarely, rarely comest thou, Spirit of Delight! " Parts of his " To a Skylark," or of Keats's " Ode to a Nightingale," or " Endymion," or maybe of a few passages from Milton's " Sampson," or his " Lycidas," or a Shakespeare sonnet.

She had come without instructions; what should she do to rouse London? It was easy for me to decide that we should follow all the other popular movements by holding a meeting in Trafalgar Square, and a procession of the East London women in the unemployed movement at the opening of Parliament. I sent her to notify the police. She met me in the evening with the news that the Square was not available that day. I went at once to Keir Hardie for advice. He told us to engage the Caxton Hall for our meeting, and promised to induce a friend to pay for the hall and the handbills to advertise it. This friend was Walter Coats, secretary to the Vacant Lands Cultivation Society. Keir

Hardie drafted the bill, then and there, and told Annie to take it to the women printers.

I next conducted Annie to the office of W. T. Stead, who, with his great tenderness for all political prisoners, wrote an enthusiastic eulogy in which he likened her to Josephine Butler. Then we went to George Lansbury at his home at St. Stephen's Road, Bow, a little house adjoining the family woodyard. He introduced us to his son, Edgar, of whom he was obviously proud, whilst we endeavoured, not very successfully, to break the ice with his daughters, who, perhaps because they were so many, were not introduced. We called on Will Crooks, who showed us photographs of rich people who admired him. He promised to help, " but some women," he said, " are no good," and told us a story in proof of his contention : A woman cleaned everything in her house, cooked her husband's supper, kindled a bright fire, and made all ready; one thing only she omitted. She did not go out to draw the water in for the night from the tap in the yard because it was pouring with rain. When she heard her husband's step, she went to the door with a bucket in her hand and said : " I thought you wouldn't mind filling this, as you can't get any wetter." The husband took the bucket, filled it, and threw it over his wife saying : " Now you go out and fill it yourself; you can't get any wetter ! " " And don't you think," said Crooks, " the poor fellow was quite right, coming in tired after a hard day's work ? "

We went to Fleet Street to interview newspaper editors, and saw, amongst others, Bernard Alfieri (of the Alfieri picture service) who was doing the illustrations of the *Daily Mirror*, a new paper then. He promised to give us publicity, and kept his word handsomely.

We called on Balfour to inform him that though we happened to be attacking the Liberal Government at the moment, our action was not prompted by any friendship towards his party. His sister received us and begged us not to interrupt her brother's meetings. " He could not stand it," she told us, almost in tears.

Annie Kenney now spent most of her time in the East End. We formed a London Committee of the W.S.P.U., consisting of ourselves, my aunt, Mary Clarke, and the landlady, Mrs. Roe.

When Mrs. Pankhurst came up to London, and found we had taken a hall holding 700 people, and announced a procession, she was angered by my temerity, and declared the whole thing would be a ridiculous fiasco. Yet since the affair had been advertised, there could be no drawing back, and her optimism soon made the best of it. Just then Flora Drummond turned up from Manchester, having begged her fare from friendly I.L.P. members there. Here was another lively pair of legs to run hither and thither, chalking the pavements and delivering handbills. She borrowed a typewriter from the Oliver Company, and thus imparted a business-like appearance to our correspondence. She too was packed in at Park Cottage, and Mrs. Martel, who now got in touch with us, was also accommodated. The Press began to hover around the house; the *Daily Mail* had already christened us the "Suffragettes."

On February 16th, 1906, the day of the Caxton Hall meeting, some three or four hundred poor women from the East End were brought by train to St. James's Park Station. They unfurled a few simple banners, which were quickly furled again by the police, and marched to the Caxton Hall, to find it filled by women of all sorts and conditions; the publicity gained by the new militant tactics had begun to do its work. When news came that the King's Speech contained no promise of Votes for Women, Mrs. Pankhurst moved, as had often been done in the Women's Franchise League, that the meeting should resolve itself into a "Lobbying committee," and go down to the House of Commons. The Franchise League audiences had always voted such resolutions, applauding with correctly gloved hands, and had then returned to their houses whilst a few of the more zealous members of the executive committee drove off to the Commons in hansom cabs. This meeting was keyed to another pitch. The woman who addressed it to-day had shed her old timidity of the nineties. Confident of her power, she swayed her hearers as the harper commands his strings, and when she rose to march out through the rain, they followed her to a woman, though many of them had never set eyes on her before. On reaching the Strangers' Entrance to the House, they found the police barring the way, with orders, issued for the first time within living memory, that no women should be admitted.

Keir Hardie and others intervened with the Speaker and the Government, and eventually it was conceded that relays of twenty women at a time might enter the Lobby, the others waiting their turn in the rain outside—a trying experience for spirits already stirred by militant words! When, drenched and shivering, the women at last got speech with some Member of Parliament and found him indifferent, Mrs. Pankhurst's appeal to their indignation was substantially reinforced. The opinion with which many of them had set out for the meeting, that the militant tactics were too aggressive to be justified, had begun to wane.

Meanwhile Keir Hardie, in his first Parliamentary utterance as leader of the Labour Party, had endeavoured to draw Votes for Women into the political arena, as no Party leader before him had ever done. The King's Speech had announced the Government's intention to abolish plural voting. Hardie replied by urging a complete reform of the franchise laws. Before that Session closed, he said, the Commons might be in legislative conflict with the Lords. An appeal to the country might be necessary. The nation was not equipped as it should be for that appeal, since one-third of the men and all the women of the country were voteless. He hoped the Liberal Government would remove " the scandal and disgrace of treating women, because they were women, no better than criminals, paupers and peers."

The W.S.P.U. had now just begun to get a foothold in London. Women of all classes, some of them suffragists of long standing, were beginning to join it, and though it was still a very small society, Mrs. Pankhurst could already use its name to conjure with. Annie Kenney found herself taken up by people of consequence. W. T. Stead had early invited her to stay at his cottage in Canvey Island, and so enthusiastic was the expression of his paternal affection that she had to appeal to Mrs. Pankhurst to tell him not to kiss her when they went together to his office. Stout Lady Carlisle, too, for a time made quite a pet of this interesting mill girl, and the Hon. Geoffrey Howard, her son, amused the girl by throwing his glass eye across the room. Movements for liberation bring with them, to some, opportunities of personal advancement and release from uncongenial drudgery; to others, loss of livelihood, lowering of status, a double load of toil. Never was this fact more frequently manifested than in the W.S.P.U. It revolutionized life for a large number of women.

CHAPTER III

T HE struggle for an independent Labour Party was still being waged, the return of those first twenty-nine Members of Parliament notwithstanding. The miners had not yet allied themselves with the Labour Representation Committee. The Labour group collected under L.R.C. auspices had, as yet, neither constitution nor programme. Many of its representatives at heart still gave their allegiance to the Liberal Party, as they had lately done in name. They had come into the L.R.C. simply because their unions had voted for inclusion. Some of them had stubbornly opposed its formation during the years in which Keir Hardie had toiled for it. Arthur Henderson had but recently left the Liberal Party. In 1897-8, during the great lock-out of the engineers, he had been found in direct conflict with John Burns and Keir Hardie; they were working at a by-election to secure the defeat of Sir Christopher Furness, a member of the Engineering Employers' Federation; Arthur Henderson was speaking in his support. The Liberal Party had rushed into office now with a roar of popular acclaim, and Liberalism carried with it the glamour of belonging to the Government Party and the possibility of office. John Burns had secured that prize, though once accounted more extreme in his Labourism than most of them. J. H. Roberts, one of the L.R.C. men, who was presently to be a reverter to Liberalism, declared the Labour Members all proud of John Burns, as coming from the working class, and yet worthy to represent the State. J. R. Macdonald, the most ambitious member of the Labour Party, had no liking for Keir Hardie's policy of isolation and perpetual opposition to all other Parties. "It is a by-word that Macdonald is always on the doorsteps of Cabinet Ministers!" Hardie exclaimed to me bitterly, in the seclusion of Nevill's Court; an outburst only possible in acutest moments of exasperation to one so reserved, so tenacious of Party loyalties.

The Labour Party, at its first meeting in the House, had elected its creator, Keir Hardie, to be its chairman and Parliamentary leader, but only after a second ballot. Too often the position, thus ungraciously granted, was to wear upon him as a fetter, deterring him from open dissent from policies opposed to the very vitals of his concepts. His fervent desire to preserve the

United Front of Labour was a law of his being, and caused him to suffer unutterable torments of internal conflict, and to endure the thwarting of many a cherished impulse.

The Labour Party chairmanship was not then invested with the attributes of control and permanency, later added to it during the tenure of Macdonald. So far from being a position in which the holder would regard replacement as an insult, the office, like the chairmanships of the Trade Union Congress and the I.L.P., was then looked upon as only tenable for three years or thereabouts; its executive functions being strictly subject to the majority vote of the Party and its executive. That the chairman should become a leader exercising virtually autocratic power, as in other Parties, and should have the personal power to choose the members of a Labour Cabinet, was a notion not suggested in Keir Hardie's day. I believe it would have met his determined opposition.

Greater·success attended the Party in that first session than for many a year to come; the fallen level of its achievement being largely due to its increasing departure from Hardie's policy. At the I.L.P. Conference in 1914, Philip Snowden complained that the policy of the Labour Party differed little from that of the Liberals, and that it had given everything, and received nothing in return. Yet, so early as March 19th, 1906, Philip Snowden, with four others: Crooks, Duncan, Wardle and Shackleton, supported the Liberal Government, in defiance of the Labour Party's decision, on an issue of capital importance, whilst seven others, including Arthur Henderson and Stephen Walsh, abstained. The occasion was a motion of Colonel Seeley to reduce the Government's Army Estimates, the Labour Party having decided to support the reduction in the interests of peace. This incident was almost intolerably painful to Keir Hardie, who, with eager and anxious mind, was intently regarding the menace of the approaching European War. His only hope of avoiding the threatened slaughter rested upon the growing solidarity of the international workers' movements, and their unity in opposition to the militarisms of the world.

The first decision of the new Labour Party was to move no amendments to the Address; in effect a refusal to place itself in active opposition to the Government. The Party had chosen certain measures for immediate advancement, and many of its members were resolved either to secure the Government's assistance for these by amicable arrangement or to leave them in the position of mere pious resolutions. This was in direct conflict with the policy of Keir Hardie, who stood at all times for a fighting independence. He desired the Labour Party to display its own policy, as an emphatic alternative to the existence of a Liberal Government, and to compel the Government to accept the passage of Labour Party measures, by the fear of losing popular support.

The Labour Party came to a further decision, which was to be expected from its democratic constitution; i.e., that the places in the ballot won by its members, should be pooled and allocated to the measures the Party, as a whole, had decided to introduce. The chosen measures included the reversal of the Taff Vale Judgement, the Right to Work Bill, the feeding of necessitous school children, old age pensions, and a little check-weighing measure, specially desired to protect their earnings, by the members of burly John Hodge's Steel Smelters' Union.

In pressing that the enfranchisement of women should be included amongst these measures, Keir Hardie probably had not at that time a single whole-hearted supporter amongst his Parliamentary colleagues; for Snowden was then but a hesitant, newly-plucked convert to votes for women on any terms. His conversion had been effected by the witchery of the genial old Isabella Ford. The narrow vote of the L.R.C. Conference[1] that February between votes for women on the same terms as men, and adult suffrage, had left both solutions without appearance of substantial support in the Labour world. In the light of later events, it is now obvious that a grave mistake was made in leaving the field of adult suffrage—the true field of the Labour movement—to those who were either hostile or indifferent to the inclusion of women. The still surviving hope that women might secure the vote by a little private Members' Bill, and the excited fear that adult suffrage would, in practice, mean manhood suffrage, the dislike by some individuals of womanhood suffrage on any terms, and jealousy of those who were able to make women's suffrage a popular issue, maintained divided councils within the Labour Party and prevented its official adoption of a Suffrage Bill. Had other councils prevailed then, the Labour Party might have given a great lead for a manhood and woman-hood Suffrage Reform Bill. The Campbell-Bannerman Government, in spite of Asquith, might have been pressed into carrying it to recover its waning popularity. The breadth of view necessary for this course was not present then amongst any of the participants in the struggle. The adult suffragists (whether most of them were anti-women suffragists, as was alleged, or not)

[1] The resolution for votes for women on the same terms as men was declared lost by 432,000 to 435,000. The postmen's delegate then announced that he had voted wrongly; the figures ought therefore to have been 446,000 for Women's Suffrage, 429,000 against.

were powerful enough to prevent Labour Party action on the limited Bill. Keir Hardie, with all his ardour to help the women to their enfranchisement, was powerless to alter this.

Mrs. Pankhurst, fresh from the Merthyr victory, which she regarded mainly as her own, and as the most essential achievement of the General Election, was oblivious of all such difficulties. She had come to claim from Keir Hardie the Labour Party's complete devotion to the limited Bill. Christabel and she had agreed that the Labour Party must have an amendment to the Address, complaining of the omission of Votes for Women from the King's Speech, and that the Party must sponsor and ballot for the Women's Enfranchisement Bill.

Mrs. Pankhurst and I went to Keir Hardie together. In the muffled voice with which he always cloaked distress, he told her, quite simply, without a word of argument or explanation, the decisions already taken by the Party. He added, and that with equal baldness, that should he himself win a place, either for Bill or for Resolution, he would use it for Votes for Women, the decision of the Party notwithstanding. From him, with his strong sense of Party loyalty and responsibility, this promise of defiance to the general agreement was a greater offering than Mrs. Pankhurst, in her impatience, was disposed to realize. She swept it aside—a pledge to act personally was of no moment; the Party decision alone was of importance. It must be reversed. She would take no denial; she would not! She would not go back to Christabel in Manchester and tell her that this had been refused.

Indeed she could not, would not accept the truth, that those striving Trade Union leaders were not Keir Hardie's puppets. This pettifogging measure for Hodge's Union—affecting some mere detail of management—this absolutely must be discarded in favour of Votes for Women, a great charter of liberation! Even to suggest such a trivial measure in preference to the cause of women was the deepest insult! It must be withdrawn; it must! She wept, implored, stormed—was it for this she joined the I.L.P.; for this that she and her husband suffered boycott?

He sat there silent, with a face of intense grief, leaving her to understand, if she would, that what she desired he could not do.

On the following April 4th the young Labour Party gave a congratulatory dinner in one of the dining-rooms of the House of Commons. With the portly, prosperous figures of Trade Union officials, the seer in his old, brown homespun jacket, whom all the world reckoned as their leader, assorted strangely, as though from the window of a commonplace taproom one saw a noble mountain in the limpid glory of the setting sun. Proposing some toast, he uttered, in colloquial phrases, and with a voice of surpassing gentleness, his plea for that crusader spirit he had himself so steadfastly maintained in his long, lonely struggle as " a party of one." He wanted, he said, to form an " Anti-Guzzling League," pledged to accept no hospitality from the members of other Parties. " We are only guys to them all the time ! We must not lose touch with our own folk."

Mrs. Pankhurst smiled at him affectionately, and a little sadly, as he resumed his seat at her side : " A man I know is too anxious to join the angels," she said.

When the result of the Members' ballot was declared, Mrs. Pankhurst was in the Lobby pleading, exhorting; not alone, as before, for the Lobby was crowded with women. It was in vain; the Labour men, save Keir Hardie, who drew no place, held firmly to their Party's official decision, and no promise from the members of other Parties could be obtained.

To add insult to injury, as it was indignantly considered, Sir Charles Dilke had given a place to adult suffrage. Since 1901 he had been suspect in suffrage camps, for in that year he had made himself responsible for a Bill to enfranchise all adult men and women. It was even said he had done it in spite, because some of the suffrage ladies had reviled him for the divorce case which wrecked his Parliamentary career. Yet undoubtedly he was sincere in desiring the complete political enfranchisement of both sexes. He had introduced his Bill session after session, but only in that eventful year, 1906, did he at last secure a place for its Second Reading. Both Suffragists and Suffragettes treated the measure as an interloper, designed with the sole purpose of frustrating their own efforts to break down the sex barrier. Their attitude gave a convenient handle to opponents, who insisted that the suffrage movement was bourgeois in leadership and opposed to any but a limited vote. Lord Robert Cecil, in his high Conservatism, reinforced this view, declaring himself a believer in women's suffrage, " but only to a certain extent." Dilke's Bill was talked out by an irrepressible anti-suffragist, Mr., afterwards Sir, Samuel Evans.

Keir Hardie, unsuccessful in the Bills, obtained a place for a Resolution, and devoted it to Votes for Women as he had promised. Meanwhile he collected £300 from donors, willing to be advised by him, as the nucleus of a campaign fund for the W.S.P.U., a very substantial assistance for that then impecunious young organization.

CHAPTER IV

IN his care for the struggling Union, and faithful friendship for its founders, Keir Hardie sought to enlist as its treasurer a woman of powerful personality who would bring to it new energy and influence. As he assured me confidently, he believed he had accurately discerned such a colleague in Emmeline Pethick Lawrence. He gave Mrs. Pankhurst a letter of introduction to her, urging her to present it forthwith at Mrs. Lawrence's flat in Clements Inn, a few minutes walk from his own rooms. I left her at their door. She returned to me from the visit with the words: " She will not help; she has so many other interests." Yet next day came an invitation from Mrs. Lawrence to meet again. It was the beginning of the six years' partnership, during which the Women's Suffrage Movement, militant and non-militant, passed from weakness and obscurity to great wealth, great numbers, and a clamant position on the political stage.

The Lawrences had but recently returned from an investigation of post-war conditions in South Africa, and particularly of Native problems, which they had discussed with Olive Schreiner, with whom a lasting friendship was cemented. Possessed of substantial means, they had the world on their side, an advantage which they placed at the service of the W.S.P.U., identifying themselves with it whole-heartedly and without reserve. Moved by the knowledge of poor childhood and unhappy womanhood, Emmeline Pethick, as she was before marriage, had left the gaiety of a prosperous home, a large, merry family of young brothers and sisters and affectionate parents, to become a " Sister " in the West London Mission, under Hugh Price Hughes. She formed a close friendship with Mark Guy Pearce, the Christian Socialist, whose influence helped to mould her young opinions. With " Sister " Mary Neal, her friend and co-worker in the Mission, she left it to form the West London Social Guild and the Esperance Club for working girls. Her expansive and ardent personality, and ability to establish sympathy with people of many sorts, made her a host of friends. Frederick Lawrence had had a Cambridge career of substantial promise. He secured honours, both in mathematics and natural science, was Fourth

Wrangler, Second Smith's Prizeman, Adam Smith Prizeman in Political Economy, Fellow of Trinity, and President of the Cambridge " Union." As a young man of fortune, he made a tour round the world on completing his studies; then took up residence at Mansfield House University Settlement, becoming its treasurer, giving financial assistance in establishing a boys' club and a women's hospital. In 1900 he became a professor at Manchester College, Oxford, and a prospective Parliamentary candidate in the Unionist interest. He withdrew from the candidature on discovering that the policy of the Conservative Party ran counter to his convictions. Most probably he was helped to that decision by the influence of Emmeline Pethick, whom he married in 1901. The bracketing of their joint names was typical of their admirable relationship. Together they founded a co-operative dressmaking business, a holiday hotel for working girls, and built a children's holiday cottage, " The Sun Dial," near their country house, " The Mascot," at Holm-wood, in Surrey. Lawrence had secured a controlling influence in the *Echo* in 1901, and had edited it from 1903 till its end in 1905. He now had a small monthly paper : *The Labour Record,* devoted to the Labour interest, the columns of which were at once opened to defence of the W.S.P.U. and its methods.

At that second meeting with Mrs. Pankhurst Mrs. Lawrence agreed to become honorary treasurer of the W.S.P.U. Our London Committee was reconstituted as the National Committee. I remained honorary secretary, Annie Kenney was formally appointed an organizer at £2 weekly. Irene Fenwick Miller, whose mother, well known as an early woman journalist, had been on the executive of the Franchise League, and who had joined the movement at the first Caxton Hall meeting, Mrs. Roe, Mrs. Clarke and Mrs. Martel were members of the Committee, along with Mrs. Pankhurst and Mrs. Drummond who were returning to Manchester. Our meetings were still held at Park Walk.

Our first move was to secure an interview with the Prime Minister. My written request being refused, I replied that we could accept no denial, and that some of our members would call upon him at the official residence in Downing Street on March 2nd. The visit proved abortive; the Prime Minister was ill. Amid the snapshotting of Press photographers, the women had seated themselves on the doorstep prepared to remain all day, but Arthur Ponsonby, the Prime Minister's secretary, persuaded them that his chief's illness was not assumed, and they consented to retire. Again we wrote for an interview, and again were refused. On March 9th thirty women proceeded to Downing Street. Two detectives opened the Prime Minister's door and ordered them away. Irene Miller knocked again and was arrested. Mrs. Drummond pulled at a little brass knob she thought a bell; the door flew open; in she ran, and was thrown out and arrested. Annie Kenney, jumping into somebody's motor-car, began to make a speech, and was taken in charge. The three were detained at Cannon Row police station for an hour. Then a message was brought that the Prime Minister would shortly receive a deputation from the Women's Social and Political Union, either individually or in conjunction with other organizations. The prisoners were released and came home jubilant.

Two hundred Members of Parliament now formed themselves into a Women's Suffrage Committee, and petitioned the Prime Minister to receive a deputation from them, in order that they might urge upon him the necessity of the immediate enfranchisement of women. He then formally announced that on May 19th he would receive a joint deputation from these Members of Parliament and all organized bodies of women desirous of obtaining the suffrage. The W.S.P.U. congratulated itself on having won the first round in the contest with the Government. On the day of the deputation, we were to hold a procession of women from the East End and a meeting in Trafalgar Square. Theresa Billington was appointed as our second organizer to assist in this work. She, too, was packed in at Park Cottage, and became another guest in the use of my once quiet little workroom, now a centre of perpetual discourse. Mrs. Martel, golden-haired and bejewelled, sat impregnable by the fireside, reading, with horrified comments, the accounts of the Crippen case. Theresa, eager to sharpen her wits on whoever could be drawn into argument, declaimed on the virtue of flouting Mrs. Grundy, and expatiated with youthful excitement on the joys of her love affair with the worthy Scotsman, Greig, whom she presently married; whilst Annie Kenney gazed at her, adoring, and punctuated: " Oh, Tess, you are so splendid! " Then Mrs. Roe would come in with the tea, and with a quizzical grimace at Theresa, and a friendly wink at me, would exclaim: " Oh, how you do go on, Miss Billington! " adding in a serio-comic voice that she hoped her daughter, Daisy, would be " good."

In view of the deputation to Sir Henry Campbell-Bannerman Keir Hardie's Resolution had assumed a new importance; it would indicate the feelings of the House towards Votes for Women, and might give the Prime Minister a cue for action should he be hesitant. Early in April Mrs. Pankhurst returned from Manchester, with intention to create a disturbance in the House of Commons by making a speech from the Ladies' Gallery on the introduction of the Education Bill. Her experience on the Manchester Education Committee would give point, she said, to this intervention. She confided her intention to Keir Hardie; he advised her either to wait until the new Parliament had had an opportunity of declaring its view, by a vote on his Resolution, or to leave the disturbing to one of her young lieutenants, whose actions would be less seriously regarded than her own. " Oh, you are only a man! " she cried, in disdain; and turned to me: " What do you say? " " Why not wait till after his Resolution has been discussed? It is less than three weeks—not long, after all these years! " She agreed to wait; but when I was alone with her she wept: " You have balked me—both of you! I thought there would have been one little nitch in the temple of fame for me! " " Oh, Mother," I answered, " do you not realize there will be many and many another opportunity? The struggle is not ended yet! "

Hardie's Resolution was set down for April 25th. It had only a second place, but the anti-vivisectionists, who held the first place, had agreed to withdraw their motion early. Nevertheless Christabel believed that the talkers out would have their way, and she therefore insisted that a protest must be made from the Ladies' Gallery. To be in readiness for this task, a dozen or more of us occupied the front seats in the gallery. An old opponent of the Cause, the so-called Liberal-Labour representative, W. Randal Cremer, excited the wrath of our little band of militants by his jocular remarks about women. Indignant exclamations issued from the historic grille, which masked our presence from the House. The Speaker gave orders that if anything further were heard from our quarter the gallery must be cleared; but when Cremer sat down all was quiet. A Government statement was awaited with expectation, and presently Herbert Gladstone, the Home Secretary, arose. He committed the decision to the free judgement of the House, and while not actually excluding Government action, he made no promise. Ten minutes before the debate must close, Samuel Evans[1] rose with the obvious intention of talking the Resolution out. He kept the House in a roar of laughter, and every now and then he turned round, with a smile, to look at the clock. The women in the gallery were now constantly stretching over to Mrs. Pankhurst to ask whether our demonstration of protest could begin. Neither she nor any of us knew that according to the established procedure of the House, before the hands of

---

[1] He was knighted later and suffragists said it was for this act.

the clock reached eleven, Keir Hardie would be entitled to move the closure of the debate, and that he was waiting to do it, the Speaker having the option to accept or reject the motion. We did not know that it was because the Speaker had refused to accept the closure resolution that the Women's Suffrage Bill had been talked out the previous year and many times before.

Suddenly one of our women looked round and saw policemen ranged against the wall of the gallery behind us. They were there in obedience to the Speaker's order to turn us out should we make any more noise. The sight precipitated the demonstration; Irene Miller shouted: "Divide! divide!" as Members do on the floor of the House. "Divide! divide! We refuse to have our Resolution talked out!" The rest of us all joined in: "Divide! divide!" Theresa Billington thrust a little white flag through the grille. We laughed as the police came rushing down over the tiers of seats to drag us out; it was fun to show our contempt for the "Talking Shop," the mace, the Speaker, and all the rest. Its Members had spent the evening laughing at us; and this was how little we thought of them! So, for an instant, I felt with the others. Then looking down again at the House I saw Keir Hardie turn and stride from the chamber. I knew by his sombre brow and the set of his shoulders we had angered this generous friend. The knowledge seemed to fall on me like a stone; I could hardly maintain a face of unconcern—yet I must, for the thing was done now, and must be carried through. I felt culpable, and that I alone was culpable; for I alone understood the difficulty of his stand for us, and realized that his rivals were taking advantage of it to aid them in decrying his whole policy. At least we should have consulted him, I thought ruefully.

The House had risen in the midst of the uproar. If there had been a chance to manœuvre the Government into committing itself to Votes for Women before it had adopted a hostile attitude, that chance was gone. Subsequent history seems to prove that the chance had never existed; yet at the time I miserably wished we had waited—and all the more when I knew that in a few moments the closure would have been moved and the intention of the Speaker put to the test.

Thrust ignominiously from the gallery, we descended into the Lobby. Mrs. Philip Snowden, some non-militant suffragists, and a dozen or more Labour Members were there. Cold looks and bitter reproaches met us as we appeared, dishevelled from the fray. The women held aloof; the men flocked round to scold us. Next morning the Press berated us; we had ruined our cause was the general verdict. Hardie remained silent a few days—they were an age to me. Then he came forward to defend us. The fact that the police were already in the gallery was sufficient explanation, he insisted, for what we had done; our action was in no way to be censured. To me he said: "I assumed that your mother knew all about the closure. I cannot understand, with her great experience of Lobbying, how such a thing could have escaped her knowledge." Opinion gradually veered round in our favour. It was said that the Speaker would in any case have refused the closure. W. T. Stead's *Review of Reviews* spoke of our "divine impatience," Spencer Leigh Hughes (*Sub Rosa*) recalled the disturbances created in the House of Lords by the peeresses of the eighteenth century, and the strategy by which the Duchess of Queensberry and her friends overcame the decision to debar them from the House. Nevertheless, attempts were made to exclude the W.S.P.U. from the deputation to the Prime Minister, the promise of which had been wrung from him by sitting on his doorstep. These efforts failed for two reasons: firstly, Keir Hardie, an important member of the Parliamentary Women's Suffrage Committee, refused to assent to our exclusion; secondly, it was realized that the W.S.P.U. would display its resentment by methods more forcible than polite.

In due course the famous deputation was received at the Foreign Office on May 19th. Upwards of 260,000 women: Suffragists, Co-operators, Temperance Workers, Liberals, Socialists, were represented. The room was crowded. The textile operatives alone had sent fifty delegates. A petition was presented from 1,530 women graduates. The aged Emily Davies, one of the two who had handed the first women's suffrage petition to John Stuart Mill in 1866, opened the case; it was closed by Emmeline Pankhurst on an unusual note. The militant women felt this question so keenly, she asserted, that they were prepared to sacrifice for it "life itself, or what is perhaps even harder, the means by which we live." The Prime Minister replied by a long argument in support of Votes for Women, but concluded that as some of his Cabinet were opposed to it, he could only "preach the virtue of patience. It would never do for me to make a statement or pledge under these circumstances." Keir Hardie replied that "patience can be carried to excess," and:

"with agreement between the leaders of the two historic parties, and with the support of other sections of the House, it surely does not pass the wit of statesmen to find ways and means for the enfranchisement of the women of England before this Parliament comes to a close."

Threat the Prime Minister shook his head in emphatic dissent. Mrs. Elmy, in her frail old voice, broke in with a reminder that she had been working for this cause since 1865; Annie Kenney jumped on a chair and shouted: " Sir, we are not satisfied! The agitation will go on! "

The W.S.P.U. delegation, Mrs. Pankhurst, old Mrs. Elmy, Annie Kenney in clogs and shawl, Keir Hardie, the crowd of poor women who had marched from the East End, and a wagon-load of children, gathered in Trafalgar Square for the first great open air public meeting for Women's Suffrage ever held in London.

Campbell-Bannerman having categorically told the deputa-tion that his Government would not initiate legislation for Votes for Women, the anti-Government policy of the W.S.P.U., as yet little more than a project, was now vigorously pursued. The heckling of Cabinet Ministers became systematic. Wherever they were announced to speak, W.S.P.U. organizers went before them to work up a hostile demonstration. Theresa Billington raised a storm by using a dog-whip on the stewards who ejected her from Asquith's meeting at Northampton on June 14th. As such things always did, the action produced retaliation against other militants. Mrs. Pankhurst was also ejected from a North-ampton meeting. At Belle Vue, Manchester, a Liverpool City Councillor was arrested for joining the women's protest, whilst Adela Pankhurst, now a Manchester elementary school teacher, was imprisoned for a week, and two other women for three days, on the absurd charge of attempting to rescue the Councillor from the police.

When interrupted at Liverpool, Lloyd George protested himself a Suffragist, and cried: " Why do you not go for your enemies? Why do you not go for your greatest enemy? " He was answered by roars of " Asquith! Asquith! " The incident accorded with the intentions of the W.S.P.U.; an interview with Asquith was demanded, and on his refusal thirty women marched with banners to his residence at 20 Cavendish Square. The police flung themselves upon the women, driving them off by the pressure of burly fists and knees, and arresting the most prominent, whilst women at the windows of Mr. Asquith's residence laughed and clapped their hands. Annie Kenney and two of the East End women, Mrs. Sparborough, an old needle-woman of sixty-four, and Mrs. Knight, lame with hip disease, who had left an eighteen-months-old baby at home, were sent to prison for six weeks, on their refusal to be bound over to keep the peace for twelve months, or in other words to give an undertaking to abstain from similar action for a year. This abandonment of the agitation they refused, and served out their time in gaol. Old Mrs. Sparborough, indeed, declared it was a delightful rest for her, save for the fact that scrubbing the stone floor each morning had awakened her rheumatism. During the fracas in Cavendish Square, Theresa Billington, crying to the police: " You shall not strike our women! " had dealt a return blow with her fist. Now, charged with assault, she refused all defence, declaring her objection to be tried in a Court of men, by " man-made laws." She was given the option of a £10 fine or two months' imprisonment. Her sentence, upon protest in Parliament, was immediately reduced by half, but her fine was anonymously paid, and she was turned out of prison.

The Press jeered: " Mock martyrs " and " Martyrettes." Keir Hardie, in the Commons, insisted that the women's agitation must be met, not by imprisonment, but by votes. The two " Liberal-Labour " Members, Maddison and Cremer, took up the cudgels for the Government—characterizing the sentences on these " female hooligans " as " extremely lenient." The Suffragettes hurled defiance at their detractors. Mrs. Pethick Lawrence wrote in the *Labour Record* : [1]

" There can be no going back. . . . We look to none but ourselves. We appeal to none but women, to rise up and stand shoulder to shoulder. . . . The women who come to us know what to expect, and are not afraid.
" First it was ridicule and contempt . . . then it was violence; to-day it is a six-weeks' sentence, to-morrow it may be six years . . . finally it may be death. We are not afraid; we are not sorry for ourselves. On the contrary we know that we have the very best thing that life has to offer—a great fight in a great cause."

But of Annie Kenney she wrote: [2]

" It seemed as though Fate had singled out just the very wrong victims for this vindictive sentence. If it had been . . . some of our more robust women! But Annie Kenney! That frail woman-child. . . . Annie Kenney, who, if I could have my way, should be shielded from every blast of bitter wind."

The haggard-looking girl from the mill had appealed irresistibly to her protective tenderness; and Annie, with her hungry, factory-oppressed soul outstretched for the comfort and culture of well-to-do life at its ease, as well as for the fame and adventure of politics, leapt to the bosom of this new friend, who could give her so much she lacked; and who received her with kind cherishing when the prison gates opened to her once

[1] July, 1906.
[2] *Labour Record,* July, 1906.

more, and she came forth shuddering from the greyness and solitude of the cell.

For months I had not seen her. In August the Lawrences invited a crowd of Suffrage and Labour people to a performance of Old English Folk Songs and Dances[1] by the Esperance Girls' Club in the gardens of " The Mascot." Annie Kenney greeted me gaily: " This is *my* home now. Would you like me to take you round the garden? Would you like me to pick you an apple or a pear? " She radiated her joyous satisfaction, a perpetual fountain of smiles and ecstasies. So she passed on to new circles and new experiences, with her thin neck and her golden hair, her twinkling blue eyes, and her mouth gasping as though to drink in every new sensation, her restless, knotted hands tearing her gloves as she dragged them on, reciting the little odd snatches of poetry she was acquiring by the way.

In 1904 Dora B. Montefiore had raised the ancient slogan: " Taxation without representation is tyranny! " and for refusal to pay her income tax had twice suffered a distraint upon her goods. On the W.S.P.U. agreeing to champion her stand, she now barred her doors against the bailiff. Her house, on the Upper Mall, Hammersmith, " Fort Montefiore " as it became known, was surrounded by a high wall with a stoutly-built doorway. The " siege " began on May 24th, 1906, and continued for six weeks. Meetings were held outside, and Theresa Billington was photographed passing a loaf over the wall. Eventually the brokers forced an entry, and a piece of furniture was seized and auctioned.

On June 30th Christabel had taken her LL.B. degree at Victoria University with honours in the first class,[2] a distinction shared with but one other student in that year. She was the only woman law student at the college, and had already obtained the prize for International Law. When she went up to take her degree there was a humorous hostile demonstration by some of the men students, one of whom, as he afterwards confessed to me, was Walton Newbold, later, for a brief period, the first Communist Member of Parliament, or, as he was fond of calling himself in those days, the representative of the Soviet Government and the Third International. That he proceeded soon to repudiate the Russian connection was characteristic.

Her degree taken, Christabel left Manchester to become chief organizer of the W.S.P.U. at a commencing wage of £2 10s. a week. Adela, on her release from prison, had also become a

---

[1] Collected by Cecil Sharp. Mary Neal was the first to organize their performance through the Esperance Girls' Club.
[2] In 1903 she had matriculated in the second class.

W.S.P.U. organizer. When Mrs. Pankhurst had told the Prime Minister that women were prepared to sacrifice their livelihood for the cause, she spoke with feeling; her waning enthusiasm for Emerson's having snuffed out what meagre degree of prosperity had ever smiled on it, the business was now closed. The quarterly fees of her registrarship were still largely drawn upon for liabilities arising from the defunct Emerson's and the W.S.P.U. Whilst she travelled about on the Votes for Women mission, her sister, Mary Clarke, who was now her deputy in the registrarship, remained at Nelson Street with Harry, keeping house on the proceeds of the daily fees, and doing it somewhat too sparely for the needs of a growing lad. Having been taken from West Heath School, Hampstead, in July, 1906, Harry's future was now the subject of occasional, inconclusive debate. His irregular schooling and poor eyesight rendered it impossible for him to sit for any examination.

The two years of my scholarship were almost at an end. I was facing the world with the last month's payment in my pocket. W.S.P.U. work had been packed into every moment left over from college work, with no spare time to prepare anything which might produce the money for a crust of bread. The teachers in the painting school had advised me to apply for a free studentship to enable me to complete the five years' course and take the diploma, but I would not, for I saw no possibility of supporting myself under those conditions. Where now should I seek for work? Of the firms to which I had previously sold designs, the ill-fated Emerson's had been a customer. I did not wish to visit them now. Moreover I was ill, tormented by neuralgic pains in my arms and hands and around my ribs. I had suggested to Mrs. Pankhurst that I should be relieved of the W.S.P.U. honorary secretaryship some months before in order that I might prepare myself to meet this pass, but she heatedly insisted that I should retain it till Christabel came to London. I did not wish to become a paid worker for the W.S.P.U., nor did Mrs. Pankhurst desire it. She thought it not well for all her family to be on the Union pay-roll. I was emphatically determined to maintain my own independence. The dream of being an artist in the cause of progress still held me. Moreover, in spite of my love for Christabel, I was, even then, not fully in accord with the spirit of her policy, which eventually always swept Mrs. Pankhurst along with it.

In those closing days of the college session, so full of anxiety for me, and those of my fellows, who were also facing a precarious future, I expected a letter from my mother, if only of encouragement. None came. We were no longer a family;

the movement was overshadowing all personal affections. I had written to her regularly every second day in all the years of my absences. Now, my last letter unanswered, I ceased to write at all, except on matters of importance. The world seemed lonely and cold. It was six weeks before any communication passed between us. I was tired to the breaking-point, and it seemed that Mrs. Roe was wondering whether I should be able to pay the rent when I left the college. Suddenly I resolved to resign the honorary secretaryship: in my uncertainty for the future, I could not give my mind to it as before. The growing work of the Union was inevitably drifting more and more towards Clements Inn, where the Pethick Lawrences were already devoting most of their time to it, and into the hands of the paid organizers. Christabel, too, was nearing the end of her college term: she would be coming to London as chief organizer.

The committee was meeting in my room at Park Walk that evening: I wrote a letter of resignation, left it on the table for Mrs. Pethick Lawrence, and took my drawing-board and materials to the rooms of a fellow student. Mrs. Despard and Mrs. Edith How Martyn, B.Sc., a teacher and member of the I.L.P. and already a close friend of Theresa Billington, were at once appointed as joint honorary secretaries in my place. The committee now consisted of the honorary secretaries and the honorary treasurer, Mrs. Pethick Lawrence, Mrs. Wolstenholme Elmy, Annie Kenney, Mary Neal, C. Hodgson, Elizabeth Robins the novelist, and Mary Gawthorpe and Mrs. Martel, who had both become organizers of the Union. Mrs. Pankhurst was greatly annoyed that I had not deferred my resignation till Christabel could be present to preside over the choice of the new honorary secretary. She feared that divided counsels would result from the appointment; her prophecy proved correct. Henceforth the committee meetings were held in the Lawrences flat at Clements Inn.

I resolved to leave Park Cottage as soon as the last days of the college term had run their course. It was quiet enough there now, for the organizers were in the provinces, but I did not wish to encounter Mrs. Roe or any of them in what might be a stiff struggle with want. I engaged two unfurnished rooms in Cheyne Walk, on the Embankment, next door to the house once occupied by Turner. I was so racked with pain that I took nearly a week to pack my small belongings. Then I hired a lad with a handcart to take my easel, camp-bed, packing-cases of books and paints, and my one little bag of clothes. These, pitched in at random, with the penny-in-the-slot gas meter and a gas ring capable of boiling two small pans, were my only furniture. I sat among my boxes, ill and lonely, when, all unexpected, Keir Hardie came knocking at my door. With quick discernment and practical kindness, he took command of the situation. He lifted the heavy things into position, and when all was, so far as it could be, in order, took me out for a meal at the little Italian restaurant where Harry and I had lunched on many a happy Sunday. I was immensely cheered, but the immediate future was dark enough. I had 25s. in the world, and my rent was 11s. a week. I cut my expenses to the lowest ebb : Egyptian lentils, and loose cocoa, sold in the King's Road, close by, with the addition of water alone, I selected as convenient and fairly sustaining; bread, milk, eggs, fruit and everything else were discarded as too expensive. After some months, Egyptian lentils became so distasteful that I was unable to swallow them any more. In the meantime they served. But where to look for work? I called at the offices of several magazines. There was always a titter when my name was announced. If the editors consented to see me, they assumed that I wanted to write about Votes for Women, and at that time they were unwilling to give much space to the subject, still less to pay for it. They seemed unable to switch on to the idea that I might be able to do other work. I called at the Bodley Head with some sketches for illustrating an old favourite, "The Open Air" of Richard Jefferies. I saw John Lane; he was exceedingly kind, but reminded me that the copyright of the work had not yet expired. He told me the publisher who held it, and even looked up the address for me to go there at once, but I was too crestfallen at the thought that I had expended my slender resources on a work that must stand or fall by the decision of one publisher, to put its fortune to the test. I thrust the sketches in a drawer. When I was almost at the end of my pence, Keir Hardie got me a commission for a couple of illuminated addresses. Later I wrote a series of articles for the *Whitehall Review*, and got other odds and ends of work which kept me going. Sometimes I made designs for the W.S.P.U. One of these was a banner, depicting Woman as Mother and Worker, which was unveiled at the Portman Rooms in 1908, and the cartoon for which was placed over the W.S.P.U. literature stall at the Hungarian Exhibition at Earl's Court that year. A stall at such an exhibition was regarded as a new and very enterprising departure for a suffrage society in those days. One of the most popular W.S.P.U. productions was the brooch presented by the Union to its released prisoners, a miniature portcullis, bearing the broad arrow in purple, white and green. I had forgotten that it was my own idea and design, till the fact was recalled to me in turning over the files of *Votes for Women* the other day. The illuminated address, also presented to prisoners, caused my youthful zeal much distress. I had executed it at short notice, but with considerable care. It was reproduced by lithography, and in the re-drawing by a workman on the stone became almost unrecognizable. The urge for quantity, speed and some sort of economy inevitably worked many a transformation. Sometimes I charged a modest sum for such works, sometimes I gave them, glad to be able to give. Always I was torn between the economic necessities of the immediate moment, the desire of further study to equip me for ambitious works, and the urging of conscience to assist in the movement. Like many another young woman of my period, I was distraught by my solidarity with that rage of militancy. There was a solidarity, too, with my family, and with the Union I had helped to form; but more than all these was the poignant, compelling appeal to my heart of the victims of social misery, the white faces in mean streets which roused my indignant pity. Even in the calm haven of the Royal College of Art, lulled by the manifest duty of work and study to justify the holding of a scholarship, I had asked Keir Hardie: " Are we brothers of the brush entitled to the luxury of release from utilitarian production? Is it just that we should be permitted to devote our entire lives to the creation of beauty, whilst others are meshed in monotonous drudgery? " Now, facing alone the hard struggle of life as an unknown artist, nervous, diffident and in poor health, came the frequent question: Why? As a speaker, a pamphlet-seller, a chalker of pavements, a canvasser on doorsteps, you are wanted; as an artist the world has no real use for you; in that capacity you must fight a purely egotistical struggle.

When I earned any surplus beyond my urgent needs, I spent it on models and studies, neither saleable nor intended to be saleable, or worked gratuitously for the movement till my surplus sped away. Somewhat later I engaged in a long statistical inquiry into the relation of infant mortality to women's employment, district rates of wages, occupational conditions and diseases, housing and over-crowding. I arrived at the conclusion that the only statistical curve in which agreement with that of infant mortality could be found was that of the number of inhabitants per square mile. Where the population was densest the proportion of infant mortality was highest; over-crowding and its attendant evils was therefore the most marked predisposing cause. I used my conclusions only in speeches, for when I had laboriously worked out my figures from the Blue Books at the British Museum, a Government report was published announcing the very fact I had discovered at so much pains. Mrs. Pankhurst,

always anxious to secure more workers, would sometimes telegraph for me to help at a by-election, or to meet her at Clements
Inn, and I would go, throwing all else to the winds.   Sometimes
I spent my last pence on the 'bus fare to meet her, and walked
back, too proud to tell my need.   Her frequent complaint that
I dressed so poorly I heard with a touch of cynicism, refusing to
discuss my financial affairs.

CHAPTER V

CLEMENTS INN

ON taking up her work as organizer of the W.S.P.U., Christabel had hastened immediately to a by-election at Cockermouth, which polled on August 3rd. She was joined by several other women speakers, all members of the I.L.P. There were three candidates: Liberal, Conservative and Labour, but it was made clear that the W.S.P.U. was in the field purely to attack the Liberal. Christabel was most pointed in emphasizing to the electors that she cared not a straw whether they voted Tory or Labour. Coming from I.L.P. women, these tactics were a shock to the Labour Party. George N. Barnes, of the Amalgamated Society of Engineers, one of the Labour Members hitherto most friendly to us, was the first to display his consternation. I was on the terrace of the House of Commons with Keir Hardie one day during the election; Barnes approached us with the words: "Cockermouth! I hear the women are independent!" Keir Hardie said "Yes" in a way he had which precluded further discussion, but that was by no means to be the last of the controversy.

From Cockermouth Christabel came to London to open a campaign in the constituency of John Burns, in Battersea. As the assumed special representative of Labour and democracy in the Government, he was selected for attack by way of exposing the hollowness of the Government's professions, since it would not practise them towards women. Pavement chalking announced the meetings; in the dinner hour at works gates, in the afternoon and evening at street corners. A big muffin bell was rung to summon the crowd. The people soon knew what it meant, and shouted in delight: "The Suffragettes! Come along!" To Christabel these campaigns seemed as the very wine of life. With what eagerness she would mount the chair and the platform and begin: "Now I'm going to tell you about our tactics!" She saturated her mind with politics. From the daily Press, assiduously studied as the first business of every day, from the memoirs and writings of prominent politicians, and the standard works on Parliament and the Constitution, she drew the material for her speeches. Street corner audiences heard from her a keen and ruthless analysis of the Government's latest proposals in home and foreign affairs, enlivened by saucy quips and scathing denunciation. It was all destructive; but how much easier to win applause by destructive condemnation than for any constructive scheme, however brilliant, however beneficent! That she was slender, young, with the flawless colouring of a briar rose, and an easy grace cultivated by her enthusiastic practice of the dance, were delicious embellishments to the sterner features of her discourse. Yet the real secret of her attraction was her audacity, fluent in its assurance, confidently gay. " Queen of the mob," J. J. Mallon named her. " Lively arabesques," Max Beerbohm called her gestures. " An enthusiast " in the *Daily Mail* wrote of her during the Peckham by-election :

" Her questioners are for the most part earthenware, and this bit of porcelain does them in the eye, quaintly, daintily, intellectually, glibly. Look to it, Mr. Gautry, or the witchery of Christabel will do you in the eye."

Elizabeth Robins, the novelist, fell in love with her, and with the movement. The result was her drama : " Votes for Women," first produced at the Court Theatre on April 4th, 1907, and her novel *The Convert*, developed from the same theme. Christabel had the admiration of a multitude; hundreds, perhaps thousands of young women adored her to distraction, and longed to be and to do likewise. For the next six years her life was crammed with occupation and incident. Speaking, writing and being interviewed, thinking out plans and tactics, and organizing their performance. To those who had known the lethargic Christabel in the days of Emerson's, and remembered the schoolgirl who could always have done much better if she would, her activity was a marvel. For a time she even managed to fit in a course of dancing lessons by way of recreation. Her physical welfare was meanwhile watched over by Emmeline Pethick Lawrence with the solicitude of a mother. For years she lived as the guest of the Lawrences at Clements Inn, and every week-end which could be snatched from meetings she spent with them at Holmwood. They took her abroad at every holiday.

Mrs. Pankhurst upheld her as an oracle, the Pethick Lawrences lauded her political genius to all comers. As for me, I detested her incipient Toryism; I was wounded by her frequent ruthless casting out of trusty friends for a mere hair's-breadth difference of view; I often considered her policy mistaken, either in conception or in application; but her speaking always delighted me; her gestures, her tones, her crisply-phrased audacity. I admired her, and took pleasure in her, as I had done when we were children together in Russell Square. I avoided crossing swords with her; for six years I refrained from dissent from her decisions, in word or deed. I could not have done this so consistently were it not that I regarded myself as one who had come into active political life only as a sacrifice to the urgency of the need, departing from the path I had marked out for myself, and to which it was then my intention to return.   There came a time when I could efface my desire for the development of another policy no longer; but this was not yet.

In October, 1906, the W.S.P.U. opened offices in Clements Inn; at first there were but two rooms: the large general office and Christabel's room.   Emmeline Lawrence worked in her own flat upstairs.   Frederick Lawrence had his editorial office for the *Labour Record* in the same building.   In 1906 he became business manager of the W.S.P.U.   When Mrs. Lawrence became the treasurer the accounts of the Union were placed under professional supervision; first under the honorary auditorship of A. G. Sayers, Chartered Accountant.   As the income rapidly increased, the auditing was taken over, on a business basis, by the firm of Sayers & Wesson.   The Government prosecutor in the conspiracy trial of 1912 testified to the fact that the accounts of the W.S.P.U. were kept with the precision of a first-class business concern. Lawrence was meticulous in matters of detail and economy, conservative in assuring a surplus to meet all contingencies; but he had large conceptions of equipment and advertisement, which would have done credit to a general of " Big Business."   He was a rigid disciplinarian, demanding accuracy and attention from all who worked under him; but he never made the mistake of placing new burdens on a staff already working to the limit of efficiency, nor did he attempt to make the shilling do the work of the pound. For each large additional venture he insisted upon new offices and a new staff; and Emmeline Lawrence, with her remarkable capacity as a treasurer, coupled with the great enthusiasm engendered by the militant tactics, was always able to call up from sympathizers with the movement such money as might be required.   " Our treasurer," Christabel once declared, " excites the envy of the entire political world."   Of a certainty every other organization in the country wondered at the income of the W.S.P.U.   It rose with increasing momentum; reaching £3,000 in 1906-7, £7,000 in 1907-8, £20,000 in 1908-9, £32,000 in 1909-10. Then there came a truce for nine months; the income decreased somewhat, but was still enormous, being £29,000 in 1910-11. Actually the donations had risen to £23,668 16s. 8d. from £18,057 8s. 10d. in the previous year; it was the income from other sources which had dropped.   In 1911-12 another truce again resulted in a certain reduction of income, which nevertheless reached the large total of £25,494 17s. 9d., the donations amounting to £19,844 5s. 3d.   The years 1912-13 and 1913-14 showed another great increase, reaching £28,502 9s. 6d. and £36,896 6s. 4d., but by this time the finances were under other auspices and another policy. By the end of 1907 the Union already occupied thirteen rooms in Clements Inn, and by the end of 1909 it had spread into twenty-one rooms. In 1910 the literature department was transferred to a shop in Charing Cross Road, other departments taking up the space it had vacated at Clements Inn, the offices in both buildings now comprising thirty-seven rooms. The salaried officials at this time numbered one hundred and ten, the greater part of the propaganda being done by volunteers. All the larger meetings were made a source of income.

In 1907-8 upwards of five thousand meetings were organized, including the first women's suffrage meeting ever held in the great Albert Hall. When the offices at Clements Inn were first opened, weekly " At Homes " were held there on Monday after-noons. In February, 1908, these meetings were transferred to the small Portman Rooms in Baker Street, and a fortnight later to the large Portman Rooms. In July of the same year a move was made to the large Queen's Hall, which was frequently filled to its utmost capacity. Literature sales rose from £60 in 1906 to £9,000 in 1910. In October, 1907, the Pethick Lawrences founded the paper *Votes for Women* and handed it over to the Union in the following year, at which time the cost of its produc-tion was covered by advertisements and sales. In 1909-10 the paper reached the zenith of its circulation, having risen in that year from 16,000 copies weekly to nearly 40,000. After this the circulation declined, from causes which will be enumerated later. It was too exclusively a one-subject propaganda organ to command the large circulation which the great efforts made to promote it, and the extensive scale of other W.S.P.U. activities might suggest. Moreover the Union, with an income and central offices far exceeding those at the disposal of the Labour Party, for instance, was a creation of rapid growth under burning enthusiasm. It had not the multitude of local organizations which may under favourable conditions be developed in a lengthy period of growth by a movement like Trade Unionism. The W.S.P.U. effort was not so much to form branches as to create an impression upon the public throughout the country, to set everyone talking about Votes for Women, to keep the subject in the Press, to leave the Government no peace from it. In these objects phenomenal success was achieved. Organizers were holding campaigns, individual volunteers working in districts where no branches existed; indeed the movement was much more largely one of individuals working directly under the headquarters, than of

branches.   By the end of 1911 there were thirty-six local
W.S.P.U.'s in London, ten of which had their own shops, and
twenty-eight centres in the Home Counties.   Here, drawing its
inspiration largely from headquarters, was the greatest concentration of the Union; in the rest of England, Wales and Scotland
were seventeen shops and fifty-eight centres, some of them very
strong and active.

In the early days the office " At Homes " were informal
gatherings of enthusiasts.   Christabel, a slight figure in green,
with rosy, engaging smiles, mounted a chair, a sheaf of letters and
cuttings in her hand, to give the news of the week.   Mrs. Pethick
Lawrence, a newly released prisoner, an organizer from the
provinces, a visitor from overseas, would take up the tale.   Old
Mrs. Sparborough would bring round the tea, with a wealth of
quaint stories and old saws: " Gin was made of junipers and
beer of hops once upon a time; now they are made to make men
thirsty ! "   In less than two years all this had been replaced by
the impressive weekly gatherings in the large Queen's Hall, which
no other organization of men or women in the country attempted
to fill save as an occasional rare event.   The staff, in the main,
had been members and enthusiasts before coming to the office.
Miss Kerr, the office manager, eminently methodical and correct,
had been running her own typewriting office.   She was the
daughter of an architect, of whom she had forgotten all save his
acerbity, the memory of which, reaching down from her youth,
had predisposed her to be a Suffragette.   The chief bookkeeper,
good-humoured, business-like Beatrice Sanders, was an I.L.P.
member, wife of William Sanders of the Fabian Society.   Mary
Home kept newspaper cuttings and research material, a pale
young woman, with a hare lip, leading a repressed life as the
only daughter of an Indian army doctor knighted and retired to
Kensington in his old age.   Learned young Æta Lamb, a frail
orphan, born in Demerara, flitted about like a disembodied spirit;
for her paleness and her shyness seldom appreciated at her worth.
A steady secretary kept in order the engagements of the fly-about
Flora Drummond.   Jessie, the youngest of the irrepressible
Kenneys, was generally engaged on matters affecting militancy.
She was as eager in manner as her sister Annie, with more system
and less pathos, and without any gift of platform speech.   There
were hosts of casual volunteers who came in to address envelopes
and wrappers for a few odd hours, the plague of good Miss Kerr,
who found it well-nigh impossible to impose upon them her
excellent order, and to prevent a distracting babel of talk and
laughter arising from their tables.   Amongst the younger element
always at the office when their work was done, was young Jessie

Spink, a shop assistant, who wore Christabel's portrait on her chest, and eventually changed her name to Vera Wentworth, becoming an organizer with ambitions towards novel writing and the university. There was Vera Holme, an orphan educated in a French convent, and now singing in the chorus of the Gilbert and Sullivan operas, who presently became chauffeur to the W.S.P.U., a noisy, explosive young person, frequently rebuked by her elders for lack of dignity. As the staff rapidly grew, the casual volunteers were eliminated from the office. There was work outside for them, paper selling, poster parading, pavement chalking, militant action of various sorts.

Since the days of the first Caxton Hall meeting women of all ages and classes, but especially of the middle class, had been flocking into the W.S.P.U., drawn by the magnet of the militant tactics and the gigantic publicity they achieved. There was a great stirring of the social conscience. The swing of the electoral pendulum from Tory to Liberal and the birth of the Parliamentary Labour Party, had taken place amid a long-continued fire of propaganda, in which the searchlight of publicity had been turned upon the evils of overcrowding, jerry-building and rack-renting, of overwork and under-payment, of dangerous and ill-regulated trades, the hardships of unemployment, the hideous insecurity of the wage worker in the face of illness and old age, the cruel insufficiency of the Poor Law. In the spring of 1906 the *Daily News* held a sweated industries exhibition in the Queen's Hall, where women out-workers, many of them mothers with babies at the breast, were seen making garments, shoes, flowers, boxes and so on, aided at times by their tiny children, at rates so low, and under conditions so miserable, as to awaken horror in the public mind. Statistics of women's wages in other industries were published. The women's Trade Union movement was rising; strikes broke out; from every side came evidence of grievous under-payment of women workers, and of the appalling miseries of widows, and the wives of invalid and unemployed men. Tragic cases of poor women, which in other days might have passed unnoticed, were seized upon to point the moral of woman's inferior social status : Daisy Lord, the young servant sentenced to death for infanticide; Margaret Murphy, the flower-seller, who, after incredible hardships, attempted to poison herself and her ailing youngest child, when she lost the purse containing the scanty proceeds of her sales at the Derby; Julia Decies, committed to seven years' penal servitude for throwing vitriol at the man who had betrayed and deserted her; Sarah Savage, imprisoned on the charge of cruelty to her children for whom she had done all that her miserable poverty would permit. By reprieve petitions, by propaganda speeches and articles, the names and the stories of these unfortunates were torn from their obscurity, to be branded upon the history of the women's movement of their day. Women raised above the economic struggle by wealth and leisure, and the relatively small number of successful professional women, mainly popular novelists, and the few actresses and musicians at the top of the tree, began to feel some glimmerings, at least, of solidarity with the starved and exploited members of their sex. To consciences stirring uneasily with the thought: " Ought I to help? " the militant movement appealed insistently : " Here is action ! With us stagnation and quiescence under the sufferings of woman are no more. It is your duty and your privilege to help us in the cause of your sex. You can go to prison and win the laurels of immortality. You can give your time and your energy. If you will neither suffer nor serve you can give your money, and thus enable other women to do the duties from which you shrink." No one so confidently voiced this appeal to the happy, the leisured and the fortunate as Emmeline Pethick Lawrence, one of themselves, herself giving, working and suffering imprisonment; in this fact lay the great secret of her power to create in the suffrage movement the practice of giving donations on a scale hitherto unprecedented in its annals.

The appeal for service and sacrifice was opportune : the energies of the women of the middle and upper classes were largely dammed. Feminist propaganda, the improvement in the education of girls during the previous decades, and the successes of those who had profited by it, had given to numbers of such women a desire for wider and more important activities and interests. The universities were open to them, but only a minority of well-to-do families were willing, as yet, to give to their daughters the higher education thought proper for their sons. The prejudice against permitting their daughters to engage in professions and employments was still extensively held. Moreover opportunities of higher paid employment were severely restricted. Except in subordinate positions, men were always preferred, and invariably better paid. The higher teaching and commercial posts were rigidly confined to men. Both branches of the legal profession were closed to women. There was strong prejudice even amongst women against women doctors, and especially against women surgeons and dentists. In architecture, engineering and scientific pursuits the presence of woman was so rare as to be all but non-existent, though such brilliant exceptions as Marie Curie and Hertha Ayrton held up a beacon light of promise to encourage the sisterhood in these fields. Women whose brothers were rich men at the head of millionaire combines, were often found as obscure typists at a paltry wage, perhaps 30s. or £2 a week, in the offices of the same firms.   Daughters of rich families were often wholly without personal means, or were permitted a meagre dress allowance, and when their parents died, they were often reduced to genteel penury, or unwelcome dependence on relatives.   To many such women, a movement which proclaimed them the equals, nay, the superiors of men, demanding for them a worthy position in Society, made an instant appeal, the more so since it offered an outlet from an empty, purposeless existence to an active, exciting part in what it continually insisted to be the most important work in the world. With the young factory worker, the shop assistant and the teacher, seeking relief from ill-paid and monotonous toil, leisured and sheltered women rallied to the call of the W.S.P.U., which promised them a wider life of romance and adventure, wherein they might be translated to persons of consequence in the public eye, and regarded as benefactors of their kind.   Women who felt themselves unjustly used under existing laws, spurred by personal suffering to a public purpose; mothers, ardently desirous of improving the world for the rising generation, eagerly joined this movement of people in haste to mend conditions.   Suffragists of long standing, impatient of the old methods, under which the franchise cause had latterly appeared to recede rather than to advance, saw hope in the new militancy.

CHAPTER VI

HOLLOWAY PRISON

WHEN Parliament reassembled on October 23rd, 1906, the W.S.P.U., as yet a small though noisy crowd, was clamouring at its doors. Again the women were only admitted in relays of twenty. Mrs. Pankhurst and Mrs. Pethick Lawrence went in with the first batch. Induced by their insistence, the Chief Liberal Whip sought out the Prime Minister, and inquired whether the Government would pledge itself to introduce Votes for Women that session, or at any time during its term of office. He returned with a polite negative. Thereupon, as had been arranged, an attempt was made to hold a meeting in the Lobby of the House. Mary Gawthorpe[1] sprang upon a seat and began to address the weary people waiting to see Members of Parliament. The police soon pounced on this lively little person, and flung her ignominiously outside. They were immediately confronted with the same unheard-of conduct on the part of the venerable Mrs. Despard, sister of General French, then in her sixty-second year, but appearing much older, tall and spare, with large ascetic features, wearing sandals and a Spanish lace mantilla on her white hair. No sooner had the stout policemen removed her than Mrs. Cobden Sanderson, daughter of Richard Cobden of Anti-Corn Law fame, took her place. Woman after woman followed suit. The order was given to clear the Lobby. The police sprang forward, thrusting with fists and knees. Mrs. Pankhurst fell to the ground, women knelt round her. Angry policemen bundled them down the steps. The scrimmage continued in the Square outside, and Mrs. Cobden Sanderson, Irene Fenwick Miller, Mrs. Pethick Lawrence, Mrs. Montefiore, Mrs. Baldock, from the East End, Mrs. How Martyn, Mary Gawthorpe, Theresa Billington, Adela

---

[1] Recently appointed organizer of the W.S.P.U., an ex-elementary school teacher and lately Vice-President of the Leeds I.L.P. She was one of the most popular speakers in the Suffragette movement. After a period of very strenuous work, speaking, organizing, and suffering imprisonment, she became seriously ill in 1910. She was totally incapacitated for many months and an invalid for several years. In February, 1912, she broke a window in the Home Office as a protest against the forcible feeding of William Ball. She was discharged after a week's remand on account of her chronic condition of serious ill-health. She became editor of the *Free Woman*, a paper taking an unconventional attitude on sex questions, and later emigrated to America, took up journalism and married.

Pankhurst and Annie Kenney were arrested. The first name aroused consternation in Government circles; for though Mrs. Cobden Sanderson had joined the I.L.P., the fact that she was Cobden's daughter would be remembered in the country.

The Press described the scene with mendacious untruths, alleging that its participants were hysterical viragoes, biting, scratching and shrieking. Officialdom everywhere treated this militancy as a pernicious form of hysteria; at Cannon Row Police Court, next day, the gaoler shepherded the friends of the accused into a side room, keeping all the women out of Court, and even bringing out some who entered during his absence, with a false promise to send for them when their case came on. I arrived to find pretty little Stella Cobden Sanderson, with her bunch of honey-coloured hair, whom I had often seen with Winston Churchill's young sister-in-law, Maggie Hosier, coming for the embroidery class at the R.C.A., gentle Mrs. Cobden Sickert, a group of Mrs. Despard's colleagues in her social work at Nine Elms, and numbers of other well-dressed women. In a very short time the gaoler returned to us, shouting: " Go home now! It is all over! Your friends have been sent to the cells! " Indignant that the case had been disposed of with a celerity which bespoke indifference and contempt, I left the crowd of women pleading to see their friends, entered the Court, and asked the Magistrate whether it was with his knowledge that all women, even those desirous of offering voluntary testimony, had been kept out of Court. He interrupted me fiercely: " There is no truth in your statements! The Court was crowded." Without more ado I was dragged out by a couple of policemen and flung into the street. There was a crowd at the door. I wanted to explain what our case was about, and why the ten women were going to prison. I stood on the steps and tried to speak, but was so shaken by rough handling that my voice had disappeared. Nevertheless I was dragged inside and charged with obstruction and abusive language. Apparently the Magistrate, Horace Smith, desired now to vindicate the conduct of his Court, for the women still waiting in the precincts were permitted to enter, and I was allowed to call some of them as witnesses in proof of my previous complaint. This, however, was brushed aside; it was no defence. The charge of abusive language was withdrawn, as I declared it untrue, and the police witness, being asked what I had said, could only answer blankly: " Votes for Women." I was sent to prison for fourteen days in the Third Division, the worst the irritated Magistrate could do for me; but the protest resulted in securing for us the consideration accorded to other people, and perhaps even a little more. Our friends were allowed to come to the cells to see us before we left, and to bring us lunch, and women were not again excluded from the hearing of Suffragette cases. Throughout the history of our struggle, it was ever thus; we had to make a fight which brought in the light of publicity, in order to secure the customary courtesies. The ten women had been given the option of being bound over to be of good behaviour for six months, or six weeks' imprisonment in the Second Division; it was a method of giving a longer sentence than the charge warranted, under pretence of leniency.

For many hours after our friends had gone we waited in the dim stone corridor connecting the filthy cells, crouching together on the stone steps by the gate at the end. Mrs. Lawrence read aloud to us from Browning, "The Statue and the Bust." In the afternoon the prison van, "Black Maria," came to take us to Holloway. We were locked in the stuffy darkness of its little compartments, each just large enough to contain a seated person, bumping against the wooden sides as the springless vehicle jolted over the stones. Some women in the van, taken up from another police court, were shrieking strange words I had never before heard, their voices in the inky blackness lending a horrible misery to the experience. The lamps had long been lit when we reached the prison. We passed between high, forbidding walls, through heavy doors, opened and shut by tall wardresses with great jangling keys hanging at their waists. They locked us into pitch-dark cubicles, with no other seat than a lidless w.c., where we waited until late in the night, whilst batches of prisoners were brought in and locked up, the new-comers thrust in with the earlier occupants of the cubicles, sometimes four or five of them together, shouting those strange words in high-pitched voices. Hearing them with mingled pity and disgust, I stood shivering in the darkness, trembling with fatigue, but afraid of coming into contact with uncleanliness by sitting down. Again and again that night we were called by the wardresses to state our name, age, occupation, religion, sentence, and whether we could read and write and sew. At last we were ranged in line to see the doctor. "All of you unfasten your chests!" the wardress shouted repeatedly. We filed in and out of the small room, where the doctor was sitting. "Are you all right?" "Are you all right?" he asked mechanically, not waiting a reply, touching us lightly with his stethoscope, but not pausing to apply his ear to it. Cases of infectious and contagious disease could easily escape him; no doubt they did. Back to the cubicles; more long hours in the cold and darkness. Finally we were marched off to a large room where, four or five at a time, we were called out to undress in view of the rest, given a short, coarse cotton chemise to cover our nakedness, and ordered to carry our clothing to an officer, who, bundling hat, shoes and all roughly together, thrust our belongings on to a shelf, to remain there till our discharge. We were marched about barefoot from place to place, here to give up our money, there to be searched, raising our arms in the air whilst an officer rubbed her hands over us and examined our hair to ensure we had nothing concealed about us. All the prisoners were quiet now; all seemed cowed; there was an atmosphere of fear. My companions had been taken some other way. They were in the Second Division; I amongst strangers in the Third. Next we went marching to the bath and dressing-room; a miserable place with piles of clothing heaped on the floor in the dim light. The baths were indescribably dirty, their paint discoloured and worn off in patches, showing the black iron beneath, the woodwork encasing them sodden and slimy. They were separated from the room outside by a half-door, revealing one's shoulders above and feet beneath. I shuddered at stepping into the water clouded with the scum of previous occupants. A wardress shouted: "Make haste and get dressed!" as she hung a towel and some clothing over the door—strange-looking garments, all plentifully marked with the "broad arrow," black on light colours, white on dark; stockings of harsh, thick wool, black with red rings round the legs; long cotton drawers, red striped to match the chemise; huge, thick petticoats—as bunchy and full at the top as those of a Dutch peasant, but without their neatness, cobbled into a broad waist-band of capacious girth, which one overlapped around one's person as best one could, and tied with tapes fastened in front; a curious sort of corset reaching from neck to knees.

"You have not put on your stays!" the wardress screamed at me, with indignant scorn. "I don't wear them." "Unless you were not wearing stays when you came in, you must put them on at once!" "Did she bring any stays in with her?" A long discussion ensued.

The prisoners were scrambling for dresses of dark, chocolate-coloured serge in the heaps on the floor. "Make haste! Make haste!" cried the officers. I pulled from the pile a skirt many feet too wide, of the same pattern as the petticoats, and a bodice with several large rents, badly cobbled together. The broad arrows daubed with white paint on the dresses were fully four inches long. The bodices were fastened with only one button at the neck, and gaped absurdly.

"Look sharp! Put on your shoes!"

We grabbed them from a rack where they had been tumbled; no chance of finding a pair! They were made of stiff, hard leather with heavy soles, like those of a navvy, and leather laces which broke as one sought to tie them. An officer handed us each a little white cap, like a Dutch bonnet, with strings under the chin, and two pieces of cotton stuff, blue and white plaid, like the dusters one buys from the draper. One of them with tapes stitched to it was to be worn as an apron, the other was the weekly handkerchief. Did I say weekly? Weekly in theory; even in the reformed period of 1921, after the appointment of a woman prison inspector, I have known prisoners to be left six weeks without a change of clothing. A wardress explained to me that this handkerchief must hang from the waist-band by one corner, no pockets being supplied. Those wide, thick stockings, none too long, were flapping about my ankles. " Could I have something to keep them up with? " " No garters here! "—an indignant shout, as though one had asked for a luxury of rare price.

We were marched through a strange sort of skeleton building, painted a drab stone colour with black ironwork, passing through great pavilions, lined with tier upon tier of cells, the doors studded with black nails and bearing in the centre a round spy-hole covered with a flap from outside. The stone corridors by which the cells were reached jutted out from the walls of the pavilion like shelves, bordered by railings of iron trellis-work, and connected by iron staircases. One could see from the floor of the pavilion to its roof, in spite of a strong wire netting stretched across at each tier of cells to catch any prisoner who might attempt to commit suicide by throwing herself over the railings.

We stopped at a little office and gave once more our names, ages, sentences, religion, profession, and so on, and received a pair of sheets, a Bible, a hymn-book, a religious tract called " The Narrow Way," and a small book, " A Healthy Home and How to Keep It," which enjoined one to take a daily bath and to sleep with open windows; excellent maxims, but impossible of performance in Holloway Prison. Waiting by the office I saw again my fellow Suffragettes with a few others of the Second Class. Dressed in dark green to distinguish them from the rest of us in the Third Class chocolate brown, they were regarded as a trifle more respectable than the common herd. A motley crowd we were; all the little women seemed to be wearing the long dresses, the tall women, the short. Those strange, clumsy garments made us look squat and awkward. Weariness and decrepitude preponderating amongst us, we formed a striking contrast to the tall, straight, well-drilled officers. Some of the Suffragettes had little brown loaves in their hands, left from their supper, they told me. Evidently there was not enough supper to go round in the Third Division, for I had seen none of it. Mrs. Baldock broke off half her loaf and begged me to take it.

The Suffragettes marched away; clack, clack, their footsteps sounded echoing through the long corridors.

At last I was in my cell. It measured perhaps seven feet by five, with a stone floor and a little barred window, not made to open, high up near the ceiling. A flickering gas jet, lighted from the corridor outside, was set in an opening in the wall, covered outside by a piece of tin and separated from me by a thick semi-opaque pane of glass. Under the gas jet was a little wooden shelf called the table. Across one corner another little shelf held the worn, discoloured old wooden spoon, which remained in the cell for prisoner after prisoner, as did the large wooden salt cellar and its contents, so long as they lasted, the tin pint measure from which one drank the time-honoured prison " skilly,"[1] a tin plate, a piece of hard yellow soap, a small scrubbing-brush, to be used for brushing one's hair, and a three-inch comb, also some cards containing the prison rules and a morning and evening prayer. Beneath these the mattress and blankets were rolled up on a lower corner shelf. Ranged on the floor under the window, in positions never to be varied, and all made of block tin, were a dustpan, a water-can with a capacity of about three pints, a small wash-basin and slop-pail, also a little round scrubbing-brush to be used for sweeping. Reared against the wall, with a pillow on top, was the famous plank bed, its cross-boards raising it about two inches from the floor when put down for the night. A thin towel, like a small dish-cloth, and a wooden stool completed the furniture. Hanging on a nail was a disk of yellow cloth, as big as the top of a cup, bearing the number of the cell, which happened to be twelve. It was the prisoner's badge, and by this number I should henceforth be known.

The door opened. " What! You have not made your bed! The light will go out soon!" " Please may I have a nightdress?" " No!" The door banged.

Sleep? Certainly not. The mattress and pillow—round like a bolster—both filled with a kind of shrub, seemed as hard and comfortless as stone. (Prisoners usually put the pillow under the mattress as the least of various evils.) The blankets and sheets were too narrow to cover one, the cell airless and

[1] A thin gruel of oatmeal and water.

cold. The night was not still. Heavy steps passed and repassed, voices sounded, occasionally a cry. All night I was cold, and every night of the imprisonment.

Long before daylight arose a tremendous clatter; great ringing of bells, great tramping of feet. The light was turned on. One learnt quickly the daily routine. One washed in the little basin and dressed hurriedly, emerged to empty one's slops at the word of command and the clangour of opening doors, rolled up the bedding, cleaned and polished the tins, with brick-dust scoured off on the floor, and with the bit of yellow soap also used for washing the person, one scrubbed the floor of the cell, the bed and the table. The sheets were changed for each prisoner; but the blankets remained in the cell.[1] So, too, the little scraps of torn rag used for cleaning the tins, the same rags being employed for all the utensils—even the drinking measure and the slop-pail. If the tins[2] were not bright enough, or the water used for scrubbing not sufficiently discoloured, the wardress would require the work to be done a second time, as she did of me on more than one occasion. I obeyed with meekness, for we had agreed to submit ourselves to the prison discipline.

Again the door opened. "Where's your pint, 12?" A thin gruel of oatmeal and water was poured into the measure, 6 oz. of brown bread tossed on to the plate. The door slammed. The food eaten, one must set to work—a sheet to hem, a mail-bag, or a man's shirt to make. At 8.30 the officers shouted: "Chapel!" The doors flew open, the prisoners emerged, and were marshalled in single file amid a running fire of rebuke: "Who is that speaking? I heard someone speaking!" "Tie up your cap strings, 27! You look like a cinder picker; you must learn to dress decently here!" "Hold up your head, 30; don't shuffle your feet!" "Don't look about you, 12!" The chapel was filled with prisoners; row upon row of careworn faces. The majority seemed quite old. The wardresses kept watch in high-raised seats. The chaplain spoke with harsh severity and many a hard word for the sinner. Old women bowed their heads and wept. At his mention of children the mothers sobbed. Tears flowed at the playing of

[1] When I was in the prison hospital under the D.O.R.A. in 1921 a woman with a baby occupied the next cell. The woman had scabies. On her release the prisoner employed in cleaning that row of cells complained to me that although the baby had stained the blankets, they had not been changed. When another prisoner was put into that cell she shouted to me that the blankets were stained and smelt as though a baby had dirtied them.

[2] An earthenware mug and plate were substituted in later years, a metal spoon replaced the wooden one.

the organ, and voices broke with weeping in the hymns. To me all this was misery. I wept with those poor souls; and when the cell door closed on me again, the shrunken forms of frail old grannies, with their scant white hair, their shaking hands and piteous, withered faces, and the tense, white looks and burning eyes of younger women haunted me. Unnerved by lack of sleep and food—for I had not eaten the morning porridge, I cried till my head ached; and shrank from the sound of foot-steps, which foretold that frequent flinging open of the door, fearing the officials would believe me sorry I had come.

"Inspection!" the wardress shouted as she unlocked the door. A pallid woman in black uniform peered in and passed in silence. "Doctor!" "Governor and matron!" "Visiting Magistrate!" they each passed by in silence. To procure a word from any of these powers, an advance application must be made to the officer who opened the doors at 6 a.m. The chaplain alone was apt to converse for a moment or two without having an express application from the prisoner.

At twelve o'clock came the clatter of tins; dinner, a pint of oatmeal porridge, unseasoned, like the breakfast gruel, but cold and stiff instead of thin and hot; two days a week 8 oz. of small, sodden potatoes of poor quality, and the two remaining days 6 oz. of what was called suet pudding, a small, stiff, waxy slice, heavy and unsweetened. 6 oz. of bread were added to each meal. The dietary contained no sugar at all, no fat save in the twice-weekly pudding. After dinner followed sewing till 3 p.m., when we were called out to fetch water for the next day. Then sewing again, and at five supper of gruel and bread, as at breakfast. The cell door was now shut for the night: prisoners might cease work. The light in my cell was too poor for me to read the small print of the Bible without strain, and as a Third Division prisoner I was not yet eligible for a book from the prison library. Twice in the twenty-four hours the prisoners had a brief opportunity, harried by the perpetual shout of "Make haste! Make haste!" to run to the w.c. in the corridor. It was protected only by a half-door without fastening, like that of a cowshed. The haste, the lack of privacy, the character of the food, the want of exercise, the solitary confinement, the airless condition of the cell told their tale on most prisoners, producing digestive and other disorders. In numbers of cases imprisonment as a Suffragette proved the onset of an illness eventually necessitating a surgical operation.

At 8 p.m. came a noisy knocking at every door, and the cry: "Are you all right? Are you all right?" The flap over the spy-hole was raised. An eye peered in. Then the light was turned out, and another cold, sleepless night began. Twice a week I went out to exercise for half an hour, in a yard surrounded by giant walls and huge gaunt buildings, chequered by the tiny, barred windows of the cells. We marched in slow file, with a space of three or four yards between each prisoner. I remember a showery day, the sun shining gaily on puddles and rain-drops, the white clouds driving briskly across a sky of strong, clear blue, and the wind whisking our bonnets and skirts in playful gusts. The pigeons, dear harbingers of freedom, dwell-ing in great numbers about that dreary prison, flew low and strutted near us. How gladly my eyes sought the varied hues of their glossy plumage. Then I turned to the prisoners, plodding round with dull gaze bent downward, treading, without heed through the water on sunk stones, though there was dry ground within reach.

How grim seemed the narrow, dull-lit cell when the door slammed again and the key turned in the lock at my back! I was without news of my fellow prisoners, till one morning the chaplain paused at my door and told me that though as a prisoner in the Third Division I was not entitled to have a library book, my sister Adela had requested that an exception might be made for me, and he had granted her request.

In the country outside was a great clamour. " Richard Cobden's daughter in prison! " From her well-ordered home on the Upper Mall, Hammersmith, beautified by the works of the William Morris circle,[1] this gracious lady, devoted to good works amongst women and children, the gentle hostess of artists, humanitarians, Socialists, and a couple of generations of Liberal politicians, had settled down to life in Holloway with genial equanimity. In the dock she had asked to be allowed to take the whole responsibility of the demonstration: " If anyone is guilty it is I. I was arrested as one of the ring-leaders, and as the eldest I was most responsible." She quoted the President of the Local Government Board, John Burns, on his trial for incitement in the 'eighties: " I am a law breaker because I want to be a law maker "; but at this the Magistrate was scandalized, and refused to permit her another word.

Keir Hardie, Lord Robert Cecil[2] and others in Parliament were demanding for us the status of political prisoners. The Government declared itself unable to interfere with the Magis-trate's decision. On October 28th Mrs. Pethick Lawrence became

[1] Her husband, the late T. J. Cobden Sanderson, of the famous Doves' book-bindery, a co-worker of William Morris, is recognized as having revived the art of gold tooling.

[2] Afterwards Lord Cecil of Chelwood.

seriously ill. In response to the insistence of her husband and a message from Mrs. Pankhurst, she gave the undertaking for six months which would procure her release. Next day Mrs. Montefiore, horrified to discover her head infested by lice, owing to the lack of precautions against the spread of vermin in the prison, precipitately gave the same undertaking and came out. A few days later my solitude was broken by a wardress who led me to a room where I met my fellow Suffragettes; and, wonder of wonders, Elizabeth Robins, the novelist. How had this brilliant creature obtained permission to visit us in defiance of rule? In our curious garb we clustered about her, her arms encircling as many of us as possible, telling us in delightful images of the agitation outside. On the eighth day of our imprisonment the matron announced to us a Home Office order to transfer us to the First Division. I was told to take up my bed linen and the sheets I had been given to hem, and thus encumbered, was bustled along the corridor by a shepherding wardress, when I met the other Suffragettes similarly engaged. We were turned into a row of dingy cells in the Remand Hospital, where we indignantly discovered that untried prisoners were treated much like the convicted, though they might presently be proved innocent of all offence. We were now offered the privileges of wearing our own clothes and getting food sent in to us from outside at our own expense. We refused to accept these concessions. No First Division dress existed, but some new ones of grey serge, of precisely the same pattern as the others, were made, to define our new position. We were served with the food supplied to prisoners of the Second Class.[1] We accepted the privileges, meagre in extent, though precious in kind, of receiving and writing a fortnightly letter,[2] and having books and a daily newspaper sent in by our friends. This, of course, was by no means the First Division treatment accorded to W. T. Stead, Dr. Jameson, and others, who had been permitted correspondence and visits without restriction. On consulting the rule card, I saw that First Class misdemeanants may exercise their profession, provided prison discipline be not

[1] Dietary of the Second Class: breakfast: 1 pint tea, 6 oz. bread. Dinner: Monday, 8 oz. haricot beans, 1 oz. fat bacon, 8 oz. potatoes, 6 oz. bread. Tuesday, 1 pint soup, 8 oz. potatoes, 6 oz. bread. Wednesday, 8 oz. suet pudding, 8 oz. potatoes, 6 oz. bread. Thursday, 8 oz. potatoes, 3 oz. cooked meat stewed together, 6 oz. bread. Sunday, 3 oz. pressed meat, 8 oz. potatoes, 6 oz. bread. Supper: 1 pint cocoa, evidently made in the boilers used for the meat, as it always had bits of meat floating in it. This dietary was supplied to Third Class prisoners also after the first month.

[2] The Second Division prisoners wrote and received a letter monthly, the Third Division monthly after the first two months.

thereby disturbed. I therefore claimed the right to send for drawing-paper, pen, ink and pencils. These being granted, I busied myself in reproducing prison scenes.

On November 6th my sentence expired. Hitherto it had been the W.S.P.U. policy, under Christabel's direction, to ignore the prison conditions, in order to concentrate attention on the vote. That course did not appeal to me. I thought it good propaganda for our movement to reveal our prison experiences. Moreover, I was far too anxious to secure prison reforms, not for ourselves, but for the ordinary prisoners, to brook any restriction. None was attempted. I found the Press eager for news of Holloway; I gave dozens of interviews and distributed my sketches for publication. Probably even Christabel could now feel content that there was no danger of losing the Votes for Women trail in a quagmire of prison reform. Keir Hardie urged me to write an article on prison and promised to place it. He sold it for me some time later to the *Pall Mall Magazine* for £10, a most needed windfall at the time. Like others in the same position, when I returned from prison or an election, I had an accumulation of rent to pay, and if I forgot to-morrow's expenses in the enthusiasm of to-day, there was nothing for it but to tighten the belt. Such is the lot of the free lance voluntary worker in reform movements.

There was an "At Home" at the office on the evening of my release. W. T. Stead appeared there in the prison dress he always wore on the anniversary of his imprisonment. Next day Keir Hardie introduced the Women's Enfranchisement Bill under the Ten Minute Rule. It could not proceed further as he had won no place for it, but he had thereby an opportunity to tell the Prime Minister that his refusal to give the April deputation any hope of Government action had inflamed the militant agitation. "C.-B." denied that he had said there was no hope of his Government giving Votes for Women during the Parliament. Vain words, for he certainly had stated that he could not act so long as his Cabinet remained divided: and Asquith, his principal lieutenant, on October 13th, had clearly informed a deputation of women who waited on him in his constituency of East Fife, that he was still an anti-suffragist.

On November 24th Mrs. Cobden Sanderson and the others who had gone to prison with us were released, though but half their term had expired. Questioned as to the reason of this unexpected clemency, the Government vouchsafed no reply. The Suffragettes declared the reason to be "not unconnected" with a by-election then in progress at Huddersfield. Certainly the Government candidate had a poster: "Don't be misled by

Socialists, Suffragettes and Tories!" The three candidates in the election all wore the penny *Votes for Women* buttons sold in the streets by the W.S.P.U. Mrs. Cobden Sanderson and the other ex-prisoners hastened up to the election and received a tremendous popular ovation.

The old non-militant National Union of Women's Suffrage Societies, which had hitherto deprecated the militant tactics, now came forward with an unexpected tribute to the prisoners. Mrs. Fawcett addressed a circular letter to old suffrage friends, which was published in the Press, and in which she wrote:

"I, in common with the great majority of Suffrage workers, wish to continue the agitation on constitutional lines; but I feel that the action of the prisoners has touched the imagination of the country in a manner which quieter methods did not succeed in doing."

Just a year later, a year in which both militant and non-militant organizations had flourished as never before, Mrs. Fawcett was writing in a precisely opposite sense in respect of very similar demonstrations. Nevertheless her approval of these particular prisoners was in 1906 so cordial, that she and her organization gave a banquet at the Savoy Hotel in honour of Mrs. Cobden Sanderson and her fellow prisoners. Some comment was made on the fact that the invitation was not extended to me. The reason given was that though I had gone to prison on the same day my sentence had been shorter. It was clear, however, that the name Pankhurst savoured a shade too strongly of militancy for the non-militants, even in that expansive moment, to extend any special courtesy to one who bore it.

Before the end of the year there were four further militant demonstrations in Parliament Square and the Lobby of the House, and twenty women were sent to prison, including Mrs. August MacDougal, an Australian journalist. The W.S.P.U. organizers were appealing for prison volunteers in the provinces, the London office for hospitality for prison delegates. An ardent little band of Manchester demonstrators obviated the need of hospitality by proceeding directly from the train to Parliament Square, carrying with them a soap-box to serve as a platform. Mrs. Wells of Birmingham first came into touch with the W.S.P.U. when Mary Gawthorpe called on her one Saturday afternoon. Electrified by the story of the militants, she at once volunteered for Holloway, and on Monday, two days later, was arrested in Parliament Square. A fortnight's imprisonment was now the general rule. Small as they were, these demonstrations, because of the imprisonments which followed, were given world-wide publicity, and awoke response in many lands. In France, for the first time in her history, a deputation of women, a hundred and fifty strong, went to the Chamber of Deputies to demand the vote.

On December 23rd a Liberal Parliamentary Committee for Women's Suffrage was formed, the all-party committee established at the beginning of the session being allowed to lapse.

Shortly after my release from prison that autumn, Mrs. Lawrence wrote asking me to go to her for a fortnight in Italy. Again I saw those fair scenes under the splendid sun: Verona, lovely among the plains; Venice, of ancient splendours; Torcello, mysterious jewel of the lagoon. During our halt on the shores of Lago Maggiore I would be off, while the others were asleep, by winding paths to some tiny terraced village, where, setting down my stool, I would make sketches of the men, women and children eagerly waiting their turn, and would cease from work only when the brief violet twilight presaged swift darkness. That care-free life from which I had turned aside allured and delighted me as of old. In Milan I went with Mrs. Lawrence to ask the Conte X for a permit to visit the women's prison. He gave it with cordiality. The prison surprised us. It seemed bright and homely after the machine-like grimness of Holloway. The cells were large rooms with casement windows, like those of an ordinary dwelling, which the inmates could open and shut at will, though there were bars outside. The furniture was that of an ordinary, plain room, the dress like that of the peasants at large. The exercise ground seemed a relic of earlier barbarism, each prisoner in a separate little yard, a soldier with his gun on guard high up in the centre.

In Venice we met the famous Scandinavian writer, Ellen Key. She told us that the twentieth century would be the century of the child. She seemed uninterested in Votes for Women. I hurried with eager steps to the old apartment in the Calle dell'-Arco, but found it deserted—the Englishwoman and the Countess were away.

CHAPTER VII

THE BREAK WITH THE LABOUR PARTY

TIME often makes nonsense of political prophecy. The Suffragette leaders inherited from the older movement the theory upon which they never wearied of insisting, that Votes for Women must be brought in as a separate Government measure, and that any attempt to deal with it in connection with an Adult Suffrage Reform Bill would end in manhood suffrage alone.[1] Never were prophets more confident, yet never were predictions more completely falsified by events, and never did Time more convincingly reveal that the effort, the earnestness and the sacrifice had been fruitful; the vaunted political prescience mere trumpery, to be torn to tatters by the realities of events. If the Suffragettes had never intervened in the elections, if they had gone there to oppose all Parties, or no Parties, given the determination of women to go to prison to advance their cause, the movement would have grown and flourished.

The severance from the Labour Party had all the bitterness and heart-break of a family quarrel. Keir Hardie cherished both movements; to him they were but phases of the same cause; but the militants were impatient, the Labour Party slow and amorphous, a mere agglomeration of Trade Unions groping towards a common policy. To Keir Hardie militancy was a divine fire; to Macdonald disreputable " antics." He had no desire to retain these termagants in the Labour movement; to his temperament it appeared that association with the W.S.P.U. must be at the expense of votes in the constituencies. Moreover his ideal of independence for the Labour Party, under the conditions then existing, was a peaceable accommodation with the Liberals whom these harridans, as he thought them, were attacking with unexampled virulence. The dislike which Macdonald had for the militants was abundantly returned by them, above all by Christabel, who regarded all Socialists, Labourists and Liberals as arrant humbugs unless they were prepared to place Votes for Women before all other issues. Like Lydia Becker before her, she considered that all other reforms should be held up till women could participate in their enactment. Very early she based her hope and her policy on the speedy return of a Conservative Government. As Macdonald was apprehensive of losing supporters by association with the militants, so she feared that even a trace of alliance with

[1] Christabel Pankhurst in the *Labour Record*, February, 1907.

the Labour movement might weaken the W.S.P.U. Moreover she could not brook a divided allegiance; she wanted to build up a body of women caring for no public question save the vote, interested in no party or organization save the W.S.P.U.

The attitude of Keir Hardie was wholly different; he wanted the Labour Party to work for Votes for Women because the cause was just, entertaining no ulterior motive. In face of principle, he never counted votes, or feared that one good cause would hurt another. He stood for humanity and progress, his ardour knowing no closed compartments.

The view of Macdonald towards militancy was that of a large section of the Labour Party officialdom. Moreover the Labour Party had come into being on economic issues; Mrs. Pankhurst herself, as a propagandist in the Labour and Socialist movement, had for many years almost laid Votes for Women propaganda aside. From its inception the Labour movement had accepted the principle of sex equality, and given verbal assent to womanhood suffrage. As a question for immediate political pressure by the Labour Party the suffrage had but lately been mooted, and scarcely even yet on a national scale. To make it a foremost plank in the active Party programme, an extensive work must be done in the branches, to move the officials. The main obstacle to be overcome within the Labour movement was the Adult Suffrage controversy. The militants insisted upon support for a limited Bill which, though technically it would establish political sex equality, would enfranchise only one woman in thirteen; the Labour Party stood, and characteristically must stand, for Adult Suffrage. The argument: "Oh yes, we shall get women admitted first, and then we shall go on together for adult suffrage," was too narrow, too tactical, for popular appeal; it might convince, but it did not enthuse; it had constantly to be re-stated and re-argued. Adult Suffrage was the main refuge of those who did not care for Votes for Women and disliked the militant tactics. The active and advanced minority of the Party, which did the main share of the Party's work throughout the country, was virtually united behind Keir Hardie for Votes for Women at any price. Therein lay the pity of the quarrel. Yet whatever the Labour Party might desire to do, when it came to a question of sheer political weight against the Government, it was, as yet, too small to be powerful; it might, and did, unseat a Government candidate here and there, but in the Commons it was the Irish Party which was able to hold the Government to ransom; with Irish support the Liberals could maintain office even though Labour Members should vote against them. This fact dominated the entire pre-war history of the Parliamentary Labour Party, on this and every other issue. It produced discouragement and divided councils within the Parliamentary Party, and criticism and discontent in the Labour movement at large.

The W.S.P.U. anti-government policy was much advertised as the policy of Josephine Butler in her fight against the C.D. Acts and of the Irish under Parnell. Towards the Labour Party it was provocative. Initiated by women who were members of the I.L.P., a constituent section of the Labour Party; by women, moreover, who appealed to Labour men and women and to Labour branches for support, it went to the electors saying: Give your vote against the Government; we care not whether you give it to the Tory or Labour candidate. It was made clear that whilst complete devotion to Votes for Women was demanded of the Labour Party, no support for the Labour Party would result, since the W.S.P.U. was pledged not to support the candidates of any Party. Persuasive speakers and canvassers were withdrawn from active work for Labour candidates, in order to pursue this new policy—a serious matter to a struggling movement to which every volunteer was an important asset.

The policy was resolved on already before the General Election of 1905-6 had brought twenty-nine L.R.C. members to Parliament; at a time, indeed, when Will Crooks and Keir Hardie had introduced the Women's Enfranchisement Bill on behalf of the handful of Labour Members who had been returned at recent by-elections. The policy was put into combatant practice, with all its bristling provocations, in the first session of the Labour Party's existence. It is true that Votes for Women had not been placed in the active Parliamentary programme of the Party that first session, but the W.S.P.U. demand had come at the eleventh hour. In spite of its ostentatious neutrality towards Labour candidates, there was at the time great support for the W.S.P.U. in the Labour Party, and above all in the I.L.P. Labour and Socialist branches gave W.S.P.U. organizers active assistance, their platforms were open to its speakers. Throughout the long struggle and its acrid denunciations this friendly spirit still in large measure remained.

The Pethick Lawrences, on joining the W.S.P.U., regarded it still as a part of the Labour movement. Emmeline Pethick Lawrence wrote in the *Labour Record*:

" The women of the Labour Party are at one with the men in their determination to hasten the day when every adult citizen in the country shall have the right to vote. Before that day comes, the bar of sex disqualification must be swept away. . . . This is a people's movement. It is the awakening of the working women of this country to their need to representation."

There were tendencies in the early days of the W.S.P.U. towards the adoption of other objects than the franchise alone; indeed towards a general assistance to reform movements. In May, 1906, on the motion of Mrs. Pethick Lawrence, the Central London Committee of the W.S.P.U. sent a resolution to the Government calling for a commission of inquiry into the unrest amongst native races in Natal. On May 14th the Glasgow branch of the Union attempted to interview the President of the Local Government Board on behalf of the unemployed, and sent him a resolution supporting the then demand of the Labour Party that unemployment should take precedence of all other questions during that session of Parliament. The demand for a Government measure for women's enfranchisement followed. In the summer and autumn of 1906 Adela Pankhurst, organizing for the W.S.P.U. in Yorkshire, mustered the local members in support of the textile strikers at Daubhill and Hebden Bridge, and two members of the W.S.P.U. were actually summoned as strike pickets; articles by Adela on these campaigns appeared in the *Labour Record*. All this was totally at variance with the policy of Christabel. She desired absolute and vigorous concentration on the vote, and on that alone; her persistent effort was directed to eradicate from the W.S.P.U. all other interests.

When the Cockermouth election revealed that the W.S.P.U. had determined upon a policy of election work without support of Labour candidates, the Manchester Central Branch, of which Christabel and Theresa Billington were members, had discussed their conduct. Not desiring yet to make a complete severance with the I.L.P., Christabel appeared to defend her policy in person. The branch capitulated to her arguments, and declared her policy " not inconsistent " with the constitution of the Party, thus countenancing a degree of personal independence in its members which Christabel herself, the most rigid of disciplinarians, would not have tolerated for an instant had the positions been reversed. This branch decision did not settle the question in the Party. Resentment was intensified by the Huddersfield by-election, where Annie Cobden Sanderson and the other released prisoners, all members of the I.L.P., drew the audiences from the candidates, and where, though the Liberal majority was lowered, the Labour vote was also reduced, the Unionist being the only apparent gainer.

Already a move had been made to counter the activities of the W.S.P.U. Margaret Macdonald had taken the lead in forming the Women's Labour League, which held its preliminary conference on June 21st, 1906. Keir Hardie opposed the formation of this body. He saw in it a rival to the W.S.P.U., moreover he wanted the women to be in the Labour Party and the Socialist societies on equal terms with men. He did not wish them relegated to a special section outside the main current of the movement, expected to help the Labour Party in elections, but powerless to control its policy. He approved the W.S.P.U. as a fighting body, created for obtaining the vote, and to raise the status of women. To such objections Mrs. Macdonald replied: " I was glad that we in the Labour Party had not separate women's organizations like the other Parties—but now that some people are running off and forming them, I think we should do the same." At an I.L.P. baby-naming ceremony about that time, the child's mother asked Keir Hardie to place the badge of the League on her baby's breast. He turned to me and asked for a W.S.P.U. badge to place beside it.

Another effort to counteract the W.S.P.U. influence was the formation of the Adult Suffrage League, with which Margaret Bondfield and Arthur Henderson were associated. Had this organization worked for Adult Suffrage, it might have performed a most useful function; but it did not. Keir Hardie wrote of it in the *Labour Leader*:

" It holds no meetings, issues no literature, carries on no agitation on behalf of Adult Suffrage. It is never heard of, save when it emerges to oppose the Women's Enfranchisement Bill. Its policy is that of the dog in the manger."

In certain Labour quarters there was bitter resentment at Keir Hardie's open support of the W.S.P.U., and at the great prominence he gave to Votes for Women itself. From the first announcement of the Government Bill to abolish Plural Voting, he had opposed the measure, on the ground that when any change should be made in the franchise, women must be included. No other Labour Member as yet adopted this view; all the others supported the Plural Voting Bill as a step in the right direction. When the measure reached the Report stage Keir Hardie joined with the high Tory, Lord Robert Cecil, in an amendment postponing the operation of the Plural Voting Bill until the General Election following the enactment of Votes for Women on the same terms as men. In support of this amendment only one Member of the Labour Party followed its leader into the Aye Lobby, this single Member stating that he had done so only because he had not the heart to leave " Old Keir " to vote alone.

In spite of all this controversy it had been announced in October, 1906, that the Labour Party would put Women's Enfranchisement amongst the measures it would ballot for in the coming session. At the Labour Party Conference at Belfast in January, 1907, the strife was renewed. Christabel, with her characteristic faculty for flinging the apple of discord, had issued to the Press, but a few days before, a statement that in the W.S.P.U. attack on the Government " no distinction is made between the Unionist and Labour Parties." The statement was regarded as provocative, even by delegates who accepted the W.S.P.U. policy. The Woolwich Trades Council had submitted a resolution for the immediate extension of Votes to Women " on the same conditions as to men." Harry Quelch, well known as one of the most truculent Marxists of the S.D.F., moved an amendment, declaring that any measure " to extend the franchise on a property qualification to a section only is a retrograde step and should be opposed." He was supported by Mabel Hope, a young civil servant, who protested that a Bill to give votes to less than two million women was not worth working for, and condemned the tactics of the W.S.P.U. as artificial. She was vociferously cheered. Keir Hardie endeavoured to save the resolution, but the amendment was carried by the large majority of 605,000 votes to 268,000.

The vote was received by Keir Hardie with an intensity of regret, comprehensible only to those who knew the deep currents of emotion surging beneath his outward calm, and were themselves steeped in the passionate feeling of the time. A little later, moving a vote of thanks to some local man, he startled the Conference with an announcement:

" Twenty-five years ago I cut myself adrift from every relationship, political and other, in order to assist in building up a workers' party. I thought the days of my pioneering were over; but of late I have felt, with increasing intensity, the injustice inflicted upon women by our present laws. The intimation I wish to make to the Conference is this: if the resolution which has been carried to-day is intended to limit the action of the Party in the House of Commons, I shall have seriously to consider whether I can remain a member further. I make that announcement with great respect to the Conference, and with great feeling. The Party is largely my own child, and I cannot part from it lightly, or without pain; but at the same time I cannot sever myself from the principles I hold. If it is necessary for me to separate myself from what has been my life's work, I do so in order to remove the stigma resting upon our wives, mothers and sisters of being accounted unfit for citizenship."

The Press immediately published rejoinders from prominent Labour men. John Hodge declared that should Hardie leave the Party he would take nobody with him. Shackleton, Macdonald and Henderson spoke not so roughly; but all were agreed that after the Conference decision the Party could by no means sponsor the Women's Enfranchisement Bill.

I read the report of the Belfast Conference with profound dismay. It would be tragic, I thought, for Keir Hardie to leave the Labour Party; a sort of vandalism to play on his sympathy for our political helplessness, in order to draw him out of the workers' movement. John Hodge, of course, exaggerated when he said that Hardie would go alone, yet I believed his exit would be abortive. His old opponents in the Party would seize upon his absence to advance their policy, on this and every question, in opposition to his own. Not only would the Labour movement lose terribly by his withdrawal; the suffrage movement might well lose also far more than he could possibly give to it by his sacrifice, the magnitude of which could not even be understood by the majority of suffragists, who did not share his ideals for the emancipation of Labour and the creation of a new social order. I wrote him, in few words, that I waited in suspense to know whether he would take the serious step of leaving the Party. I knew that I had influence with him; I would have him know I recognized the gravity of the act he contemplated, and would not demand from him a sacrifice, which, if made at all, should be made solely of his own will.

At Clements Inn, where I went to sound the pulse of things, I heard great talk of a new party of "People of Goodwill" to arise from this crisis in the Labour movement. I saw no possibility of unity for such a Party. A Socialist advance guard, with plenty of scope for Keir Hardie's personal lead, might have held its ground, either as a Left Wing of the Labour Party or an independent group. A heterogeneous mass of "good" people, without a concrete economic policy, could gain no foothold, I thought, as a Parliamentary Party. The two old Parties existed for their typic policies; the Labour Party, often unconsciously, and not always unitedly, had yet its inherent social and economic policy—being the party of Labour. The existence of an organized Labour movement made the possibility of creating a vague social reform party more remote than would otherwise have been the case. As to the suffrage movement, it was a gathering of people of all sorts, united by one simple idea, which necessitated the surrender of no prejudice of race or of class. With all its splendid verve and enthusiasm, it was too narrow a field for Keir Hardie.

Amid the prevailing excitement Christabel was silent. She was not disposed to be enthusiastic about anything which might draw the Suffragettes and the Labour movement into closer union. It was far from her wish that Keir Hardie, with his unpopularity in Tory circles, should be intimately associated with the W.S.P.U.; yet confident in her belief that he would not leave the Labour Party, she held her peace, allowing the excitement of her colleagues to expend itself. To me she openly expressed disdain for "all this fuss." "He will do nothing!" What interest she had ever possessed in the Socialist movement, in which she had been reared, she had shed as readily as a garment.

The Labour Conference had dissolved; the Parliamentary Labour Party assembled at Westminster to consider the situation. It decided to leave its members free to vote and act as they thought fit in relation to the Women's Enfranchisement Bill and Adult Suffrage.

I met Keir Hardie after the Party meeting; he told me its decision, adding: "and I am to be chairman." I saw he anticipated I should be glad of this at least. In spite of my relief that his resignation was avoided, a blank dreariness fell upon me. I knew the state of feeling in the Conference and the Party rendered impossible, for the present, any solution more favourable to the Women's Enfranchisement Bill than this; but I realized, very keenly, that the decision precluded the Party from doing anything to advance either women's suffrage on the present terms, or adult manhood and womanhood suffrage. I realized the absurdity of leaving the franchise question thus in a cleft stick, but I had not yet the heart to flout the opinion of the W.S.P.U. and the entire women's suffrage movement by advocating that the Labour movement should make a serious effort to secure the type of suffrage in which it believed. Keir Hardie was himself not displeased by the result of his protest, without which, he told me, the Labour group would simply have instructed its members to vote against the Women's Enfranchisement Bill. I did not speak to him then of my dissatisfaction and distress, which were so great that they sent me to prison at the next militant demonstration three days later.

At Clements Inn they expressed, and very forcibly, all, and more than all, the discontent which was mine. Pethick Lawrence, in the *Labour Record*, stated that the Labour Party decision meant " the final severance of the Women's Movement from the Labour Movement."

It was after a W.S.P.U. meeting in Exeter Hall, on the following March 8th, that I talked the thing out with Keir Hardie. He had been a speaker there, and had said that if the women's claim were not granted within two years a movement would develop which would be satisfied with nothing short of complete adult suffrage. " Adult Suffrage! " The very phrase was as a red rag to a bull to the rest of the platform. Moreover the W.S.P.U. watchword was the vote " this session." It was treason to suggest that we might actually wait two years! An atmosphere of hostility arose. Mrs. Pankhurst, in the chair, was hardly able to treat the erring speaker with civility. She pointedly observed that he had expressed merely his individual view. No hand was held to him as he left the platform, unconscious that he had offended, though the manner of Mrs. Pankhurst appeared to him strange. Coming out of the meeting at his side, I explained to him the anger aroused by his speech, and the disappointment I shared at the Labour Party's decision. I told him that, though I had dreaded the thought that he might leave the Party, I could not logically deny Christabel's taunt that he had receded from his Belfast declaration; for the Labour Party, in effect, had simply abandoned the franchise issue, and thus placed itself in line with the old political parties. Indeed it might come to be attacked by the Suffragettes as the Liberals were attacked to-day—prophetic words! In my sorrow I said that my friendship with him might even become a competitor with my loyalty to the suffrage cause. He listened in silence, with an occasional sad monosyllable of comprehension. We paced the Thames Embankment as I revealed to him the emotions which had seethed about him on the platform, and were surging within me now. A queue of ragged, homeless men were lining up in the darkness for tickets for the night shelter. "Do you ask me to desert these?" he asked, with the gruffness of deep emotion in his voice. I left him on a note of tragedy. He wrote to me after we parted, expressing a sorrowful understanding. With returning day the prospect seemed not so dark. The Belfast crisis was soon obliterated by other happenings. My sad farewell to Keir Hardie faded like the shadow of a dream. Yet the friction which occasioned it continued.

Mrs. Pankhurst, torn as she then was between her old associations with the I.L.P., her friendship for Keir Hardie, and the opposing leadership of Christabel, swung, as it were, between the poles. At the I.L.P. Conference in Derby that Easter, 1907, the W.S.P.U. appeared in force. A monster meeting was held in the market place at which Mrs. Philip Snowden and other prominent I.L.P. women spoke with Mrs. Pankhurst. A resolution equivalent to that which had been lost at the L.R.C. Conference raised the contentious issue. Keir Hardie declared that the I.L.P. must now choose whether or not it would retain some of its most valuable women members. If he were a woman, and this motion was lost, he would be ashamed to belong to a Party which had turned its back on him. He urged the Party to " stand by the women," and so " keep the women for Socialism." The resolution was carried by a great majority. The opponents of the W.S.P.U. now sought to secure a declaration that the action of I.L.P. members of the W.S.P.U. in publicly dissociating themselves from support of I.L.P. Labour candidates was detrimental to the interests of the Party. Margaret McMillan,

of Deptford Camp School fame, rose and offered a message of
peace from Mrs. Cobden Sanderson, Mrs. Snowden, Mrs. Despard
and other I.L.P. women, declaring that they would pledge
themselves not to intervene in elections except to help Labour
candidates.   Apparently she had mistaken the terms of the
message, which seems from Mrs. Snowden's subsequent account
of it, to have had no practical bearing on the question.   At the
time, however, this message held the floor.   Mrs. Pankhurst,
with impassioned fervour, indignantly repudiated the pledge,
declaring that she would never surrender the independent anti-
Government election policy of the W.S.P.U.   Rather she would
resign her membership of the I.L.P., though she pleaded in
moving accents, rousing her hearers to a high pitch of sympathy,
that on every other point she had been loyal to Socialism and to
the Party.   The previous question was immediately moved, and
carried by an overwhelming majority, thus sweeping aside the
attempt to censure the W.S.P.U.   Now, on the suggestion of
Keir Hardie, the Standing Orders Committee proposed a resolution of congratulation to the suffragette prisoners.   Mrs. J. R.
Macdonald, raising her small voice in vain against the popularity
of Mrs. Pankhurst, J. R. Macdonald, Bruce Glasier, Russell
Williams, the Labour candidate in the late Huddersfield election,
all protested against the sending of the telegram.   Keir Hardie
appealed on its behalf and won the fight by 181 votes to 60.   It
was a tribute to the courage of the militants, a testimony to the
appreciation of Mrs. Pankhurst in the I.L.P.; a triumph for the
desire of Keir Hardie to keep her and her fellow militant Suffragettes within the Party.   Yet a few months later Mrs. Pankhurst
and the other W.S.P.U. members had quietly withdrawn from
the I.L.P., without warning or further controversy.

This clean cut between the W.S.P.U. and the Labour Party
was calculated to stimulate the growth of a large non-party body,
and to attract especially the support of wealthy Conservatives
opposed to Labour views.   Yet it is probable that the majority
of those who supported the W.S.P.U., in their enthusiasm for
the courageous militants, would have supported it none the less
had it been working with the Labour Party, which, with all its
shortcomings, remained throughout the long struggle the only
political party willing to declare for women's suffrage.   The
old N.U.W.S.S.,[1] when it decided in 1912 to support Labour
candidates against Liberals, lost no substantial number of its
supporters, though instead of springing from the Socialist movement, like the W.S.P.U., its ranks had been mainly recruited
from women whose associations were with the old political

[1] The National Union of Women's Suffrage Societies, Mrs. Fawcett's organization.

parties. In the hands of the National Union, the pro-Labour election policy attracted little attention: in those of the more efficient and active W.S.P.U. it might have proved a powerful weapon. It is conceivable that it might have influenced the Government so far as to shorten the term of the franchise struggle. On the other hand, it is possible that the victory could in no circumstances have been more speedily effected. The question how far the W.S.P.U. election campaigns, directed as they were solely against the Government, actually influenced votes was frequently canvassed, but incapable of proof. That they were highly effective as general propaganda for the cause was freely admitted. The following brief extracts, torn in most cases from a long and eulogistic context, indicate the Press view that votes were turned.

" I think there can be no doubt the Suffragists did influence voters."—*Manchester Guardian*, January 20th, 1908, commenting on the Mid-Devon election.

" No good purpose could be served by shutting one's eyes to the part which Women's Suffrage is playing on this occasion."—*Daily News*, February 11th, 1908, on South Leeds election.

" The antagonism of the women lost many votes."—*Daily News*, April 24th, 1908, on North-West Manchester election.

" I am convinced that they influenced many waverers to oppose Mr. Churchill."—*Standard*, April 25th, 1908, on North-West Manchester election.

" Mrs. Pankhurst and a large body of Suffragettes are turning many waverers against the Liberal candidate."—*Morning Post*, July 6th, 1908, on Pembroke election.

" The really big meetings you find where the women are in possession . . . it is absurd to suppose that the enormous output of work at this election will not affect votes."—*Manchester Guardian*, 28th July, 1911, on South-West Bethnal Green.

" This Peckham election has been a revelation to me of the perfectly wonderful forces which the W.S.P.U. are bringing to bear on by-elections. . . . As a purely impartial observer . . . I submit . . . to the Liberal Party that it is time they started doing something for the women. The mandate might not have been there in 1906, but it most certainly is there now."—St. John Ervine in the *Nation*, March 28th, 1908.

" . . . Mrs. Pankhurst. As in South Hereford her speeches and tactics won hundreds of votes. We have watched every step in the campaign."—*Hereford Times*, August 8th, 1908.

" . . . anyone who has had any experience of recent electoral contests knows that the invasion of the orators from Clements Inn has repeatedly been a deciding factor in the fray. . . . I do not believe the public has the remotest idea of the immense impression Mrs. Pankhurst and her followers have produced in this work."—*Christian Commonwealth*, 23rd September, 1908.

CHAPTER VIII

THE year 1907 opened in strenuous guise. The Suffragettes were already in the full flight of their activity. Spurred by their example, and the general arousing of interest in the cause, the old National Union of Women's Suffrage Societies was waking from a long inertia. On February 4th it so far emulated the manifestations of the militants as to organize a procession of women from Hyde Park Corner to the Exeter Hall. Owing to the inclement weather this event, the first public open-air demonstration the non-militants had ever held, was generally referred to as "the Mud March." Its authors were so proud of it that they forgot such efforts were already habitual in the W.S.P.U. Keir Hardie and Israel Zangwill, the novelist, had been invited to address the demonstrators. Both were hissed by a section of the audience; the former because he urged women to place the question of their enfranchisement before all Party considerations; the latter because he declared himself a supporter of the militant tactics, in that amazingly witty address afterwards printed under the title: "One and One are Two":

> "Let those lady suffragists who sit by their cosy firesides at least give them [the militants] their sympathy and encouragement. 'Qui veut la fin veut les moyens' and undoubtedly the means are not the most ladylike. . . . Damage the Government—that is the whole secret. Are these tactics sound? In my opinion absolutely so."

This was the burden of the entire discourse. It was too much to be silently endured at their own meeting by the staid non-militants and Liberal women. Yet to others, above all to the Suffragettes, that tall figure, with snaky locks falling heavily about his long pale face, in his droll mock-seriousness was a magician of irresistible fun.

Militancy broke out again on February 13th, the day after Parliament opened. The Caxton Hall had been hired for what was called a "Women's Parliament," and was really a rallying ground for those who were to march up to the House of Commons to get themselves arrested. The tickets for the gathering were sold out long before the day, and the Exeter Hall, which the non-militant mud marchers had scarcely been able to fill, was hired for the overflow. The motion to carry a resolution to the House protesting against the omission of Votes for Women from the King's Speech, was received with cries of: "Rise up, women!" and answering shouts of: "Now!" Almost everyone in the hall turned out for the march. Parliament was guarded by an army of police to prevent the women approaching its sacred precincts. The constables had their orders to drive them away, making as few arrests as possible. Mounted men scattered the marchers; foot police seized them by the back of the neck and rushed them along at arm's length, thumping them in the back, and bumping them with their knees in approved police fashion. Women, by the hundred, returned again and again with painful persistence, enduring this treatment by the hour. Those who took refuge in doorways were dragged down the steps and hurled in front of the horses, then pounced upon by constables and beaten again. There was a tremendous press of people. Members of Parliament were themselves inconvenienced by the guardians of the Law, and one of them, Claude Hay, asked the Home Secretary whether it had been necessary to surround the House with police as though it had been a fortress. Yet in spite of all precautions some of the women got inside, and one of them was only kept out of the Chamber by Members of Parliament rushing forward to slam the doors in her face. Mrs. Despard had led the first march in the afternoon: by evening party after party went out behind whoever felt exuberant enough to gather another company and dash out to the fray. As I was leading out a little band, I was surprised to see Christabel slip quietly into the line behind me. She told me later that she thought it would be necessary for her to go to prison in London, and on the spur of the moment she had decided to take this opportunity while sentences were short. She feared that if her absence were protracted, her influence might be undermined. As night advanced the violence grew. Finally fifty-four women and two men had been arrested, and the mounted police were left galloping alone in an empty Square. The *Daily Chronicle* next morning published a cartoon of a mounted policeman, entitled: "The London Cossack." The Press as a whole condemned the brutality with which the women had been used.

On the whole the women received the experience proudly and with surprising sang-froid, prepared to encounter whatever might advantage their cause, casting respect for authority to the winds with an impetuosity by no means confined to the Socialists who were led by their economic creed to criticize social institutions. Women brought up in Conservative traditions, and those who had hitherto taken no interest in political theory, were often most vehement in this militancy, which was primarily a vindication of their status as women.

At Westminster Police Court Christabel asked to be tried first, saying that she was the organizer of the demonstration. She adopted a high tone of rebuke:

" I wish it to be understood that several of our members have suffered seriously, and the whole of the responsibility lies with the authorities, who instructed the police to use every measure to clear the women away. . . . It is no fault of the authorities that there are no lives lost."

She warned the Government that more would happen unless women were given " their undoubted right to vote." Curtis Bennett, the Magistrate, replied : " These disorderly scenes must be stopped." He dealt out sentences ranging from 10s. or seven days to 20s. or fourteen days, to everyone, except Mrs. Despard and myself, who each had three weeks, and Edward Croft, a workman, who received 40s. or a month for trying to defend a woman in Parliament Square.

We were now regarded as misdemeanants of the First Division, and wore our own clothes whilst accepting the prison food. Conditions were rapidly changing. It is true the cells were unaltered and the food exceedingly bad. A vegetarian dietary, which had been introduced for those who wished it, consisted of potatoes and bread, with carrots and onions on alternate days, and occasionally a by-no-means-fresh egg, with milk and bread morning and evening; all this served in the unappetizing prison fashion. Yet the old rigid discipline was breaking down. The Suffragettes communicated with each other by tapping the Morse code on the hot water pipes which ran through the cells, by shouting so that their voices could be heard in other cells, by talking in the exercise yard. Occasionally they even broke forth into singing, and the chorus rang through the cells. Each week a procession headed by a brass band, which played for an hour or more at the prison gates, came to welcome a batch of released Suffragettes, whereat every woman in the prison rejoiced.

I was busy making drawings of prison life, and on the alert for information which would aid me to press for reforms. Fainting on the way to exercise, I was removed to the Remand Hospital, and discovered that there were no trained nurses, and only one woman with midwifery experience. I saw in the hospital Millie Marsh, a domestic servant of eighteen years, awaiting trial on a charge of perjury. She was alleged to have shielded her lover, who was accused in a notorious cheque fraud. The girl was convicted, though there was a strong element of doubt in the case. As soon as I was free I agitated for the remission of her sentence on the score of her youth. Mrs. Despard lent her aid and our efforts were successful. On our release, Mrs. Despard and I were given a welcome breakfast at the Eustace Miles Restaurant. Captain Arthur St. John then and there formed the Penal Reform Union, which under his secretaryship accomplished good work for a number of years. As a result of the reform movement inaugurated by Suffragette imprisonments, Dr. Mary Gordon was appointed as the first woman inspector of prisons. She assisted in the introduction of a number of improvements, but afterwards became officialized in her view. During the early years of her office, hospital-trained nurses and matrons were introduced into prison hospitals.

I, too, had gone to prison by impulse, and had left hanging on the easel an almost finished coloured cartoon of Queen Boadicea riding to battle in her chariot, which I was doing as a poster to illustrate a new series of coloured children's books then projected by W. T. Stead. I wondered if, by chance, I had left the window open, and if the rain had driven in. I pictured the wind whisking the frame from the easel, and the taut paper on which the drawing was made disastrously split. Nothing of the kind happened; I finished the work, and delivered it after my release. Stead paid me great compliments, but he had already changed his mind about the coloured series. He asked me to make some black and white drawings for his penny booklets. As I was about to leave he suddenly seized me in his arms, and hugged me. I felt like a small, weak child in his huge grip. I struggled with all my might to get free, and rushed out of the building without a word. His manner of displaying his paternal interest in young women enraged me. Apparently it was a relic of his youth when the woman who appeared asking an editor for work was a rare bird. Judging from previous conversations, it appears his imprisonment had been the most deeply-felt experience of his life. The mere sight of a fellow political prisoner seemed to throw him into an excitable state. He was a highly emotional and impulsive individual. I saw him only once again at a meeting in the Essex Hall. He waylaid me in the gangway: " Why have you not been to see me? " " I have been busy," I answered. He stared at me keenly: " That is not the reason ! " " No, it is not," I said, and passed on to my seat, wondering why a man who had been so zealous a friend of women's movements should behave like an uncouth bear.

During our imprisonment that February the constitutional suffragists made an unsuccessful attempt to secure the spectacular lead. Mrs. Fawcett and four of her colleagues had appealed in vain to be allowed to plead for Women's Suffrage at the Bar of the House of Commons. The opponents of the cause had begun to think it necessary to organize against it, and a Women's Anti-

Suffrage Society had been formed. For the first time in the history of the movement the Member who obtained the first place in the ballot, W. H. Dickinson, a Liberal, had given it to Women's Suffrage. In the Second Reading debate on March 9th, Sir Henry Campbell-Bannerman declared himself " not very warmly enamoured " of the Bill, because it would only enfranchise a small minority of well-to-do women. Philip Snowden denied this allegation, quoting the I.L.P. inquiry, which showed the majority of the women municipal voters were of working class. Shackleton, the textile workers' representative, said he would vote for the Bill, though he disliked its limitations. The Speaker, acting of course by agreement with the Government, refused to accept the closure resolution, and the measure was talked out by a Liberal, Mr. Rees. No protest was made from the Ladies' Gallery; it had been closed for the day. The Bill thus wrecked, Sir Charles McLaren set down a Resolution, but using a well-known Parliamentary trick, Maurice Levy blocked the Resolution by introducing a dummy Bill on the same subject. Lord Robert Cecil retaliated by blocking a Government motion. The Prime Minister promised an amending rule to make such antics impossible if Lord Robert would only withdraw his Bill. He did so, but the promise was never kept. The humorous Mr. Levy received a knighthood—a reward for this action, the suffragists declared.

On March 20th a second " Women's Parliament " assembled in the Caxton Hall. It was rendered picturesque by a company of cotton operatives in clogs and shawls, led by Annie Kenney. Christabel called on the women to rush into the House: " If possible seize the mace and you will be the Cromwells of the twentieth century ! " The aged Lady Harberton led the first attempt. A thousand extra police were drafted into the Square. Herbert Gladstone and Lloyd George came out to watch the scenes. Seventy-five women were arrested, and one man, Orage, editor of the *New Age*. Most of them got fourteen days imprisonment, two " old offenders " received a month, together with Mary Leigh, who scandalized the Magistrate by hanging a Votes for Women banner over the edge of the dock. He did not think it " a decent thing to wave a flag in a Court of Justice." Naici Peters, a Norwegian painter, and a friend of Ibsen, and Emilia Cemino Folliero, a painter from Rome on a visit to Mrs. Cobden Sanderson, had attended the Women's Parliament, and found themselves in prison with the rest, marvelling, perhaps, that such a strange experience could have befallen them during a holiday in the English capital. La Cemino was a middle-aged woman, who had spent her youth as a governess, until she gained a competence to enable her to devote her time to painting. She called often to see me, urging me to flee from the Suffragette storm, which was utterly destructive to artistic work. She insisted on reading my palm, gazing at me the while with her knowing black eyes, and trying to probe me. She was a gossip *par excellence*. She told me that unusually late in life I should have "one sweet son." Then affected to break off in consternation: "Oh, poor girl, poor girl! I must not tell you more! Too sad! Indeed too sad!" Why had she gone to prison, this woman with interests apparently bounded by the chit-chat of the drawing-rooms of her circle? "Well, it is right," she said, "I do not like your Labour views, and the women with their votes will go in that direction. They will make things harder for us artists—but it is right. Yes, it is right." She begged me to return with her to Italy, we should live together in an old castle and paint as happily as the day was long; but I would not go with her.

Keir Hardie frequently talked in those days of the menace of war and Conscription, for which he said Haldane's Army Bill, then before Parliament, was intended to pave the way. Calling at Nevill's Court one Saturday in April, when he was at work on an analysis of Haldane's Bill, I found him ill and awaiting a visit from his doctor. I wandered off to the Temple, and sat on Oliver Goldsmith's grave, thinking of the strange tangle into which our lives had been wrought. When I returned, Hardie seemed much more ill than before, and after doing what I could for his comfort, I left him, with anxiety, to such care as the wife of another tenant in the building might be able to spare for him. Thereafter I called for an hour or two each day. His condition seemed daily more serious. Frank Smith was there, acting as nurse and secretary; in his nervousness and concern for his old friend, spilling two spoonfuls of medicine to fill one.

On Thursday the Budget was introduced. There was a surplus of five millions, but Asquith announced a reduction of direct taxation instead of the social reforms expected from the Liberal revival. Old age pensions had been promised at the General Election; there was merely a proposal to set aside a meagre £2,000,000 to make a beginning with old age pensions in the year 1908-9. Keir Hardie was terribly disappointed by this postponement. His voice broken with weakness, he insisted upon dictating a long statement in reply to the Budget; a "brutal budget" he called it. He finished in a state of complete exhaustion. I was relieved next day to learn that the doctor had had him removed to St. Thomas's nursing home. A few days later he wrote me to come there. I found him at ease, his bed outside in the garden by the river, facing the House of Commons. He was listening with pleasure to a panegyric on Pantheism from T. J. Cobden Sanderson, who, fingering the narrow scarlet ribbon he wore attached to his eyeglass, launched forth in a poetic disquisition on his views of life and ideals for the industrial production of the future.

Yet Keir Hardie was gravely ill. Far from recovery, he announced his intention to move to his home at Cumnock. I wrote to Mrs. Pankhurst my fear that he was going there to die. Shocked by this thought, she came immediately from Manchester, simply to see him on the railway platform as he started for Scotland. Unable to stand without aid, and deathly pale, he seemed to have fallen into an old man during the brief weeks of his illness. He was startled by seeing her, and deeply moved that she had taken this journey to bid him farewell. She too was agitated by grief. As his train steamed out, we wept, clinging to each other, as we had done in the misery of our great loss nine years before. Memories of Keir Hardie's beautiful rugged presence, his gallantry and his kindness, smote upon me with unbearable poignancy. Life would be shorn indeed without this friend who had stood by us through good and ill.

He grew no better. He tried a hydropathic cure at Wemyss Bay. Mrs. Pankhurst, Mary McArthur, Frank Smith, a score or more of people who loved him, went up there to see him—too many indeed. He made no progress. Finally a voyage round the world was decided on. He sailed in July, leaving behind no great hope of his ultimate recovery.

PART II

BOOK VI

CHAPTER I

MRS. PANKHURST, rushing about the country on speaking tours, received frequent official complaints that her work was too often performed by her deputy. Under this pressure, she resigned the registrarship on March 21st, 1907, giving up her home in Manchester at the same time. To provide for her son, she apprenticed him to a Glasgow builder, a member of the I.L.P. whose main business lay in the erection of barrack dwellings for the working class. A room was hired for the boy in a workman's lodging-house, and he went to the buildings each day to wait on the men and learn from them what he could, a hard life for a delicate lad. He accepted it with his quiet, gay gentleness, immersing himself in the movements of Socialism and Suffragettism (then closely intermingled in Glasgow).

That summer I set off for Cradley Heath, in the Staffordshire " Black Country," to study the conditions of women employed in the making of nails and chains, whose earnings in those days, before the establishment of the Trade Boards, averaged no more than 5s. per week. Lodging with a little old dame who kept a confectioner's shop, I went out each day to paint pictures of the women toiling at the forges in the dilapidated domestic workshops, and wrote articles about the work in the evening. Never have I seen so hideous a disregard of elementary decencies in housing and sanitation as in that area. Roads were too often but beaten tracks of litter-fouled earth; rubbish heaps abounded; jerry-built hovels crumbled in decay. The country was utterly blighted; there were none of the usual amenities of town life, only its grosser ugliness. The men in the chain trade earned unusually high wages, but they had virtually no outlet save the public-house.

The women were working eight or ten hours a day at the domestic forge to earn a miserable four or five shillings a week, doing such domestic work as they could by the way. Their faces were drawn with toil, their garments flecked with small holes burnt by the flying sparks. Often a white-faced baby, scarcely taken out of the dark hovel from week to week, sat in a tiny chair beside the anvil, watching its mother's hammer; sometimes a child got a speck of red hot coke in its face, but in general the sparks flew the other way. The women told me they worked thus to gain some money of their very own, but actually they were simply following the tradition of the district; all the women made chain, as a matter of course. There were no recreations except perhaps an annual fair. The cinema had not yet reached those parts. There were no libraries, no public baths, only the most miserable shops. One must walk far to find green country. The women were the drudges of the industry; they made only the common " slap " chain, as it was called, for which speed was required but not great accuracy. The Trade Union prohibited them from the better work. It wounded me to see a mother, or sometimes an old grandmother, blowing the bellows at a paltry wage for a lad in his 'teens, already doing skilled work, and occupying an industrial status to which his mother could never attain.

I was preparing to leave Cradley when I received a telegram from Mrs. Pankhurst calling me to join her at the Rutland by-election, where she was short of speakers. The contest was typical of many others in rural constituencies. The labourers and their wives were delighted that the Suffragettes, of whose doings they had read in the newspapers, should appear in their quiet villages. Our speakers, driving by in traps hung with posters, were hailed by women at cottage doors and workers in the crops, who came running across wide fields to receive a leaflet. The country people were readily moved to sympathy by tales of the sweated women of the cities; the hardships of widows and orphans were but too common to them; there was no difficulty in inducing them to accept the simple plea that women should have the vote. Only in the towns, Oakham and Uppingham, where political feeling was keener, and where, in the absence of any Labour movement, a section of workmen looked towards Liberalism for emancipation, some resentment was shown against the women who were aiding the return of the Tory. It was common knowledge that a well-to-do Liberal was paying a band of youths to disturb our Oakham meeting. Police reinforcements were drafted from Leicestershire to keep the peace. The tradesman who hired the lorry, which served as our platform, was presently warned that the vehicle would be destroyed. He told us to go elsewhere, but no one else in the town was bold enough to provide us with a vehicle. Finally a man storing a wagon for a distant farmer told us that if we would fetch it ourselves from a barn where it was housed, we might have the use of it. There were active young women in our party, who thought nothing of such a condition. We held our meetings till the end of the contest, though on the last nights our voices were almost overwhelmed by horns and rattles. Crowds of sympathizers always escorted us home, but as we reached our door there was generally a scuffle with a band of youths waiting there to pelt us with sand and stones. One night at the Uppingham meeting hard boiled sweets were thrown up by some of the lads. Merry little Mary Gawthorpe was speaking. "Sweets to the sweet," she retorted gaily, but at that moment a pot-egg, thrown from behind, struck her on the head and she fell unconscious. She received an ovation when she spoke the next night.

The election over, I moved to Leicester to work amongst the women in the shoemaking industry. Mrs. Hawkins, the W.S.P.U. secretary, was also active in the Bootmakers' Union. She introduced me to a small producers' co-operative factory. As the women working there rose from their monotonous task, repeating year in year out the same operation, perhaps machining toe-caps—always toe-caps, they would crowd around my easel full of interest. I was astonished by their oft-repeated comment : " I should never have the patience to do it ! "

At night I held meetings for the local W.S.P.U., amongst whom only Mrs. Hawkins, as yet, dared mount the platform. The members were then almost all working class. One of them was a collector of laundry accounts, struggling to support a younger sister and brother. She had published a first novel, and was casually employed by a local newspaper, which obligingly permitted her to give good reports of our work.

Differences and discontents were brewing in the W.S.P.U. which largely hinged upon questions of personality. There were two opposing groups on its executive: Christabel, Mrs. Pankhurst and the Pethick Lawrences and their supporters, *versus* Theresa Billington (who had become Mrs. Billington Greig) supported by Mrs. How Martyn, Mrs. Despard and others. The Pankhurst-Pethick-Lawrence combination regarded Mrs. Billington Greig as the prime malcontent in the opposing group. Returning to London I had received a telegram from Christabel urging me to attend a W.S.P.U. Members' Meeting, followed by a letter asking me to write her a report of it. She added:

" I feel as though some of us would have to round on the enemy. . . . I am sorry to worry you about my affairs. You, poor child, have not had much family assistance in your worries. This is more than my affairs though—it concerns the Union as a whole. T.B. is a wrecker."

The members' meeting proved unimportant enough; but the buzz buzz of talk continued that at the approaching Annual Conference of the Union some tremendous coup would be made by the Billington Greig faction. I had seen enough of such frictions and manœuvres in the I.L.P. to know that they usually fizzle out when the conference takes place, and I did not take the W.S.P.U. differences very seriously. Mrs. Pankhurst wrote to me on June 23rd from the Jarrow by-election, a characteristic letter, wherein she referred to the friction. To-day the letter is most interesting for the insight it gives into her then entirely confident belief that the franchise struggle was nearing its end, and the great confidence she had in the efficacy of the W.S.P.U. intervention in by-elections.

" . . . I have just written to J.K.H.[1] about Teresa B.G. He promised me he would help with Mrs. C.S.[2] if it became necessary, and judging from what I hear the time has come to act. . . .

" I haven't worried J.K.H. about the election. I know it irritates him. If only the North-Eastern Suffrage Society had held aloof and had not supported Pete Curran we should have got a (Labour) Party declaration before the end of the election, and that would have made our dear J.K.'s position much easier. They are dying to have our support, for they see the men are with us in this election more than they were at Huddersfield.

" It won't be long before they and the Tories too will be forced to take the question up in a practical way. By the time J.K. comes back from his holiday things will be ready for him to take us up and win.

" As for the T.B.G. affair, we have just to face her and put her in her place. She has gone too far this time."

I was in Wigan among the " pit brow " girls when she wrote me that in view of the intrigues concentrating upon the forthcoming Annual Delegate Conference, the democratic constitution of the W.S.P.U. was to be abolished, and that she had assented to the desire of the Pethick Lawrences that she herself should become " the autocrat " of the Union. Regarding the proposal as ill-judged and unnecessary, I wrote at once : " Do not fear the democratic constitution. You can carry the Conference with you. There is no doubt of it." I might as well have urged the wind to cease from blowing !

Before the date of the Conference arrived, Mrs. Pankhurst had called upon the members to support her as the dictator of the Union, announcing that its committee would henceforth be appointed by herself and would serve during her pleasure to support her decisions. The majority of the committee and

---

[1] Keir Hardie.
[2] Annie Cobden Sanderson.

membership supported Mrs. Pankhurst. The minority retired. Holding a Conference on the date which had been intended for the Annual Conference of the original W.S.P.U., they elected a new committee, with Mrs. Despard as president, and opened new offices. Claiming to be the original organization they also called themselves the W.S.P.U., until the beginning of 1908, when they adopted the new title of the "Women's Freedom League."

How far large questions of principle were involved in the much-discussed split may be gathered from the fact that each of the two organizations which emerged from it retained the original statement of the objects and policy as its own. Save on the question of democracy *versus* autocracy, there was for a time little marked distinction between the policies of the two organizations. From February, 1908 until 1912 the Freedom League practised the original anti-Government election policy. Its discipline did not interfere with those of its members, who, like Mrs. Despard, were apt to depart from it. Court protests against the trial of women "by man made laws," a favourite idea of Theresa Billington, were carried out by the League, with many more or less militant variants of the original tactics, on a smaller scale than those of the W.S.P.U. When later the W.S.P.U. militancy became intensified, that of the Freedom League remained stationary. The Freedom League never approached the W.S.P.U. in membership, means, or influence, but occasionally it intervened with a bright, effective strategy.

After the split there was a general tightening of discipline in the W.S.P.U. All members were called upon to sign the following pledge, which, as a matter of fact, though I never contravened it, I did not sign:

" I endorse the objects and methods of the Women's Social and Political Union and hereby undertake not to support the candidate of any political party at Parliamentary elections until women have the vote."

There had been a clashing of temperaments and personalities; the split had ended it; democracy has drawbacks as well as advantages. The destruction of the democratic constitution prevented the W.S.P.U. from becoming a long-lived organization; the Freedom League remained when the W.S.P.U. was no more. Under the autocracy members and officials could be dismissed as readily as an employer discharges her cook. There was no democratic procedure, either to impose a check upon precipitate impulse or to hinder decisive action.

The spirit of the W.S.P.U. now became more and more that of a volunteer army at war. It was made a point of honour to give unquestioning assent to the decisions of the leaders, and to obey the command of the officials, paid or unpaid, whom they had seen fit to place over one. Processions and pageantry were a prominent feature of the work, and these, in their precision, their regalia, their marshals and captains, had a decided military flavour. Flora Drummond was called the General and rode at the head of processions with an officer's cap and epaulettes. To Emmeline Pethick Lawrence the Union mainly owed its spectacular conceptions, its colour and symbolism.

The W.S.P.U. now consisted of the headquarters at Clements Inn, and organizers responsible to it, working in London and the provinces. Local unions were sometimes formed by the organizers. More often they sprang up independently; indeed, for a time after the split they were discouraged by headquarters. They were built on the usual democratic model, electing their officers and committees like any trade union branch. Wholly independent of headquarters, paying no fixed dues, and united to the Union only by sympathy with its policy, they were extraordinarily loyal and devoted. I know of no case of secession from the parent body by any local union, though some of them pursued a somewhat different policy. Flora Drummond was called the secretary for the local unions; her office was of an entirely informal character. The local unions applied to her department when requiring assistance in obtaining speakers or in other ways, and from it speakers were sent to their members' meetings when headquarters desired to expound a policy or appeal for workers.

From 1907 till the autumn of 1912 the committee of the Union nominally consisted of Elizabeth Robins, the novelist, the veteran pioneer, Elizabeth Wolstenholme Elmy, Mary Gawthorpe (till late in 1911), Annie Kenney, with Emmeline Pethick Lawrence as treasurer, Emmeline Pankhurst, founder and honorary secretary, Mabel Tuke, joint honorary secretary, Christabel Pankhurst, organizing secretary. Frederick Pethick Lawrence was not mentioned as a member of the committee. He was, however, one of the four who held the deciding voice.

Mrs. Pankhurst, though nominally the ruler of the Union, was far from being that; the main work and policy of the W.S.P.U. was directed by Christabel and the Pethick Lawrences. Mrs. Pankhurst was usually in the provinces, moving from campaign to campaign, lodging to lodging. When, for a brief respite, she came to London, she felt herself almost an outsider. She had a desk in the office of Mrs. Tuke, but the work of the Union proceeded whether she were present or absent. It could not be otherwise if she were to be free to fulfil her special mission in the country. She often resented the position, and many times unburdened her mind to me with tears. Christabel, the apple of her eye, was aloof from her, absorbed in her work and friendship with the Pethick Lawrences, whose activities dovetailed with hers, and in whose home she lived. The mother was lonely and jealous for the companionship of her daughter. She who hated solitude, was alone at the Inns of Court Hotel. Yet on the platform she was accorded the foremost honours by everyone in the W.S.P.U., from the Lawrences to the most detached member. Social and speaking engagements seldom left her to her own resources; but whenever chance or fatigue caused this to happen, she deplored her lot, feeling herself a widow at heart. Repose was impossible to her : each new call to action found her as eager, nay, if possible more eager, than she had been to welcome its predecessor. The movement became more and more the passion of her life, the fount through which her turbulent emotions found outlet. Herein lay the source of her power.

Mabel Tuke, the joint honorary secretary, was one of the many unlikely women found in the W.S.P.U. In the winter of 1905 Mrs. Lawrence had met her on the voyage home from South Africa, a young widow, mourning the recent loss of her husband and only child. Later she was the guest of the Pethick Lawrences, and during Mrs. Lawrence's absence in 1906 had acted nominally as honorary treasurer. Actually it was Frederick Lawrence who undertook this responsibility. It was then that he began to take a large controlling part in the affairs of the Union and assumed the direction of the office and business management. Mrs. Tuke was from this time a constant habitué at Clements Inn and at " The Mascot." Her work in the Union was the writing of letters of thanks and the paying of calls. She was regarded as a very charming emissary for introduction as " a Suffragette " to the guests at a luncheon or dinner party, in the hope of disarming their prejudices against " those dreadful militants," and inducing them to come to a big meeting to hear " the leaders." Mr. Lawrence named Mrs. Tuke " Pansy," and so she was called by all her intimates in the W.S.P.U. Pale and melancholy in appearance, with large, mournful brown eyes, she was an example of the excessively feminine woman, always in poor health and requiring someone to wait on her, so common in the leisured classes of the nineteenth century, giving a disproportionately large share of her interests to personal adornment and the social round; the life against which Florence Nightingale had rebelled in her day, but to which most women of her class were still wedded. Constituted as she was, we regarded " Pansy " as a heroine to endure the turbulent atmosphere of militancy. I remember her in some of the " raids," as the marches to Parliament were called, running to and fro between Westminster and the office, white and tearful, imploring news of the dreadful happenings in Parliament Square. She frequently declared that she could never endure imprisonment. With much surprise I learnt that she was by no means a pacifist, even in peace time, when pacifism is always respectable. In those days we all said that women voters would be a great influence for peace, but when I deprecated militarism and expressed desire for universal disarmament, she met me with bitter hostility, asserting her pride that the motto of her family was: " My soldiers are many." She was reactionary in many respects, and, save for the fact that her apparently unconsoled bereavements invested her, in my mind's eye, with a romantic halo, I might perhaps have disapproved of her as much as she did of me.

In June, 1907, J. E. Francis of the " Athenæum Press," started a weekly paper, *Women's Franchise,* published at his own risk, in which he offered space to the W.S.P.U., the National Union of Women's Suffrage Societies, and the Men's League for Women's Suffrage. The League had been formed a few weeks before by Mrs. Pethick Lawrence's brother-in-law, Mortimer Budget, Goldfinch Bate and others. When the division arose between the Pankhurst-Lawrence and the Billington-Despard factions, Francis refused to take sides, and published the material sent by both factions. Immediately afterwards the Pankhurst-Pethick-Lawrence faction ceased to send notes to the *Franchise,* and the Pethick Lawrences inaugurated a new W.S.P.U. organ entitled *Votes for Women.* To the W.S.P.U., and even more to its contributors, the paper was a great asset, as a paper always is to those who express through it their beliefs and desires. The Lawrences and Christabel had their regular pages in it. Mrs. Pankhurst wrote only an occasional brief appeal. She never could bring herself to write; her book, " My Own Story," was produced by Rhita Childe Dorr from talks with Mrs. Pankhurst and from Suffragette literature. I had a series of articles on the early history of the movement in the first year of the paper, and on the militant movement in the second year. Mr. Lawrence kindly asked me to report the meetings as a part-time contributor, but the task presented itself to my mind as a monotonous bondage, of no great service to anyone. Speeches, I thought, were seldom suitable for reproduction, or meetings for report. I did not accept. The W.S.P.U. and its members made tremendous efforts to extend the circulation of the paper. It was advertised by four-in-hand coaches, women on horseback, poster and umbrella parades, boats, kites, pavement chalking and canvassing. Members canvassed shops for advertisements, stood in the gutter to sell it in Piccadilly, Fleet Street, the Strand and anywhere and everywhere of prominence in London and the provinces, and paid for its posters to be exhibited at shops and stations.

I was still in Wigan when a telegram called me to a by-election at Bury St. Edmunds. It was another rural constituency where, in default of a Labour movement, such independence as was beginning to form amongst the workers, regarded Liberalism as its only outlet from the dominant influence of the brewer, the parson and the squire. The Tory candidate belonged to the great brewing family of Guinness. Finding it intensely saddening to be helping to bolster up the Tory influence, I was in ill-assorted companionship with some of the other speakers, who, no more than I, had shed their previous opinions on joining the militant movement. Theirs was the Conservatism of the suburban middle-class, barnacled with the prejudices of their circle, instinctively hostile to other classes and other races, and to social reform of any kind. One of these, Miss A——, was a virulent feminist, who actually asserted that married women were "contaminated," and should be segregated. I was booked for a group of meetings with her; our car broke down; we stood in the road looking for someone to give us a lift. A big primrose-coloured car drove up. We knew it belonged to the Earl of Beaconsfield, who was assisting the Conservative candidate, but as the chauffeur offered a lift, I accepted it as a mere courtesy of the road. Our meeting proved to be in a Liberal stronghold, and when the audience saw us dismount from the primrose car a cry was raised that we were in the pay of the Tories. Miss A—— struggled in vain for a hearing. When she abandoned the attempt, I eagerly protested that we were not Tories, but women of all parties banded together for the vote, and that I and my family were far more advanced than Liberals; we were Socialists and had been supporters of the Labour Party. The interrupters were disarmed, the meeting turned to enthusiasm. The argument for the Parliamentary representation of women was not far distant from that for the representation of Labour; and if I did not make the latter appeal directly, I was, at any rate, direct enough to win the group who had previously abused us to lead the cheers.

After the declaration of the poll a great concourse waited in the main square of Bury St. Edmunds, the Suffragette carriage amid the Press. A cheer was raised; the Tory majority had been more than doubled. Miss A—— stood up, waving a flag. The victorious candidate came forward to address the people:

" What has been the cause of this great and glorious victory? "
A shout went up from the crowd: " Votes for Women ! "
" Three cheers for the Suffragettes ! "   There was great laughter
and cheering.   " No doubt the ladies had something to do with
it ! "   The candidate bowed to us with a sweep of his arm.
Miss A—— was radiant.   My gaze turned from the jubilant,
well-dressed Tories on the balcony, across the laughing, non-
Party masses of the crowd, to a little group of frowning workmen with red favours.   My thoughts were sad.

When we returned to London, Miss A—— complained at
Clements Inn that I had told an audience I was a Socialist and
had looked " as glum as could be " when the glorious victory
was announced.   Christabel interrogated me; I told her of the
car incident; it had been necessary to convince the people we
were not Conservatives.   " You should have said we used to be
Liberals," said Christabel with her engaging smile.   " I do not
agree," I answered.   We knew each other's tenacity.   The
subject dropped.   In the industrial districts, where progressive
movements were strong, the election policy might be a testing
of democratic principles; in the backward country districts we
seemed to be helping to strangle the small spark of progress.
Yet the campaign was building up a solidarity of women for
women, which was gradually broadening the interests even of
the narrowest, who were learning from contact with women of
wider experience in the movement, and still more, perhaps, from
the women they canvassed, the homes they visited, the crowds
they addressed.

Glad to be free of the by-elections, I sped north to Scar-
borough, to study the conditions of the Scotch fisher lassies
working the east coast in the trail of the herring, beautified by
their outdoor life, singing and chattering like a shoal of sea birds,
over the fish they were cleaning and packing.   I lodged with
a fisherman's wife in the old town; a jolly woman, with quaint
stories, grave and merry.   I wept when she told me of how
the Scotch herring fleet, setting off to reach home by Christmas,
had been caught by a squall and wrecked within sight of her
windows, the toys the fishermen had bought for their children
thrown up with their bodies on the shore.   She made me
laugh, in spite of myself, over her first adventure in domestic
service as a child of fourteen.   Her young master, before departing for his office each morning, would tell her that she must on
no account permit her mistress to do any housework.   The young
mistress had usually no desire to offend in that direction, but
one day confided her intention to make a cake.   It was a cake
of a very special kind, comprised entirely of eggs and butter, and

so light that it must only be beaten by the tips of the fingers, which proved an exceedingly messy proceeding. Finally it was stowed in a hot oven for half an hour. When the door was opened the poor young mistress gave a cry of dismay. The servant burst into laughter. Next morning she ran away home to her mother, the milkman helping her with her box.

I left that good friend, as she had become, and went north to the Border counties, found a home with a lonely widow at Churnside in Berwickshire, and went painting amongst the neat, quiet women farm labourers of the locality, and the casual potato-pickers imported by the day from the slums of Berwick-on-Tweed. Working for contractors under rough gangsmen, these last were a crowd of tattered womanhood, lost to all reticence and respect. Their eyelids inflamed, as though painted with blood, their faces ingrained with dirt, their garments a collection of rags. Old crones with bent backs, girls with lewd speech and hideous laughter, their faces bruised and cut from last night's levity, toiled on without pause, grubbing the tubers from the ruts. When the potatoes were being sorted and piled in the " pit," I heard their stories, sordid and grey, with the Workhouse as the inevitable harbour of old age.

When the cold weather set in, I moved on to Glasgow. I found a lodging in a two-roomed flat in a barrack-dwelling in Bridgton, with a decent, middle-aged working couple, who had a little adopted daughter of three years and a family of prize-winning Yorkshire terriers. I occupied the parlour and slept in one of those bed-cupboards in the wall, so common in " the land o' cakes "; the rest of the household gathered in the kitchen. I secured permission to paint in a near-by cotton mill. The mule-spinning room, where I started my work, was so hot that I fainted in the first hour, and the manager, who had not so much as asked my name, but liked the notion of an artist painting pictures of the mill, gave permission for a little window to be kept open near me. The girls told me they were all made sick by the heat and bad air when they first began work in the mills. The ring-spinning room, where the little half-timers were employed, was worst of all; I found it impossible to work there.

Painting in the mill all day, writing hard at night, or speaking for the W.S.P.U., I spent my Saturday afternoons and Sundays with Harry. He was eighteen now, and had grown to nearly six feet, a graceful, slender youth. He piloted me about the city, talking in his eloquent way. His employer had become a Buddhist, and the boy, in search of a perfect altruism, was investigating the philosophies of the East. He spoke but little of his work, and made fun of its hardships, but what I learnt from him and others disquieted me. The thought of him climbing high scaffolding on dark, cold, winter mornings, by the bleak Clydeside, was distressing.

It was near Christmas when I returned to London. Mrs. Pankhurst and Christabel called on me one evening; I had not seen them for many months. I took them to the little restaurant where I used to go with Harry during his Hampstead school days. I had picked up a letter laid for me on the hall table as I went out; and as I sat opposite to them in the restaurant, I opened it and read it on my knee. It roused in me a sudden storm of misery, which seemed to be killing my inner life, transforming an inner shrine which had been as a pleasant garden of singing birds, to a waste and barren place. Snakes and writhing creatures, fire and destruction, passed before my eyes; yet neither of the two sitting before me perceived my anguish. I was content that it should be so. They asked me to go with them to Teignmouth in Mid-Devon, where an election was pending. I refused, feeling that I must be alone with my grief, but after three days, with a desperate longing to flee from it, I followed them to Teignmouth on Christmas Eve. It was dark when I arrived; a furious gale was blowing, the blast so fierce that the streets were deserted and the front door of the hotel could not be opened. My two and Mary Gawthorpe were together, as merry as crickets. I could not escape from my misery, and regretted that I had come. On Christmas Day I made a sketch of little Mary Gawthorpe. On Bank Holiday, to my mother's disgust, I insisted on returning to London, unable to control my restless misery in face of their cheerful chatter. I could not foresee that my sorrow would presently be dispelled as suddenly as it came.

The election proved to be the scene of unexampled rowdiness. The roughs of Newton Abbot, the principal town in the constituency, were notorious. The banding of them into a " League of Young Liberals " now cloaked their undisciplined savagery with the respectable mantle of politics. Their first act of war was to push a policeman through the window of the Suffragette committee rooms. After the declaration of the poll, the successful Tory was escorted from the town by a strong force of police. The occupants of the Conservative Club were besieged by a noisy mob, and kept prisoners the whole night. Next morning the body of a well-known Conservative, Sergeant-Major Rendall of the Royal Marines, was found in the mill race, with injuries suggestive of foul play. Mrs. Pankhurst and Mrs. Martel were the only Suffragettes who remained for the declaration of the poll. Local people advised them to hasten away, but they ridiculed any suggestion of danger. They were set upon and beaten in the street. A woman shopkeeper succeeded in dragging Mrs. Martel inside her shop to safety, but Mrs. Pankhurst was left outside with the mob. She was thrown to the ground, and a barrel was brought to roll her in. The police appeared just in time to save her, but she had received an injury to her ankle which was a recurring source of pain and disability for many years.

It was some weeks later that my brother Harry walked into my rooms at Cheyne walk. The builder, having suspended business under financial stress, had told the lad he had better go " home," and so he had come to me. The fare from Glasgow had absorbed all he had in hand from his 'prentice pittance. I was relieved to know him free of the buildings, however it might have happened. But I was uncomfortably short of money and waiting impatiently for payments for my work. I counted my cash, dividing it to make it last for us both on short commons for nine days, hoping that before that time had expired a cheque would arrive. As ever, he was dear; his shy, sweet smile and gentle voice caressed me, but the grief within me seemed to cast a shadow between us. I could scarcely control my speech to hide my misery. Moreover, I feared to arouse in him despair and pessimism, for his future appeared to me precarious in the extreme; I saw him as a skater on thin ice, who at any moment may descend into an anxious sea of discouragement.

A week later Mrs. Pankhurst returned to London to find her son; for her it was a worrying disappointment. I read his discernment of her trouble. Christabel suggested that Harry should qualify himself to become a secretary. His scattered schooling, always hindered by eye-trouble, had by no means prepared him for such work; Mrs. Pankhurst decided that she would allow him a pound a week to keep him in lodgings, he must get a readers' ticket for the British Museum, and she would pay for a couple of weekly classes in shorthand and typewriting at the Polytechnic. Then she was off again to the provinces. We sisters got his eyes tested and furnished with the spectacles he had needed since childhood; for the first time in his life he was able to read without distress. He attempted to apply himself to the work marked out for him, but the Suffrage and Socialist movements attracted him like a magnet. In April he was up at the North-West Manchester by-election, driving a coach for the W.S.P.U. Returning to London, he was out each night, chalking pavements, heckling Cabinet Ministers, speaking at street corners. I heard of him lecturing to the I.L.P. on the virtues of a return to the land.   I urged on Mrs. Pankhurst that a way should be found to give him a systematic training.   In an unfortunate moment, I said that to fit himself to lecture on agriculture, he should have some experience of it.   She immediately sought the advice of Joseph Fels, the proprietor of Naptha soap, a follower of Henry George, who had established small holdings and a farm of his own at Mayland, in Essex.   We knew him through Keir Hardie, of whom he was a firm admirer. It was arranged that Harry should become a pupil at the Fels' farm.   He was put to lodge with a neighbouring cottager under deplorable conditions; how deplorable we none of us learnt till much later, for his lips were sealed by determination not to worry his mother.   Far from the strength of maturity, born of a sedentary stock, and with a delicacy which had remained with him from a coddled infancy, he was wholly unfit for the hard toil and exposure to all weathers which, even more acutely than in Glasgow, were now his lot.

CHAPTER II

IN 1906-7 the Suffragette imprisonments totalled 191 weeks;
in 1907-8, 350 weeks. Other activities grew proportionately:
membership, funds, meetings, election work and the heckling
of Cabinet Ministers. On October 5th a thousand suffragists,
militant and non-militant, marched to the Synod Hall, Edinburgh. Sir Henry Campbell-Bannerman, for whose enlighten-
ment the procession was arranged, refused to receive a deputation,
but on October 22nd he replied to a heckler in Dunfermline that
women desirous of enfranchisement should " go on pestering."
Pester they did! Of the taunts and sayings received by them in
the process, some were long remembered: Asquith, at Tayport
on October 29th, declared that Votes for Women would do
" more harm than good," and that Parliament was not elected
on a basis of universal suffrage, for " children are not represented
there." Lloyd George, on November 22nd, told a deputation
from the non-militant Glasgow and West of Scotland Association
for Women's Suffrage that he would oppose " very strenuously "
any limited Women's Suffrage Bill. Haldane, in Glasgow, on
January 8th, 1908, told the women who were being thrown out
that men did not like to be fought with " pin pricks," and that
though women might " wage war " he should advise them not
to do it with " bodkins," adding: " I am bachelor-proof against
these belles! " When Mrs. Pankhurst was ejected from Asquith's
meeting in Aberdeen, on December 19th, Mrs. Black, the
president of the Women's Liberal Federation, and the Reverend
Alexander Webster, who held a high position in local regard,
were insulted and hustled for endeavouring to prevent disorder.
The *Aberdeen Free Press* observed: " Many a Liberal left the
meeting with the uneasy feeling that the suffragists had got the
best of it."

Cabinet Ministers had long ceased to address open meetings;
their audiences were now only admitted by tickets, carefully
distributed amongst their supporters. The W.S.P.U. early
resorted to the printing of forged tickets. The Liberal organizers
then excluded women from the meetings, issuing only a few
special women's tickets to guaranteed supporters, and bearing the
name and address of the holder. To circumvent this move, the

Suffragettes set themselves to enter the meetings by strategy, climbing in through windows and lying concealed. Men sympathizers took up the heckling in their absence, though not until 1910 was the Men's Political Union formally constituted to make a prominent feature of this work. The heckling of Ministers was not confined to public meetings, they were catechized at both private and public social functions. The business of tracking their movements was a serious business at Clements Inn; a secretary kept a list of their forthcoming engagements, culled from obscure newspaper paragraphs by eager scrutineers, and also obtained on many occasions from confidential sources. Elegantly gowned women, mingling unsuspected among the guests in famous houses, suddenly seized Ministers by the shoulder and raised their cry. One of the most successful at this curious task was Mrs. McLeod, a middle-aged woman, whose small brown face never seemed to impress itself upon the memory of the detectives guarding the persons of the Government. She would turn up among the élite, with an air of helpless incompetence, affecting to discover that she had left her ticket behind; gazing at the attendants with those baffling Celtic eyes, arguing in her soft drawl, she escaped suspicion. As Suffragettism spread, the women who accosted Ministers at parties and receptions were, more and more often, duly invited guests.

With the opening of 1908 militancy was renewed at Westminster. Nurse Smith and Edith New, a teacher, chained themselves to the railings of the Prime Minister's residence in Downing Street, whilst the Cabinet was in session, and with three others were sent to prison for three weeks, in the Second Division. Prison treatment now reverted to its original rigours. First Division treatment for Suffragettes was at an end. Protests were made in both Houses of Parliament, Earl Russell warning the Government that the blood of the martyrs is the " seed of the church." On January 29th, as the royal procession advanced to the opening of Parliament, four members of the Women's Freedom League rushed forward with a petition, but were hustled away by the soldiery. On the two following days eleven members of the same organization visited the residences of Asquith and other Cabinet Ministers. For refusal to quit the doorsteps, they were arrested and sent to prison for terms varying from two to six weeks. A deputation of the non-militant National Union of Women's Suffrage Societies was received by Asquith on January 30th. He made no secret of his own uncompromising hostility, and clearly stated that the Government would neither introduce a Votes for Women Bill on its own account, nor give facilities for such a Bill introduced by a private Member. This hostile pronouncement was the more important since it was common knowledge that Asquith was about to become Prime Minister, owing to the impending retirement of his chief.

Another "Women's Parliament" in the Caxton Hall was called by the W.S.P.U. for February 11th; another deputation to the Prime Minister announced. Whilst the police were out guarding the House against the expected women, two furniture vans approached, and as they were passing the Strangers' Entrance to the Commons, twenty-one women sprang out and made a dash for the doors. Two of them actually succeeded in gaining the portals. The incident tickled the fancy of the Press; the strategy of the furniture van was likened to that of the Trojan horse. Meanwhile, as before, a body of candidates for arrest emerged from the Caxton Hall, and after a painful buffeting were at last taken into custody. Next morning forty-eight women received two months in the Second Division, on refusal to be bound over; two "old offenders" a month in the Third Division, in lieu of fines. Amongst the prisoners were Maud Joachim, niece of the great violinist, and Georgina and Marie Brackenbury, nieces of the General of that name. Muskett, the prosecuting solicitor, announced that though in these cases the Government would proceed as before, under the Crimes Act, which authorized penalties up to £5, or two months' imprisonment, further powers were in reserve, and might presently be employed. There was still upon the Statute Book an Act of Charles II, dealing with "tumultuous petitions," under which persons, to the number of more than twelve, attempting to approach either Parliament or the Sovereign, might be punished by a fine of £100 or three months' imprisonment.

This challenge was immediately taken up by the W.S.P.U. The Caxton Hall Parliament was still in session, awaiting the arrival of Mrs. Pankhurst from a by-election in South Leeds. Coming from a great procession and demonstration of 100,000 people on Hunslet Moor, exhausted by strenuous campaigning, she was strung to a high emotional pitch. She announced that she would lead a deputation of thirteen women to challenge arrest under the Act of Charles II. Her hearers were moved to tears. There were agitated cries: "Mrs. Pankhurst must not go! We cannot spare her!" Hands were outstretched to bar the way, but Christabel firmly repressed these protests. The thirteen set forth, Mrs. Pankhurst still lame from the attack in Mid-Devon. Seeing this, Mrs. Drummond called to a stranger driving by in a dog-cart: "Will you take Mrs. Pankhurst to the House of Commons?" He consented politely, and Mrs. Pankhurst mounted the cart. A police inspector almost immediately compelled her to dismount, and presently, with eight other women, she was arrested. The scene was one of intense silence and peculiar restraint; there had been no need on this occasion to struggle for arrest. Yet the prosecution grotesquely alleged that the deputation had proceeded singing and shouting and knocking off policemen's helmets. Sympathy with the militants was growing, in Parliament and out. On the adjournment of the Commons, Sir William Bull, a Unionist Member, took up the cudgels for Mrs. Pankhurst's deputation, and protested against her arrest. Other Members asked why Ginnell, the Nationalist Member for Westmeath, then in prison for inciting to cattle-driving in Ireland, should be treated as a First Class misdemeanant, whilst the Suffragettes were again incarcerated as ordinary criminals. Lord Robert Cecil raised a laugh against John Burns, by pointing out that when he was imprisoned in the 'eighties, the Government of the day intervened to secure preferential treatment for him. At the trial next day nothing further was said of the Charles II Act. Mrs. Pankhurst and her companions were sent to prison for six weeks in the Second Division on refusal to be bound over.

The Women's Enfranchisement Bill had not lacked a place in the Members' Ballot. A Liberal Member, H. Y. Stanger, had put it down for Second Reading for February 28th. There was an atmosphere of hope; the militants confidently anticipated the moment when their agitation should bring the Government to the point of action. It was believed that the Government would make a statement of its intentions in the course of the debate. Herbert Gladstone, the Home Secretary, made the pronouncement:

" On the question of Women's Suffrage, experience shows that predominance of argument alone, and I believe that this has been attained, is not enough to win the political day. . . . Then comes the time when political dynamics are far more important than political argument. . . . Men have learned this lesson, and know the necessity for demonstrating the greatness of their movements, and for establishing that *force majeure* which actuates and arms a Government for effective work. That is the task before the supporters of this great movement. . . . Looking back at the great political crises in the 'thirties, the 'sixties and the 'eighties it will be found that people . . . assembled in their tens of thousands all over the country. . . . Of course it cannot be expected that women can assemble in such masses, but power belongs to the masses, and through this power a Government can be influenced into more effective action than a Government will be likely to take under present conditions."

The speech seemed to indicate that the Government was not

hostile, and waited only a larger manifestation of demand. The Second Reading of the Bill was carried by 271 votes to 92, but the Speaker, doubtless on consultation with the Government, had only agreed to accept the Closure on condition that the sponsor of the Bill would move for its reference to a Committee of the whole House, instead of allowing it to pass automatically to a Grand Committee. This meant that the Bill was blocked as effectively as though it had been talked out. So completely did Members of Parliament accept the dominance of the Cabinet, that not a voice was raised against this smothering of an important Bill, for which a majority of the House had voted; no protest was made against the destruction of the Private Members' meagre legislative opportunities. Even the suffragists, militant and non-militant, made no great complaint; the militants were convinced that the franchise could only be secured by a Government measure, or a measure receiving Government aid; the non-militants, in their patience, were prepared to accept every rebuff; one of their prominent officials observed to me that after all we need not be surprised if women had to wait another fifty years for the vote. The great progress of the movement, under the militant spur, was a continual astonishment to the easy-going non-militants.

In March, Mrs. Pethick Lawrence called for a week of self-denial to raise funds for the cause. Women deprived themselves of tea, cocoa, milk or sugar, of one or two meals a day. Some rose earlier that they might walk to their work; some sacrificed a proportion of their earnings; others took in washing, or made and sold cakes, sweets, soap, clothing; some stood in the gutter turning barrel-organs, swept crossings, or became pavement artists. Evelyn Sharp, May Sinclair, Violet Hunt and other women writers rattled collecting-boxes at street corners. John Galsworthy, E. V. Lucas, Nevinson and others gave autographed copies of their books. A sympathizer let her house in the West End for £1,000 a year, and promised this rent to the W.S.P.U. until the vote should be won. Mr. and Mrs. Pethick Lawrence promised £1,000 a year. Twelve women, including Mrs. Bernard Shaw, Hertha Ayrton, the scientist, and Dr. Garrett Anderson gave £100. The collections and donations were announced at a meeting in the great Albert Hall, and shown on a scoring apparatus, manipulated by Pethick Lawrence, amid deafening cheers. The Government provided an appropriate surprise by releasing Mrs. Pankhurst the day before the expiry of her sentence, and thus enabled her to be present. That huge meeting, hitherto unprecedented in suffrage annals, was a revelation to her and to itself. "The old cry was: 'You will never rouse women '; but we have done what they thought, and what they hoped to be impossible. We women are roused!" she rejoiced; they echoed her with shouts.

At Easter, Campbell-Bannerman resigned; Asquith became Prime Minister. There was a general move up in the Cabinet, and the Ministers who had changed their posts were obliged to vacate their seats and face re-election. The W.S.P.U. was active in all the nine contests; but its greatest effort was in North-West Manchester, against Winston Churchill. Christabel settled there for the election. Manchester showed its preference without uncertainty; Churchill could not procure such audiences as the Pankhursts. Prominent Liberal women refused to assist him, and one of the most prominent, Margaret Ashton, wrote to the Press that she would work no more for the Liberal Party until it grew prepared to give her a vote. The *Manchester Guardian* complained that the Liberal women, " deprived of their natural leaders," were " as sheep without a shepherd." Churchill made desperate efforts to retrieve his position :

" Trust me, ladies, I am your friend and will be your friend in the Cabinet.

" I will do my best, as and when occasion offers, because I do think sincerely that the women have always had a logical case, and they have now got behind them a great popular demand amongst women."

His protests were useless; Christabel and the W.S.P.U. would accept nothing short of an undertaking on behalf of the Prime Minister and the Government to pass the Women's Enfranchisement Bill into law without delay. Churchill was defeated; Joynson-Hicks, in offering thanks for his victory, said :

" I acknowledge the assistance I have received from those ladies who are sometimes laughed at, but who, I think, will now be feared by Mr. Churchill—the Suffragists."

The Press, both Conservative and Liberal, admitted that the opposition of the Suffragettes had largely contributed to Churchill's defeat. Christabel returned to London wearing it as a feather in her cap. Mrs. Pethick Lawrence presented her with a statuette of the Victory of Samothrace as a memento of the event. On moving to Dundee for a safe seat, the defeated Minister arrived to find Mrs. Pankhurst holding a great meeting in the Kinnaird Hall. One of his first acts was to address a meeting of Liberal women :

" No one can be blind to the fact that at the next General Election Women's Suffrage will be a real practical issue; and the next Parliament, I think, ought to see the gratification of the women's claims :

I do not exclude the possibility of the suffrage being dealt with in this Parliament."

The Suffragettes he described as " hornets,"

" allying themselves with the forces of drink and reaction, carried shoulder high, so I am informed, by the rowdy elements always to be found at the tail of a public-house-made agitation."

The reference was to the Peckham by-election, where the issue had been the Government's Licensing Bill, and the Tory had been returned, and where, when the poll was declared, Flora Drummond had been hoisted shoulder high by the crowd. The W.S.P.U. ignored these strictures as of no account, tearing the rest of the statement to tatters, because it contained no promise of a Government measure. The Freedom League had also opposed the Government in Peckham : one of its members, " La Belle " Maloney, as she was afterwards called, determined either to make Churchill apologize or to silence him. She appeared at all his open-air meetings with a huge muffin bell, and having delivered her ultimatum, effectively prevented him from speaking. On the eve of the poll, the manager of the gas works attempted to secure him a hearing inside the yard of the works, but Miss Maloney got in with her bell. The manager appealed to his men : " Hands up those who want to hear Mr. Churchill," but only a few hands were raised. " Hands up all who want to hear me ! " cried Maloney, and carried the vote with acclaim. Churchill turned tail and left her to triumph.

The militants had now effectively placed the Liberals in the public pillory, as the Government which would not give women the vote, and had attempted to silence the women's agitation by violence and imprisonment. Prominent Liberal men and women openly resigned their Party positions on this account, and even those suffragists who had hitherto put Liberalism first, smarted under the charges of disloyalty to their sex which were hurled against them when Campbell-Bannerman was replaced by a leader who ostentatiously proclaimed his hostility to Votes for Women. At a Women's Liberal Federation meeting in the Queen's Hall, Florence Balgarnie, a suffragist and a Liberal of long standing, declared that Liberal women had too long been " the hewers of wood and drawers of water for the Liberal Party." Her words were echoed by other prominent Liberal women. Churchill's experience in Manchester gave warning of a strike from election work, a highly important matter, since the law had limited the sum which may be spent on elections. For the annual conference of the Women's Liberal Federation, its Cuck-field branch had set down a resolution that unless Women's

Suffrage were granted before the dissolution of Parliament, the time would have arrived for a definite refusal to work at Parliamentary elections. Another resolution called for the immediate cessation of election work. There was great fluttering in the Liberal dovecotes, wire-pulling, pleading and negotiation. On May 20th, the day before the conference, Asquith consented to receive a deputation of sixty Liberal Members of Parliament, asking him to grant the few days required for carrying into law the Stanger Bill, which the Government and the Speaker had effectively blocked. Asquith refused the request, but stated that, "barring accidents," he regarded it as a "binding obligation" on his Government to bring in an effective reform of the electoral system before that Parliament came to an end. Whilst Women's Suffrage would have no place in the proposed Reform Bill, opportunity would be given for the moving of a Women's Suffrage amendment. This amendment the Government would leave to a free vote of the House, on condition that it was framed on democratic lines, and had behind it the "strong and undoubted support" of the women of the country, and also of the men electors.

PREMIER'S GREAT REFORM BILL! VOTES FOR WOMEN! glared the election placards. "Our great Prime Minister, all honour to him, has opened a way to us, by which we can enter into that inheritance from which we have been too long debarred," cried Lady Carlisle, presiding over the conference next morning. The Cuckfield resolution was lost by an overwhelming majority; the loyalty of the women Liberals was assured for another year at least. The constitutional suffragists accepted Asquith's promise with reserve. The W.S.P.U. denounced it as a "trick." Seven Freedom Leaguers were arrested on his doorstep, demanding immediate facilities for Stanger's Bill, or a promise that Women's Suffrage should be included as an original part of the proposed Reform Bill.

The Liberal Press hailed the vote as won:

"The meaning of Mr. Asquith's pledge is plain. Women's Suffrage will be passed through the House of Commons before the present Government goes to the country."—*Star*.

"A more mature and experienced leader than Miss Christabel Pankhurst would have understood that the pledge which Mr. Asquith has given is quite exceptionally definite and binding."—*Daily News*.

A week later, on May 26th, Asquith, interrogated by a Liberal Anti-Suffragist as to what would happen if a women's suffrage amendment to the proposed Reform Bill were carried, replied:

"My honourable friend has asked me a contingent question with regard to a remote and speculative future."

The W.S.P.U. roared " We told you so ! " in triumphant rage; its members shouted in a burst of enthusiasm : " Miss Christabel Pankhurst has never been wrong ! " Denunciation of the Government had risen to a fever heat of popularity.

Since the spring, the W.S.P.U. had been preparing to take up Herbert Gladstone's challenge by a series of great provincial demonstrations and the largest meeting ever yet seen in Hyde Park, to be held on Midsummer Day. The constitutional suffragists, not to be out-done, though starting later, cut in before, and on June 13th held a procession of 13,000 women to the Albert Hall, carrying banners made by the Artists' League for Women's Suffrage, and including contingents from the Women's Co-operative Guild, National Union of Women Workers, Women's Freedom League, I.L.P. and Fabian Society.

The W.S.P.U. organized its own much greater demonstration without calling on other societies to co-operate. Pethick Lawrence was the main architect of the scheme, which cost upwards of £4,813, this sum not including either salaries, office rent, or the money spent by local unions. A new suite of offices was opened, more clerks engaged. Mrs. Pethick Lawrence conceived the idea that the Union should have its own colours : purple, white and green, which, selected in the middle of May, had achieved a nation-wide familiarity before the month was out. The authorities consented to take up a quarter of a mile of Park railings, in order to add more space to the large area round the Reformers' Tree, ordinarily set apart for the numerous meetings held in the Park. A huge wall poster, measuring thirteen feet by ten feet, containing photographs of the twenty women who were to preside at the twenty platforms, a map showing the meeting-place in the Park, and the route of the seven processions to march thereto, was displayed in London and the provinces. Thirty special trains were run from seventy towns to convey the demonstrators. A quarter of a million mock tickets to Hyde Park were distributed, and as many handbills of various kinds. There were nine chief marshals, seven group marshals, thirty group captains, forty banner marshals and captains, hundreds of railway station marshals, captains and stewards, to meet provincial demonstrators, as well as sergeants, band superintendents and park stewards, and over three thousand standard-bearers, all wearing badges and regalia in the colours. There were ten huge silk banners, five hundred smaller ones, thousands of flags and a large number of brass bands, each item paid for by some ardent donor, the price announced and its payment appealed for in *Votes for Women*. Banners, bunting, regalia and ribbons striped in the three colours, were all specially made for the event by a firm specializing in such work. There was no great artistry about them; it was mass production in double-quick time. I was asked to prepare designs for borders and heraldic devices for the factory to apply, and did so in haste. The Kensington W.S.P.U. provided its own banners, one of which was designed by Lawrence Housman. So vast was the demonstration that the appearance of an individual banner counted for little; but it is true to say that the creation of a Michael Angelo would have ranked low in the eyes of the W.S.P.U. members beside a term served in Holloway.

London was divided into districts wherein shops and committee rooms were opened. Meetings, literature distribution, pavement chalking, proceeded as vigorously as though it had been an election. Decorated 'buses drove through the streets, a steam launch laden with Suffragettes halted beside the Terrace of the House of Commons, and Members of Parliament at tea were invited to the demonstration by General Drummond: " You will have police protection there also, and we promise there shall be no arrests."

We worked as though it had been a test campaign for winning the vote: everything else was laid aside. I was voluntary organizer of the Chelsea, Fulham and Wandsworth district, training a band of young speakers by the way, and like many other volunteers, glad to be able, at the time, to pay my own expenses. Crowds of young people went chalking and fly-posting; Harry and some of the others worked continuously for four days and three nights at the end. London had probably never before been flooded with such intensive propaganda for any cause. At each new open-air pitch our first meeting was a fight with noisy uproar, our second mainly sympathetic, our third a triumph of unanimity, ending in cheers. The manager of the Chelsea Palace called at our shop in the King's Road, and asked me to provide a Suffragette to speak for five minutes at each performance. The cinemas announced the demonstration, and gave scenes from the campaign. Leading London shops gave displays in the colours, an evidence of the popularity of the movement.

Each procession to the Park was headed by a four-in-hand coach, in which rode notable people: Izrael Zangwill, Mrs. H. G. Wells, Mrs. Thomas Hardy, Miss Lillah McCarthy, Mme. Sara Grand, Professor Ayrton and others. The Fabians and the I.L.P. joined the Trafalgar Square procession, Keir Hardie and Bernard Shaw amongst them. Women processionists had been asked to come in white dresses, wearing favours of purple, white and green. So dressed, by the thousand they came from amongst the great public, their numbers far exceeding the membership of the Union.

Our Chelsea procession, not by any means the largest, numbered 7,000 women in white, with at least double that number of men and women swarming along the road on either side of it. So we flocked to Hyde Park. The ground was already thronged with an unprecedented mass of human beings; we had difficulty in making our way to the platform with our banners. As far as the eye could reach was a sea of human beings. Instead of the sombre darkness of other crowds, the predominating gay hues of the women's clothes and the white straw hats of the men suggested a giant bed of flowers. Under that golden sunshine, that sky of cloudless blue, it was a gala day indeed. From a furniture van—Pethick Lawrence had called it a conning-tower, but it looked a tiny speck in the mass—bugles sounded for the commencement and ending of the speeches. Then came the great shout: " Votes for Women ! " three times repeated. All went with a swing. Only a few young rowdies at the platforms of Christabel and Mrs. Pankhurst attempted ineffectually to mar the great good humour of the day.

We were buoyed by delighted triumph in this success, and belief of an early victory for the cause. Self was forgotten; personality seemed minute, the movement so big, so splendid. What an achievement! This without doubt was the greatest meeting ever known. The Press described the gathering with evident admiration, devoting great space to it. A few brief extracts will suffice:

" Its organizers had counted on an audience of 250,000. That expectation was certainly fulfilled; probably it was doubled; it would be difficult to contradict anyone who asserted that it was trebled. Like the distance and numbers of the stars, the facts were beyond the threshold of perception."—*The Times*.

" There is no combination of words which will convey an adequate idea of the immensity of the crowd around the platforms."—*Daily News*.

" The Women Suffragists provided London yesterday with one of the most wonderful and astonishing sights that has ever been seen since the days of Boadicea. . . . It is probable that so many people never before stood in one square mass anywhere in England. Men who saw the great Gladstone meeting years ago said that, compared with yesterday's multitude, it was as nothing."—*Daily Express*.

Immediately after the meeting we rushed to Clements Inn. Christabel, in eager excitement, dispatched the Hyde Park resolution to Asquith by special messenger, asking what action the Government proposed to take in response to the demand of so great a gathering. The answer was curt; the Prime Minister

had " nothing to add " to his statement of May 20th.   The reply
of the W.S.P.U. was to summon a public meeting in Parliament
Square for the night of June 30th.   To prevent the meeting,
an official warning was issued to the public not to assemble in
the Square, and 5,000 foot police, and 50 mounted men were
assembled.   Naturally there could be no platforms.   Women
spoke from the steps of the Government buildings and offices
in Broad Sanctuary, they lifted themselves above the people by
the railings round the Abbey Gardens and Palace Yard, or raised
their voices standing among the crowds on road or pavement.
They were torn by the harrying constables from their foothold
and flung into the masses of people.   Friendly sections of the
crowd kept rushing the Suffragettes forward, crying: " We'll
get you through to the House of Commons! "   Then roughs
appeared, organized gangs, who treated the women with every
type of indignity.   Out in the press, I was obliged to drop
my handbag with keys and purse, to have my hands free to
protect myself.   The roughs were constantly attempting to
drag women down side streets away from the main body of the
crowd.   Lloyd George, Winston Churchill, Herbert Gladstone
and other Members of both Houses watched the scene.   The
ill-usage by the police and the roughs was greater than we had
hitherto experienced : it was harder than ever to secure arrest.

Enraged by the violence and indecency in the Square, Mary
Leigh and Edith New took a cab into Downing Street, and flung
two small stones through the windows of the Prime Minister's
house; the first act of damage ever committed by the Suffragettes.
Next day at Westminster police court twenty-seven women were
sent to prison in the Second Division for terms varying from
one to two months.   The stone-throwers were tried at Bow
Street.   They had sent a message to Mrs. Pankhurst that as their
action was unauthorized, she should repudiate them if she
thought fit; she went to the cells to congratulate them.   In the
precincts of the Court I met Mary Leigh's husband, a quiet, small
man.   " It is heartrending! " he said in a choked voice.   The
prisoners were in the dock with white dresses and white faces.
I was relieved to hear the sentence : two months in the Third
Division, fearing it had been more.   They were welcomed on
release by a team of women in white dresses who drew their
carriage to Clements Inn.

We were now in the throes of a heat-wave; news came from
Holloway that the Suffragettes were fainting in the exercise yard
and the ill-ventilated cells.   The *Manchester Guardian* protested
in a leading article on July 10th : " Their stringent imprisonment
. . . violates the public conscience."   Dr. Mary Gordon secured

the provision of sun-bonnets for women prisoners at exercise, and notebooks and pencils for the Suffragettes, a privilege soon withdrawn.

Demonstrations, by-election campaigns, the heckling and harrying of Cabinet Ministers increased in intensity. On July 28th Lloyd George was interrupted by thirty determined women when he addressed a Peace Conference in the Queen's Hall. He protested in rage: "If women do not show more intelligence than these very sorry samples . . . they are creating a feeling of disgust . . . put a handkerchief over it . . . I think the gag should be tried."

The more he abused them, the more he became a special target of Suffragette wrath. At Swansea he cried: "We shall have to order sacks for them next. . . . I wonder how much she has been paid for coming here? . . . This business is becoming a profession." Mrs. Pethick Lawrence wrote to the Press declaring that none of the women who interrupted Lloyd George had been paid.

In the W.S.P.U. defiance was paramount; the stronger its expression, the louder were the cheers at the "At Homes" in the Queen's Hall. "I want to be tried for sedition!" had become a frequent saying of Mrs. Pankhurst.

CHAPTER III

FOR the opening of Parliament on October 13th another Women's Parliament was projected, and a new device to advertise it was hit upon: a handbill was issued broadcast: " Men and Women, HELP THE SUFFRAGETTES TO RUSH THE HOUSE OF COMMONS." A Votes for Women kite floated over the House, a steam launch, with posters announcing the forthcoming demonstration, patrolled the river.

Detectives were watching the offices at Clements Inn. On October 8th a call was received from Inspector Jarvis. Christabel met him gaily: " What about the thirteenth? Have you seen our new bills? " She offered him a copy of the handbill, explaining, with vivacity, that the word " rush " was not large enough; it must appear in more prominent type. At midday on Monday, October 12th, a summons to appear at Bow Street that afternoon, in respect of the " rush " handbill, was served upon Christabel, Mrs. Pankhurst and Mrs. Drummond. They ignored the summons and proceeded to the Queen's Hall. Suspense and excitement ran high. Lady Constance Lytton was in the audience, not yet fully free from scruples against militant tactics, but ardent to go to prison, longing to be convinced. It was expected that the police would come to arrest the trio on the platform, but a message was received that the Magistrate, Curtis Bennett, had adjourned the summonses till next morning. To enhance excitement, the three again refrained from appearance, sending a message to the Court that they would not be in attendance at their offices till 6 p.m. next day, " When we shall all three be entirely at your disposal." The Magistrate immediately issued a warrant for their arrest, but the police were unable to execute it till the appointed hour, when the three appeared and were taken immediately to the cells at Bow Street.

Lady Constance Lytton rushed about from the Court to the Commons, pleading for bail for the three. She ran the Magistrate to earth near Olympia, but he declared that the prisoners, by their late hour of surrender, had made it impossible to let them out. At last, at 11 p.m. Lady Constance and Mrs. Lawrence returned to Bow Street, laden with rugs and cushions from Clements Inn, to find that James Murray, the Liberal M.P. for East Aberdeenshire, had already arranged for beds and every

288

sort of comfort to be sent in from the Savoy Hotel. An elaborate meal had been served by three waiters in the gaol superintendent's room, brightened by tall wax candles, flowers, silver and bonbons.

Meanwhile the battle for Parliament Square was raging; cordons of police, five feet deep, were drawn across all the approaches to the Square, and mounted men galloped within the enclosure thus preserved. Without, surging against the massed ranks of the police, all London seemed to have gathered. It was "like Mafeking night without the disorder," the newspapers said. Deputation after deputation of women came struggling up to the cordon, only to be hurled back and swept away in the crowd. Mary Leigh flung herself upon the horsemen, seizing a bridle in either hand. Again the police had been ordered to make as few arrests as possible. Twenty-four women and twelve men were sent to prison for from three weeks to two months. Ten persons were taken to hospital. Haldane, John Burns, Walter Long, and Lloyd George, with his six-year-old daughter, Megan, were amongst the spectators.

Margaret Travers Symons, Keir Hardie's secretary, and as such having entry to the House, was also watching. She sent for one of the Welsh Liberal Members, and asked him to take her to look into the Chamber through a little window, known as the "peep hole," close to the glass doors by which Members enter. As her companion turned to escort her back to the outer Lobby, she rushed into the Chamber, crying: "Attend to the women's question!"

Next morning Christabel tried in vain to get the case against herself and her two companions sent for trial by jury, but secured an adjournment to take legal advice. She seized with avidity an opportunity to score a point against a Labour Member of Parliament, Will Thorne, who was by no means friendly to the W.S.P.U. He had told the unemployed in Trafalgar Square that instead of accepting the Suffragette invitation to "rush" the House of Commons, they should rush the bakers' shops: "You ought to rush every bally bakers' shop in London rather than starve. . . . You would be better off in prison."[1] When Superintendent Wells was questioned from the dock on this speech, the Government felt itself compelled to move: Will Thorne was also summoned to Bow Street, and ordered either to be bound over in sureties to keep the peace, or to go to prison for six months. He chose the more comfortable alternative.

The Suffragette case was resumed at Bow Street on October 21st. It evoked tremendous interest. Lloyd George and Herbert Gladstone were brought as witnesses on subpœna and

[1] *The Times.*

examined by the prisoners in the dock. Lloyd George obviously disliked the ordeal and constantly appealed to Curtis Bennett to forbid the questions fired at him by Christabel. Wrote Max Beerbohm in the *Saturday Review*: " His Celtic fire burned very low; and the contrast between the buoyancy of the girl and the depression of the statesman was almost painful. Youth and an ideal on the one hand, and on the other middle age and no illusions left over." Whilst the two Ministers were in Court, Marie Brackenbury was put into the box, and asked whether Horace Smith, the Magistrate who sent her to prison for six weeks, had afterwards told her at a dinner party that he had only given her that sentence because the Government had told him to. " You must not put that question," Curtis Bennett thundered, but the witness answered : " He did ! " In spite of this revelation, apparently most irritating to the Magistrate, Herbert Gladstone seemed to be enjoying himself immensely. When Christabel read to him his advice to Suffragists to organize larger demonstrations, he called it " a most excellent speech." He smiled when she asked how it was that since his conditions had been fulfilled, the Government had taken no step to give women the vote. Of course he was asked what he had meant by *force majeure*, and reminded of his father's historic utterance :

" I am sorry to say that if no instructions had ever been addressed in political crises to the people of this country except to remember to hate violence, to love order, and to exercise patience, the liberties of this country would never have been attained."

For two days the Court was turned into a Suffragette meeting by a crowd of witnesses, including a colonel of the Dragoon Guards, Miller Macguire, the Army Coach, Lady Constance Lytton, and James Murray, who said he had the greatest admiration for the Suffragettes' " earnestness of purpose, ability and general management of the whole scheme." Next morning the Magistrate brought the case to an end. Christabel was angry and disappointed. She had tried every artifice to drag the proceedings on till after the forthcoming Albert Hall meeting. She wept with rage. She detested the prospect of going to prison; it was a hateful waste of time. Even during her brief fortnight in the First Division, with her secretary coming every day for dictation, she had found the experience a deadening and depressing one; each day of the imprisonment, she told me later, she had less to propose and less to say. Now she would be incarcerated for a longer period; and First Division contact with the outer world had been abolished for Suffragettes. Her anger at going to prison lent force to her scorn and defiance. The case had been brought, she said, "out of malice, to lame in an illegitimate way a political enemy." The evidence of Miss Brackenbury was proof that the judicial system was being corrupted for Party ends. Because the Government believed that the defendants would be acquitted by a jury, they had conducted the case in the police court, "the Star Chamber of the twentieth century," above the doors of which should be written: "Abandon hope all ye who enter here!" When the Reform Bill hung in the balance, Joseph Chamberlain had threatened to march a hundred thousand men on London. "The Gladstone of those days was less absurd, hesitating and cowardly than the present Gladstone and his colleagues."

"Everyone knows that with a timid Government like the present, having at its disposal the entire Metropolitan Police Force, if one woman says she is going to 'rush the House of Commons,' there will be an immense number of police to prevent her doing it. Nobody thought the women would 'rush' the House of Commons, but everyone knew the women would be there to show their indignation against the Government. . . .

"Remember that we are demanding the franchise, and if the present Government cannot reconcile order with our demand for the vote without delay, it will mark the breakdown of their statesmanship. . . . They are disgraced. It is only in this Court that they have the smallest hope of getting bolstered up."

Mrs. Pankhurst, in her voice of mournful melody, moved the Court as the tragedienne sways the theatre:

"If you had power to send us to prison, not for six months, but for six years, or for our lives, the Government must not think they could stop this agitation. It would go on!"

The Magistrate ordered three months in the Second Division for the two older defendants, ten weeks for the younger, in default of finding sureties to be of good behaviour for twelve months. The trial was over. We saw them led away to the cells. Another milestone had been passed.

Mrs. Lawrence had insisted that I should take Christabel's place in the office during her absence. Beside keeping things going, it seemed to me my particular task to struggle for better conditions for the prisoners; and in addition to the large correspondence and details of organization, to make a continuous effort to get letters and articles into the Press. Farrell, an Irish Member of Parliament, and others were in prison for inciting to boycotting and cattle-driving. They were receiving the full privileges of the First Division: permission to do their professional work, to carry on their correspondence without restraint, to see such visitors as they chose, to have their own food, clothing and furniture, medicines and medical attendant. Mrs. Pankhurst was campaigning in Holloway for the same rights. She announced that Suffragettes would no longer submit to be searched, nor would they undress except in private, and that she herself would refuse to observe the rule of silence. The Governor conceded the first two demands, and ignored the third. She addressed a petition for First Division treatment to the Home Secretary, and received a negative reply. On November 1st, as the Suffragettes trudged round the yard in single file she linked arms with Christabel and walked beside her, talking in low tones. A wardress ran up to them: " I shall listen to everything you say ! " " You are welcome to do that, but I shall insist on my right to speak to my daughter." More wardresses were summoned; Mrs. Pankhurst was ordered to return to her cell. Her comrades rushed to her, crying: " Three cheers for Mrs. Pankhurst ! " The officers drove them in. The Governor came to Mrs. Pankhurst's cell to pass judgement on her offence; he asked her to promise not to break the rule of silence. She refused; he sentenced her to strict solitary confinement. A wardress was stationed outside her cell to prevent all communication with the other prisoners, who were informed that she was a " dangerous criminal." This news was brought out to us by Flora Drummond, who was discharged after nine days, the authorities having discovered that she was pregnant.[1] We answered with processions to Holloway, marches round the prison, singing the " Women's Marseillaise,"[2] and meetings at the gate. The Home Secretary blandly replied to Parliamentary inquiries that Mrs. Pankhurst was confined to her cell on account of ill-health. It was true enough that she was ill: unable to tolerate inaction and solitude, she always suffered in Holloway. Having applied in vain that I or her own doctor might see her, I wrote to C. P. Scott of the *Manchester Guardian,* asking his intervention. He kindly came at once to the office, induced the Home Secretary to let him visit Mrs. Pankhurst in Holloway, and procured for her the concession that Christabel might spend an hour with her each day and that they both should be allowed to see the newspapers. I induced Blumenfeld, editor of the *Daily Express,* to open a column called " Express Letters to the Suffragettes," wherein he published articles in the guise of letters from Elizabeth Robins and other popular authors which he was able to obtain cost free. His interest in the project unfortunately

---

[1] A boy was born in due course and named Keir Hardie. When the man after whom she had called her son lay dying, Mrs. Drummond was in his constituency working for his opponent.

[2] Words by Miss F. E. Macaulay set to the French air.

evaporated before the prisoners were released. Journalism knows no constancy.

The concessions C. P. Scott had obtained were not extended to the other Suffragettes. On the contrary, they were treated with increased severity. Mary Leigh was put in solitary confinement on the charge (false, her companions averred) of inciting to disobedience, or, in prison parlance, to " mutiny." The others protested on her behalf, and were punished by five days' close confinement and the complete withdrawal of the much vaunted associated labour. When this became known outside, enthusiasm for the prisoners increased; larger and more jubilant processions assembled at the prison gates at eight in the morning to convey each batch of released prisoners to a welcome breakfast. Mrs. Lawrence was fertile in picturesque ideas. The Scottish prisoners were escorted by lassies dressed in kilted tartans, the Irish by a piper and colleens in a jaunting car.

Early in October the Prime Minister visited Leeds. As he emerged from the station, Jennie Baines, a little woman with ashen face and blazing eyes, threw herself upon him, crying: " Votes for Women and down with tyranny ! " She was hurled aside by the police; but, followed by a great crowd, she marched to the Coliseum, where Asquith was to speak, and held a meeting at the doors. Having carried a resolution to interview him, she leapt from her platform, crying: " If these tyrants will not come to us, we must go to them, and compel a hearing ! " She was arrested with five others, who each received five days' imprisonment; but was herself committed for trial at the Assizes on the charge of unlawful assembly. She was defended by Pethick Lawrence, who attempted to subpoena both Asquith and Herbert Gladstone; but they obtained a Rule of the Divisional Court exempting them from attendance. Mrs. Baines was found guilty, with a recommendation to mercy, and received six weeks in the Second Division. Successively a Salvation Army lieutenant, an evangelist to a workmen's mission, a temperance worker and a member of the Stockport I.L.P., Unemployment Committee, and Committee for the Feeding of School Children, she was one of the early members of the W.S.P.U. A wage earner from eleven years, she remained so after marriage, although the mother of five children, for her husband, a shoemaker, earned but 25s. a week.

On October 28th Muriel Matters, of the Women's Freedom League, startled the House of Commons by delivering a speech from the Ladies' Gallery. An attendant rushed to eject her, but found she had chained herself to the historic grille by which the occupants of the Ladies' Gallery were discreetly hidden from the

Members—a precaution not thought necessary in the case of the
" Strangers' Gallery," reserved for the use of men.   The padlock
was a yale, the chain was strong.   The attendant gagged the
disturber with his hands, whilst his colleagues made ineffectual
efforts to dislodge her.   Another woman began to speak; she
too was chained.   It was necessary to clear the gallery and dis-
member the grille.   The offenders were brought out with the
heavy pieces of wrought brass to which they were fastened, and
kept in a committee room till a smith was procured to file
through the chains.   Meanwhile a man in the Strangers' Gallery
shouted: " Why don't you do justice to women? " and another
flung a bundle of leaflets into the Chamber.   Women attempted
to hold a meeting in the Lobby, and when flung out, climbed
up to speak on the pedestal of Richard I's statue.   Whilst the
police were clambering after some of them, others rushed into
the House.   As a result of these episodes, fourteen women
received a month's imprisonment, and the Speaker ordered that
the galleries, both for men and women, should be closed.

The grille was restored, but even the temporary dismember-
ment of a fixture which seemed so strikingly typical of the long
enslavement of women was widely regarded as a triumph.
Nevertheless the closing of the galleries aroused the law-abiding
Suffragists to protest against the militants.   Mrs. Fawcett a year
before had arranged the Savoy dinner to Mrs. Cobden Sanderson
and the others who had made the first disturbance in the Lobby.
Now she joined the executive of the N.U.W.S.S. in addressing
a manifesto to the House of Commons, placing on record her
Union's strong objection to such " disturbances of the peace."
Members of Parliament were appealed to neither to " change
their opinions " nor " abstain from voting because of the disorder "—an exhortation which seemed to indicate the opinion
that they had reason to do so.   Beatrice Harraden, Dr. Louisa
Garrett Anderson (Mrs. Fawcett's niece), Dr. Flora Murray, and
other members of the N.U.W.S.S. protested against the manifesto.
Mrs. Hylton Dale resigned her vice-presidentship:

" She cannot remain even an honorary official of a society which,
while enormously benefiting, and in fact being revitalized by the
splendid courage and self-sacrifice of the militant section, the founders
and leaders of which are now in prison, yet denounces that militant
section."

The National Union now announced its intention to withdraw from the joint organ, Women's Franchise, in which the
Women's Freedom League was also a participator.

The galleries of the House remained closed throughout the
winter, the question of maintaining order being referred to a

Select Committee.[1] The manifesto of the non-militants had emphasized their trust in Asquith's promise of a free vote for a women's suffrage amendment to his projected Reform Bill; yet conflicting statements by members of the Government were inflaming the opinion that the promise was mere humbug, and the stipulation that the franchise for women must be a democratic one a mere ruse to defraud them of a franchise of any sort. Lloyd George had declared he would " strenuously oppose " any measure failing to give votes to the working man's wife. Immediately afterwards Augustine Birrell told a deputation that he would oppose any measure to give votes to married women, that he would only support the grant of votes to widows and spinsters qualified on the Municipal basis, and that he did not think the question ripe for solution on any terms.

Lloyd George, so successful in strategy amongst men, now made one of his many attempts to become the hero of the suffrage cause, which invariably miscarried, because those recalcitrant women persisted in saying that he came to them empty handed with only a bevy of fair, indefinite words in his mouth. On this occasion he wrote to the Women's Liberal Federation, suggesting that he should address them on Votes for Women, and bring a message from the Government. His offer was eagerly accepted, and an Albert Hall meeting arranged. The W.S.P.U. was implored not to interrupt him; it replied that unless an assurance were forthcoming that the pronouncement would contain a pledge of Government action, Lloyd George must expect the usual heckling. The promoters of the meeting argued in vain. A statement urging a peaceful hearing for the pronouncement was published under the signatures of influential women. Withdrawal from our position was never so much as considered at Clements Inn. Obviously the intended disturbance was calculated

[1] On April 20th, 1909, the Attorney-General moved the Second Reading of the " Houses of Parliament Bill," also called " The Brawling Bill." Its object was to avoid the publicity entailed by summoning an offender to the Bar of the House. It proposed giving magistrates power to inflict a fine of £100, or six months' imprisonment, for disturbing the House. The trial of Mrs. Baines was quoted to prove that the Officers of Parliament could be protected against subpœna. Members declared that the measure would become an " aunt sally " for the Suffragettes to shy at; someone suggested it had been drafted at Clements Inn. Keir Hardie observed that the methods of the Suffragettes had been prompted by their opinion that it was useless to appeal to the honour of the House. The " Brawling Bill " proceeded no further. On April 27th five women chained themselves to the statues of Walpole, Somers, Selden and Falkland in St. Stephen's Hall. The act was a challenge to the " Brawling Bill," and proved to be its death-blow. The galleries were shortly afterwards re-opened to men signing a pledge to refrain from disturbance. The same pledge was exacted of women; but admission was only granted to women who were relatives of Members of Parliament who must obtain places for them by ballot.

to evoke a tempest of wrath against us. I had control of the arrangements, and was anxious to organize matters so that the tide might be turned against our opponents. By luck we had secured all the seats in the front row of the arena. I arranged that all the women occupying them should wear facsimile prison dress as a reminder that our women were suffering under Government coercion. I asked all the hecklers to return to Clements Inn when ejected from the Albert Hall, in order that I might summon the Press to witness their condition after the ill-treatment which I well knew, by experience, they would receive.

I was confronted in the office by a growing resentment against this ill-treatment amongst the rank and file militants. Helen Ogston, a B.Sc. of St. Andrews, and daughter of an Aberdeen Professor, a tall, handsome girl, who had made her first trials as a speaker in my Chelsea campaign, came to unburden herself to me. She had enlisted for the Albert Hall contingent, but she insisted that she must protect herself from indecent assault. "Surely you do not desire women to submit to that without protest?" I could not say I wished it; indeed I was distressed at sending them to face it. She would carry a dog-whip, she declared, and strike the first man who dared to mishandle her. "Oh, don't go slashing about with a whip!" I begged her. "You cannot control whom you may hit in a crowd with a thing like that. Take your umbrella with you, and only use it in case of necessity!" "You know—of course you know I do not want to strike anyone . . . for any other reason."

I was called away; she had not promised to abandon the dog-whip. I feared she would make matters worse with it, for herself and the others. I expected to see her again, but she did not come. There was so much to do; events swept on; it was too late to send for her. When the Albert Hall meeting began and the hecklers in the front row snatched off their cloaks and revealed themselves in the hideous prison garb the speakers knew what to anticipate. Moreover a few moments made clear that hecklers were stationed in every part of the hall. Lloyd George's pronouncement proved to be only a repetition of Asquith's original offer. The interruptions were pertinent; any practised speaker could have dealt with them without being deflected from his speech; but the determination of the stewards to eject every interrupter, their violent method of doing it, and the excitement of the audience caused a noisy disturbance to follow the smallest interjection.

It was Saturday afternoon; the office was deserted; I waited impatiently for the women to return. They came in ones and twos, bruised and dishevelled, hatless, with hair dragged down and clothing torn; some had their very corsets ripped off, false teeth knocked out, faces scratched, eyes swollen, noses bleeding. Someone rushed in with the news that Helen Ogston had used a dog-whip; she had kept several men at bay! The news-bearers were in ecstasies. " Bravo! " cried the others. I telephoned for the Press; the reporters arrived almost immediately. I introduced them to the dishevelled company: " This is how our women return from questioning Mr. Lloyd George." " It is reported that one of them has used a dog-whip," a Pressman said. I asked him: " What would you do if you were treated like this for asking a question? " The pathetic groups of battered hecklers were still arriving; the Pressmen showed a genuine concern. " Tell the truth about the violence done to these women," I urged.

Helen Ogston arrived; I took her aside. " So you did it," I said to her with regret. " A man put the lighted end of his cigar on my wrist; another struck me in the chest. The stewards rushed into the box and knocked me down. I said I would walk out quietly, but I would not submit to their handling. They all struck at me. I could not endure it. I do not think we should submit to such violence. It is not a question of being thrown out; we are set upon and beaten." " Never mind," I said, " we shall see it through."

Mr. Lawrence returned to the office. He did not think a grave new departure of this sort ought to have been made without consultation. I saw him and accepted responsibility. Mrs. Drummond also saw him, and came back to us with one of her yarns, never taken too literally by any of us. " He said : ' Damn the dog-whip! ' and I said ' Damn you! ' " she told us. Mrs. Lawrence was away; she returned in time for the Queen's Hall meeting on Monday. With a generosity not always found in leaders, she championed Helen Ogston and called her on to the platform to give her own version of the story. The girl was received with incredible enthusiasm. Women flocked on to the platform to embrace her. " Let me touch the hand that used the dog-whip! " a woman cried.

The reporters undoubtedly did their best for us. The *Evening Standard* representative at the Queen's Hall addressed a personal protest to the paper signed " your representative," in which he declared himself prepared to swear to " the grossly brutal conduct " and " unnecessary violence " of stewards wearing the official yellow rosette. The *Manchester Guardian* also admitted that ejections had been effected " with a brutality which was almost nauseating." On the whole Helen Ogston's action, which I had feared might make things harder, seemed, on the contrary, to arouse the sympathy of people who, for the first time, learnt from it of the ill-usage to which the hecklers had been subjected. Christabel, however, thought otherwise. She told me on her release that too much fuss had been made about the violence; she was ever a stoic in such matters. For a time we had reprisals. When Helen Ogston appeared at Maidenhead men dressed up as women appeared with whips and drove the speakers from the platform; but she had a splendid reception in Aberdeen. When I spoke for the Ipswich and County Women's Suffrage Society the anti-suffragists had printed a song about the dog-whip; the singing of this song, the rattling of tin cans, the hurtling through the air of whips, walking-sticks and other missiles were the greetings I received. The Ipswich suffragists begged the Chief Constable to intervene, but he would not. The music had to be faced; but in this case, as was usual, one could win through at last, if one kept doggedly on. A by-election at mid-Essex was in progress at the time. The constitutional suffragists fell victims to disorder, which might, more justly, have been directed against us. We saw them swept from the market-place, whilst we, at a neighbouring pitch, were able to hold our own; indeed we militants were usually fortunate with the crowd. After that Albert Hall uproar, Lloyd George announced that women would be excluded from all his meetings. He was perpetually at the poles—now the saviour of women, now their contemner. To suppress disorder Lord Robert Cecil introduced a Public Meetings Bill, which provided for a fine of £5 or a month's imprisonment for " disorderly conduct " at a public meeting. With the aid of the Government it was rushed into law by December 21st; eleven days after its introduction, one and a half hours being spent on all its stages in both Houses. The Act remained practically a dead letter.

Whilst I was immersed in all this, Harry wrote to me that a friend had recommended him for a post as French gardener at a sanatorium kept by a woman doctor whose name I knew. Whether his training at Mayland had qualified him for such a position I was unaware; but I was doubtful. I wrote urging him to make no change until his mother's release, but he replied that he had already accepted the post. Very shortly the woman doctor came to the office to see me; a large, imposing lady. She complained that Harry was not qualified for the intensive French gardening she desired; he had only been employed in " rough farming " at Mayland. He had not gone out to cover the frames one night of unexpected frost : " My garden might have been spoiled ! " Moreover her patients would ruin him; their behaviour was absurd. Middle-aged women received his opinions as momentous. A woman of forty had actually closed a discussion with : " I shall ask Mr. Pankhurst." His health, too, so gravely needed attention. Listening in a crushed silence under her tirade, I interrupted, alarmed : " What is the matter with him ? " She seemed to relent, and brushing my inquiry aside, proposed that he should remain at the sanatorium as a patient for the nominal fee of £1 a week and should work under and learn from the gardener she intended to procure from France. The decision might stand over till Mrs. Pankhurst's return. When that happened, Mrs. Pankhurst thought the doctor ought to abate her demands and keep the lad free of charge in return for his services. His elders failing to agree, he was sent back to Mayland. This, however, is to anticipate; at the time of which I write, Mrs. Pankhurst was still in prison.

On the eve of Christabel's release Mrs. Lawrence apostrophized her as the young Siegfried :

" . . . Maiden warrior, we give you rapturous welcome. Go forth with the fiat of the future, strong in the gladness and youth of your dauntless spirit to smite with your sword of destiny the forces of stupid and unreasoning prejudice and blind domination. . . ."

Great was the rejoicing when at the opening of the prison gates, not Christabel only emerged, as we expected, but Mrs. Pankhurst also, the remainder of her sentence being remitted. Had this concession too been procured by the editor of the *Manchester Guardian*? Mrs. Lawrence had asked the women to wear in the welcome procession a special winter costume in the purple, white and green. As ever, her desire received eager response. A landau surmounted by a banner : " To victory " was drawn by white horses led by young Suffragettes and accompanied by women out-riders. At the welcome breakfast Christabel said : " During the first few days in prison you have serious doubts whether you will ever see the outside again. You know it, but you do not feel it." Mrs. Pankhurst foreshadowed the new and harder struggle she intended to force in prison : with the ostensible object of securing political treatment; with the real object of rendering the prison ordeal so terrible that it would prove a compelling argument in the winning of the vote. She was resolved to return to prison in the new year to begin this struggle, whilst Christabel was determined never to go to prison again. At the Queen's Hall that night there was a trooping of the purple, white and green; the organizers and officials of the Union lined up and saluted. Christabel was presented with a silk standard bearing a gilt shield inscribed with the dates of her imprisonments. Mrs. Pankhurst presently received a necklace in the colours and an address on vellum, bound and executed at the Doves' Bindery of Cobden Sanderson.

The winter of 1908 saw the enfranchisement of the Women of Victoria and the rejection by the British House of Lords of the legal appeal of five Scottish women graduates, who claimed that the law entitled them to exercise the university franchise. This case had originally come before the Lords Ordinary of Scotland in 1906, and had been decided against the women. They had appealed to the Lords of the Extra Division in 1907 and from them to the House of Lords.

CHAPTER IV

THE HUNGER STRIKE. THE FIRST STONE THROWERS

WHEN the first Cabinet Council of 1909 met in January, four members of the W.S.P.U. were arrested for knocking at the door. Next day Muriel Matters, of the Women's Freedom League, sailed over the House of Commons in a dirigible balloon painted: Votes for Women, whilst twenty-six members of the League were arrested for endeavouring to interview Cabinet Ministers at Downing Street and the House of Commons. The sentences ranged from fourteen days to a month. Members of the W.S.P.U. carrying placards: " Deputation to the House of Commons next Wednesday," were dispatched to the Prime Minister as " human letters " in care of a post-office messenger-boy. A facsimile prison van, bearing the initials " E. P." instead of " E. R.," drove through the streets, advertising the forthcoming militant deputation, women in prison dress occasionally springing out to chalk announcements on the pavement. The offence for which Mrs. Pankhurst and her companions had gone to prison was being repeated with opulent disregard of anything the Government might do.

On February 24th, 1909, the sixth Women's Parliament met in the Caxton Hall. Mrs. Pethick Lawrence, Lady Constance Lytton, Daisy Solomon, daughter of the late Prime Minister of the Cape, Caprina Fahy, daughter of Gilbert the sculptor, were amongst the twenty-eight women arrested and sent to prison for a month or two, for attempting to reach the House. Those who were known to the police as leaders were soon taken into custody; the others were treated with great violence, constables seizing them and hurling them bodily into the crowd. One had a thumb dislocated, another an ankle sprained. No complaints were made; the stoic policy again held sway. Lady Constance Lytton observed:[1]

" The word went round that we were to conceal as best we might our various injuries. It was no part of our policy to get the police into trouble. . . . The most difficult thing to disguise was the wounded nose of Miss Dugdale."[2]

Constance Lytton was put in the prison hospital. Desiring no privileges not shared by her companions, she agitated constantly till she was transferred to the ordinary cells. To secure this

---

[1] *Prisons and Prisoners*, by Lady Constance Lytton. (Heinemann.)

[2] Daughter of Captain Dugdale, R.N., and niece of Viscount Peel.

object, she slept on the floor at night, and even began to cut across her chest the motto: Votes for Women. One of the Freedom League members, Mrs. Meredith MacDonald, fell in the exercise yard, and broke her thigh-bone. For eighteen days her injury was untreated; she begged in vain for an X-ray examination. At the expiry of her sentence she was discharged to a hospital, where an operation was performed; but owing to the neglect of her injury she was lamed for life. A committee took up her case, and after eighteen months delay, the Government agreed, under pressure of legal proceedings, to pay her £500 and legal costs.

On March 30th the Caxton Hall witnessed a seventh Women's Parliament. Twenty-one women were arrested and received from one to three months' imprisonment. On April 16th Mrs. Lawrence was released. Women in white drew her carriage to the welcome breakfast. She was presented with a motor-car for the use of the Union. £8,000 was raised by the W.S.P.U. Self-Denial Week.

Lady Carlisle's son, Geoffrey Howard, had won a place in the Parliamentary ballot. He devoted it to a Bill to give Manhood and Womanhood Suffrage on a three months' residential qualification, which would raise the electorate to 30,000,000. He hoped that his Bill might " clear the way " for the Government's proposed Reform Bill, and test the feeling of the House on a democratic suffrage for women. There is no doubt his professions were genuine, but he was repudiated as a traitor to the women's cause. All the Suffrage Societies denounced his Bill. On the day of its Second Reading, the militants handcuffed placards opposing it to the railings of Palace Yard. Again was witnessed the strange spectacle of the suffrage societies passionately struggling for the enfranchisement of their sex, but, with equal insistence, limiting the demand to a small minority. The Liberal Party in power averred continually that if brought to the point of granting any franchise to women, it would by no means accept the narrow franchise which the suffragists were demanding under the firm delusion that it would be easiest to obtain. Mrs. Fawcett wrote on behalf of the non-militants:

" Mr. Howard's Bill is not what we want, and suffragists disclaim any part or lot in it."

She appealed to Members of Parliament to vote for the amendment of A. E. Goulden, a Conservative:

" That the extension of the franchise to women now disqualified solely on account of sex should precede consideration of the further changes proposed in this Bill."

In spite of the Labour sympathies of its President, the Women's Freedom League protested: "the country is not ripe for Adult Suffrage." Christabel Pankhurst was equally emphatic in denouncing not only Adult Suffrage but every form of franchise for women save that opposed by all the Liberal Party organizers, in the belief that it would advantage their opponents in the constituencies. She wrote:

"It has been suggested that a husband and wife living together shall be deemed to be joint occupiers where either of them would otherwise be the sole occupier. Those who understand present-day political conditions will realize that such a proposition is hardly less likely to wreck our movement than the proposals contained in Mr. Geoffrey Howard's Bill."

It was precisely the form of franchise she here repudiated which was eventually carried into law under changed conditions. The strange circumstance that, so far from proposing such an accommodation for married women, the suffrage societies vehemently opposed it, is only explained by the fact that faced with the cold-shoulder of Governments and of Parties, they were continually thrown back upon efforts to procure enfranchisement by a private Members' Bill supported by groups in all Parties. Christabel Pankhurst had been foremost in denouncing the private Members' Bill method. She had called for concentration in making Votes for Women a Party question and in compelling the Government to introduce a Bill. Yet again and again she, like the rest, returned to the old method. Private Members of Parliament were "like the back buttons on the frock coat," she declared; they once fulfilled a function, but now they were incapacitated; yet denouncing Geoffrey Howard's Bill, she again held forth hope in the little old one-clause-Bill, to make the word man include woman, which might be slipped through as a private Members' Bill. Repudiating now her own frequently and hotly argued thesis, that only a Government measure could succeed, she recalled that the Married Woman's Property Act was introduced as a private Members' Bill though afterwards taken up by the Government. When Howard's Bill came to be voted on, Asquith observed that he did not desire perhaps to go quite so far as this Bill in the enfranchisement of men, and that he was still opposed to Votes for Women on any terms. The Conservative whips officially told against the Bill, yet its Second Reading was carried by a majority of thirty-five votes. The measure, of course, went no further; the Speaker insisted that it be sent to a Committee of the whole House, the now firmly established expedient for avoiding the scandal of the "talk out." Had the suffrage movement been of another timbre, the carrying of this vote for womanhood suffrage would have been seized upon as a lever for demanding an Adult Suffrage Reform Bill; but the time for this was not yet.

Before her imprisonment, Mrs. Lawrence had asked me to prepare decorations for a W.S.P.U. Exhibition to be held in the Prince's Skating Rink, Knightsbridge, a hall measuring 250 feet by 150 feet. I had but three months in which to execute this immense piece of work. It took me three weeks of ceaseless tramping to find premises large enough to contain the designs. At last I found a lofty and narrow room in Avenue Studios, Fulham Road, where the cartoons, with some adjustment, could be made, and a very large, but not lofty workshop over a stable, some distance away, where the larger work could be carried out by extending it on the floor. Three women who had been students with me at the Royal College of Art joined me for the modest stipend I asked for myself: 30s. a week. We did not want to take more from the movement. Four men ex-students of the college were paid, at their own request, 10d. per hour, the pay of a working decorator. They all entered into the work with the ebullient enthusiasm of the young artist employed for the first time on a big piece of work. I made all the designs to quarter scale. My women colleagues assisted me in enlarging them, and in painting the human figures. The men in the workshop laid all the grounds of the canvasses, and executed the ornament from the full size black and white cartoons which we prepared in the studio, and my quarter-size coloured designs. They were obliged to do the greater part of their work kneeling on mats, whilst we in the studio had ladder towers to reach the upper part of the cartoons. The decorations surrounded the hall, and were themselves twenty feet in height. Their theme was:

" He that goeth forth and weepeth bearing precious seed shall doubtless come again with rejoicing bringing his sheaves with him."

Over the entrance was the colossal figure of a woman, more than thirteen feet high, sowing the grain. A flight of doves bearing an olive branch hovered above her. On either hand were the blossoming almond trees of early spring. Facing her at the far end of the hall, a woman bearing the corn advanced over a green, flower-sprinkled lawn, angels with bright wings, playing on stringed instruments, flew beside her in the rays of the sun. On the side walls were such motives as the pelican, emblem of sacrifice, piercing its breast to feed its young, the dove of hope with the olive branch of peace, and the broad-arrow, the insignia of imprisonment, gilded, and draped with the laurels of victory. The whole was enclosed by pilasters and round arches of interlacing vines. This large work was an exhilarating experience. One felt alive, indeed, as the small designs grew and covered huge surfaces. It was a tremendous rush to get finished in time. From waking to sleeping, I scarcely paused except to overlook the work of my assistants.

In the midst of our labours Mr. Lawrence appeared one day to know what sort of stalls we were making. That was a shock; I had no idea that stalls were in my province. It was well he had come in time. He and I rushed off together to the rink, mapped out the number of stalls required and gave the order to a bazaar fitter.

I worked through two nights at the end; the second night was almost too much for me. When Amy Browning, my right hand, appeared in the studio the last morning, I came down from my tower and almost fainted on seeing that its wheels had crushed two young mice we had tamed. After making a cup of tea, whilst my companion fired off on me those friendly, caustic shafts which youth employs for the restoration of one's equilibrium, I was ready to go down with her to the rink to see the canvasses arranged in position. The men students worked until late at night fixing them. One of them had suffered a mental break-down some years before. He slept in the facsimile prison cell which was to be shown at the exhibition. The experience reawakened his abnormality, and he terrified some of the stall-holders by his wild talk. I was thrilled by the sight of the work we had executed under such cramped conditions, extended in that vast hall. It bore the ordeal surprisingly well, and assumed an appearance of grace and brilliancy which gave me great pleasure, in spite of my acute consciousness of certain defects of detail. The creamy-white walls, the soaring figures, the tracery of the arches formed a delightful background for the bright crowds at their commerce. A spirit of gaiety pervaded the exhibition. It was a fortnight's holiday from militant action for the Suffragettes. At the exhibition polling-booth we voted on topical questions of the moment, including the Daylight Saving Bill, a fantastic idea to most people at that time. Not even its promoter expected it to become law. A history of the militant movement was displayed in a long series of Press photographs; there were cartoon models of the Cabinet Ministers and the Suffragettes: Asquith in the dock, Mrs. Lawrence in the witness-box, with Public Opinion on the bench, and other such subjects executed by the Brackenburys and other artist members of the Union. Side-shows included Cicely Hamilton's clever " Anti-Suffrage Waxworks," plays by Beatrice Harraden and Christopher St. John, lessons in

ju-jitsu, which was recommended as useful for employment in
Parliament Square. The pioneer medical woman, Dr. Garrett
Anderson, lately elected Mayor of Aldeburgh, opened the fair,
the little daughter of Sir Edwin Lutyens presenting her with
a bouquet. The Press was kind, the public interested. £6,000
was added to the funds.

Whilst I had been working on the decorations, Harry, back
again on the Fels' farm at Mayland, was suddenly taken ill with
serious inflammation of the bladder and brought to the nursing-
home of Sisters Townend and Pine in Pembridge Gardens.
Mrs. Pankhurst was acutely distressed. The decision to make
an examination under chloroform shocked her intensely, and
seemed to her the precursor of a fatal result. When, however, the
boy came round safely from the anæsthetic, and the graver
symptoms subsided, her buoyant temperament rebounded to the
opposite pole. Dr. Mills advised that Harry should not return
to Mayland, urging that he was too delicate to endure the
exposure and hard toil on a farm. It was only much later that
I learnt from the doctor of this warning. Mrs. Pankhurst
brushed it aside; her boy was not delicate; she would not believe
it! How tall he had grown, how well proportioned; what
broad shoulders, that graceful droop of his head notwithstanding.
There was nothing so healthy as an active, open air life. This
passing trouble was over: he would be stronger to face the cold
next winter. She must get him some warm belts. Of course
he must go back to Mayland; indeed, there was nothing else to
be done. She had no time just now to seek another employment
for him. The movement needed her; she had so many engagements. Young people must learn to face difficulties. Indeed,
it was best for them. " Keir Hardie never went to school."
How often she had said it!

She had a brief respite in London for the exhibition. It was
delightful to have her tall son, convalescent now, beside her, so
proud of his mother, so solicitous for her comfort. " What a
charming boy. . . . I did not know you had a son. . . . Your
daughters . . . your movement . . ." Hope, enthusiasm, ardent
affection surrounded her. Her restless spirit almost touched
contentment.

Before the exhibition was over I left London, longing for
leafy lanes and flowery fields and a period of quiet study. " Go
to Ightham; you will meet old Benjamin Harrison; he will show
you his records of Eolithic man," Keir Hardie urged me. There
I went, and met the genial village grocer, a pioneer of the belief
that men using flint tools existed in the tertiary period. He
showed me, arranged in cigar boxes, his fine collection of flint

instruments found by himself in the Weald of Kent, and sent to him from all over the world by fellow investigators. He had preserved an old cartoon from *Punch* depicting him as the advocate for the " missing link " with a tail. I was back again in London for the next scene in Militancy, and then settled down painting by day, writing by night, in a cottage on Cinder Hill near Penshurst, where I saw the mutilated effigy of old Stephen de Penchester in his coat of mail.

When the Government had threatened the Suffragettes with the Tumultuous Petitions Act of Charles II, the W.S.P.U. had challenged prosecution by sending a deputation of more than twelve petitioners to the House of Commons in violation of the Act. The motive, of course, was to advertise the Cause and to find a pretext for incurring imprisonment to that end. In June, 1909, it was decided to vary the procedure, conforming to the restriction imposed by the Act of Charles, whilst exercising the right of petition assured by the Bill of Rights of 1869. To draw attention to this move, Marion Wallace Dunlop, a sculptor, gentle and steadfast, proceeded to St. Stephen's Hall, and there, with a specially prepared forme, attempted to print on the stone wall this extract from the Bill of Rights:

" It is the right of the subject to petition the King, and all commitments and prosecutions for such petitioning are illegal."

A policeman discovered her at the work, but she was simply turned out of the House, and allowed to go free. Learning that her handiwork had been erased, she returned and reprinted the inscription, for which act of defiance she was sent to prison for a month in the Second Division. According to the new policy announced by Mrs. Pankhurst, she demanded the treatment of a political prisoner, informing the Governor that she would go on hunger strike till her demand should be conceded. Neither young nor strong, but possessed of a cheerful courage, she remained unmoved by the Governor's assurance that the Home Secretary was resolved to make no concession and that she would be left to die. Dainty food failed to tempt her. " What are you going to have for dinner? " asked the doctor. She replied: " My determination." He answered: " Indigestible stuff, but tough no doubt." When she had fasted ninety-one hours she was suddenly set free. Her release was received with great rejoicing in the W.S.P.U., and intense relief by the few who were aware of her ordeal. She had staked her life on the reluctance of the Government to let a woman die, and had won the test—a brave deed. Her leap in the dark had lead to freedom. Dozens of women were ready to follow, believing

the way had been found to the vote itself, worshipping courage
as the supremest quality.

> " Our Comrades, greatly daring,
> Through prison bars have led the way."[1]

Meanwhile on June 29th an eighth Women's Parliament had
gathered in the Caxton Hall, and Mrs. Pankhurst had led a
small deputation, including the aged Mrs. Saul Solomon, who
was making her third attempt to secure arrest, and Miss Neligan,
an old school mistress of seventy-six, one of the pioneers of the
higher education of women. Whilst Keir Hardie, within the
citadel, was urging their admittance, they were conducted by tall
Inspector Jarvis, now a familiar figure in these events, through
the police cordon drawn across the road by St. Mary's Church, to
the very door of the House. Here stood the stout, red-faced
Inspector Scantlebury, the head of the police force attached to the
House, with a company of his men. He handed Mrs. Pankhurst
a letter from the Prime Minister—a curt refusal to accord an
interview. " I am firmly resolved to stand here till I am
received ! " she cried, with blazing eyes, and threw the missive
to the ground. Inspector Jarvis then began to push her away,
and his subordinates laid hands on the other women. To end
the struggle and protect her elder companions from the violence
usually preceding arrest, she struck the Inspector lightly on the
cheek with her open hand. " I know why you did that," he
said, but the hustling continued. " Must I do it again? " she
asked quietly. He answered : " Yes." She struck him on the
other cheek, and he called to his subordinates : " Take them in."

Other small deputations followed in constant succession,
until late in the evening, but in their case no blows were struck,
and the usual long, painful buffeting continued. Members of
Parliament and their friends, as usual, watched from behind the
police cordon. Lawrence Housman, author and artist, raised a
protest in the Lobby and was flung out. At last the Square was
cleared. The crowd had now grown sympathetic to the women;
it was not wise to allow the people to congregate about the
House. The police lines were drawn across every approach; yet
women suddenly appeared in the Square. They had lain concealed in thirty offices hired for the night. Whilst official
vigilance had been concentrated in the Square, the windows of
several Government offices had been broken. The thing had
been carefully done, to avoid the risk of injuring any person who
might be within. The stones, wrapped in paper and tied with
string, were knocked against the glass, and then dropped in

[1] " Women's Marseillaise," F. E. Macaulay.

through the holes they had made. This was the first official window-breaking by the Suffragettes, and only Government panes were as yet attacked. The new departure was a protest against the violence done to women who offered themselves for arrest. Since we must go to prison to obtain the vote, let it be the windows of the Government, not the bodies of women which shall be broken, was the argument; for a window-smasher was at once taken quietly into custody.

In spite of the window-breaking, a great change was revealing itself in the Press; no longer were the women represented as demented harridans; expressions of admiration for their fortitude crept into the descriptive reports, and even the anti-suffrage editorials were not without their tributes of respect. The *Daily Telegraph* said:

" It was a pitiable sight—the earnest faces of these frail, high-spirited young women roughly handled by the worried police. . . . The record of these attempted ' raids ' has been one of remarkable persistency."

The Liberal *Daily News* called for Votes for Women as the only solution.

" The sympathy of the crowd was with them."—*Standard*.

" An unparalleled phenomenon! Valiant courage and undaunted spirit. ' More than in women commonly seen.' "—*East Anglican Times*.

" One cannot overlook their earnestness."—*Scotsman*.

" The Prime Minister has shockingly mismanaged the business from the beginning."—*Yorkshire Post*.

This last remark was very widely echoed.[1]

One hundred and eight women had been arrested, including the Hon. Mrs. Haverfield, Lord Abinger's daughter, Mrs. Mansel, niece of Lord Wimborne, and Alice Paul, M.A., of Pennsylvania, who was later to form a militant " Women's Party " in the United States. Mrs. Pankhurst and Mrs. Haverfield were put in the dock together; theirs was treated as a test case. Mrs. Haverfield was defended by Council, who claimed that she had been wrongfully arrested in the exercise of a constitutional right. Muskett, appearing for the Government, felt some uneasiness on the point of law, and asked Sir Albert de Rutzen, the Magistrate, to allow him time to prepare his reply. Sir Albert observed that the advisability of such consideration had already presented itself to him before he came to the Court that morning. He adjourned the case for ten days. On its resumption Lord Robert Cecil

---

[1] At a meeting of the London County Council shortly afterwards Captain Hemphill complained that the Government had charged London £10,000 for the protection of " trembling legislators " against the Suffragettes.

appeared for the defence. He cited a wealth of historical precedent, but the old gentleman on the Bench had in the meantime become persuaded that the Bill of Rights was a musty old document, unsuited for application to present affairs; it must on no account be allowed to interfere with the work and convenience of the Prime Minister, and the preservation of public order. He brushed Lord Robert's arguments aside, and very gently explained that though the right of petition undoubtedly belongs to every subject, " the ladies " were wrong not to obey the police who told them to go away. There was nothing to prevent them from sending their petition by post. It was common sense, of course; indeed the upholders of law and order have always common sense on their side, but fanatics continue their stormy way to create another order. The punishment would be £5 or a month in the Second Division, but the Magistrate stated a case for appeal. This appeal was not heard till December 1st. In the meantime all the prisoners were liberated, with the exception of fourteen, who were charged with window-breaking and attempted rescue.

The fourteen were sent to prison forthwith, and at once began the fight for political status. They refused to change into prison clothes, and were forcibly stripped by a crowd of wardresses. The midsummer heat was intense, and the offensive atmosphere of the cells, which had no direct contact with the outer air, was an old-standing grievance. The revolting fourteen smashed the windows of their cells. Having immediately adopted the hunger strike, they were already weak from fasting when the visiting Magistrates sentenced them to from seven to ten days' close solitary confinement in punishment cells, where there was little light and the ventilation still less than in the cells they had left. The floors were of stone, in some cases never dry; the only seat was a tree stump, rising through the floor, even the plank bed being removed during the day.

In Parliament Keir Hardie, Philip Snowden and Willie Redmond[1] voiced indignant protest against their treatment. Herbert Gladstone replied by charging the hunger strikers with kicking and biting the wardresses; and afterwards announced that he had held an inquiry at the prison, and had determined to prosecute two of the released women, Theresa Garnet and Lilian Dove Willcox, who were re-arrested on August 4th. Theresa Garnet was acquitted of the charge of biting a wardress. She had been wearing the brooch I had designed for presentation to W.S.P.U. prisoners, and she was able to demonstrate that the marks on the officer's hand, mistaken for those of teeth, were made by the points of the portcullis. Nevertheless the

---

[1] Brother of John Redmond, the Irish leader.

two hunger strikers were convicted on other trumped-up charges of assault alleged to have been made in the scuffle to remove the prisoners' clothes. On these charges they were sent back to Holloway for seven and ten days. The wardresses again tore off their clothes, and flung them into punishment cells till their release, after a further three days' fast. Keir Hardie continued his protests, receiving sufficient support, in Parliament and out, to induce the Home Secretary to propose that his persistent interrogator, two Liberal Members of Parliament, and one of the released prisoners (Mary Allen) should accompany him to Holloway to examine the cells. Though the part of the prison displayed had been somewhat arranged for the occasion, Keir Hardie saw enough to convince him that the Suffragettes had not overstated their case.

The W.S.P.U. had pledged itself not to make any further attempts to exercise the right of petition pending its appeal. The Women's Freedom League meanwhile took up the point. On being refused an interview with the Prime Minister, relays of pickets, waiting with a petition for him, were stationed outside Parliament whenever it was in Session. The League also appealed to the King, requesting him to receive their deputation in person, since the Prime Minister had for two years refused an audience. During a protracted correspondence they were continually referred to the Home Secretary, instead of to their objective, the Prime Minister. On the intervention of the King's private secretary, Lord Knollys, Herbert Gladstone received them at the Home Office and accepted a memorial begging an audience with the King. Four pickets were stationed also at Downing Street. Asquith accepted a petition from one of them. Afterward the four were arrested and imprisoned for three weeks. A few days later eight more Downing Street pickets were arrested, including Mrs. Despard and Mrs. Cobden Sanderson. They were defended by the witty Irishman, Tim Healey, and given the option of 40s. or seven days, sentence being stayed pending appeal. The pickets maintained their vigil from July 5th till October 28th, when the House rose. Already on July 26th it was stated in Parliament that over a hundred members of the League had picketed for an aggregate of three thousand hours.

CHAPTER V

FORCIBLE FEEDING

ON emerging from the hunger strike, the stone throwers were presented with gold brooches set with flint stones. The rebellion of the prisoners had set the W.S.P.U. movement on fire. "It is no longer a movement; it is a whirlwind," declared the *Daily News*. The thought that women were facing death in the cells painted life, for their friends and supporters, in heightened colours; actions seemed right and necessary, which at ordinary times would not have been conceived. The spirit of adventure and sacrifice awoke in quietly mannered people, who hitherto had never stepped from the beaten track of conventional usage. Eager for sacrifice they found joy in it: "The wonderful days . . . can one never pin down on paper the joy and emotions of 1906-14?" Isabel Seymour wrote to me.

Cabinet Ministers were vehemently pursued by accusing suffragists—women and men. "Shame on you for putting women in dark punishment cells; why don't you give us the vote and end it?" they cried when Asquith unveiled a statue in the Embankment Gardens. Five women were arrested in an attempt to rush the doors of "Lulu" Harcourt's meeting in Leigh, Lancashire; four of them were torn from the grasp of the police and rescued by the crowd. Two days later, in Edinburgh, Adela Pankhurst and Bessie Brand, daughter of the High Sheriff, were arrested at the head of a crowd surging against the doors of Winston Churchill's meeting. Two women were arrested when Herbert Samuel spoke at Bedford, four at Nottingham. At Northampton Marie Brackenbury climbed to the top of a forty foot scaffolding to address the vast crowd she had led there to hoot him. Inside the meetings the turbulent women were reinforced by men heckling on their behalf.

The Government had troubles of its own; it was fighting what had hitherto been a losing legislative battle with the House of Lords. Its Bills on Education and Plural Voting in 1906, Scottish Small Holdings in 1907, Licensing in 1908 had all been wrecked. Yet its efforts to raise a popular outcry had proved abortive, countered as they were by the Labour Party, with its appeal to working-class solidarity, and by the persistent hostility of the Suffragettes, appearing everywhere to denounce its professions of democracy as a sham. Though the Lloyd George Budget of

1909, with its taxation of land values and licensing duties, was widely advertised as a " War Budget against Poverty," little enthusiasm for it could be worked up. Even at Limehouse, where the Chancellor made one of his strongest bids for popular favour, the militant W.S.P.U. and its men supporters were present to mar the effect of his appeal. Inside the hall a heckler climbed a fifteen foot pillar and fired interjections from that altitude, defended by comrades below. The interrupters were attacked by the promoters of the meeting with so much violence that between them they sustained a fractured collar-bone, a broken wrist, a broken nose, a sprained ankle and several black eyes. The heckler himself received such injuries when brought down at last that the police carried him to a doctor. Yet this was not all which occurred to disturb the Limehouse oration. The voices of women were heard, persistently shouting through a megaphone from a house near by. Twelve Suffragettes got themselves arrested, and sent to prison for terms ranging from ten days to two months, for attempting to rush the doors, and so gained further publicity for their disturbance. When ordered to change into prison clothes, they linked arms and set their backs against the wall for resistance. Dozens of wardresses dragged them apart; window breaking, the punishment cells, the hunger strike followed as before. Mrs. Leigh and Mrs. Baker were denied even the hard Holloway mattress and left to lie on the plank. Release followed after four to six days' fast.

At Exeter three women were arrested for leading a crowd to the door of Lord Carrington's meeting and released after a hunger strike. At a Liberal fête where Churchill was to speak in Canford Park, near the Dorsetshire residence of Lord Wimbourne, Annie Kenney had her clothing slit with a knife from neck to hem, whilst two girls, mistakenly thought to be Suffragettes, were dragged out of the Park under a pig-net. At Rushpool Hall; Saltburn-by-the-Sea, a Suffragette was hustled to the pond for a ducking, and one of the guests, Miss de Legh, who cried " Shame," was sufficiently ill-treated to recover damages for assault. On August 20th, when Lord Crewe spoke at St. Andrew's Hall, Glasgow, Adela Pankhurst, and others, were arrested at the doors, a huge crowd following them to the gaol. Next morning their case was heard before the time, and the bail escheated, whilst they were actually in the building asking the way to the Court and the bailee was appealing for two minutes in which to find them. The Chairman of the Bench met them at the door as he hurried away. No more was heard of the case. The women were apt to be more leniently treated where popular support was aroused. At Birrell's meeting in the Manchester

"White City" two hundred stewards and fifty police were present to keep order. The Suffragettes entered the American Cake-Walk and the American Dragon Slide, situated on either side of the hall, and from these places of entertainment flung small stones through the windows into the meeting, and made their voices heard. A policeman dashed on to the cake-walk to arrest them, but mounted the wrong platform; to the screaming amusement of the onlookers, the machine compelled him to cake-walk backward, whilst the offending women were equally obliged to cake-walk forward, a ludicrous spectacle indeed! For the women the fun soon ended; they were sent to Strangeways Gaol, placed in handcuffs for twenty-four hours, and released after a four days' fast. Six women were arrested outside Churchill's meeting in Leicester and released after a hunger strike. When he spoke in Dundee Isabel Kelley climbed a scaffolding, and lowered herself with a rope, twenty-five feet, on to the roof of the Kinnaird Hall. She lay there concealed for seventeen hours, then let herself down through a skylight, and rushed into the Hall.

Whilst Haldane was speaking in the Sun Hall, Liverpool, Mary Leigh, brandishing a hatchet, high up among the chimney-stacks of a neighbouring house, tore up slates and hurled them clattering on to the roof of the hall, while her comrades shouted through a megaphone. They were arrested, and imprisoned pending trial, but escaped by the hunger strike. This was the first act of damage, other than window breaking, yet perpetrated by the Suffragettes. There was more of the sort to follow. A "bower-bedecked" special train was to carry the Prime Minister and several prominent colleagues "to challenge the Lords" at a great gathering in the Bingley Hall, Birmingham, to be opened with a "Song of Freedom," led by a band of trumpets. Extra-ordinary measures were taken against disturbance. A fire hose and a tarpaulin were stretched across the roof of the Bingley Hall. The streets surrounding it were sealed by barricades several days before the meeting. The precautions were ridiculed by the local Press:

"Those who imagine that the organizers of the great Bingley Hall demonstration have had the wicked Peers in their minds all the time, are far out of it. Day and night they have been thinking of the Suffragettes, in the certain and scarifying knowledge that the Suffragettes have been thinking day and night of them. If the whole story . . . could be written, what a comedy it would make!"— *Western Mail.*

All precautions were vain; thirteen men supporters of "those hornets," the Suffragettes, were inside the hall putting their questions, and getting ejected with such violence that life-long

Liberals rose up to protest. The " hornets " themselves had taken lodgings within the sealed-up streets. One of them hurled a stone from a neighbouring house and broke a window in the hall : her voice was heard in the meeting. The police burst into the house and brought out several women. Immediately the sound of an electric horn issued from another dwelling. The " hornets " had funds to enable them to purchase such means of annoyance, and they were spending them. The stewards of the meeting, without any vestige of legal right, it should be observed, broke into the house and secured the instrument; yet quiet was not obtained. On a roof at the other side of the hall, Mary Leigh and a tall, golden-haired girl, Charlotte Marsh, with axes in their hands, tore up slates and threw them on to the roof of the hall. A crowd of policemen and stewards of the meeting shouted at them to desist; a ladder was produced, but the two on the roof shouted : " Take care ! " and hurled a slate into the road to prevent approach. The fire hose was dragged forward. The fireman refused to use it, but the police played it on the two, who took off their shoes to avoid slipping on the wet slates, and continued hurling their missiles. Pieces of slate were flung back at the women; they were hit several times, but did not pause in their work till the Prime Minister drove away. Then they ceased hurling, and permitted themselves to be brought down. They were marched to the cells in their stockinged feet, with drenched clothes and blood streaming from their wounds. Eight other women were arrested for window breaking; one of them for flinging an iron bar through the window of an empty carriage in the rear of the train carrying Asquith back to London. The women spent the night in the cells. Mary Leigh got four months' imprisonment, Charlotte Marsh three, the others from a month to fourteen days. The scenes of the night had not enhanced the local popularity of the Government; the people thronging the streets resented being hustled and chased by mounted police, and shouted in anger : " You curs ! You would ride over your own flesh and blood ! "

An outcry was raised against the new Suffragette policy of stone throwing and damage to private property, which had appeared in such sensational guise. The *Daily News* appealed to Mrs. Pankhurst to check these " disgraceful developments." She replied that to turn back now would be " folly, weakness and wickedness "; to ask her followers to desist would be betrayal of her " sacred trust." Christabel, in a letter to *The Times*, avowed and defended the new tactics. Mrs. Lawrence upheld them in *Votes for Women*. She explained, as was the fact, that the difficulty of keeping up the heckling of Cabinet Ministers by ordinary means was daily becoming greater. The women were kept out of the halls, and if they attempted to hold a protest meeting in the street they were taken into custody and held at the police station until the Minister and his following had departed for the night.   Therefore they had been faced, she declared, by the " inevitable choice, either to admit the game was up and give in," or discover a new method.

After this lapse of time when all is won, and all is over, I must frankly say that I did not think the old methods had yet been exploited to their full capacity.   I believed, then and always, that the movement required, not more serious militancy by the few, but a stronger appeal to the great masses to join the struggle. Yet it was not in me to criticize or expostulate.   I would rather have died at the stake than say one word against the actions of those who were in the throes of the fight.   I knew but too surely, that the militant women would be made to suffer renewed hardships for each act of more serious damage.   Yet in the spate of that impetuous movement, they would rush enthusiastic to their martyrdom, and bless, as their truest saviours, the leaders who summoned them to each new ordeal.   I realized how supremely difficult is the holding of calm thought and the sense of perspective at such a time, how readily one daring enthusiast influences another, and in the gathering momentum of numbers all are swept along.   Posterity, I knew, would see the heroism of the militants and forget their damage, but in the present they would pay severely.   There never was any doubt of the responsibility of the militant leaders for the doings of their followers; they accepted that always, without flinching, making themselves an open target for Government attack.   Christabel, especially, when not actually the instigator, was, as a rule, aware of every intended militant act, down to its smallest detail; for the W.S.P.U. was conducted with the rigid discipline of an army.   When the roof tactics were first discussed, Jennie Baines asked for hatchets. " What would you do with them? " Christabel asked.   " Well, we could be hacking and chopping, couldn't we? " replied the fiery-spirited one; and so the idea developed.

The Government was not slow to take advantage of the new tactics to inflict harsher punishment upon their instruments. These women should not be permitted to terminate their imprisonment by the hunger strike, as thirty-seven women had already done, four of them twice in succession.   The Birmingham prisoners commenced their fast on September 18th.   The Home Secretary ordered the medical officer of the prison to feed them forcibly by means of a rubber tube passed through the mouth or nose into the stomach.   The fact appeared in the Press on September 24th.   It was received with horrified consternation by everyone connected with the militant movement; by no one more than by Keir Hardie, in whom emotional distress now invariably caused the reaction of physical illness. He immediately tabled a Parliamentary question. Masterman, replying for the Home Secretary, described the forcible feeding as " hospital treatment." Hardie, white with wrath, retorted: " A horrible, beastly outrage." Philip Snowden cried: " Russian barbarism! " The supporters of the Government shouted with laughter. Keir Hardie wrote to the Press:

" . . . Women, worn and weak by hunger, are seized upon, held down by brute force, gagged, a tube inserted down the throat, and food poured or pumped into the stomach. Let British men think over the spectacle. . . .

" I was horrified at the levity displayed by a large section of Members of the House when the question was being answered. Had I not heard it, I could not have believed that a body of gentlemen could have found reason for mirth and applause in a scene which I venture to say has no parallel in the recent history of our country. One of these days we shall learn that Mrs. Leigh, or some other of her brave fellow prisoners, has succumbed to the ' hospital treatment,' as a man did in 1870."[1]

At Clements Inn evidence was immediately sought as to the effects of forcible feeding. This was mainly to be discovered in the records of prisons and insane asylums. The Lancet, September 28th, 1872, reported the case of a man forcibly fed under sentence of death. He struggled, his throat was lacerated, he became exhausted and died the following day. Dr. Anderson Moxey, M.D., M.R.C.P., commented: " If anyone were to ask you to name the worst possible treatment for suicidal starvation, I should say unhesitatingly ' forcible feeding by means of the stomach pump.' " He quoted the experience of three well-known experts in support of his view. The W.S.P.U. consulted Dr. Forbes Winslow as an authority experienced in dealing with the insane. He made a written statement that he had long discontinued the use of the stomach pump, which he held to involve the risk of injury to heart and lungs and of sudden death even in cases of mild heart disease. He knew of a case in which the tongue had been twisted behind the tube and partially bitten off. If persisted in, the results of forcible feeding would be:

" seriously to injure the constitution, to lacerate the parts surrounding the mouth, to break and ruin the teeth. . . . In normal individuals the very fact of resorting to forcible feeding is to injure the digestive organs, to aggravate any bronchial condition which may exist and to cause dangerous chronic symptoms."

[1] In 1910 two ordinary criminals were forcibly fed: the man died during the first operation, the woman committed suicide.

Mansell Moullin, M.D., F.R.C.S., wrote to *The Times*, as a hospital surgeon of thirty years standing, to protest against the use of the term " hospital treatment," which he described as a " foul libel." Dr. Harry Roberts wrote to the *Manchester Guardian* :

" To the ordinary reader the full horror of what this implies is probably not obvious. . . . This latest piece of official cruelty will quite possibly end in the insanity of some of the victims."

Dr. Forbes Ross of Harley Street, in the *Observer*, declared :

" As a medical man without any particular feeling for the cause of the Suffragettes, I consider forcible feeding by the methods employed an act of brutality beyond common endurance."

A memorial to the Prime Minister against forcible feeding, signed by a hundred and sixteen physicians and surgeons, headed by Sir Victor Horsley, F.R.C.S., was organized by Dr. Flora Murray. In spite of ridicule and evasion, Keir Hardie and a small group of others continued protesting in Parliament. Herbert Gladstone endeavoured to shelter himself from responsibility behind the Prison Commissioners and Medical Officers, whereat the *British Medical Journal* described his conduct as " contemptible." H. N. Brailsford, the Liberal pacifist, who was later to throw in his lot with the I.L.P., and Henry Nevinson, so honourably known as the chronicler of every struggle for freedom in his day, and constantly to be seen in the ranks of the Suffragette demonstrations, resigned their positions on the *Daily News*. They explained in *The Times* :

" We cannot denounce torture in Russia and support it in England, nor can we advocate democratic principles in the name of a Party which confines them to a single sex."

The ex-Premier of South Australia, the Hon. H. B. T. Strangways, sent £10 to the W.S.P.U. declaring forcible feeding an " atrocity "; the Rev. J. R. Campbell wrote to Asquith, " as a whole-hearted supporter of the Budget," that forcible feeding would create " a public scandal." There were several important resignations from the men's and women's Liberal Associations.

Only when an action at law, against the Home Secretary and the governor and doctor of Birmingham prison, was commenced on behalf of Mary Leigh, could direct testimony be obtained from the prisoners. It now transpired that Mrs. Leigh had been handcuffed for upwards of thirty hours, the hands fastened behind during the day and in front with the palms outward at night. Only when the wrists had become intensely painful and swollen were the irons removed. On the fourth day of her fast, the doctor had told her that she must either abandon the hunger strike or be fed by force. She protested that forcible feeding was an operation, and as such could not be performed without a sane patient's consent; but she was seized by the wardresses and the doctor administered food by the nasal tube. This was done twice daily, from September 22nd till October 30th. All her companions were forcibly fed, one being released before her, and the others, save one, shortly afterward. Charlotte Marsh was held almost to the end of her three months' sentence, the usual one-sixth remission being denied, although her mother was urgently appealing for her release, on account of her father's serious illness. He had sunk into unconsciousness, and would never wake to know her any more, when his daughter was tardily set free.

Mary Leigh's action was heard on December 9th before the Lord Chief Justice. Dr. Ernest Dormer Kirby, who attended her on release, Sir Victor Horsley, Hugh Fenton, senior surgeon of the Chelsea Hospital for Women, and Mansell Moullin testified for the defence. The Lord Chief Justice ruled that it was the duty of the prison medical officer to prevent the prisoner from committing suicide; the only question for the jury was whether the right steps had been taken. His summing up clearly argued this proposition in the affirmative, and the jury obediently found the verdict expected of them.

The authorities had by no means suspended forcible feeding in the interim. They even re-arrested Evelyn Wharrie, who had been arrested on the night of the Bingley Hall meeting, but discharged by the Magistrate, because she had broken her cell windows during the night on remand. Convicted of this offence she was now re-imprisoned. Four of the Manchester released prisoners were also made to serve a second term for breaking their cell windows, and were forcibly fed, though the damage in some cases was valued at less than 1s.

CHAPTER VI

HARRY

CERTAINLY there was no peace for me at Penshurst, or for anyone else who had touch or sympathy with the militant movement. Keir Hardie came down to see me. He told me that the thought of forcible feeding was making him ill. The levity in the House had surprised and saddened him. " I cannot stay here if it continues," I told him. " I shall have to go to prison to stand by the others." " Of what use to make one more? " he asked me ruefully. " Finish what you are working on at least! " So I resolved. Then a great blow fell.

I returned from my work in the little wood, with my canvas on my back, to find a telegram announcing that my brother had been brought to London, seriously ill. I found him at the nursing home in Pembridge Gardens, completely paralysed from the waist downwards, and suffering intolerable agony. He had been obliged to cease work and return to bed the previous day, and had waked in the morning to find himself unable to move. The people with whom he lodged had sent to Mrs. Maclachlan, a member of the W.S.P.U., who lived near, with the message: " Mr. Pankhurst is dying." She had brought him in her car to the nursing home. He had contracted that terrible and obscure disease, known as infantile paralysis, which sometimes occurs in adults, and in which the grey matter of the spinal cord is the seat of acute inflammation; and destruction, more or less great, occurs in the spinal motor nerve path to the muscles. We could only wait till the inflammation had abated to know how far the lesions extended, and whether there could be any hope that he might regain the use of his limbs.

Mrs. Pankhurst was to sail in a few days' time for a lecture tour to America. So ruthless was the inner call to action, that, finding her son thus stricken, she persevered with her intention. It must be added that she would thereby have the opportunity of earning money which might be needed for her boy, but there was never a moment of doubt as to where she should be substituted—on the platform or by the bedside of her son. The movement was paramount. She left us two together, not knowing what might be his fate.

Each day Dr. Mills tested the boy's progress. He lay there

extended in his nudity, proportioned like the ancient Greeks, lovely as an image of the young Adonis, showing no trace of illness, save only in his clear, smooth pallor. " A beautiful boy," the doctor murmured in shocked distress each day as he left his room. Gradually he recovered the power to move his toes; then that, too, ebbed away. He could raise himself with his arms by a pulley above his head; that was all; pain he felt in all acuteness, but all movement from the waist downward was destroyed for ever.

In his long, sleepless nights of agony he often asked me: " Shall I be able to walk again? " I lied to him faithfully: " Yes, yes." Then, later, when weeks had passed, learning a desperate cunning, I added, as though this were the whole, unpleasant truth I had wished to keep from his knowledge: " You must not be impatient; it will be rather long." Soon I should have to tell his mother that he would never be able even to sit up unaided; to tell her and to warn her: " He must not know it; he is not strong enough to bear it yet."

She returned to learn the truth my letters had not disclosed to her. " He would be better dead! " she cried in startled consternation. " No, no! " I urged her. " His mind is active; he will occupy himself; he will be happy." Together we pledged ourselves to do what remained for his welfare. I was to stay with him, and when he was strong enough I should continue my work, helping him to find interests he could pursue, thus stricken as he was. A youth with his powers in the bud, though prostrate of limb, he would compensate in mind; his kind philosophy would defy despair; desperately I willed it; it must, it should be so.

Friends of the movement, going to India for a year, generously placed at our disposal their house and studio, and their servants. Convalescent now, Harry was to be moved there next day. Then suddenly he was less well. The move was postponed. Dr. Mills met me with clouded face. The bladder trouble of last year had recurred. Steadily it gained on him, bringing its toll of wearing agony. Consultants were called in; they gave no hope. Recovery was impossible; he might live perhaps three weeks.

In those long nights of pain and fever, delirious or alert, he talked to me of his childhood; his father's death; the shock to the little son to see dear Father's face so changed when they carried him to his bedside on that last day. He told of his hard life down at Mayland. The superintendent thought him a " muff," and treated him with a rough contempt. He had striven to prove his grit: toiled at hard tasks, endured the bitterest cold. Once it had been his lot to gather a crop of turnips into sacks, and carry them on his back to the gate of the field, in readiness for the cart which would come hastening to take them to the train with barely the time to load. He had filled the sacks and sewn them up before he realized they were too heavy for him to shoulder. He feared to delay by undoing them to reduce their contents, shrank from the bitter reception awaiting him should he fail. Staggering and straining, almost exhausted, he managed at last to get them to the gate at the appointed hour. Even now he groaned in agitation at those memories, as though battling again with those hard conditions. He described, whilst I hid my face and set my teeth to hide my sorrow, the sordid poverty of his lodging; the degenerate husband, the crushed and weary wife, whom the lad in his gentle kindness had tried to help, the ill-nourished children, the animals woefully neglected. One night, as he had lain in bed there, he heard a strange bleating. He went outside and found the goat had given birth to her young in the snow. He spoke of it with a cry in his voice. Deeply shocked, and moved by the mystery of new life in this harsh adversity, he opened the shed and made a bed for her. Suffering continual distress for the poor creatures at his lodging, his own hardships were increased by his sensitive reserve. " Oh, Harry, it was too much for you! " " Don't cry, dear; it has made a man of me." His arm was round me. " It has killed you, my darling boy! " Oh bitter, unspoken thought!

One night when the pain seemed to be crushing him down, as he told me later, he confided to me his love for " Helen." He had arrived in Manchester for the by-election in April of the previous year. The Suffragette committee rooms were in darkness. " Is Mrs. Drummond here? " he questioned. A voice which made him tremble answered he knew not what. He was in love. . . .

When she appeared to his sight he saw she was of his own age, fair and tall, with a bright little face, well poised on a graciously curved throat. He regarded her as the most adorable of beings. Driving the Suffragette four-in-hand at the election, he always contrived a place for her beside him. What days of bliss! But when the election was over she returned to her boarding school at Brighton. He had written to her and received an answer; and once he had gone down there and spent the night on the cliffs, in the hope of catching a glimpse of her. He had seen her for an instant, as she passed by in a troop of girls. Her parents were wealthy, he had been told, and now, more than ever, so sorely stricken, he despaired of ever being able to reach her. I soothed him to rest, determined to bring her to him.

Next morning I telegraphed to Mrs. May. She came, ugly as an old toad, but human and understanding. Did she know who the girl was? Could she find her? In an hour Helen was with me. I begged her: " Think of him as your young brother. Tell him you love him; he has only three weeks to live." Gallantly she played her part, if part it were. To me, who watched them with anxious absorption, her constant tenderness was very real. All day she sat with him, and at night slept on a sofa to be near the telephone, lest I should summon her. I never did so, but always she was prepared.

Great joy transfigured him, endowing him with extraordinary fortitude; for several days he firmly refused to permit the injection of anodynes, having conceived the idea that they would undermine his character, and render him unworthy of his love. It was with difficulty that Dr. Mills overcame his determination, and only by persuading him that his character would be unharmed. His transcendent happiness comforted the poignancy of my sorrow; he had reached the highest pinnacle of joy. His illness enclosed those two young creatures within a haven of dream; the hard realities of life were shut away. They planned a delightful convalescence; they would go to Venice and take me with them. " Dear Sylvia," they were very kind to her; they called her to sit beside them and share their happiness. She was content; life has no greater gift than this, she told herself. He has achieved the highest point of being: life cannot long endure thus perfect, thus unclouded.

His mother was not glad of his love; she reproached me for having acted without waiting to consult her. This girl, she repined, was taking from her the last of her son.

One night in delirium, or in dream, he imagined that Helen had been stolen away and imprisoned by her father on his account. He cried out in a man's angry tones against himself: " That young scoundrel! " Then clinging to me in misery, with unseeing eyes, bewailed her loss, piteously moaning: " Little Helen . . . little Helen . . . just a few of us . . ." In vain I told him it was a dream, assuring him she would return to-morrow; he did not hear me. Together we wrestled with his loss till he fell back exhausted. Returning day effaced all memory of his dream, renewed his confidence and joy.

Although the doctors declared his malady increasing, and precluded hope, not one of us could believe this radiant boy was dying. We said it with our lips; our minds refused to know it, until those final days, when all his frame was racked with torture, and only the stifling aid of drugs enabled him to drift into unconsciousness. The end came in the new year—lightly at last, with one small, stifled gasp, as though to wake. . . .

In those sad and yet precious months of illness his life from childhood passed before me in his talk; his gentle, loyal character, unsullied by flaw or smirch, revealing itself with limpid clearness. Reserve and shyness fell from him; his mind gained in maturity. As though subconscious memories were at work, his gestures and phrases strangely recalled his father. Ever more closely he twined himself about my heart; my life seemed merged in his.

When the great blank fell, some remnants of his glory clung about me.

His mother was broken as I had never seen her; huddled together without a care for her appearance, she seemed an old, plain, cheerless woman. Her utter dejection moved me more than her vanished charm. We rode that sad way in the funeral coaches, stricken with regret—regret that we had not saved our boy. I saw him, beautiful, gentle; little forgotten incidents forcing their way into my mind of the toddler with flaxen hair, the eager child watching the trains, the schoolboy meeting me on his holidays, the youth with his dreams. We stood in our hopeless impotence beside the grave. The sods fell down. We parted in the misery of our regret.

Before Mrs. Pankhurst left London she asked me to arrange for a headstone, for she and the Doctor had never been able to bend themselves to the sad task of placing a stone over their first little son. " Choose something you like," she said; then with insistent passion: " Sylvia, remember, when my time comes, I want to be put with my two boys! "

" Blessed are the pure in heart," were the words I chose to be written over them—for that sweet purity and gentleness was all they had.

After our great bereavements life seems grey. I went to the little cottage on Cinder Hill; gathered the paintings and the writings, with all their interest gone; collected my little furniture from the rooms on the Embankment, which Aunt Mary had taken over for a time; and found myself a studio in Linden Gardens, close to the nursing home; and there endeavoured to gather up the broken threads of my life. " Let me still come to see you! " Helen said. " No, dear girl, you must forget; go; and be happy, or I shall blame myself that I have cast a shadow over your future."

Later Harry's small belongings were sent to me. Amongst them I found some little slips of vellum on which he had written :

" I saw thee, beloved,
And having seen, shall ever see,
I as a Greek, and thou,
O Helen, within the walls of Troy.
Tell me, is there no weak spot
In this great wall by which
I could come to thee, beloved? "

CHAPTER VII

" JANE WARTON "

ON December 1st, 1909, the appeal of Pankhurst and Haver-field against the decision of Sir Albert de Rutzen in July of the same year, had been heard in the Divisional Court. The Lord Chief Justice decided against the appellants.[1] He declared that there was an undoubted right of petition; but this was a claim, not merely to petition, but to be received in deputation. Mr. Asquith's refusal he considered not unnatural, " in view of what we know did happen on previous occasions." The Chief Justice was mistaken as to the facts, for when Sir Henry Campbell-Bannerman received the militants at the Foreign Office in 1906 there had been no disorder; Asquith had at no time received a deputation of the W.S.P.U.; disorders had followed his refusals. This adverse decision virtually wiped out the ancient right of petition; for a petition sent through the post could be of little value to the agitator. Yet a favourable decision would by no means have profited the militants. An orderly deputation to the Prime Minister, even once per session, would quickly have become a matter of form ignored by both Press and public. It could by no means advance the Cause as the so-called " raids " on Parliament had done. The cases against the forty-nine women tried with them were withdrawn, but the fines recorded against Mrs. Pankhurst and Mrs. Haverfield were officially applied for. Then receipts for their amount were sent to Clements Inn, two days before the return of Mrs. Pankhurst from the United States.

When I had left Cinder Hill in October to hasten in anxiety to the nursing home, Mrs. Pankhurst and Christabel had been in Newcastle, where, said Christabel, the W.S.P.U. was to display its " power and force " on the occasion of a visit there by Lloyd George on October 9th. Lady Constance Lytton, but lately hesitating as to the ethics of the mildest militancy, was now a burning enthusiast, eager to be convicted as a stone thrower, that she might place herself on a level with the women who had been forcibly fed in Birmingham prison, and suffer the same penalty. She knew that owing to her defective heart and extreme delicacy, she would probably lose her life; but believing that her rank would lend a special value to her sacrifice in the eyes of the world,

---

[1] The appeal of Mrs. Despard and other members of the Freedom League was also dismissed by the Lord Chief Justice, January 14th, 1910.

she eagerly welcomed the risk. She travelled up to Newcastle with Mrs. Brailsford. Christabel accompanied them to preside over the militant arrangements, and later to speak at a great meeting. The authorities had taken the usual tremendous precautions against disturbance, including the erection of street barricades. Mrs. Brailsford struck the barricade with an axe, masked till that moment by a bunch of chrysanthemums. One dull thud of the axe on the barricade was the symbolic act of revolution she had resolved on; it was sufficient to procure arrest. Constance Lytton, eager to be in custody as soon as possible, threw a stone at the radiator of a motor-car, which, to her pleased surprise, turned out to be that of Sir Walter Runciman, with whom the Chancellor of the Exchequer was staying. She and Mrs. Brailsford got six weeks' imprisonment, on refusal to be bound over. A number of window breakers were also imprisoned, including a sister of Mrs. Pethick Lawrence. All adopted the hunger strike. Mrs. Brailsford and Constance Lytton were released as medically unfit, the others were forcibly fed.

On October 18th Winston Churchill told a deputation of the Women's Freedom League that Votes for Women was "marching backward," and would not figure in the election address of any Party or prominent man. He himself would render no assistance till militancy were discontinued. Next night Adela Pankhurst and others were arrested in and around the Kinnaird Hall, Dundee, where he was speaking. They were released after five and a half days' hunger strike. It was believed that popular demonstrations outside the gaol had decided the authorities against forcible feeding.

Four Suffragettes were now forcibly fed in Strangeways Prison, Manchester. Emily Wilding Davison found the ordeal so hideous that when, by accident, the wardress locked her into a cell where there were two plank beds, she conceived the idea of using them to fasten herself in. She laid them on the floor, end to end, jammed the wooden stool and her shoes into the intervening space, and crouched down, holding all in position. Threats and coaxing failed to move her. By order of the visiting Magistrates, who happened to be in the prison at the time, the cell window was broken, the nozzle of a hose pipe poked in, and the great stream of water turned on. Already weak from five days' hunger strike and three days' forcible feeding, she clung to the bed boards, gasping for breath. When the water was six inches deep a voice cried: "Stop!" Warders were now brought to remove the door from its hinges—a simple operation. Apparently the authorities had taken fright, for the offender was hastily carried to hospital, plunged into a hot bath, and put to bed with hot water bottles. The news at once appeared in the Press, and evoked unusual indignation. The *Liverpool Courier* demanded the removal of those responsible for this "abuse of authority." Herbert Gladstone ordered Emily Davison's release. When questioned in Parliament he admitted that the visiting justices had been guilty of "a grave error of judgment." Yet afterwards he publicly complimented "all concerned" on the "tact, humanity and firmness" with which the Suffragettes had been handled in Strangeways Gaol. Emily Davison brought an action[1] against the Magistrates. Judge Parry decided in her favour, but awarded her only 40s. damages, on the ground that the incident had procured her release, provided her with copy for the Press and advertised her cause. Emily Davison was a coach and teacher at University Extension tutorial classes. She had taken a London B.A. and a first class in the Oxford Final Honours School in English Language and Literature. She had had to struggle for these distinctions, having supported herself by teaching in the meantime, her mother keeping a little confectioner's shop at Long Horsley, near Morpeth, in Northumberland. Far from the inner circle of the Union, she was one of the most daring and reckless of the militants. She was tall and slender, with unusually long arms, a small narrow head and red hair. Her illusive, whimsical green eyes and thin, half-smiling mouth, bore often the mocking expression of the Mona Lisa. There was little in her appearance to suggest her cool, unflinching courage, or the martyr's fate, which finally was to be hers; and of deliberate choice.

Though the Government was punishing with severity the disorderly conduct of the Suffragettes, signs were not wanting that such behaviour on the part of its own supporters would be welcome to it. A "League against the Lords" was formed for the purpose of heckling and harassing Conservative speakers; Liberal newspapers termed its interruptions: "The Voice." A gang of men organized by the League gathered in Parliament Square to hoot the Peers driving to a session of the House of Lords, but there was little of fire or vigour in these doings. They were tame indeed beside the furious activity of the Suffragettes. During the Lord Mayor's Annual Banquet in November, two women, who had got in with pails and brooms as charwomen, broke a stained-glass window in the gallery outside the banqueting hall and shouted their war-cry through the hole. They were imprisoned and forcibly fed, and one of them contracted gastritis. A few days later Theresa Garnett struck Winston Churchill with a riding switch in the Great Western Station,

[1] Heard on January 19th, 1910.

Bristol, and with four others arrested that day, was forcibly fed. When " Lulu " Harcourt held a series of meetings in Rossendale Valley he was accompanied by a campaign of window breaking. The doors and windows of the house where he was staying were pasted over with posters depicting forcible feeding. The next night eight men, with hose pipes attached to the main, were set to guard the premises, but the pipes were cut, and the windows broken nevertheless. On Churchill's visit to Lancashire, £150 at Preston, and £250 at Southport, was spent in precautions against the Suffragettes; yet wherever he went there were disturbances and arrests, from which forcible feeding resulted. At Southport Dora Marsden, B.A., and others lay concealed for twenty-four hours on the roof of the hall where he spoke, and called " Votes for Women! " through the skylights. Enraged Liberal stewards sent them rolling down the steep roof. Two of them were saved by colliding with a cistern. A policeman seized Dora Marsden by the foot: " If I had not caught you, you would have gone to glory! " They were arrested and brought into Court, but the Magistrate, with an unusual sense of realities, dismissed the case. When Lloyd George spoke at Reading two women appeared from under the platform. In London a man flung a forcible feeding tube in his face. At Louth women's voices were heard in the roof. " Some Rats have got in; let them squeal! " cried Lloyd George. Two women were dragged from the rafters and charged under the Public Meetings Act. Again a Magistrate was independent enough to discharge them, this time with a compliment to their pluck.

In Liverpool, on December 20th, Selina Martin and Leslie Hall, disguised as street hawkers, spoke to Asquith as he stepped from his motor-car to enter a meeting, and one of them tossed a ginger beer bottle into the empty car. No damage was done, but both women were arrested. Bail was refused. They broke the cell windows and hunger struck, were handcuffed, placed in punishment cells, and forcibly fed. Selina Martin was carried face downward by the arms and legs—" frog marching," as it is called—her face being allowed to bump on the steps. The doctor jeered at Leslie Hall, telling her she was " mentally sick," and that feeding her was " like stuffing a turkey for Christmas." These two girls were sentenced on December 27th and held in prison till February 3rd.

In December the Lords had rejected Lloyd George's famous " War-on-Poverty " Budget—a flagrant defiance of the Commons' historic prerogative to control finance. Yet the country was not roused, as repeatedly it had been, with lesser occasion, in the Gladstonian period. Asquith called a General Election in

January, declaring that he would not resume office until furnished with powers to overcome the veto of the Lords. Reminded of his promise to introduce a Reform Bill during the Parliament thus brought to a premature close, he made the following declaration, which largely rehabilitated him in the somewhat damaged confidence of the Liberal women:

" Nearly two years ago I declared on behalf of the present Government that in the event of our bringing in a Reform Bill, we should make the insertion of a women's suffrage amendment an open question for the House of Commons to decide . . . our friends and fellow-workers of the Women's Liberal Federation have asked me to say that my declaration survives the expiring Parliament, and will hold good in its successor (cheers), and that their cause, so far as the Government is concerned, shall be no worse off in the new Parliament than it would have been in the old. I have no hesitation in acceding to that request. . . . The Government . . . has no disposition or desire to burke this question. It is clearly one on which a new House of Commons ought to be given the opportunity to express its views."

The W.S.P.U. denounced the statement as worthless. Calling upon every righteous man to vote against the Government, it sustained a vigorous campaign to this end in no less than forty constituencies. Militant action was suspended during the election, but the soldiers of previous militancy were still being forcibly fed in Liverpool prison. Lady Constance Lytton, devoted in her loyalty to the commands of Clements Inn, was chafing against the dictum which restrained her from an immediate act of solidarity with the hunger strikers. Visiting Mary Gawthorpe, who was already incapacitated by her long illness, she voiced her anxiety and distress. Mary Gawthorpe burst into tears, crying in confirmation of her thought:

" These women are quite unknown—nobody cares about them except their own friends. They go to prison again and again, to be treated like this until it kills them."

The words decided Constance Lytton, although she feared her action might be " displeasing to the leaders." She disguised herself, in poor clothes, and assumed the designation of " Jane Warton, seamstress." At a meeting addressed by Mrs. Baines near Walton Gaol, she spoke up from the crowd, begging the people to go with her to the governor's house and demand the hunger strikers' release. She ran ahead, exhorting the people as she went, and anxious to make certain of arrest she dropped some stones she had brought with her over the hedge of the governor's garden. She was sent to prison for fourteen days in the Third Division, whilst Elsie Howey, a brave young Suffragette who broke a window, just to keep her company, got six weeks. " Jane Warton " was forcibly stripped and clothed in prison dress, and put in a punishment cell. She had not been medically examined on entering the prison, and on the fourth day of her hunger strike she was forcibly fed, without examination. She alleged that Dr. Price, the senior medical officer, struck her contemptuously on the cheek, and left her in a state of collapse. At the second forcible feeding she vomited over his clothes. He was angry: " If you do that again I shall feed you twice! " At the third feeding she vomited continuously, but he pressed the tube down more firmly, and poured in more food. This produced an attack of shivering so serious as to alarm him. He ordered the wardresses to lay her on the bed board, and called to his junior, who was passing, to test her heart. The junior, in jovial mood, listened through his stethoscope for a brief instant, and exclaimed: " Oh, ripping! Splendid heart! You can go on with her! " The senior was not reassured; he pleaded with her, " not as a prison doctor, but as a man," to abandon the hunger strike. On the eighth day of her imprisonment her sister, Lady Emily Lutyens, was apprised by the Press Association of a rumour that she was a prisoner in Liverpool. The Home Office being prepared to release her, Emily Lutyens took the midnight train to Liverpool to bring her sister away next morning. She was informed by Dr. Price that he had never seen " such a bad case of forcible feeding ": Lady Constance being " practically asphyxiated every time." She had lost weight at the rate of 2 lb. a day, and had grown so thin that she could not bear to sit in a chair, and for some time after took her meals kneeling on a cushion. The gravity of her condition was not, however, realized by her family. She went about, wrote letters to the Press, and even spoke at the Queen's Hall a week later. Then came a collapse. Dr. Marion Vaughan was summoned, and ordered her to bed under care of a nurse, testifying that she was suffering from mitral disease of the heart, which was in a dangerous condition, and considerably larger than normal. Not until June was she able to return to ordinary life. She was then appointed a paid organizer of the W.S.P.U., at the commencing wage of a junior organizer, £2 a week, which enabled her to take a small flat in Grey's Inn Road, where she lived alone. She would doubtless have refused a higher salary; yet, on reflection now, it seems an almost unduly modest pittance for one whose extreme delicacy demanded peculiar care and comfort, and the price of whose services must inevitably be the speedy termination of all activity.

A controversy between Sir Edward Troup of the Home Office and her brother, Lord Lytton, ensued as to the veracity of her statements, and the widely differing treatment meted out to Lady Constance Lytton and to "Jane Warton," who both had refused to answer medical inquiries, but neither of whom, the prisoner averred, had refused medical examination. Herbert Gladstone retired from the Home Secretaryship at this juncture, Winston Churchill becoming "prison secretary" in his stead. In the autumn of 1910 Constance Lytton had a paralytic seizure and was bedridden for six weeks. In November, 1911, she was arrested for window breaking, but her fine was paid after four days. Heart attacks were now becoming frequent. On May 5th, 1912, she had a stroke and thereafter was confined to bed and remained in a state of total or partial incapacity until her death in May, 1923. She wrote of herself as:

"One of that numerous gang of upper-class, leisured-class spinsters, unemployed, unpropertied, unendowed, uneducated . . . economically dependent entirely upon others. . . . A maiming subserviency is so conditional to their very existence that it becomes an aim in itself, an ideal. Driven through life with blinkers on, they are unresentful of the bridle."

Tall and excessively spare and slender, her features were refined and sensitive, with an expression of gentle melancholy. In her girlhood she had desired to study music as a profession, and later had wished to become a journalist; but these aspirations not finding favour with her parents, were obediently repressed. Her life-long delicacy, and prolonged existence as a dependent daughter, had bred a morbid self-depreciation and fear of giving offence, and maintained an almost childish ingenuousness of character, though she was by no means without intellectual endowments. Her first attraction to the W.S.P.U., when she was already thirty-nine years of age, had been that through its agency she might go to prison and thereby help the cause of prison reform, which, with the prevention of cruelty to animals, aroused her strongest interest at that time. She felt that even a being so feeble as she might aid the weakest and most forlorn. In the W.S.P.U. her self-confidence grew, yet she wept a night long in prison for fear that a most trivial incident might have offended her sister, and like a great child unburdened her trouble to the wardress for comfort and reassurance. Ever seeking opportunities to serve, she was assiduous in helping the prison hospital cleaners, waiting on the sick, even rubbing the chest of a wardress troubled with a cough. She refused many ameliorations because they were not extended to her companions. Profuse in her expressions of admiration for her Suffragette colleagues, she laid equal emphasis on the kindness and care of her relatives in the illnesses consequent on her suffrage work and imprisonments. A trivial incident reveals her spiritual isolation during the long periods of enforced inactivity. Miss Brackenbury visited her at the house of Emily Lutyens, where she was lying helpless, and asked her little nephews: "Are you not proud of your splendid auntie?" They answered: "No, we think she has done very wrong!"

When she published the story of her experiences she asked that a medallion I had designed for the W.S.P.U. might be placed on the cover, and insisted on sending to the *Women's Dreadnought*, of which I was editor, half the small sums she received in royalties from the book. So slender were her means at this time, that, although she was a regular subscriber to that penny weekly paper until her death, she could not afford to send an annual subscription, but paid for it by instalments.

CHAPTER VIII

THE TRUCE AND THE CONCILIATION BILL

HAVING called an election to strengthen his hands, Asquith, on the contrary, had lost a hundred seats to the Conservatives, and resumed office without a majority. Having but 275 Liberal seats, against 273 Conservative, 82 Irish Nationalist and 40 Labour, his Government was dependent upon the support of the Irish for its existence. In Ireland John Redmond was regarded by the growing Sinn Fein and old Fenian elements as a time-serving, almost pro-English palterer; in London he was considered as the imperative taskmaster of procrastinating Asquith, in the attack on the House of Lords, which barred the way to Home Rule. The small Labour Party, standing, almost unconsciously, for profound economic changes, was in a position of difficulty and discouragement; a Party too small to accomplish anything in Parliament of itself; its members unwilling to occupy the Ishmaelite position in the House which had been that of Keir Hardie as a Party of one.

The King's Speech of 1910 contained but a single legislative proposal: the restriction of the veto of the House of Lords. All other questions were thrust aside, the Liberal Suffragist Members showing their solidarity with the Government by refusing to ballot for a Votes for Women Bill.

Other auguries were unpromising. At the Labour Party Conference in February a composite resolution from several branches, declaring that any attempt to exclude women from the proposed Reform Bill would be met by the " uncompromising hostility of organized Labour to the whole Bill," was confided to Margaret Bondfield. She withdrew, however, the last four words, on the protest of Henderson that they might " wreck a great scheme of electoral reform, if, by some accident, the women were left out." The intention of the resolution was thus completely negatived. The incident was denounced by the suffragists as typical of " adult suffragist treachery." It is, indeed, a curious fact that the women who secured political office when the citizenship of women was achieved had none of them taken a prominent part in the struggle for the vote; the first woman Cabinet Minister having remained during the greater part of her public life uninterested in the question.

An ominous harbinger of further hostilities was the

announcement by the new Home Secretary, Winston Churchill,[1] of a new prison rule specially framed for Suffragette prisoners, which would avoid both the latitude of the First Division, and the grosser hardships and humiliations of the ordinary prison discipline. Yet militancy, suspended for the General Election, had not been renewed. Rumours were abroad that the Government was disposed to relent, and desirous of obtaining a peaceful atmosphere, in order to do so gracefully. In close converse with Christabel, the Pethick Lawrences and Constance Lytton, H. N. Brailsford was quietly and persistently gathering a "Conciliation Committee" of Members of Parliament, drawn from all Parties, under the chairmanship of Lord Lytton, to promote an agreed Bill.

In this peaceful interlude Mrs. Lawrence went abroad for a brief holiday, inviting Annie Kenney and me to join her at Innsbruck and proceed to Oberammergau for the Passion Play. We travelled in easy stages through mountain roads, fringed by white, upright stones which brought to my mind the haunting fancy that they might stand for the tombstones of the workers by whose hard toil these roads were made. At Parten Kirchen we visited a cottage workshop among the meadows. A woman sat by the door painting a swag of flowers on a basket. In pleasant, informal companionship, a group of workers were producing the painted toys and furniture characteristic of the locality. We learnt that the organizer of the industry had been the "black sheep" of his village till he discovered his aptitude for this craft. That took my thoughts back to the drear wastefulness of our English prisons, and my impatience to have the vote struggle over and done with that we might move on to constructive work caused an unrestful undercurrent in my mind.

In the beautiful vale of Oberammergau the Passion Play was a tremendous spectacle; a thousand men, women and children appeared on the vast stage, habituated from childhood to the practice of this and kindred plays. The choir was magnificent. Some of the most famous Biblical pictures the art of Europe has produced guided the composition of the tableaux. Yet it was not the Passion Play, but the life of its people which most greatly rejoiced me. It was a village of craftsmen; wood carvers, potters, fresco-painters, wherein was no poverty. The carving school was famous. A circulating library brought books from Munich, the Art Club lent reproductions of great pictures to hang for a period in the home, or for

[1] Herbert Gladstone had resigned to become Governor of South Africa, not sorry to be released from an invidious position.

copying in fresco on its outer walls. The visitors who flocked thither at all times, and especially during the Passion Play, were a substantial source of income. The village committee allocated lodgings to the guests, payments were pooled and distributed, a proportion being kept for common needs and the provident fund. Co-operative shops sold the wares of the craftsmen, though each might dispose of them privately should he choose. We stayed at the house of Anton Lang, the potter, who was playing the part of Christ. Our host and his wife and sister spoke excellent English. They were eager to learn of the English Suffragettes, and especially of Constance Lytton, whose adventure as " Jane Warton " had sent its thrill thus far.

At Parten Kirchen we had learnt of King Edward's death. Behind the clamant domestic controversies of his reign, looming as an ominous shadow, in wait to cloud all other issues, reared Foreign Policy. Two ideals strove for mastery : imperialism and aggressive armaments, *versus* arbitration and conciliation, with the ultimate goal of international citizenship in the United States of the World. Between these poles a multitude of rival policies contended : the neutrality of Britain, a moderate navy and small army, *versus* participation in alliances which would make this country the decisive factor in a world balance of power, a policy entailing a great navy and an army organized for expansion in case of war. This last was the policy of the Liberal Cabinet. Insatiable Conservative hot-bloods demanded more battle-ships. A section of the Liberals—Brailsford, Ponsonby, Trevelyan and others—strove to turn the Government towards internationalism, or neutrality at least; and thereby found themselves, willy-nilly, in frequent alliance with Keir Hardie and the pacifist section of the Labour Party, which most of them were eventually to join. As a constitutional sovereign, and perhaps with somewhat more of personal impulse than was indispensable to his office, King Edward had borne the ceremonial part in cementing the French and Russian alliances, which were to counter German expansion in industry, commerce, territory and raw materials. Victoria had differed vehemently with the foreign policies of her Ministers; Edward, for his agreement with the Governments preceding the greatest war in history, was termed " the peacemaker."

At his death Parliamentary controversies were for the moment suspended. We learnt this in Oberammergau, and news presently reached us from Clements Inn that all W.S.P.U. propaganda had been stopped until after the Royal funeral; a great procession had been postponed for a month. *Votes for Women*, black bordered, displayed the portrait of Queen

Alexandra as its cover, and the following week that of Queen Mary.   Christabel, daughter of Republican Dr. Pankhurst, vied with the Conservative organs in her expressions of devotion to the Throne.   In her repetition of the legend of the peacemaking achieved in the reign of Edward, it was as though she knew nothing of the struggle convulsing the groups of political thinkers through which she had passed; had heard no protests against the race of naval armaments, no cries of alarm at the division of Europe into two armed camps.   She had been untouched by Keir Hardie's impassioned protests against British aid in stabilizing the Tsarist Government, which had extermin- ated the popular uprising of 1905-6 with torture and massacre, and in two years had executed upwards of 3,000 political prisoners, and butchered 19,000 people by its " Black Hundreds."   The struggle for freedom in Russia she dismissed as a " men's movement."   The representatives of the suppressed Duma who came to London appealing for the support of British democrats, were to her merely " old Liberals."   She made no effort to see beyond them.

Early in June the Conciliation Committee announced its decision to promote a Bill to give votes to women householders and women occupiers of business premises of a rateable value of not less than £10 a year.   Marriage was not to be actually a disqualification; yet it was expressly stated that husband and wife might not vote for the same property, though two men might qualify as joint householders or occupiers under the existing law. The Bill invited many lines of attack : it would enfranchise little more than a million women, approximately one woman in thirteen, and these mainly elderly widows and spinsters.   It excluded several classes who could have voted under the then franchise laws had they been men.   By abandoning the technical equality of the original Bill, a precedent would be created for inequalities under an adult suffrage measure.

The committee had mainly aimed at placating the prejudices of the Conservatives; its other members, anxious, in Zangwill's witty phrase, to secure, " not Votes for Liberals, or Votes for Labour, but Votes for Women," were content to accept any sort of measure.   Their abnegation was not, however, successful. Many members of the Liberal and Labour Parties outside the committee were not prepared to assent to such a franchise, as they believed that a majority of the elderly widows and spinsters, the largest class covered by the Bill, would give their votes to the Tories.   These objectors preferred to enfranchise the younger married women whom they held to be more progressive. Whether Lloyd George, the main opponent of the Conciliation

Bill, was sincere in his professions; whether he was the arch anti-Suffragist he was considered by the W.S.P.U.; whether he deliberately plotted to kill both the Conciliation Bill and all other Suffrage opportunities, in order to rescue the Prime Minister from a dilemma without estranging the Liberal Suffragists, only he could know. It is probable that he veered to a certain extent from point to point; and that there were times, at least, when he was genuinely desirous of assisting the Suffrage question, provided it were not necessary for him to stake too much on the issue. Be that as it may, it must be emphasized that the Conciliation Bill, in spite of its name, was in reality a highly controversial measure, and that it made the mistake of flouting the political interests of the Party in power, which alone could ensure its passage. The measure was even drafted so as to preclude widening amendments, though Asquith, in offering a free vote on a Suffrage amendment to his projected Reform Bill, had made the possibility of amendment a stipulation. The Liberal opinion of the case was never clearly visualized and considered by the Suffrage leaders, militant or non-militant. One and all, they held firmly to the belief, largely a legacy from the early days of the movement, that the narrower their demand, the greater its chances of success. Without exception they approved the Bill, and the Women's Liberal Federation, the I.L.P., the Women's Labour League, the Fabian Society and the Women's Co-operative Guild fell into line behind them. The anti-Suffragists, and the Adult Suffragists who did virtually no work for suffrage of any sort, were the only dissentients.

To secure the atmosphere of conciliation required for the Bill, the W.S.P.U. now formally announced a truce from militant action, though the Government was still to be attacked in the by-elections. As I told Mrs. Pankhurst at once, I was opposed to the terms of the Bill, both because I regarded it as too narrow for justice, and also because I believed its narrowness would not avert, but rather contribute to its failure. Mrs. Pankhurst herself had always opposed such measures in the past; she had clung tenaciously to the original Bill of 1870. The Conciliation Committee had not succeeded, as yet, in producing any sign of the Government's alleged change of heart, though militancy had remained in abeyance. The W.S.P.U. had hitherto persistently declared that it would never cease from militancy till a Government measure had been obtained. Now that the Court and the Government were peculiarly anxious to avoid all signs of dissension, in view of the approaching Coronation festivities, it seemed to me that no promise of a truce should have been issued till concessions from the Government had been secured. Christabel, who had entered now into aristocratic Conservative circles, believed a display of loyalty without concessions to be essential, though her great loyalty of those days was later to be flung to the winds. Mrs. Pankhurst admitted the truth of my contentions, but declared the matter was decided, and unity essential. I felt the force of the latter argument, and saw that she herself had only accepted the situation under the pressure of Christabel.

All the Suffrage Societies worked strenuously for the Bill; the W.S.P.U., as ever, on by far the largest scale. Again it filled the Albert Hall[1] three times in succession, as well as the largest provincial halls, and held a monster procession, to which it invited all other Suffrage Societies, and a Hyde Park demonstration with forty platforms. Every week several hundred meetings were held in London. Memorials were presented from prominent doctors, social workers, educationists, writers, musicians and representatives of the Church and the stage. Resolutions in support of the Bill were passed by the Australian Senate and House of Representatives, and by 182 City, Town and Urban District Councils.[2] No public body ever recorded a vote against Women's Suffrage. Yet the Bill had that session no Parliamentary place and could not be debated save by Government favour. Asquith was bombarded with appeals. On June 21st he first received a deputation of Liberal women and Constitutional Suffragists, then two deputations of anti-Suffragists. The Liberal women threatened that if he would not implement his pledges, they would go to the constituencies, not to support him in his struggle against the veto of the House of Lords, but to complain that he had " vetoed the House of Commons." Mrs. Fawcett warned him that if the hopes resting on the Conciliation Bill were defeated, the militants would break forth again. She often repudiated militancy, but in dealing with the Government she never failed to make it her principal argument. Asquith gave the deputation no answer, replying that he would declare the intention of his Government to the Commons. He then received the anti-Suffragists, and informed them that so far as he

---

[1] On November 15th, 1910, Lord Lytton, in a letter to Mr. Asquith, showed that in the past twelve months six meetings for Women's Suffrage had been held in the Albert Hall, thirty-four in the Queen's Hall, whilst all other movements together had held but three meetings in the Albert Hall and thirteen in the Queen's Hall.

[2] These included:

Birmingham passed by 31 to 15.	Glasgow passed unanimously.
Manchester passed by 44 to 19.	Edinburgh passed 24 to 2.
Liverpool passed by 43 to 10.	Dundee carried unanimously.
Sheffield passed by 38 to 6.	Dublin carried unanimously.
Leeds passed without division.	Cardiff by 24 to 4.

was concerned they were " preaching to the converted," but his Cabinet must decide the issue. Finally he granted July 11th and 12th for the Second Reading of the Conciliation Bill. When that time came Lloyd George asked the Speaker whether the Bill was so framed as to admit of widening amendments, and on receiving a negative reply, he spoke and voted against it. Churchill and Asquith did the same. Nevertheless the Bill was carried by 299 votes to 189,[1] a majority of 110. The Conciliation Committee desired the Bill to proceed automatically to a standing committee, in order that it might pass another legislative stage without hindrance. The Speaker, on this occasion, made no move to prevent this; but to smother the Bill in the old way, an opponent proposed to commit it to the whole House as before. Haldane strongly supported this course, insisting that it would mean no delay, and urging that unless so important a measure had been debated by the whole House at every stage, the Lords would have an excuse for throwing it out. The ingenuous might have assumed from the speech of this Minister that if the Bill were referred to the whole House the Government would give time for the House to deal with it. Unfortunately for his reputation as a sincere man, Haldane subsequently quoted as a proof of desire to suppress the Bill the decision of the House to follow his advice. This decision was made by 320 votes to 175, Ramsay Macdonald and four other members of the Labour Party voting with the majority against the Conciliation Committee. Asquith presently stated that the Government could give no further time to the Bill that session, nor in any session to any Bill the title of which was so framed as to preclude amendment. The Conciliation Committee's anxiety to secure Conservative votes had given a loophole, as was emphasized by Lloyd George, to refuse further facilities for the Bill. The Committee had no alternative but to recast the measure.

The W.S.P.U. was now threatening renewed militancy and enrolling volunteers for the next " raid." At the City Temple two members of the Men's League, Duval and Jacobs, assailed Lloyd George with the familiar cry. Refused the benefits of the new rule 243A, they hunger struck and were forcibly fed. Yet, with this exception, the truce continued.

Since May the leaders of the Liberal and Conservative Parties had been sitting in secret conclave, with a view to achieving an

---

[1] The official report gave 190 " noes," but an analysis of the voting was given by the *Nation* as follows:

For		Against	
Liberal 161	Unionist 87	Liberal 60	Unionist 113
Labour 31	Nationalist 20	Labour 2	Nationalist 14

agreed settlement of the House of Lords controversy, in order that political strife might not mar the unity of the Coronation. Tariff Reform, Conscription, and above all Home Rule were also discussed. It was rumoured that the British Constitution was being recast under pressure of the Irish Party. It is truer to say that the Conservatives were demanding their price for the surrender of the Lords' veto. At the end of July Parliament adjourned till November. On the eve of its resumption a rumour was circulated that the Conference was discussing a Franchise Bill. The sleepless suspicions of the W.S.P.U. were aroused. Deputations were sent to interview Birrell and Grey; both these Ministers replied that facilities for the Conciliation Bill would not be granted in 1910, and urged concentration on 1911. This was as match to the tinder; the truce was immediately abandoned.

CHAPTER IX

A NINTH " Women's Parliament " was called for the Caxton Hall on November 18th. It was dramatically timed. Ten days before, Asquith had disclosed the breakdown of the House of Lords Conference; the Parties had refused to agree. Whilst the women were assembling in the Caxton Hall, he announced his intention to dissolve Parliament ten days later, and to take all the time of the House for Government business. Keir Hardie requested two hours to discuss a resolution that the Government should leave time for the Conciliation Bill. Asquith promised to answer him in a few moments, but left the House without doing so.

Meanwhile three hundred women, in detachments of twelve, were approaching. Mrs. Pankhurst, Dr. Elizabeth Garrett Anderson, one of the earliest women doctors, first of the Women Mayors and sister of Mrs. Fawcett, Hertha Ayrton, the scientist, Mrs. Cobden Sanderson, three aged women : Miss Neligan, Mrs. Saul Solomon, and Mrs. Brackenbury, and the Princess Dhuleep Singh. Mrs. Pankhurst and this first company were allowed to reach the House and even taken to the Prime Minister's room; unable to see him, they returned to the Strangers' Entrance. Members of Parliament flocked out to speak to them—Lord Castlereagh moved an amendment on the lines of Keir Hardie's motion. It was debated for an hour; only fifty-two Members voted for it, but it drew from Asquith a promise to state on the following Tuesday his Government's intentions respecting Votes for Women. In the throes of the constitutional crisis, with the struggle of Nationalist Ireland *versus* Ulster driving the country towards civil war, Votes for Women was in the forefront of the stage: a triumph indeed for the militants. Outside in the Square were scenes of unexampled violence. I had promised to report the affair for *Votes for Women,* and I was obliged to avoid arrest as I was writing a history of the militant movement[1] under contract with the publishers. With Annie Kenney I took a taxi and drove about, the driver nothing loath to make his way into the throng. Finding it unbearable thus to watch other women knocked about, with a violence more than common even on such occasions, we jumped out of the taxi, but soon

[1] *The Suffragette.* Gay & Hancock.

returned to it, for policemen in uniform and plain clothes struck us in the chest, seized us by the arms and flung us to the ground. This was the common experience. I saw Ada Wright knocked down a dozen times in succession. A tall man with a silk hat fought to protect her as she lay on the ground, but a group of policemen thrust him away, seized her again, hurled her into the crowd and felled her again as she turned. Later I saw her lying against the wall of the House of Lords, with a group of anxious women kneeling round her. Two girls with linked arms were being dragged about by two uniformed policemen. One of a group of officers in plain clothes ran up and kicked one of the girls, whilst the others laughed and jeered at her. Again and again we saw the small deputations struggling through the crowd with their little purple bannerettes: "Asquith has vetoed our Bill." The police snatched the flags, tore them to shreds, and smashed the sticks, struck the women with fists and knees, knocked them down, some even kicked them, then dragged them up, carried them a few paces and flung them into the crowd of sightseers. For six hours this continued. From time to time we returned to the Caxton Hall, where doctors and nurses were attending to women who had been hurt. We saw the women go out and return exhausted, with black eyes, bleeding noses, bruises, sprains and dislocations. The cry went round: "Be careful; they are dragging women down the side streets!" We knew this always meant greater ill-usage. I saw Cecilia Haig go out with the rest; a tall, strongly built, reserved woman, comfortably situated, who in ordinary circumstances might have gone through life without ever receiving an insult, much less a blow. She was assaulted with violence and indecency, and died in December, 1911, after a painful illness, arising from her injuries. Henria Williams, already suffering from a weak heart, did not recover from the treatment she received that night in the Square, and died on January 1st. Even some of the old ladies who accompanied Mrs. Pankhurst in the first deputation but were separated from her in the crowd, were subjected to ill-usage. Mrs. Saul Solomon was thrown to the ground in front of the mounted police. She complained of violent and indecent treatment, and suffered the result of it for many months.

H. N. Brailsford and Dr. Jessie Murray collected evidence from witnesses and sufferers, who testified to deliberate acts of cruelty, such as twisting and wrenching of arms, wrists, and thumbs; gripping the throat and forcing back the head; pinching the arms; striking the face with fists, sticks, helmets; throwing women down and kicking them; rubbing a woman's face against the railings; pinching the breasts; squeezing the ribs. A girl under arrest was marched to the police station with her skirts over her head. An old woman of seventy was knocked down by a blow in the face, receiving a black eye and a wound on the back of the head. The Conciliation Committee requested a Government inquiry into the conduct of the police, but Churchill refused. He said that instead of dispersing the women by a baton charge, or permitting the disorders to continue for a long time, it had been his desire to have them arrested as soon as they gave lawful occasion. It was his predecessor, not he, who had given orders to make as few arrests as possible. His own directions had not been " fully understood or carried out."[1] This explanation was received with derision by those who had witnessed the scenes. It was contradicted by its author's own subsequent statement:[2] " No orders, verbal or written, directly or indirectly emanating from me, were given to the police."

One hundred and fifteen women and two men had been arrested on " Black Friday," as the day was afterwards named. When they appeared at Bow Street the majority of the charges were withdrawn in view of the General Election. Only the women accused of window breaking or assaults upon the police were proceeded against.

The Women's Parliament remained in session awaiting the Premier's statement on Tuesday. It was:

" The Government will, if they are still in power, give facilities in the next Parliament for effectively proceeding with a Bill, if so framed as to admit of free amendment."

Shouts of disgust greeted this repetition. It was stigmatized as " worthless." " I am going to Downing Street: come along, all of you! " commanded Mrs. Pankhurst, and off they went, taking the police unawares. Only a line of constables two deep could be mustered to bar their entry to the official street. The Inspector, outnumbered, endeavoured to parley with Mrs. Pankhurst; we two, standing on the roof of our taxi, shouted to the women in the rear: " Push forward! " Mrs. Haverfield, in the van, cried: " Shove along, girls! " In a moment the police ranks were broken. The little purple bannerettes went surging forward. Police reinforcements were hurried to the scene. In the midst of the fight Asquith himself appeared, unaware of the struggle, and found himself surrounded by angry women. The police hurried him into a taxi as a woman dashed her fist through one of its windows. Birrell was also encountered by several women, and in hastening away from them, twisted his

---

[1] House of Commons, March 8th, 1910.
[2] House of Commons, March 13th, 1910.

knee. Mrs. Pankhurst and over a hundred others were arrested. During the night parties of women broke windows in Cabinet Ministers' houses. The total arrests amounted to 159. On Wednesday another attempt to reach the House resulted in 18 arrests, and window breaking on Thursday accounted for a further 21, making a total of 285 arrests in the three days of militant action.

Again all charges were withdrawn, except for assault and window breaking. Seventy-five women were now in prison, and ten of them had admitted striking the police in defence of other women. Mrs. Haverfield was imprisoned for leading the police horses out of their ranks, a characteristic action. She was an accomplished horsewoman, and during the South African War had formed a remount camp of horses left on the veldt to die. She habitually wore a hunting-stock and a small black riding hat. When first she joined the Suffragette movement her expression was cold and proud; one felt that bitterness, rather than love, was the impelling motive of her militancy. I was repelled when she told me that she had felt no affection for her children. During her years in the Suffrage movement her sympathies so broadened that she seemed to have undergone a rebirth.

After the "battle of Downing Street," Mrs. Cobden Sanderson, exhausted by the fray, remained near the end of the street when the crowd had dispersed. Winston Churchill, encountering her, called up a policeman and ordered: "Drive that woman away!" The shock to her was great; she had often been his hostess and was on intimate terms with his wife's family. Immediately afterwards young Hugh Franklin, nephew to a member of the Government, Herbert Samuel, came up, and learning the reason of her distress, declared: "I will whip him for this!" A few days later Churchill spoke in Bradford; Franklin was present with others to heckle. As they were flung out Churchill taunted them, decrying their zeal as "money-fed." The charge was deeply resented by these men, who often at great personal sacrifice were doing this wholly without pay, and receiving, at most, their bare travelling expenses. One of them, Alfred Hawkins, a young workman, sustained a double fracture to the knee at this meeting, and was lamed for life. He eventually secured £100 damages against the promoters of the meeting. In the train back to London, Franklin rushed into Churchill's compartment with a whip, but was prevented from striking him. He was imprisoned for six weeks, and being refused the ameliorations of Churchill's new prison rule 243A, he hunger struck and was forcibly fed.

Amongst the seventy-five Suffragettes now in Holloway was

Mrs. Pankhurst's sister, Mary Clarke. On ceasing to be Mrs. Pankhurst's deputy in the Registrarship, she had become an organizer for the W.S.P.U., and thereby found release from the regretful memories of an unhappy marriage. Facing the rude violence of the seaside rowdies at Brighton, where she was stationed, she displayed a quiet, persistent courage, which made peculiarly large demands on one so sensitive. Exerting her frail physique to its utmost, she was grievously ill on the eve of " Black Friday," and her Brighton comrades had begged her not to go. She had promised to take the easier course of arrest for window breaking, and had telegraphed to Brighton from the Police Court: " One month: I am content to pay the price of victory."

Preparing to leave for America, and revising the final chapters of *The Suffragette,* I spent Christmas alone at Linden Gardens. Early on the morning of Boxing Day I saw at the window my mother's face, haggard and drawn. I ran to admit her: " Something has happened! " " Aunt Mary is not very well," she faltered. " She is dead, I know."

Yes; she was dead, our gentle confidante, too frail to weather this rude tide of militant struggle. Released from prison two days before, she had spoken at the welcome luncheon in London, hastened to Brighton to address a welcome meeting there the same night, and returned on Christmas Eve to her brother's house in London. She was with Mrs. Pankhurst and others of the family at the midday Christmas dinner, and quietly left the table. When Mrs. Pankhurst went to look for her she found her unconscious. She had burst a blood vessel on the brain.

Stunned by this sudden blow, we spent the next days together, my mother coming to Southampton to see me sail.

Engrossed in work for my book, and desiring no other relaxation than to gaze on the tremendous grandeur of the seas, I paid little attention either to passengers or officers. I remember a sensation of pity for the third-class passengers, coming on board at Queenstown, and made to pause in mid-gangway to have their eyeballs examined by the doctor. On the last day the doctor, who had occasionally spoken a brief word in passing, astonished me by a proposal of marriage, mainly motived, I gathered, by the desire to save me from the militant movement. That was how it affected some people of protective tendencies. I questioned myself, most searchingly, as to whether I had inadvertently said or done anything to encourage this undue interest in my welfare, but was able to exonerate myself from culpability.

The jagged silhouette of New York City showed like a

ruined castle on the horizon. It was intensely cold, with great blocks of ice jamming the harbour. That learned nurse, Lavinia Dock, Mrs. Stanton Blatch, and Mrs. Winters Brannan of the Women's Political Union met me with a flock of Pressmen, who kept me busy with interviews for three entire days. They were exceedingly young, almost like schoolboys, I thought. I received them in relays, four to six at a time. " Don't you take notes? " I asked them, anxious for accurate reports. " We are not stenographers! " they replied indignantly, but I rang for the " bell girl," and sent for notebooks and pencils from the stationer's stall in the hotel. The young men amiably permitted me to suggest the questions and dictate the answers. The result was excellent; the interviews, which appeared all over the country, were so good that whilst the Civic Forum Lecture Bureau had only booked two engagements for me on my arrival, telegrams for dates began pouring in, and during my three months' stay I could satisfy only a small proportion of those who were asking me to speak, though I travelled almost every night, and spoke once, twice or thrice a day. I had arrived at the height of the interest and sympathy felt by America in the English movement. Everywhere the Press was wholly benign towards me, except in Chicago, where the difference arose from my own action. It happened that I had there a day to spare. I attempted to spend it quietly writing, and to postpone my interviews with the reporters till the morrow. This incensed some of them extremely. Some battered persistently on my door, others invented the most atrocious interviews, which were published with faked photographs in which I appeared an appalling hooligan. A newspaper containing one such caricature was flung over the head of the chambermaid as she entered my room. Seeing it, I capitulated immediately, but the Press men and women did not entirely relent. Arriving after an all-night journey at Desmoines, Iowa, having entirely lost my voice, I was met by a group of women, who told me that at noon I must address the Senate and the House of Representatives in joint convention. The only woman who had previously done so was Susan B. Anthony, on Married Woman's Property, forty years before. I whispered that my voice was gone, but Dr. Dewey, an osteopath, assured me that she would put it right for me, and she absolutely fulfilled her promise in a miraculous manner. A Bill to enfranchise the women of Iowa was then pending, and in view of this I felt very deeply the responsibility laid upon me. The Speaker bowed low and led me to the dais to speak; the legislators were cordial. The women assured me I had helped them. Later I spoke before the Michigan Legislature at Lansing, and to the Judiciary Committees of Illinois and New York State; in each case a Suffrage Bill was before the House. I went East through Canada to St. John's, New Brunswick, West to California, South to Tennessee, speaking in the principal cities at public meetings in great halls and theatres, men's and women's city, literary, social, political, dinner, and luncheon clubs, at many universities and colleges, and to the inmates of a women's prison. Everywhere I met crowded halls and tremendous enthusiasm, the audiences streaming on to the platform at the close of the meeting to shake my hand in the American way and send their greetings to the British movement.

I visited the Indian University in Arksansas and the Negro University in Tennessee. When it was announced that I was to address the latter, I was astonished to find every newspaper I opened on my journey thither, protesting against my action. Wherever I went my hostesses took me to see the prisons. I saw the terrible Harrison Street Gaol, Chicago, where the cells were almost in darkness. In Tennessee I saw the tank, a great cage, enclosing a number of smaller cages, in which the prisoners were confined. Each small cage had two wooden shelves, one above the other, which served as beds. For exercise the occupants of the small cages were let out into the large cage, to stand about, or prowl to and fro like animals at the zoo. There was no privacy for any of them, day or night. In each small cage was an open w.c. without a lid. The inmates had no power to flush it; this was done for all the closets at once by a lever outside, when the warder chose to work it, as he did once or twice a day, so he told us. A spare old man, his face as white and delicately featured as though of finely-chiselled ivory, stood with closed eyes, his folded arms resting upon the upper shelf. A heavy thud startled me as we took our leave. The old man had fallen. "He is ill!" I urged, but our guide hurried us away. "He is only drunk!" he insisted. I thought otherwise and came away torn by anguished, impotent revolt against this cruelty. Tragic indeed was the sight of the women prisoners, housed in a single room, whites and negroes together, with a wooden shelf round the wall, which served for seats by day and beds by night. A pale negress, with a face of beautiful despair, recalled wonderful Lydia Yavorska in Maxim Gorky's *Lowest Depths*.

Conditions varied; in some gaols the prisoners had nothing but the walls and the bars to contemplate; in others they had occupation. In one prison I heard the terrible cries of drug takers, deprived of their habitual poison. In another I saw a miner from Wales, who had killed a man in a quarrel, and who, having covered with paintings of his native valleys the three walls of the cell he shared with another inmate, had now taken to learning musical instruments. Among the features common to many prisons, which I found particularly bad, was the fact that the cell windows received light and air only through a barred gate opening on to a corridor, lit, as a rule, by a sky-light. Two or three inmates often shared a cell, and in its confined space were sometimes employed at knitting machines, brushmaking or other work. Some prisons were like mediæval dungeons in their darkness and absence of arrangements for cleanliness of person or clothing.

I saw great wealth and luxury, the fevered quest of some men to spend money, and of some women to get culture, the squalid poverty of the new immigrants, the nightmare industrialism of Pittsburg. I visited dozens of factories and laundries, and found in some of them most horrible conditions. Yet American women constantly told me there was no need for them to take an interest in politics, because American conditions were so good. I met Jane Addams at Hull House, Lillian Wald at Henry Street, Mrs. Raymond Robbins and Rose Schneidermann, who were immersed in the Garment Workers' Strike, and Mrs. Glendower Evans of Boston, who spoke of Robert La Follette as "my big boy." I took a midday cup of chocolate with Booth Tarkington, the novelist, whose sister informed me that he never rose before 1 p.m. I met Max Eastman, then apparently a very shy young fellow, and his sister Crystal. I lost my heart to the lovely Lewisohn sisters, expending their wealth and talents for the creation of a school of dance and drama for the young people of New York's East Side at Henry Street Settlement.

At St. Louis, the Gateway to the Southern States, my train missed its connection. I had many hours to wait. I walked through the sordid streets about the station, overcome by a tremendous loneliness. I saw wretched garments on sale there, priced for the poor, made in the sweat shop. I passed the windows of pornographic "Dime Museums," and saloons where two-course lunches were offered free to customers who would drink. Sometimes, as I watched from the railway carriage windows the interminable plains, mournful with the withered brown stalks of last year's maize; or tossed in the stuffy berth at night, a wondering sadness fell on me that Fate should be rushing me on in this strange way. Sometimes I felt like a poor caged bird beating its wings ineffectually for escape. Depression, almost despair, dwelt with me crossing the desert of New Mexico, where, hour on hour, nothing but red sand met the eye, marked by the tiny imprint of birds' claws, with here and there a group of whitening bones.   Sometimes, at rare intervals, we passed a cluster of sun-dried huts on a little strip of cultivated land—an Indian reservation; sometimes a dark Indian, his figure crouching low, would be seen swiftly running across the sand—the desert, all that civilization had left to them.   I was alone, so utterly alone on this vast continent, longing to make and to do—condemned to travel and to speak.   Yet in the great meetings a vision of Hope for Humanity always guided me— resplendent, triumphant!

At Minneapolis with a day to spare, I arrived in such exhaustion that I slept almost continuously for thirty-six hours. I heard Niagara, but at a neighbouring junction received a telegram that I must leave the train immediately and travel by another route on account of the snow.   I had to quit my berth, drag on a coat, and jump out with my garments in my arms, whilst the porter threw out my bags.

Life in the States seemed a whirl, with harsh, rude extremes, rough and unfinished, yet with scope and opportunity for young people and with more receptivity to new ideas than is found in the old countries: I thought that some day I might become an American citizen.

CHAPTER X

THE second election of 1910 left the position of Parties virtually as before. Yet the fact that a further appeal to the country had brought no change, had actually strengthened the position of the Government. The limitation of the Lords' veto, and the establishment of quinquennial Parliaments were the main item of the King's Speech. The W.S.P.U. had easily been persuaded to return to the truce, in the interests of the Conciliation Bill, which had been re-drafted to apply only to women householders, the £10 occupiers' qualification being omitted. To comply with the stipulations of Asquith and Lloyd George, the title now left the Bill open to amendment. Its supporters had won the three first places in the ballot, and were able to give it the best available place. Though militancy was in suspense, the W.S.P.U. still attacked the Government candidates in the elections. Tax resistance and resistance to enumeration under the Census of that year were mild forms of militancy now in vogue. The Women's Freedom League had hoisted the standard of " no vote, no tax " in the early days of its formation, and Mrs. Despard and others had suffered a succession of distraints, to the accompaniment of auction sale protest meetings. In November, 1910, the W.S.P.U. first adopted the same policy, and the Women's Tax Resistance League was formed about this time. In May, 1911, two women were imprisoned for refusal to take out dog licences. A little later, Clemence Housman, sister of the author-artist, Laurence Housman, was committed to Holloway till she should pay the trifling sum of 4s. 6d., but was released in a week's time, having paid nothing.

On May 5th the Conciliation Bill passed the Second Reading by 255 votes to 88, a majority of 167 made up of 145 Liberals, 53 Conservatives, 26 Labour members and 31 Nationalists. Reversing the policy of former years, its sponsors immediately moved that it be referred to a committee of the whole House, thus leaving it, as before, dependent on Government pleasure for further progress—a challenge to Asquith to provide the facilities he had promised. The title of the Bill now permitted amendment and was therefore regarded as meeting his conditions. The Bill applied now only to women householders. The £10 occupiers (usually poor lodgers in unfurnished rooms) were

351

thrown out as a sop to Liberal democratic ideas. During the debate Parliament Square was packed with women, who were allowed, in view of the truce, to gather there unmolested. There was tremendous rejoicing in suffrage ranks. Desire was so ardently mother to belief that even the W.S.P.U. was confident of success. Petitions rolled up in support of the Bill. The Lord Mayor of Dublin, with the Irish mace and double-handed sword of justice borne before him, and accompanied by the Town Clerk and other civic officials, appeared in person to present a petition in support of the Bill at the Bar of the House of Commons. The hope of victory, and with it the readiness to erase old controversies, was abroad; the W.S.P.U. gave a dinner to the Lord Mayor of Dublin, and invited the leaders of the other principal suffrage societies, including Mrs. Fawcett, Mrs. Despard and several Members of Parliament, to propose the toasts. The Conciliation Committee continued agitating for facilities for its Bill in that session of Parliament.

On May 29th Lloyd George stated in the House that the Government could do nothing in 1911, but in 1912 a day would be granted for the Second Reading of a Bill capable of free amendment, and if it should again pass the Second Reading, a week for its further stages. The W.S.P.U. was not satisfied. Eventually Asquith wrote to Lord Lytton :

" The week offered will be interpreted with reasonable elasticity, and the Government will oppose no obstacle to a proper use of the closure. . . . The extra days for Report and Third Reading would not be refused.

" The Government, though divided in their opinion on the merits of the Bill, are unanimous in their determination to give effect, not only in the letter, but in the spirit to the promise in regard to facilities which I made on their behalf before the last General Election."

At this there was great rejoicing. Christabel, now entirely confident, declared in *Votes for Women* :

" It is a pledge upon which we can base the expectation of taking part as voters in the election of the next and every future Parliament."

The Liberal *Nation*[1] said :

" From the moment the Prime Minister signed this frank and ungrudging letter, women became in all but the legal formality voters and citizens."

Again the W.S.P.U. had invited all other suffrage organizations to join in a great procession—" The Women's Coronation Procession," as it was called. For the first time the old non-

[1] June 24th, 1911.

militant faction accepted an invitation from the militants: upwards of forty thousand women marched five abreast, taking three hours to pass a given point. It was a triumph of organization, a pageant of science, art, nursing, education, poverty, factory-dom, slumdom, youth, age, labour, motherhood; a beautiful and imposing spectacle. Marian Wallace Dunlop, the first hunger striker, and Edith Downing had arranged a pageant of Empire and of History, beginning with the abbesses and peeresses summoned to Parliament in the reign of Edward III. At the head of the procession walked seven hundred ex-prisoners. Elizabeth Wolstenholme Elmy, " the oldest Suffragette," in a balcony in St. James's Street, was saluted as we passed.

Mrs. Saul Solomon rode in a bath-chair carrying a flag: " Join the deputation! " a reminder of militancy. I shared her scepticism. Leaving the ranks of the prisoners as we reached the Albert Hall, I stood on the steps to watch the mighty procession roll on, feeling sadly aloof from all this jubilation, convinced that the end was not yet. One banner only was mine—a memorial of Mary Clarke.

Yet undoubtedly the movement had reached a stage of triumph. The *Daily News* observed in a leading article on my history, *The Suffragette*, published that week:

" Of one thing there can be no doubt at all: the pioneers of 1905 found woman suffrage an academic question; they have made it a vital issue of national affairs."

Now for the first time since the beginning of militancy, the anti-Government election policy was suspended. Candidates were asked two questions: " Will you support the Conciliation Bill? " " Will you vote for any amendment the Conciliation Committee believe will endanger the passage of the Bill into law? " On the candidate's answers to these questions the Union decided whether to oppose or support. Masterman, the Liberal candidate in Bethnal Green, was opposed because he said he would support an amendment to give votes to the wives of electors, a paradoxical reward for so righteous an intention. Visitors from other countries found it difficult to comprehend the fear of Adult Suffrage, and the tenacious clinging to the narrowest franchise, which were outstanding characteristics of the British women's suffrage movement. Many, like Ella Anker of Norway, found themselves unable to reconcile themselves to the British movement on that account.

During the truce to Suffragette militancy the National Insurance Act was passing through Parliament. The suffrage movement on the whole opposed it, if for no other reason than on the ground that all social legislation required the women's point of view. " I won't lick stamps! "; " Regimenting the workers "; " Burden on industry "—all the conflicting catch cries of the factions opposing the Bill were heard on suffrage platforms. I could not content myself with destructive criticism of this far-reaching legislation, but worked in conjunction with Keir Hardie, preparing amendments to increase the proposed benefits. He kept me informed on the progress of the Bill, and passed my amendments on with his own to the Labour Party Committee on this subject, himself moving some of them. When the Bill passed beyond Labour intervention to the House of Lords, I appealed on one occasion to the well-known old anti-Suffragist, Lord Balfour of Burleigh, to take up certain amendments in the interest of the lowest paid workers, mainly women. I did so owing to an opening given by one of his speeches. He replied with great cordiality, asking me to meet him, and on discussion agreed to a part of what I asked. I felt like a pigmy walking beside his huge figure.

In that year the *Merthyr Pioneer* was started by the I.L.P. in Keir Hardie's constituency. Without imposing the heavy personal burden he had long carried for the *Labour Leader*, this paper provided him with a congenial outlet. At his request I wrote a weekly article for it under the initial *S*. For years before and after that he talked to me of starting another weekly paper of his own, a cherished project never realized.

I was working then on what was to prove, though I did not realize it, a last, unfinished effort at a big picture—a crowd of girls Morris dancing. I made for it a large series of elaborate studies, and broke off from it, temporarily, as I thought, when Mrs. Lawrence asked me to arrange another W.S.P.U. exhibition in the Portman Rooms. The skating rink decorations were used again with a specially designed architectural setting, the main room being surrounded by a colonnade. When my full-size models, drawings and plans had all been cast in plaster at the bazaar fitters, it was exciting to me to see the work assembled and erected, looking as solid and permanent as stone. The stalls and a roundabout, propelled by hand, had been made from my working drawings by a carpenter. I had taken them from the picture of an old village fair in a beautiful eighteenth century book of costumes, by the famous illustrator Pine, in aquatint coloured by hand, which Keir Hardie had given me. I hope indeed he had picked it up at less than its value. It was stolen from me some years later. The stall-holders were all in late eighteenth century costume: gentlewomen, fisherwomen, market women, weavers, workers of all sorts, a gipsy fortune-teller with her two green birds, a roast chestnut seller, a town crier, a "zanny" with his odd fool's cap. The wearers of these costumes paid for them to be made by voluntary workers at the Brackenbury's studio in Kensington. Anti-suffrage coco-nut shies, representing the Cabinet Ministers, Lord Curzon, Mrs. Humphry Ward and other notable opponents, Old London cries, arranged after tremendous research by willing enthusiasts, and delightfully sung by Lady Sybil Smith and her friends, concerts of their music arranged by Dr. Ethel Smyth and Liza Lehmann, made a week of gay amusement enjoyed by all because it was all for the Cause and a gathering-ground for comrades. After two nights and the day between preparing the show with the bazaar fitters, I went home and fell asleep on my studio floor, and so missed the pleasure of seeing Keir Hardie riding on the roundabout to the cheering of the throng. Seven thousand people visited the fair.

Mrs. Pankhurst was now in America, enjoying a triumphal progress. She entered her meetings under arches of flowers and flags. Harriot Stanton Blatch, of the Women's Political Union, announced her as "the woman in all the world who is doing most for the suffrage." The National American Women's Suffrage Association invited her to address its annual convention at Louisville, Kentucky. Newly enfranchised delegates from California assured her that the Militant Movement in Britain had inspired and assisted their struggle.

CHAPTER XI

THE House of Lords contest virtually ended when, on July 20th, 1911, Asquith informed Balfour that, if necessary, Peers would be created to compel the enactment of his proposals. The Tories howled him down in the House four days later, but the scene, which was named the " pot house brawl," had no more importance than a schoolboy's rag. The Suffragettes, of course, commented : " This is how men politicians behave; they must not complain if we do likewise ! " To the Irish, North and South, the abolition of the Lords' final power of veto meant the removal of the constitutional barrier to Home Rule. To replace that old barrier, Ulster Unionism, lead by Sir Edward Carson, immediately erected the threat of armed resistance. To Reformers of many schools the shearing of the veto meant the hope of democratic legislation, but to the women's suffrage movement it suggested no widening of demand, only insistence that to make sure of obtaining the Protection of the Parliament Act against the suspensory power of the Lords, the Conciliation Bill must be passed in 1912. The suggestion by Lloyd George, in reply to a Parliamentary question on August 16th, that the facilities promised by the Government might be used for a wider measure, aroused indignant protests and cries of " treachery ! " These were presently allayed by another letter from Asquith to Lytton, on August 23rd, promising that the pledge of facilities for the Conciliation Bill would be " strictly adhered to, both in the letter and in the spirit." Clements Inn was again reassured, but presently a new trouble arose.

On November 7th a deputation lead by Arthur Henderson, from that very shadowy organization, the People's Suffrage Federation, urged the introduction of a measure for Adult Manhood and Womanhood Suffrage. Asquith replied that the Government Franchise Bill, first promised in 1908, and to which he had again pledged himself on the eve of both the elections of 1910, would be introduced in 1912. He was still opposed to the inclusion of women, but the House would be left free to insert a women's suffrage amendment should it so desire. His words were simply a repetition of his previous statement, but they were received with a tempest of indignation. Rightly or wrongly,

Suffragists and Suffragettes believed that the introduction of the Government Bill was timed with the sole purpose of frustrating the chances of the Conciliation Bill. The old cry: " They are trying to introduce Manhood Suffrage as a barrier against women," was raised with unprecedented fury. Suspicion was confirmed by rumours emanating from Parliamentary circles. Christabel declaimed:

" War is declared on women! . . . The Government's latest attempt to cheat women of the vote is of course inspired by Mr. Lloyd George. The whole crooked and discreditable scheme is characteristic of the man."[1]

Another militant deputation headed by Mrs. Pethick Lawrence, was arranged for November 21st. She wrote to Asquith announcing it, but was surprised to receive a polite reply, inviting the W.S.P.U. to meet him with other Suffrage Societies on November 17th.

Asquith received the Suffragists with the genial airs of an indulgent father. Lloyd George, scowling beside him, seemed thoroughly out of humour. The deputation was by no means united in its demand; indeed the attitude of the societies was highly conflicting. Christabel Pankhurst was the first speaker called upon. Asquith regarded her benignly, occasionally capping one of her quips against himself with a humorous corroborant. She demanded a Government measure conferring equal rights upon men and women, which must be carried through in 1912 to gain the benefit of the Parliament Act, and become law before the next General Election. The Conciliation Bill she dismissed with contempt; it was worthless now; Lloyd George had destroyed its chances by creating division amongst its supporters. Moreover, now that the Government had decided to give Manhood Suffrage, household suffrage for women was not sufficient; the proper solution was Womanhood Suffrage, and that could only be carried as a Government measure. Mrs. Fawcett took an entirely opposite line. Adult Suffrage, in her opinion, was " an altogether unpractical solution." There was " no demand at all for it in the country." She did not ask for a Government measure, treating the refusal to give it as final. She still regarded the Conciliation Bill as " the one bright spot," and the offer of facilities for it as of " utmost value." As to the proposed Reform Bill, she raised no objection; her only anxiety was that an amendment giving women less than Adult Suffrage should be accepted by the Government. The Conservative women were Conservative first and foremost; they were opposed

---

[1] *Votes for Women*, November 10th, 1911.

to any wider measure of votes for women than the Conciliation Bill. The Liberal women took yet another line: they welcomed the Reform Bill. They expressed their confidence that Lloyd George had the power to win the day for a Votes for Women amendment, and pleaded with Asquith to let it be " carried over his head."

He answered in genial strain, beginning with compliments to Christabel; she had come, he said, " offering terms of peace, with a dagger in one hand and a pistol in the other." Yet he could " understand and respect " her point of view. She wanted the Government to make themselves " the official sponsors of equality between the sexes; but I am the head of the Government and I am not going to make myself responsible for the introduction of a measure which I do not believe to be demanded in the interests of the country." " Then you can go and we shall get another head! " Christabel burst forth. " If you can get rid of me, well and good "—his smile was a trifle grim. Nevertheless he insisted repeatedly that notwithstanding his own opinion, Parliament should be left free to decide the issue. The Government would allow a free vote, both on the Conciliation Bill and on an amendment to the Reform Bill. If either were approved by a majority of the Commons, the Government would provide facilities to carry it into law.

" I give you my assurance on behalf of the Government that they will accept the decision then come to, and will accept the measure and give facilities for it. That ought to satisfy you."

" We are not satisfied! " cried Christabel.

He answered: " I did not expect to satisfy *you*! "

Mrs. Pethick Lawrence had stigmatized the offer of an amendment to the Reform Bill as a " trick " to destroy the Conciliation Bill. Lloyd George spoke briefly:

" Don't you commit yourselves too readily to the statement that this is a trick upon Women's Suffrage. If you find next year, as a result of this ' trick,' that several million women have been added to the franchise . . . then those who have committed themselves to this ill-conditioned suggestion will look very foolish! "

" We shall not mind that if we get the vote! " Christabel retorted.

The suffrage movement was now torn by dispute as to the intentions of the Government. The W.S.P.U. held firmly to belief in a deliberate betrayal, denouncing Asquith's fair offers as a mere device to gull women with vain hopes, and divert public sympathy from the Suffragettes, and declaring militancy to be the only possible reply to such trickery. The opinion that the

Government was dealing falsely was widely shared by militants and non-militants, Suffragists and anti-Suffragists, and was generally corroborated by the Conservative Press. Mrs. Pankhurst cabled from America: " Protest imperative! " Clements Inn had already determined on a renewal of militancy. The decision was widely applauded. Numbers of people who had not before approved of militancy encouraged it now. Numbers of new recruits volunteered for prison, desirous of obtaining their " Holloway degree," as Constance Lytton had named it.

A tenth Women's Parliament was summoned to the Caxton Hall on November 21st. The usual deputations went forth. Three men were arrested, including the well-known Russian writer, Dr. Soskice, and two hundred and twenty women, including Mrs. Brailsford; Mrs. Travers Symons, Keir Hardie's secretary; Lady Sybil Smith, daughter of Lord Antrim; Mrs. Mansell Moullin, wife of the well-known surgeon. The Duval family contributed no fewer than five prisoners: the mother, three daughters and the son. Mrs. Pethick Lawrence was arrested for striking a policeman in defence of another woman. The violence of the police on " Black Friday," the year before, had caused an extension of window breaking as a painless method of securing arrest. A prisoner stated in the dock: " It is better to break windows than to allow men to damage women as we were damaged last year."

Stone throwing was now carefully organized. Motors were driven at dusk to quiet country lanes where flints could be obtained. Would-be window breakers met Marion Wallace Dunlop, or some other trusted member of the W.S.P.U., at somebody's flat, and were furnished with hammers or black bags filled with flints. I had the W.S.P.U. Christmas Fair in hand, and could not risk arrest, but three of the new recruits, who wanted to break windows, and had difficulty in summoning themselves to the act, begged me to bear them company in a taxi to a point where they would jump out and throw their stones. Two of them were arrested, the third came back; she had broken her window without being caught. Next day many stone throwers received shorter sentences than had previously been given for simple obstruction; punishment for window breaking ranging from seven days to two months. Twenty-one women charged with damage amounting to more than £5 were sent for trial by judge and jury. Two of them were discharged, the others imprisoned for two months.

As Lloyd George was driving away from a meeting at the Horticultural Hall, from which members of the M.P.U. had been ejected, a youth named MacDougal, in an unpremeditated gesture of excitement, flung his dispatch case at the car. It entered a window and struck Lloyd George, though without injuring him. MacDougal was imprisoned for two months and forcibly fed. An older comrade, a workman named William Ball, broke a window at the Home Office on December 21st by way of protest. He also was forcibly fed. On February 12th his wife received a letter stating that he was to be certified as a lunatic and removed to Colney Hatch. The letter was delayed, and on hurrying to the prison she learnt that her husband was already in the asylum. An agitation arose, Ball's discharge was secured, and on removal to a nursing home the unfortunate man slowly recovered. Protests in and out of Parliament resulted in the production of a Government White Paper stating that Ball's temporary insanity was in no way attributable to his treatment in prison.

The non-militant suffragists were enraged at the renewal of militancy, though their faith in the sincerity of the Cabinet was not great. Mrs. Swanwick, then editing the non-militants' organ, the *Common Cause*, in a letter dated Christmas Day, 1910, wrote to me of: " Lloyd George and Churchill, who are merely out for an excuse to shelve our question." Churchill, a weathercock towards this cause, as to many others, was probably an opponent at heart. Of Lloyd George I never thought that; to me he appeared to be making an unsuccessful attempt to gather the sweets of two worlds; to win laurels as the heroic champion of Women's Suffrage, without jeopardizing his place in a Cabinet headed by an anti-Suffragist Prime Minister. He was not by any means confident, like Christabel, that if he and the other professing Suffragists in the Cabinet were to deliver an ultimatum to Asquith, it would be Asquith who would resign, and they who would be left to carry on the Government.

Yet the question obviously intrigued him. He announced, with much importance, that he had placed his services at the disposal of the " great and growing Suffrage Party." Even the resumption of militant tactics would not deter him. He and Sir Edward Grey would support an amendment giving votes to women householders, and the wives of householders, and he would campaign for it in the country. The triumvirate of Clements Inn indignantly repudiated his offers, and refused to countenance anything short of womanhood suffrage. Brailsford attempted the hard task of establishing an understanding. Lloyd George was nothing loath, but Christabel fiercely opposed all negotiations. " Brailsford has Lloyd Georgitis," she told me sarcastically. This was a most prevalent affection, in her opinion; indeed she regarded the Chancellor as a veritable magician.

He had asked, she told me, to see his old friend, Pethick Lawrence, but that would never do, she confided to me: " Mr. Lawrence could never stand up against Lloyd George! " Indeed it was clear she did not believe anyone in the world, save herself, could be trusted to negotiate with the " Welsh Wizard." I was amazed at this. I had heckled Lloyd George in Glasgow and thought his oratory over-rated. Moreover, Pethick Lawrence, in the editorial columns of *Votes for Women*, was displaying complete solidarity with her views. A few days before he had given £1,000 at an Albert Hall meeting, declaring that he had increased his gift from £100 because of the Government's attempt to trick the women.

Lloyd George's promised campaign was opened at Bath on November 24th. Negotiations with the W.S.P.U. having failed, the effort was rendered ridiculous by the exclusion of all save a few carefully selected women. Men hecklers were present in force. His honesty impugned, Lloyd George accused the militants of being far less pro-Suffrage than anti-Liberal, and of desiring the passage of the narrow Conciliation Bill, because it would " pack the register " against the Liberal Party. They were furious, he said, because the Conciliation Bill had been " torpedoed," and the way was now clear for a broad and democratic amendment, which would include the working man's wife. In speaking thus, he ignored his obligations as a Member of the Asquith Cabinet, which had repeatedly promised facilities and a free vote of the House for the Conciliation Bill. Lord Lytton immediately wrote to him protesting against the suggestion that all possibility of passing a measure to enfranchise women householders only, had been destroyed. He, Lord Lytton, had assured the Suffrage Societies that if the wider amendment to the Reform Bill he favoured were defeated, Lloyd George would then give his support to a narrower amendment to enfranchise women householders. All the Suffrage Societies save the W.S.P.U. had accepted this assurance. Lloyd George replied by putting the blame for all misunderstanding upon the militants; his intentions, he protested, were such as Lord Lytton had expressed. He had merely attacked the militants for inconsistency because, having demanded votes for a million women only, they now denounced, as not wide enough, an amendment which would enfranchise six or seven million women. His explanation did not allay the anger and suspicion he had aroused. His phrase " torpedoed " became a slogan in the attack upon him.

Asquith now added fuel to the fire of Suffragist anger; to a deputation from the National League for Opposing Women's

Suffrage, led by Lord Curzon, on December 14th, he observed
that to grant Votes to Women would be " a political mistake
of a very disastrous kind." He advocated " militant operations
of a constitutional character " to prevent it.

Cabinet Ministers were now heckled and harassed by the
militants on every possible occasion. Asquith at the City Temple
was obliged to leave without having uttered a single audible
sentence. Ramsay Macdonald, who was on the platform, complained :

" The consequence of this demonstration must be felt in the
House of Commons. If I felt that the cause had come to this, I
would go into the Lobby every time against it."

On the other hand, Keir Hardie supported the policy of the
W.S.P.U., and the *Labour Leader* prophetically remarked :

" . . . the militant fighters for women's freedom have made
franchise reform a living and pressing issue. In a few years from
now we shall forget what they did at this or that meeting . . . we
shall only remember their prolonged and dauntless struggle."

On December 15th occurred a militant incident of a new
type : Emily Wilding Davison was arrested in the act of thrusting
into a pillar-box a piece of linen, alight and saturated with
paraffin. She had already set fire to several other boxes, even
calling a constable to arrest her, and had previously announced
her intention to the Press. She declared that she had taken
this action on her own initiative. She was committed for trial
and sentenced to six months' imprisonment. Her deed was
reported as a news item in *Votes for Women,* but the usual
eulogy of all militant acts was in this case omitted from the
editorial columns. Her action, cold-shouldered by Clements Inn
at the time, was the precursor of a new and terrible struggle.

Not in the Suffragette movement alone were storms of
rebellion gathering; Lloyd George complained that revolt was
spreading through the country " like foot-and-mouth disease."
Rebellion grew apace in Ulster, its every manifestation openly
encouraged by the English Conservative Press and the prominent
leaders of the Conservative Party. " I can imagine no lengths
of resistance to which Ulster will go which I shall not be ready
to support," said Bonar Law at Blenheim; in Ulster he promised
" help from across the channel." " I utterly decline to be
bound within a strait-waistcoat of constitutional resistance,"
announced F. E. Smith, afterwards made Lord Birkenhead for
his services to Unionism. The Earl of Selborne wrote in the
Oxford and Cambridge Review that the " men of our race " would
fight for their liberties " with rifles in their hands." Violence

in the docks and rioting in the streets gave tangible proof that incitements and organization in powerful quarters were bearing their intended fruit. The drilling of volunteers, the distribution of arms, the decision of the Ulster Unionist Council to appoint a rebel provisional Government should the Home Rule Bill become law followed in their turn. Grave acts of sedition these according to habitual estimate, but the Government made no move against the powerful offenders. The W.S.P.U. raised its voice in protest at the imprisonment of its militants, whilst the rebels of Unionism went scot-free.

In 1911 industrial unrest, which had long been gathering, broke forth in what was to prove a great series of unprecedented unheavals. According to official statistics, which never over-state such discrepancies, wages in the five principal industries had risen only 0·31 in the years 1900-11, whilst the wholesale price of foodstuffs had advanced 11·6 during the same period. The swing of the Labour pendulum from the 'nineties until the advent of the thirty-nine Labour Members at Westminster in 1906, had moved steadily, and with growing momentum, towards Parliamentary action; it had now reverted towards industrialism. Despite the desire of the higher Trade Union officials for a reduction of disputes, strikes were rapidly increasing, both in number and extent. In 1908 there had been 399 disputes; in 1911 there were 903. A new spirit of rebellion was abroad in industry, and a revolt against officialism in the Unions themselves. " Industrial Unionism," " The One Big Union," " The Sympathetic Strike," " The Political Strike " were the battle-cries of various " Left Wing " sections which adopted their theories and terminology from Karl Marx, the American Daniel de Leon, the American Industrial Workers of the World and the French Syndicalists. In 1905 James Connolly[1] had founded a De Leonite Socialist Labour Party in Glasgow, with Industrial Unionism as its watchword; its tenets: " They who rule industrially will rule politically." The function of industrial unionism is " to build up an industrial republic inside the shell of the political state,"[2] which industrial republic will, in due time, crack the shell and take the place of the existing order. The influence of the Socialist Labour Party spread from the engineering workshops of the Clyde to those of Sheffield, Manchester and other areas. Stimulated by the confusion arising from the multiplicity of craft unions catering for

[1] James Connolly founded in 1896 the Irish Socialist Republican Party, was associated with James Larkin in the Irish Transport Workers' Federation, and was executed for his part in the Irish Rebellion of Easter Week, 1916.

[2] James Connolly. *Socialism Made Easy.*

engineering workers, it developed the Shop Stewards' Movement. In 1908 a break-away from the mild indefiniteness of Ruskin College for working men at Oxford, produced the Central Labour College in London and the Plebs League for Independent Working Class Education. Their influence was extensive, especially in the mining areas of North-East England and South Wales. The South Wales Socialist Society, meeting amid the mines of the frowning Rhondda Valley, was the controlling influence of the Left Wing movement in South Wales. Its most determined and doctrinaire leader was Will Mainwaring. All the others took their cue from him, and shrank from incurring his acid criticism, of which every speaker coming into those parts was made to feel the sting. Amongst this little coterie was A. J. Cook, afterwards secretary of the Miners' Federation of Great Britain; a wholly impossible appointment it would have seemed in those days. He was an object of genial derision to his colleagues, who ridiculed his alleged imperfect knowledge of industrial history and economics. Yet his popularity with the mob exceeded theirs, for, more than once, he found himself in prison for his oratory, whilst his cautious critics did not come into conflict with authority. In 1912 this group produced the *Miners' Next Step*, a little pamphlet much applauded and much denounced. In London arose a Syndicalist movement directly inspired by the similar movement in France, Guy Bowman being one of its most active pioneers. Tom Mann joined it in 1910; in 1891, from the witness chair of the Royal Commission on Labour, that volatile, good fellow had advocated the nationalization of industry under Parliamentary control; he now flew to the opposite extreme, declaring that to manage industry by State machinery would be "more mischievous" than the existing method; the industries must be run by the industrially organized workers, and the "General Strike of national proportions," which would be "the actual social and industrial revolution," must be prepared "as rapidly as possible."

In 1910 there had been an outbreak of unofficial strikes, many of them successful, and some of them against agreements made by the employers and the Trade Union officials. During an unofficial coal strike police and soldiers were drafted to the Rhondda Valley. Wherever they appeared, disorder followed. The agile Welsh youths mischievously incited the heavy London policemen to chase them, puffing and blowing, up the precipitous mountain steeps. The police retaliated with violence, not upon their elusive tormentors, but on whoever was unfortunate enough to be available as a substitute. In at least one punitive raid, houses were entered, and women and old people beaten. In this unofficial fight Keir Hardie was the only sure champion of the workers. Wherever they were suffering, his voice was raised; now to battle for them in the strikes, official or unofficial; now in the Whitehaven disaster, where the mine was sealed up to save further damage to the workings, with the men entombed therein, dead or alive; now in the Pretoria Pit fatality in Lancashire. The tragedies of industrial life agitated him intensely; his protests were no mere flights of oratory. His advocacy did something to check the tide of Labour sympathy flowing away from the Labour Party. Another influence tending to rally working class loyalty to it was the Osborne Judgement of the House of Lords, in 1909, whereby political action by a Trade Union was declared illegal. Yet it was on the workshop, not on Parliament, that the thoughts of the workers now mainly centred. In May, 1911, the tailors and tailoresses struck work. The seamen followed in June. In July came the first great dock strike since 1889. The Port of London was at a standstill, troops were concentrated at the docks, and Winston Churchill threatened to use them to replace the strikers. Finally the Government induced the employers to negotiate, and the dispute was settled. The seamen and dockers were scarcely in before the railwaymen were out. Unofficial strikes began in Liverpool, Manchester and other towns. The executives of the Unions gave the employers twenty-four hours' notice to meet them, or face a national stoppage. The Government offered the Unions a Royal Commission to discuss their grievances, and informed them that in the event of a strike the troops would be used to prevent the suspension of commerce. The Trade Union officials resented the ultimatum, and brought out 200,000 men. Churchill and Haldane had guaranteed military aid to the railway companies, and soldiers were now supplied for the protection of strike-breakers, on the mere request of the companies, without the hitherto customary requisition of the civil authorities. Being called out, the troops in some cases fired. A man unconnected with the dispute was fatally injured in Liverpool, two others at Llanelly. At the latter inquest Major Stewart declared that he had been empowered by the War Office to fire without waiting instructions from the local magistrates. The situation having grown serious, the Government called the employers to meet the Unions, in conjunction with Henderson and Macdonald, who were afterwards bitterly assailed in working class quarters, for having conceded too much to the employers. Trouble in the mining areas had become almost continuous. Low piece-rate earnings in difficult working places were a perpetual source of hardship. In 1911 the Miners' Federation demanded a national minimum wage and threatened a strike for it. In February, 1912, a million men were brought out, and for a month the mines were at a standstill; all industry was affected. The Government was compelled to legislate; but the desired national minimum wage was set aside in favour of district minima, to be set up in each coal-field by a joint board of employers and employed. The compromise was strongly resented by the men in the pits and throughout the Labour movement. Keir Hardie himself made no secret of his opinion that the Labour Parliamentary negotiators had not made full use of the victory achieved by the strikers. In May, 1912, the dockers of the Thames and Medway were out again, complaining that the agreements won by the previous strike were not being observed. The Government and the Port of London Authority persistently refused all concessions. The strike was maintained to the point of starvation. Processions of 100,000 people marched to Tower Hill. Misery was intense, homes were sold up, children died. Dr. Barbara Tchaykovsy organized the "Children's White Cross League." Thousands of sympathizers lent their aid, but the area and extent of the poverty was too great for volunteer help to avail; the people were starved into submission.

Passionately would Dr. Pankhurst have protested, staking his legal knowledge and reputation against the employment of the troops; ardently would Mrs. Pankhurst, in the old days, have joined in the relief of distress. To-day the W.S.P.U. was at grips with what was becoming a life and death struggle of its own. Moreover, its spirit was wholly changed from that which had animated the earlier lives of its founders. *Votes for Women* merely referred to the tragedies of Liverpool and Llanelly as an item in the cost of the strike: "Several lives have been lost." It declared that Suffragettes had more reason for revolt than working men, for the latter had votes, and so "could gain improvements in their condition without resorting to strikes." When Tom Mann, Guy Bowman, and Fred Crowsley were imprisoned for an appeal to the soldiers not to shoot their fellow workers on strike, the W.S.P.U. coldly commented that this offence was more serious than any committed by the Suffragettes, and should have been more seriously punished. Later, when Christabel became acting editor of the paper, its tone grew still further aloof from the realities of industrial life:

"We would ask the Government if they propose to make the organization of strikes punishable by law."

To such an amazing proposition the history of Trade Unionism of course supplied the obvious negative answer.

In spite of such utterances the W.S.P.U. was regarded with admiration and friendship, not only by many of the Left Wing of the political Labour and Socialist movement, but also amongst the industrial rebels. Its editorial columns were scarcely read in such quarters, its speeches little noticed, but its militant actions aroused the enthusiasm of those who were impatient of the slow pace of their own movements. *Votes for Women* expressed its gratitude to the Queen for decreeing that her train should be borne by women instead of pages, but Flora Drummond and other little-reported speakers and organizers of the Union were busy fanning every flame of discontent which showed itself in the Labour Party, on the score of its failure to maintain with adequate rigour the proletarian class war. With Christabel such manœuvring was merely intended to embarrass the Labour Members of Parliament in their support of an anti-Suffrage Liberal Government, but many an earnest young militant Suffragette had her family and her sympathies ardently attached to some Left Wing workers' movement. She might be as Red at heart as she pleased, provided she left the control of Suffragette policy to her W.S.P.U. leaders. The local W.S.P.U. organizer was usually a person who could be trusted not to offend a well-to-do Conservative audience. Adela Pankhurst was regarded by Christabel as a very black sheep amongst organizers, because the warmth of her Socialism did not always permit her to comply with this requirement. Undoubtedly the example of Suffragette militancy (arising as it had done from the I.L.P.) had a profound influence in accentuating militant tendencies in the Left Wing working class movements.

Some of the sporadic discontents rising and falling in the Labour Party gathered for a brief period about the unstable personality of Victor Grayson, a young graduate of Manchester University, elected as an Independent Socialist Member of Parliament for the Colne Valley at a by-election in 1907. The W.S.P.U. was much in evidence at the election, and Grayson made a great feature of his championship of the women. Mrs. Pankhurst was charmed by him. In Parliament he at once forgot all about the W.S.P.U., and directed his ephemeral energies towards the unemployed. After making a Parliamentary uproar in defence of the workers, and denouncing the Labour Members as traitors to their class, he refused to speak on the same platform with Keir Hardie. H. M. Hyndman joined Grayson in this refusal, being incensed by Hardie's opposition to his militarist propaganda, and to the anti-German war scare in which Hyndman and Blatchford then figured. At the I.L.P. Conference of Easter, 1909, the reverberations of this incident caused the resignation from the I.L.P. executive of its four most prominent members: Hardie, Macdonald, Snowden and Bruce Glasier. From Keir Hardie's resignation arose at least one important, unforeseen consequence. Whilst attending the International Socialist Congress at Copenhagen in 1910, he was impressed by the existence of successful Socialist daily newspapers amongst the relatively small populations of the Scandinavian countries, and had determined to initiate such a paper in this country. He spoke of it on the voyage home, and Sime Seruya, a Socialist-Suffragette, who was of the party, offered £1,000 towards the venture. He laid his proposal before the executive of the Independent Labour Party, offering to raise a fund for a daily paper, to be the property of the I.L.P. He strongly stipulated that the paper should not be the organ of the Labour Party, or subject to its control. He desired it to be the leader and the educator of the Labour Party; its spur, not its mouthpiece. Nevertheless the I.L.P. executive, of which W. C. Anderson was then chairman, without informing Hardie of his intentions, offered to the Labour Party executive half the seats on the directorate of the proposed paper. Hardie was greatly incensed; he told me that he should write to those who had subscribed to the project, telling them he was opposed to the publication of a Labour Party organ, and that, so far as he was concerned, he advised them to withdraw their donations. Lacking his enthusiasm, the scheme failed for some time to advance. Eventually a Labour Party organ, the short-lived *Daily Citizen*, appeared in November, 1912. This paper by no means accorded with the views of Keir Hardie. He told me in 1914 that he was ashamed to open it, calling it a " jingo rag." Meanwhile the *Daily Herald* had been started in the spring of 1912; in the first place, as the organ of the printing workers on strike. George Lansbury, who had been elected to Parliament in the second election of 1910, was early induced to lend his support to the *Daily Herald*, and by his energy and power of gaining the confidence of people of diverse sorts, became its principal mainstay. Since his election he had become prominent as a supporter of the Suffragettes, and in the debate on the Conciliation Bill had declared: " I glory in the women's fight! " Indeed it was very largely from supporters of the women's movement that he was able to raise the money to keep the *Herald* going. Its editors were at first changing constantly: H. Seed, Sheridan Jones, brother-in-law of Cecil Chesterton and a Liberal anti-Socialist who wrote pamphlets against the nationalization of the mines, Rowland Kenney, and Lapworth, a supporter of the I.W.W. from the United States, who raised the paper to great popularity with the

Left Wing industrialists. Finally, when he regarded the utterances of Lapworth as too bitter and drastic, Lansbury himself became editor, with the help of Gerald Gould. The cartoons of Will Dyson were by no means always guiltless of vulgarity and sameness, but they had a striking style of their own, and they attacked and ridiculed Capitalism in the person of " Mr. Fat and his wife," in a manner delightful to a large proportion of *Herald* readers. They assorted well with the editorship of Lapworth, but somewhat curiously with that of Lansbury. Dyson was paid £1,000 a year for his work, and held the directors to his contract when the *Herald* became a weekly. " Let them all come," was Lansbury's motto, especially in the early days of the *Herald*. Labour Party Parliamentarians of the Left and Right, anti-Parliamentary Syndicalists, Suffragettes, Indian Home Rulers, Irish Sinn Feiners—whoever had a substantial group of readers to be catered for, could obtain at least a few paragraphs in the *Daily Herald*. If the policy of the paper were more unstable than a weathercock, that must be attributed to the catholicity of its sympathies.

BOOK VII

CHAPTER I

WITH industry in a ferment, with Civil War threatening from Ireland, the W.S.P.U. faced 1912, determined at all costs to maintain Votes for Women in the centre of the political stage. Rumour persistently asserted that, despite Asquith's oft-repeated pledges, the Government would not permit the Parliamentary majority for Votes for Women to take effect, and that Asquith would resign if the promised free vote of the House should result in a victory for the Suffragists. As Christabel afterwards disclosed, the W.S.P.U. had already been privately informed that John Redmond would muster the Irish Party in opposition. He had always been an opponent, but had hitherto left the Irish Members free to vote as they chose on the question. It was said he urged his followers to join him in opposition now, in order to ward off the possibility of Asquith's resignation and the break-up of the Cabinet, and, in any case, to prevent the extension of votes to women before the enactment of Home Rule, lest women's enfranchisement might be followed by a General Election and the balance of Parties be changed. It may be that at the root of this sophistry was the fear, then commonly expressed by politicians in Roman Catholic countries, that the women's vote would be directed by the priests. It is difficult to understand why the W.S.P.U. did not at once publish its information that the Irish Party was to oppose votes for women, for herein lay the best justification for W.S.P.U. insistence that Asquith's offer of neutrality was valueless.

The possibility of a Government split, or the resignation of the Prime Minister, if Votes for Women in any form should secure a majority in the Commons, was now canvassed in every newspaper. The Liberal *Daily Chronicle*[1] announced:

" A hopeless Parliamentary tangle with the Cabinet tied in a knot in the middle of it . . . we cannot have one Cabinet on Home Rule and two Cabinets on Women's Suffrage. . . . The situation created, places the Prime Minister in a very difficult and embarrassing position. . . . The House of Commons is responsible. Members of Parliament

[1] 11th January, 1912.

voted in the past light-heartedly in favour of Women's Suffrage. When Second Readings of a private Bill are carried time after time the Government is forced to take cognizance of the result."

This was an obvious plea for Members of Parliament to vote against this tiresome question. Indeed many Liberal Members, hitherto counted as Suffragists, were already openly urging this course as a temporary aid to Party harmony. The Liberal *Westminster Gazette* and *Daily Chronicle* further suggested that Votes for Women, if carried by Parliament, should be submitted to a Referendum. In all probability it would be defeated; thus Asquith's dignity would be maintained. The *Chronicle* article was said to be inspired by a Cabinet Minister. A member of Mrs. Fawcett's organization denounced Lloyd George as the culprit. Mrs. Fawcett exonerated him and named Winston Churchill. That chameleonic character, who in his by-election of 1908 had said: " Trust me, ladies; I am your friend, and will be your friend in the Cabinet," had now assumed an attitude of fastidious truculence. He informed[1] the Women's Freedom League that he would vote against the Conciliation Bill because it would be unfair to the Liberal Party, and that he would vote against the amendment favoured by Lloyd George because the country was not prepared to enfranchise the six or seven million women it would include.

Whilst the Referendum " red herring " was industriously trailed and furiously pursued by the W.S.P.U., the prophetic suggestion was made in *The Times* political notes that a Votes for Women amendment to the Reform Bill would be contrary to all precedent, and that the Speaker might declare it out of order. Little attention was paid to this pregnant utterance, but a couple of days later the point was replied to in *The Times*:

" This difficulty has been present throughout to the mind of the Cabinet, and is not insurmountable. . . . Votes for Women amendments were moved and voted on in the Reform Bills of 1867 and 1884."

There should the matter have ended, but the wisdom of politicians is inscrutable to simple minds.

The suffrage agitation continued apace. Great meetings were held in the Albert Hall by all the protagonists. First the W.S.P.U., then even the Antis, with a platform of seven Cabinet Ministers, five dukes, fifteen earls, five viscounts, forty-four barons, thirteen Members of Parliament and one woman. The National Union of Suffrage Societies brought Lloyd George to the Albert Hall. Heckled by the militants, he insisted that the Government's pledges would be kept, indeed he was emphatic that they could not be broken " without deep dishonour." He

[1] Letter dated 24th February, 1912.

positively asserted that a democratic amendment for Women's Suffrage would be carried.   Next came a joint meeting of the Labour Party, the I.L.P. and the Fabians.   Keir Hardie, glad to be done with the limitations of the Conciliation Bill, demanded Adult Suffrage for women and men; failing this he would vote against the Reform Bill.   Henderson also categorically declared [1] that he would vote against the Bill unless women were included. Macdonald, asked whether he would turn the Government out if women were not included in the Bill, answered " Certainly."

When Parliament met, the Reform Bill was at last in the King's Speech.   The Conciliation Bill obtained a third place in the ballot, but attention was diverted from it to the Reform Bill, and the proposed Women's Suffrage amendments thereto.   The W.S.P.U. issued a statement that it had " ceased to be interested " in the Conciliation Bill, or in any scheme short of a Government proposal.   There was an indescribable rage of excitement. Every Ministerial utterance was suspect.   Thousands of lynx-eyes sought a trick in every phrase, and eagerly scanned the pages of *Votes for Women* for the punctilious analysis of the subterfuge they would assuredly find there.   Masses of women beyond the membership of the Union looked to its leaders, above all to Christabel Pankhurst, to steer the franchise cause through the shoals and quicksands which beset its path.   " Miss Christabel Pankhurst has never been wrong! " was the members' oft-heard cry.   She exhorted them to the fight with passionate references to Joan of Arc as " the greatest woman in history.   We know that, like hers, our voices are of God.   They are!   They are! " It was firmly believed that militancy, and only militancy, could advance the cause; only because the truce had lasted too long had the Cabinet now dared to introduce its Reform Bill for men only.

Mrs. Pankhurst had returned from America; she would lead the next militant action.   On February 16th, at a welcome dinner to released prisoners who had been stone throwers the previous November, she declared: [2]

" The argument of the broken pane is the most valuable argument in modern politics. . . . That we are to-day awaiting the issue of dissensions in the very heart of the Government itself . . . is due to Mrs. Pethick Lawrence and her deputation of November 21st."

Unversed in subtleties, Mrs. Pankhurst saw one clear fact: women had toiled for the vote for fifty years, and for six years had fought and suffered for it with seldom-exampled passion; the Government had replied by offering more votes to men, who did not even care for them.   The assertion was true; the minds of

[1] January 29th, 1912.
[2] Connaught Rooms, Kingsway.   February 16th, 1912.

such class-conscious young workmen as were unable to qualify for the household franchise were then almost wholly occupied with economic issues. To this denial of political justice, women, in the W.S.P.U. opinion, could only reply by revolution. Mrs. Pankhurst declared that the only legitimate criticism of the militants could be that their weapons had not been sufficiently strong. "The argument of the stone, that time-honoured political weapon . . . is the argument I am going to use!"

Whilst Mrs. Pankhurst was uttering those words, a new incitement was being delivered. A Member of the Government, the Right Hon. C. E. Hobhouse, addressing an Anti-Suffrage meeting in the Colston Hall, Bristol, observed:

"In the case of the Suffrage demand there has not been the kind of popular sentimental uprising which accounted for Nottingham Castle in 1832, or the Hyde Park railings in 1867. There has been no great ebullition of popular feeling."

That speech was like a match to a fuse. "We can win the victory of Votes for Women by far less drastic methods of protest than those indicated by Mr. Hobhouse," replied Mrs. Pethick Lawrence in *Votes for Women*; but there were others in the Union who held an opposite opinion, as was presently to appear.

A handbill calling the public to a protest meeting in Parliament Square on March 4th was issued with the signature of Mrs. Pankhurst, who also wrote to the Prime Minister, announcing that she would bring a deputation to elicit from him a statement upon the Referendum. Warned by the window smashing of November, the police were preparing for the event. On Friday, March 1st, at 4 p.m., whilst a conference was actually being held at Scotland Yard to devise measures for the protection of shopkeepers, an unadvertised outbreak occurred. In Piccadilly, Regent Street, Oxford Street, Bond Street, Coventry Street and their neighbourhood, in Whitehall, Parliament Street, Trafalgar Square, Cockspur Street and the Strand, as well as in districts so far away as Chelsea, well-dressed women suddenly produced strong hammers from innocent-looking bags and parcels, and fell to smashing the shop windows. There is nothing like a hammer for smashing plate glass; stones, even flints, are apt to glance off harmlessly. The hammers did terrible execution. Shop assistants rushed out; traffic was stopped. Policemen blew their whistles and called the public to aid them. Damage amounting to thousands of pounds was effected in a few moments. Lyons, the A.B.C. and Appendrodt's suffered in several branches. The great shipping firms in Cockspur Street; Cook's, Burbury's, the Kodak, Swan & Edgar, Marshall & Snelgrove, Jay's, Liberty's, Fuller's, Swears & Wells, Hope Brothers, the Carrara Marble

Works and a host of other famous shops were victims. Jewellers were not spared. In fashionable Bond Street few windows remained. Police reserves were hurried out, shopkeepers were warned all over London, police stations were besieged with complaints. Mrs. Pankhurst had meanwhile driven to Downing Street in a taxi and broken some windows in the Prime Minister's residence, in company with Mrs. Tuke, her first act of militancy, and Mrs. Marshall, wife of the solicitor to the W.S.P.U. Two hundred and nineteen women were arrested, but many window breakers escaped. On Monday morning " the Mænads," as *The Times* called them, turned their attack on Knightsbridge, Brompton Road and Kensington High Street. Again the outbreak was unexpected; few constables were about, and in Knightsbridge the military police from the barracks arrested the destroyers before the civilian police arrived. That day the British Museum and all the picture galleries in the centre of London were already closed, the shop fronts in Trafalgar Square and neighbourhood were covered with hoardings or wire screens. Nine thousand police were stationed in the Square. As in November, the sentences on the window smashers ranged from seven days to two months, but the prisoners committed to the sessions for damage over £5 were more severely dealt with, sentences ranging from four to eight months. The Coal Strike had begun on March 18th. In the midst of the great industrial struggle the W.S.P.U. had thrust itself into the limelight again!

On March 5th the police appeared at Clements Inn and arrested the Pethick Lawrences on warrants charging them with conspiracy " to incite certain persons to commit malicious damage to property "; Mrs. Pankhurst and Mrs. Tuke, who were already in prison, were also named in the charge. There was a warrant, too, for the arrest of Christabel, but she was absent from the Inn. When, late that night, she learnt what had occurred, she determined to escape. Making no other attempt at disguise than to substitute a close-fitting pink straw hat for the large floppy one she habitually wore, she crossed to Paris next day and took rooms there, styling herself " Miss Amy Richards." There she edited *Votes for Women* and directed W.S.P.U. activities. Her whereabouts were kept secret. Owing, said the Government, to " the fanatical loyalty of her friends," the police discovered no trace of her, though they sought her assiduously, watching the offices, raiding the houses of prominent supporters, opening letters, tapping telephones, and though the Press joined in the search. The Suffragettes laid many a false trail for the bewildering of Scotland Yard. A young lady dressed in a characteristic long green coat succeeded in inducing the police to besiege her in a lonely flat in the middle of the night. A Member of Parliament informed the Home Secretary that the fugitive was in the United States. There were reports of her appearance in several countries. Many an article and cartoon, many a humorous verse and story were devoted to her disappearance. " Gentlemen of the police, she is here—in our hearts! " cried Israel Zangwill, the wit of the Suffrage movement. Christabel meanwhile poked fun at her pursuers in the columns of *Votes for Women*. She was enjoying herself immensely. The London newspapers reached her in Paris only a few hours late. A small circle of devotees went to and fro with messages and copy, and in general obeyed her behests to the letter. She was mistress of the militant movement, without a single colleague of equal authority to be converted to her views. The differences which had lately arisen in the trium- virate troubled her no more. She wrote with complete confidence of an early victory; of freedom after dark hours of subjection, and quoted Omar Khayyám with enthusiasm:

" Awake, for morning in the bowl of night
·Has flung the stone that puts the stars to flight! "

In London there was excitement, turmoil, uproar. Suffra- gettes were mobbed in the streets. For the first time in its history *Votes for Women* came out with great blank spaces. The printer had censored it with ruthless hand. Of Christabel's article appeared only the title: " A Challenge! " *The Times* called for sentences of penal servitude upon the W.S.P.U. leaders. In the House of Commons Members demanded drastic punishment and the compensation of the shopkeepers out of W.S.P.U. funds. Asquith replied that he was consulting the Law Officers of the Crown as to the best means of bringing home the damage, not only to " the wretched individuals concerned," but to those who were responsible for their acts. An indignation meeting of outraged tradesmen was held in the Queen's Hall, Boosey, its proprietor in the chair. A lady shopkeeper,[1] whose windows had been broken, was hustled and howled at for moving an amendment calling for Votes for Women to stop the disorders Her amendment was ruled out of order. Hostility in business circles was unbounded. Mrs. Ayres Purdie, a certified auditor, who specialized in income tax recovery business, had taken an office at Craven House, Kingsway, a month before, displaying on her window the sign: " Women Tax Payers' Agency." She now received notice from her landlord that she must take down her sign or quit the premises, for " women should keep quiet; men did not want them to go about shouting that they paid taxes."

[1] Miss Atherton of the Fine Arts Society, New Bond Street.

Agg Gardner, who had obtained a place for the Conciliation Bill, was asked to withdraw it. Sydney Buxton, the Postmaster-General, always an anti-Suffragist, declared he would vote against the Conciliation Bill on account of the militants. Lord Willoughby de Broke replied advising Buxton to show consistency by refusing also to vote for Home Rule, as a protest against cattle driving and boycotting, which were then rife in Galway. Lord Willoughby de Broke afterwards observed that Suffragette militancy had made him more favourable to Votes for Women than before. Lloyd George's secretary, Crawshay Williams, wrote to *The Times* calling for the defeat of the Conciliation Bill, " to demonstrate the folly of militant tactics," and canvassed Members of Parliament against it. George Lansbury told a provincial audience that he took his hat off to the ladies, and wished the working classes had as much spirit. Keir Hardie remained steadfast in his support. James Connolly[1] wrote from Ireland:

" When trimmers and compromisers disavow you, a poor, slumbred politician, I raise my hat in thanksgiving that I lived to see this insurgence of women."

The W.S.P.U. weekly meetings in the London Pavilion were thronged; great gatherings were held in the London Opera House and in the Albert Hall, where a record collection of £10,000 was taken, and Annie Besant declared that posterity would crown with honour the martyrs of the present struggle.

For a brief period there were high times in Holloway; it had become a veritable Liberty Hall. McKenna, the new Home Secretary, had modified, it is true, the famous Rule 243A, introduced by Winston Churchill to avoid the recurrence of the hunger strike when militancy was resumed in 1910. Even in its modified form McKenna refused to apply it fully to the majority of the Suffragette prisoners. Only a minority of them were allowed to have food sent in from outside, and those who had it got only one parcel, weighing 11 lb., brought once a week by the W.S.P.U. motor-car. But food was a minor question; it was the prevailing freedom which transformed imprisonment. The D x wing was given over to the Suffragettes; cell doors were unlocked; prisoners could go about in the pavilion as they pleased, and visit each other's cells. They wore their own clothes; a dancer, who had come from Paris to go to prison, sent for her ballet skirts and gave lively exhibitions of her art for the delight both of the prisoners and the wardresses, who agreed that Holloway had become a jolly place indeed, and in after years often recounted the pleasures of that brief interlude. The Brackenbury sisters modelled little

[1] Executed for his part in the Irish Rebellion, Easter, 1916.

animals of squeezed bread and presented them to the officers; funny drawings and humorous writing appeared daily. At exercise in the yard a group of the Suffragettes were singing Dr. Ethel Smyth's " March of the Women," the hand of its composer thrust through a cell window, conducting the chorus with a tooth-brush. This vivid personality had joined the Union in 1910, subjugated by the charm of Mrs. Pankhurst, whom she described as " an artist in life," and " possessed of personal magnetism on a gigantic scale."

Ethel Smyth was a being only these islands could have produced. Individualized to the last point, she had in middle age little about her which was feminine. Her features were clean cut and well marked, neither manly nor womanly, her thin hair drawn plainly aside, her speech clear in articulation, and incisive rather than melodious, with a racy wit. Wearing a small, mannish hat, battered and old, plain-cut country clothes, hard worn by weather and usage, she would don a tie of the brightest purple, white and green, or some hideous purple cotton jacket, or other oddity in the W.S.P.U. colours she was so proud of, which shone out from her, incongruously, like a new gate to old palings. She lived in a pleasant, modern cottage, built to her own fancy, named " Coigne," at Hook Heath, near Woking, alone with a shaggy, grey, Old English sheep-dog she named " Pan," and a silent, middle-aged housekeeper, a woman with yellow hair and pallid face, who might have been trusted to keep the secrets of a Bluebeard's chamber.

In her youth Ethel Smyth had run away from home to study music, and had been a student in Leipzig. She frequently deplored that she had not received an earlier training. Hermann Levi said of her that she was the most musical human being, save Wagner, he had ever met. The great devotion of her life had been to the librettist of her opera " The Wreckers ": Henry Brewster, dead some years before this. She spoke of him frequently as her great inspirer, and of his books as her Bible. She had a passion for ships. I stood with her on the quay at Southampton, bidding good-bye to Mrs. Pankhurst, on board for America. At the moment of parting the siren blew hugely. The adored Mrs. Pankhurst, smiling and waving to us from the deck, was forgotten by the musician, who snatched a note-book from her pocket and scribbled eagerly, exclaiming in her ecstasy: " A gorgeous noise! "

She had no great singing organ; yet, seated at the piano, she could do with her voice and fingers most marvellous things—the work of a full choir and symphony orchestra! Certainly their essentials. Indeed her music never sounded so limitless, so universal, when given by all the voices and instruments for which she wrote them, as by their author alone. Somehow she produced the great turgid effect of them all—and something more—the spirit of her strange, wild, suffering, striving heart, whose secrets none could fathom. " Hey Nonny No! " that great chorus of hers, which has no parallel, never was heard with such great power and weirdness as when she gave it, playing to some casual group of Suffragettes in that small cottage. Voices of sailors drinking in a tavern, rude, rough fellows, wild, adventurous spirits; voices of merriment; coarse, large laughter; hideous laughter; mad, wild laughter; voices of women, foolish, fierce, merry, sad and grieving; voices of horror; voices of Death— all these enwrapt in the rude, wild blast of the storm one heard in that chorus, given by that one magic being. The sketch of her by John Sargent, singing and playing thus, gives a graphic remembrance of her.

In her first enthusiasm for the Suffragette movement, she rapidly produced a trilogy for choir and orchestra called " Songs of Sunrise," including " The March of the Women," for which the words were written by Cicely Hamilton, " Laggard Dawn," the voices of people waiting for the dawn to break, and " 1910, a Medley." The words of the two last were her own; highly characteristic and amusing, but by no means comparable with the music. Yet who, save she, would have attempted to set to music a Suffragette raid in Trafalgar Square? Such was the Medley:

Suffragettes : " Sounds of the battle raging round us! Up and defy them! Laugh in their faces! "
Policemen : " Move on! Move on! "
Unfriendly men : " Putting back the clock for years! I know Mrs. Humphry Ward."

.   .   .   .

Suffragettes : " We knew we should get it! "

The daughter of a General and of Tory stock, it was odd to find this tremendous genius immensely concerned with the genealogy of her family. She had written and published privately a brief history of it, including a speech of one of her forebears to the soldiers who were to disperse, and, if need be, to shoot, the franchise agitators prior to 1832. Of her imprisonment she wrote : " It was impossible to keep my self-respect without throwing in my lot with my colleagues in my Union." Therefore she broke a window in the house of " Lulu Harcourt," selecting this Minister for correction because he had told a suffrage deputation he would agree to Votes for Women if all women were as " well-behaved and intelligent " as his wife.

Another prisoner at the time was the wife of W. W. Jacobs,

the novelist. She had told Fordham, the Magistrate, that her stone throwing was prompted by a sense of duty to her children, as she desired that her daughters should grow up to equal duties and responsibilities with her sons. The Magistrate declared her contention so absurd that she must be demented, and announced that he would remand her for a week to have the state of her mind inquired into.

The Conspiracy Case dragged on at Bow Street, bail was refused, the four defendants were brought each day from prison to the dock. On March 21st Mrs. Pankhurst and the Pethick Lawrences were committed for trial. Mrs. Tuke, for inscrutable reasons, was acquitted. The redoubtable Bodkin, of the *Daily Herald* cartoons, displayed unusual forbearance towards her, observing that, if the Magistrate's decision were a merciful one, he hoped it would be given effect to. The Magistrate, Curtis Bennett, was equally complacent. The prosecution had been rightly taken, he said, and the evidence was sufficient to commit, but he feared Mrs. Tuke was in a very serious condition of health. Therefore she was discharged. Her illness was short-lived. She was presently back again at the office, having acquired, owing to the absence of others of more knowledge and experience, a greater authority than before. She even presided at a meeting in the Albert Hall, though her inexperience as a speaker ill-fitted her for the task.

The comparative leniency of her treatment was strikingly exemplified by a tragic case which occurred a few days later. On the Sunday following the Hobhouse speech, the police raid on Clements Inn and the arrest of the Pethick Lawrences, Nurse Ellen Pitfield resolved on a symbolic act of protest. An ill-paid midwife, she had sustained on " Black Friday " a wound which remained open. Arrested during the struggle that day, she was next morning committed to prison for two months. Her wound never healed, cancer developed, and after two unsuccessful operations she was declared incurable. A friend who saw it told me that the gaping wound in her thigh was like that of a poor, neglected sheep. Knowing herself a dying woman, she now entered the General Post Office, almost deserted on Sunday, and there set light to a basket of wood shavings she had brought with her. Having done so, she ran outside, broke a window, and gave herself up to a policeman. The little blaze had already been extinguished by the watchman, who came out of his box when he heard the smashing of glass. For this symbolic pretence at arson, she was committed for trial, bail being refused. On March 19th she was sentenced to six months' imprisonment, though she had been carried to Court from her bed in the prison hospital, and the prison doctor testified that she was now so ill that she would never walk again. The Men's Political Union organized a petition for her release which was effected in May. Sympathizers subscribed to send her to a nursing home, where she died in August. She had been arrested five times, and was forcibly fed in 1909. She had said on her release then:

" There are only two things that matter to me in the world : principle and liberty. For these I will fight as long as there is life in my veins. I am no longer an individual, I am an instrument."

On March 28th the Conciliation Bill came up for Second Reading. The *Manchester Guardian* had disclosed that the Irish would vote against it. Keir Hardie, Lansbury and others made no secret of the fact that Members were canvassing against the Bill, on the plea that Asquith would resign if it were carried, and Lloyd George's secretary, Mr. Crawshay Williams, organized a round-robin against the Bill. *Votes for Women* accused Lloyd George of being the true author of these machinations. Crawshay Williams protested that he had acted on his own initiative without consulting his chief, but the W.S.P.U. insisted that his action had been prompted by the knowledge that it would be pleasing to Lloyd George. The Master of Elibank, the Chief Government Whip, urged Members to vote against the Bill, declaring that its passage would mean a Cabinet split. When the Bill came on, Asquith, despite his oft-repeated promises of neutrality, made a fierce attack on it, sardonically observing that the result of the division would provide a measure of the advance which the question had made in public estimation since the last debate. Sir William Byles revealed the situation very clearly. He feared, he said, that the question was becoming " a dangerous one." If he found it would imperil the stability of the Government he would " leave the question severely alone till the danger is past." The Bill had been carried in 1911 by a majority of a hundred and thirty-nine; it was now defeated by fourteen votes. Thirty-six Irish Nationalists voted or paired against it. Only nine defied their Party Whip and voted for it. Willie Redmond, a life-long supporter, was absent unpaired. A large number of Labour members were compelled to be away on account of negotiations arising from the great industrial disputes; only twenty-five of them out of forty-two were present to vote, and only two of the absentees had paired with opponents. The defeat was therefore described by some people as a chance vote, but there is no doubt that had more Labour Members been present to support the Bill, more Irish, if not also more Liberals, would have been whipped to oppose it. Sir Thomas Whittaker, one of the Liberals who voted against the Bill, said he was "animated by a strong desire to manifest admiration and give personal support to the Prime Minister." *The Times* observed:

"The House of Commons followed Mr. Asquith in his arguments, which are admirable, and has saved him from the effects of his promise."

The manœuvres by which the Bill had been defeated were an ill omen for the fate of amendments to the Reform Bill.

Whilst the Labour Party support had been weak indeed, it was the large turnover of Irish votes which had wrecked the Conciliation Bill. English Suffragists were angry and disappointed; the Irish Party had long been considered staunch, in the main, for the suffrage cause.

In Ireland the defection of Irish Members, who had given their pledges to Irish women, was received with consternation. It was unworthy of the freedom-loving Irish race, men and women declared, to follow the hated, overbearing Saxon in opposing the liberties of one's fellow creatures. Professor Oldham of University College, Dublin, refused on this account to speak at a Nationalist Demonstration, and he wrote to John Redmond, complaining that he had smirched the honour of the Irish Party. Irish women had hitherto taken part in all Nationalist political functions; they were now excluded. Members of the Irish Women's Franchise League parading the streets with sandwich boards, bearing the demand for Votes for Women in the Home Rule Bill, were attacked by stewards of the Nationalist demonstration. Redmond received a deputation of the League, and plainly told them he would oppose Votes for Women for Westminster and for Dublin, but refused to permit his statement to be published. A little later women delegates were excluded from the Nationalist Convention called to consider the Home Rule Bill, and Women's Suffrage amendments were abandoned by those who had promised to sponsor them, in response to the platform appeal for unity. The daughters of Gavan Duffy and the great-granddaughter of O'Connell, waiting with other women at the doors, were prevented from entering the Convention by a police cordon. They received no answer to their plea for a hearing. That night the Franchise League painted "Votes for Women" on the offices of the United Irish League. Prominent in all this were Hannah Sheehy Skeffington and her husband, who became the non-combatant martyr of Easter Week, 1916.[1] In 1911 I had

---

[1] Arrested by the military when putting up notices appealing to the people not to loot, he was shot without even a semblance of a trial. It is said that, left for dead, he crawled across the yard in his agony, and was finally dispatched some hours later.

seen him at the office of his weekly paper, *The Irish Citizen*, a small man in knee-breeches, jumping about as though on springs, with a red beard covering the greater part of his face. " Skeffy," he was widely called in affection and in derision. He was a citizen of the world, a comradely man, with broad views and a quick intelligence—essentially a pioneer.

At this juncture it was reported that Chinese Women Suffragists, having been offered by the Nankin Assembly only an academic expression of approval of Votes for Women, had rushed into the chamber, breaking windows and assaulting the Members. Soldiers were brought in, but the shadow was replaced by the substance. Votes for Women was established. It was a short-lived victory in a land where revolution and counter-revolution succeeded each other in a bewildering whirl, yet the news played its part in stirring up British indignation : the unchanging East had given votes to its women, whilst the women of Britain, who had worked for the vote for half a century, were denied. The New York Suffragists now held their first big procession, in which was a banner : " Catching up to China ! "

The repercussion of the great stone-throwing raids had reached me in the United States. At the first shock of it many American supporters were estranged. People about me drew away, becoming reserved and distant, or uttering a grieved rebuke. Enthusiastic college girls of Michigan University, Ann Arbor, where I arrived while the news was fresh, ran about with me, trying to gain information from the Press, and joined me in sending a telegram to Clements Inn. There was always enthusiasm at the great meetings, and as I travelled from town to town, many a cable of sympathy was sent from the audiences, but individuals were cautious of committing themselves. Already the November militancy had exercised a deterrent effect upon some people. In the previous year, when the truce was in force, and the prophets declared the vote almost won, the past militancy had been everywhere popular. With the newly-appointed governor of a women's prison, I had then planned to decorate the prison chapel, and to train the prisoners to aid me in the work. I had anticipated great joy in this task for me, and great enlargement of interest for the prisoners. I was to give my services gratuitously, having earned enough to do so by lecturing. The date of the enterprise was to be fixed on my return visit, and in the meantime the governor was to broach the matter to her committee. Yet when I returned she was evasive; nothing had been arranged. Perhaps it was that the ardour with which she had entered on her new duties had faded; evidently she had lost interest in the scheme. I thought the renewal of militancy the cause. The incident affected me greatly. It would be useless, I told myself, even to attempt any serious project till the vote were won; the prejudices of other people would always intervene. Then came the March outbreak and the conspiracy charge; I neither could nor would now withdraw to another country, nor immerse myself in any large work unconnected with the movement.

I clearly foresaw the coming struggle—painful and long. The W.S.P.U. had set itself to more serious militancy; the Government would retaliate with more drastic punishment. The psychology of politics necessitated that there should be no flinching, that above all the tide of popular sympathy and support must not be allowed to recede. The movement must not dwindle to a small group, however determined and heroic. To save the militants from years of imprisonment, or death by the hunger strike and forcible feeding, to prevent the cause from being beaten back for a generation, as has happened to many a cause, a large popular agitation for the vote itself must be maintained at fever heat, and the fate of the prisoners always kept in the public eye. The four most prominent had been seized; others would follow. Every one of us would be needed. I determined that on my return home I would give all my time as a voluntary worker in the active movement, doing whatever I saw required to be done which would not be attempted without my intervention. What I had earned in America would maintain me for some time. I would add to it by writing occasional articles.

Mrs. Pankhurst had already been released on bail [1] when I arrived in London, the remainder of her sentence for window breaking being remitted until after the conspiracy trial. She was now recuperating with friends in the country. Sister Pine, at the nursing home, gave me Christabel's address, and lent me a nurse's uniform that I might cross over to see her unobserved. Consumed with anxiety lest I should betray her whereabouts, on arrival in Paris I changed my clothes in the railway station, walked swiftly through the streets, turning sharply to see if I were followed, then hired a conveyance, drove for a distance, walked again, hired another conveyance, and finally drove to my destination: Christabel's flat in the Hôtel Cité Bergère.

I found her entirely serene, enjoying the exciting crisis of the W.S.P.U. and her new life in Paris, the shops and the Bois. After the strenuous office routine of Clements Inn—correspondence, meetings, interviews—Paris meant relaxation. Her articles dashed

[1] April 8th.

off at great speed, she was ready for sight-seeing, for which I had
no heart, keyed as I was for the struggle, and awed by the suffering for so many in imprisonment and loss of health, friends, employment, which I knew the heightened militancy would produce.
As to the movement, she was gay and confident: everything was
organized; everything in order. I asked her what I might best
do to help. " Behave as though you were not in the country! "
she answered cheerfully. " When those who are doing the work
are arrested, you may be needed, and can be called on." To me
the reply was ludicrous; with our mother facing a conspiracy
charge, and the movement limitless in its need. " You don't
expect me to behave as though I were afraid? " I asked her. She
conceded amiably: " Well, just speak at a few meetings." I saw
that, consciously or unconsciously, she did not welcome my intervention. She was so absolutely convinced that her own policy was
the only correct one, so intensely jealous for it, that instinctively
she thrust aside whoever might differ from her tactics by a hair's-
breadth. " I would not care if *you* were multiplied by a hundred,
but one of Adela is too many! " she had said to me but recently.
Now it was clearly evident to me that I too might become superfluous in her eyes. I made no comment. I had always been
scrupulous neither to criticize nor oppose her, to show no open
divergence of opinion in relation to the movement. I was still
prepared to uphold her, and for the sake of unity to subordinate
my views in many matters to hers, but her refusal to ask any
service of me would leave me the more free to do what I thought
necessary in my own way. I accepted that position without
regret, desiring only to be of service. I could not express to her
my views on policy; she desired only to impose her own. That,
too, I accepted, as one accepts that the rose bears thorns. Yet, in
our mutual reserve about that which most greatly occupied our
minds, I found talk on indifferent matters intolerable. She was
insistent that I should desire to see some pictures; I suggested a
visit to the Panthéon to see the paintings of Puvvis de Chavannes.
From thence I accompanied her to a favourite little shop, where
she purchased a dress, and I yielded to her pressure to do the
same. Then I left by the night boat, unable to endure another
day.

There was work enough to occupy me in London. Propaganda was never more difficult. Audiences were hostile, speakers
were swept from the open-air platforms with cries of: " You
ought to be hung! " Moreover there was an outcry in the Union
that propaganda meetings were useless, the one thing essential
being the destruction of private property to arouse the public, and
the terrorizing of Cabinet Ministers. Both in speaking and

organizing, I set to work to combat this view, and to secure the extension, not the slackening, of propaganda work.

Two hundred prisoners were denied the privileges of Rule 243A. The discipline in the prisons was being tightened. The hunger strike for political status broke out in Aylesbury, then in Holloway, and Winson Green, Birmingham. Forcible feeding followed. I addressed a letter and a report containing the statements of prisoners who had been forcibly fed under aggravated conditions in 1909-10 to Members of Parliament and the Press, showing that harmful as forcible feeding must be in any event, in dozens of cases it had been accompanied by wanton cruelty: confinement in dark, damp punishment cells, handcuffing, frog marching, and beating. Sir Charles Henry, the brother-in-law of my friends Alice and Irene Lewisohn of New York, called the attention of the Home Secretary to my letter, and urged that the prison authorities and officials should be protected from charges of this nature. Sir Charles Henry was a virulent anti-Suffragist, and a reactionary on most questions; his wife was a constitutional Suffragist. McKenna replied that my letter was " a tissue of falsehoods," and my charges " carefully made in such general terms as to prevent the possibility of legal proceedings being taken against those responsible for the falsehoods."

Keir Hardie defended me, saying he had particulars of the cases referred to in his pocket, and that a copy had been sent to McKenna himself. I was anxious to be prosecuted; any failure to particularize fully was due to the need of condensation for the Press. I addressed to the Press a further, more detailed statement. Whilst I was writing it, Miss Lilla Durham, who had just been released from Holloway, called in to tell me that on March 3rd, 1912, she had been frog-marched in that prison. I vainly challenged McKenna to prosecute me for libel. Lady Selborne publicly urged him to do so.

Among the few in the House of Commons who defended the hunger strikers was William O'Brien, who had fought for political treatment in prison and won it from a Tory Government. Finally, when most of the prisoners had been released, the hunger strike terminated by the grant of Rule 243A to the remainder.

CHAPTER II

ON May 15th began the conspiracy trial at the Old Bailey, that Court of mockery and doom, where I had heard poor Margaret Murphy sentenced to death. The feeble, foolish paintings in its entrance hall, " The Golden Age " and the rest, so talked of at the R.C.A. when I was a student, because our Professor Moira was one of their painters, seemed like a silly gibe at the unhappy people dragged within those walls. The Judge in his silk and scarlet, the old men in their blue robes and their red robes fringed with fur, and the heavy gold chains about their necks, the under Sheriffs, with their white lace ruffles and bouquets of flowers and herbs to ward off gaol fever, were all part of a grim burlesque; a caricature of the Middle Ages flaunting a sour, inhuman visage. Police witnesses, constables in uniform and detectives in plain clothes, crowded the Court, scanning the faces of Suffragettes to learn their features for future reference. Among the wigged functionaries of the legal sphere wherein no woman might yet intrude, sat Sir Rufus Isaacs, the Attorney-General, with handsome Jewish face and dark hawk's eye. Beside him " Bodkin," " Sir Archibald " as he presently became, making those fatuously insulting remarks so often pilloried in the *Daily Herald*. Ruddy and bald, with an egg-shaped head, he was the very image of " Alley-Sloper," depicted in the comic papers the servants were reading in the kitchen when I was a little girl in Russell Square. Tim Healey, for the defence, a Chaucer-like figure with his square cranium, his deep, rich brogue and flashes of sudden satire. In the dock the two women, each with her special charm, serenely determined to make a platform of it: the one impervious to small points, searching to fathom the inner mysticism and eternal verities of the situation in which they found themselves; the other swifter and more impassioned than a tigress, sensitive to the waves of emotion surging about her; by turns petulant, imperious and appealing. She recalled the fact that in 1868 her husband had stood beside the father of the Judge, pleading the legal claim to women's enfranchisement in the case of Chorlton *v.* Lings. She was now in the flood-tide of the last great energies of her personality, before the disintegrating ravages of old age should

386

begin to steal upon her. The man in the dock, to the public eye an unattractive foil to the two women beside him, blunt and precise, fastidious and orderly in mind, correctly conventional in attire; yet displaying an unusual selflessness, having chosen a part which few men of equal ability and position would have been willing to adopt; a part undertaken by reason of a general sense of fairness, an instinctive, often-displayed impulse to support the weak and oppressed; above all from a great devotion to the woman who was his life's partner, and an abounding faith in her instincts and judgement of profound issues. Till near the end of the six days' hearing these three were repressed, for long intervals almost effaced by the tedious formalities of the Court.

Melhuish, the gloomy ironmonger of Fetter Lane, gave evidence of the purchase of hammers used in the "raid." Shopkeepers, borne down by business considerations, gave testimony to the destruction of windows. In droning accents letters were maundered through which the two women in the dock had sent giving advice and instructions to prison volunteers, not to bring money, furs or jewellery to the demonstration; what to do on arrest; what to bring to the police court the next day; the conduct to be followed in prison. A code was produced, never used as it happened, which had been discovered at Clements Inn, giving names of Cabinet Ministers, railway stations, important places in London, and such phrases as: "Don't get arrested unless success depends on it" and "How many are prepared for arrest?" Militant speeches and articles were quoted; the most violent from Christabel:

" They say we are going to get heavy sentences. I say we might as well be hung for a sheep as a lamb. Let them give us seven years if they like, I am ready for it . . . we shall do our bit . . . even if it is burning down a palace."

The W.S.P.U. printer and banker were called by the prosecution, the latter testifying that the finances of the Union were "conducted on extremely good business lines." A woman was led weeping into the box, Lilian Ball, a pitiable witness for the prosecution, a Tooting dressmaker, who went as a Suffragette stone-thrower to Holloway. Prepared for a sentence of seven days only, she received two months' hard labour. Concerned for her delicate little boy, she had made a statement to detectives who visited her in prison, in the vain hope that her sentence would be reduced. She testified that she had been called by a W.S.P.U. circular to a certain place, where she had been given a bag of stones and advised which window to break.

The defendants made no denial of the charges; the burden of their argument was that the Government had dealt falsely with the Votes for Women Cause. Accepting the charge as they did, the hostile speech of Justice Coleridge, with its attempts to rebut their accusations against the Government, was not necessary to secure a conviction. Party feeling in a Judge is peculiarly unbecoming. The jury displayed a more generous spirit. Whilst finding the defendants guilty, they added:

" We desire unanimously to express the hope that taking into consideration the undoubtedly pure motives that underlie the agitation which has led to this trial, you will be pleased to exercise the utmost leniency in dealing with the case."

·The Judge pronounced sentence of nine months' imprisonment, and refused, in harsh terms, the application of the prisoners to be treated as First Class misdemeanants.

I sat through the trial, weighed down by a deep sadness that all this struggle should still be necessary for the winning of so simple and obvious a reform. I knew that the three in the dock would not accept the provisions of Rule 243A, but would hunger strike, if necessary, for full political treatment. Under the gloom of this prospect I went, after the trial, to Merthyr Tydfil, to take part in the W.S.P.U. demonstrations held to impress the I.L.P. Annual Conference, which that year had been postponed from Easter on account of the industrial upheaval. I was so stunned and shocked, that when I spoke at the great drill hall meeting it seemed that each word I uttered was wrapped in cotton wool which must be painfully unfolded. At last all went black, and I dropped into my seat lest I should fall from the high platform to the auditorium.

We received a tremendous welcome both from the delegates and the people of the locality, but we made no members for the W.S.P.U. To join it entailed a pledge to abstain from working for any Parliamentary candidate, and not a woman who sympathized with us would debar herself from working for Keir Hardie. The Conference declared its opposition to any Reform Bill in which women were not included, and demanded a Government measure giving Adult Suffrage to men and women. I was rejoiced to see the agitation going forward on those large lines. Indeed, if anything could relieve the load of anxiety and foreboding by hopeful anticipations, it was the big, friendly movement in Merthyr.

Unless the demand for First Division treatment were granted within a week the hunger strike was to begin. Asquith was bombarded with memorials from one hundred Members of

Parliament, presented by Atherley Jones,[1] the son of the great Chartist; from principals, wardens, lecturers, tutors and fellows of Oxford, Cambridge and London Universities; from Suffrage and other organizations in Germany, France, Italy, Austria and most other European countries; from India, the Dominions, and the United States; from international notabilities, including Jean Jaures, Romain Rolland, Maurice Maeterlinck, Madame Curie, Professor Westermark, Victor Adler, Peter Kropotkin, Olive Schreiner, Ellen Key, Upton Sinclair, Selma Lagerlöf, George Brandes. The agitation was successful. Before the week had elapsed the three leaders were transferred to the First Division, but, as had previously been resolved, they now immediately announced that, failing the grant of equal privileges to the rank and file, whom they were convicted of inciting, they would join the other seventy-nine Suffragette prisoners in the hunger strike. Again there was tremendous excitement; marches round the prison, meetings, memorials, Parliamentary questions. However much one felt it was to the large public we must appeal, one could not refrain from giving every available moment to efforts to influence Members of Parliament and the Government. Josiah Wedgwood has since told me, with his jocular habit of exaggerating, that I *almost* wept on his breast in my anxiety for my mother. Certainly there were many beside myself who were keyed to a pitch of distraction. Sir John Rolleston moved the adjournment of the House, and bitterly remarked that until a female prisoner being forcibly fed were displayed at Madame Tussauds, the representation of the history of our times, there and elsewhere, would not be complete. The waxworks proprietors have not yet adopted the suggestion of Sir John Rolleston, but I hazard the prophecy that such a representation will in time come to find a place in the House of Commons itself.

Keir Hardie, complaining of the cruelties practised on hunger strikers, was assailed with a shout: "The Home Secretary has denied it!" "I am not concerned with the denials; I am only concerned with the facts!" he answered. The phrase became a slogan.

" Be they leaders or rank and file, forcible feeding will be adopted if they do not take their food,"

McKenna declared on June 20th. On June 23rd George Lansbury made a scene in the House, which caused the *Herald* to come out with the headline, " Thank God for Lansbury! "

[1] He made a very warm public defence of the conspirators, admitting that he had a " hereditary interest in political prisoners " and referred to his father's incarceration in 1848.

Some Suffragette prisoners, on account of the illness of relatives, had petitioned for release, and had been met with the stipulation that they must give a life undertaking to abstain from all militant action.   Asquith, in the House that day, broke testily upon the protests :

"There is not one single prisoner who cannot go out of prison this afternoon by giving the undertaking asked for by the Home Secretary."

Lansbury sprang to his feet at the end of the front bench below the gangway :

"You know they cannot; it is perfectly disgraceful that the Prime Minister of England should make such a statement."

He strode up the gangway to Asquith :

"That was a disgraceful thing for you to say, sir. . . . You will go down to history as the man who tortured innocent women. . . . You ought to be driven from public life. . . ."

The House, so easily excited, was in an uproar.   Lansbury shouted above the din that the women were "fighting for principle," that Members would "be better employed in doing the same," and that the House had "lost all respect."   At last the Speaker induced him to obey his command to leave the Chamber.   Immediately afterwards Isabel Irvine broke a glass panel in the central lobby, and, according to the *Daily Chronicle,* a report ran through the House that an army of Suffragettes with hammers had seized all the doors and would presently appear to attack the Members.   To a very wide public Lansbury was for the time being by far the most popular man in the House of Commons.   To thousands in the Suffrage movement he had become a hero and a saint.

Meanwhile, on June 22nd, forcible feeding had begun in the three prisons where Suffragettes were confined.   Mrs. Pankhurst, ill from fasting and suspense, grasped the earthen toilet ewer and threatened to fling it at the doctors and wardresses, who appeared with the feeding tube.   They withdrew, and the order for her release was issued next day.   Mrs. Lawrence was forcibly fed, but only once, and two days later she was released.   Her husband, in Pentonville, was forcibly fed for five days.   To punish Pethick Lawrence, to make him taste the hardships of prison, and to get at his money, had long been the cherished wish of certain opponents, enraged that a man of means should be helping the detested Suffragettes.   Not content with his imprisonment, and the actions for damages pending in the Courts, they succeeded also in getting him expelled from the

Reform Club, of which he had been a member for twenty years.

The three released leaders retired to the country to recuperate; the rank and file maintained the bitter fight in prison. Emily Wilding Davison, the victim of the fire-hose incident of 1909, who had barricaded herself in a Manchester prison cell to avoid the misery of forcible feeding, again found it so unendurable that she threw herself over the railings of the staircase. She was caught by the wire screen across the lower floor, but hurled herself from the screen to the iron staircase below and received grave injuries; yet hurt as she was, she was forcibly fed more than once before release.

Even Government medical witnesses had testified that artificial feeding under any circumstances was an operation involving elements of danger, and requiring care and medical experience, yet at this time forcible feeding was actually performed by wardresses who lacked even the rudiments of a nurse's training. These tyros resorted to pummelling and tickling to overcome the resistance of their patients.

By July 6th all the hunger strikers had been released, forty-five of them before the end of their sentences. The sad controversy respecting the treatment of Lady Constance Lytton as Jane Warton still dragged on. She was now stricken with paralysis.

Meanwhile, wherever a Cabinet Minister showed himself, the Suffragettes and their men supporters were sure to be heard. A reception to the Prime Minister at the National Liberal Club was postponed on this account. At an India Office reception, Asquith and other Ministers were many times accosted with the familiar question. One of the interrogators reported that John Burns himself attempted to eject her, pinioning her arms, and thrusting her along before him, shouting: " Clear the way there! " pushing past the guests and stumbling over ladies' trains. A waiter called to him: " There is no door that way! " He answered, " There shall be a door! " but reaching the end of the corridor he was obliged to return with his prisoner. When Lloyd George spoke at the Kennington Theatre, Charles Gray, a student for the Congregational ministry, attempted to accost him. In the rush to remove Gray, both he and Lloyd George were thrown to the ground, for which cause Gray was sent to prison for two months' hard labour. Tim Healey, at a W.S.P.U. meeting in the Albert Hall, accused the Government of " specious and continuous hypocrisy " towards the Suffragists. Lloyd George denounced the W.S.P.U. as " a copious fountain of mendacity." At his meetings in Wales Suffragette interrupters were furiously maltreated, the Chancellor inciting his supporters to the task.   At Wrexham he cried:

"I remember little eisteddfodau at which prizes were given for . . . the best hazel stick.   One of those sticks would be rather a good thing to have just now."

The hazel sticks did not fail, and both inside the meeting hall and by the crowd assembled outside, men and women were beaten, kicked and stripped almost naked.   The hair of the women was torn out in handfuls.   The few police on duty struggled to save the victims from fatal injury.   Liberal and Conservative papers alike testified to the extraordinary ferocity displayed.   To interrupt at Lloyd George's native village, Llanystymdwy, after what had happened at Wrexham, meant courage indeed.   Yet women bravely endured the ordeal.   The *Globe* devoted a leading article to the occasion, entitled "Chivalry," declaring the treatment meted out to the Suffragettes had been "shameful" and "degrading to manhood."   "It was a revelation of the latent beast in man," wrote one of the women.   They were dressed in thick, strong clothing, but it was torn to ribands, and two of them at least were left without a shred upon their bodies.   The Press and the women themselves testified that the police had with difficulty saved their lives. Llanystymdwy was long a by-word.

Votes for Women declared that the W.S.P.U. regarded the heroines of Llanystymdwy "with devotion."   Yet some of the sheltered habitués of Clements Inn objected to the attitude of the girls who had faced the fray; it was too bold and defiant for their approval, and lacking in appropriate womanly distress. Quietly they were replaced by a more orthodox type of young woman.

CHAPTER III

I had prevailed upon the local W.S.P.U.'s to organize a series of great meetings throughout the summer in all the principal parks and open spaces around London: Ealing and Wimbledon Common, Regent's Park, Gladstone Park, Blackheath, the historic site of Wat Tyler's encampment, Peckham Rye, Clapham Common, Finsbury Park, Streatham Common and so on, to culminate in a great Hyde Park demonstration on July 14th, the anniversary of the fall of the Bastille, and Mrs. Pankhurst's birthday. The local demonstrations and the Hyde Park meeting itself were worked up by open air speeches, chalking, canvassing and poster parades, of unexampled thoroughness. It was the greatest propaganda campaign since that for the Hyde Park meeting of 1908, and this time all done by volunteer workers, with comparatively little expenditure even for printing. The 'buses and tubes printed and displayed free advertisements, and even granted reduced fares to groups of fifteen or more persons booking to the Park. Such funds as we had, were raised by a joint appeal to assist the holding of popular demonstrations issued by Lady Sybil Smith, who acted as treasurer, and myself.

Sybil Smith was a being of great charm. Her tall and slender figure remained as lithe and straight as a young girl's when the flaxen hair she had in the days of those meetings had turned white. Gay and vivacious, her swift mind leaping from point to point, her speech like a bright cascade of scintillating ideas and merry quips, she had often a pretty little air of diffident self-depreciation, which seemed to belong to the young bride of eighteen whom she had never left behind. She was a Tolstoyan in theory, and inherently incapable of class pride or prejudice. An enthusiastic mother, she had seven children whom she adored, yet regarded with a detachment which strove to understand and aid the development of each young individuality. Her abounding vitality knew no limit to its sympathies. Her voice had been highly trained: Ethel Smyth said of her that as a singer she was "completely equipped with music." She was ever ready to use it in the service of the movement, looking then, in her long straight gown, like a nymph from a Greek vase. Elsa Dalglish, a landscape painter, with the considerable capacity for hard work in other spheres the artist often displays, was financial secretary to the campaign. I was careful to work in harmony with Mrs. Drummond, and to declare the campaign conducted under her auspices, as the local unions were regarded as being in her department. Having no particular projects of her own, she was glad enough to see someone coming along with ideas and funds to set things humming. The Hyde Park meeting, although there were no processions to draw the people there, as before, was the largest ever held by any movement of those times save the phenomenal gathering of 1908. Moreover, it was by far the most enthusiastic. To the 1908 meeting the tremendous advertisement had drawn a large sight-seeing element, and a proportion of hostile rowdies; this was a great demonstration of support. The majority of the other Suffrage Societies, the I.L.P. and the Fabians co-operated, only the N.U.W.S.S. holding aloof. There were twenty platforms, far too few for the vast throng. At each platform were twelve banners in the colours of its organization, mounted on staves, thirteen feet high, topped with scarlet caps of liberty and supported by women in white. The banners and caps were adapted from those carried in the great franchise demonstrations of the 'sixties. A hundred and fifty brass bandsmen were grouped at the foot of a huge laurel-wreathed flag pole, from which waved the colours of the W.S.P.U.

Memories of the day drift back to me. The blaze of colour in the Park. The scarlet caps, gorgeously flaming red on their long poles. The wide banners, floating above the concourse, like boat sails on a sea of people; boat sails floating in concentric circles, gaily emblazoned as for some huge regatta, with all the colours of the comrades, for every organization had its colours now : purple, white and green, often repeated for the W.S.P.U.; orange and green for the Irish; strong, almost startling bars of black and white for the Writers'; green and gold with the red dragon of Wales; the sombre black and brown of the Tax Resisters, which somehow always brought to my mind Wat Tyler and the peasants who fought to abolish serfdom five hundred years before, though it was always of John Hampden the Tax Resisters spoke; brilliant red and white for Labour, with Keir Hardie speaking from the lorry in a white suit and red plaid tie; Lansbury, a huge figure on a high W.S.P.U. platform; a host of women speakers. The swelling music of " The March of the Women," strong and martial, bold with the joy of battle and endeavour, yet with a lasting undertone of sadness characteristic of that rebellious soul, there in her fierce energy conducting in the fine white and lilac academic robes of Durham University;

everywhere the scarlet caps of Liberty seeming to burn with delight in the radiant sun.

Here was the reward of hard labour; the pleasure to the eye of the fine spectacle; the sense of achievement in having seen it grow from the first mental conception; above all, the knowledge that this demonstration of large scale support would give the lie to the idea that the movement was dwindling and could be crushed. Beforehand there had been the work and the struggle, to accomplish the big thing at little cost; to bring everyone round to it in face of a silent element of hostility, sensed rather than seen. Clearly remembered still are the humours and the work in the little white studio in a Kensington garden, lent for the making of 252 great caps and banners and the hundreds of smaller flags; the gay-spirited volunteers, coming to me with a cup of tea and their difficulties, when I rushed in to visit them; the bunting, cottons and fringes always running short. What a hunt for the white bullion fringe for the pink, white and green banners of the Actresses' Franchise League, who fiercely refused to accept a trimming of the traditional yellow! After half London had been searched for it, the desired white fringe was found in John Barker's hire department, left over from Queen Victoria's funeral. In the last thirty-six hours the studio garden grew crowded with caps and banners strung up on their long poles. Two lovely girls sat out there through the blue twilight and black night, with the lamplight on their faces, till the fresh, clear dawn, with the rosy glow in the sky, sewing away at the red dragons of Wales, which I, in the studio, was drawing on scarlet flannel, with lighted candles stuck in bottles around me to reinforce the gas. Such aids to sight were scorned by the dark, bright eyes of Zelie Emerson, that merry little American, whose youthful desire for adventure had brought her across the Atlantic to join the movement. Elsa Dalglish hovered about, arranging with orderly precision the details for the morrow. When I rose in broad sunshine from finishing the last dragon, my legs were swollen to an extraordinary size. " Look at you, you'll never be able to speak! " the others exclaimed at the sight of them. I laughed: " There is no procession; don't make a fuss! "

The only jarring note in the local demonstrations had been the complaints of questioners who believed us to be advocating a limited vote, and reproached us for not demanding womanhood suffrage. This impression was intensified by the terms of the old, stock resolution, sent out from headquarters, demanding a measure giving votes to women " on the same terms as men," and wholly ignoring the new situation created by the Reform

Bill. For Hyde Park I drafted a resolution repudiating "the introduction of any measure to extend the Parliamentary Franchise which does not sweep away both the sex and marriage disqualifications at present erected against women," and calling upon the Government " to introduce into the Reform Bill provisions for securing political equality for men and women." As soon as the London campaign was on foot, I had urged the provincial unions to join the effort. In Aberdeen, Edinburgh, Dundee, Newcastle, Sunderland, North and South Shields, Hull, Jarrow, York, Manchester, Bradford, Halifax, Sheffield, and other towns large demonstrations were held, and at many of them I rushed up to speak, or to spend some days organizing.

In the midst of all this came a message from Christabel : Would I burn down Nottingham Castle? The request came as a shock to me. The idea of doing a stealthy deed of destruction was repugnant. I did not think such an act could assist the cause. Though I knew she did not consider it so, I had the unhappy sense of having been asked to do something morally wrong. I replied that I should be willing to lead a torchlight procession to the castle, to fling my torch at it, and to call the others to do the same, as a symbolic act. I was presently sent to speak at a by-election in Nottingham, but no procession had been arranged, and we were obliged to struggle with a hostile audience to procure a partial hearing.

After Hyde Park I was asked to go to a by-election in the Crewe division, where the W.S.P.U. lacked speakers. Zelie Emerson accompanied me. The disintegrating effect of the many incarcerations was here apparent; obviously the solitary ruler of the Union in Paris was not always receiving a correct impression of its activities. The organizer was inexperienced, temperamentally unsuited to the work, and poorly supplied with assistants in a large, scattered constituency. " Town Hall, Crewe," was a good address to put in *Votes for Women* as the W.S.P.U. committee rooms, but it proved to be a small upstairs office in the town hall building, situated in a side street, without even a notice in the window. The National Union of Suffrage Societies and other propaganda organizations, even the anti-Suffragists, had shops on main thoroughfares in Crewe, and some also in Nantwich and Sandbach. I could imagine the frown of Mrs. Pankhurst had she seen the small show made by her Union. " This Liberal candidate is going to get in : it is no use wasting our efforts on him," the organizer told me blandly, with that assumption of political prescience which had become the fashion amongst women in those days, unaware that the intervention of a Labour candidate must affect the

Liberal vote. As a matter of fact the Liberal was thrown out, the Tory secured the seat, and the Labour Party was exceedingly pleased with the poll of its candidate as a first attempt. I bandied no words with the organizer, but immediately telegraphed to Manchester and London for more workers, and sent an unvarnished account of the facts to Paris. A reply came in haste, asking me to do what I thought necessary. Whether we were changing votes or not, we had soon managed to secure for the W.S.P.U. the centre of the stage in that election, and were holding meetings practically all day. With her furious energy and resource, and the American genius for advertisement, Zelie Emerson was a battering-ram to be turned on many a difficulty. The principal evening meetings were held in the market-place, thronged to capacity, the speakers shouting each other down. Leaving this over-crowded square to the timid, we risked becoming an isolated side show, by raising up our voices on a great dusty stretch of waste land, "the Catholic bank"; but before we did it the town had been chalked from end to end, announcing the remove. Votes for Women, militant tactics, the hunger strike, forcible feeding—these were notorious; to hear of them we drew such audiences that presently the market-place was deserted. Candidates, Tariff Reformers, Free Traders, and all the others who flocked to elections in those days, had followed us to the new pitch. The election literature had been written in Paris. We supplemented it with leaflets bristling with local facts of hardships suffered by women in industry and in the home; facts brought to us as women by women, of which the candidates never heard. A big shop, with a great curved frontage, at the junction of three main roads, fell vacant in the centre of the town. We took it for our committee rooms, filled its windows with enormous posters, quickly produced by a number of workers, demanding political equality, and announcing a "Women's Day in Crewe," with a great procession and demonstration, for the eve of the poll, and a similar function the day preceding in Nantwich, where Zelie had opened a centre. We wired to Clements Inn for banners and tri-colours, Zelie and I determined and convinced, whoever might be doubters, that the women of Crewe should and would march and carry our banners, though the W.S.P.U. had no branch and no membership in the town. The band for the procession was a difficulty. Brass bands, as I learnt for the first time, are voluntary associations, usually of workmen, playing as a spare-time hobby. The six bands of Crewe refused to march with us, because they had Liberal Members. Nantwich, Sandbach, Whitchurch, Middlewich, Tarporley also failed; even to Manchester we telegraphed in vain. At last from the little village of Winsford a sturdy band was procured. Mrs. Drummond came up on the day of the procession, to act as Marshal. "Women's Day" took the constituency by storm. Mothers came in their best clothes, children in white starched frocks, as though for a school treat. We invited the women to muster in the big town hall; enough of them to fill it three times over had to remain outside. As we formed up for the march, men and women flocked into our ranks, clamouring to wear the Votes for Women gum labels we had had printed. Many tore off their Party badges to wear the purple, white and green, but the Tory and Labour, and even the Liberal colours were plentiful in our ranks. A crowd of Liberals had gathered to howl us down when we reached the meeting-place. Silenced by our overwhelming numbers, they were thrust aside in the press. We had made our appeal to the people to unite with us; the people had responded.

Keir Hardie and the others of the Labour Party who, like ourselves, were quartered at the dingy old Temperance Hotel, were enthusiastic about the "Day." They believed we had greatly turned the temper of the constituency against the Government—and that the result would be the transfer of Liberal votes to them, the more so as we had made womanhood suffrage and the needs of the working woman the keynote of our demand. In that election, at least, we were far more popular with the Labour Party workers, both local and imported, than were Mrs. Fawcett's "Constitutional" Suffragists, although the latter had come to the election with their new policy of supporting Labour candidates against the candidates of the Liberal Government.[1] At Holmfirth and Hanley, where they had initiated this new policy, Labour had appeared at the bottom of the poll, and the Liberal had been returned. Hanley had been a Labour seat. It is true that the Liberal single tax candidate, R. L. Outhwaite, was hardly an orthodox Government representative, and his special land programme undoubtedly affected the result; yet it had to be confessed that the "Constitutional" Suffragists' propaganda had hitherto produced no very striking result. Nevertheless their policy, which was suggested to the N.U.W.S.S. by H. N. Brailsford and also now adopted by the Women's Freedom League, had much to

[1] The declared policy of the N.U.W.S.S. was:
   (1) To shorten the term of office of the Cabinet as at present constituted, especially by opposing anti-suffrage Ministers.
   (2) To strengthen any Party in the House which adopted women's suffrage as part of its official programme.

recommend it. Making appeal to the forward element in the electorate, amongst which support for women's suffrage was usually to be found, it was provided with logical arguments: the women were helping the Party most prepared to support their cause; they were not supporting reaction against progress; they were not assisting the return of the Tory Party, which, according to the votes cast by its Members in the House, was obviously more hostile to our cause than were the Liberals. Had the policy been prosecuted with the driving force which the W.S.P.U. had hitherto been able to throw into its campaigns, it might have had a devastating effect upon Government candidatures. The National Union was not, however, an organization which could be looked to for that. Though at last compelled by competition to come out into the open, it was still essentially a movement of the drawing-room. The picturesque movement of the militants, and the struggle of the prisoners held the centre of public interest. The constitutional Suffragists, who condemned the militants, sometimes with more severity than the "Antis" themselves, were regarded by popular audiences as but half-hearted Suffragists. Intrinsically the main drawback to the new policy was the weakness of Labour Party support. Keir Hardie told me that when the constitutional Suffragists had asked his advice about helping the Labour Party, he had said: "Keep your funds; run your campaign in your own way; the Labour Party is not pledged to do anything for you." A story was in circulation, which I had from Mrs. Pankhurst, that when Keir Hardie's remark was repeated by the Suffragists to Ramsay Macdonald, he answered: "Take no notice of Keir Hardie; he is only an old grandfather." Whether the anecdote had a basis of truth, or was merely a picturesque canard, I cannot say. Macdonald had convinced Mrs. Fawcett and her colleagues that the Labour Party attitude on Women's Suffrage was satisfactory to them, but the Party had taken no step to advance a Suffrage Bill of its own; its vote on the Conciliation Bill had been poor, and as yet it was unpledged in respect of its action on the Reform Bill, and had come to no decision as to how it should vote if women were excluded. Macdonald's own intentions were none too clear. His utterances displayed the ambiguity of an accomplished politician. In attacking the "criminality" and "tomfoolery" of the militants, he even suggested that Women's Suffrage might "disappear from practical programmes."

The Reform Bill was introduced on July 17th by an anti-Suffragist Minister, J. A. Pease. As had been foreshadowed, it made no provision for extending the Parliamentary vote to women. Arthur Henderson declared that if women were not included by amendment he would vote against the Bill on its Third Reading; but when he was questioned by F. E. Smith as to the intentions of the Labour Party itself he replied: "I have had no instructions from my leader," and advised the interrogator to ask Macdonald "what course his Party propose to take on the Third Reading." David Mason, a Liberal Member, opposed the Bill because women were left out. Men who were sincere, he said, must admit that Women's Suffrage was the greatest question then before the country. It was dishonest for Members to tell their constituents they were supporters of Votes for Women and then to take part in "a double shuffle" in Parliament to escape from their promises. Ministers who claimed to be Women's Suffragists should resign from the Government if it persisted with a Franchise Bill which did not include women. Members who desired the enfranchisement of women should not support this Bill at any stage, for the women's amendments would probably be defeated, and the Bill carried without them. Lord Robert Cecil adopted the same line. To enfranchise more men, and leave the women outside, was an "intolerable proposal." He was "amazed" at the conduct of Liberal Members, an enormous majority of whom were pledged to give women the vote: "they will go gaily into the Lobby and will not care about their pledges, so long as they keep the Government in office." The Second Reading of the Bill took place in July. Again it was moved by an anti-Suffragist, Lewis Harcourt. Balfour and Bonar Law, with the careful subtilty of statesmen not to commit themselves to policies which might prove embarrassing should they ascend to office, condemned the proposal to admit women to the franchise by way of an amendment, Balfour declaring that to do so would be "the grossest and gravest abuse of our Parliamentary system." The so-called Suffragist members of the Government were silent, save Montague, who said it would be "a mischievous thing" to postpone all other franchise reforms till a Government were agreed on Women's Suffrage, the benefits to be derived from which were "commonly exaggerated." Asquith displayed his satisfaction at the defeat of the Conciliation Bill, casting off all pretence of neutrality:

"This Bill does not propose to confer the franchise upon women; whatever extensions of the franchise it makes are to male persons only. . . . The House at an earlier stage of the Session rejected with, I think, sufficient decisiveness the proposal to confer the franchise upon women. I dismiss at this moment, as an altogether improbable hypothesis, that the House of Commons is likely to stultify itself by reversing the considered judgement at which it has already arrived."

This speech, in view of his promise to remain neutral, and the manner in which his much-advertised promise of a free vote on a suffrage amendment had been used to win support for the Government, was denounced by Philip Snowden as the most " disgraceful episode " of the Prime Minister's career.   The Liberal Press expressed the same opinion more mildly.   The constitutional Suffragists sent Asquith a letter of remonstrance; he answered that his speech did not conflict with his pledges. The Women's Liberal Federation, still anxious to trust their Prime Minister, sent an organizer to work for the Government candidate at Hanley, whose return both Suffragists and Suffragettes were opposing.

Militancy was now assuming a new and serious aspect.   In December, 1911, and March, 1912, Emily Wilding Davison and Nurse Pitfield had committed spectacular arson on their own initiative, both doing their deeds openly and suffering arrest and punishment.   In July, 1912, secret arson began to be organized under the direction of Christabel Pankhurst.   When the policy was fully under way, certain officials of the Union were given, as their main work, the task of advising incendiaries, and arranging for the supply of such inflammable material, house-breaking tools and other matters as they might require.   A certain exceedingly feminine-looking young lady was strolling about London, meeting militants in all sorts of public and unexpected places, to arrange for perilous expeditions.   Women, most of them very young, toiled through the night across unfamiliar country, carrying heavy cases of petrol and paraffine.   Sometimes they failed; sometimes succeeded in setting fire to an untenanted building—all the better if it were the residence of a notability— or a church, or other place of historic interest.   Occasionally they were caught and convicted; usually they escaped.   They exercised every possible care to avoid endangering human life, but works of art, the spiritual offspring of the race, were attacked without ruth.

I regarded this new policy with grief and regret, believing it wholly mistaken and unnecessary, deeply deploring the life of furtive destruction it would impose upon the participators, and the harsh punishment it was preparing for them; for these unknown girls there would be no international telegrams; the mead of public sympathy would be attenuated.   The old, defiant, symbolic militancy performed in the sight of all, punished with a severity out of all proportion to its damage, if damage there were, had roused an enormous volume of support; had brought the Cause to the fore, and would keep it there.   What the movement required, that it might reap what had been sown, was, in my

2D

opinion, a broader and more confident appeal to the people, and the effort, which assuredly would be crowned with success, to make the movement a genuine mass movement. Secret incendiarism, diluted enthusiasm, whittled away supporters, hardened opposition, compelling the propagandist to begin the task of conversion anew. On the other hand the heroism of the militants, and the Government's extraordinary treatment of the Cause, which had now become widely popular, largely neutralized any harm that incendiarism would work. Masses of people were prepared to declare that against a Government so stubborn, women had no alternative but to resort to the desperate means adopted by men in past franchise struggles. Though I deplored the new policy, I uttered no repudiation. To stop it was impossible; to attack it would but have caused another fissure in the movement. I would not add one word to the chorus condemning those courageous girls who trusted implicitly in the wisdom of the Union. I would not advocate secret militancy, I would take no part in it, but repudiation I would leave to others.

The first attempt at serious arson was that to set fire to Nuneham House, the residence of the anti-Suffragist Minister, Lewis Harcourt. On July 12th two militants, with cases of inflammable oil, pick-locks and glass cutters, hired a canoe at Abingdon. One of the two, Helen Craggs, who did all the talking at every stage, referred to the other as " Miss Smyth," but insisted that the boat-keeper should book the name as " Smith." At one a.m. next morning a policeman discovered the women crouching among the ivy by the wall of Nuneham House. Helen Craggs said they were camping out, and had come to look round the house, as it was too hot to sleep. Her embarrassment being obvious, he ordered both women to accompany him to the police station. They attempted to run away. Helen Craggs was captured, but her silent companion, who was traced as having appeared in the neighbourhood as " Miss Smith," escaped across the fields. The boat-keeper was positive the name " Smyth " had been mentioned; a vocal card for Dr. Ethel Smyth's " March of the Women " was found in a book amongst the luggage in the canoe. Dr. Smyth had been arrested for breaking the windows of Harcourt's London house in March; what more likely than that she had pursued her vendetta by attacking his country residence? She was arrested at Hook Heath, and brought to Oxford for identification. She was able to prove a complete alibi. Moreover the witness obstinately refused to identify her. That was a silent woman—but this! Indeed she was very voluble, very indignant. She wrote to the

Press, in high disdain, ridiculing the police for their folly. The alteration of a single vowel in one's name seemed to her " one of the less happy devices " for " securing anonymity." Had she desired that, she might have called herself Brown, Jones or Robinson; certainly not " Miss Smith." Yet if only the police had looked but a little further along the same line they would have discovered the missing culprit, for her name in actual fact was Smyth. Helen Craggs received a sentence of nine months' imprisonment, and was released after a hunger strike of eleven days.

The next sensational attempt at arson occurred in Ireland. The Irish Women's Franchise League had already taken to militancy. On July 13th Mrs. Sheehy Skeffington and seven others broke windows in public offices in Dublin, and were sent to prison for two months, with costs and damages which they never paid. They were treated as first-class misdemeanants, being permitted their own furniture, books, letters and news-papers, and to write to the Press. One of them had a typewriter in her cell; a teacher gave postal lessons to her pupils. The concessions indicated that the authorities were anxious not to inflame the Irish militants. If there were any hope of influenc-ing Redmond and the Irish Party it could only be by the efforts of Irish women. In view of the high tension of nationalist feeling, English women were obviously out of court in that respect. Yet, though the Irishwomen were active and vigilant, the W.S.P.U. would not leave the Irish question to them. When the Conciliation Bill was defeated Christabel sent a poster parade to Parliament Square : " No votes for women, no home rule." As a propaganda manifestation, the demonstration might be well enough; as a serious policy it was fantastic; for not a single Member of Parliament who desired Home Rule would vote against it by way of reprisal. H. N. Brailsford presently joined issue with Christabel on this question, protesting :

" Mr. Redmond sullied the Irish flag by opposing one movement of liberation in the supposed interests of another. His methods are not a model to imitate."

Christabel replied that the Home Rule Bill was an insult to women because it proposed to continue the voteless condition of Irish women under Home Rule, and to deprive the Irish Parlia-ment of the power to alter it for three years. Brailsford was brusquely told : " This is a Women's Movement; the tactics whereby it is advanced must consequently be decided by women." The breach between the W.S.P.U. and Brailsford was now clearly evident, a grievous pity, for he had been a sincere and zealous friend to the Cause and had made a notable sacrifice for it.

When Asquith visited Dublin, on July 18th, Irish Suffragists met him by boat at Kingstown, and shouted to him through megaphones. They rained Votes for Women confetti upon him from an upper window as he and Redmond were conducted in torchlight procession through the streets, but when they attempted poster parades and an open-air meeting close to the hall where he was speaking, a mob attacked them with extraordinary violence. Countess Markievicz and others were hurt; every woman who happened to be in the streets was assailed. Many unconnected with the movement had to take refuge in shops and houses. The Ancient Order of Hibernians was abroad, determined to punish womanhood for the acts of militant women from England. Mary Leigh had rushed to the carriage in which John Redmond and the Prime Minister were riding and had dropped into it a small hatchet.[1] She was mobbed, but escaped, and afterwards she and Gladys Evans had made a spectacular show of setting fire to the Theatre Royal, where Asquith was to speak. They had attended a performance at the theatre, and as the audience was dispersing, Mary Leigh, in full view of numbers of persons, had poured petrol on to the curtains of a box and set fire to them, then flung a flaming chair over the edge of the box into the orchestra. Gladys Evans set a carpet alight, then rushed to the cinema box, threw in a little handbag filled with gunpowder, struck matches and dropped them in after it. Finding they all went out as they fell, she attempted to get under the wire fencing into the box. Several small explosions occurred, produced by amateur bombs made of tin canisters, which, with bottles of petrol and benzine, were afterwards found lying about.

Charged with these amazing offences, the two were defended by Tim Healey, who observed that when hands of horror were held up at the doings of the Suffragettes, it should be remembered that every member of the Ancient Order of Hibernians, which had made a guard of honour for Asquith and attacked the women in the streets, had in the time of Gladstone been liable to a cell in Kilmainham Gaol, whilst anyone having intercourse with them had been in danger of two years' imprisonment. He urged that the sooner the public made up its mind to a settlement of the

---

[1] The authorities finally handed it over at her request to Mrs. Asquith, who desired it as a memento. Having heard the hatchet variously described, I recently wrote to Lady Oxford and Asquith, requesting that I might see it. She replied that it had been left in Downing Street when her husband ceased to be Prime Minister. Most curiously she called it not a hatchet, but a " scythe," and insisted that it had been deliberately aimed at herself—undoubtedly a mistake; for the Prime Minister was the objective of Mary Leigh : his wife politically unimportant in her estimate.

women's question, the sooner such incidents as this would become past history. Mary Leigh was bravely defiant:

> " I have stood in the dock before this day, and if I live to come out of Mountjoy Prison, and I am still without the vote, I will take my stand in the dock again; it is better for me to have the number of a convict than any star or order."

The jury disagreed on the question of identity, and the case was reheard with another jury, when the Judge so strongly pleaded for a conviction that the prisoners were found guilty. Declaring it his duty to pass a sentence calculated to have a deterrent effect, Justice Madden sentenced both Mary Leigh and Gladys Evans to five years' penal servitude. He expressed the hope that when militancy were discontinued the term would be reduced. " It will have no deterrent effect upon us," responded Mary Leigh in defiant tones. Jennie Baines, against whom nothing was alleged save that she had shared with the prisoners lodgings wherein inflammable material was discovered, was sent to prison for seven months.

There was then a by-election in North-West Manchester. We were closing a meeting in Deansgate for a march to Piccadilly when someone rushed in with news of the Dublin sentences. It was heard with a shock of dismay, and an indignation intensified by the fact that a few days before two men had been sentenced in Dublin to but six months' imprisonment for burning down a pavilion attached to the Peamont Sanatorium, against the position of which there had been some public agitation. These men were released after but five weeks of their sentences had been served.

This Manchester election was a reunion of old friends; do what it might, the city regarded the W.S.P.U. as a plant of its own growing. I was touched by the manifest affection of the crowds; the throngs pressing up to the lorry at the close of the meetings, with hands outstretched to mine, and tender words of " Dear Dr. Pankhurst." His memory green with them still, old folk, campaigners with him for thirty years or more, shed tears for him to-day. Our meetings were far larger than any others held during the election; the only questions asked of us were what could be done to bring votes for women sooner, and how the prisoners fared. Asquith, in the customary letter of support to the candidate of his Party, referred to the Reform Bill as an issue of the election, and thus thrust the suffrage question into the arena for decision by the electorate. In previous elections other questions: the Licensing Bill, the Education Bill, the Budget, the House of Lords, Home Rule, had been cited as the matters which the aye or nay of the electors would affect; the Prime Minister had now asked for judgement on the Reform Bill. The Liberal majority of 445 at the previous election was replaced by a Conservative majority of 1,202. There was no Labour candidate.

My sister Adela was also a helper in this election; one of the last W.S.P.U. campaigns in which she took part. From over-work and exposure to all weathers, followed by an attack of pleurisy, she presently suffered a complete loss of voice. Prolonged rest from speaking was ordered. Miserable at the prospect of inaction, and dependence upon others, she conceived the idea of becoming a gardener—perhaps the least suitable occupation she could have selected. The desire was a reaction from the know-ledge that though a brilliant speaker, and one of the hardest workers in the movement, she was often regarded with more disapproval than approbation by Mrs. Pankhurst and Christabel, and was the subject of a sharper criticism than the other organizers had to face. Mrs. Pankhurst now offered to send her for a course at Studley Horticultural College, but exacted a promise that she would never speak in public again in this country. Having taken her course at Studley, Adela obtained a position as gardener, only to find that the woman gardener was expected to do the work of two men previously employed, and that the scientific culture of plants she was desirous to follow was under the circumstances of the place an impossible dream. She moved to another situation, with no better result. The manual work was too hard for her, the life uncongenial. She was fretting to return to the movement, but she had given her promise. Vida Goldstein had spent some time in this country speaking for the W.S.P.U.; through her, Adela went out to Australia, to become an organizer of the Women's Party there. Long inclined to despondency, she left the country in much grief, but in Australia made many friends, achieved great popularity, and for many years was happier than she had ever been in her life. After a time she left the Women's Party to become an organizer of the Australian Socialist Party.

I returned from the Manchester election to stand with a little crowd of unofficial members beside Nurse Pitfield's grave, think-ing sadly of her lonely and long unheeded suffering, resenting the callousness of society and of movements towards the heroes of the rank and file, who work and suffer most, and give their willing cheers to platform idols. To keep the prisoners in mind, I had now induced the Kensington W.S.P.U. to organize with me a march with black flags from King's Cross to Tower Hill. Already I had laid plans for the East End campaign.

In Dublin the suffrage prisoners were on hunger strike; the

English were denied political treatment, and the Irish were striking in sympathy with them. All were released without resort to forcible feeding, save Mary Leigh and Gladys Evans, who were repeatedly warned that on no consideration would they be set free. A young W.S.P.U. organizer stationed in Dublin obtained interviews with the Lord-Lieutenant and Sir James Dougherty, secretary to Augustine Birrell, the Secretary of State. In a letter to Clements Inn the organizer alleged that the Lord-Lieutenant had told her that Asquith and Lloyd George were alone responsible for the forcible feeding, and that he had been to London to intercede with the Prime Minister without success. She further insisted that Sir James Dougherty had led her to believe Mary Leigh was to be sent to a criminal lunatic asylum. Her letter containing these assertions was published in *Votes for Women*, and evoked an official denial. In the meantime a high state of tension had been created.

A demonstration in Phœnix Park to demand the release of Leigh and Evans was announced by the W.S.P.U., and a well-known W.S.P.U. member and I were called to speak there. It was agreed between us that at the close of the meeting we should lead the crowd to the prison gates to cheer the hunger strikers within. I assumed that my companion would notify the organizer of our project. The meeting in Phœnix Park, so far from being a demonstration of sympathy with the prisoners, was mainly a great roar of hostility. When the resolution was put, only a few hands were raised in support of it in any part of the field. To end on a note of this kind seemed to me disastrous, particularly if the position were so serious as we had been told. A diversion must be created; if there were any sympathizers in the gathering they would display themselves. I cried to the crowd that I was going to Mountjoy, where women were facing death in the cells in which many a martyr of Irish freedom had been confined. Seizing the tricolour, I sprang from the high platform. The sympathizers, the rowdies who had been shouting me down, and masses of people from all the platforms followed—to see, if not to assist. The W.S.P.U. organizer and speakers stuck to their platforms, and one of them, on the very platform I had left, continued speaking, pleased that the rowdies had been drawn off. Whether the other speakers had been informed of my project I never knew; to me, at that moment, it seemed essential to act without discussion. Strange women pressed round me, eager to know what all this was about and why I carried those colours. " They'll be our colours now ! " they declared when I told them, and gathered close, whilst two of them put their arms about me. " The police will be on us next ! " they said. I continued exhorting the people; they formed in ordered ranks. The police appeared as we neared the prison; the Inspector shouted to me that it was forbidden to carry a flag through the streets. That was enough; the people were all on my side. They closed around to protect me; the police charged; men and women were thrown to the ground, and after some moments of struggle, I was dragged inside the prison. Left alone in a cell, I reflected, with a shade of ruefulness, that this flying visit to Ireland was likely to have somewhat serious consequences. I had struck my blow, and must follow it up. I should be missing at the Tower Hill demonstration next Saturday, but that was of very small consequence in comparison with what might mean the abandonment for a considerable time of the East End movement. I had committed myself, for the time at least, I thought, to carry out a similar action in Dublin, where my difficulties would be heightened by my nationality. Yet if these women were really in danger of being left to die, mass demonstrations, accompanied by the mob turbulence, so easily roused in Ireland, seemed to me an excellent means of exciting pressure on their behalf outside. The door of pleading and negotiation had been abruptly slammed by the publication of the organizer's account of her conversations, embarrassing to the officials concerned, whether true or false. I wondered what the others of the W.S.P.U. were doing; whether any of them had followed; whether they had been acute enough to make the most of the occasion by cementing the adhesion of those enthusiastic women who had clung to me in the march, and by leading the crowd to a spot where a meeting could be held.

As I sat making my plans, one of the higher police officials entered, followed by the organizer and the speaker with whom I had concerted the march. To my astonishment the organizer commenced to reproach me, complaining that my action was jeopardizing her work. She begged me to accept the offer she had obtained for me, that if I would promise to return by the night boat to England I should be released forthwith. Her companion urged me to accept the view, that the organizer being in charge of the campaign should have her way. I realized that with opposition from those to whom I should naturally look for support, the action I contemplated would be difficult indeed. Without a word to the women, I turned to the police official: " I did not ask to be dragged in here! I came to Dublin intending to leave for England by the first boat after the meeting, and I desire to return at once."

The fear that Mary Leigh would be sent to a lunatic asylum was presently laid to rest. After a hunger strike and forcible feeding, lasting nine weeks, she was released on a convict's licence, or " ticket of leave," on September 21st. Gladys Evans was held till October 3rd. This brave young woman was a shop assistant, for three years employed at Selfridge's. Her father was one of the proprietors of *Vanity Fair*, and for some time editor of *The Bullionist*. She had emigrated to Canada in 1911, but in March, 1912, on learning of the Conspiracy Trial of Mrs. Pankhurst and the Lawrences, she had hastened back to give her services to the Union.

Though released, the two prisoners were by no means free. Police at the back door, the front door and on the roof were set to watch the house where they were staying. When Gladys Evans attempted to go out on October 23rd she was arrested for failure to report her address according to the rules laid down for " ticket of leave " prisoners, although this obligation was not mentioned on the licence given to her when she left the prison. Remanded in custody for a week, she recommenced her hunger strike, and when brought into Court was discharged with a caution. Both she and Mrs. Leigh continually declared that they would not report to the police. On November 5th Evans was re-arrested, on the pretext that she was preparing to leave that police district without notification. After a three days' remand, the Magistrate discharged her, stating there was no evidence of intention to act illegally. The second charge still pending against Mary Leigh of throwing a hatchet into Asquith's carriage had been postponed. It was brought up on December 10th, but she refused to come to Court, on the plea that the nine policemen watching the house would arrest her. An undertaking being given not to molest her, she appeared next day. The Crown prosecutor alleged that the hatchet had inflicted a cut on John Redmond's ear an inch long, which healed in five days. Mrs. Leigh replied that the wound was not caused by her, for she had not thrown the hatchet, but had simply " put " it into the carriage as a symbol; it had hit no one. There was evidence that Redmond's ear had been scratched accidentally by a hat-pin in the press at the doors of the meeting. The jury disagreed. Justice Gibson refused to try the case again, and advised the prosecution to let it drop. If it came before another judge, his notes, showing that the evidence of the Crown witnesses was contradictory, would be supplied to him. He bound Mrs. Leigh over to come up for judgement if called upon at the next commission, but not later. She was, he said, " a clever, earnest, and in her own way a good woman." The attitude of the Judge having made a re-trial virtually impossible, the case was dropped. Nevertheless, on December 19th, the two women were again re-arrested for failure to report to the police. They were sentenced to fourteen days' imprisonment, but released on bail, pending an appeal to the High Court, wherein the Magistrate's decision was upheld; but it was never enforced. Now at last the two were able to return to England, and the case was closed.

An incident of this period was the imprisonment of Mark Wilks for fourteen days, for refusal to pay his wife's income tax, she being a Women's Freedom League Tax Resister. Another was the march from Edinburgh to Downing Street, holding meetings and obtaining signatures to a petition by the way, of the " Brown Women," as they were called, from their uniform. This effort was independent of all suffrage societies, and its organizer, Mrs. de Fontblanc, declared that but for the militants it would never have been undertaken. She wrote:

" We cannot sleep in our beds knowing what these women have suffered in this fight."

BOOK VIII

CHAPTER I

THE SEVERANCE FROM THE PETHICK LAWRENCES

IN October, 1912, the W.S.P.U. was rent by a breach with the Pethick Lawrences, as a result of their refusal to agree to new developments in policy, insisted upon by Christabel and Mrs. Pankhurst. The unity between these four people had been apparently so complete, and their joint command over the organization so absolute, that the event was a tremendous shock to the Union and to the movement as a whole.

In the same month I started the East End campaign from which was to arise a new movement.

As though to emphasize that the old order was no more, the W.S.P.U. departed from the offices at Clements Inn and the shop in Charing Cross Road, both of which had been engaged for it by the Pethick Lawrences. The new phase of its existence was inaugurated at Lincoln's Inn House, Kingsway, a massive-looking new building, its architecture derived from the palaces of the Italian Renaissance, the ground floor having a vaulted and pillared hall. The old premises had been dowdy and commonplace in comparison.

Christabel's presence in Paris had been publicly announced at the end of September. In the internal crises of the W.S.P.U. which it was her intention to precipitate, she deemed it essential that the members and the public should be made aware that she was the editor of its organ and the guardian of its policy. Before the departure of the Pethick Lawrences for Canada, differences between herself and them were already pronounced. She believed that the fissure had extended during their absence. It was her intention to introduce new and more extreme tactics. Property was now to be destroyed, by arson and otherwise, on an extensive scale, the destroyers evading arrest whenever possible. The Labour Party[1] was to be attacked as a component part of the Government majority, its candidates opposed, its speakers heckled and harassed, as though they had been Cabinet Ministers.

The Pethick Lawrences did not accept the new militancy; they had other views as to the plan of campaign. "If you do not accept Christabel's policy we shall smash you!" Mrs.

---

[1] The Irish Party was also nominally attacked, but as its activities were mainly in Ireland this attack was not systematic.

Pankhurst had already said to them, in a moment of excitement, before their departure for Canada. The observation represented her attitude to all comers. Christabel believed that the Government intended to strip Mr. Lawrence of all his worldly possessions. This would be embarrassing. His financial responsibility had been emphasized in the conspiracy trial. It had been pointed out that whilst two signatories were required for drawing upon the W.S.P.U. account, one of the signatories must be either Mrs. Lawrence or himself. " The Government would have ruined Mr. Lawrence and he would not have liked it," and " they had come under other influences whilst they were in Canada," Christabel said to me, imperturbably, in a passing reference, when I saw her in Paris much later. The Lawrences were convinced that it was Christabel, and not they whose attitude had changed. Be that as it might, on arrival in England they refused to accept the new militancy. Thereupon Mrs. Pankhurst required them to leave the Union, suggesting that they should resume the ownership of the paper, *Votes for Women,* which they had founded. The Lawrences desired that Christabel should come to London to discuss matters with them. She did so. To cover her movements, Mrs. Pankhurst travelled first class from France; Christabel taking a second class passage on the same steamer. Arriving in London, she walked through the dark streets, fearing to take a conveyance lest the driver should recognize her.

To many, not least to Mrs. Lawrence, it seemed that the breach had been caused by Mrs. Pankhurst, impetuous and fiery on such occasions, rather than by Christabel, sweet-tongued and cool, although immovable. Yet the decision was that of Christabel. Nevertheless the change was not uncongenial to Mrs. Pankhurst. She had always been jealous for the companionship of her daughter. To plan with her now, and to direct the plans made together, was a delight to her. The W.S.P.U. was henceforth more fully and personally her own than it had ever been since the early days.

The Union was an autocracy: none of the four most concerned thought it necessary to consult its membership. The following notice was the only announcement made:

" At the first re-union of the leaders after the enforced holiday Mrs. Pankhurst and Miss Christabel Pankhurst outlined a new militant policy, which Mr. and Mrs. Lawrence found themselves altogether unable to approve.

" Mrs. Pankhurst and Miss Christabel Pankhurst indicated that they were not prepared to modify their intentions, and recommended that Mr. and Mrs. Pethick Lawrence should resume control of the paper *Votes for Women* and should leave the Women's Social and Political Union.

"Rather than make schism in the ranks of the Union, Mr. and Mrs. Pethick Lawrence consented to this course.

"In these circumstances Mr. and Mrs. Pethick Lawrence will not be present at the meeting at the Royal Albert Hall on October 17th.

> "EMMELINE PANKHURST.
> "CHRISTABEL PANKHURST.
> "EMMELINE PETHICK LAWRENCE.
> "F. W. PETHICK LAWRENCE."

I went from the East End to the office when I heard the news, with the old instinct to stand by my two when they might be in trouble or difficulty, not knowing what inner cause had led to the disruption, but with the unhappy belief that the secret militancy, which I regretted so much, was at the root of it. The staff, for the most part, accepted the position as the leaders had made it. Mrs. Tuke and Annie Kenney were keenly partisan for Christabel; the "Gentle Pansy" displayed the expression of the "little terrier dog" which had surprised Keir Hardie when first he saw her. Annie Kenney declared at the W.S.P.U. "At Home": "If all the world were on one side, and Christabel Pankhurst on the other, I would walk straight over to Christabel Pankhurst!"

My thoughts flew back to the abolishing of the original democratic constitution in 1907, which had left the decision wholly to the small group of four, and ultimately to one, and had made possible the present impetuous course. The breach was deplorable, I thought, and wished both sides might have surrendered some points. They differed less with each other, I thought, than I had often differed in view from them. The keener the pursuit of a cause, the more the sense of perspective is apt to be undermined; the more are details magnified; this I knew, and like the rest of the membership accepted the accomplished fact. Frederick Lawrence wrote me as to the ownership of my little design on the cover of *Votes for Women*. I said I should be pleased for him to continue using it. Mrs. Pankhurst, with frowning brows, reproached me when I told her this. Yet outwardly all was dignified reserve on both sides. If any recrimination took place in the open, it was the work, not of the four concerned, but of their partisans.

At the great Albert Hall meeting of welcome—to one leader only, as it turned out—Mrs. Pankhurst propounded the new policy, declaring that the Government must be made to realize that property would henceforth be as gravely endangered by the Suffragettes as by the Chartists of old. If she were prosecuted for incitement, she would not remain in prison, " First Division or no First Division," whilst the militant men of Ulster were at large. That was her special contribution to the new policy: the hunger strike, not for political treatment, but for release.

Enthusiasm ran high; the most militant people were more militant than ever, yet the shock of the " split," and the doubts arising from the new policy, reacted upon the collection. The two previous Albert Hall meetings had raised between them over £16,000; this one £3,600. The financial set-back was but temporary. The income of 1913 beat all previous records with the tremendous total of £36,896. The incomes of 1911 and 1912 were £25,484 and £28,502 respectively. As before, the accounts were kept and audited with precision,[1] though the auditors were several times changed; firstly because of the division, the auditor, A. G. Sayers, being a personal friend introduced in the early days by the Lawrences; secondly because the Government persecution, which followed on the extreme militancy, eventually necessitated many and frequent changes of auditor, as well as of printers and office staff. Books, in the latter days, had to be kept in duplicate, on account of probable police seizures, and clerks were at work in undiscovered private houses as well as at the known headquarters.

Immediately after the announcement of the split, appeared a new W.S.P.U. organ: *The Suffragette.*

The Pethick Lawrences acted with great loyalty and

[1] It is necessary to emphasize this fact on account of statements, both published and unpublished, which have been circulated in respect of the accounts, due, of course, to the tremendous income, which far exceeded that of any propaganda organization of its time. The following letter is of interest in this connection:

" A. G. SAYERS, SEATON AND BUTTERWORTH,
    " CHARTERED ACCOUNTANTS,
        " 62 BROOK STREET, W.I.   14*th February*, 1929.

" DEAR MISS PANKHURST,—Your letter addressed to the extinct firm of Sayers & Wesson has reached me in the ordinary course. I had already seen in the Press briefly a record of the absurd statement made by this lady. The fact is as follows, that when the W.S.P.U. was started, a Committee of the Society called at my office in Hanover Square and said that as they would be dealing with public moneys, every penny must be accounted for, and the accounts properly kept and audited; they therefore put themselves entirely in my hands in this matter. I am not quite sure whether a member of your family was present at this meeting or not, but such is the fact. . . . I can recall at this moment my final interview with your mother, at which she said to me that as I had to choose between going on with one organization or the other, and as I had been introduced to the movement by Mr. and Mrs. Pethick Lawrence, she quite understood that I was discontinuing the supervision of the accounts when the split took place. It comes back to me how in the midst of the most agitating part of the movement I went to Paris to meet your sister and arranged financial matters with her. . . .

                                        " Yours faithfully,
                                            " A. G. SAYERS."

generosity during the difficult period which followed. They uttered no criticism of the W.S.P.U. and its actions, even in respect of those policies which had led to their withdrawal from the movement. When the struggle was ended, they proved beneficent friends to several of those who had been partisans of the opposite side. Before their return from Canada, the Government had already put bailiffs in their house at Holmwood, with a view to recovering by distraint the costs of the conspiracy trial. Though the auctioneer advertised the simple and entirely modern furniture as " Early English," and the plate as " A1," and though friends rolled up to bid in large numbers, only a little over £300 was raised by the sale. £800 still remained to be found. A High Court action for damages by Robinson & Cleaver, and ninety-three other firms, whose windows had been broken, brought judgement for another £2,000. In each case the whole cost was recovered from Frederick Lawrence because Mrs. Pankhurst and Christabel had no property which could be seized. Lawrence refused to pay, and the Government made him a bankrupt; a costly and unpleasant proceeding, which he bore personally, not desiring the fighting funds of the movement to reimburse him for these losses.

At first the new militancy mainly displayed itself in :

(1) Attempts to destroy the contents of pillar-boxes by red ochre, jam, tar, permanganate of potash, varnish and inflammable substances, including phosphorus. Such attempts were widespread throughout the Kingdom. On December 9th, 1912, the Home Secretary stated that 5,000[1] letters had been damaged, but of these all save thirteen letters and seven postcards had been delivered. Special wrappers stating the cause of the damage were affixed. Only one conviction had been secured. The prisoner, a Liverpool University student, had both hands badly burnt by a preparation containing phosphorus. One of the Holloway officers, who had been stationed in Walton Gaol at the time, told me long afterwards : " It was terrible to see how that poor mortal had been burned ! "

(2) The giving of false fire alarms. In 1911 there had been 176 false calls, followed by 22 convictions; in 1912 there were 425 such calls, followed by 27 convictions. In 1913 the number increased, and a reward was offered for information leading to a conviction.

(3) Arson, which was not developed on a large scale till the opening of the new year, and the destruction of works of art and historic relics.

[1] The Suffragettes claimed the damage to be much greater.

CHAPTER II

THE East End campaign began modestly. I induced the local W.S.P.U.'s to assist in organizing it: Kensington, Chelsea, and Paddington made themselves responsible for shops in Bethnal Green, Limehouse and Poplar respectively, and Unions, even so far afield as Wimbledon, sent speakers and canvassers. W.S.P.U. headquarters agreed to be responsible for the rent of a shop in Bow. An intensive campaign like that of an election, to include deputations to local M.P.'s, was to culminate in a demonstration in Victoria Park. Sybil Smith remained treasurer of the modest sums we collected for handbills and other needs, Elsa Dalglish financial secretary.

I regarded the rousing of the East End as of utmost importance. My aim was not merely to make some members and establish some branches, but the larger task of bringing the district as a whole into a mass movement, from which only a minority would stand aside. The need of our cause I believed to be such a movement. This was the meaning of Herbert Gladstone's challenge to the Suffragists in 1908, and the still more pointed challenge of Hobhouse in February, 1912, which had caused so much excitement. Not by the secret militancy of a few enthusiasts, but by the rousing of the masses, could the gauge be taken up which not merely some Cabinet Ministers, but history itself had flung to us. The East End was the greatest homogeneous working-class area accessible to the House of Commons by popular demonstrations. The creation of a woman's movement in that great abyss of poverty would be a call and a rallying cry to the rise of similar movements in all parts of the country. The members of the suffrage movement, militant and non-militant, had always been largely of the middle class, though the W.S.P.U. had begun otherwise. The W.S.P.U. attack on the Labour Party was now giving new impetus to the taunt: "Vote for Ladies!" The influence of that taunt, militating against real support of the suffrage movement in working class circles, was ever a strong undercurrent. I was anxious, too, to fortify the position of the working woman when the vote should actually be given; the existence of a strong, self-reliant movement amongst working women would be the greatest aid in safe-guarding their rights in the day of settlement. Moreover, I was looking to the future; I wanted to rouse these women of the submerged mass to be, not merely the argument of more fortunate people, but to be fighters on their own account, despising mere platitudes and catch-cries, revolting against the hideous conditions about them, and demanding for themselves and their families a full share of the benefits of civilization and progress.

I set out with Zelie Emerson down the dingy Bow Road, a once prosperous residential thoroughfare, now hideous in decay. In spite of their grime, we found pleasure in visiting the old shops to let, finding in some of them a picturesque antiquity, relic of a lovelier age of handicraft, behind a newer frontage, ugly and ageing from neglect. I was glad that conditions of rent and tenure permitted us to hire an architecturally charming little old place, lately a baker's, with a bow window painted and grained in quiet and pleasant brown. We polished and cleaned the place till it shone. I mounted a ladder and wrote the familiar legend, Votes for Women, upon the fascia, taking great pains to write it in early Roman characters and to gild it with true gold leaf. To see me up there was the astonishment, if not the scandal of the neighbourhood. Beside us in the middle of the road was the old Bow Church, its sculptured masonry crumbling under corroding soot; around us everywhere dirt, dilapidation and poverty. Soap works and tanneries exhaled the most appalling smells. How my head ached from them!

A motley crowd swept upon us, urchins who shouted and banged the door from sheer, exuberant mischief, which the sharp expostulations of the uninitiated were powerless to affect. I knew the secret which would win them, the talisman which always guided me in the East End: " Let us be friends. Come and see what we are doing. We want to work with your mothers to make things better. Take these papers home with you."

Strange women of the underworld came to us eagerly: " I have seen the Suffragettes in Holloway. They have made things better there! I remember you. I saw you when you was there." One of these poor ones came asking for me in my absence and left her address. I went to seek for her, and knocked at the door with the given number in a neighbouring alley. From the window, close beside me, an old man leant out, wrapped in a filthy blanket, displaying his naked breast and shoulders. He shouted and swore at me, and looked so evil and menacing that I fled precipitately; but chiding myself for cowardice, returned to knock again. Thereto came no response, but fearing the woman might be in trouble, I went again later in the day. Again the old fellow appeared at the window, extending a bare arm from his blanket to shake his fist in my face with horrible epithets. From others I learnt he was the landlord of a common lodging-house, expressing his objection to being disturbed during the day. The woman, who usually slept there, had merely left the address in case I should want to see her. For some time she was an eager attender at the meetings, then ceased to come. I learnt she was again in prison.

One morning two young men, pretending to be drunk, entered the shop and asked for free literature and penny pamphlets, insisting that they should be rolled up in paper and tied with string. The young Suffragette in charge humoured them by compliance, but they suddenly seized each a packet of the tea labelled: "Votes for Women," which was on sale for our funds, and dashed off down the street. The Suffragette gave a shout, and her sturdier companion,[1] who was writing posters in an inner room, sped off in pursuit. One offender she caught and handed over to a policeman. When I arrived, and learnt of this, I was distressed indeed; a sad way, I thought, to commence our work of loving comradeship by sending a man to prison for so trivial an offence! I had scarcely heard that the youth had been charged in my name, as responsible for the premises, when there entered, much agitated and far advanced in pregnancy, a young woman with ashen face, whose dark eyes gazed pathetically into mine. It was her husband who had just been arrested. Before their marriage he had been several times in prison for petty thefts and youthful rowdiness, but she had "kept him straight," and would again, she pleaded. I tried to reassure her: "I know he only did it in fun. We'll get him off; don't worry." Yet I was much concerned, not knowing then that I had the option to refuse to prosecute him. We went together to the Court. I asked leave to go into the witness-box, and pleaded for him, saying I was persuaded it was all a joke, and if he were released to his wife she would keep him from mischief. The Magistrate expressed cordial agreement; the prisoner was set free. I often saw him in our marches afterwards.

Women in sweated and unknown trades came to us, telling their hardships: rope-makers, waste rubber cleaners, biscuit packers, women who plucked chickens, too often "high," for canning, and those who made wooden seeds to put in raspberry jam. Occupants of hideously unsavoury tenements asked us to visit and expose them. Hidden dwellings were revealed to us, so much built round that many of their rooms were as dark as

[1] Emily Dyce Sharp.

night all day. Exorbitant rents were charged in wretched barracks for so-called " furnished rooms," containing nothing but a dilapidated bedstead with the poorest of covering, and a couple of chairs. In one such, I met a fragile orphan girl earning 7s. a week and her food, minus 3d. insurance, for washing-up in a city restaurant until nine each night, and paying 6s. a week in rent. It was " hard to keep straight," she said. I procured for her an offer of better work, but when I returned she was gone. I could find no trace. Her words haunted me. In a one-roomed dwelling were a crowd of little children, and a man lying ill on a heap of rags. He had been a blackleg in the dock strike, and the strikers had thrown him from the embankment. His leg had been broken and had not recovered. His wife had just been released from prison, where she had served a sentence for begging. She had been standing in the gutter offering bootlaces for sale, but several people had given her pennies without troubling to take the laces. The policeman declared her trading merely a blind to cover appeals for alms.

Women flocked to our meetings; members joined in large numbers. I at once began urging them to speak, taking classes for them indoors, and inducing them to make a start outdoors by taking the chair for me at a succession of short meetings in the side streets where the workers lived, or by the market stalls in the shopping hours.

At first we had a difficult time of it; even in Bow and Bromley, Mr. Lansbury's constituency. The Trades Council and L.R.C. were none too friendly, and its secretary, Joe Banks, bitterly hostile. Though we found friends at once, we had much rowdiness to contend with. It was overcome after a time, but in the early weeks it was very violent. At our first meeting in Bow we were harassed by a swarm of urchins, who ran before us, from Old Ford to Bow Road, throwing small stones in our faces. In Bethnal Green, where Elsa Dalglish and Zelie Emerson were in charge, the crowds were rougher; fishes' heads and paper soaked in the public urinal near the principal open air meeting place were the commonest missiles. As the only person called Pankhurst in sight, I was inevitably the principal target for the filth and violence. The greater the rowdiness, the more valiantly friends rallied round to protect me; I was never free from numerous bruises, my feet and ankles especially were black and blue from being kicked and trampled upon, but I escaped serious injury. One night whilst the rowdies were pushing the lorry which served as our platform far from the pitch, and supporters were striving to retard its progress, I heard an exclamation of pain, and saw the face of

Elsa Dalglish looking up at me with an expression of agonized patience. She seemed to be falling against the lorry: " You are hurt! " " They are pushing the wheel over my foot." We raised an outcry. Some of the men succeeded in halting the throng and lifted her up to us. Her foot was badly crushed, but she bravely continued the work with scarcely a break, hobbling to the shop with her stick. There were dozens of meetings every night. Crowds of speakers came down from other districts. The most practised were chosen for the Victoria Park demonstration. Then, to my delight, came a protest from the East End speakers, headed by Melvina Walker; they were not to be left out; one or more of them must be heard on every platform. This was the very spirit I desired.

At this point Lansbury resigned his seat in Parliament and severed his connection with the official Labour Party, the Poplar Labour Representation Committee becoming for several years an independent body.

Suffrage demands upon the Labour Party had now crystallized into the Brailsford, the Keir Hardie and the Lansbury policies. The Brailsford policy was that the Labour Party should vote against the Third Reading of the Reform Bill (which had been suspended since its Second Reading in July) unless before the Third Reading women had already been included in the Bill by the " free vote " which Asquith had promised. It had been generally assumed that the Labour Party was pledged to this course, but Lansbury, Hardie, and Macdonald now made known that the Party had not come to any decision. Macdonald, on being pressed for an explanation, stated that his Albert Hall pledge to turn out the Government had only meant: " We shall support Women's Suffrage, even if by our support of that we shall turn out the Government."[1]

Keir Hardie's policy was that the Labour Party should vote against the Reform Bill in every division, unless and until women were included.[2]

The Lansbury policy, which was in fact the policy of Christabel Pankhurst, was that the Labour Party should go into opposition, and vote against the Government in any and every division, on all questions, until the Government should introduce a measure for women's suffrage. This was embodied in a resolution[3] circulated by George Lansbury to Labour and Socialist

[1] Letter to F. E. Matzen, October 12th, 1912.

[2] " I should like to have seen them decide to oppose the Bill now. I believe the effect would have been an amendment being carried." Keir Hardie, speaking at Newcastle, December 22nd, 1912.

[3] " The . . . branch of the . . . being determined that the political enfranchisement of the women workers shall be granted without delay, condemns the Govern-

organizations. The prime weakness of all these policies was that, as the Liberals and Conservatives were almost evenly balanced, the Government, backed by eighty odd Irish Nationalist votes, could afford to disregard those of the forty odd Labour Members. No Government with a clear majority of forty votes over all other Parties would go out of office on a "snap" division, or allow itself to be coerced by the minority against its will. It is true that the moral effect in the country of Labour Party opposition to Government measures might in some circumstances have been impressive. It would have been impressive undoubtedly in the case of the Reform Bill, but, as it happened, that other overdue question of popular self-government, Home Rule for Ireland, to which the Labour Party was deeply pledged, was also in a critical and claimant position on the political stage. The Lansbury policy demanded a vote against Home Rule. There is little doubt that many even of those branches which signed the Lansbury declaration would have protested had the Labour Members actually voted against freedom for Ireland. The ostensible policy of the Labour Party was to vote upon each question on its merits, but this policy was not adhered to. Philip Snowden and others complained that the Party frequently refrained from voting in support of its principles where there was a possibility of making an anti-Government majority. The old complaint from within the Party that its policy was subservient to Liberalism was louder than ever, but those who made it desired more vigour and independence from the Party, not on one, but on many questions. Few, and certainly not Lansbury, would have accepted the complete application of the policy he had espoused. It would have compelled the Labour Members to vote with the Conservatives in every division. A policy destructive of all measures save one is apt to be anti-social; the Suffragists found it so when the Irish practised it against Votes for Women. Brailsford undoubtedly had pure justice on the side of his argument when he strove to deter the W.S.P.U. from following that unpleasant example. Yet women were outside the constitution, and desperate circumstances beget desperate methods.

In the height of these controversies, Ramsay Macdonald was making bitterly phrased attacks upon the W.S.P.U., which,

ment for introducing a Franchise Bill for men only, repudiates the sham pledges by which the Government are trying to trick the advocates of Votes for Women, protests against the Government which is guilty of such a policy being kept in power by the aid of Labour Votes, and finally calls upon the Labour Members of Parliament to vote constantly and relentlessly against the Government, from now onwards, until they have either driven them from office or compelled them to introduce and carry a proposal giving votes to women on equal terms with men."

according to his view, appeared to be " a cynical skit on the mind of woman, devised by some imp of a person who holds women in low esteem."[1]

Just at this time Philip Snowden moved his Amendment to the Home Rule Bill, which would have extended votes for the Irish Parliament to Irish women already qualified as municipal voters. His proposal was defeated by 314 votes to 141, the Government Whips being put on against it. Twenty-seven Labour Members voted with him, five against, the rest were absent from the division. The W.S.P.U. replied to the loss of the Amendment with a window-smashing raid, in which £500 worth of glass was broken. The meagre attendance of the Labour Members did not escape comment. The demand for ruthless opposition to the Government and to the Irish who had joined in destroying the Amendment was more clamant.

The Lansbury resolution was debated at a conference of the Parliamentary Labour Party and its national executive, the conference declaring the resolution out of harmony with the decisions of the annual delegate conferences. Lansbury publicly complained that when his resolution had been thus defeated he was told by the Parliamentary Labour Party that he should either fall into line with the majority, or leave the Party. On this he resolved to resign his seat in order to stand as an independent candidate, making Votes for Women his foremost plank. It was by no means only upon this issue that he differed from the Party majority and its executive, of which he was not then a member; indeed he was in opposition on many points. He had campaigned against the National Insurance Act, to which the Party majority had given a qualified support. He openly complained on public platforms that the Party was too chary of fighting the Government, either in Parliament or in by-elections. For these and other matters he was often called to order at the Labour Party meetings. The influences about him at the *Herald* office upheld his insurgent attitude : the editor, Charles Lapworth from America, a revolutionary industrialist, out of sympathy with Parliamentarism of any sort, Robert Williams, then a very Red orator, and a crowd of Left Wing enthusiasts of many schools.

On the eve of the Victoria Park demonstration the young organizer I had encountered in Dublin appeared in the Bow Road shop, with some companions carrying parcels. She announced that she had come to take charge, and that the premises must be cleared for her, as Lansbury was resigning his seat and a by-election was imminent. The little place was filled

[1] Letter to the *Daily Citizen*.

to overflowing with flags and banners to be used in the Park next day—all these must be removed. The workers who were fitting up the banners resented the suggestion and looked to me to do battle, but I was determined to avoid friction with one who had been appointed from Paris, whatever she might propose. I induced her to see that to make a fiasco of a demonstration widely advertised in the name of the W.S.P.U. would be an inauspicious opening to the campaign she desired to direct. She agreed to dump her parcels, and give us till Monday to prepare for her advent. Then I induced my co-workers to take service under her, and retired to another district, promising to assist the organizer in any way should she send for me. I thought her entirely unsuited to the work before her, but was anxious to cast no difficulties in her path. I must confess that this cavalier conduct somewhat depressed me, but, like many another, I schooled myself with the admonition: the Cause alone is important. In truth I was still more depressed by the opinion that Lansbury had acted too precipitately.

George Lansbury was not at the demonstration; he was in Boulogne, arranging his forthcoming election campaign with Mrs. Pankhurst and Christabel. It was not the first discussion he had had with them on the subject. His resignation won him tremendous popularity at the time, and the lasting support of wealthy Suffragists; one of them, a retiring woman whose aid was always given by stealth, provided the *Herald* with a regular subsidy which enabled it to keep going for many years. She, with Muriel, Countess de la Warr, H. D. Harben and others, made possible the purchase by the *Herald* of the Victoria House Printing Press. Harben, a Fabian, had been a Liberal candidate, but had sent in his resignation as a protest against the Government's treatment of the women's suffrage question.

On the Monday afternoon following the Victoria Park demonstration Lansbury spoke at the usual W.S.P.U. "At Home" in the London Pavilion, and there announced his intention to resign his seat in support of what he then deemed " *the* movement in the world,"[1] and " the biggest fight socially that is going on in our country."[2] Only after making this public declaration, which was immediately reported in the Press, did he consult his sponsors, the Poplar Labour Party, a fact which caused great dissatisfaction amongst its members, and especially its officials.

Lansbury's defeat was perhaps inevitable. The Labour Party did not then attract a majority of the electors, as was clear from

[1] Reported *Votes for Women*, October 25th, 1912.
[2] Reported *Votes for Women*, November 15th, 1912.

their minority on the local governing bodies, and Lansbury had only won the seat in 1910 by Liberal aid. He had been the Liberal election agent from 1886 to 1892.[1] Lloyd George had gone out of his way to recommend him: "I hope you will vote for my friend Lansbury"; but of this 1912 by-election Lloyd George afterwards said: "Blair [the Conservative] was my candidate." Lansbury had been prominent in opposing the Lloyd George National Insurance Act; if his present candidature meant anything it meant strenuous opposition to the Liberal Government. Certainly many Liberals voted against him. In any case the resignation was premature. Neither his own Party nor the electors were sufficiently prepared for it. I, speaking continuously in his constituency, both in public meetings and to Labour organizations, would urgently have advised him first to allow a further period of propaganda. I knew that the district was as yet little, if anything, in advance of the rest of England upon our question. Indeed it was at that time far behind Manchester and the industrial North in general. I knew that in the Labour and Socialist movement of the constituency, in spite of Lansbury's own strong advocacy of the women's movement during the past two years—it was barely that—there was the same indifference and hostility to be found as elsewhere, and the same suspicion in the Marxian and Left Wing elements of a "middle-class movement" and a "ladies' vote." Some at least of the prominent members and officials of the local Labour movement resented the W.S.P.U. attack on their official Party as bitterly as it was resented elsewhere. They objected to Lansbury's championship of the Suffragettes, as others had resented their championship by Keir Hardie. They regarded the resignation of their Member as an affront to themselves, and blamed the Suffragettes as the unworthy cause of it. Whilst I had been at work in the constituency, I had striven to conciliate the local Labourists, and to demonstrate that our object was to rouse working women to the cause of their own political and economic liberation. The present emergency was a severe strain on the measure of good will I had established.

The election having been called, it was important for Suffragists of all schools that it should be won. Lansbury was in close accord with the W.S.P.U. The other suffrage organizations merely came down to hold independent meetings and sell their papers. The proper course for the W.S.P.U. was to place itself in contact with and work under the local Labour Party which was responsible for Lansbury's candidature. The proper course for the Labour Party was to assume control of the campaign,

[1] *My Life*, by George Lansbury, pp. 63, 75, 114. (Constable.)

putting the W.S.P.U. workers to the best possible use.   Unfortunately both organizations were possessed of wholly incompetent officials, who immediately took up an attitude of acute hostility towards each other.   Banks, the Labour secretary, was truculent and obstinate; the W.S.P.U. organizer was mainly concerned to uphold the superiority of her organization, resentful of advice, ignorant of election methods.   She had no sympathy with the Labour movement.   She was supremely unaware of the long, hard struggle and self-sacrificing effort on the part of poor, earnest volunteers, by which the movement had achieved a Party in Parliament, and had won this particular seat.   In every movement the professional organizer, stepping into office with little novitiate of voluntary work and struggle, is all too apt to trample upon the feelings of older pioneers.   Mrs. Pankhurst, who could ably have dealt with the opposing elements, took no part in the organization of the campaign.   She devoted herself purely to speaking at the meetings arranged for her.   The W.S.P.U. organizer followed to the letter the tactics she had seen the Union employ in the elections where it had no candidate to support. Great meetings were held, and as far as possible all the halls and the most popular open-air pitches were cornered, little more quarter being shown in this respect to the Labour Party than to the Conservatives.   Selling the *Suffragette* and advertising the W.S.P.U. meetings completed the Union's activities. The Labour Party, mainly dependent on the voluntary effort of busy working people, was left to carry on the canvass as best it could.   It was deprived of many of its regular volunteers; some drawn off to hear the unusual number of notable speakers invading the constituency, others disaffected and leaving the " donkey work " to the Suffragettes.   The canvass was not completed; voters who had moved out of the constituency were not traced.   Summoned for the open-air meetings a day or two after the contest began, I found the organizer inveighing against "the men."   On reaching the pitch assigned to me, I met a group of disconsolate W.S.P.U. speakers, the Labour Party having captured the stump. Yet all around the district were streets untouched by any meetings. Thereafter I refused to speak at the time-honoured meeting places, and went only to new spots; but what was one who broke new ground among so many contending for the old pitches?   The foolish friction continued.   Suffragists of all sorts, united in nothing save the demand for some sort of franchise for women, and otherwise differing from Marxism to the most extreme Conservatism, flooded the constituency.   Even on the Labour platforms was heard a babel of conflicting policies from Labour and Liberal Members of Parliament, individualists, collectivists, faddists of every school. Out of the confusion the questions which probably emerged most clearly were: whether women were justified in destroying private property to win the vote; whether Lansbury did well to resign his seat; and the pros and cons of the Insurance Act. In spite of all rivalries amongst the organizers, there was great enthusiasm for the candidate. Meetings were thronged with delighted crowds. Unfortunately auditors flocked from all parts of London, and a large proportion of the electors failed to gain admission. The children had a delightful time; special meetings were arranged for them. Evelyn Sharp told them fairy tales with an election moral. Lansbury made triumphant progresses through the constituency, surrounded by bands of little boys and girls, who punctuated with cheers the songs in which they called their elders to vote for him.

Blair, the Conservative candidate, had difficulty in securing halls for his meetings, and never once was his Party able to carry a meeting to its natural conclusion, indoors or out. Heckling invariably ended in disorder; the speakers were howled down and hustled away.

The most ridiculous episodes of the campaign took place on polling day. The Labour Party had very few vehicles at its disposal, whilst the W.S.P.U. had many cars sent by its prosperous supporters. These stood idle outside its committee rooms in the Bow Road throughout the breakfast hour, whilst Conservative cars were rushing voters to the poll. Banks refused to send the lists of voters to the W.S.P.U., demanding the cars be sent to him; the organizer replied: " Mrs. Pankhurst would never allow the Union to work under the men! " When Mrs. Pankhurst arrived late in the morning she dispatched the cars to the Labour Party. The W.S.P.U. organizer had disbanded her workers on the eve of the poll, retaining only a few to stand at the booths with placards. In the evening Lansbury sent to me, begging me to get a party of women together to assist in persuading electors, drenched by the torrential rains, to turn out again to vote. I gathered what workers I could, but the time was short. The need for such efforts was quite genuinely unknown to the organizer of the W.S.P.U.

When the news came that Lansbury's majority of 863 had become a minority of 731, the Lincoln's Inn House representatives were astonished. As we drove to Lansbury's house, in St. Stephen's Road, the organizer exclaimed: " What will Christabel say? " then opened her mouth and cried noisily like a child.

I was intensely depressed, and could hardly bear to meet the Lansburys. The white-faced distress of the wife caused me the greater pain. Her exceptionally large family had long debarred her from activity in the Labour movement; her part had been the harder one of lonely sacrifice and harsh economy. Though I had no share in the decision, I was oppressed by the sense that Lansbury had been badly advised, led away by generous impulses, and ill-served by the arrogant folly of the officials supporting him on both sides. Of course the defeat was met with tremendous enthusiasm. An enormous crowd cheered, and cheered, in a glow of exalted comradeship, but such gatherings are, after all, small consolation upon the morrow. Next day the Central Labour Party executive issued a manifesto condemning Lansbury's resignation and his demand that the Labour Party should vote continuously against the Government in the interests of Votes for Women. Macdonald, in a statement of his own, declared the executive attack to be " not half so strong as the circumstances warrant," and adding that Lansbury had

" proved his absolute incapacity . . . to take a stand on anything . . . he had men on his platform whom Labour Members ought not to have invited to speak for them . . . he left no stone unturned to get Liberal support."

Lansbury replied that he had " stood up " to " Mr. Macdonald and his executive," and would have " continued that line had it not been that we were told in set terms that those who would not hang together had to get out."

The word was now given by W.S.P.U. headquarters to retire from the East End; the shops we had opened were shut. Yet I persuaded Mrs. Pankhurst not to let the campaign close in an atmosphere of defeat, and urged that we should organize a deputation of East End workers to the Government—preferably to Lloyd George. The idea was accepted. Mrs. Pankhurst indicated that the W.S.P.U. would remunerate me for continuing the work. " I'll do the work; I don't want any pay! " I said. The answer perhaps a little wounded her, and caused her some anxiety; it was a sign of independence. She knew that I was opposed to some of the W.S.P.U. policies, though I no longer spoke of them, knowing expostulation would be vain. We continued the East End work much as before. Later the W.S.P.U. decided to give the deputation a national character; some Newhaven fish-wives, Lancashire pitbrow girls, textile operatives and others, in the costumes of their trade, were gathered from up and down the country, to add to the East End majority. Finally, out of the thousands who had volunteered, and the hundreds prepared to speak, twenty were chosen. The deputation was named " Mrs. Drummond's deputation of working women." I was wholly content that it should be so, and wrote in the *Suffragette*: " Good luck to Mrs. Drummond and her deputation!" I was weighted by a profound seriousness; this was no light-hearted adventure for me. I realized that I was steadily moving further from my chosen mission, and the artist's work which gave me a satisfaction and pleasure I found in nothing else. I was watching the movement with the anxious intensity of a nurse by the bedside of a loved patient fighting for life.

The deputation was to take place on January 17th, the day before the Women's Suffrage amendments to the Reform Bill were to be debated. The political atmosphere teemed with adverse rumours. Since the autumn many newspapers, including the Labour Party organ, the *Daily Citizen,* had predicted defeat for the women's amendments, the withdrawal of the Reform Bill, and the substitution of a Bill to abolish plural voting. The *Daily Herald's* "Special Commissioner" now announced that two Cabinet Ministers, "Lulu" Harcourt and Winston Churchill, were lobbying against the women's amendments, and declaring their intention to resign if they were carried. Christabel was alternately calling upon Lloyd George and Sir Edward Grey to threaten resignation if the women's amendments were not carried, and accusing the two Ministers of trickery and partnership in the anti-Suffrage plot to wreck the amendments. At the same time she was declaring that the amendments had never had a chance of being carried. She called for dismissal of the Liberals, and the substitution of the Conservatives. She asserted that opposition to Votes for Women would be impossible to a Conservative Government in spite of the well-known fact that the Conservative Party, in Parliament and out, contained fewer supporters and more opponents of Votes for Women than any other.

In spite of most urgent appeals to desist from many quarters, Suffragette destruction continued until only five days remained before the debate on the amendments; then Mrs. Pankhurst announced that militancy would be suspended "until after the amendments are defeated," in order that there might be "no excuse" for blaming the W.S.P.U. for the event. The decision,[1] so tardy and so phrased, was received with bitterness by the non-militants, who were then pinning their faith to the amendments, though Mrs. Fawcett afterwards said that the amendments could not in any event have been carried, because they lacked Government support.

Whilst militancy was thus suspended for the moment, several women remained in prison, two of them serving sentences of eight months. Some were hunger striking and being forcibly fed; amongst these May Billinghurst, a cripple, unable to walk.

[1] *The Suffragette,* January 24th, 1913.

Archdeacon Wilberforce, Dr. Clifford, Mrs. Bramwell Booth, wife of the Salvation Army " General," Countess de la Warr and others, vainly endeavoured to create an atmosphere of conciliation for the amendments by arranging suffrage services of " mediation and intercession " in Westminster Abbey and St. Paul's.

On the morning of the deputation I took my little band of East End speakers to Lincoln's Inn House, and saw them depart for the Treasury with the rest. Received by Lloyd George and Sir Edward Grey, the workers spoke up earnestly for the vote, the East End women giving their poignant facts of wretchedness and need. Lloyd George questioned them keenly. Annie Kenney, Christabel's spokeswoman, brushed all this aside: " You, Mr. Lloyd George, and you, Sir Edward Grey, must resign! " She declared that the Prime Minister's pledge was a " trick," and even if it were not, the anti-Suffrage Ministers had " smashed it to bits." Lloyd George interrupted; there were sharp passages between the two. Flora Drummond strove to recover harmony by a few jokes. Lloyd George insisted that the Prime Minister's pledge had been and would be kept—nay, more than kept: a guillotine closure specifically providing time for the suffrage amendments had been resolved on. There was " not a scrap of truth " in the rumours " assiduously circulated " that anti-Suffragist Ministers would resign if the women's amendments were carried; all Ministers were pledged to accept the decision of the House. Sir Edward Grey reiterated that the Women's Suffrage amendments would have a fair opportunity. Lloyd George promised to receive the deputation again " for further consultation " when the amendments had been debated.

A bare four hours after the working women had left the Treasury, with compliments and felicitations, that Thursday morning, the Speaker hurled what was known as his " bombshell." Bonar Law had questioned him as to whether certain Government amendments, unconnected with Women's Suffrage, would so change the character of the Reform Bill as to render it a new Bill which must be re-introduced. The Speaker deferred an answer upon this point, but stated clearly that if any of the Women's Suffrage amendments were carried, the Bill would be so changed that it could not be proceeded with, and must be re-introduced as a new measure. Excitement was intense. The Press predicted the withdrawal of the Reform Bill. The debate on the amendments began in an atmosphere of unreality. On Monday the Speaker reiterated that the Women's Suffrage amendments would necessitate a new Bill. When introduced this Bill had not proposed the enfranchisement of any new classes of voters (as had been done by the Reform Acts of 1832, 1867 and

1884). It had only proposed the abolition of plural voting and to shorten the term of registration. Therefore amendments applicable to the earlier Reform Bills would be out of order in this case. Asquith protested that this ruling had not been anticipated by the Government; indeed the very point at issue had been considered by the Government, in the light of the Women's Suffrage amendments moved in 1867 and 1884. In the latter case Lord Randolph Churchill had taken objection to the amendment, on the ground now raised by the Speaker, but the Chairman of Committee, after consultation with the Speaker, had over-ruled the objection. Though taken by surprise, the Government would loyally accept the ruling, but, as " a mere matter of common honour and common sense," the Bill could not be proceeded with now that the promised opportunity for a free vote on Women's Suffrage had been destroyed. By way of compensation to the women, the Government, in the coming session, would grant time for the passage of a private Members' Bill to enfranchise them, if drafted so as to be capable of amendment. The Government would leave its supporters free to vote upon it as they chose. Thus in substitution for the amendment, which, if once carried, the Government had promised to sponsor as its own, all that was offered was time for a private Bill, which was to be left to battle through all the stages, and to face the House of Lords, without, to say the least of it, any assistance from the Government. It was less than had been offered for the defunct Conciliation Bill. Lloyd George had hitherto insisted that an amendment to a general Reform Bill was the perfect manner of enacting Votes for Women. He was now equally emphatic that the private Bill method was the best. He and Sir Edward Grey now both asserted that the amendment had been faced with " machinations "[1] which had destroyed its chances. Lloyd George said: " No one who has watched the proceedings of the last days and weeks can have imagined that we were going to have a clear issue on Women's Suffrage in this Bill." Sir Edward Grey added: " It is felt that to put into a Government Bill something to which many Members of the Government, and notably the Prime Minister, are opposed, is to create a situation which is very embarrassing." Yet to the working women's deputation both George and Grey had denied the existence of these machina-

---

[1] T. P. O'Connor, in the *Chicago Tribune*, told a graphic story of these machinations against the Women's Suffrage amendments, the passage of which " would be bound to humiliate and weaken Premier Asquith . . . the most powerful and trustworthy friend of the Irish Cause." In compassing the defeat of the amendments, said O'Connor, " Redmond never wavered . . . though placed in a position of peculiar difficulty " by a public pledge to leave his Party free to vote as it chose on the issue.

tions. Balfour replied that Lloyd George himself had not only indulged in machinations against Women's Suffrage, but had openly boasted of his success. If he had not " torpedoed " the Conciliation Bill we should have had precisely what he now recommended. " It was he, and he only," who had prevented the question coming before the House in a clear and specific form. Keir Hardie demanded a Government measure. As lately as the previous Saturday, he said, he had defended the Prime Minister against the charge of bad faith; he had no longer any confidence in the honesty of the Government's intentions. The Prime Minister's new offer was, in his opinion, " mere chaff." " What else is left to the women," he asked, " but militant tactics? " Of course he was denounced for that saying. Balfour, the anti-Suffragist F. E. Smith, and other Tories, joined the Liberals in declaring that by a private Members' Bill, and certainly not by a Government measure, would the women's cause best be advanced. They were considering, of course, their own position, should the next election bring them to power: Balfour even complained that it was a dangerous precedent to provide Government time for the passage of a private Members' Bill. In truth, the Suffrage movement was not yet strong enough to compel, though it had gained the power to embarrass, a Government; that was the hard, though hopeful lesson of the situation.

The W.S.P.U. met in the Holborn Hall that night; the burden of its speeches was: " We told you so! The W.S.P.U. has never been wrong! "

To me all this was maddening. I was weary of the canvassing of rumour, the atmosphere of House of Commons intrigue. That 450 Members pledged to support Women's Suffrage, in a House of 670, should be unable to keep their word unless whipped thereto by a Government, was an absurdity. It was also enraging to me to hear Suffragists argue, as they did, that there was no demand in the country for Womanhood Suffrage. The amendments ought to have been carried. I was not prepared to consider the Speaker alone responsible for the impasse: if, though it were difficult to believe, he had acted upon his sole initiative, and had hidden his intention until now, there were abundant means whereby the difficulty might have been circumvented. The Bill was a poor mouse of a Reform Bill, a miserable substitute for Adult Suffrage, to offer to the country after a lapse of thirty years since the last Act. A new Bill could be introduced and carried through all its preliminary stages at a sitting, if the House willed it. Parliament, after all, was supposed to exist in order to legislate. All that had happened was a mere pretence. The situation called, not for cleverness, not for " political arithmetic," but for defiant deeds—or so I felt. I fled from the meeting; I could endure no more speeches. Hurrying home to Linden Gardens, I groped in the darkness of the little courtyard, grasping for the largest stones; as it happened, I gathered, not flints, but lumps of mere cement. At the House of Commons I sent a card in for Keir Hardie, and whilst I sat in the deserted St. Stephen's Hall, ostensibly waiting for him, I considered what object should be my aim; not a stained glass window, nor a statue, not the work of some artist's loving toil. My eye caught a recently hung picture; it looked feebly unattractive; its subject made no impression. It was covered by a great expanse of glass; that would serve; the picture, in any case, would not suffer. I hurled one of the big lumps I had in my pocket. It made a tremendous noise, but it glanced off the glass, leaving no scratch, and was shattered on the paving. Policemen rushed on me from all sides, clutching me at the back of the neck, the shoulders, arms, everywhere; dozens of clutching hands. When they had dragged me to a small police room in the inner precincts, their apparent anger evaporated; they laughed and treated the incident as a good joke. I waited, wondering, without apprehension, what would happen next. When the House rose shortly afterwards, Keir Hardie came, smiling with delighted approval, to tell me I was free. He was glad that I had acted so promptly, he said, and wished that every woman had done the same. Curiously I had thrown my stone at the newly-placed picture of Speaker Finch attempting to adjourn the House in obedience to a message from the King, and being held in the Chair by Members, in order that Sir John Elliot's resolution against tonnage and poundage might be proceeded with, on March 2nd, 1629, the period of the Great Rebellion. Chance had guided my aim very aptly. Mr. Speaker had decided to take no action against me. Keir Hardie escorted me through the House, proudly meeting the out-streaming Members, as though I had been a distinguished guest. Again he expressed the wish that there had been a big militant outbreak that night. We did not then know that Mrs. Despard and three others of the Women's Freedom League had been arrested for attempting to hold a protest meeting in Trafalgar Square.

All the suffrage societies were now repudiating the new offer of a private Bill, and demanding a Government measure. Correspondence was passing between Lloyd George and the W.S.P.U., ostensibly from Mrs. Drummond, but actually from Christabel. On such occasions Annie Kenney and others would cross the Channel even twice daily to obtain her instructions.

Lloyd George was now called upon to make good his promise

to receive the deputation. He offered to see Mrs. Drummond and a few others privately; he would not meet a public deputation. His offer was declined. As a matter of fact the W.S.P.U. desired, not another deputation, but a militant protest. A meeting was held in the Horticultural Hall on Tuesday night. We set out from it to march to the House in the pouring rain. As we neared St. Stephen's Church, one of a group of policemen following us seized Mrs. Drummond roughly round the waist, lifted her and flung her to the ground. She lay still, apparently stunned, and breathing hoarsely. I feared she was seriously hurt. After some moments she appeared to regain consciousness. We helped her to her feet, mud-stained and dishevelled. I kept my arm round her, trying to shield her from further violence. A few of us were allowed to pass through the police cordon near the House. Then the police sprang at us, pushing and dragging us about. Again Mrs. Drummond was flung to the ground. I called to Superintendent Wells that she had been hurt, and told him either to arrest her quietly or let her proceed in peace. Only after further ill-usage was she finally arrested. I was most anxious and indignant on her behalf. It was time to be done with all this police brutality, I thought; it had gone on too long. When arrested and dragged into the charge room, spurred by an intolerable sense of outrage and disgust, I swept the inkpot from the recording desk, in an impulsive gesture, and struck with my open hand, dripping with ink, the face of Superintendent Wells—not to hurt him, but to mark him with the sign of my contempt. " *THE BLACK HAND!* " glared the newspaper placards.

To epitomize the absurd situation to which the Government and the Suffrage question had been brought the *Westminster Gazette* published a cartoon of Asquith, Lloyd George, Harcourt and Grey, feeling their way in a dense fog: " Cherchant la Femme."

Thirty of us appeared at Bow Street next morning; some charged with obstruction, others with window breaking and damage to pillar-boxes. I applied for an adjournment " to take legal advice," purely to gain time to make arrangements for the East End campaign. When my case came up a week later I tried to concentrate attention on the cruel treatment of Mrs. Drummond and police violence in general. I obtained an admission from Superintendent Wells, whom I put in the witness-box, that if a policeman threw a woman down " he was exceeding his orders and his duty." He promised that my statement that Mrs. Drummond had been so treated would be investigated. Sir Albert de Rutzen, the old Magistrate with his half-shut eyes, who always reminded me of a tortoise, ordered me 40s. or fourteen days. I said I would accept neither fine nor sentence, and began a hunger and thirst strike, but the W.S.P.U. paid all our fines anonymously without consulting us, and we came out of prison. It was the policy of the Union now to do this wherever possible.

Whilst we had been battling in Parliament Square that Tuesday night, Irish Suffragettes were arrested for breaking windows in Dublin.

It was now recalled that women had obtained the Municipal vote by a private Member's amendment to a Government Bill, and the Liberal organ, *The Nation,* suggested that the Speaker's ruling had been prompted by gout and bad temper.

The brief truce before the withdrawal of the Reform Bill and its amendments, was followed by destructive militancy on a hitherto unparalleled scale, petty injuries and annoyances continuing side by side with large-scale damage. Street lamps were broken, Votes for Women was painted on the seats at Hampstead Heath, keyholes were stopped up with lead pellets, house numbers were painted out, chairs flung in the Serpentine, cushions of railway carriages slashed, flower-beds damaged, golf greens all over the country scraped and burnt with acid. A bowling green was cut in Glasgow, the turf in Duthie Park, Aberdeen. A mother and daughter, bearing an ancient name, spent much of their time travelling in trains in order to drop pebbles between the sashes of carriage windows, hoping the glass would smash on being raised. Old ladies applied for gun licences to terrify the authorities. Bogus telephone messages were sent calling up the Army Reserves and Territorials. Telegraph and telephone wires were severed with long-handled clippers; fuse boxes were blown up, communication between London and Glasgow being cut off for some hours. There was a window-smashing raid in West End club-land; the Carlton, the Junior Carlton, the Reform Club and others being attacked. A large envelope containing red pepper and snuff was sent to every Cabinet Minister; the Press reported that they all fell victims to the ruse. Boat-houses and sports pavilions in England, Ireland and Scotland, and a grand-stand at Ayr race-course were burnt down. Mrs. Cohen, a Leeds member of the deputation to Lloyd George, broke the glass of a jewel-case in the Tower of London. Works of art and objects of exceptional value became the target of determined militants. Thirteen pictures were hacked in the Manchester Art Gallery. Refreshment pavilions were burnt down in Regent's Park and Kew Gardens, where the glass in three orchid houses was smashed, and the plants, thus exposed, were broken and torn up by the roots. Empty houses and other unattended buildings were systematically sought out and set on fire, and many were destroyed, including Lady White's house near Staines, a loss of £4,000, Roughwood House, Chorley Wood, and a mansion at St. Leonard's valued at £10,000. There were fires at several houses in Hampstead Garden Suburb, at the Suburb Free Church, at Abercarn Church, Monmouthshire, in the Shipcoat Council Schools, at South Bromley Station on the London underground, and in a wood yard at Walham Green. Hugh Franklin set fire to an empty railway carriage; he was imprisoned and forcibly fed. An old cannon was fired near Dudley Castle, shattering glass and terrifying the neighbourhood. Bombs were placed near the Bank of England, at Wheatley Hall, Doncaster, at Oxted Station, and on the steps of a Dublin Insurance Office. Lloyd George's new house in process of erection at Walton-on-the-Hill was injured beyond repair by a bomb explosion. The story of a motor-car passing through the village at 4 a.m., two broken hat-pins, a hairpin, and a golosh indisputably feminine, found on the site, were the only traces of the incendiaries, Emily Wilding Davison and others, all of whom escaped undiscovered. That this was the work of the Suffragettes was usually made evident by literature deposited in the vicinity. In most cases the culprits had altogether disappeared and no clue to their identity was left. Where a capture was effected, the punishment varied considerably: up to nine months for breaking windows or the glass covering pictures; eighteen months or two years for arson. Miriam Pratt, in an unsuccessful attempt to burn an empty house, dropped her watch. Her uncle, a police constable in whose house she lived, identified the watch and gave evidence against her.

Olive Wharry carried out a secret hunger strike, which was not discovered for thirty-one days, when her state of exhaustion necessitated release. I heard the news with a shock of horror, fearing the exploit would teach the authorities that prisoners could survive under starvation much longer than they had thought. On her release she looked, it was said, " all eyes and teeth." At the studio, in Campden Hill Gardens, of Olive Hockin, an artist, a police raid revealed what the Press called a " Suffragette arsenal": clippers for cutting telegraph wires, bottles of corrosive fluid, hammers, flints, false motor-car identification plates. She was sent to prison for four months in the Second Division. On threatening to hunger strike, she was transferred to the First Division, and agreed to serve her sentence on condition of being permitted to carry on her professional work. The First Division, so obstinately refused to petty offenders of old, could now be had for the asking.

"A new kind of woman has been created by the present Government . . . the 'Outragette,'" said the *Weekly Dispatch*.

During the week in which the Reform Bill was withdrawn the Labour Party Annual Conference met at Lambeth Baths. The official suffrage resolution accepted the Prime Minister's offer of a free vote on a private Members' Bill, merely stipulating, as Arthur Henderson had urged in the House, that the Government should become responsible for the Bill after it had passed the Second Reading. An amendment by the Women's Labour League and the Fabian Society was carried by a two to one majority, demanding that the Parliamentary Labour Party should oppose any franchise measure in which women were not included. The amendment was received with great gratitude by Mrs. Fawcett and her organization, but its importance must not be over emphasized. Philip Snowden, in a speech to the N.U.W.S.S., candidly observed that the decision did not mean the Labour Party would vote against the abolition of plural voting, which was all he thought the Government likely now to attempt in that Parliament. Nevertheless, the decision was an advance, and a bigger one than many people could discern in the then white-heat of controversy. It was a tragic waste of energy that the National Union of Suffrage Societies and the Women's Freedom League should be supporting Labour candidates, whilst the W.S.P.U. was directing against the Labour Party the same attack made upon the Government, which had the power to grant the vote and would not. The Labour Party, after all, could be counted on to vote for Women's Suffrage, on a straight issue, as had been proved on many occasions. It is true that on this, as on every other question, the proportion of absentee Labour Members was larger than could be approved by its friends, but it was not on this account that the Suffrage Bills had been lost. Certainly Ramsay Macdonald, its chairman, was slow indeed to treat Votes for Women as a measure of first class importance—if he ever arrived at that point. The conciliatory diplomacy on which he prided himself was conspicuous by its absence in his dealings with the Suffragettes. Nevertheless the Labour Party was the one pro-Votes for Women Party in the House, though the Adult Suffrage controversy had disabled it from the active sponsorship of a Bill. Moreover, the Labour Party was too small in numbers to compel the Government to action. It was a sad absurdity, which few outsiders could comprehend, that the chief virulence of the W.S.P.U. attack was concentrated upon Keir Hardie, who had long ceased to be chairman of the Party. In the issue of the *Suffragette* following the Labour Conference appeared a hideous caricature of him, smoking a tremendous cigar, labelled " Liberalo Patrona," and clinging to the arm of Asquith, whilst at the same time raising his hat to a Suffragette, who dismissed him with an indignant gesture. Under the drawing appeared these words:

" The Prime Minister to Labour Party with fat Liberal cigar: ' Tut! tut! My dear fellow! You go on sticking to me, and don't allow yourself to be worried by the coldness of primitive creatures who expect politicians to keep their pledges.' "

I did not see this cartoon at the time. The campaign of insult against this staunch old friend wounded me deeply. Like himself, I made no protest, from loyalty to those I would not criticize in the hour of adversity. Once when a woman strove to drown his voice by cries of " fool " and " traitor " he replied in irritated terms, but, ever quick to defend the militants, at the close of the meeting he apologized for what he had said.

At the annual conference of the I.L.P. the following Easter, a resolution was carried demanding a Government measure for Votes for Women, and pledging the Party's Parliamentary representatives to oppose and vote against any Franchise or Registration Bill from which women were excluded. The resolution did not go far enough for Lansbury and the W.S.P.U. Suffragettes attempted to shout down Keir Hardie at a Free Trade Hall demonstration; they interrupted the conference with their outcries, locked in the delegates, who were subsequently liberated by the police, and threw sausages at Keir Hardie and Snowden.

Asquith in January had withdrawn the Reform Bill, saying that " as a mere matter of common honour and common sense," it could not be proceeded with after the Women's Suffrage amendments had been declared out of order. Nevertheless in March he introduced a new measure to secure the main plank in the Reform Bill, and the only one his Party cared for: the abolition of plural voting. Snowden declared this a deliberate attempt to evade the Government's pledges to women, but only three Labour Members voted against the Plural Voting Bill! The ill-starred measure was again thrown out by the Lords.

CHAPTER III

AFTER the working women's deputation to Lloyd George, Lincoln's Inn House finally withdrew its representatives from the East End and closed all financial aid to the movement there. Such branches as had been formed were hitherto under the tutelage of imported organizers and secretaries, appointed either by the local unions, or from Lincoln's Inn House. When the imported officials withdrew I immediately established branches, with their own local officials, in Bow, Bromley, Stepney, Limehouse, Bethnal Green and Poplar.[1] A few pounds remained from our previous " popular campaign fund." With this as a nucleus, I determined to open premises in Bow, which would serve as a rallying centre for the East End branches. Our old shop in Bow Road had been empty since we left it, but Zelie Emerson urged me: " Come to the Roman Road; all the people go there! " She was right; the Roman Road was seething with life. Women crowded the narrow thoroughfare, pressing against the costers' barrows laden with oranges, cabbages, garments, crockery and what not. A cheery kindliness held the throng, in spite of its poverty. My serious mood was lightened by the sparkling gaiety of the girl beside me. We were hungry, and bought hot buns at the baker's, and thought them the nicest food we had ever tasted. There was only one shop to let in the road: number 321—a little place with a parlour behind the shop, a tiny scullery-kitchen, and three small rooms upstairs. The shop window was broken across the centre and held together by putty, the flooring was in holes. The landlord would do nothing to put the place in repair, but he would let it for 14s. 6d. a week. We took it on the spot. It had lately been a second-hand clothes dealer's, and was bug-ridden, like many another East End hovel. Repeated fumigation and papering never entirely eradicated the pests. In spite of such drawbacks, the place was a centre of joyous enthusiasm. Mrs. Wise, at the sweet shop next door, brought in a trestle table for a counter, and helped us to hoist the purple, white and green. Her boy volunteered to put up and take down the shutters night and morning; her girl came

[1] The Paddington local W.S.P.U. worked in Poplar for some time longer.

438

in to sweep. Friends rallied round; women of the neighbour-hood scrubbed the floors and cleaned the windows; tables and chairs and crockery were given by poor people's self-denial. Jessie Lansbury, the young wife of Lansbury's eldest son, Willie, a Bow working girl, was made honorary secretary of the branch. There were paper-selling captains, shop, chalking and handbill captains, and a library secretary, for we were already collecting a lending library. Zelie Emerson was the honorary organizer to keep all the others going. Elsa Dalglish was preparing a jumble sale to assist the exchequer.

On February 14th, a week after the shop was opened, we held a meeting in the Bromley Public Hall, Bow Road, and from it led a procession round the district. Some stones were solemnly thrown at the window of a bank. My stone missed, but someone else managed to send one through the glass. To make sure of imprisonment, I broke a window in the police station, and was convicted for this and the bank window. Daisy Lansbury was accused of catching a policeman by the belt, but the charge was dismissed. Zelie Emerson and I went to prison for six weeks on Friday, and began the hunger and thirst strike, but Mrs. Pankhurst had our fines paid anonymously, and we were released at noon on Saturday. We rushed back to the shop and found it crowded with members, scrubbing the tables and arranging to march to Holloway prison to cheer us next day.

On the following Monday, February 17th, we held a meeting at the Obelisk, a mean-looking monument in a dreary, almost unlighted open space near Bow Church.

Our platform, a high, uncovered cart, was pitched against the dark wall of a dismal council school in the teeth of a bitter wind. Already a little knot of people had gathered; women holding their dark garments closely about them, shivering and talking of the cold, four or five police constables and a couple of Inspectors. We climbed into the cart and watched the crowd growing, the men and women turning from the footpaths to join the mass. One of the Inspectors stretched up to ask me in a whisper whether I intended to form a procession. I answered "No." Zelie Emerson spoke first, witty and engaging. I sat beside her, half numbed by the cold, thinking of many things in a dull way, and wondering how the damp cold would affect my throat, which had been troubling me of late, and whether I should be able to make myself well heard when my turn came.

As she stopped I was suddenly all alert. My voice rang out loud and very clear. I felt the tense expectancy about me; the thrill of sympathy responding to my words. In concluding I said I knew it to be a hard thing for men and women to risk imprisonment in such a neighbourhood, where most of them were labouring under the sternest economic pressure, yet I pleaded for some of the women of Bow to join us in showing themselves prepared to make a sacrifice to secure enfranchisement. Then amid a stunned surprise that I had said no more, for the people expected a call to action, I got down from the cart, slow and stumbling, for my feet were stiff with cold.

Half the crowd was disappointed that nothing had come of the meeting; half was wondering if something would happen yet. The police too were waiting, and would have prevented what I intended had I spoken of it. I walked slowly away toward the Bow Road, the crowd irresolute, half turning to follow, half waiting to see if someone else would speak. A few of the women pressed round me. At the corner was a brightly-lit undertaker's shop with cheap, showy monuments in its window.

I took a heavy flint from my pocket and hurled it as hard as I could. It broke the glass with a loud report, passing through it as easily as though it had been butter, I thought, recalling my bad shot in St. Stephen's Hall. Three stones went flying from close beside me; they sounded like the firing of guns. I was seized by two policemen; three other women were seized. We were dragged, resisting, along the Bow Road, the crowd cheering and running with us. Suddenly a young man darted forward with a shout: "Votes for Women!" and flung a stone through a window in the Bromley Public Hall. The people applauded: "Bravo! Votes for Women!" The police leapt upon him, wrenching his arms, hauling him along by the collar, a short, thick-set figure, struggling and breathless. It was Willie, George Lansbury's eldest son, who had promised his wife to go to prison instead of her because she had tubercular tendencies and could not leave their little daughter only two years old.

The crowd, always growing in numbers, surging around and ahead of us, roaring its cheers and its epithets, massing around the doors of the big new police station. The police fought their way through and thrust us inside. The Inspector shouted: "File out, you men, and keep them back—and shut the doors!"

There were four others inside with me: Annie Lansbury and her brother Will, pale, delicate Mrs. Watkins, a widow struggling to maintain herself by sweated sewing-machine work, and young Mrs. Moore. A moment later little Zelie Emerson was bundled in, flushed and triumphant—she had broken the window of the Liberal Club.

I looked at the others who were new to this. They all seemed satisfied and glad. Mrs. Moore sat with her fair young face a little raised and lighted by an ecstatic smile. Cheers were resounding from outside, and the policemen hastened to and fro from the windows to the doors.

Next morning we were at the Thames Police Court. "What can you expect from East End people like that?" the Magistrate snarled at me, when I asked a police witness whether the crowd had been sympathetic to us. "If you behave like common riff-raff, you must be treated like common riff-raff!" he said in sentencing Willie Lansbury, Zelie Emerson and me to two months' hard labour without the option of a fine, and the others to a month. He was angry to find us returning again so soon; piqued, perhaps, that he had been so cordial to me when first I came there to plead for the poor fellow who took the tea.

That was the beginning of the mass movement for Votes for Women in East London. A tremendous flame of enthusiasm burst forth; great meetings were held, and during our imprison-ment long processions marched eight times the six miles to Holloway and several times also to Brixton, where Willie Lansbury was incarcerated. The people set out from Bow at eight or nine at night, and arrived home in the small hours; hard efforts indeed for weary working people after a day of toil.

Zelie, Mrs. Watkins and I determined to do the hunger strike; the others elected to serve their sentences. Mrs. Watkins, who suffered from chronic heart complaint, was soon released. Zelie and I had to endure a very much longer term, though to get free the sooner, we refrained from water as well as from food; ours were the first thirst strikes.[1]

After hours of waiting at the police court and a long journey in the crowded van, which went round by Pentonville to deposit the men prisoners, we were locked at last each into a little unheated reception cell. I was wearing the fur coat I had bought to withstand American winters, and a cloth coat wrapped about my knees, yet I was cold. I thought of the others, who had all seemed to me thinly clad. I roused myself and began to sing, hoping to cheer them, but there were no answering voices. Were the walls too thick for the others to reply? I paced the cell in anxiety, singing still, and read the messages scratched on the wall—cynical, obscene, tragic. "I only did it for my poor children!" "Oh, God, when shall I know my fate?"

I sang till I lost hope of reply. When I got to my cell at

[1] The thirst strike was not, I think, generally adopted by hunger strikers until the latter part of 1913. In *The Suffragette* it was referred to as a "new and terrible form of protest" by myself and Mary Richardson, who was arrested with me on July 8th, 1913. Mrs. Pankhurst is first mentioned as refraining from water after her arrest on July 24th, 1913. Except where forcible feeding was employed, the longest term endured without food was by Olive Wharry, thirty-one days; the longest term without food and water, fifteen days by Freda Graham.

last, a hospital cell, as I knew by the sound of babies crying, and the iron bedstead in place of the plank, I climbed to the window and called out loudly: " Are there any Suffragettes here? " There was no response. I tapped the walls on either side, as prisoners do; still no one answered. My companions had evidently been taken to another part of the prison. I was sorry for that: I wanted the others near me to aid them in their struggle.

Rule 243A being in force, we were exempt from the search and permitted to wear our own clothes. Writing materials were not allowed, but I was well supplied with paper and pencils; I wore a bag of them round my waist, under my skirt, and had an additional thick wad of paper as a lining to my brush-and-comb tidy. As it was known that we should hunger strike, we were at once placed in hospital cells, which differed from the ordinary cells in having an ordinary bed with a spring mattress instead of the plank. In spite of the hunger and thirst strike I was able to write fairly steadily, for the greater part of most days, until near the end of my imprisonment, lying on the bed in such a position that what I was doing could not be observed through the spy hole, and always on the *qui vive* to conceal my work between the sheets. I kept a calendar scratched with a hairpin on the white-washed walls of my cell, and printed favourite verses there to keep myself occupied during the periods when my secret writing was likely to be interrupted. For this the governor, a tall, sandy-haired man with a long red face, several times sentenced me to various terms of " close solitary confinement," but as exercise and books from the library had already been withdrawn as a punishment for the hunger strike, the additional punishments were only a matter of form. I permitted myself the great luxury, for such it became, of rinsing out my mouth only once a day, lest the tongue should absorb moisture. I was careful never to swallow a single drop. I was always cold, but I felt only a trace of hunger, and less as the days passed. Thirst strikers crave only for water. Food such as I had never before seen in Holloway was daily placed in my cell: chicken, Brand's essence, fruit. The varied colours diverted my eye in the drabness of the cell, but I had no more inclination to eat the still life groups on my table than if they had been a painting or a vase of flowers. Nevertheless the first night I took the precaution of putting the eatables on the floor under the table, with the stool in front, in case I should go to them in my sleep; then realized the absurdity of such measures, for I could not sleep.

On the third day the two doctors sounded my heart and felt my pulse. The senior told me he had no alternative but to feed

me by force.   Then they left the cell.   I was thrown into a state
of great agitation, heart palpitating with fear, noises in my ears,
hot and cold shivers down my spine.   I paced the cell, crouched
against the wall, knelt by the bed, paced again, longing for some
means of escape, resolving, impotently, to fight to prevent the
outrage—knowing not what to do.   I gathered together in the
clothes-basket the prison mug and plate, my out-door shoes—
everything the cell contained which might be used as a missile,
and placing the basket on the table beside me, stood with my
back to the wall, waiting to hurl these things at the doctors as
soon as they should appear.   Presently I heard footsteps approaching, collecting outside my cell.   I was strangled with fear, cold
and stunned, yet alert to every sound.   The door opened—not
the doctors, but a crowd of wardresses filled the doorway.   I
could not use my missiles upon them; poor tools!   Yet nervously
the hand that lay on the basket clutched a shoe and it fell amongst
them as they closed with me.   I struggled, but was overcome.
There were six of them, all much bigger and stronger than I.
They flung me on my back on the bed, and held me down firmly
by shoulders and wrists, hips, knees and ankles.   Then the
doctors came stealing in.   Someone seized me by the head and
thrust a sheet under my chin.   My eyes were shut.   I set my teeth
and tightened my lips over them with all my strength.   A man's
hands were trying to force open my mouth; my breath was
coming so fast that I felt as though I should suffocate.   His
fingers were striving to pull my lips apart—getting inside.   I felt
them and a steel instrument pressing round my gums, feeling for
gaps in my teeth.   I was trying to jerk my head away, trying to
wrench it free.   Two of them were holding it, two of them
dragging at my mouth.   I was panting and heaving, my breath
quicker and quicker, coming now with a low scream which was
growing louder.   " Here is a gap," one of them said.   " No, here
is a better one.   This long gap here! "   A steel instrument
pressed my gums, cutting into the flesh.   I braced myself to
resist that terrible pain.   " No, that won't do "—that voice again.
" Give me the pointed one! "   A stab of sharp, intolerable
agony.   I wrenched my head free.   Again they grasped me.
Again the struggle.   Again the steel cutting its way in, though
I strained my force against it.   Then something gradually forced
my jaws apart as a screw was turned; the pain was like having the
teeth drawn.   They were trying to get the tube down my throat,
I was struggling madly to stiffen my muscles and close my throat.
They got it down, I suppose, though I was unconscious of any-
thing then save a mad revolt of struggling, for they said at last:
" That's all! " and I vomited as the tube came up.   They left

me on the bed exhausted, gasping for breath and sobbing convulsively.

The same thing happened in the evening, but I was too tired to fight so long.

The governor came to my cell that day or the next accompanied by the crowd. I was accused of striking the principal wardress with the shoe which fell from my hand. The others gave evidence that I had done so. "Did I hurt you?" I asked. She answered "No." I said no more. The governor sentenced me to some days of solitary confinement.

Day after day, morning and evening, the same struggle. Sometimes they used one steel gag on my jaw, sometimes two. "Don't hurt more than you can help," the senior sometimes said when his junior prodded with the sharp point of steel. My gums, where they prised them open, were always sore and bleeding, with bits of loose, jagged flesh; and other parts of the mouth got bruised or pinched in the struggle. Sometimes the tube was coughed up three or four times before they finally got it down. Sometimes, but not often—I was generally too much agitated by then—I felt the tube go right down into the stomach; a sickening, terrifying sensation, especially when it reached the breast. My shoulders were bruised, my back ached during the night. I scarcely slept. Often I fainted once or twice after the feeding.

Infinitely worse than the pain was the sense of degradation; the very fight that one made against the outrage was shattering one's nerves and one's self-control. Daily there grew on me more strongly the realization that the other human beings who were torturing me came to the task with loathing and pity and would have refrained from it if they could. Sometimes when the struggle was over, or even in the heat of it, in a swift flash I felt as though my entity had been broken up into many selves, of which one, aloof and calm, surveyed all this misery, and one, ruthless and unswerving, forced the weak, shrinking body to its ordeal. Sometimes, breaking forth, it seemed, from the inner depths of my being, came outraged, violated, tortured selves; waves of emotion, fear, indignation, wildly up-surging. Whilst all these selves were struggling, resisting, shrinking from the tortures, would rise in them a fierce desire to scream. The ruthless one permitted: "Yes, let them hear it! Others too often suffered dumbly, hiding their wrath and agony! Yes, let them know." Occasionally after the torturers had left the cell, that poor body and its voices, which seemed not part of me, protested, wailing in rage and misery. The ruthless one allowed it. "Yes, let them hear!" Then a small fear would creep up, lest all those voices, of those maddened, agonized sensations, those huge, untamable emotions, should overwhelm alike the ruthless and the calm self, and, with great effort, I would silence them—lie still and, when I could, clean off all the filth left from the outrage—and put myself to write on my precious store of paper, cautiously lest I might be surprised. At first I kept a regular diary, but as the toll of days lengthened into weeks I lost heart in it; the events it chronicled were too hateful to be dwelt upon. I gave it up and used my paper for more inspiring things, with fear that it might be filled up too quickly. With this thought I wrote verse as the most concentrated form of expression, and the greater part of a play dealing with the Biblical story of David and Bathsheba. I hoped to complete it after release, but in the stress and turmoil of those days it was thrown away by someone tidying up my papers. Sometimes to crush down despondency I would draw on my slate. Once it was an illustration to Omar Khayyám's "Awake for morning in the bowl of night has flung the stone that puts the stars to flight," which helped to divert my mind from the torture. Another time it was Ezekiel xxxiv., where it is told that the shepherds have eaten the fat and clothed themselves in the wool, but they have neither cared for the sick nor sought the lost, but with force and with cruelty have ruled them, so that the flock, for lack of a shepherd, has been scattered and has become meat to all the beasts of the field. Reading the words I saw in my mind's eye a group of shepherds feasting together on the edge of a cliff beside a fire at which they had roasted a young lamb. A ram had caught its horns in the branches of a tree overhanging the chasm. Many of the flock had fallen and were lying dead on the rocks below. The shepherds were dressed like the shepherds of old, but their faces were those of the Cabinet Ministers. Here was another picture for my slate, but a slate is a dismal thing to draw on; one cannot long retain one's zest in making drawings to rub out.

At night I scarcely slept, and when free from pain those dark, quiet hours were more peaceful than the day. I would lie still, thinking of things for which there is too little time in the hurry of one's life. Passages from the Bible I had read during the day brought resplendent visions.

"How beautiful upon the mountains are the feet of him that bringeth good tidings, that publisheth of peace."

Sometimes I tossed in feverish impatience and anxiety. I felt once that a dear friend was beside me in the cell, and afterwards there smote upon me sometimes a fear that this dear friend was dead.

Not a whisper of news came to me from the outer world, nor even from within the gaol itself. My mother was arrested and imprisoned in Holloway for a day; I did not know. Third-class prisoners were brought into my cell to scrub; old women; pale women; a bright young girl who smiled at me whenever she raised her eyes from the floor; a poor, ugly creature without a nose, awful to look upon. The wardress watched them always so closely not one could get a word with me.

From the moment my door was thrown open at six in the morning I could not cease to think of the doctors' coming, and after I was dressed I could not sit or stand for a moment, but would pace up and down, trembling and shivering, with heart beating fast. Often I vomited during the struggle and while the tube was being withdrawn, but at other times I could not. Always I brought up huge quantities of phlegm. My back and head ached almost constantly. I was tasting the stuff administered at one meal when they came to pour in more. I longed to vomit for relief, but just as when I was a child at sea, I longed in vain. Mary Leigh had told me that after the feeding she lay still, and thought of a boat heaving on the waves till she was sick. I desired vainly to emulate her. The weeks were passing; if I could bring up all they poured in, I thought, I could hasten the day of my release. Every hour I remained seemed a shameful consent, an encouragement to the maintainers of outrage. I lay on the bed, with my head hanging down, retching and struggling. At last I discovered that by thrusting my hand down my throat I could make myself sick. Now, as soon as I could pull myself together after each feeding, I struggled till I had brought up what had been forced into me, choking and straining, the cords of my streaming eyes feeling as though they would snap. The flesh round the eyes and the eyeballs themselves grew daily more painful; the eyes shrank from the light. I noticed that the officials who came to my door stopped to stare at me.

Exercise had been denied; the doctor was now urging me to take it, but I refused to go unless I could exercise with my comrades, and this he declared impossible. At last, three weeks and three days after I entered the prison, the wardress told me I could take exercise with Miss Emerson, who was asking for me.

When I staggered into the yard, I saw a little figure moving towards me, so changed from her plump rotundity, with that pinched, wistful face that my heart smote me for being the cause of her imprisonment. She told me that she had refrained from food for fourteen days before the officials had discovered it, since when she had been fed by the nasal tube. She seemed startled by my appearance and told me my eyes were bloodshot. She whispered that she had a means of sending out letters, and that

if I would slip one into her hand at exercise next morning she
would get it posted.   That night I wrote to my mother:

"I am fighting, fighting, fighting. I have four, five and six
wardresses every day, as well as two doctors. . . . I resist all the time.
My gums are always bleeding. . . .

"I was told that Dr. Ede says Mrs. Branson had a defect in her
heart.   Can something be done?

"I am afraid they may be saying we don't resist.[1]   Yet my
shoulders are bruised with struggling. . . ."

I wrote also to Keir Hardie.[2]

Again I went out to exercise and gave the letters to my little
comrade.   Perhaps it was the sight of the sky above the height
of those towering walls; the sun, even upon those stones; perhaps
the painful impression of her shrunken form—on returning to
the cell I was torn with a passion of self-contempt that I had
endured the torturing indignity for so long.   I scourged myself
with the thought that by occupying myself with writing, I was
reconciling my being to this odious nightmare existence.   That
evening the forcible feeding seemed more disgusting than ever.
When, with ruthless self-torture, I had brought about the sickness
and dragged myself up from it, I sat leaning upon the table,
abandoned to tears of despair; my voice, high-pitched and strange,
cried out, growing louder and louder, till it filled the place with
sound, that it was a scandal four of us should be serving five
months in all for one little £3 window; that the Government had
had their pound of flesh, and far, far more, oh, far, far more; that
this torture had been going on year after year; woman after
woman had been broken and destroyed, and all because a handful
of men stood against us, like a solid wall in their sullen, cruel
obstinacy, and would not give way—some for the sake of their
jobs, some for the sake of their pride.   I heard myself crying:
"No, no, no, no; I will not endure any more of it.   I will not
endure any more of it. . . ."   I knew not and cared not whether,
if I should strive, I could silence that voice or not.   I listened as
to a thing apart. . . .

I rested a while, half dozing, half faint, with a rushing noise
in the ears, yet thinking clearly; somehow it seemed with preter-
natural clarity, as though a wall had been rent away.

Then, nerved by deliberate purpose, I began to pace up and
down the cell: five steps to the window end, abruptly turning,
five steps back to the door; pacing on and on. . . . I felt very
sick, and faint, terribly faint, but I would not stop.

[1] The Home Secretary had frequently stated that the prisoners did not resist.

[2] The letter was returned to me from Clements Inn after my release on the
pretence that the address was indistinct.

After two hours perhaps, all went black. There was a terrible pain in my chest; my legs gave way under me. I must have cried out, for the principal officer, she who had accused me of hitting her with the shoe, came into my cell. She took my hands, chafing them, and drawing me to her. "Darling, darling," I heard her say. She helped me to bed. She was so kind, and I so terribly suffering, that I could not gainsay her, though my purpose was interrupted. "I will do it in the morning," I silently resolved. A doctor came. A wardress watched me through a panel they opened in the door as she passed on her rounds.

In the morning, between six and seven o'clock, I rose up, determined that I would not cease from walking till my release. I walked till they came to feed me, and told the doctor what I intended. There was the old struggle. Then I sprang up and began again, dashing across and across my cell with outstretched arms, throwing my weight against the wall as I turned. I felt sick, terribly, terribly sick and faint, but I would not faint. I plunged my hands for an instant in cold water and dashed it over my face, moistened with a wet hand my parched tongue, then dashed on. Hitherto I had suffered with extreme constipation, like everyone who was forcibly fed—how many, indeed, were obliged to undergo serious operations as a result! Now the violent exertion caused the food to pass from me within an hour after the meal, and gave me some relief. Every official who came to the cell door seemed shocked at the sight of me. There was no glass in the cell, but it occurred to me that by holding the towel behind my head I could see myself in the polished tin reflector behind the gas. I paused an instant to look: my face was white, my eyes horrible, like cups of blood. At times all went black, and I fell, but did not lose consciousness, and after an instant I rose again and continued the march. . . . Again the misery of the evening struggle. . . . Again I marched.

Late in the evening steps paused outside my cell. "She says she is going to walk about till she goes, sir. Shall we tie her on the bed?" The doctor answered: "No; she'll soon get tired of that."

I walked on through the night, my footsteps loud in the silence, and as the hours passed I tottered across the cell, constantly falling, and should have fallen more often still, save for the near proximity of the opposite walls. At times I felt as though my force would entirely ebb, but when the morning came I got more strength. My legs were sore and swollen, my joints were stiff.

The principal officer came to me with tired, flushed face, and dark rings under her eyes. "You make me ill," she said, her voice trembling. "I have heard you walking all night." I looked at her dumbly, unable to answer. I was only hobbling now, and knew that soon I should not be able to walk at all. I felt my pulse; it was fluttering like the trembling of a little wing. A thought came to me: "Home Office doctors." I knew that they had been sent for in some cases. I believed if they saw me now they would report it dangerous to force food on me any more. I asked the next officer who came to the cell that I might see the governor and doctor together, and lay down to calm myself, that I might be able to speak to them. I had walked for twenty-eight hours.

The doctor and governor came. The doctor spoke of my "extraordinary struggles." He little knew how the words reassured me. I feared that my little muscular strength had made me a contemptibly easy victim, as compared with more active people. They said that though it was Sunday they would allow me to petition the Home Secretary for an independent medical examination, and would send a medical report on their own account; but they insisted I must take a cup of milk twice that day and also on Monday morning. I agreed, and on Monday evening two doctors came. I had had two comparatively peaceful days, and seeing them with the two prison doctors, four people together in my cell, seemed to excite me. I was strangely cheerful, I felt entirely well, and when they asked me questions about my symptoms I could not remember how I had felt. However, they told me I should be released, but, they said, the papers could not come through till Wednesday. They made me promise to continue taking two cups of milk each day till then.

Thereafter I became horribly depressed. I no longer attempted to write, but lay on the bed, unable to stay my tears. I told the doctor of the nervous trouble from which I had suffered for many years after my father's death, and that I feared my nervous system would be completely deranged. On Wednesday there was no news. In vain I asked the governor to let me communicate with my Uncle Walter Goulden, who might go to the Home Office to expedite the answer. That evening an officer came to fetch me to Zelie Emerson's cell. She was ill and asking for me. They hoped that I might quiet her. I knew by the dry, burning touch of her skin that she had fever. She complained of terrible abdominal pain. Shocked at her condition, I took her in my arms, uttering foolish words: "Oh, my little sweetheart! Oh, my little sweetheart!" Her wrist was bandaged. She told me she had tried to commit suicide by cutting an artery. She had dug into the flesh with her small, blunt penknife, till she reached the artery, but when she had tried to cut it, she found it, she said, too tough, and like an indiarubber band. They had come to the cell while she was working at it.

I determined to recommence the hunger strike at once, believing that I was being played with, ashamed to have fallen into a trap. I told the doctor of my intention. He argued with me; but though I had rejected the cup of milk, he did not attempt to feed by force. I lay on the bed, feeling too weak and ill to move. At 5 p.m. a wardress came and took me through long passages to a cell in another part of the prison. I felt very tired and stiff, and though she put her arm round me to help me, all went black, and there was a rushing in my ears. At last we reached a cell where the doctor was waiting. He told me I was released, and seeing I was faint made me lie on the bed and gave me brandy. Anxious to recover the writings I had concealed there, I asked to go back to my cell to collect my things, but the wardress said she would pack them for me. All were in fact returned to me except the diary. That, I believe, was sent to the Home Secretary. I asked to say good-bye to Zelie Emerson, but was refused.

Two wardresses took me home in a taxi. At starting I asked to be allowed to send a telegram for someone to meet me, as I lived alone. "You cannot do it unless the governor gives permission." One of them went back to ask, but returning, jumped in and shouted: "Drive on!" The wardresses left me at my door about eight in the evening. It was Good Friday, the studio empty and cheerless. I staggered out into Linden Gardens, walking unsteadily with my hand on the wall for support. I saw a taxi and drove to the nursing home in Pembridge Gardens. Miss Pine did not recognize me when she opened the door. She cried out when she saw my eyes. She put me to bed at once. It was difficult to realize that that small, top-heavy-looking white face, with the awful eyes, in the mirror opposite, was really mine. For weeks after, when anyone came into the room, a hot flush seemed to rise from my feet and pass over me to my face. When the nurse washed my arms and hands there was a pain between my toes.

In a few hours Keir Hardie was bending over me, his face haggard and seamed with sorrow and insomnia, his hair long and unkempt. "I have caused you this grief, O tender heart!" I inwardly reproached myself, trying to dispel his distress. My mother came later; she too seemed shocked. I was tortured by anxiety for those I had left behind; above all, for Zelie Emerson. What was the matter with her? I wanted to march next day to Holloway, but fainted when I tried to stand. Dr. Murray told me I was very ill. My blood-red eyeballs were due, she said, to the rupture of small blood-vessels under the conjunctivæ.

McKenna spoke of my twenty-eight hours' walk to Keir Hardie: "Sylvia *is* a plucky girl!" "He seemed as pleased," Keir Hardie told me, "as though one of his young employees had been distinguishing himself." "The brute!" I answered. During the War when McKenna was at the Board of Trade I was elected to a deputation which interviewed him. When we were leaving he approached me with outstretched hand: "I must shake hands with you. You are the pluckiest girl I ever knew." I refused his hand. It may have been churlish. I did it not from resentment for the past, but because I was at the time strongly opposed to his Government. Moreover, the vote was not yet won. Yet I bore no resentment towards the prison officials; they did their odious work, on the whole, with no more violence than they found necessary to accomplish it. At times they were kind, even solicitous, but they were desirous of retaining their employment. Some wardresses were said to have resigned owing to forcible feeding. £250 was distributed amongst them early in 1913, as a recompense for the extra strain on them involved by forcible feeding. To many of them our conduct may have seemed mere madness, but many conveyed, in one way or other, that they understood, and sympathized.

I could not march, but my mind was clear and active. The struggle seemed always to render me more alert. I wrote at once a long Press statement, which received very wide publicity, endeavouring to reveal, through my own experiences, the psychological as well as the physical effects of forcible feeding. There was now a widespread revolt of public feeling against the "Cat and Mouse" Act. Bernard Shaw displayed, in his attack upon it, a serious persistence never, I think, shown by him in any other cause. Again and again he wrote and spoke against it:

"If you take a woman and torture her you torture me. These denials of fundamental rights are really a violation of the soul. They are an attack on that sacred part of life that is common to all of us, that part which has no individuality, that which is real, the thing of which you speak when you talk of ' the life everlasting ' . . . the denial of these fundamental rights to ourselves, in the persons of women, is practically a denial of the life everlasting."—Kingsway Hall, March 18th, 1913.

The *Medical Times* (March 1st) declared:

" Rather than be a party to such an outrage we would resign the most lucrative appointment ever held by a member of the ' noble ' profession."

In the Commons a Conservative Member, moving a reduction of the Home Office vote, declared forcible feeding " the most barbaric and cruel thing that could possibly be devised." He called attention to the startling case of Lilian Lenton, a young girl who had come up from the provinces to join the working women's deputation, and had been arrested on suspicion of complicity in the burning of the Kew refreshment pavilion. Being refused bail, she rejected food in prison, and was forcibly fed on one occasion only.   Marshall, the W.S.P.U. solicitor, had seen her the previous afternoon when she appeared well and gay, making light of a two days' fast.   Yet during the first attempt at forcible feeding the tube was accidentally passed into the trachea, and the food poured into her lungs.   Alarming symptoms developed.   Frantic telephone messages were received at the Home Office by one of the officials in charge.   " He was told," said McKenna, " that the thing might be a question of minutes."   He gave the order of release.   The girl[1] was rushed out, suffering from pleuro-pneumonia, with a temperature of 102°.   Lord Robert Cecil urged deportation of Suffragette offenders.   McKenna retorted by inquiring what was to happen should the prisoners hunger strike on the boat?   " We are endeavouring, slowly but surely, to break down the movement," he said; but he was not prepared to let women die for window-breaking and obstinacy, as he put it.   Sir Frederick Banbury, the old anti-Suffragist, protested with a sneer that there was no question of death.   McKenna insisted that forty or fifty women would be proud to die for their cause.   Forcible feeding had been in force under his predecessor; he wanted to avoid it. With that object he desired the power to " license out " the hunger strikers for short periods, and take them back to serve

[1] On her recovery Lilian Lenton eluded the police and went her militant way. A woman was wrongfully arrested in Doncaster for attempted arson. To save her Lilian Lenton, being the woman actually concerned, gave herself up (as May Dennis) on June 9th. She was released after a hunger strike on June 17th. Detectives were watching the house to which she went. A van stopped at the door, a boy sitting on the tail-board entered the house. He reappeared, eating an apple, and resumed his seat. The van drove away. As it happened, it was not the same boy. The one eating the apple was Lilian Lenton. She disappeared till October 7th, when she was again re-arrested for trial on her Kew charge. Forcible feeding again failed. She was released in eight days, and again disappeared. On May 4th, 1914, she was re-arrested on the Doncaster charge, and brought to trial four days later; but forcible feeding failed again. She was released on May 12th and once more disappeared.

their sentences after recovery. Already, on January 31st, a Member had made this suggestion. McKenna had then replied that he would not propose such legislation unless it would meet with acceptance by all Parties in the House. Such acceptance was now forthcoming. The Prisoners' Temporary Discharge for Ill-Health Bill, which became notorious as the "Cat and Mouse" Act, was introduced on March 25th. Under it hunger strikers were licensed out for short terms, the currency of the sentence[1] being meanwhile suspended until their return to prison. The Second Reading was carried by 296 votes to 43. The "ayes" included 170 Liberals, 48 Conservatives, 14 Labour Members, 64 Irish Nationalists; the "noes" 6 Liberals, 30 Conservatives, 7 Labour men, and no Irish. Keir Hardie moved an amendment declining to strengthen the law against hunger strikers till the Government had redeemed its pledge to carry through its subsequent stages any Votes for Women measure, which a free vote of the House had accepted on Second Reading. His proposal was defeated amid laughter. He was supported by only four members of his Party, and fifteen of them went into the opposite lobby in support of the Bill as it stood. His grief and wrath that his Party had given its assent to this Act was one of the cumulative distresses which led to his premature death. The rancour aroused by the Suffragette attack provided in his lofty judgement no least excuse for this.

The Bill had been recommended by McKenna as an alternative to forcible feeding, but he firmly refused to surrender the power to forcibly feed prisoners subjected to the new Act. He would only require forcible feeding, he said, for the more serious criminals, and even instanced the case of a murderer, but refused any limitation of his powers to employ it as he chose. An amendment not to apply the "Cat and Mouse" Act to prisoners who had been forcibly fed was lost by 229 votes to 49. Even the *Daily Mail* protested:

"It will not do. No one who has read the reports of their sufferings . . . such as, for instance, Miss Sylvia Pankhurst's story in yesterday's *Daily Mail*, can have any other feeling than this—that however necessary it may be to use such methods in the case of the insane, their application to women, who, in the full possession of their senses, choose to offer violent resistance, is barbarous and uncivilized. It converts a sentence of a month's or two months' imprisonment into a sentence of unbearable torment, degrading to the community which inflicts it. What we suggest is that Mr. McKenna should cut forcible feeding completely out of his scheme."

[1] In the case of the long existent convict's licence (called the "ticket of leave," which only applies to persons under penal servitude) the period of liberation is part of the sentence, which is expiring meanwhile.

This was the attitude of the entire Press. In Parliament and out, no one had an excuse to urge for forcible feeding, yet forcible feeding was retained. Sir Arthur Markham, who, next to Keir Hardie, was the most persistent opponent of the " Cat and Mouse " Bill, dubbed it " mean, cruel, unworthy of the House of Commons and framed with diabolical ingenuity." Keir Hardie said :

" The endurance and heroism that these women are showing in prison equals, if it does not excel, anything we have witnessed on the field of battle, or elsewhere. When they have fought for their freedom, give them a chance. Do not torture them in prison, and feed them as you would a half-worried rat in a cock-pit, and let them out, and then take them back once more to prison to undergo all these horrors and tortures."

Passions ran high on both sides : that was the meaning of the " Cat and Mouse " Act, above all of its retention of forcible feeding. The House of Commons was almost hysterical in its susceptibility to any affront to its prestige, the political party officials unbounded in their resentment towards any attack on themselves and their parties. Their pledges and principles, their entire sense of proportion were sacrificed as burnt offerings to the gratification of their wrath. The long inequality of the sexes had bitten deeply into them; they had grown up with it in every relation of life. What from men might have been received as a commonplace of political controversy, from women was an intolerable impertinence, an unpardonable offence. Indeed that is usually the attitude of the strong towards the weak, and the women, as non-voters, were powerless in politics. On the other hand the W.S.P.U. was as provocative, both in word and deed, as a body of people could be. Outside the circles of Party officialdom the public, on the whole, regarded the situation with a more generous sanity.

CHAPTER IV

MILITANT incidents were now chronicled in the *Suffragette* under the title: "The Women's Revolution." Mrs. Pankhurst proudly accepted responsibility for every sort of destruction, and continually challenged the Government to prosecute her. "We have blown up Lloyd George's house at Walton Heath!" she told a great public meeting in Cardiff, on February 23rd, and was arrested next day for conspiring to that end. She was brought up at Epsom Police Court and committed for trial at the Summer Assizes. Bail was offered if she would refrain from militant incitements in the meantime, but she refused to give an undertaking for so long a period, electing rather to go to prison and hunger strike. She flung her defiance: "I shall be a dying person when I come to be tried!" The Government quailed before her determination. A message was brought to her cell that her demand to be tried at the Central Criminal Court at the beginning of April was conceded. Having won her point she rushed back to her militants to tell them that though the path they were treading was long and weary, every step was bringing them nearer to the goal. At her trial (on April 2nd and 3rd) she was sentenced to three years' penal servitude. The jury strongly recommended her to mercy. The Judge admitted she was not actuated by selfish motives, but begged her to think dispassionately, "if only for one short hour." "I know, unfortunately, you will pay no heed to what I say!" he deplored. She answered proudly: "I feel I have done my duty. I look upon myself as a prisoner of war!" A little girl, only twelve years old, had been brought from Walton Heath to give evidence of the explosion. "I do not want to question that child; she ought not to be here—though she is legally marriageable, it is true," Mrs. Pankhurst said. Twice during the trial she referred with feeling to my own condition as the result of forcible feeding, and concluded, addressing her words not to the Judge but to the militant movement: "To the women who have faced these terrible consequences I want to say: I am not going to fail them, but to face it as they face it."

She was perhaps more entirely satisfied of the importance of her mission now than she had ever been; though it had been her perennial gift to believe herself engaged in the most important

455

work of the world. Whenever, throughout her life, she experienced any weakening of that opinion, she was at once a prey to misery and depression. From such unhappy periods she was now almost exempt. Her sole doubt was lest she might die at too small a price. In Holloway once more, she refrained from food, not yet from water. Impatient of inactivity, and tortured by imaginative terrors as much as by physical suffering, she desperately clung to what then seemed but a slender hope that she would live to see the victory. Refusing all medical examination, she deprived the authorities of their usual criteria for ascertaining the ebb of her vitality. "You are not doctors: you are torturers!" she protested. Women pickets watched at the prison gates for her release. One of them, arrested for obstruction, passionately complained: "When the queen is in prison her subjects must wait outside!" No attempt at forcible feeding was made. The "Cat and Mouse" Act was not law yet, but on April 12th, the ninth day of her hunger strike, the Home Secretary exercised his power to release her on the Special Licence which is applicable to convicts under sentence of penal servitude. She was to be liberated for fifteen days, on condition that she should not go outside the house to which she first went on release, "Except so far as may, on her application, and on her submitting, if required, to medical examination, be allowed in writing by the Directors of Convict Prisons." Her licence was to be forfeited should she fail to preserve it, and to produce it when called upon by a magistrate or police officer. So little respect did she show for the document, that she tore it to shreds when it was placed in her hands. She was taken at once to the nursing home in Pembridge Gardens, but the detectives picketing outside caused crowds to collect, and created so much noise and excitement that she feared to disturb other patients and destroy the livelihood of her friends. She removed to the house of Hertha Ayrton in Norfolk Square, Sister Pine accompanying her and being henceforth her devoted attendant whenever she was out of prison. On account of this removal, Mrs. Pankhurst's licence was revoked, and a warrant issued for her arrest, but the officer presenting it was accompanied by Dr. Smalley, the medical inspector of prisons. He found her in bed, an emaciated figure, haggard and sallow, with blazing eyes, indignantly defying his right to examine her. He declared her unfit to return to prison. The "Cat and Mouse" Act had now been passed, and the *Daily Mail* calculated that, having regard to its suspension during her periods of release on licence, Mrs. Pankhurst's sentence of three years might be expected to terminate in 1930.

Whilst she remained thus, a prisoner still, though released from prison, vainly attempting to recuperate, a clamour was raised in Parliament for the suppression of W.S.P.U. meetings. The demand was reinforced by the appearance of bands of rowdies who shouted down the speakers and attempted to drive them from the platform. Some spontaneous rowdiness always greeted each new demonstration of militancy, but these gangs of disturbers were obviously controlled by certain individuals who gathered about the anti-Suffrage societies. As it happened, they were also attached to the anti-Socialist societies. Indeed they were professional objectors, who were recognized as interrupters at London meetings for a number of years. On April 15th Sir Edward Henry, the police commissioner, wrote to the acting secretary of the W.S.P.U., that owing to the character of the speeches delivered from W.S.P.U. platforms, no police arrangements could obviate disorder. The Home Secretary had therefore directed the Metropolitan police to prevent the meetings being held. The prohibition was extended also to meetings of the Women's Freedom League,[1] which destroyed no property, and had now even ceased to heckle Cabinet Ministers. Meetings of the various men's societies for Women's Suffrage, and some of the women's non-militant organizations, though not officially prohibited, were often broken up also by the police. Neither the W.S.P.U. nor the other societies accepted the prohibition; not a Sunday was allowed to pass without their attempts to hold meetings in Hyde Park. The police prevented their platforms entering the Park, but their speakers declaimed from the ground. As usual, it was Keir Hardie who protested in the Commons, and who was largely responsible for the formation of the Free Speech Defence Committee, now formed to resist such encroachments upon the right of free speech. McKenna refused to withdraw the prohibition, and insisted that every speaker would be arrested, but the threat was not followed up, and the action of the police against the meetings was half-hearted. The attacks of the organized rowdies were more formidable. Through George Lansbury and John Scurr, who took charge of this work, dockers were brought up from the East End to Hyde Park, Sunday by Sunday, to fight against the straw-hatted young roughs. I was annoyed that Lincoln's Inn House provided money for these East End contingents. It

[1] As a protest the League held a meeting without police permission in Trafalgar Square, and Mrs. Despard and others were imprisoned for short terms. In the summer of 1914 the Home Secretary indulged his anti-Suffrage prejudices by prohibiting the display of posters advertising the non-militant National Union of Suffrage Societies in the Underground railway trains.

was, I believe, little more than enough to supply the men with refreshment on the way, but even the smallest subsidy was out of harmony with the genuine mass movement I desired.

At Wimbledon Common and other places where the local W.S.P.U.'s had carried on a steady propaganda, spontaneous local support prevented all rowdiness. Though the prohibition of W.S.P.U. meetings was overcome after a fashion, it helped, more than ever, to efface constitutional Suffrage work in the public mind, and to concentrate attention on militancy. Of the vast open air Suffragette pageants in central London, which had astonished the world, but one more, and that of a new and tragic character, was to be held. In the East End there was no attempt to apply the prohibition; we had too much popular support in that area. It was the East End now which would throng both the East and the centre with its crowds.

The Government's determination to crush out the militant movement was not confined to the suppression of meetings. On April 8th Annie Kenney had been charged with incitement, and summoned under an ancient Statute of Edward III to show cause why she should not enter into recognizances, and find sureties to be of good behaviour. An adjournment was asked, on the ground of the unusual character of the summons. Next night another great Albert Hall meeting was held, the last in that hall, for it was afterwards barred to the W.S.P.U. A record collection of £15,000 was taken. Carried away by the prevailing excited enthusiasm, George Lansbury outdid the women speakers in militant incitement, crying in the full flood of his oratory:

" There are limits to human endurance. . . . When you are tricked and deceived, when Parliament betrays its sacred trust, you have a right to rebel. It is the only course left open to you. I ask that all of us here will stand shoulder to shoulder with the militant women; hold them up in the fight they are waging. Let them burn and destroy property! Let them do anything they will; and for every leader that is taken, let a dozen step forward to take their places . . . this is a holy war! "

He, too, was summoned under the Statute of Edward III with Flora Drummond, the chairman of the meeting. This old Act had been passed after the peace of Bretigny to deal with discharged soldiers returning from the wars, and unwilling to settle down as peaceful citizens. It directed that of these disturbing elements all who were of " good fame " should be made to find sureties for their " good bearing towards the King and his people," whilst the others should be punished. The Statute was in Old French; an exchequer clerk copying it about the year 1515 had inserted the word " not " before " good fame." After several adjournments Mrs. Drummond and Annie Kenney were discharged to face a more serious indictment. Lansbury was ordered to enter into his own recognizances to find bail of £2,000 for his good behaviour, or go to prison for three months. He appealed on that little word " not " which the old exchequer clerk had inserted, and for the present went free.

In the interim the police had raided Lincoln's Inn House, arresting Miss Kerr, Miss Rachel Barrett, who had become acting editor of the *Suffragette*, Miss Lennox, the sub-editor, and Miss Lake, who only in the previous January had been appointed business manager of the paper. These five people, with Mrs. Drummond, Annie Kenney and Edwy Clayton, an analytical consultant chemist, were charged with conspiracy to commit malicious damage. Meanwhile the police were raiding George Lansbury's Victoria House Press, which was printing the *Suffragette* for the first time that week, Speaight, the previous printers, having become alarmed. All the copy was seized except Christabel's leading article, which had not yet arrived. The paper was nevertheless re-written and rushed out at the last moment. When the prisoners were brought up at Bow Street next day, the rubicund Bodkin announced, with great unction, that the W.S.P.U. organ " must be put a stop to, as a continued danger to society. . . . If there is any printer who can be found after this warning to print and publish the literature of these women associated with the W.S.P.U., he will find himself in a very awkward position as the aider and abettor of these persons." He added that whoever spoke in favour of the Union or contributed to its funds would also be " in a very awkward position if discovered." A couple of days later, the manager of the Victoria House Press, S. G. Drew, was arrested. On May 2nd he was put in the dock with Annie Kenney and the others as a fellow conspirator, but was released on finding sureties of £2,000 and undertaking not to print the *Suffragette* or any other literature of the W.S.P.U. Excitement ran high.

The *Manchester Guardian* solemnly protested against the threats of Bodkin, declaring that the law had no power to suppress newspapers in advance, but only to punish if and when the contents of a particular issue should prove illegal. Bernard Shaw uttered one of his quips :

" The Suffragettes have succeeded in driving the Cabinet stark mad. Mr. McKenna should be examined at once by two doctors. He apparently believes himself to be the Tsar of Russia, a very common form of delusion."

A host of papers and organizations echoed the same opinion. In reply McKenna denied all intention to suppress the *Suffragette*; Bodkin's warning, he said, had only been to persons who might be guilty of printing incitements to crime.   The next issue was printed by the National Labour Press in Manchester, the property of an I.L.P. trust.   The manager, Edgar Whiteley, a taciturn, acute business man, drove a hard financial bargain with the W.S.P.U., and took Counsel's opinion on the contents of the paper to be sure of incurring no risk.   It was scarcely printed and dispatched when detectives appeared to warn him.   He replied he had read every line of it, and could assure them it was innocuous.   Next day, when the *Suffragette* was put on sale in London, he was arrested and charged with conspiring with Christabel and Mrs. Pankhurst to commit wilful damage. Gordon Hewart, K.C.,[1] who prosecuted for the Government, declared it an act of conspiracy merely to print a paper inviting support, by money or otherwise, to the policy of the W.S.P.U. Excitement was intensified.   Whiteley was removed from the contest by a personal undertaking not to print further issues pending his trial.   The Labour Press directors, our old I.L.P. comrades, Bruce Glasier, T. D. Benson and others, decided : " It won't be our fault if the paper does not appear this week ! " and prepared themselves for arrest.   J. R. Macdonald announced, through the *Daily Citizen*, his opposition to the suppression of any newspaper, and his willingness to become manager of the National Labour Press in order to face the coercion of the Government.   He promised to exercise a rigid censorship over the contents of the *Suffragette*.   Keir Hardie telegraphed that he would act with Macdonald.   Perhaps he thought the sole censorship of his colleague might prove somewhat too drastic. Now with the I.L.P. leaders all nerved for martyrdom, Christabel, in her irrepressible spirit of provocation, and her determination that no one else should catch a ray of limelight from a W.S.P.U.-made crisis, whisked away the printing order from the National Labour Press, and placed it with that benevolent autocrat, J. E. Francis of the Athenæum Press.   She was by no means willing either to deposit from W.S.P.U. funds the large indemnity against legal damages now demanded by the Labour Press, or to submit to the censorship of her one-time political elders.   What her rebel spirit must have suffered, however, under the genial Francis is only imaginable by one, like myself, who has endured his exactions.   They entailed a perpetual readiness to produce a printed reference, or highly certified documentary evidence, for

---

[1] The same whom we had had a share in defeating when he stood as Liberal candidate for North-West Manchester in the by-election of 1912.

any and every unimportant statement of fact which his keen but inconsistent eye might chance to select. Even at the very twelfth hour, when the paper had been passed by himself and the editors, and printing had actually begun, his cry: " Stop the machines! " might bring all to a standstill. His demand for the expulsion or re-writing of any passage, or a whole article, which might happen to offend his ethical or literary sensibilities, was always probable. The columns of the *Suffragette* grew attenuated under Francis.

Whiteley was eventually found guilty of conspiracy, and sentenced to six days' imprisonment, which amounted to immediate discharge. Meanwhile the Home Office had issued a statement that it was open to anyone to print and publish the *Suffragette* " provided that, after publication, no incitement to crime or destruction to property was to be found in its columns."

Drew obtained release from his undertaking not to print the *Suffragette* or other W.S.P.U. literature, and the substitution of a pledge not to print incitements to crime, but the police had not done with him; the comedy of errors proceeded. The W.S.P.U. presently escaped from the exacting tutelage of Francis at the Athenæum Press to the Utopia Press owned by Robert Blatchford's *Clarion* group, A. M. Thompson (Dangle, of the *Clarion*) becoming the censor of militant utterances. The Utopia Press was able to set up the paper, but had not facilities for machining it; the completed metal formes were sent out to be machined, a common expedient amongst printers. Drew agreed to do the machining at Victoria House. The *Clarion* people were not attacked, but some months later Drew was pounced upon for his part in the production and finally sent to prison for two months in July, 1914. One of the passages cited against him was a Biblical quotation: " They that walk in darkness shall see a great light! "—the *Suffragette's* comment upon a Sutton Mansion in flames. The prosecution declared that the damage occasioned by Suffragette arson in 1913 had amounted to £510,150.

The conspiracy trial of Annie Kenney and the others, from which Drew had been discharged, had meanwhile ended on June 17th, 1913. The police had taken a pantechnicon-load of documents from Lincoln's Inn House, and Bodkin, in sepulchral tones, suggested that when the load had been examined " even graver charges " might be formulated. A bizarre collection of evidence was selected from the mass, both for convicting the defendants and for entrapping the public interest. Plans were disclosed for the burning of timber yards and Labour Exchanges. The salaries of the persons in the dock were enumerated from Annie Kenney's £4 4s. per week, and the £3 10s. of Mrs. Drummond, to the £2 a week of the lowest paid. I always regretted the differences, and should have preferred an equal wage for all. An auditor testified that a hundred people were employed by the Union, their salaries averaging 24s. a week. A man who had been engaged to provide the *Suffragette* with a professional make-up deposed that in the first four issues the paper had a circulation of 17,000, though 30,000 copies had been printed. By the end of January the circulation had fallen to 10,000 copies, of which 7,500 had represented sales, the rest a free circulation to Members of Parliament and others. The expert attributed the fall to the pillar-box raids. In part it may have been so, but in part also it was due to police intimidation of the wholesale newsagents, and to the attack on the Labour Party, which caused a withdrawal of readers in Labour circles. He observed that after he had expressed his opinion on the fall in circulation, Mrs. Pankhurst had told him she was sorry she had engaged him, as a woman could do his work. Miss Lake was engaged to replace him at £2 a week. A printer testified that when, on arranging to print the *Suffragette*, he had suggested to Mrs. Pankhurst that he might incur risk by printing the paper, she had replied that, on the contrary, his firm would be in an exceptional position, as her daughter, the editor, had received a legal training, and was a specialist in constitutional law. I have not à shadow of doubt that her faith had convinced her of his immunity from risk.

"No bail!" snapped Curtis Bennett, the Magistrate, at the close of the first day's proceedings; his characteristic taciturnity thrusting aside the intercession of the mild-voiced solicitor, Marshall. "I said no bail!" he repeated, ignoring the reply from the dock: "We will hunger strike!" Yet when the women were brought fasting to the Court on the resumption of the case their common prostration compelled another adjournment for them to recuperate on bail.

Clayton had assisted the militants by providing them with a preparation for the firing of pillar-boxes, and by advising on arson of larger scale. The evidence against him rested solely on a card and memorandum in his writing, which had been placed in a book on the Bristol franchise riots, discovered by the police in a flat occupied by Annie and Jessie Kenney in Mecklenburg Square. On the card, which revealed his name and address, Clayton had written : " Burn this." Perhaps it was to exonerate herself from the imputation of disregarding this request that Annie Kenney told the Court the documents belonged to her sister Jessie, she herself having no knowledge of their existence. After this ill-judged disclosure it was surprising that Jessie Kenney was not also prosecuted. The sentences on the W.S.P.U. staff varied from six to eighteen months. Clayton got twenty-one months.

He had been purely a voluntary worker for the Union, happy, as he wrote, to give his services to a cause he believed just. His business ruined, he was reduced to great poverty, and was eventually assisted by Francis of the Athenæum Press, who paid him a small wage. Justice Philimore warned the prisoners that if he were consulted, as Judges often were in such matters, he would say they should not be released on any consideration. They were taken to separate prisons : Maidstone, Lewis, Canterbury, Bristol, Warwick, Holloway, and Clayton to Wormwood Scrubbs. All hunger struck, and all were released on licence, after strikes varying from two to eight days. Annie Kenney, Rachel Barrett and two of the others were all quietly re-arrested within a few days of the expiry of their licences, but thereafter Annie Kenney served less than one month of her sentence, Annie Lake served forty-eight days, and the others only from ten to fourteen days in all. Mrs. Drummond was not convicted. At the second hearing her doctor testified that she must undergo an operation. Eventually the case against her was withdrawn in order to prove, averred the Magistrate and Bodkin, that the health of prisoners was taken account of in these cases. Mrs. Drummond insisted that she was engaged in purely constitutional activities : " The police know my work ! " This, as the case of Nurse Pitfield and others indicated, was the true reason why her health was respected. The Government did not believe her engaged in the business of militant activities, otherwise they would have given her no quarter.

CHAPTER V

EMILY WILDING DAVISON AT THE DERBY

ON May 5th and 6th came up for debate the non-Party Private Members' Bill, which the Government had suggested as a substitute for the long promised amendment to a Reform Bill. This Bill had been drawn up by a non-Party Committee, with the Solicitor-General as Chairman, which was derisively referred to as "the Cabinette." The Bill proposed to enfranchise women householders and the wives of householders. No one expected it to be carried; it was recognized that the Prime Minister's Opposition, which had defeated the Bill of 1912, would destroy this Bill also, in spite of the promised "free vote." The unhopeful auguries were more than fulfilled, for the hostile majority was actually larger than before, the "ayes" being 219 and the "noes" 266 on this occasion. Balfour, in *The Times*, explained that he and other Conservatives had absented themselves from the division because the measure was too broad for them. The Ancient Order of Hibernians, in Dublin, passed a resolution thanking the Irish Members who had voted against the Bill, which they called "a senseless obstacle to Home Rule," and censuring the little company of five faithful Irishmen who had voted for it. It had been rumoured on this occasion that the Prime Minister would dissolve Parliament had the Bill passed the Second Reading. The Parliamentary situation of Votes for Women thus remained at a deadlock.

As soon as the more acute effects of forcible feeding were allayed, and I was able to walk about without fainting, I set to work to develop the East End movement and to secure the setting up of an influential committee for the repeal of the "Cat and Mouse" Act. The latter object was not secured—indeed the Act remains on the Statute Book to this day—but the committee accomplished important work in mobilizing public opinion, and thereby providing the only possible check upon the employment of extreme measures against the hunger strikers. The committee met at the Wimpole Street house of Mansell Moullin,[1] the surgeon, his wife being honorary secretary. Sir Victor Horsley[1]

[1] In June, 1913, Horsley and Mansell Moullin complained that the Home Secretary was urging the Royal College of Surgeons to take action against them, for having attacked several of its members in the person of the prison doctors. The R.C.S. replied to the Home Secretary that the Royal College of Surgeons declined

was honorary treasurer. The honorary acting secretary was Millie Gliksten, the eldest of four Suffragette sisters, one of whose brothers was a millionaire timber merchant, not in sympathy with the Cause. When the sister who was employed at the family timber works went to prison for admonishing a policeman with her umbrella, she was supposed to be taking a holiday. Millie Gliksten agreed to do the Cat and Mouse Committee work, provided I would draft Press letters and appeals and resolutions and keep her supplied with plans. She had great capacity for affairs, but was eminently modest. This arrangement was strictly between ourselves because we thought the work would be more effective if not associated with any prominently militant name. The committee, when it came into being, made a special point of this. My anonymity gave rise to some humorous incidents. Miss Gliksten once inadvertently told Sir Victor Horsley she had asked me to draft a manifesto. He made no comment, but when the document was produced he observed severely: " I notice that Miss Pankhurst has lifted an entire sentence from my last appeal." He had forgotten the appeal had merely been submitted to him for signature. Not having it by me, I had accidentally fallen upon my previous phrase.

In the East End the poor women of the slums were rushing to the movement as though all their life and their hope depended upon it, spending in and for it every moment that could be snatched from their toil, making innumerable efforts and sacrifices for its sake. A thousand members were quickly enrolled in the small district of North Bow alone. Throughout the East End activity and interest extended far beyond the actual membership. Numbers of women undertook the distribution of literature, canvassing and chalking in the streets where they lived. Unionist Ulster was at that time signing its Declaration of Independence. In the East End we prepared a " Women's Declaration of Independence," and hundreds of women canvassed the streets for signatures. A Women's May Day was planned for the last Sunday in the month (May 25th). Already before I could return the women were decorating thousands of natural boughs with almond blossoms made of pink paper, as emblems of the Spring. These, with the gay colours of the W.S.P.U. and the other Suffrage societies, red caps of Liberty, children in white with garlands of flowers, the great banners of the local Trade Union branches, and standards lettered by East End friends, made the long procession the brightest show ever seen in the grey East

to accede to the Home Secretary's request, observing that the documents supplied by him were conflicting, and that the College had no power to hold such a judicial inquiry as would be necessary to decide the points at issue.

End. There were fifteen platforms in Victoria Park, and a vast and friendly crowd. There was peace in Hyde Park that afternoon, for the organized rowdies had been drafted to the East End. They stationed themselves at my platform. The familiar red-faced gentleman in the white waistcoat prompted their yells with voice and hand. " She's got to go, boys! " he cried at last, and just before the meeting was ended, his henchmen began dragging the lorry from which I was speaking towards the gates. Those out of earshot thought it was part of the programme, and cheered and waved to us as we went. What did it matter? I laughed at the joke. At the gate the poor rowdies were scared away by the police mustered outside.

A few days later the East End branches were formally united in the East London Federation of the W.S.P.U. Its executive consisted of the honorary officers, who were subject to re-election at the annual delegate conference, and two representatives of each branch. Lady Sybil Smith remained the treasurer. She did not attend the meetings, or take any share in directing our actions, but confined herself to the business of raising finance and super-vising the accounts of the financial secretary, who was responsible for disbursements. She was kept in touch with the work, not from ceremony, but of necessity. Her appeals for funds were accompanied by brief reports of our activities with which I supplied her. Through her intercession our East End speakers were heard in many of the drawing-rooms of Mayfair and Kensington. She and I often appeared together; she to delight the audience with her songs, I to tell them of the suffrage struggle and the East End campaign. In December, 1913, home affairs compelled her to resign the treasurership, and she arranged, with our agreement, that Mrs. D. A. Thomas, wife of the South Wales coal magnate, should take her place temporarily. In April Mrs. Thomas was succeeded by Evelina Haverfield, who, since the income of the Federation was now substantial, arranged for the books to be under the supervision of a certified auditor, Mrs. Ayres Purdie. Mrs. Haverfield accepted the same position of non-interference as her predecessors. The business of our treasurers was, in short, to aid us in raising a supplementary fund, to enable us to do a larger propaganda than we could have done by the contributions of our poor membership alone, and to supervise the accounts. George Lansbury's son, Edgar, and afterwards Norah Smyth, followed Mrs. Haverfield as treasurer. After the forma-tion of the Federation, our first paid organizer was appointed, and Mrs. Watkins, who had hunger struck in February, was installed as caretaker of the Roman Road shop.

Since April 12th Mrs. Pankhurst had remained out of prison

on licence. Wearying of Norfolk Square, she was removed to Dr. Ethel Smyth's cottage at Hook Heath; the inevitable detectives followed and took up their stand at the gate. Dr. Ethel Smyth excelled herself to divert her militant friend, but Emmeline Pankhurst pined to be in the movement; confinement was a wearing fetter upon her spirit. Her health remained poor. She declared she could never be well with the menace of re-imprisonment always overshadowing her, and the intolerable insult, for such she deemed it, of detectives ever spying upon her movements. At last she summoned herself to action. On the Monday following the Women's May Day she had resolved to attend the W.S.P.U. meeting in the London Pavilion. The Union car was sent from London to fetch her. Accompanied by Dr. Flora Murray, who had driven down in anxious solicitude for her patient, and by Ethel Smyth and the devoted Sister Pine, she attempted to start, but one of the two big detectives at the gate squared his back against the door of the car, demanding to know where she was going. She fell back, half fainting, into the arms of Ethel Smyth. Sister Pine, like a faithful old bull-dog, scowled as though anxious to set her teeth in the flesh of the Scotland Yard men; the delicate, tender-hearted Flora Murray was a very monument of distress; the musician excited and eager. As the W.S.P.U. chauffeur would take her instructions only from Mrs. Pankhurst, the detectives procured a taxi from Woking and conveyed their prisoner to Bow Street, where the Magistrate re-committed her to prison. She was released on May 30th after a four days' strike, this time on a " Cat and Mouse " licence of seven days. She proceeded to a flat she had taken in Westminster Mansions. I saw her there, worn and aged, I thought, but not so much exhausted as I had feared, though the heat in the cell had been intense, and she had lain on the floor to find shade. Her old zest for the fight was returning. She spoke to me in tender terms of Dr. Pankhurst, of whom she had been silent for many years, telling me that in prison she had dreamt of his kind face smiling upon her.

Then, swift as a shaft of light from a thundrous sky, followed a tragic happening. Emily Wilding Davison rushed out on to the Derby race-course, and was fatally injured in stopping the King's horse. She had long believed that the deliberate giving of a woman's life would create the atmosphere necessary to win the victory, and bring all the suffering of the militants to an end. That had been her intention when, in prison a year before, she had flung herself over the corridor railings. A statement she then wrote revealed that she had made three successive attempts to kill herself, twice being caught by the wire netting forty feet below, and finally throwing herself on to the iron staircase. Already in that fall she had received injuries from which she had never entirely recovered. Her statement, sent at the time to the *Suffragette*, was not published until after her death, for there had been a general desire at Lincoln's Inn House to discourage her in such tendencies; some of her colleagues even suggested her attempt had been a sensational pretence. She was condemned and ostracized as a self-willed person who persisted in acting upon her own initiative without waiting for official instructions. All such criticism was now for ever silenced; she had risen to the supreme test of her faith. There remained only the memory of her brave gallantry and gay comradeship, her tall, slight, awkward figure and the green, elusive eyes in the small, jauntily poised head.

On the eve of the Derby she went with two friends to a W.S.P.U. bazaar in the Empress Rooms, Kensington, where, amid the trivial artificiality of a bazaar-fitter's ornamental garden, and the chatter of buying and selling at the stalls, she had joined in laying a wreath on the plaster statue of Joan of Arc, whom Christabel had called " the patron saint of Suffragettes." With a fellow militant in whose flat she lived, she had concerted a Derby protest without tragedy—a mere waving of the purple-white-and-green at Tattenham Corner, which, by its suddenness, it was hoped would stop the race. Whether from the first her purpose was more serious, or whether a final impulse altered her resolve, I know not. Her friend declares she would not thus have died without writing a farewell message to her mother. Yet she had sewed the W.S.P.U. colours inside her coat as though to ensure that no mistake could be made as to her motive when her dead body should be examined. So she set forth alone, the hope of a great achievement surging through her mind. With sure resolve she ran out on to the course and deliberately flung herself upon the King's horse, Anmer, that her deed might be the more pointed.[1] Her skull was fractured. Incurably injured, she was removed to the Epsom Cottage Hospital, and there died on June 8th without regaining consciousness. As life lingered in her for two days, Mansell Moullin performed an operation, which, in surgeon's parlance, " gave great temporary relief," but the injured brain did not mend.

A solemn funeral procession was organized to do her honour. To the militants who had prepared so many processions, this was the natural manifestation. The call to women to come garbed

---

[1] At the previous opening of Parliament the W.S.P.U. had sent five women to present a petition to the King. They were now in prison.

in black carrying purple irises, in purple with crimson peonies, in white bearing laurel wreaths, received a response from thousands who gathered from all parts of the country. Graduates and clergy marched in their robes, suffrage societies, trade unionists from the East End, unattached people. The streets were densely lined by silent, respectful crowds. The great public responded to the appeal of a life deliberately given for an impersonal end. The police had issued a notice which was virtually a prohibition of the procession, but at the same time constables were enjoined to reverent conduct.

Mrs. Pankhurst intended to drive in the procession. Her licence had expired, and anxious lest she should be arrested on emerging from her flat, I went there to accompany her to the starting point. The detectives advanced to arrest her as she came out. She expressed her desire to attend the funeral; then silently accompanied them.[1] I was shocked that with just a few of us to see it she should be taken away, thus quietly, without protest!

I marched with the hunger strikers to the burial service at St. George's, Hart Street, the church of C. Baumgarten, a good friend of suffrage, and afterwards to King's Cross, where the last of what was Emily Wilding Davison steamed away to be buried at her mother's home in Morpeth. Her tall shape flitted across my eyes; I could see her in imagination as she ran out unflinching across the course. The thought of her great courage and of that terrible agony which had ended her held my mind as in a vice. The ordinary round of duties and interests had lost, for the time, their meaning. I went with Norah Smyth to her brother's cottage at Ugly Green, amid the quiet of broad fields and towering elms. There, in the effort to realize and convey that heroism and its portent, I wrote some brief sentences, which someone returning to London thrust for me into the letter-box of the *Daily Mail*, chosen as the typical organ of the unheeding world.

" O DEED MAJESTIC! O TRIUMPHANT DEATH!

" The crowded, trivial race-course and the glaring sun.

" The swift rush out into that horror of horses' hoofs; a frantic, clinging impact.

" Then, unseen, the column of flame that rises up to Heaven as the great heart bursts—the ascending spirit is set free.

" O deed of infinite majesty! Great heart that none could ever know!

" Mean, sordid things they write of her in printed sheets whose objects fill our minds with petty things.

[1] She was released within forty-eight hours.

" Parliament sits—a House of Mockery! It proses on without a word of that great act, or the great Cause for which she gave her life.

" The world goes on as though it could not heed.

" They carry the poor broken body through the streets, women in white with lilies, clergy in their robes, poor people who have gone without some needed thing even to come thus far to follow her.

" All those four miles the roads are thronged with crowds who wait, silent and with bared heads, to see her pass.

" One should be there—another woman whom they dragged back from following her, back to the gaol where with starvation and weakness she fights strong powers that be.

" O dullard minds in power that cannot see great Freedom's history making; great tragic acts under their very eyes!

" Parliament sat to govern us the while, and not a man arose to speak of it.

.   .   .   .

" In the wide stillness of the night, in the grey fields, under the quiet moon, that deed goes on. The beating of the horses' hoofs, the rushing of the horses—she and they.

" Upward the spreading column pours in the soul's ecstasy of light.

" All through Eternity that deed goes on; in the quiet fields, as in the hurrying world, and on the trivial race-course in the glaring sun.

" O deed majestic! O triumphant death! "

Strangely enough, the editor desired to publish this eccentric manifesto; but uncertain of its authenticity, written as it was in pencil on the leaf of a note-book, he sent a messenger with it to Linden Gardens. The place untenanted, he returned it to me by post for confirmation. No longer wishing it to appear, I laid it aside.

BOOK IX

CHAPTER I

EAST LONDON FEDERATION FORMED—" CAT AND MOUSE " ACT
IN PRACTICE

IN the East End we were preparing for action. We had invited the Men's Federation for Women's Suffrage, the Free Speech Defence League[1] and others to co-operate with us in a Trafalgar Square demonstration on June 29th. The Men's Federation got permission for the Square: the police would have denied it to us. The Defence League named as its speakers Keir Hardie,[2] Josiah Wedgwood and Frank Smith. Keir Hardie was unable to keep the engagement. It is curious that the demonstration, with his name as a speaker, was put in the W.S.P.U. meetings list in the *Suffragette*; yet had he appeared he would doubtless have been shouted down by militants from Lincoln's Inn House. Josiah Wedgwood, then a Liberal Member of Parliament, was ignored by Lincoln's Inn House as of no importance.

We marched to the Square from the East End. I had agreed with my own co-workers that at the close of the meeting I should call upon the crowd to make a hostile demonstration at the Prime Minister's residence in Downing Street. The meeting proved a large one, but, as I thought, unpromising for such an effort. There was no cheering, no excitement. The people looked dull and tired. I was oppressed with a heaviness as of lead by the anxieties of the struggle, seeing as in a mirror the desperate efforts of the few militants, the tremendous power of the Government, the huge inertia of the public. How quietly had come and gone the innumerable crowds which had met in that Square to plead, and to protest, meekly accepting denial and disregard! This crowd seemed like the rest, patient, quiescent, without a spark of fire. Yet something must be done: I must not flinch from the effort. I begged the people

---

[1] Formed the same year to resist the many Government attacks on free speech. Secretary, Frank Smith; Josiah Wedgwood, M.P., chairman.

[2] Hardie had also been billed to speak at a joint demonstration organized by the local W.S.P.U.'s in North West London that summer. Then also he was called abroad.

to go to Downing Street and manifest their support for the
Suffrage Cause in some unmistakable way; to hoot the Cabinet
Ministers; to imprison them in their houses by a demonstration
of popular anger at their neglect. I expected to lead the way,
and to be arrested, alone most probably, or perhaps with a few
others. I had scarcely finished speaking when, even before I
knew it, a swarm of people responded to my appeal, without
waiting to be led or marshalled. Detained a few moments by
some question of detail, importunately brought to me, I saw
when I passed to the back of the plinth, that the bulk of the
crowd was half-way down Whitehall; its vanguard, bearing a
cap of Liberty on a long pole, had already rushed into
Downing Street, and was engaged in a tussle with the police.
Following in haste, I met Zelie Emerson and others coming
back with the news that five men had been arrested, the street
cleared by the mounted police, and a cordon drawn across it.
We had made a beginning in popular turbulence; it was, I
thought, enough for the day.

On the following Thursday I was in the studio at Linden
Gardens, when two big detectives stepped into the courtyard
and handed me a paper through the open window. It was a
summons under the Statute of Edward III to appear at Bow
Street on Saturday as " a disturber of the peace of our Lord the
King." I realized that I had now received the cue for my
" Cat and Mouse " act.

I determined not to respond to the summons. We had
arranged a meeting in the Bromley Public Hall in the Bow Road
on Monday night. I would slip away from London now, and
get to the meeting in disguise. Let the detectives arrest me
there, if they could. It was easily done; the police had not
expected this move. I ran up the steps unmolested and into the
hall. As soon as the people saw me, they sprang to their feet,
cheering and waving their hands, whilst a crowd of friends
slammed and barricaded the doors. The knowledge that a
warrant had been issued for my arrest had packed the hall long
before the time, and hundreds of people were gathering outside.
The cheers ringing out into the street soon spread the news that
I was within. A strong force of police and detectives mustered
at the entrance. When the speeches were done, the people
formed a body-guard to protect me, crowding together in a
dense mass, and thus jammed together we pushed our way out,
in spite of a horde of detectives crowding about the door to
take me. Dozens of men and women held their arms around
me and each other in the centre of the crush. Detectives,
fighting their way through the crowd, grasped at me over the

shoulders of the people around me. My light dress was a target for their eyes, even in the darkness. Men and women thrust the police away, and we pressed on; but in the pitch black night detectives, big men in plain clothes, began to mingle with my protectors, trying to tear me from them. Wrenched this way and that, I could scarcely tell friends from foes. My feet were constantly trampled on. The dozens who held me amongst them began to run—faster, faster. . . . I called to them: "Friends, not so fast." They could not hear me in the struggle. I was losing breath. We were leaving the main body of the crowd behind. The police, seizing their advantage, were closing round us, dragging at us; separating us; tearing me away. "By God, you shan't have her!" a man cried. The police struck at him with savage blows, and hurled him away. I was seized; two, three, four policemen grasped me, and hurried me along. Others beat the crowd aside. I was faint, and my feet slipped. I was carried into the police station. In the later small hours, when the crowd, which long struggled outside, had at last dispersed, I was taken in a cab to the cells at Bow Street and kept there till morning.

I was ordered three months' imprisonment. Lansbury's appeal against the same charge was still pending. John Scurr and Mrs. Cohen of Leeds, who had also been apprehended under the same old statute, were, like him, at large on bail, awaiting the decision of the Higher Court. I might have claimed a like respite, but I accepted the sentence; conviction on this charge was the same as another to me. I was looking to the struggle of the "Cat and Mouse" Act to stimulate mass action in the East End, which should shed its influence throughout the country.

I felt sick and cold when I got to Holloway, bruised from the struggle. In spite of me, I resented the dreary confinement of the cell, yet, beneath all, I was happy and confident; already my hope was beginning to be realized. I did not undress at all during my imprisonment, but remained, as it were, momentarily awaiting release. Yet I composed myself to write, lying on the bed and hiding my work. As before, I had a bag of paper and pencils round my waist under the skirt. There were resolutions and leaflets to draft, new plans to devise. "I get all my good ideas in Holloway," I gained the habit of saying during the next year, for there were long vistas of solitary hours in which to think, and the brain was ever alert. I was writing at that period unpaid weekly articles for the *Clarion*, the *Merthyr Pioneer* and the *Glasgow Forward*, as well as some paid articles for American publications, and many letters to the Press. As before, food was constantly in the cell: tea and bread and butter, chops and steaks, jellies and fruit. These offered no temptation; but for water, had I allowed myself to dwell on the thought of it, I should have craved intensely. Indeed there is nothing which tastes so sweet as the first draft of water after the thirst strike is over. It has a peculiar, delicate flavour, only noticed then, for accustomed to other and stronger tastes, the palate grows dulled to it. I used to say in those days that the Biblical manna must have been hail. In the thirst strike there is always a horrible taste in the mouth, which grows more parched as the days pass, with the tongue dry and hot and thickly coated. The saliva becomes thick and yellow; a bitter tasting phlegm rises constantly, so nasty that one retches violently, but is denied the relief of sickness. The urine, growing thicker, darker, more scanty, is passed with difficulty. There is no action of the bowels during the imprisonment. Each day one's bones seem more prominent, the flesh falling away, the skin shrivelled, the hands and feet a dull purple with bright red streaks. One is always cold, and if one accepts the hot water bottle the wardress offers, it seems to burn, not to warm, the one place it touches, and to leave even that place cold as before when moved away. Pain settles in the small of the back and in the chest; occasionally a sharp stinging pain in the right breast. Griping pains seize one suddenly in the stomach and abdomen. The pulse becomes swift and irregular. There are palpitations and pain in the region of the heart. If one rises from bed, one grows faint and giddy, and there comes at last a constant ringing in the ears, when one is lying flat, which changes, if one stands up, to a deafening roar, with a sensation of pressure in the ears, as one breathes. The consciousness of pulses in the head, throbbing in unison with the beating of the heart, distresses and disturbs. If one refuses to lie still and take things quietly, all the symptoms are intensified, and become a nightmare-like torture of pain and misery. The nights, from the first, are sleepless and painful. When the wardress opens the cell door at half-past five in the morning, one is still awake. After that one may fall into a hazy, half-sleeping, half-waking state, which may last perhaps for an hour or two, perhaps for the greater part of the day.

This is what the prisoner feels; the medical version of the experience was:

" The tissues are depleted of moisture, the muscles waste, the bowels and kidneys cease to act normally. The poisons are unable to pass out of the body, and are retained and absorbed. When absorption occurs, the patient feels shivery. She has headaches, nausea, and more or less fever. More than one of the prisoners has come out jaundiced, and in a toxic condition. In one person toxicity may affect the nervous system; in another the digestive or respiratory tracts."

Illness grew on me rapidly; I had not recovered from the forcible feeding of February and March, and I was worn out when I entered the prison on Tuesday. By Friday I determined to remain quiescent no longer, for I was to speak at the Bromley Public Hall on the following Monday, and must bestir myself to get out. I commenced to walk about my cell; faintness over-powered me. I fell or stumbled to my knees, drowned in darkness and pain and rushing noises. By Saturday, to stand for a few moments made me fall fainting to the ground. I did it repeatedly, the sooner to be free. I had fainted when they came to bring me the order of release on Sunday evening.

The members had begged me, if ever I should be under the "Cat and Mouse" Act, to come down to them in the East End, in order that they might protect me; they would not let me be taken back to prison without a struggle as the others had been, they assured me. On the night of my arrest Zelie Emerson had pressed into my hand an address: "Mr. and Mrs. Payne, 28 Ford Road, Bow." Thither I was now driven in a taxi with two wardresses. As the cab slowed down perforce among the marketing throngs in the Roman Road, friends recognized me, and rushed into the roadway, cheering and waving their hands. Mrs. Payne was waiting for me on the doorstep. It was a typical little East End house in a typical little street, the front door opening directly from the pavement, with not an inch of ground to withdraw its windows from the passers-by. I was welcomed by the kindest of kind people, shoe-making home-workers, who carried me in with the utmost tenderness. They had put their double bed for me in the little front parlour on the ground floor next the street, and had tied up the door knocker. For three days they stopped their work that I might not be disturbed by the noise of their tools. Yet there was no quiet. The detectives, notified of my release, had arrived before me. A hostile crowd collected. A woman flung one of the clogs she wore at the wash-tub at a detective's head. The "Cats," as a hundred angry voices called them, retired to the near-by public-houses; there were several of these havens within a stone's throw, as there usually are in the East End. Yet even though the detectives were out of sight, people were constantly stopping before the house to discuss the movement and my imprisonment. Children gathered, with prattling treble. If anyone called at the house, or a vehicle stopped before it, detectives at once came hastening forth; a storm of hostile voices rose. Here, indeed, was no peace. My hosts carried me upstairs to their own bed-room, at the back of the house, hastily prepared; a small room, longer, but scarcely wider, than a prison cell—my home when out of prison for many months to come.

I was able to get to the Bromley Public Hall the next night. It could hold but a small proportion of the audience; thousands were gathered outside. A nurse gave me brandy to help me to speak. I could not stand, but sat in the chairman's big arm-chair. The people cheered till they were hoarse, and cried: "Down with the 'Cat and Mouse' Act!" I read the terms of my seven days' licence. The people shouted: "We'll never let them take you back!" "Votes for Women this year!" "Votes for Women this year!" Though there was no need for it this time, they set their backs to the doors to keep the police out, and made a body-guard to take me home. Each night great meetings were held at the end of Ford Road.

I had accepted, on release, only a drink of warm water. Now, under care of doctor and nurse, I took but two ounces of liquid food at a time, the doses, after a day or two, being gradually increased until solid food was reached. In such matters I left myself in the hands of doctor and nurse; but before their arrival I was at work—articles, letters, resolutions. My secretary, to take shorthand notes and receive for typing the manuscripts written in prison; the organizers, to set going on new plans—these were the first necessity. In the excitement of being free, I felt no weakness once I was lying on my back, though I could not sit up without faintness. Dr. Flora Murray would come, and find papers all around me: "My friend, you are very ill; you must not do this!" I would not argue with her anxiety, but I had no intention to obey. I had put myself on the rack to spur the movement, and every moment I was free, every atom of vitality the ordeal had left me must be turned to account.

As soon as I began to drink again after the thirst strike my skin became fiery red. The first night out of prison, sleeping draughts proved useless. Pulses throbbed intolerably; I was hot and cold by turns. Thoughts raced through my brain; plans for work, hopes, fears, worries. With everything at hand to ease them, pains seemed more acute than in gaol. Next day I felt as though I had been crushed by a steam roller; too weak to raise myself without help, it was usually a week before I could stand without distress. It is long before the digestive functions of the thirst striker become normal. The bowels obstinately refuse their task, acute flatulence persists indefinitely, headaches become chronic. Dry, eczema-like patches appear on the skin.

The extremities remain very red for some days and are often swollen and burning like a great chilblain.   Heart and nervous symptoms often persist for a long time.   Among the " Mice," operations for appendicitis and other afflictions became frequent. A house was set apart for them as a nursing home in the West End, and spoken of amongst us as " Mouse Castle " and the " Mouse hole."   Curiously, no other hunger striker was in and out of prison so often as I, and not one of them carried a continuous load of work as I did, yet I was one of the few who escaped incapacitating illness.   I think I was actually the better for the work, though I toiled to the point of exhaustion.   Indeed I had never been mentally so serene, so exalted above all vexations.   It was usually the second day after my release, in any case the day after the first meeting (always timed to occur as soon as possible after I was free), that I had an absolute collapse; twenty-four hours of blinding headache and acute illness of the whole frame. After that I would rise to work again, and with occasional days of incapacity, I could keep on till my next imprisonment for ten to fourteen hours a day, so long as I was lying on my back. For five years afterwards I suffered substantially from the effects of these efforts.

In that little room I slept, wrote, interviewed the Press and personalities of all sorts, and presently edited a weekly paper. Its walls were covered with a cheap, drab paper, with an etching of a ship in full sail, and two old-fashioned colour prints of a little girl at her morning and evening prayers.   From the window by my bed I could see the steeple of St. Stephen's Church and the belfry of its school, a jumble of red-tiled roofs, darkened with smoke and age, the dull brick of the walls and the new white-wash of some of the backyards in the next street.   There were certain odd hints and memories of the vanished country, still remaining from the time ere London slumdom had crept up to Bow, which was once far out of town.   It is said that the slum houses were built with rubbish tips for foundation; that well may be, for vermin seems to infest their very bricks and mortar. Mrs. Payne told me that as a young bride she hung her bed with pink curtains, but plunged those curtains into a bucket of water the night of her marriage on account of the bugs she was horrified to find crawling over them.   When I lit my candle on sleepless nights, I would see a dozen or more of them on the wall, though disinfectants were always burnt in the room during my absence.

Our colours were nailed to the wall behind my bed, and a flag of the purple, white and green was displayed from an opposite dwelling, where pots of scarlet geraniums hung on the whitewashed wall of the yard below, and a beautiful girl with smooth, dark hair and a white bodice would come out to delight my eyes in helping her mother at the wash-tub. The next yard was a fish curers'. An old lady with a chenille net on her grey hair would be passing in and out of the smoke-house, preparing the sawdust fires. A man with his shirt sleeves rolled up would be splitting herrings; and another hooking them on to rods balanced on boards and packing-cases, till the yard was filled, and gleamed with them like a coat of mail. Close by, tall sunflowers were growing, and garments of many colours hung out to dry. Next door to us they bred pigeons and cocks and hens, which cooed and crowed and clucked in the early hours. Two doors away a woman supported a paralysed husband and a number of young children by making shirts at 8d. a dozen. Opposite, on the other side of Ford Street, was a poor widow with a family of little ones. The detectives endeavoured to hire a room from her, that they might watch for me unobserved. "It will be a small fortune to you while it lasts!" they told her. Bravely she refused with disdain: "Money wouldn't do me any good if I was to hurt that young woman!" The same proposal was made and rejected at every house in Ford Road.

Mrs. Payne was a dark, pale woman, of middle age, with one of the most benevolent faces I have ever known. An orphan brought up by her grandparents, who had taught her to make shoes with them, she had been, as a girl, the first soldier of the Salvation Army in Old Ford. The Army, then in its early days, was regarded with hostility by the churches, and by the established order in general. It was beset by organized bands of roughs, called the Skeleton Army, from whom the police gave it no protection. Mrs. Payne—Jessie Avory as she was then (and it is curious that her father's family for many generations had been ivory cutters)—encountered the Skeleton Army before she formally enrolled herself as a soldier. She had gone to the Salvation meeting-room, and offered her services. The Captain had put her at the door to give out handbills. When the Skeleton Army came up, with pots of ale and long clay pipes in their hands, she recognized them as youths whom she saw each week when she carried the finished shoes to the factory. She stood in the doorway: "You shan't come in!" and held them at bay till the Captain pulled her aside. Then the lads rushed in, knocking him down. Jessie Avory contended for the Army with her fists and her prayers. The religion she imbibed from it was crude and primitive, tempered by her own kindliness. "They preach hell fire," she confided to me, and admitted, half ashamed, that this seemed too cruel to her. Her husband, slightly afflicted with epilepsy, was a genial good fellow, and a great talker, aggressively an atheist, but with a tremendous respect and admiration for his wife. She was in fact the "better half," and had maintained him in work and sobriety by the force of example and affection. She had borne two children, one of whom had died of some childish ailment; the other, mentally deficient, had lived to be twenty-seven years, a dear burden to her mother, to whom the care of her had been an exacting, but ever patiently followed toil. As a young wife, finding many women of her street in debt and paying exorbitant interest to money-lenders, she had lent them, from the savings of her industry, the money to secure release from extortion. They agreed to repay her by instalments. The promise was broken, but she cherished no bitterness for her loss.

The sacrifice made by these good people in giving me hospitality was no small one. Shoe work had been voluntarily suspended for three days; and even after that Mrs. Payne was kept busy cooking for me and the nurse, for Zelie Emerson and others. Opening the door to the perpetual succession of callers was a work in itself. After the first week or two I induced her to let me pay for my room; but it was a very modest sum she consented to accept. Visitors were constant. An old age pensioner walked over from Poplar to bring me two fresh eggs laid by her neighbour's hens. Poor people brought fruit and flowers, purchased in the shops with hard-earned pennies, grown on the allotments, or fetched by bicycles from the country. My room was always gay with fresh blooms, and many I passed on to our members who were ill. Letters rained upon me. Troubles with landlords, employers, Government departments and insurance societies were brought to me for solution and exposure. Enthusiasts came with plans of propaganda and attack. A woman wrote that she did not see why I should ever go back to prison since every woman could buy a rolling-pin for a penny. A music-hall proprietress begged me to write a playlet with five-minute scenes of forcible feeding and the " Cat and Mouse " Act, but desired to transform what I produced for her into a roaring farce, and suggested that I should allow her to re-write it and use my name. Of course I refused.

It was Mrs. Payne who begged me to send for the Bishop of London, to impress upon him the urgency that poor women should have the vote. He came, and admitted himself a recent convert to a limited franchise. He said we had not yet secured sufficient popular support. I reminded him that the people had fought for me. " Oh, yes," he protested, " but this is the dear, chivalrous East End; it will always fight for the bottom dog!"

Our East End fight on July 7th seemed to have spurred the whole militant movement to new life. The first Monday afternoon after my release, July 14th, Mrs. Pankhurst and Annie Kenney, both liable to re-arrest, eluded the vigilance of the police and appeared at the London Pavilion, to be greeted with rapturous excitement. Both had spoken; Annie Kenney had sold her two temporary discharge licences for the funds for £6 each; police and detectives were at the door. They rushed at Annie Kenney as she emerged, seized her and hustled her off in a taxi, despite the efforts of some of the women to protect her. Meanwhile Mrs. Pankhurst walked out unobserved and returned to her flat. On the following Thursday Rachel Barrett was arrested outside the Memorial Hall, where she had spoken. On Friday, still on licence, I had a great meeting in Poplar Town Hall. On Saturday a veiled woman dressed in Mrs. Pankhurst's clothes emerged from her flat supported by others. The police got possession of her after a struggle and set off with her in a taxi, only to find that the prisoner they had taken was not Mrs. Pankhurst, who had slipped away in their absence. I, too, had escaped them. Nora Smyth had once or twice come to take my nurse for a drive. On Saturday it was I who stepped into the car in the uniform of Nurse Hebbes; she had lent it gladly to further my escape; every woman with whom we had contact in those rare days speedily became as ardent in the struggle as the old hands.

On Monday, July 21st, Mrs. Pankhurst succeeded in entering the Pavilion, but detectives seized her inside the building. "Women, they are arresting me!" Her cry was heard in the auditorium. Women rushed out to rescue her. The police dragged her into a side room. The lights were switched off and blows exchanged in the darkness, one of the detectives striking out with a stick. Police reinforcements arrived. Mrs. Pankhurst was taken back to prison; five persons were charged with assault. The meeting resumed. Life, for the rest of the world, goes on as before when the prisoner is removed. Annie Kenney, released the previous Friday, and a number of Scottish bailies, who had come south to interview the Prime Minister, also addressed the meeting. Their deputation of forty councillors, bailies and provosts, being refused an audience, had held a meeting on Asquith's doorstep, but had not been arrested like women. Their organization, the Northern Men's Federation for Women's Suffrage, had been founded at the funeral of Emily Wilding Davison. Mrs. Arncliffe Sennett was its guide and inspirer. Its policy was to turn votes against the Government on the Women's Suffrage issue.

That same Monday evening I was to speak again at the Bromley Public Hall. My licence had expired. A long, close-fitting dark coat with a high collar, a hat pulled down over the eyes, as women wore them then, and a touch of rouge on the cheeks were enough to transform my appearance, for I never could bear my throat or eyes constrained, my face was still blanched from the hunger strike, and cosmetics were most alien to me. Almost suffocated by the beating of my heart, I passed through the lines of detectives waiting to seize me, and up the stairs with the people streaming into the hall. The seats were full, the gangways thronged. A detective snatched at me as I hurried to the platform. His action betrayed his presence; men and women hurled themselves upon him; he was hustled out and down into the street. A crowd of stalwarts shut and guarded the main door. I had torn off the dark coat and hat; the air was rent with cheers. Whilst I was waiting to speak, a paper was passed to me—a note from Zelie Emerson that she had found me a hiding-place in the hall. I shook my head. She knew that I was determined to go out amongst the people as before. I saw her face flush, and her lips tremble. She went out, pouting and frowning, with tears on her face. A shadow seemed to fall on me. " Poor girl, she is not fit for this ! " I thought with compunction. In speaking, all else was forgotten. To me it was a great struggle, not for the vote alone; for the uplifting of these masses, the enlarging of their horizons. I spoke to them as I felt: " They say that life is sweet and liberty is precious; there is no liberty for us so long as the majority of our people lead wretched lives. Unless we can free them from the chains of poverty, life, to us, is not worth preserving, and I, for one, would rather leave this world. . . ."

I jumped down amongst the people, hatless, in light dress, easily discernible amongst the dark-clad people. Pressing together, we passed out and slowly descended the stairs. The police were massed outside the only entrance, dozens of detectives with heavy sticks, and a hundred or more of uniformed men, ready to pounce as our mass inevitably narrowed at the doorway. Suddenly they were deluged by a tremendous torrent of water. Zelie Emerson, with her quick ingenuity, had arranged for our stalwarts guarding the doors to turn the fire hose upon the " Cats " ! Helter-skelter they went ! A group of us ran out to the right as the stream followed the scurrying policemen leftward. Down the dark road we ran. " Where are we going? Where are we going? " I asked as we ran. My companions waited each for the others to answer, for none of them knew. It had been intended that we should take shelter in a member's house near by, but she was not with us, and no one knew the address.

We rushed down an alley. It was blind. We heard footsteps hurrying in the rear. Like trapped wild things, we thrust ourselves against every door : one of them gave. We found ourselves in a dark, disused stable. We shut the door and huddled against it, holding our breath; then discovered there were bolts, shot them, and retired to the darkest recess to hide lest the door should be forced. Footsteps and voices approached. We saw through an upper grating the light of a bull's eye lantern playing about the window. The police! They tried the doors. . . . The old bolts creaked, but they held. The minions of the Law passed on.

All was quiet. We waited hour after hour, wondering what to do. Mrs. Watkins, Mrs. Ives, our Hackney secretary, I and a woman we did not know and could not see in the darkness. It was Mrs. Connell, wife of the man who wrote the *Red Flag*, but we did not know it. She kept begging us to let her go home, and offered to get help, but we feared her exit would betray us, and refused. At last, between three and four in the morning, I relented. She promised to ask help from Willie Lansbury, in St. Stephen's Road. Less than half an hour after we let her go we again heard footsteps. Our hearts quaked—but there followed a gentle tapping. My name was whispered in a voice I thought I knew. We opened with caution and suspense. As we hoped, it was Willie and Edgar Lansbury. They had a cart piled high with sacks of firewood, which happened, by chance, to have been loaded the night before. They hoisted me on to the pile and hid me under a blanket they had seized from one of their beds. Off we went, while the women scuttled away in the darkness. As we drove down St. Stephen's Road we met the Chief Constable of Bow with a posse of constables, playing their lanterns on every nook and cranny. The search continued still! The cart swung in at the gate, striking the post in the hurry. The burly Chief Constable turned suspicious eyes on the back of the cart and the two young men, leaping down in hot haste, and shutting the gates with a bang, but what could he say or see? He had no warrant for breaking into enclosed premises. I was safe for the nonce, and soon in bed.

And now what an excitement! The detectives were searching every likely spot. They infested St. Stephen's Road, watching especially the two adjoining houses where the Lansbury families lived. Very easily were they outwitted. The wood cart was unloaded. I was tied up in a sack, squatting huddled with my knees touching my chin on the floor of the cart. Sacks filled with wood were packed around me. "Are you all right?" they asked. "Oh, yes!" I said, my knees pressed together as tightly as could be. I did not know that presently I should long for an inch to shift my limbs in, but long in vain, for the sacks were far too heavy for me to move them, even a hair's breadth, try as I might. Burning pains shot through my limbs like red-hot wires. I was breathless for lack of air. "What happens if one faints trussed up like this?" I wondered. Twice or thrice I called to the driver, but the jolting of the cart prevented him hearing the feeble cry, which I feared to make too loud. At last, after hours it seemed, the slow jogging horses ended their journey at Wood-ford. The man unloaded the wood-sacks, one by one, carried them into the house on his back, and carried me too in my turn. I found myself in the house of the Lansburys' cousin, Mrs. Brine.

A few nights later I was to speak at Canning Town Public Hall. I ventured alone and slightly disguised by tram to Stratford, met Mrs. Watkins, and went with her to the hall, entering with our stewards three hours before the advertised time of the meeting, and waiting amongst them in a dressing-room— no protecting crowds to make a fight for it, only a few weak women together, trying to keep up our spirits, and I with the sick thought of the iron grasp on the shoulder. Then again rose the cheers and the shouting; the people hissing the detectives, howling around them, thrusting them from the hall; and after the meeting again the great press of people about me, the horses charging the hurrying crowds in the darkness, the eager hands of women grasping, shrill screams, dark alleys—a friendly home at last.

Next morning I was driven away to the country house of Mrs. Evans, a rich American enthusiast. A few days I spent in her lovely gardens, slightly aloof from a gay house party, of whom only a small, intimate circle had the least notion of my identity.

On Thursday in that week was held a Caxton Hall conference convened by the "Cat and Mouse" Repeal Committee, which we had been preparing for many weeks, and attended by delegates from social, political and religious bodies and Trade Unions and by members of the legal and medical professions. The Labour view was represented by a direct conflict of opinion: Keir Hardie was present and said that the "Cat and Mouse" Act was "sub-stituting murder for suicide," and that the only alternative was to give women the vote. J. R. Macdonald wrote that the militants had only themselves to blame for it, and that he did not think any representative Government would repeal the Act without putting some other effective measure in its place: " I am rather surprised that the only proposal you make is to give women the vote."[1]

The conference had been intended as a weighty, non-militant, deliberative body, but thirty-one women and four men were already being " moused " under the Act, and so keen was the anxiety of the delegates on their behalf that militant decisions inevitably cropped up. The Prime Minister had been requested in advance to receive a memorial from the conference. As usual, he had refused. The conference nevertheless determined to take its memorial to the House of Commons and endeavour to see him. Sir Edward Busk, Mr. Mansell Moullin, Mrs. Cecil Chapman,[2] wife of the London Magistrate, Margaret McMillan, the great educationist, and others were elected to go. Asquith was away in Yorkshire. McKenna would only consent to receive Sir Edward Busk alone for a fifteen minute interview the next morning. The deputation refused to accept denial and waited, insistent. Mrs. Pethick Lawrence resorted to the old W.S.P.U. methods. Beginning to address the Members and visitors in St. Stephen's Hall, she was thrust outside with all her companions. She continued to speak and was arrested. Margaret McMillan was thrown down the steps; Lady Sybil Smith and Evelyn Sharp endeavoured to force their way back into St. Stephen's, and were arrested and sentenced to fourteen days, in default of being bound over, and at once began the hunger strike. Mrs. Lawrence demanded political treatment, and awaited a reply before adopting the same course.

There was a flutter of excitement in aristocratic circles at the incarceration of Lady Sybil Smith. Her husband had paid her fine on the previous occasion, but now there was no such possibility. According to Evelyn Sharp's account: " She sat in her cell looking perfectly lovely, in a delightful tea-gown and golden slippers," and obstinately refused all persuasion to taste the daintiest food. This would never do! The unique device employed was to induce the Magistrate, Sir John Dickinson, to issue a fresh commitment of four days only, in respect of the three prisoners. McKenna protested that no exceptional treatment had been shown to Lady Sybil Smith.

On Saturday, July 26th, the Suffrage " Pilgrims," organized by the National Union of Women's Suffrage Societies, held a mass meeting in Hyde Park. For weeks they had been marching towards London, from north, south, east and west, holding meetings by the way. The idea had been borrowed from

---

[1] Reported in *Votes for Women*, August 1st, 1913.

[2] She was an official of the New Constitutional Society for Women's Suffrage, which, though itself non-militant, supported the militants.

Mrs. de Fontblanc's "Marchers' Qui Vive Corps," the "Brown Women," who were still holding local marches. The demonstration, according to Nevinson, best and most generous recorder of Suffrage scenes, was large, but "nothing in comparison with the enormous Suffrage demonstrations of 1908 and 1910." Indeed the N.U.W.S.S. never captured the interest of the multitude. It was so staid, so willing to wait, so incorrigibly leisurely. Mrs. Fawcett has recorded [1] that during her most active years she only addressed meetings during four months of the year. The demonstration—again let me quote Nevinson:

"was like an untouched army sweeping with banners flying into a field strewn with evidences of hard-fought battles. One could not help remembering the tragedies that lay at the back of this success. . . . One would not have noticed it so much, and certainly the welcome to the Pilgrims would have been more enthusiastic, but for the reminders of 'Law Abiding' and 'Non-Militant,' proclaimed on the banners and scarves on every side."[2]

Behind all this the secretly perpetrated militancy of the W.S.P.U. continued; every day brought its tale of buildings burnt, windows smashed, pillar-boxes fired. Two men threw mouse-traps at the Members of Parliament from the Strangers' Gallery of the House of Commons, and one of them struck fear into their hearts by firing a toy pistol into the air. The hunger strikers were dragged in and out of prison. Kitty Marion got a release licence of two days only, Lilian Lenton of one day. A. M. Thompson, in the *Clarion*, wrote:

"The women are winning again. What they lost by window smashing has been restored to them and multiplied a hundredfold by the Government's 'Cat and Mouse' Act. That, by God, we can't stand!"

An unparalleled scene in Trafalgar Square on Sunday, July 27th, concluded that hectic week. Again the Men's Federation had obtained police permission for the plinth on our behalf, and though it was advertised that I should speak, and it was common knowledge that I should again lead the crowd to Downing Street, the permit was not withdrawn. Norah Smyth came down to my hiding-place to bring me a wig. Mrs. Evans dressed me up in an aggressively American shepherd's plaid coat and skirt, stuffed with newspaper across the chest, and a transparent veil, which assisted in disguising without hiding the face. There was a great procession from the East End, and the largest crowd I had yet seen in the Square, overflowing on to the surrounding

---

[1] *What I Remember*, by M. G. Fawcett.
[2] *Votes for Women*, August 1st, 1913.

streets, and the steps and terrace of the National Gallery beyond. Nevinson wrote:[1]

> "The Square was crammed as I have never seen it since the Unemployed riots of the 'eighties, or since Bradlaugh's demand to take his seat as an elected Member. . . . There was no mistake about the feeling of the crowd. Even the Government papers have not questioned it. I doubt if any Trafalgar Square crowd of that size has been so unanimous and so deeply moved."

Mrs. Evans and a party of us motored to the Square and mounted the plinth together. My knees trembled so much from weakness and suspense that I could scarcely walk. I seated myself on the pedestal of one of the Landseer lions. Stout Superintendent Wells was behind me; I heard him ask: "Has Miss Pankhurst come?" A detective answered "No."

When my turn came I rushed to the edge of the plinth and tore off my wig, while friends closed round me, fiercely suspicious of any outsider who dared approach. Throughout the vast throng was a waving of hands and a roar of cheering. The people were with me, it seemed, to a man and to a woman. With a storm of acclaim the resolution was adopted to carry our "Women's Declarations of Independence" to Downing Street. (I had a great roll of them one of the stewards had handed me as I spoke.) When I leapt from the plinth the people caught me and took me with them. We had swept from the Square and across the road into Parliament Street, the whole great concourse moving after us, before the police could bring up their massed forces waiting in the side streets. Detectives were everywhere in the crowd, but the people always knew them, despite their civilian dress, and hustled them away. There was a strange, deep, growling sound in the crowd about me I had never heard before: the sound of angry men. At the top of Whitehall, mounted policemen met us; we rushed between. The people protecting me gathered in a thick bunch with their arms about each other, thrusting the horses aside.

"'Coppers' behind us! 'Coppers' behind us!" hoarse voices shouted. We had gone too fast; the police had broken into the crowd and were dragging at us from behind. A company of policemen came running to meet us up Whitehall. They closed with us, striking at men and women. A thin, bald-headed man, in poor clothes, was knocked down beside me. He rolled on the ground. I cried out, but we were swept on—over him, I feared. "Keep back! Keep back!" the people in front were shouting. There was someone else on the ground. We tried in vain to stop,

[1] *Votes for Women*, August 1st.

and called to those behind us; impelled from the rear, they could not pause. I saw something dark on the ground, felt something soft. It was a woman, I thought. I was borne forward by the arms and shoulders. I raised up my feet that I might not step on what was beneath me—it was all I could do.

A taxi-cab stood in the road before us. Friends about me opened the door, begged me to drive away and elude the police. I answered: " No, I am going with you to Downing Street! " The cab door was slammed, and on we went. Reinforcements from Scotland Yard, a great company, came dashing upon us, beating their way through the people protecting me, striking and knocking them down, arresting some. Finally I was seized, and as I was dragged past the end of Downing Street, I saw it was guarded by a double cordon of police with a mass of mounted men behind. We were feared, it seemed. I called to the crowd to go there. At Cannon Row police station the charge room was crowded by policemen and their prisoners; eleven men and thirteen women under arrest. Irritated that I had not succeeded in doing more, I snatched up a tumbler and broke a window, in the vain hope of getting in touch with the people outside.

Soon I was back in Holloway, and at first so horrified by the return there that I felt I could have knocked my head against the wall. I had determined this time to strike against sleep, as well as against food and water, in the hope of gaining an earlier release. I tramped about the cell as I had done in March; the same old cell. The night wardress opened the door: " You must not make that noise! " I knew that on one side of me was the staircase, on the other the lavatory and sink, but I took a blanket from the bed and threw it on the floor to deaden the sound of my steps lest other prisoners might be disturbed. Then I walked on. The gas light in the recess behind the glass, dim as it was, hurt my eyes. I covered it with one of the prison rule cards, but still the light of it made me dizzy as I turned. I watched the patch of sky through the heavy bars; a sombre grey, charged with sullen, yellow fire, the lights of the London streets. I stumbled over the blanket; it wrinkled and caught my feet. I grew sick and faint, and often sank to my knees, clutching the bed or the chair. Sometimes I slept an instant as I crouched there, for sleep seemed to be dogging me as I walked. It was cold, cold, and as morning came, colder still. The sky turned violet; a strange, brilliant, almost startling colour it seemed, between those heavy bars. Then it died to the bleak, grey white of early day. I still walked, but sometimes I could not forbear to rest on the hard wooden chair. Then my head would nod heavily to one side, and I would pull myself up and walk again. I was racked with pains, my legs ached, my feet were swollen and burning. I thought of the martyrs of the past who walked on red-hot plough-shares for their faith. The pain in my back was overwhelming, my throat was parched. . . .

On Wednesday I began to faint. I had pressure and noises in the head. I asked to see a Home Office doctor. He came on Thursday. On Friday I had fever; I knew it by my burning skin, and the cold shivers passing over me. I lay on the bed; there was no question of sleeping now. That evening I was released. It may be that by all the additional agonies I had piled upon myself I had not shortened my sentence by a single hour.

Indeed the Government was conditioning the punishment to the offence; to prisoners who kept quietly out of the way, the " Cat and Mouse " Act might be a menace rather than a reality; to those who persistently repeated their offence the Act was merci-less. Mary Richardson, asked by the prison doctor whether she would refrain from militancy on her release, answered : " I shall be militant as long as I can stand or see; they cannot do more than kill me." He told her :

" It is not a question of killing you . . . you will be kept till you are a skeleton, and a nervous and mental wreck, and then you will be sent to an institution where they look after mental wrecks."

The words were denounced as a threat. In fact it was simply a warning; the doctor spoke the thing which he foresaw, knowing the intentions of those from whom he took his orders.

Unknown to me in prison, that Sunday's march on Downing Street had created a sensation. It was the first large-scale demon-stration of real popular turbulence the Suffrage movement had shown. Nevinson expressed his opinion with emphasis :

" . . . the barbarity of the ' Cat and Mouse ' Act has struck very deep into the mind of the ordinary man and woman. . . . A great deal also is due to Miss Sylvia Pankhurst's action in throwing herself upon the genuine chivalry and good sense of the workers in the East End. I think that was a stroke of genius. We have all the working classes now, not only favourable, but zealous. After the battle of Valmy, when the national troops of the French Revolution held in check the hirelings of official Europe, Goethe said to his friends : ' To-day marks a turning-point in history, and we can say we were present at it.' We who were in the Square last Sunday can say the same."

Discounting something for journalism, and more for sym-pathy, the words were true enough, for the demonstration had been unlike all the old " raids " on the House of Commons, in which a picked band of women, recruited from all parts of the country, had gone forward to struggle with the police, watched by a crowd mainly composed of sightseers. Now at last we had seen an entire crowd in action. Mrs. Pankhurst, at the London Pavilion next day, expressed a similar view :

" The fight is nearly over; the end is at hand—a few months more and the spirit of the crowd that followed Sylvia Pankhurst down Whitehall . . . will have found some definite expression which the Government will no longer be able to deny."

I did not see these or any such comments till long after. At that Monday meeting Annie Kenney had been re-captured, four other arrests being made in the struggle. Mrs. Pankhurst had sold her " Cat and Mouse " licence for £100. She had been released the previous Thursday. She had refrained from water during her four days in prison, and at the last had walked up and down until exhausted. She was in a jaundiced condition, a tendency which persisted for many years. It was erroneously reported in the Press that the operation of transfusion of blood from another person had been performed on her.

That same Monday (July 28th), Lansbury's appeal[1] was rejected by three Judges of the King's Bench Divisional Court; on Wednesday he surrendered to his bail, and was removed to Pentonville Prison. He refused to eat and was released on Saturday. He has since revealed[2] that he had begun his hunger strike some days before, in order to shorten his imprisonment. He was taken from prison to the house of Joseph Fels, in Cornwall Terrace, Regent's Park. A procession of 10,000 people, organized by the Poplar Labour Party, marched from the East End to welcome him. He was not re-arrested, though he gave no undertaking. He presented, however, a petition to Parliament asking for intercession with the Crown on his behalf, and representing that he was " not guilty of any crime or offence, or likely to commit any crime or offence," though " for particular reasons affecting his own personal honour " he did not " feel at liberty " to find sureties. This petition was cited by the Government as an expression of his intention not to break the law, and as the reason of his non-arrest. Wedgwood had made in the House what was something like an apology, though Lansbury may not have been responsible for its terms.

Before his appeal was heard, Lansbury's connection with Christabel and Mrs. Pankhurst was already at an end; his

[1] Like myself, John Scurr and Mrs. Cohen of Leeds had also been convicted under the Statute of Edward III. Their imprisonments had been stayed pending Lansbury's appeal, but they were never made to serve them. Scurr had said : " I do not regard property as sacred at all. . . . The sooner they commence destroying property, anywhere and everywhere, the better."

[2] *My Life,* by George Lansbury. (Constable.)

temperament was too volatile; theirs too ruthless for its continuance. He soon abandoned the claim that the Labour Party should oppose all Government measures without exception. Indeed he forgot that he had ever made it. By the time he published his life[1] story, in 1928, he thought he had simply demanded that the Party should move an amendment to the Reform Bill, and vote against the Bill unless women were included. Moreover, Christabel's cry had now definitely crystallized into: " Wanted, a Tory Government! " Lansbury would not support the Tories; with all his vacillations, he preferred to go on working and waiting for a strong Labour Party. Christabel lacked both the patience and the sympathy with Labour ideals which could have made that course acceptable to her, short of clear proof that it could achieve immediate success. Yet for a brief period she had been attracted by Lansbury's Left Wing insurgence. So recently as June a by-election had occurred at Leicester. The Lansbury faction desired the Labour Party to contest the seat, the Party officials refused. It was alleged the Party officials had made a bargain with the Liberals to safeguard Macdonald in possession of the second Leicester seat. Lansbury and his *Daily Herald* thundered against such arrangements, and joined with the Social Democratic Federation in running Edward R. Hartley, an original member of the I.L.P. The W.S.P.U. enthusiastically welcomed this candidature, Christabel declaring in the *Suffragette* that it would " lead the way in a great attack by Labour against a decadent Liberalism and all its evil works." The W.S.P.U. canvassed the electors assiduously and excelled itself in pageantry, sending forth a procession led by children with rose wands and tableaux of " woman bond and woman free " and forcible feeding. Hartley polled 2,000 votes, a remarkable achievement for an Independent last moment candidate, but failed to defeat the Liberal. Christabel henceforth declared the policy of running Labour candidates to be " over-rated " and " too sectional." What was required, she said, was to mobilize the Labour vote in support of the Tories until the Liberal Government would agree to give women the vote. When Lansbury's faction ran John Scurr as Independent Labour candidate at Chesterfield in the following August, the W.S.P.U. gave no support. When Lansbury went to prison the *Suffragette* referred to the fact in distant terms: Lincoln's Inn House no longer invited his services as a speaker.

The Free Speech Defence Committee, of which Wedgwood was chairman and Keir Hardie a prominent member, had announced another Trafalgar Square demonstration on August

[1] *My Life*, by George Lansbury, p. 120. (Constable.)

10th. Those of us who had been charged under the Act of Edward III were invited to speak. In conveying the invitation to me, Frank Smith asked for a pledge that I would not ask the people to march to Downing Street. I refused to accept this condition, and issued a leaflet: "To Lovers of Freedom," stating that after the "Free Speech" meeting had done its talking, I should be in the Square to go with those who cared to Downing Street. The leaflet was scarcely out when Keir Hardie visited me. He had just returned from the International Women's Suffrage Conference at Budapest, where he had received a great ovation. The Leicester and Chesterfield contests had focussed unrest in the Labour ranks. F. W. Jowett in the *Labour Leader* was complaining that the Party's subservience to Liberalism was " injuring the movement "; Snowden, in the same paper, had written that the Party could not take an independent line because four-fifths of its seats were dependent on Liberal votes. To many it appeared that the Labour advance of 1906 was being followed by a continual retreat. The Party's banner, I thought, was being dragged in the dust. I flashed all this out to Keir Hardie, and asked unhappily: " Why do you allow yourself to be tarred with Macdonald's brush? " I told him of my answer to Frank Smith. I saw his dislike of it, though he said no word to dissuade me, and doubtless it was he who had insisted I should be invited. In spite of his gentleness it was almost a quarrel— on my part, not on his. I did not see him again till the following summer; indeed I had told him it was too painful, too incongruous he should come in the midst of the warfare waged against him and the Labour Party by the orders of my sister. I saw myself now in the position towards him in which I had so often seen my mother; he trying to help her, she flouting his efforts. I did not want him to help me to get free, or even to try. It might have been better to leave the " Free Speech " meeting alone—my manifesto had gone out; it was too late now to draw back.

Next day it was Mrs. Pankhurst who came to my bedside. The Government was permitting a holiday respite to her and Annie Kenney, it seemed; at any rate they had been at large for some time, and both had delivered speeches in public after the expiry of their licences without any attempt at arrest. She complained that she had intended to visit me the previous day, but learnt that Keir Hardie was coming and feared to encounter him. She spoke as though he were a person a Suffragette should be ashamed to meet. So far had divergence of opinion on tactics, not on principles, destroyed her old friendship. I answered her reproaches with sadness: " He will not come again."

CHAPTER II

I WAS present at the "Free Speech" demonstration as I had declared I should be. Eluding the police at Ford Road, I drove to the Square and sprang from a taxi into the East End procession as it swung round from the Strand. The marchers hoisted me to the plinth, and a crowd of them jumped up beside me as a body-guard. When the resolutions had been put, and the "Free Speech" meeting was officially ended, I would have addressed the people from the wide north plinth; but John Scurr continued speaking there, begging the crowd not to go to Downing Street with me, but to await the reply to some question shortly to be asked in Parliament; if the answer to that question were not satisfactory he said, "Then let us burn; let us destroy . . ." So he ran on.

Unable to keep the crowd waiting indefinitely, I was obliged to speak from the narrow east plinth instead of facing the main body of the crowd. A woman calling herself an Anarchist was following up Scurr's appeals on the main plinth with excited warnings. Her cry: "I have seen a little woman in a blue costume lying on the pavement . . ." rang in my ears as I jumped down to the people. As before, the crowd took me to its breast and bore me on towards Downing Street. There were eighteen arrests and the windows of a motor 'bus were broken. As before, I was snatched away. . . .

I was released after four days. Again there were great meetings in the East End, both during the term of my licence and after it had expired. I was anxious to press the fight home, and called on the people to show no fear of the police, but to arm themselves with weapons as effective as the police truncheons. Then they would be permitted to act with impunity, like Sir Edward Carson. Men and women were now, in fact, coming to the meetings with sticks in their hands, and beginning to retaliate against the blows of the police. I began to see also a weapon, hitherto unknown to me, which they called a "Saturday night," made of tarred rope, closely twisted, with a heavy bundle of knots at the end, and sometimes weighted with lead. Against our crowds in their present temper, the detectives were not desirous of engaging too serious a fight. They generally made a rush for me, but allowed themselves to be jostled aside, and I went free.

The scenes at the London Pavilion were of another character. It was a crowd of well-to-do women, and a very small sprinkling of men, mostly of the leisured or professional class. The efforts at resistance and rescue were quite incapable of securing a prisoner's escape, save by strategy. Yet such scenes in the heart of fashionable London were annoying to the Government. During the sessions of the International Medical Congress, Mrs. Pankhurst was permitted to go at large unmolested, and to address the congress itself.

When Parliament was prorogued, on August 15th, she and Annie Kenney crossed to the Continent, and on October 16th Mrs. Pankhurst sailed thence to the United States. Held up at Ellis Island, she was presently informed that she would be returned to England as a person guilty of " moral turpitude." Appealing against the decision, and refused bail during the interim, she threatened to hunger strike on the Island. The American authorities immediately capitulated and she was set at liberty; Mrs. Belmont, known as the millionaire Suffragist, stood bail for her. Harriot Stanton Blatch, Jane Addams, and other well-known people had appealed on her behalf. President Wilson had intervened. She was permitted to proceed on her tour, wherein she was accorded a greater welcome than ever by Press and public. Arthur Brisbane wrote a striking eulogy of her mission and personality.

All the people about me were urging me to go away for a time. I was becoming more and more frequently incapacitated with attacks of pain. I decided to go to Finland to meet there the first women elected to a modern Parliament. I slipped away in disguise, and landed at Esbjerg in Denmark. The Danish Women's Federation soon found me out, and pressed me to lecture in Copenhagen, Aarhuus and Svendborg. I was astonished to see how fully these big, enthusiastic audiences, where I was the only speaker, could follow a long discourse in English. The Press was most cordial. We were greatly amused that Norah Smyth was invariably taken for me when we first appeared on the platform, being regarded as a typical Englishwoman, because she had a long stride, a nose with a high bridge, and hair screwed tightly in a knot. We visited the Old Age Pensioners Home, a combination of hotel and sanitorium, where the old people enjoyed a freedom and comfort, and a dignity of status undreamt of in the most humanely governed English Workhouses. The prison for short sentence prisoners was like a garden-suburb rather than the gaols I have seen in other countries. There were no cells, no bars, no high walls or locked gates. Trades were taught, and the inmates were encouraged to practise them and begin earning a living before release. The peasant schools and the peasant agricultural schools were an encouraging revelation. A remarkably high percentage of the youth of Denmark attend these adult boarding-schools for one, two, or three half-year terms. The peasants' co-operatives, their highly skilled and co-ordinated farming, the absence of poverty, and the high general culture and prosperity awakened in me great joy and hopefulness. Admirable Denmark; it seemed to me the happiest and most fraternal, and therefore the noblest country in the world! In Sweden, which we touched at Gothenburg, we encountered the slums again. Here I addressed a great meeting organized by Greta Carlberg, a most earnest toiler for social betterment.

In Christiania, where I had another big meeting, we met the first Norwegian woman factory inspector, Betty Kjelsberg, and Castberg, the Minister of Justice, who was sponsoring a Bill to give the children of unmarried mothers the same claim on their father as those born in wedlock, and the right to bear his name. Frederica Moerk, who presently stood as a candidate for the Norwegian Parliament, kindly acted as our guide. We visited the Socialist Folketshus. Kindness itself was Olave Kringen, the foreign correspondent of the *Social Demokraten*, who took us under his genial wing when I presented a letter of introduction from Keir Hardie. Kringen was a rare, delightful character, a huge elderly man, with a mushroom-like straw hat of enormous size, a short jacket and a waistcoat of grey brocaded silk, plentifully bespattered with the stains of bilberries, upon which, with other sweet-flavoured Norwegian berries, he insisted upon regaling us. After an excellent lunch provided by his housekeeper, he whisked us off, bespattered as he was, to the smartest confectioner's in the town for an introduction to Norwegian pastries, and thence to booksellers and picture galleries. His childlike gaiety was occasionally overshadowed by the fact that his wife was serving a sentence of imprisonment on a matter of principle. He had a surprisingly close knowledge of English affairs. All the Norwegian newspapers gave me excellent interviews and reports. The *Morgenbladet*, the proprietor of which, Niels Vogt, was then Norwegian Minister in London, published an article from me on forcible feeding. The Finnish women Members of Parliament were preparing a great welcome. Not knowing of this till my return to England, I abandoned the visit to Finland in favour of a rest in the Norwegian mountains. I hoped to stay in a peasant's house, in order to come into intimate touch with the life of the people, but every-one I inquired of answered: " Impossible, the houses are too small." Finally we stayed at a farm where boarders were occasionally taken, and went about sketching the people, the majestic scenery and the old wooden buildings with their intricate carving of Fafnir, Sigurd, and the other creations of Norse mythology.

Taking my Danish meetings on my return Englandward, I was to speak at Aarhuus on one of the last days. Jaded and nerve-racked, I was lying on the bed to rest before the meeting. A tall, pale girl came into the room, with hesitant gait, peering about short-sightedly through her spectacles, and spoke my name; then, seeing me prone, would have retired with apologies. Immediately charmed by her, I prevailed on her to stay. Mysteriously her presence soothed and restored me. Her features were blunt and sallow, her gait without grace, but a serene natural clarity of judgement, and an unsullied goodness and sympathy lent her a remarkable attraction. Her English was perfect. I listened to her with delight; she seemed to reveal to me the youth of a future time. Of peasant stock, an orphan living with her grandparents, she had been incapacitated from manual work by an early spinal affliction which had left her permanently fragile. We parted on the understanding that she should come to work with us in the East End. It was not my wish to make a militant of her; I desired her personal influence and Danish outlook amongst our people. She soon followed us. She had the gift which made her welcomed and trusted by all, but our conditions were too harsh for her. The hideous poverty of the slums distressed her beyond measure, as though she had come from another and happier planet. Her old ailment reasserted itself and she was obliged to return to Denmark.

CHAPTER III

WHILST some of us snatched a respite, others maintained the old, hard struggle. Mrs. Baines, charged
with blowing up an empty railway carriage in a siding,
hunger struck on remand and was released in a dangerous condition suffering from chorea. Medically advised that another strike
might mean her death, she was prevailed upon to emigrate with
her family to Australia, where she became active in the causes
she had cared for here, and a coadjutor with Adela Pankhurst.
Mrs. Wyan, refused release under the "Cat and Mouse" Act, and
claiming complete discharge, declined to give the governor any
address. He dispatched her to the "Mousehole." She refused
to enter, and continued her strike on a chair in the road outside,
where the wardresses deposited her. The police removed her to
the Kensington Workhouse, and only then did she desist from
her strike and return to her friends.

Annie Kenney returned from her continental holiday to
speak at the London Pavilion on October 6th. The police tore
her from the stage. In a rush to protect her, ten people were
arrested. She was released on October 13th with a five days'
licence, but was not re-arrested till May 22nd, 1914—her last
term in prison. During the intervening period, though she was
carried to several meetings on a stretcher, she only twice
delivered a speech. She served, in fact, but twenty-eight days of
her sentence of eighteen months' imprisonment.

On October 5th "The Elms," an unoccupied house at
Hampton on Thames, was destroyed by fire, the value being
estimated at £1,500. Mary Richardson, already a "Mouse"
under sentence for several charges, and Rachel Peace were discovered in the vicinity. They were arrested, hunger struck on
remand, and were forcibly fed.[1] These were the first women
forcibly fed under the "Cat and Mouse" Act. They were not
to be the last.

On learning that the process from which she had so

---

[1] On October 7th an inquest was held on Albert Davis, aged twenty-one, serving
a sentence of fifteen months for theft. He took little food, was forcibly fed, and
died from exhaustion. The incident was widely commented upon in relation to
Suffragette cases.

grievously suffered was again being practised, Zelie Emerson
went up to Holloway with Mrs. Moore and Mrs. Watkins from
the East End, carrying a South African sjambok. She knew
that the doctor was due at the prison each morning at nine
o'clock and would be forcibly feeding the Suffragettes soon
after. She waited for him to emerge from his house close by,
then accosted him: " Good morning, Dr. Forward; you are
forcibly feeding our women." " You know I cannot help
myself," he answered. " You could resign! You are a
disgrace to your profession! " She seized him and beat him till
the whip broke. " You forcibly fed me for five weeks! You
should be forcibly fed yourself! " To do him justice, he made
no attempt to retaliate or to have her arrested, which would
have been easy, for she stood her ground, explaining what she
had done to a group of road-sweepers who had watched the
scene. I learnt of the incident only after my return from
Norway; it was past, I did not speak of it. I appreciated her
brave protest on behalf of other women, which might well have
meant a return to the same torture; yet I regretted that Zelie
had done it. Dr. Forward was not, in my judgement, a bad
man, or a cruel one. It is true he was not courageous, but one
cannot make heroes by compulsion. The power to view events,
even the most tragic, in detachment from the personal interests
and environment is rare. The unquestioning assumption that
those in authority must be right is all too common. Refusal
to obey the Home Secretary's command would have meant
dismissal for the prison doctors. If anyone were to be whipped,
I preferred it should be a member of the Government.

Returning from Norway, I landed and reached East
London with infinite precaution. The large Bow Baths Hall
was now available for our meetings, for swimming was suspended for the winter season. Strange that two great popular
needs should thus be placed in a state of mutual conflict in
a great working-class area! Our Federation had arranged a
meeting of welcome in the Baths on October 13th. I reached
the hall in disguise, and as soon as I was inside, the doors were
guarded that no detective might enter. What a triumph it
seemed to be back amongst my people! What rejoicings and
cheers! We grasped each other's hands in our fellowship of
love and enthusiasm. Our hopes were high; we would re-create
the East End; we would sweep poverty and slums from out the
land. I had been speaking perhaps ten minutes when the
people were thrown into an extraordinary state of agitation.
" Jump, Sylvia! Jump! " they cried, with arms outstretched.
And jump I did. The heavy red curtains at the back of the

stage had been torn aside by detectives rushing to seize me. The caretaker had let them in by a side door, and they had slipped behind us unawares. A furious fight was raging between them and the speakers on the platform, reinforced by men of the audience, who were leaping down from the side galleries to prevent their advance. The detectives were fighting with sticks, the men with the chairs and benches. The people closed round me. Someone put a hat and coat on me; someone changed the hat for another; the hat was changed again. In the press we moved slowly outward. The battle of the platform continued, the table flung to the ground, the chairs smashed. Mrs. Ives, our Hackney secretary, a very small, delicate woman, was held by the coat collar and beaten with a truncheon. She sustained a broken collar-bone. Mary Leigh was knocked senseless. Miss Forbes-Robertson, a sister of the actor, who had come from the other end of London, had her arm broken. Sister Townend had her knee put out of joint. Scores of East End people received injuries, accepted stoically as part of the fight. The police had their share of blows. The *Daily Chronicle* published a list of " casualties " next day.

Outside it was dark and raining. The police were rearing their horses and driving the people before them. Our mass scattered, re-formed, and scattered again. Beside me, holding my arm, was " Kosher " Hunt (a noted East End prize fighter; ten policemen, it was said, had once failed to take him to prison, having to send for reinforcements). In the commotion a uniformed constable recognized me. I saw him start, and raise his arm to stop me passing, then he drew back—from fear or pity? I thought the latter. In the dark we fled; Hunt and I alone now, with a group of friends shadowing us for our safety. He put his muffler round my neck to disguise me, and hurried me down dark by-ways to a friendly home, where we waited till one of our company discovered Willie Lansbury; he was regarded as the master of resource. Had he not run away to sea as a boy? Did he not desert his ship, and afterwards go to the offices of the Maritime Board and recover his pay before the officials had discovered he was a deserter? His friends said so, were it true or not. At any rate, he had the gift of decision. Out with him I went through the night, hurrying round the north outskirts of Victoria Park; then by 'bus to the city; a taxi to Hampstead; and so to the flat of the Gliksten sisters, safe for the night.

The detectives were as angry at my escape as the people were pleased. They were loath to believe that I had really left the hall, and whilst some were attacking the people outside, others remained to search. Zelie Emerson, leaving the hall in triumph, gibed at them merrily: " Puss, puss! " One of them struck her a heavy blow with his lead-weighted stick. She fell to the ground unconscious. As soon as she was able to stand again, she insisted upon accompanying Sister Townend to have her knee examined by Mansell Moullin. " But what is the matter with *you*? " exclaimed the surgeon when he saw Zelie Emerson's own more serious injury, remarking that had the blow struck her but a little further back, she must have been killed. The Mansell Moullins insisted that she should stay at their house and remain in bed for some days at least, but going to her room next morning they discovered she had risen beforehand and returned to the East End.

Next night I was to speak in Poplar Town Hall. I was dressed in poor clothes, with the garments of an infant stuffed with paper, as a " baby " in my arms, to aid the disguise. A party of us went together on the top of the 'bus in the dark. Poor conspirators, we fell into talk. As we rose to dismount I saw two big men descending before us. With a palpitation of the heart, I knew that I was discovered. I gave the " baby " to one of the others, not telling the reason why. The road was thronged, but a strong force of police preserved a clear island about the entrance to the hall. The others went forward. I must follow alone through the massed ranks of my captors. As soon as I was amongst them, detectives seized me and thrust me into a taxi kept in readiness. I cried out at the top of my voice, in the fantastic hope that the people in the hall upstairs might be able to rescue me. The stewards at the door took up the shout. " They have got her! " The people rose up: " They have got her! " They rushed for the doors, but John Scurr, who was speaking, insisted that it was a false alarm, and ordered the people to sit down; he feared a panic on the staircase. It did not matter: I had to return to prison sooner or later. A man and his wife, who had rushed towards me when I was seized, were arrested, and the man was afterwards fined £5; a tremendous sum to exact from poor working people.

I was interested to see the excitement of the detectives who were conveying me to Holloway, chuckling and congratulating themselves. As soon as they were well out of Poplar, their leader called to the driver to stop, and ordered one of his companions: " Go and 'phone to the chief that Sylvia Pankhurst is arrested! "

I had another nine days of the hunger and thirst strike, writing during the earlier days, torturing myself by refusing all rest in order to hasten my release, as the time approached when I must be out to fulfil my engagements. Uplifted by the belief that we were making progress, I experienced no doubts, no regrets, certainly no self-pity. On my release I went to Poplar; the members there had urged that I should stay with one of them this time. I was carried to the usual great release meetings on a stretcher.

In the industrial world revolutionary Marxism contested vigorously against the old Trade Unionism, and the opportunist political Labourism of Macdonald. Rank and file movements, striving to convert the Trade Unions into instruments of revolutionary action, were enlarging their propaganda in all directions. The ferment in Ireland had risen to fever heat. Unionism, Nationalism, Labour: all were in the high throes of conflict. In Ulster Carson twitted the Government for its failure to enforce the law and preserve order. "Drilling is illegal," he cried. "Volunteers are illegal, and the Government knows they are illegal. The Government dare not interfere!" There were Unionist riots resulting in loss of life in Londonderry; the city was virtually an armed camp; an arsenal was discovered there in the house of a clergyman. In September the W.S.P.U. announced a campaign in Ulster to press for the enfranchisement of women under the rebel Unionist Government. A letter was dispatched by the W.S.P.U. organizer to Carson embodying the demand. Immediately the secretary of the Ulster Unionist Council announced to the similar Council of Women, that the draft articles of the provisional Government provided for votes for women under the Ulster Parliament on the basis of the local government register. This promise, which was ruthlessly swept away by Sir Edward Carson in the following March, was hailed as a great and splendid victory. Christabel wrote:

"The W.S.P.U. will henceforth oppose the Government and the Nationalist Party with more vigour than ever, because if the Government and Mr. John Redmond should be successful in forcing the Home Rule Bill upon Ulster, women would be robbed of the voting rights which Sir Edward Carson and his colleagues are prepared to grant to them under the provisional government."

The non-militant Suffragists rejoiced with the W.S.P.U., forgetting the scruples they had so often expressed against militancy in their pride that the rebel Unionist Women of Ulster were to be granted a vote under a Government of Civil War.

Amid the appalling Labour conditions, common both to the Catholic and Protestant areas of the distressful isle, the Irish

Transport and General Workers' Union, formed by James Connolly, was making startling advances, under the headlong, passion-provoking oratory of James Larkin, a tall, red-haired young man, who had learnt in America the methods and phraseology of the I.W.W. The employers, headed by a certain Murphy, much abused in the *Daily Herald,* took fright at the new Trade Unionism, and proclaimed a lock-out of all Union workers. Delia, Jim Larkin's sister, was energetic in organizing the women, who in large numbers were locked out, or struck in support of the men. The Irish Constabulary, long notorious for their cruelty, treated the strikers with great brutality, breaking up meetings and using their truncheons on men, women and children. Men were killed. English Liberal newspapers protested; James Connolly was imprisoned for incitement. Larkin declaimed:

" We will follow Sir Edward Carson's example, and from to-morrow morning, in all our offices and halls, we will enrol, organize and arm a volunteer force. Sir Edward Carson has armed his men with Italian rifles; do you arm yourselves with Irish weapons : black-thorns, bottles and hurleys."

Larkin was arrested and public meetings were prohibited in Dublin. Constance Markievicz, who was helping in the strike soup kitchens, had already inaugurated her boy scouts : the first contingent enrolled to fight for the Labour and Republican causes. The lads were to be engaged in serious warfare when the rebellion finally broke out in 1916. The result of the strike was the enrolment of the Citizen Army at Liberty Hall, the Transport Union's headquarters. This force also was to bear its part in the rebellion. Captain White was heard of in the formation of the Citizen Army; also Sir Francis Vane, a descendant of that upholder of religious tolerance who was executed in 1642, having been excluded from the Indemnity Bill at the restoration of the Monarchy, and of whom Oliver Cromwell said : " Oh, Sir Henry Vane, Sir Henry Vane; the Lord deliver me from Sir Henry Vane ! " Francis Vane was in appearance a type unusual to-day, though often seen in sixteenth and seventeenth century pictures, with a long, smooth, oval head, tall and thin. For brief periods he appeared as a stormy petrel in British politics.

In the long-drawn misery of the Dublin lock-out its victims pleaded vainly for sympathetic action by British transport workers, and received instead a " food ship " from the Trade Union Congress—a mere handful of crumbs in the vast desert of their need. Ere finally they were starved into submission, the canker of bitterness had bitten deeply into them. Terrible conditions of sweating were brought to light: girls of fifteen and sixteen working twelve days in a linen factory for 10d., embroideresses paid 2d. for nine hours' work, others embroidering twelve cushions for 2¾d.; they struck when the management proposed to reduce the rate to 2¼d. Girls earning 6s. a week were locked out for wearing a Union badge. The dispute spread rapidly from trade to trade. The Union funds were exhausted; the ill-paid workers had no resources to fall back upon.

The *Daily Herald* took a prominent part in calling for sympathetic action and appealing for funds. Children were brought over from Dublin to English homes, the first party of six children being housed with the mother of one of them at the Pethick Lawrences' country cottage in Surrey. Lansbury announced an Albert Hall meeting on November 1st in support of the strike, and to demand Larkin's release, with Connolly to bring first-hand information from Dublin. Lansbury asked me to speak. My latest " Cat and Mouse " licence would have expired, and I should be arrested if I were caught, but that was no deterrent. The Dublin lock-out was to me a poignant incident in our common struggle for a fairer and more humane society. I was glad to accept the invitation, as an opportunity to show solidarity with the Dublin workers, and to keep the women's side of the struggle to the front. Moreover, it seemed to me there would be much piquancy, and I hoped some embarrassment, for the Government, in my appearance side by side with two fellow hunger strikers, Connolly and Lansbury, both at perfect liberty, whilst I was pursued under the " Cat and Mouse " Act. I reached the platform without mishap. It was a tremendous meeting, crammed with Labourists, Socialists, Suffragists, reformers of every school; the miseries of Dublin had stirred the public heart. Connolly, a thick-set, quiet-mannered, serious-looking man, who might have been taken for a comfortable farmer by his appearance, gave a temperate, informative address, in striking contrast to the excitability of Lansbury and the other speakers, and an evidence of the old adage that " still waters run deep." Because of my immediate liability to arrest, I had a bigger burst of applause than even Connolly, but there was no great difficulty in escaping in a crowd of 10,000 people. I went out with Lansbury and the other speakers, and though the mounted police chased us about, I got away clear, and was at Hackney Baths next night, where the police were again overcome by the solidarity of our gallant crowd.

My presence at the Albert Hall meeting had aroused the ire

of Christabel. The *Daily Herald* made matters worse by observing:

> "One great result of the militant Suffrage Movement has been to convince many people that the vote is not the best way of getting what one wants . . . every day the industrial rebels and the Suffrage rebels march nearer together. Thus one found Mrs. Despard, Mr. Pethick Lawrence and Miss Sylvia Pankhurst at the Albert Hall, demanding the release of Jim Larkin."

It was suggested that our East London Federation had formed an alliance with George Lansbury's " Daily Herald League." I wrote to the *Suffragette*, stating definitely that neither I nor the East London Federation had formed an alliance with the " Daily Herald League," or any other Party, and that I had gone to the Albert Hall to point out that " behind every poor man there stands a still poorer woman." This was, in fact, an old saying of Mrs. Pankhurst, as Christabel may perhaps have remembered. Lansbury, as a matter of fact, was never consulted about our East London Federation policy. We went ahead and made our own decisions. He spoke at a large number of our meetings, many of which were in, or bordering on, his constituency, and which, owing to the excitement and enthusiasm engendered by our militancy and its results, were larger and more alive than he and the Labour and Socialist bodies could then muster without us. Of that there can be no question, for the " Cat and Mouse " Act stirred our meetings of those days by a very storm of emotions, wholly removed from the relatively stolid temper of ordinary political propaganda.

Lansbury might be swept by excitement into saying militant things, and even on one occasion took a hand in the disturbance made by our women at the Poplar Borough Council, but he was never a militant: he was temperamentally incapable even of taking the initiative in so relatively mild an act as to lead a prohibited march to Trafalgar Square. Moreover, he was running a movement of his own, in which Votes for Women was by no means the main objective. That amorphous body, the Herald League, like the staff of the *Herald* itself, included persons not favourable either to Women's Suffrage or the Suffragettes.

Lansbury discussed Christabel's attack with me and urged that I should not retaliate. " I think you are going to be biggest," he said in his genial way, which I received as an adjuration to generosity of spirit. So far as any verbal retaliation went, his persuasion chimed with my own thought. I was determined to avoid dissension and division if I could, but I was convinced I was right to keep our working women's movement in touch with the main body of the working-class movement; that was essentially the difference between the Paris policy and mine; it was a difference Christabel would not tolerate. Lansbury said I was right, but he did not invite me to speak at the Albert Hall meeting he presently organized to celebrate the release of Larkin, who was soon set free in response to popular agitation. I should have accepted the invitation had it been given. I was wholly convinced that our East London work, and its influence on the movement throughout the country, were performing a necessary service to the Cause. Time, I believed, would prove the wisdom of our policy; I was content to avoid discussion in the meantime. Moreover, I reflected that the only large Suffragette demonstrations in the centre of London in that year, 1913, had been ours in Trafalgar Square: that such demonstrations were valuable seemed to me self-evident.

Since the expiry of my last licence I had now spoken at three meetings, and each time we had vanquished the police. The members were elated by our success, and we were all eager to extend the area in which the crowd could be depended on for support.

The Times of August 20th, 1913, had stated that Colonel Wallace had sent a letter to every Orange Lodge in Ulster, urging all members " to enrol in the Volunteer Company nearest their residence." In the same issue was obligingly published the report of a speech delivered by me at an East End meeting:

" We have not yet made ourselves a match for the police and we have got to do it. The police know ju-jitsu. I advise you to learn ju-jitsu. Women should practise it as well as men. If there is any man here who has been in the Army or knows anything about drilling, will he please communicate with me and we will start drilling! "

Sir Francis Vane responded to this appeal, declaring that he would provide us with Army officers to drill our people, and that he would himself take the lead. I did not contemplate, for winning the vote, a mortal struggle to overthrow the existing Government by force, such as was presently developed in Ireland. I envisaged always a popular movement of the character which had preceded the Reform Acts. Yet with militancy springing up on every hand, it seemed then that we were on the eve of great social changes and contests. I knew not whither the future might lead us. For the present I saw that our movement was awakening masses of women, and men also, to a strong desire for better conditions. I saw that the police now shrank from attacking us in the East End; I wanted that shrinking accentuated. I was anxious that the Government should have no excuse to ignore us, for obviously its persecution provided the most effective spur to the popular turbulence which appeared necessary to success. I was always convinced that the element of martyrdom provided the highest and keenest incentive to our movement. I knew that the hallowing influence of sacrifice cemented the comradeship of the great mass movement which had grown up. Yet, as in August I had urged the people to take sticks to parry police truncheons, I was now prepared to rise to the circumstances and phraseology of the time by calling for the formation of a

"People's Army; an organization men and women may join in order to fight for freedom. And in order that they may fit themselves to cope with the brutality of Government servants."

The term "Army" was in our case rhetorical rather than militarist. Vane drafted a pledge for the "People's Training Corps":

"I promise to serve the common cause of Justice and my Comrades under our duly elected Officers. I will be a friend to all and a brother to every member of the People's Army. I am a sincere believer in a Vote for every Woman and every Man."

The inauguration of the Army was to take place in the Bow Baths on November 5th. Vane offered his assistance in getting me to the meeting. I was disguised as a very sporting lady, some sympathizer having provided the costume, and drove to Bow in an open car with some friends of Vane, and one of his boy scouts on the step. We arrived far too soon; one might as well give oneself up to the police as enter an empty hall, I thought, and suggested we should go to George Lansbury's to wait. We had scarcely entered when a police whistle sounded: a crowd of big detectives with big sticks came rushing out of the public-houses and gathered about the door, calling a taxi to take me away. How should I get to the meeting? Should we gather a crowd to engage the detectives and fight our way through them, or try some strategy? Everyone looked to Willie Lansbury; in his family also he had the reputation of being cool-headed. He speedily offered a solution. His sister Daisy, not too much unlike me, was to go out dressed as the sporting lady, and I, in her coat and hat, was to pass over the garden wall to Willie's house. The family step-ladders were always kept conveniently in position for that purpose. Then Daisy, her father, Vane and all who could be mustered were to rush out with her, whilst Willie and I would emerge from the next house unobserved. We could not aid the deception in either case by a veil; that had been tried too often by others, and would rouse instant suspicion. We must act quickly or the Baths would be emptied of people, for the news was spreading like wild-fire. The moment of stepping out required some resolution; almost I felt the big hands grasping my shoulder. But the plan worked. A short, sharp struggle around Daisy, in which some vigorous enthusiast gashed a detective's face, then they were driving away with her—whilst I was running with Willie up the steps of the Bow Baths, a seething mass of people rushing in and out in strange confusion. Zelie Emerson on the platform, brandishing her "Saturday night" and flushed with triumph, was calling them to order. The meeting proceeded, thrilled to a great excitement. Daisy Lansbury soon returned to us. Four huge detectives, crushing her between them, grasping her wrists in approved "Cat and Mouse" Act style, had suddenly discovered: "This one's too fat!" Obviously it was true, for she was a healthy, substantial young person, and I, from much fasting, was as thin as a rake. They stopped at Bethnal Green police station. "You've got Miss Lansbury!" the sergeant told them. They abandoned her in disgust and she raced back to tell us. What roars of laughter! The hall was rocking with glee. Indeed what roars of laughter!

The wires had been set in motion for reinforcements. Willie Lansbury came to me with serious face: "They have got such a posse of police outside as has never been seen in Bow. Three hundred mounted men! Our people will not be able to stand against the horses." "Never mind; we shall manage it some-how," I answered; and so we did, by the sheer pressure of numbers, and the valiant fight of the crowd. There was another great struggle in the Roman Road, many of the policemen being unhorsed, and injuries, though none were fatal, received on both sides. Zelie Emerson was again struck on the head, this time by a uniformed constable. Again she fell to the ground uncon-scious. These blows were telling upon her. Escaping in the chaos, I entered the Lansbury workshop through a neighbour's home at the rear, and so passed across the timber yard into the house. Next day I again escaped in a wood cart, but this time more comfortably, the bundles of wood being piled high, leaving a cavity in which three of us sat concealed. We halted at the Rising Sun Inn on the Woodford Road, where Norah Smyth was waiting with a car. Vane had taken no part in the fight, but he assumed the title of "leader" of the People's Army. He interviewed the local Trade Unionists with a view to forming them into corps for use in trade disputes, and named Army officers whom he said would drill the corps. Then he retired to Italy. On November 24th he wrote to Norah Smyth:

" I am sorry that the two officers I mentioned have failed you—
but to be just I had told Captain Hayter that he would not be
required until after Christmas when he promised to join you in this
scheme. You see I did not know your rapid methods, and my
interview with the Trade Unionists led me to suppose that they
would move slowly but surely. . . . I had a card from Mr. Lansbury
asking me to come back as soon as possible. But I cannot until after
Christmas. . . ."

After a meeting in the Bow Palace Music Hall we marched
back to the house in Ford Road, and when I spoke to the people
from the window, it seemed that almost everyone in the crowd
was waving a heavy stick in triumph at having come safely home.
Vane wrote at once to congratulate us, sending an "address" to
be read to the troops as their "leader," and giving instructions
and advice. He added: "I have no doubt Captain Ivrea will
come in on my staff, as will Captain Hayter when we have got
a little further." Smyth answered him: "Major Roskell (whom
we call Mr. Rendall, as he did not wish his name mentioned) is
drilling us at present. . . . Mr. Nevinson hopes to help us after
Christmas."

Vane post-carded Smyth a little later that he had an article on
his Army in the *New Witness*, but he took no steps to make a
reality of it. None of his officers ever appeared. Captain White
was another broken reed who offered much and did nothing.

I was again in prison. We had arranged a meeting at the
Shoreditch Town Hall, but this time as soon as I saw the audience
I scented failure. "Bad generalship," I said to myself, realizing
that the meetings were following each other too quickly for our
workers to make the required preparation. The district was new
ground to us; the meeting, not too well advertised, instead of
being packed and overflowing with enthusiasts, was barely filled.
One by one our workers came to me, urging disguises and
strategies—getting out by the back door, hiding in the building.
"Better be taken amongst the people than caught like a rat in a
trap," I answered. I went out to the inevitable. The police
were drawn up in two strong cordons, reaching from the door of
the hall to the police station close by. I was seized and swept in
with some men and women who still clung to me. One of them
received the heavy sentence of two months' hard labour.

Mrs. Pankhurst and I were again following each other in and
out of prison. She had landed at Plymouth from the United
States the previous Thursday, December 4th. The W.S.P.U. had
been holding a campaign in the town. There was a meeting at
the dock gates, and a W.S.P.U. tug went out to bring her from
the ship, but the police boat arrived there first. Detectives carried

her from the ship and took her by motor across Dartmoor to Exeter prison. She was held there, as she was told by the prison officials, to ensure that she should not attend a welcome meeting arranged for her at the Empress Hall, Earl's Court. In her absence the audience raised £10,500; she had brought £4,500 in donations from America. She was released on Sunday evening at the Station Hotel to the care of Dr. Flora Murray and Sister Pine, who were waiting there to receive her. On Tuesday she went to Christabel in Paris, detectives watching her departure. Returning the day before the expiry of her licence, she was re-arrested on the ground that she had broken its terms by not giving the police twenty-four hours notice of her departure. Detectives and a wardress entered the boat train to apprehend her, and extraordinary police precautions were taken at Victoria Station to prevent a rescue. Police were lined up on the arrival platform, and, to the anger of other passengers, detectives commandeered all the taxi-cabs, and, packed into thirteen of these vehicles, escorted their prisoner to Holloway. All this was because the W.S.P.U. had advertised that Mrs. Drummond was drilling a body-guard for Mrs. Pankhurst. Arrested on Saturday night, December 13th, she was set free the following Wednesday.

I had been released on the 15th after a six days' strike. My most painful efforts had not sufficed to get me out to attend a meeting at the Bow Palace to protest against the refusal[1] which the Poplar Borough Council had maintained since the autumn to permit us the use of the public halls. A scene of extraordinary violence had followed the Palace meeting. Zelie Emerson had called for a procession to march to the houses of the hostile Councillors. When the procession turned out of Bow Road into Tomlin's Grove, where lived Councillor Le Manquais, who had voted against us, the street lamps had been extinguished. The police turned their horses upon the crowd " with a sudden movement which surprised everyone," as testified by the *Manchester Guardian* reporter, whose account of the affray may best be quoted:

" The shouts of police officers directing their men to clear the streets were mingled with the yells of women and children, who rushed here and there to seek safety. The main body of processionists rushed helter-skelter up and down the street in front of the mounted police, shrieking wildly and frantically at their pursuers. Women and children were thrown to the ground in the mêlée, many being

[1] The ground of the refusal was the destruction of furniture in the police raid on October 13th. It included the Bow Baths, Poplar Town Hall and Bromley Public Hall, the only meeting halls in the Borough, except the relatively small elementary school class-rooms, a small mission room, and Bow Palace, a dingy, cheerless place too costly for frequent use.

trampled on in the semi-darkness. . . . The majority of the processionists sought an exit into Bow Road, and here they were followed by a detachment of mounted police, who speedily broke up any formation there was in their ranks. . . . The street . . . was excessively crowded when the procession entered it. On one side runs a blank wall, and there was no shelter for women and children except in the houses on the opposite side of the street."

Just as the procession reached Tomlin's Grove the police arrested Zelie Emerson and eight other persons, two of them men who were merely passing by on their way home to tea. At the same moment twenty mounted men came riding down upon the processionists from the far end of Tomlin's Grove, and twenty others from the Bow Road. The people had no sticks in their hands, having no " Mouse " to protect, and there were many children and elderly women in the crowd. They rushed panic-stricken into the small gardens in front of the houses, but the police hunted them out. An old woman who saw the police beating women and children in her garden was so much distressed that she fell in a fit, and died without regaining consciousness. A lad of eighteen was trampled upon and carried away to the infirmary. A publican, who happened to be passing, was knocked down and kicked by the police, and sustained a fractured rib. The procession had been led by the band of the Gas Workers' Trade Union. The bandsmen were not spared; their instruments were snatched from them and thrown over the wall. The big drum was smashed, and the drummer so badly used that for several months he was on his Union list for sick benefit. The police were taking their revenge for many defeats; they had often done the same to break the spirit of the people in trades disputes. Many of the injured, including five children, were carried into the police station, where, after a doctor had attended them, the adults were charged with assaulting the police. Inside the charge room Inspector Potter struck a labourer, named Atkinson, who had already been severely handled, and gave him a black eye. An action for assault was afterwards brought on Atkinson's behalf, but though the Inspector was committed for trial, he was afterwards acquitted in defiance of overwhelming evidence. Several of the arrestees were fined, but Zelie Emerson, with face cut and arm in a sling, and others obviously suffering from their injuries, were discharged by Mr. Leycester, who apparently thought they had been punished enough. The prosecuting solicitor announced that if Zelie Emerson were arrested again, application would be made to deport her, and this intention was repeated by McKenna in the House of Commons.

At the end of the year 1913 there was only one Suffragette

left in prison; all who had received long sentences had secured temporary release under the " Cat and Mouse " Act. Hundreds of fires had been caused, but only on eight occasions had the perpetrators been caught, thirteen persons being convicted of arson. Mrs. Humphrey Mackworth (afterwards Lady Rhondda) had been convicted of setting fire to a pillar-box. Mrs. Rigby, wife of a Preston medical man, and an early member of the W.S.P.U., had set fire to Sir William Lever's bungalow at Rivington Pike while actually a " Mouse " serving sentence for placing explosives in the Liverpool Exchange. Dr. Dorothea Chalmers Smith was convicted of house-breaking with intent to commit arson. Nevertheless the majority of those convicted were young women without influential connections, or for family reasons bearing assumed names, and thus deprived of influence. In order to protest against the hardships of the " Cat and Mouse " Act, women had made a practice of attending Church services and chanting prayers for the hunger strikers. In some cases they were ejected, in others allowed to proceed. In a few cases the clergy assisted the demonstration. Archdeacon Buckley, for instance, commented on the " moral courage " of the women who had offered prayers at Llandaff Cathedral. The Rev. R. G. Douglas, of St. Andrew's, Bexhill, prayed before his congregation for the hunger strikers, mentioning seven of us by name, " and for all others in prison, or seriously ill for conscience sake " that they might have success and be comforted. The East London Suffragettes had also adopted the " Church protest " method, as these demonstrations were termed, in most cases unmolested and with the sympathy of the congregation, but they had been beaten by the people attending a Roman Catholic Church in Poplar.

East and West, the Suffragettes were everywhere in evidence. They distributed leaflets and made speeches in restaurants, theatres and cinemas. At Bernard Shaw's " Androcles and the Lion," there were cries of " McKenna! McKenna! " when, on failing to persuade a Christian heroine to renounce her faith, the Captain of the Guard uttered the words: " Any person who perishes in the arena is not a martyr, but is committing suicide." Disturbances began to be made at the trials of W.S.P.U. prisoners. When Rachel Peace was sentenced, a hammer was flung through a glass screen by a woman in Court, and a juryman cried: " Cannot these women be searched for weapons? We are none of us safe! "

The deputation of Scottish Bailies to Downing Street had been followed by a similar visit of clergymen, under the auspices of the Bishops of Lincoln and Kensington, who appealed against the " Cat and Mouse " Act, and urged the enfranchisement of women. A deputation from Hampshire men was on the Prime Minister's doorstep a few days later. In October the Bishop of Winchester had appealed, through *The Times*, for "a truce of God "; to the militants "for the relief of an inflamed and most unwholesome condition of our common life "; to the Government for an amnesty and the introduction of a Suffrage Bill as a " first-class measure." In November yet another society was formed in the hope of turning voters against the Government: the " Suffrage First Committee," with Pethick Lawrence as honorary secretary and H. D. Harben as treasurer. Cabinet Ministers, Liberal, Labour and Irish Nationalist Members of Parliament were continually heckled and harassed. Asquith was attacked with a horse-whip while motoring in Scotland. A dead cat was flung at Augustine Birrell.

Keir Hardie was much abroad, endeavouring to arouse the European workers, and especially the Germans, to international solidarity against war. Churchill had announced the acceleration of Naval building and the substitution of oil for coal as the fuel to drive the warships. The Government's Chief Whip had resigned to become an oil magnate. Whilst the war against which he was striving drew nearer, Hardie was heckled and howled at by W.S.P.U. women, who believed him to be deserting realities for a mythical danger. Yet his remained the only voice in Parliament always vigilant in championship of the Suffragettes, never raised against them in rebuke. Petitions to be heard at the Bar of the House of Commons were presented on behalf of thirty Women's Suffrage Societies with a membership of 100,000, and from women's working-class organizations with a membership of 42,000. Women tax resisters were growing in numbers. The Duchess of Bedford and the novelists Beatrice Harraden and Flora Annie Steele were amongst those against whom a distraint was levied. The sale of a tax resister's goods at Hastings led to riotous scenes, in which the club of the non-militant Suffragists was wrecked, and in respect of which damages were obtained from the local corporation. At Bristol Suffragettes burnt the Sports Pavilion newly erected for students of the university, who retaliated by twice wrecking the W.S.P.U. shop. No arrests were made on either occasion, though the police arrived on the scene whilst the students were in possession. In spite of the great destruction wrought by the Suffragettes, such acts of retaliation against their premises were few.

The utterances of the Government remained blankly unfruitful. The Prime Minister received the N.U.W.S.S. shortly after its " pilgrimage." Mrs. Fawcett reproached him: " Your promises and pledges to us remain unredeemed." She suggested

that a new Reform Bill be introduced, and that to overcome the
Speaker's ruling a Votes for Women clause should be put in the
original Bill, but afterwards referred to a full vote of the House.
Lloyd George met a deputation of the same society on October
23rd.   He declared himself more of a woman suffragist than he
had ever been, but insisted that, " in a Parliamentary sense," the
movement had " gone back."   There was more enthusiasm for
it than before, he admitted, but militancy, he said, had transformed indifference into hostility.   This Parliament had been
" ruined " so far as Suffrage was concerned, but he thought that
at the next election, if the case were well presented, the opposing
candidates would find " on the whole it will be better for them
to reconsider their views."   He considered an " instalment " of
Women's Suffrage, such as the Conciliation Bill, would be worse
than nothing; he desired a wider measure.   Mrs. Fawcett replied
that the movement had made a tremendous advance; there were
twenty Suffragists to-day for every one a few years before.   With
a touch of her dry humour, she pointed out that the Irish
Members of Parliament had not voted against the Conciliation
Bill in March because of the hatchet thrown by Mrs. Leigh the
previous July, as the Chancellor's account of affairs had inferred.

Sir Edward Grey, who was interviewed by the Northern
Men's Federation, in his constituency, was of opinion that the
movement had advanced.   In 1906 there had been no demand
from the country for Votes for Women.   Indeed the Prime
Minister's pledges were a register of the advance which the
movement had made.   He believed the way was now blocked
against any further enfranchisement of men till women were
included, but he too insisted that militancy had transformed
apathy to opposition.   Nothing could be done in this Parliament,
but if in the next Parliament there were an earnest majority in
support, he regarded it as absolutely certain that Votes for
Women would become law.

The Trade Union Congress, with only seven dissentients, had
resolved :

" That this congress protests against the Prime Minister's failure
to redeem his repeated pledges to women, and calls upon the Parliamentary Committee to press for the immediate enactment of a
Government Reform Bill, which must include the enfranchisement
of women."

Now that the adult suffrage controversy was swept away, the
congress was whole-hearted in this intent.   On the other hand
the Labour Party Conference in the new year decided to support
the Government measure for the abolition of Plural Voting.   Keir
Hardie again urged his old policy of blocking this Bill, but

Macdonald and Henderson carried the day against him with their plea that in some constituencies the measure would turn the scale in favour of Labour candidates. When the Reform Bill had been withdrawn a year before, Asquith himself had said [1] that the Government thought it would be dishonourable to substitute this measure for the Reform Bill under which the women had been promised a free amendment; yet three months later the Government had introduced it, and now the Labour Party had given its assent. The W.S.P.U. attacked the Labour Party with renewed fury. It is true that had the vote of the conference gone the other way, the W.S.P.U. would have given the Labour Party no credit and no quarter. Christabel would have declared a vote against the Government on the single issue worthless, as she had done before. The National Union of Suffrage Societies had condemned the Government's introduction of the Plural Voting Bill as " discreditable," but it made no protest against the Labour Party's support of the measure. The National Union was supporting Labour candidates against the Government; perhaps Mrs. Fawcett thought the abolition of Plural Voting would assist her election policy. There was nothing heroic in her judgements; their infirmity was that they were redolent of the wire-puller's committee room. Her mistake in dealing with Ministers was always that she asked and expected too little from them; perhaps because she had been the wife of one of them. The Plural Voting Bill, which had seen the light of so many sessions, was again thrown out by the Lords, and never reached the Statute Book. Shortly after the Labour Conference decision, the N.U.W.S.S. invited Henderson to speak for them at the Albert Hall. The W.S.P.U. turned up in force to shout at him. Mrs. Fawcett,[2] in her memories of those years, has written : " For some reason never disclosed they [the Suffragettes] had a vendetta against Mr. Henderson." When the incident actually took place she must have been fully aware of the reason. In her account of the movement in the *Encyclopædia Britannica* she wrote : " The militants bitterly resented criticism and made organized efforts to prevent its expression by trying to break up meetings of the law-abiding Suffragists." The only explanation of these statements is that, years having dimmed the writer's memory, they were written without reference to documents, for the meetings of the non-militant Suffragists were never attacked, except when addressed by Members of Parliament forming the majority which kept the Government in power.

[1] January 27th, 1913.
[2] M. G. Fawcett. *What I Remember.* 1924.

CHAPTER IV

THE year 1914 opened with an important leading article of the *Manchester Guardian*:

" What is needed is that a Liberal Government should be formed with a clear intimation that Women's Suffrage will be part of its programme. And the sooner that happens the better for Liberalism. There is nothing which would so quicken its life."

This observation was the more striking to those who knew that before the days of militancy a deputation of the W.S.P.U. had waited upon the editor requesting publicity for Women's Suffrage, and had been told: " It is the settled policy of the *Manchester Guardian* to ignore the question."

A cherished project of mine was the Suffrage School, held for one week in Bow, one week in Kensington (by co-operation with Elsa Daglish and the Kensington W.S.P.U.), at which lectures were given on many questions constantly referred to at large on Suffrage platforms: the history of the franchise; the history of the women's movement; the history of trade union legislation; the industrial position of women; the legal disabilities of women; sex teaching for mothers and in relation to child life and the schools. Theodora Bonwick, to whose memory the National Union of Teachers has since erected a School Journey Hostel, was one of the teachers. One of the students was a young clerk, whom Zelie Emerson urged me to engage as my secretary. Efficient and earnest, she was the first of what presently became a large office staff. The East London Federation had now some five or six full time paid organizers. More than twice that number of whole, or almost whole, time volunteers, besides hundreds of part time volunteer workers, and masses of ardent supporters, the bulk of the population indeed in certain districts, and friends in all parts of the country. Our organizers were paid 30s. weekly, not as a wage, but a subsistence allowance, to make it possible for the recipient to give her time to the Cause; we did not desire to make a profession of Suffrage work. Yet many of the women about us were working in factories for from 11s. to 15s. per week. The Post Office then employed girl telephonists at a wage of 5s. a week, with an annual increase of 1s.! The Trade Board for the sugar, preserving, and confectionery trades fixed minimum rates (which tended to be the average) of 13s. a week for women, 26s. for men; and no Trade Board had yet given more than 13s. 6d. a week to adult women. Women's wages in the clothing trades averaged weekly 13s. 6d., under public bodies 14s. 6d.; in cap-making, 10s. to 12s.; in brush-making, 8s. to 9s.; in fancy leather and bag trades, 12s. to 14s.; and in light iron castings, 10s. The women textile operatives, the highest paid of the factory workers, earned an average full time wage of 15s. 9d. per week, whilst girls under eighteen in millinery and clothing workshops often earned less than 3s. for a full week's work. Women wage earners were indeed in evil case.

At the close of the Suffrage School in Bow we held a meeting in the King's Hall, Covent Garden, on January 4th. I was staying at the house of some members in the Old Ford Road. We thought the detectives had not discovered my whereabouts, but they were concealed in the inevitable public-house almost opposite. The night before the meeting I left the house with Norah Smyth, intending to walk to Hackney by Grove Road, which passes through a section of Victoria Park, but is separated from it by high railings on either side. On reaching the other side of the park I was accosted by two detectives, who had followed us unobserved. Without a word I took to my heels and ran back towards the Old Ford Road, where I knew every door would be opened to give me shelter. They were big, heavy men, not good at running; I might have eluded them, but the button came off my shoe and caused me to run lamely. They caught me while I was still between the park railings, and dragged me back into Hackney. A crowd collected, sympathetic to me, menacing towards the two big men dragging me along. I was astonished that the people apparently took them for " White Slave " traffickers, of whom there was much talk at the time, romances concerning them appearing at the cinemas. The narrow width of Victoria Park had cut off Hackney from us as though it were another country; whilst all adjoining Bow was with us, here I was unknown. There was no time to explain; I simply begged the crowd to help me into a shop, hoping that in some way I should be able to get free and take refuge there. As the struggle began, a uniformed constable pushed his way into the crowd. " Go with him, my dear; you'll be all right with *him*! " the women kindly urged me. At that moment an empty laundry cart was driving past: in a trice the detectives had stopped it and flung me in. They ordered the driver to take them to the police station and obtained a taxi for Holloway.   I remained there till January 10th, decidedly piqued at having been caught so easily.

For some time messages had been reaching me that Mrs. Pankhurst and Christabel desired to see me in Paris.   I was loath to go, for as the ports were watched I was likely to be arrested on embarking, and I was unwilling to expend my energies in another hunger and thirst strike except as the price of a rousing struggle.   I realized that, like so many others, I was to be given the *congé*.   In November Elsa Dalglish had been persuaded at Lincoln's Inn House that her duty was to resign the honorary financial secretaryship of the East London Federation, and to " concentrate " on the honorary secretaryship of the Kensington W.S.P.U.[1] as the East End work was on " wrong lines."   I was unwilling to argue points of view, which I knew would not be reconciled, unless by the development of events.   I was anxious to avoid a rupture in the full impact of our struggle with the Government, and, as far as possible, to stand together in the fight.   Yet so insistent were the messages from Paris, that a few days after my release, and as soon as the welcome meetings were over, I agreed to go.   The arrangements for the journey were made by Lincoln's Inn House.   I was smuggled into a car and driven to Harwich.   I insisted that Nora Smyth, who had become financial secretary of the Federation, should go with me to represent our members.   My uncle, Herbert Goulden, always kind and thoughtful, to my surprise appeared to accompany me to the boat.   He knew, I suppose, the reason for which I was summoned to Paris, though we did not discuss it.   I was miserably ill in body, and distressed by the reason of my journey.   A small private cabin had been booked for us in an assumed name.   I reached it without mishap, but my uncle came down to tell us that detectives were on the boat.   So ill that I almost wished I might die, I was tortured throughout the night by the thought that I should be seized on emerging from the cabin, and dragged back on the return voyage next morning.   The detectives, however, were not seeking me, but on the trail of diamond thieves, and I landed at the Hook of Holland unmolested.   The journey, which in other circumstances would have been delightful, seemed only excessively tiring.

As soon as we reached Paris the business was opened. Christabel, nursing a tiny Pomeranian dog, announced that the East London Federation of the W.S.P.U. must become a separate

---

[1] I had been honorary secretary of the Kensington W.S.P.U. for a short time and had asked Elsa Dalglish to take the position, thinking that we could thus link up our popular campaign work from East to West.

organization; the *Suffragette* would announce this, and unless we immediately chose to adopt one for ourselves, a new name would be given to us. Norah Smyth was known both to Christabel and Mrs. Pankhurst. She had served as unpaid chauffeur to Mrs. Pankhurst; she had been the companion of Helen Craggs at Newnham, and had assisted the W.S.P.U. headquarters in other ways. Dr. Ethel Smyth said of her to Mrs. Pankhurst in my hearing: "She is just the class we want." She happened, in fact, to belong to a distant branch of Ethel Smyth's own family. Having experienced both aspects, she had chosen to work with the East London Federation as the branch of the movement which appealed to her as most useful. Like me, she desired to avoid a breach. Dogged in her fidelities, and by temperament unable to express herself under emotion, she was silent. I said she had accompanied me to represent our members and to report to them. Therefore she should be told the reason for our expulsion. Christabel replied that I had spoken at Lansbury's Larkin release meeting, which was contrary to W.S.P.U. policy. Lansbury was a good fellow, of course, but his motto was: "Let them all come!" The W.S.P.U. did not want to be "mixed up with him." She added: "You have a democratic constitution for your Federation; we do not agree with that." Moreover, she urged, a working women's movement was of no value: working women were the weakest portion of the sex: how could it be otherwise? Their lives were too hard, their education too meagre to equip them for the contest. "Surely it is a mistake to use the weakest for the struggle! We want picked women, the very strongest and most intelligent!" She turned to me. "You have your own ideas. We do not want that; we want all our women to take their instructions and walk in step like an army!" Too tired, too ill to argue, I made no reply. I was oppressed by a sense of tragedy, grieved by her ruthlessness. Her glorification of autocracy seemed to me remote indeed from the struggle we were waging, the grim fight even now proceeding in the cells. I thought of many others who had been thrust aside for some minor difference.

We drove in the Bois; Christabel with the small dog on her arm, I struggling against headache and weakness, Mrs. Pankhurst blanched and emaciated.

We returned to our conversations. "Moreover," urged Christabel, "your Federation appeals for funds; people think it is all part of the same thing. You get donations which might come to us." "That is what *we* say!" Norah Smyth interposed at last; it was a practical point of interest to the financial secretary. "We know people have sent money to Lincoln's Inn House on account of our big demonstrations, for which we have the bill to pay!" "How much do you want? What would you think a suitable income for your Federation? You can't need much in your simple way!" Christabel challenged her. "All we can raise for our work, like you!" "Suppose I were to say we would allow you something," Mrs. Pankhurst interposed; she was obviously distressed by the discussion. "Would you——?" "Oh, no; we can't have that!" Christabel was emphatic. "It must be a clean cut!" So it went on. "As you will then," I answered at last.

Afterwards, when we were alone together, Christabel said that sometimes we should meet, "not as Suffragettes, but as sisters." To me the words seemed meaningless; we had no life apart from the movement. I felt bruised, as one does, when fighting the foe without, one is struck by the friend within. My mind was thronged with the memories of our childhood: the little heads clustering at the window in Green Hayes; her pink cheeks and the young green shoots in the spring in Russell Square; my father's voice: "You are the four pillars of my house!"

The Federation was unaltered. We had defended the W.S.P.U. against outside attack; we still would do so. Our place in the Union had been merely nominal: indeed the local unions were united by no tie of organization, only by sympathy and support to Lincoln's Inn House. There was no real change, yet the sadness remained. Any resentment I might otherwise have felt, then and always, was allayed by commiseration for Christabel: how terrible to be away over there, giving the orders leading to imprisonment and torture for other women! I would not take that part. A thousand times easier to be in the struggle and share its anguish. I knew the call of a compelling conscience, stronger than all the shrinking of unwilling impulses, dominating the whole being, permitting no reprieve from its dictates. Under that force I believed she, too, was acting. When the War came I was glad of the "clean cut" she had insisted upon.

Norah Smyth and I left Paris immediately. She had arranged with the others that we should travel by a circuitous route through Normandy, taking some days for the journey to give me time to regain strength before running the risk of arrest on touching English soil. I left it all to her. Provided with disguises procured on the journey, we landed unrecognized at Southampton, and were motored to London by a man supporter accustomed to carry Christabel's visitors. He had been notified by her messengers where to meet us in the town. On reaching London we at once summoned a general meeting of the Federation. The members at first declared they would not be "thrown out" of the W.S.P.U., nor would they agree to a change of name. I persuaded them at last that refusal would open the door to acrimonious discussions, which would hinder our work and deflect attention from the Cause. The name of our organization was then debated. The East London Federation of the Suffragettes was suggested by someone, and at once accepted with enthusiasm. I took no part in the decision. Our colours were to be the old purple, white and green, with the addition of red—no change, as a matter of fact, for we had already adopted the red caps of liberty. Mrs. Pankhurst, annoyed by our choice of name, hastened down to the East End to expostulate; she probably anticipated objections from Paris. "*We* are the Suffragettes! that is the name *we* are always known by," she protested, "and there will be the same confusion as before!" I told her the members had decided it, and I would not interfere.

When the W.S.P.U. sent out a brief announcement of the separation, the newspapers jumped to the conclusion that a split had occurred, because the W.S.P.U. had resolved on a truce from militancy, which I had refused to accept. The *Daily News* observed exultantly:

"There could scarcely be a more crushing condemnation of militancy than its formal abandonment by all save one of its inventors and patentees."

The W.S.P.U. protested:

"There is no change in the policy of the W.S.P.U. . . . The statement already issued by the Union is a recognition of the fact which for a long time has existed—viz., that Miss Sylvia Pankhurst prefers to work on her own account and independently."

Christabel followed this up with a letter over her own signature:

"The true position is that since the W.S.P.U. does not exist for the mere purpose of propaganda, but is a fighting organization, it must have only one policy, one programme and one command. The W.S.P.U. policy and the programme are framed, and the word of command is given by Mrs. Pankhurst and myself. From the very beginning of the militant movement this has been the case. Consequently those who wish to give an independent lead, or to carry out either a programme or a policy which differs from those laid down by the W.S.P.U., must necessarily have an independent organization of their own."

The subject was further developed in the *Suffragette*, coupled with a reference to a new organization for men and women, " The United Suffragists,"[1] which had just been formed, and in which it had been announced that militants and non-militants were to join hands: " Now that something like fifty Suffrage organizations have come into existence those who are connected with the W.S.P.U. . . . are determined not to have their energies and subscriptions divided and sub-divided." The attitude which led to such expulsions as my own and the denunciation of old supporters like Zangwill was upheld:

" As victory grows nearer and the fight, therefore, grows sterner, distinctions have to be drawn and a stringency displayed which were less needful in the early days of the militant movement . . . the course becomes specially dangerous and careful piloting is needed. . . . The Suffragettes as the fighting force—the advance guard—necessarily stand alone. Theirs is a glorious isolation—the splendour of independent strength."

In the following issue appeared a warning against " Liberal intrigue ":

" It is as the result of Liberal intrigue and inner weakness that the Labour Party has come to naught and is to-day powerless and despised. Here is a tragic end to twenty-five years of effort and sacrifice, generously spent by those who brought the Labour Party into being! "

Strange that the woman who wrote thus should depart absolutely from the Suffrage movement on the outbreak of war. Yet in those days she appeared inflexible in that one purpose. To me it seemed that her isolation in Paris was the main cause both of her growing intolerance and of her sudden retirement. Yet, withal, one must say: she was the true begetter of the militant movement, though others bore a greater share of the physical suffering of its travail, and the labour of

---

[1] Barbara Ayrton Gould, daughter of Hertha Ayrton the scientist, and step-sister-in-law to Israel Zangwill, was the honorary secretary. She had visited me before its formation, suggesting that she should join the East London Federation and become assistant treasurer or occupy some other office. I told her I had no doubt the Federation would welcome her, but she afterwards wrote that " there was a general desire " for a new organization of men and women and she was helping to form it. The United Suffragists mustered a large proportion of those who had been thrown out of the W.S.P.U., or had left it on account of recent developments. Emmeline Pethick Lawrence, Nevinson and Evelyn Sharp were members of its committee. Its long list of vice-presidents included William de Morgan, potter and novelist, who had become a subscriber to the W.S.P.U. in 1912, Bernard Shaw, George Lansbury, Israel Zangwill, Lady Olivier, whose husband later became a Member of the first Labour Government, Sir Harry Johnston, the explorer, Beatrice Harraden, St. John Ervine, Sir Ronald Ross, the Ranee of Sarawak and several well-known authors, physicians and ministers of religion.

many equally devoted workers maintained its life. Carrying the majority of the W.S.P.U. membership with her, she had travelled far from its starting point in the I.L.P. and her interest in the Women Textile Workers' Labour Representation Committee. Her early speeches had dealt almost entirely with the industrial status of women; her later utterances with the political tactics required, in her judgement, for winning the vote. She who had deprecated and shunned every mention of her sex, now hinged the greater part of her propaganda upon the supposed great prevalence of venereal diseases and the sex excesses of men. "Votes for women and chastity for men," became her favourite slogan, elaborated in articles in the *Suffragette* and a collection of these called *The Great Scourge*. She alleged that seventy-five to eighty per cent. of men become infected with gonorrhœa, and twenty to twenty-five per cent. with syphilis, insisting that "only an insignificant minority—twenty-five per cent. at most"—escaped infection by some form of venereal disease. Women were strongly warned against the dangers of marriage, and assured that large numbers of women were refusing it. The greater part, both of the serious and minor illnesses suffered by married women, including the vague delicacy called "poor health," she declared to be due to the husband having at some time contracted gonorrhœa. Childless marriages were attributed to the same cause. Syphilis she declared to be "the prime reason of a high infantile mortality." The mutilation of a "White Slave Traffic" Bill in 1912, the notorious Piccadilly flat case in 1913,[1] cases of assault on young children punished with leniency by the Courts, were seized upon, week by week, to illustrate the text that "Man is not the 'lord of creation,' but the exterminator of the species." The injuries of women in the sex relationship were now put forward as the main reason and basis of militancy. The tremendously advertised *Great Scourge* was on the whole well received. The *Medical World* cast some doubt upon its statistics, which had been largely culled from American writers:

"Were eighty per cent. of the male population infected with gonorrhœa, the state of the country would be too appalling to contemplate . . . but even if there is some exaggeration, the figures are far too high!"

[1] Queenie Gerald, charged with living on the immoral earnings of other women, was sentenced to three months' imprisonment on July 10th, 1913. Men prominent in social and political circles, whose names were kept out of the case, were said to be frequenters of the brothel, which was alleged to be of luxurious type. Sadist practices were said to be carried on. The case created a tremendous sensation. Keir Hardie wrote a pamphlet on it, which was published by the National Labour Press.

The Royal Commission on Venereal Diseases, appointed in 1913, reported in 1915 a prevalence of such diseases which was certainly serious, but very much smaller than that asserted in *The Great Scourge*. Sir William Osler placed syphilis as fourth amongst the "Killing Diseases,"[1] and the Commissioners estimated that not less than ten per cent. of the population in large cities was infected with syphilis, congenital or acquired. Thirty to fifty per cent. of sterility amongst women they attributed to gonorrhœa. Later researches suggest that even these estimates were exaggerated. Post mortem examinations of still-born infants by Holland and Lane Clayton showed 8·7 per cent. of syphilis. Other investigators found from eight to eighteen per cent. In the British Army in 1912 a strength of 107,582 men showed an average of 593 men incapacitated from venereal disease.

How exaggerated was the alarmist view of syphilis as the prime cause of the high infant death-rate has been revealed by the great reduction in infant mortality which has happily been secured. The establishment of mother and infant Clinics and Welfare Centres, and other social improvements, did much to reduce the then terribly high rate of infantile mortality. Our East London Federation was subsequently to bear a notable part in this work.

Apart from any intrinsic merit, a great advantage of *The Great Scourge* propaganda in W.S.P.U. eyes was that, like the vote itself, it cut across the usual line of Party programmes. It did not offend the sensitive class consciousness of those frail hot-house blooms, the Conservative supporters of Women's Suffrage, whom the W.S.P.U. was eager to encourage. By its sensational nature, this propaganda encouraged the fevered emotions, and sense of intolerable wrong, required to spur women to the more serious acts of destruction. Christabel was now, in effect, preaching the sex war deprecated and denied by the older Suffragists. Mr. Lawrence had often said he had thrown in his lot with the militant women in order that the Suffragette struggle might not become "a sex war." Not from the speeches of

---

[1] The death-rate per million of men over fifteen years of age from venereal diseases was given as follows:

I. Upper and middle classes	.	.	.	.	302
II. Intermediate between I and III	.	.	.	280
III. Skilled labour	.	.	.	.	264
IV. Intermediate between III and V	.	.	.	304
V. Unskilled labour	.	.	.	.	429
VI. Textile workers	.	.	.	.	186
VII. Miners	.	.	.	.	177
VIII. Agricultural labourers	.	.	.	.	108

Mrs. Pankhurst, who never lost her gift of sympathy with her audiences, but from the columns of the *Suffragette* the deduction was clear : women were purer, nobler and more courageous, men were an inferior body, greatly in need of purification; the W.S.P.U. being the chosen instrument capable of administering the purge. Masses of women, especially of the middle class, were affected by this attitude, even though they remained outside the ranks of the Union. The pendulum had swung far, indeed, from the womanly humility of Victorian times. No matter; it must right itself.

The propaganda for sexual purity made strong appeal to the clergy and social workers, brought by the nature of their work into close contact with the sad effects of prostitution and the sexual abuse of girl children. Mrs. Fawcett, always strictly temperate in her observations, testified to the fact that Votes for Women had made great advances amongst the clergy during the years 1913-14, the period in which the W.S.P.U. had shrieked this propaganda of " chastity for men " in every key of vehemence and excitement. A number of clergy were ardent supporters of the W.S.P.U., speaking from its platforms, contributing to its organ, hailing the militants as heroines and martyrs.

In the East End, with its miserable housing, its ill-paid casual employment and harsh privations bravely borne by masses of toilers, life wore another aspect. The yoke of poverty oppressing all, was a factor no one-sided propaganda could disregard. The women speakers who rose up from the slums were struggling, day in day out, with the ills which to others were merely hearsay. Sometimes a group of them went with me to the drawing-rooms of Kensington and Mayfair; their speeches made a startling impression upon those women of another world, to whom hard manual toil and the lack of necessaries were unknown. Many of the W.S.P.U. speakers came down to us as before : Mary Leigh, Amy Hicks, Theodora Bonwick, Mary Paterson, Mrs. Bouvier, that brave, persistent Russian, and many others; but it was from our own East End speakers that our movement took its life. There was wise, logical Charlotte Drake of Custom House, who, left an orphan with young brothers and sisters, had worked both as barmaid and sewing machinist, and who recorded in her clear memory incidents, curious, humorous and tragic, which stirred her East End audiences by their truth. Told with her brief, inimitable keenness, they would have made the fortune of a realistic novelist. " You ought to breed," was her first spoken greeting to me, when she came to my side as I was being carried to speak on a stretcher on release from one of my hunger strikes. Wife of a labourer, and mother of five children, she had read books on physiology in order to teach her four children. Melvina Walker was born in Jersey and had been a lady's maid; many a racy story could she tell of the insight into " High Life " she had gained in that capacity. For a long period she was one of the most popular open air speakers in any movement in London. She seemed to me like a woman of the French Revolution. I could imagine her on the barricades, waving the *bonnet rouge*, and urging on the fighters with impassioned cries. When she was in the full flood of her oratory, she appeared the very embodiment of toiling, famine-ridden, proletarian womanhood. So whimsical and erratic she was at times, in those early days, that I used to say to the others, as a joke : " When the revolution comes, my first duty will be to order the arrest of Mrs. Walker." Then I would set myself to straighten out the tangled troubles she had made for herself; little storms in a teacup, easily dispelled ! Mrs. Schlette, a sturdy old dame, well on in her sixties, came forward to make a maiden oration without hesitation, and soon was able to hold huge crowds for an hour and a half at a stretch. Mrs. Cressell, afterwards a Borough Councillor; Florence Buchan, a young girl discharged from a jam factory, the reason being given by the forewoman : " What do you want to kick up a disturbance of a night with the Suffragettes? "; Mrs. Pascoe, one of our prisoners, supporting by charing and home work a tubercular husband and an orphan boy she had adopted—but a few of the many who learnt to voice their claims.

I had scarcely returned from Paris when a by-election occurred in Poplar. We had already a permanent office and meeting room there in the East India Dock Road. In the small-hours of the morning, when, as we had learnt, the detectives had generally gone off duty for a rest, I was smuggled in. There I was able to work against the Right Hon. Sydney Buxton, speaking to women's meetings indoors, and to great open air crowds from the window each night. On the eve of the poll I marched openly in a procession and spoke at the dock gates. The crowds were enormous. Detectives were present in great force, but allowed themselves to be held by the people at a safe distance. It was thought inadvisable, no doubt, to break the heads of the electors the night before they went to vote.

When our severance from the W.S.P.U. was complete, Zelie Emerson came to me in her most coaxing way. " I want you to start a paper." The *Suffragette* gave little attention to the special needs of women such as ours. Obviously we required an organ, and now that we had been cut off from the W.S.P.U., we were free to publish one. Our funds, however, were inadequate to the venture. Some of the provincial I.L.P. branches produced small propaganda sheets, paid for by advertisements, and distributed freely from door to door. I agreed to venture on such a sheet. Zelie Emerson consulted printers, and obtained from them estimates and dummy sheets, headed by the title which had occurred to me : *The Woman's Banner*. Finally we chose a sheet much larger than I had contemplated : eighteen inches by twenty-four inches, folded to make a four-page paper. We calculated that each inch of advertisement would pay for itself and an inch of news-matter. The idea was delightfully simple, but the plan did not work. Zelie secured only three inches of advertisement. At last she begged me to produce a specimen advance number, in order that she might have something better than a mere dummy to show. Nothing daunted, I agreed, and in the excitement of going to press, Zelie secured some large advertisements of Neave's Food and Lipton's cocoa to run for three months, her only success in the advertisement line. The paper was emphatically not an advertising medium. The local shopkeepers assured us that they never advertised, which was generally true. Central London firms would have nothing to say to us. A general meeting of the Federation was called to approve the scheme and select a title for the new paper. I think it was Mary Paterson who suggested the "Workers' Dreadnought." It would not have been my choice, but the members generally acclaimed it, and I fell in with their view. I wished it had been "The Workers' Mate," a name which occurred to me later. "Mate" was a favourite term of address with our people in the East End, and to my mind a most genial and sympathetic one. With the thrifty instinct of careful working-class mothers, our members insisted that the paper should be sold, not given away. We compromised by the decision that it should be sold during the first four days after publication, the copies left over being distributed from house to house in the latter part of the week. The price was a halfpenny, other propaganda sheets in those days being usually a penny. The advance number of eight pages was published on March 8th, the first regular issue on March 21st, 1914. Twenty thousand copies were published weekly until after the commencement of the War, when, at the end of August, owing to the rising cost of paper, the issue was cut down to the actual sales. The *Dreadnought*, which had grown meanwhile in both size and sales circulation, continued until July, 1924. It was my earnest desire that it should be a medium through which working women, however unlettered, might express themselves, and find their interests defended. I took infinite pains in correcting and arranging their manuscripts, endeavouring to preserve the spirit and unsophisticated freshness of the original. I wanted the paper to be as far as possible written from life; no dry arguments, but a vivid presentment of things as they are, arguing always from the particular, with all its human features, to the general principle. No case of hardship came its way but the *Dreadnought* was eager to give it publicity, and if possible to muster help for its alleviation. How great was the need it sought to meet, how sure its appeal, could be measured by the response. From all over the East End, and much further afield, people in dispute with, or suffering under employers, landlords, insurance agents, Government departments, local authorities, hospitals and asylums, lawyers, and railway companies brought their difficulties for publicity and solution. The brother of a young girl charged with infanticide wrote to us giving vital facts not brought out when she was committed for trial. We sent them to the proper quarters. Even a detective wrote to us in reply to Suffragette complaints against the staff of the Criminal Investigation Department, admitting and deploring the presence of some bad characters in the force, and giving instances of the evil wrought by them. Our volunteer working women reporters, when investigating conditions, produced far truer accounts than any Fleet Street journalist, for they knew what to ask and how to win the confidence of the sufferers. Many times we were threatened with libel actions. Only once was I persuaded to have recourse to a lawyer, and on that occasion we had to pay some £20. As a rule I replied that if I could be convinced we had published an untruth, I would willingly apologize. Usually I was not convinced. It was on account of the risk, both of libel action and Government prosecution, that the paper was vested in me, not in the committee of the Federation. This gave me a freedom as editor which I should have hesitated to exercise had there been risk of action against others. To me the *Dreadnought* was a heavy burden, for upon me fell the responsibility of collecting in donations whatever was lacking to finance[1] it. It impoverished me by greatly reducing such time as I had for earning an income for my own needs. Moreover, I gladly gave the greater part of my earnings, whether from writing or for speaking for other organizations, to forward the work. Yet my personal needs were small; I rested only when incapable of working. Recreation outside my work never occurred to me. The paper was a tremendous interest, and

[1] Norah Smyth, as time passed, more and more shared this burden, gradually giving to the paper and the organization almost all she had inherited.

during the latter part of my year under the "Cat and Mouse" Act it probably saved my life, for I was compelled, in some measure at least, to husband my strength to produce it. There could be no sleep strike in prison till what I had set myself to write for the *Dreadnought* had been completed.

The first issue was printed by J. E. Francis at the Athenæum Press. We went to him because of his courage in printing the raided *Suffragette*. Ethel Moorhead, a Suffragette imprisoned for arson in Calton Gaol, Edinburgh, had just been released with double pneumonia, through food being poured into her lungs during forcible feeding. Apparently the prison officials had refused to undertake the feeding; hers was, in fact, the first case in Scotland, and Dr. Devon, one of the Scottish Prison Commissioners, had previously opposed forcible feeding, in his book, *The Criminal and the Community*.[1] A so-called expert from the criminal lunatic asylum in Perth had been imported for the operation, accompanied by a male warder, who, according to the prisoner, put hot wires into her ear, apparently to lessen her resistance while she was on the operating table. She was fed from Saturday till Tuesday, when the food entered the lungs, and was released on Wednesday in a dangerous condition. Her statement was published two days before the *Dreadnought* was printed. I desired to republish it. Francis passed the proofs of the paper, but after Emily Dyce Sharp, my sub-editor, had left the press he replaced the Moorhead statement by some uncorrected over-matter, and sent me by post a letter, which I received after the paper was printed, stating that he had expunged the statement because the Government had not had time to reply to it. I was wounded to the quick by his action, feeling it a gross lack of solidarity towards a fellow prisoner to ignore her statement in our paper. I immediately removed the paper to an East End printer, telling Mr. Francis that I considered he had acted dishonourably towards us. Nevertheless, he generously consented to print the paper again some years later when all other printers were afraid. I have no doubt his intention was to exercise a wise discretion for the sake of all concerned.

On February 24th we held a meeting from the window in Ford Road, and afterwards eighty recruits to the "People's Army" were drilled by Norah Smyth and four squad captains. The demonstration ended with cheers. Three evenings later an attempt was made to repeat the performance. The police appeared in large numbers and broke up the ranks. The squads

---

[1] "It certainly was indiscreet. . . . It is one thing to place the liberties of men, and another thing altogether to place their lives in the hands of officials."

moved up the street and continued their drill. After a time they came down the street, running with linked arms. The police deliberately put themselves in the way so that the runners collided with them. When she dismissed the ranks Norah Smyth was arrested and charged with kicking a policeman. She was ordered to pay £15 or go to prison for a month; she chose imprisonment, but her sister paid her fine, writing her that she was " sorry for the poor policeman."

No militant movement can afford to stand still. In prison and out, new tactics were my constant preoccupation. It was generally when I was torn from the rush of activity to the quietude of the cell that they were conceived. The " no vote no rent" strike occurred to me in the autumn of 1913. It appealed to me intensely as an action which would develop the solidarity of the people. I had dreams of a great re-housing of the East End population, not an impossibility, given a rousing of the public conscience, though a costly project it must be admitted. By a replanning of the area, the same number of people might obviously be accommodated under tremendously improved conditions; not in cheerless barracks, but in houses with gardens, with a communal nursery and playground for groups of families, central heating for blocks of streets, turned on and off at will in each room, and other amenities, the thought of which made so strong an appeal to me, that I had difficulty at times in restraining myself from attempting the inauguration of a campaign for them, then and there. I did so, for I was convinced that the appropriate time for this and other great ventures would be after the winning of the vote. A huge rent strike, or the threat of it, might be the precursor of a national effort for the re-housing of the East End. In the meantime, it might be of overwhelming importance in the franchise struggle. It was an instrument which would arouse consternation in the Government and the well-to-do. Already I knew that the turbulence of East London was causing anxiety in official circles. Once started, the " no rent" strike might swiftly become irresistible, gathering uncounted thousands, spreading by example from district to district, till a crisis were reached. The " People's Army," reinforced from every rent strike household, would prevent evictions. Moreover, if the strike were large, there could be no evictions, for no alternative accommodation could be found. Many successful rent strikes had already taken place in this country and others, occasioned by some sudden increase of rent or other grievance. Some of them even took place while our propaganda for the " no vote no rent" strike was in progress. We announced that the strike should not begin till a formidable number of pledges to join it had been received. The pledges came in slowly. A house-to-house canvass revealed the deep-rooted fear amongst the women of "losing the home." That calamity had befallen most of them at some time through illness, unemployment or trades disputes. The risk of it was so terrible as only to be faced in some desperate crisis. I saw that whilst we might continue to propagate the idea, it could only be realized as the result of some crisis. Later on, in the first weeks of the War, I saw the rent strike break out, not for the vote, but from sheer force of economic pressure. Across a neighbouring street was suspended a strip of calico, roughly lettered:

"Please, landlord, don't be offended, don't come for the rent till the War is ended."

Owing to the immediate rise in prices (afterwards controlled), the sudden stoppage of many forms of employment, the calling up of Reservists and the tardy coming of separation allowances, the rent strike was rapidly spreading. It ceased when the first acute economic pressure was mitigated.

The hour was not yet ripe for the rent strike; we could not rest on our oars, but must press forward with other demonstrations.

Just as the Men's League for Women's Suffrage, the Men's Political Union and the Men's Federation had been formed to help the W.S.P.U. at successive stages, there sprang up, quite spontaneously and without any suggestion from us, two men's societies in the East End: the Rebels' Social and Political Union and the East London Men's Society. One of these men's societies had engaged Trafalgar Square for March 8th on our behalf because the police had refused it to us. The advance number of the *Dreadnought* made its first appearance that day. Determined to be present, I escaped the detectives in the East End, and made my way to Appendrodt's restaurant, at the Trafalgar Square end of the Strand, hoping to rush thence into the East End procession. As the marchers approached, only the rear band was playing, the East London Cowboys' Drum and Fife Band, a group of enthusiastic lads in bizarre costume, who now joined all our processions (what a rabble the smart people must have thought us!). I ran out when I heard the sound. Too late! The tail of the crowd had already passed the shop. A detective grasped my arm, shouting: "Seize this woman!" A dozen more sprang at me. "Friends!" I called as they seized me. Policemen closed round on all sides. Mounted men galloped to their aid. The people came running back at my cry. The horsemen turned to repel them, and the crowd of detectives rushed me towards Charing Cross, with policemen on horse and foot as a body-guard around them. "Get her on a 'bus! Get her on a 'bus!" detectives shouted. A 'bus was just starting. They tried to drag me on. The conductor barred the way with his arm and thrust them back: "No, no! You shan't get her on here! I won't help you to take her!" I blessed him inwardly for his words. Truly indeed, the workers were with us. An Inspector hailed a taxi standing empty, but some of the men from the procession, who had managed to get ahead of us, persuaded him to drive on: brave fellow; he might have endangered his licence. They dragged me to another taxi. There was a struggle around it; a woman had reached the cab and clung to the radiator. I was thrown down on to the step of the cab and hauled in head foremost. "This will have saved a great deal of trouble and many broken heads," a detective told me. "It is not all over yet," I replied. I was right; the people set off for Downing Street, opposed by police in extraordinary numbers, and curiously enough, accompanied by a fire engine. The horsemen finally drove the crowd back to Trafalgar Square. Five women and five men were arrested. "Half Scotland Yard," said the Magistrate irately, when they were brought before him, "had turned out to keep a lot of desperadoes in order!" The famous "Saturday nights" and heavy sticks taken from the people were produced in Court and photographs of them appeared in the Press.

So I was back in Holloway again. Mrs. Pankhurst followed me there in two days' time. I was unaware of it. I did not see or hear of her in any of these imprisonments, though we were often inside together.

Soon after I had left her in Paris she returned to London unobserved. An announcement was then sent to the Press that she had taken up her residence at 2 Campden Hill Square, W. (the home of the Brackenburys) and would speak from the window on February 8th. The "women's body-guard," carrying small Indian clubs, was there to protect her. After the meeting the body-guard rushed out escorting a veiled woman. The police fought to seize her. In the struggle she was flung to the ground and received a blow on the head. The body-guard said she was deliberately struck by a policeman; the police protested that she was accidentally hit by one of the clubs of the body-guard. The veiled woman turned out to be a certain Mrs. F. E. Smith, Mrs. Pankhurst having escaped in the meantime. A few days later Mrs. Pankhurst spoke from the house of Dr. Schutze in Glebe Place, Chelsea, and escaped in the same manner.

On March 9th she was billed to speak in the St. Andrew's Hall, Glasgow. She succeeded in reaching the platform and spoke in the midst of the "body-guard." The platform was draped with barbed wire, ingeniously hidden by ivy, on which the police tore their hands in attempting to storm the platform. Buckets of water were emptied upon them and flower-pots thrown. A woman kept some of them at bay for a while by firing blank shots from a revolver. Under cover of the struggle, an attempt was made to hurry Mrs. Pankhurst away at the side, but detectives seized her and dragged her out with much violence. In conveying her to the police station they forced her on to the floor of the cab amongst their feet, refusing her a seat with the gibe: "You are only a prisoner!" The scenes aroused great excitement. Crowds assembled outside the police station. Next day she was taken by motor to a small Lanarkshire station, where the London express was stopped to take her in. Some of the faithful body-guard, watching the trains at Carlisle, discovered the carriage in which she was travelling. They greeted her at every halt, and finally one of them was permitted to sit with her for a few moments. So loudly had her little body-guard been advertised that the police again took extraordinary precautions against it, and a posse of police was stationed at Holloway to repel any possible attack as she was taken in. The scrimmages to avoid arrest were hard enough for younger women; they were over strenuous indeed for Mrs. Pankhurst. The manner of her arrest and the violence done to her aroused protests in Glasgow, which reverberated for many weeks. There were deputations to the Magistrates and City Council.

She and I were both released on March 14th. As always, there were pickets at the prison gates; and, as always, the East End stalwarts had marched those six long miles to circle the prison with cheering and song, setting out for the long march homeward at half-past eleven at night. Bruised and shocked by her Glasgow experience, Mrs. Pankhurst made no further public appearance till May 21st. She journeyed in secret to East Fife to oppose the Prime Minister when he came forward to stand for re-election as Minister for War when the officers at the Curragh threatened resignation in support of Ulster. Her journey was vain, for Asquith was returned unopposed. She had been announced to speak during the teachers' conference at Lowestoft, but Annie Kenney emerged from a long seclusion to take her place there, arriving and leaving the hall by successful strategy.

Immediately on release I was carried to great East End welcome meetings on a stretcher. In prison I had planned that we should march to Westminster Abbey to pray for the vote on "Mothering Sunday," March 22nd. I wrote to the Dean, explaining our intention, and asking that the service might be adapted to the occasion. To me the act was symbolic: our voice must be heard in every place. I had made no recovery since the last imprisonment. The news that I was more ill than usual had travelled amongst our members. The thought of going to the Abbey to pray had conjured up visions of death in their minds. At the time of starting, they crowded in painful anxiety about the door of the little house in Ford Road. All the people of the neighbouring streets were out. The thoroughfare was jammed from wall to wall with human beings. A spinal chair had been borrowed for me from the Cripples' Institute, but the dozens of protecting hands stretched out to protect it from the hostile forces, whose appearance all anticipated with horror, made so crushing a weight on the frail thing that the wheels were immediately buckled.

We could not start. Partridge, the blacksmith, a Labour Councillor and a good friend to us, was fetched from the Old Ford Road. He straightened the wheels with his strong hands, but again the same thing happened! "Carry her! Carry her!" hundreds of voices shouted. Men came forward and hoisted the carriage on their shoulders. On we went, with that ardent rebel, the Rev. C. A. Wills, in his surplice, marching on ahead, roads and pavements thronged, and windows crowded by those who could not walk. We passed a taxi, drawn up at the side of the "Roman," with a detective sitting inside; but his companions remained in the public-houses; we were too many for them that day. At Gardner's Corner we met the Poplar contingent; at the Bank the Men's Federation and the Welsh Suffragists with their scarlet dragons. At Ludgate Circus I turned to see the crowd coming down Ludgate Hill; not a procession with numbered ranks, as of old, but a swarm covering roads and pavements as far as the eye could reach. For some reason the demonstration was greatly minimized by the Press.

When we neared the Abbey the police asked Wills to lead the procession to the side entrance by St. Margaret's Church, but as we approached there the Abbey gates were shut in our face. Wills sent in a message of protest. "The Abbey is full," came the reply. "May we enter the gates and pray in the yard?" he asked. The answer was an emphatic "No." "Then we will pray where we stand," he said, and proceeded with that office. Two policemen stepped up; the custodian desired that the clergyman would interview him within. "Tell him to come outside. I have commenced the service!" Parson Wills rebuked him, sternly. . . .

All pain had left me. The air seemed intensely restful and

still. When my turn came I spoke without effort, feeling that the people and I were united in a great triumph of love. . . .

I was lifted into a motor ambulance my thoughtful friends had provided unknown to me. Now that the day was over, how ill I was! All the way in the spinal carriage the swaying springs had made me sick, so sick! I had borne it then, as occasion compelled. Now I could only hide my face and long for this hour to pass.

. . . .

The Poplar Borough Council had resolved that the public halls should not be let for Votes for Women meetings, but the Rebels' Social and Political Union engaged the hall for a social evening, in order that I might speak. The Council retorted by a new resolution, exacting from all suffrage societies, and organizations believed to be in sympathy with Suffragettes, a pledge that militancy would not be advocated in the public halls, and no one wanted by the police would be permitted to speak. This resolution was not by any means applied to the Conservatives, who at this time were preparing a great Hyde Park demonstration in support of Ulster militancy, and organizing for it in Bow and everywhere. Deputations from our Federation and the Trade Union and Socialist organizations waited upon the Council to protest.

The matter was set down for debate on March 27th, the Council meeting being open to the public. The members had been asked to be present to show their interest. That was all I knew of it. Zelie Emerson commanded the occasion in her own audacious way. Lansbury championed the free use of the halls to almost empty benches. Aldermen and Councillors trooped in to closure the case by voting next business. Then the storm burst. Cries of " Shame! " The shooting of pop-guns, the throwing of bags of flour, blue powder and more solid missiles began the fray. The barrier between the public and the Councillors was broken down by a rush of women. The Councillors engaged in a hand-to-hand conflict to force them back. Whilst missiles still fell from the gallery, wild women dashed round the room, over-turning ink-pots and tearing agenda papers, seizing the Councillors' chairs as weapons of defence. When attacked, some brandished " Saturday nights " of knotted rope. Alderman Bussy, a well-known opponent, grappled with a couple of women. Councillor Thorne, another Anti, was surrounded by several more. The police were sent for, but refused to enter the building. At last the Mayor adjourned the Council for a quarter of an hour. The Labour members, then a minority, remained in the chamber; the others retired with clothes besmirched. Zelie Emerson presided in the seat of the Mayor, calling on Amy Hicks to address the company. Zelie was herself holding forth when the Councillors returned, and continued her remarks unconcernedly till she had finished what she had to say.

When the Mayor was in his chair again, the Council carried a motion excluding the public from the Council meetings for three months. George Lansbury declared the motion was out of order, and on the Mayor's refusal to hear him, swept to the floor the Town Clerk's books and papers, and all the documents he could lay hands on, to the accompaniment of delighted laughter and cheers from the Suffragettes. The meeting broke up in confusion, the Mayor scuttling out holding up his robes. " This meeting will go down in history ! " an attendant confided to Zelie Emerson, who departed triumphant, cheeks flushed and black eyes shining.

" Don't be cross ! " she said with a modest smile when she and a dozen others returned to tell me the news. I was startled indeed, but perforce must laugh. " And Christabel called them ' the weakest ! ' " said Norah Smyth.

CHAPTER V

ON Sunday, April 5th, we held a great procession from Canning Town to Victoria Park, which passed down Ford Road and carried me with it in a long chair. The crowds were immense, and there was no attempt at arrest.

A few days later a Hungarian journalist, Joseph Szebenyei, interviewed me for a Hungarian newspaper. He wrote an article for the *Dreadnought*, telling that at the International Women's Suffrage Congress in Budapest the previous summer, harsh speeches had been delivered against Suffragette militancy. Yet he had never heard a name cheered as those women had cheered the name of Pankhurst. "It is the old story," he wrote, " of the mother being turned out of the house, whilst the children, with weeping and crying, run after her to kiss the folds of her dress." His picturesque phrase indicated with truth that the Suffrage movement of the world had been stimulated by Suffragette militancy. He urged that I should lecture in Hungary. The proposal seemed fantastic, but Zelie Emerson and he conspired to arrange an invitation from a well-known London agency for me to lecture in Budapest, Vienna, Dresden, Berlin and Paris. My expenses were to be paid, and I was to receive a proportion of the proceeds, which would cover Zelie's expenses as my companion on the journey. Easter was at hand, and police vigilance was always relaxed on the eve of a holiday. I should probably be able to get away undetected. What turned the scale with me in favour of going was that Szebenyei had told me rent strikes and market riots were common in Budapest. I fancied I might learn something of value to our own struggle from such popular movements. Moreover there would be a wealth of other interesting matter to be recorded for *Dreadnought* readers. I agreed to go, on condition that Paris should be omitted from the programme, lest anything I might say should jeopardize Christabel's position there as a political refugee. Brussels was substituted. In the midst of the tour, the German police refused to permit the Berlin and Dresden meetings. To make good this loss, the agency again urged me to take a meeting in Paris, but I refused.

As we had hoped, our disguises escaped detection. Arriving in Paris, with some hours to spare, we called on Christabel at her flat in the Avenue Grande Armée. Her maid, Marthe, opened the door and almost collapsed as I entered; then she raised her arms and screamed in excitement and delight. A film of the procession to the Abbey had just been shown in the Paris cinemas, and Marthe had recognized me; having shed my disguise, I was wearing, as it happened, the clothes I had worn on " Mothering " Sunday. " Miss Richards " was out, but every moment expected. Marthe implored us to wait, and brought in the evening meal, disappointed that we only consented to take a plate of soup, and treating me with embarrassing homage. She was evidently unaware of my relationship to her employer, for when my sister presently arrived, we heard her ecstatically exclaiming: " La dame! La dame Anglaise du cinema! " and pouring forth her tale that the English Suffragette she had seen on the films was actually within. The cold monosyllable which met her transports caused the good creature to retire discomforted. My sister's greeting to us was distant and preoccupied. We had committed an indiscretion perhaps by this intrusion. An impassable wall had risen between us. My explanation of our journey evoked no interest. The brows of the warm-hearted, impulsive little Emerson were ominously ruffled. I saw by the curve of her lip that some barbed shaft was about to issue. Our train left at midnight, yet I affected to discover we had no time to linger another moment, and hurried her away.

We travelled straight through to Budapest for the first meeting, both struggling on the border-line of falling incapably ill; each endeavouring to keep cheerful for the sake of the other. Though I was temporarily the weaker, the afflictions of my companion were the graver. When the morning found us in Hungary, our spirits rose. It was splendid, after all, to be free, and in this wide country! We were passing through a vast plain, apparently flat as a table, every inch of it cultivated; the deep green of winter wheat, the lately sown land, and the newly ploughed, marked off with precision, as though by a ruler. There were no hedgerows; the furrows ran right down to the edge of the narrow white roads. In every direction were signs of great labour, though the workers were few; now and then some women in blue and red garments, weeding and hoeing, mere mites in the huge surroundings, or a long train of carts, laden with brush-wood, drawn by slow oxen. Occasionally the train stopped at a little station, thronged with men in soft felt hats, peasant women in wide pleated skirts, soldiers with silver cockades, men selling beer and boys water, a penny a glass. The train filled. The passengers were of two distinct types: the bourgeois, inclining to stoutness, something Eastern displaying itself in the full lips and the large, dark, almost motionless eyes; and the peasants, like the people who work on the land all over Europe, their eyes deeper and sadder than those others, their sunburnt features worn and refined.

The courier from the lecture agency had told no one the hour of our arrival, but one enterprising journalist discovered us, having met every train for a couple of days. That first evening, and a great part of our whole brief stay in Budapest, was occupied with the Pressmen. Next morning was Easter Sunday: we entered the Basilica, gorgeous with bronze and gold, its air heavy with incense, and the bells calling to the populace outside, making a strange, musical echoing within. It was crowded with people of all classes, waiting for the great Mass. A preacher was declaiming against Socialism and Liberal ideas. We took a carriage, and drove through the great streets, with their avenues of trees and splendid buildings domed and turreted, with roofs of coloured tiles and gilded spires. Everywhere was a gay throng; fashionable people in clothes of Vienna cut, peasants in flowered shawls and bodices with pleated skirts of every gorgeous hue. Returning to the hotel we found the proprietor of the principal film company waiting to arrange a picture of us, and presently the Hungarian Suffragists appeared to take us to the Corso, to be filmed with them selling their paper, *A Nö* (*The Woman*). Vilma Glucklich, Rosika Schwimmer, Adele Spady, the sister of Willie Pogany, whom we knew as an artist in London, and other good comrades, gave us a rousing welcome. They took us to their excellent offices in the same building as the then powerful newspaper, *Pesti Lloyd*, and afterwards to tea on the Corso. I was impressed by the enterprise and bright élan of the Hungarian movements of women. The Women Clerks' Union had enrolled 4,000 out of the 6,000 women clerks of Hungary, the greater part of whom worked in Budapest. Its club had a magnificent position in the centre of the town, overlooking the great square of the Vigado, the Corso, the Danube, and the city of Buda upon the hills.

We saw neither a rent strike nor a market riot, but we visited some of the extensive new working-class suburbs erected by the Government. One of these comprised 30,000 houses, far surpassing in comfort and architectural beauty any dwellings of the kind I had hitherto seen. It set my mind busy on my dreams for the East End. Our guides took us proudly to investigate the State arrangements for the welfare of orphaned, deserted and destitute children, boasting, not without reason, that they were the finest in the world. There were eighteen reception bureaux, to which parents, or others, might bring the children. No child

was refused.　At the central receiving station we saw a baby
brought in, and, according to rule, it was first examined by one of
the doctors, a woman as it happened, to determine whether it
must be kept under medical care, or be sent to the children's
hotel till permanent arrangements could be made.　Only when
the nurse had dressed the child and carried it away were
particulars taken down from the old woman who had brought
it in.　Parents, whether fathers of children born out of wedlock,
or otherwise, who were judged able to pay for their children's
keep, were expected to do so, but out of 54,478 children cared for
in the year 1910, payments had only been exacted in 139 cases.
The children were boarded out with carefully chosen foster-
parents, under the supervision of women inspectors.　Where
possible, mother and child were placed in the same household,
57·4 per cent. of the children under a year old being with their
mothers.　57·9 per cent. of the foster-parents were small land-
owners.　On leaving school the children were apprenticed to
various employments, unless they chose to remain on the farms
of their foster-parents.　The State also made small subsidies to
poor mothers with babies under a year old.　A woman whose
husband, a factory worker, earned £45 a year received 8s. 4d. a
month for her child.　This small payment was not so small in
actual value as it would be here and now.　I ascertained that in
some cases the children of widows who would have desired to
keep them were boarded out with others; the reason given was
that the State grant per child was not enough for the upkeep of
a home, and would serve only to cover the additional cost of a
child in a home already established.　Thus for the orphaned and
deserted child the scheme was well enough; for the child with a
mother it fell far short of humane requirements.　The mother of
one child might be received into the home of the foster-parents;
if there were several children the family must be disbanded.
Desirous of investigating further, I went unannounced to the
administrative office in Buda, and obtained permission to accompany one of the inspectors on her rounds through Kispest, a
small factory town a short distance from the city.　The children
I saw seemed happy and kindly cared for, apparently the well-
loved sons and daughters of their foster-parents.

" Do you wish to see our prison? " the Budapest Suffragists
asked us.　It was a sad experience.　In the gloomy building there
were no women officials; the warders, of soldierly appearance,
wore swords at the hip.　The cells were a little larger, but darker
and less clean than those of Holloway.　In the first of them five
girls of fifteen to sixteen years were confined, some of them convicted as thieves, some as prostitutes plying their trade without a

ticket from the police. The odious system of State Regulation was in force. One of the girls was in bed; the others stood up in a row before us as the warder opened the door. So dejected they looked, and one so hopelessly sorrowful that I was constrained to take her hand, miserably wishing I had the power to help her. She burst into shuddering sobs. I guided her to a bench, then saw that all the others were weeping too. I made them be seated, attempting, so vainly, to comfort and encourage them. They seized my hands, trying to kiss them; even the girl in the bed stretched out her arms. Distressed that I had occasioned their tears, I pressed their hands, poor children, but would not let them touch mine with their lips; their humility grieved and embarrassed me. As we left them the Suffrage ladies told me they would think that I had scorned their kisses. I knew of nothing to dispel that thought save to blow kisses to them from the door. In the next cell was a yet more unhappy sight: a group of girls, from fifteen to seventeen years of age, their clothes ragged and dirty, their faces pallid and suffering, with dull, tired eyes, half hidden by matted hair; prostitutes all. "They are already ill," the warder said. We were hurried away to another part of the gaol, where old women, five or six in a cell, were imprisoned as thieves or receivers of stolen goods, and young lads as tramps. In the exercise yard where the women filed round, as in Holloway, a warder mounted guard over them with sword and gun.

Passing an elementary school, we asked leave to enter. The head teacher received us with cordial enthusiasm. On a shelf in his room was a statuette of a peasant in the attitude of despair, his head bowed and a gun falling from his hand. The teacher told us the figure represented the agony of the peasants, forced to lay down their arms after the revolution of 1849. His grandfather had been the model. "I am a revolutionist like you," he added. "I would fight for Freedom if I could." Wherever we went, men and women, seeking in some form or other a finer and higher life, reached out to us.

My Budapest meeting was in the great hall of the Vigado, where the International Women's Suffrage Conference had been held the year before. The large audience, for the time being at least, was at one with me in my story of our struggle. After I and the translator, who followed me, had concluded, they rose in a body to applaud, and flocked to the platform, shaking hands and begging for autographs. The newspapers were all but unanimous in their eulogies, thanking me for having come to explain what before had been obscure to them, and praising the "incredible greatness" of the hunger strikers in their "heroic fight for human freedom." *Vilag* (*The World*) concluded a long article :

" Therefore good-bye, dear Sylvia; take your political childishness to other countries, where other earnest, long-bearded men, with the smell of beer and wine in their clothes, will smile at your hysterical programme. Wherever you go sympathetic thoughts will follow you home on the thorny path of your struggles, and everywhere there will be some who for *your* childishness would gladly change their political ripeness—that ripeness which has made clubs and public houses out of the Parliaments of Europe."

. . . .

A great reception awaited us in Vienna. " Our Liberal papers," said the *Arbeiter Zeitung,* " look upon Miss Pankhurst as a distinguished foreigner, with whom an interview is a great honour." More than a dozen Pressmen greeted us at the station, and most of them gave very favourable reports. Again we were filmed for the cinemas. Our rooms at the hotel were soon filled with flowers sent in by admirers of our movement. We were surrounded by a cosmopolitan crowd. A cousin of Hertha Ayrton, living in Vienna, took us to lunch in the Prater, the Hyde Park of Vienna, but lovelier and more charmingly rural. In the afternoon the Suffragists held a reception for us; a tremendous crush, attended by Americans, English, French, Russians, Poles, Germans, and the tall, well-dressed Viennese. An Austrian lieutenant presented us with a wonderful basket of blue gentians and red and white tiger lilies, with ribbons in the British and Austrian colours. Ernestine Furth thanked us in the name of Austrian women for coming to Vienna. That night the Grosses Konzerthaussal was thronged by a splendid audience, applauding with tremendous enthusiasm; the translation seemed scarcely necessary. I was busy exchanging autographs till the management came to extinguish the lights. The following days were passed in visits and sight-seeing. We saw the old Gothic cathedral with richly sculptured walls and jewel-like windows, soaring in such quaint fashion, from the pavements of the modern city. We visited the splendid picture galleries. The cousin of an English Suffragette lent us a box at the opera. The magnificent music of " Die Walküre," rarely staged with magic effects of light and cloud, the like of which I had never seen, made treasured memories to take back to the dull walls of the prison cell. More precious than all was an afternoon gathering violets in the lovely beech woods in the hills, for my life in the drear East End and confinement in a cell had made me like a caged wild thing when I was liberated among the trees. Poor town-bred children; what joys you miss !

Russian and Polish women came to us, urging a visit to their countries. A Pole from Lemberg in Galicia told us how the boys and girls there were organizing as scouts to fight for national liberty, and of the women of all classes studying to become volunteer teachers of the children to whom the Government vouchsafed no education.

A deputation, gloriously young, and exalted by their joyous idealism, came to us from the League of Youth, an organization formed to battle for the rights of young men and women. They were two girls of eighteen, one of them lovely as a flower, with a sort of delicate bloom upon her which made me hold my breath, a lad of twenty-four, boyish and shy, and one of thirty-two, invincibly young, though his hair was thinning prematurely, and he gave his age with an apology for his loss of youth. They said that youth should live apart, untrammelled by the anxious materialism of age, for youth is the best part of life, to which the race must look for its inspiration and ideals. Youth, they said, chooses for itself such characters as Joan of Arc, Michelangelo, Shakespeare, Beethoven; it desires to be beautiful, noble, and great, not merely to be rich. Two communities of youth had already been established, at Wickersdorf and Tieberg in South Germany, where young people from twelve to twenty-four years of age might live, making their own laws, but free from material want and gainful labour. Only such elders as those, still youthful in heart, whom the young had themselves chosen as guides, might enter there. The means for these communities were at present found by the parents, but the League of Youth would have it that in time to come the State must maintain such communities for all the youth of the land. The guides chosen by the young would then be represented in Parliament. An offshoot of the League of Youth was the Green Anchor, a society formed to help the young in their conflicts with the old, sending the guides to plead with parents and guardians for the liberties of youth, and helping young people in difficulties, with money, friendship and advice. The Austrian Government objected to the League of Youth, and declared its aspirations dangerous to the State. *The Mission of Youth in the Fight of Our Time,* a paper edited by Dr. Wyncken, the founder of the movement, had been suppressed. Meetings of the League had been prohibited in Vienna, and its members now held secret conclaves in the woods. My visitors had each been interviewed by the police; they all expected to be in prison soon.

My meetings in Germany had been prohibited. Albert and Lena Lowey were then in Dresden studying in that happy community, the Eurhythmics school of Jaques-Dalcroze, where we spent a glorious day. They were able to arrange a private meeting in the house of Mrs. Lindsey Neustatter, who was afterwards fined because the meeting was less private than the police thought fit.

Taking a last drive on our last day in Brussels my eyes turned to Zelie seated before me. How changed she was; her face nervously strained, her figure shrunk. Her clothes hung loosely on her; they were the same that she had brought from America; she had cared to get nothing new. The interests common to young women of her age were discarded. She leant back against the cushions, striving piteously to relax and be at peace—to recover the power of enjoyment. My heart smote me. She smiled at me, a pathetic little smile. "What a couple of poor creatures we are!" I said, with an effort to seem gay.

We were in Bow again with the familiar work-driven, sorrow-drawn faces about us. Before leaving for Budapest I had successfully ventured out one morning of dense fog, to see an empty house in the Old Ford Road. It had been in turn a school and a factory, and had a hall capable of seating about three hundred people at the rear, connected with the house by a smaller hall with a flat roof. We decided to take it as the headquarters of the East London Federation, reserving a part of it as a home for Norah Smyth, myself and the Paynes. The others were already installed on my return. The landlord would give nothing for decoration, but Norah Smyth painted and papered the house, and the Rebels' S.P.U. painted the hall under the leadership of Willie Lansbury, and made the seats which our women stained, bringing them up to the flat roof, where we hoisted our colours on an enormous pole. It was delightful to me to be out there under the sky with them. We were able now to organize a lending library, a choir, lectures, concerts, a "Junior Suffragettes' Club," and so on. The place became a hive of activity and the first house of call for everyone in distress. When a girl in grievous trouble was found fainting in Victoria Park, it was here that the park-keeper brought her. A child, unhappy in a Poor Law home, appeared at our door. The asbestos workers on strike, because two of their number had been discharged for joining a trade union, were led to us by a little girl of fifteen, with her red hair in two little plaits. She told us, her delicious little face aglow with laughter, that they had christened her "Sylvia" in the factory. She packed the asbestos, carried the heavy saggers in which it was fired, did the " governor's " washing, peeled the potatoes, scrubbed the floors and ran the errands for 6s. a week. A girl two years her junior worked from 8 a.m. to 8 p.m. for 4s. a week. A lad of fifteen told us, with tears, that he was doing for 8s. 6d. a week the work for which a man, until recently, had been paid 18s. Strikes, especially of women, and some of them only lasting a few days, were breaking out on all sides of us. All day our hall was often requisitioned for strike meetings; we were appealed to for speakers and help in every sort of way. It is estimated that in 1914 there were five hundred strikes and lock-outs a month, but the smaller disputes always go unrecorded. The tension in Ireland, the militancy of the Suffragettes, was reflected in the labour world. There were strike leaders in prison also.

Our Federation took its place in the annual Labour May Day Demonstration. It is curious now to recall that the secretary of the First of May Demonstration Committee declared us ineligible and ordered us not to come. Our platform, banned by the police, but taken in the name of a men's organization formed for the occasion, attracted by far the largest crowd in the park.

Our house-warming at the " Women's Hall," as the members elected to call it, was on May 5th. Next day Zelie Emerson sailed for America. As a result of forcible feeding and the fracture to her skull, her health occasioned growing anxiety. Mr. Mansell Moullin had advised me, at all costs, to get her away from danger and excitement. I had the greatest difficulty to induce her to go, and suffered many a painful hour of distressful heart-searching on her account. I was grieved to lose her.

CHAPTER VI

GREATER DESTRUCTION——SUFFRAGETTE MILITANCY TURNS
UPON ULSTER

THE destruction wrought in the seven months of 1914 before the War excelled that of the previous year.[1] Three Scotch castles were destroyed by fire on a single night. The Carnegie Library in Birmingham was burnt. The Rokeby Venus, falsely, as I consider, attributed to Velazquez, and purchased for the National Gallery at a cost of £45,000, was mutilated by Mary Richardson. Romney's " Master Thornhill," in the Birmingham Art Gallery, was slashed by Bertha Ryland, daughter of an early Suffragist. Carlyle's portrait of Millais in the National Portrait Gallery, and numbers of other pictures were attacked, a Bartolozzi drawing in the Doré Gallery being completely ruined. Many large empty houses in all parts of the country were set on fire, including Redlynch House, Somerset, where the damage was estimated at £40,000. Railway stations, piers, sports pavilions, haystacks were set on fire. Attempts were made to blow up reservoirs. A bomb exploded in Westminster Abbey, and in the fashionable church of St. George's, Hanover Square, where a famous stained-glass window from Malines was damaged. There were two explosions in St. John's, Westminster, and one in St. Martin's in the Fields, and in Spurgeon's Tabernacle. The ancient Breadsall Church, near Derby, was destroyed, and the ancient Wargrave Church. The organ was flooded at the Albert Hall, the damage amounting to £2,000. The bombs and other material used were of a much more professional and formidable character than those of the early period of secret militancy. One hundred and forty-one acts of destruction were chronicled in the Press during the first seven months of 1914. In respect of these there was a total of thirty-five arrests. There were one hundred and seven cases of arson, but only nine arrests. On the other hand, window smashing and outrages in picture galleries and museums,

[1] Amongst 261 of the more serious acts of destruction attributed by the Press to the Suffragettes in the years 1913 and 1914, an estimate of the loss appeared in 78 cases only. For these 78 cases the estimated loss totalled £722,850. The remaining 183 cases must have shown a much higher total had the damage been given. They included the destruction of two ancient churches, piers, grandstands, timber-yards, factories and private houses, including Lloyd George's new house and Sir William Lever's bungalow.

made under the public eye, almost invariably resulted in the arrest of all the perpetrators.

The destruction of church property becoming more serious and frequent, and the Suffragette prayers and interruptions in churches more unrestrained, the feelings of some of the clergy became acerb. The Rev. C. H. Percival, Vicar of All Saints, Branksome, Bournemouth, went so far as to say he would "honour the man or woman who took the law into his or her own hands against the Suffragettes." Dean Inge, when a woman wrote to him to protest that a verger had struck her in the face while she uttered her prayer, replied: "I am glad to have your name and address, which may be useful to the police." He averred that the "shameless monkey-tricks" and the "infamous crimes" and "unparalleled wickedness" of "the scoundrels" with whom she appeared to be in sympathy had "ruined for a generation" a political reform of which he had long been in favour. Thus may the prophets be misled. On the other hand, the Bishop of Kensington wrote in the *Daily Graphic*: "The present outbursts of militancy are mainly due to the persistent disregard of the claims of women." Canon Scott Holland, in a strong plea for the Suffrage, wrote that forcible feeding was "hideously cruel," and "maddens people into criminal acts of indignant retaliation." The Bishop of Durham, when interviewed by a W.S.P.U. deputation, said: "I will do all I can to help, and will do it as soon as possible." The Bishop of Leicester, Dr. Peake, in reply to a deputation, said that forcible feeding was a detestable practice, politically, legally and medically indefensible, but pointed out that four bishops and five hundred clergymen had already protested against it.

In February forty women, much distressed by accounts of the Holloway prisoners, went from one of the W.S.P.U. meetings in the Knightsbridge Hall[1] to the Bishop of London, to urge his intervention against forcible feeding. He promised his help, and eventually made two visits to Holloway, after which he reported that forcible feeding was performed "in the kindliest spirit," and pleaded for a cessation of militancy, promising in that event to lead a Votes for Women deputation to the Prime Minister. "A whitewash brush has been put in your hand, my Lord Bishop!" was the W.S.P.U. reply. In fact his statements had made light of the effect which forcible feeding had had upon the prisoners, though the Judge who presently sentenced

[1] The Monday afternoon "At Homes" had removed there from the London Pavilion, the management of the former hall having objected to the platform struggles with the police.

one of those whom the Bishop had seen, commented on her piteous condition of weakness. Mary Richardson called on the Bishop. I also wrote to him and he came to the East End to see me. As a result of these interviews, he wrote to McKenna, telling him he had spoken with us, and adding: " I am convinced we are not justified in treating delicate women in this way." He advised that to avoid forcible feeding the prisoners should be released " for a time " under the " Cat and Mouse " Act, and before forcible feeding were again attempted, a committee of five leading doctors and surgeons (two of them women) should be invited to report. This letter he kept private for a time, not wishing to embarrass the Home Secretary, but reserved the right to publish it, which he did in the following July.

Shortly after writing it, the Bishop introduced a Bill to raise the " age of consent," pointing out that in six of the rescue homes managed by the London Diocesan Council there were eighty-eight girls under sixteen years of age, and in thirteen of these homes two hundred and five girls between sixteen and eighteen years. The Bishop's Bill was so greatly mutilated by Government amendments, that he finally withdrew it, declaring that, as altered, it would even destroy some safeguards of the existing law. His warmth towards the suffrage question continued to increase. Though he protested it was " tactless " of Suffragettes to place a bomb under his chair in St. Paul's, he supported Lord Selborne's Bill for Women's Suffrage, which was debated in the House of Lords[1] on May 5th and 6th. When Suffragettes invaded the Bishop's garden party on July 11th, interrogating him and his guests, selling literature and distributing leaflets, he preserved an attitude of complacency for some time. When at last he became exasperated, and desired to have one of the intruders removed, some of his guests took the part of the woman, and one elderly clergyman even assisted her in resisting removal.

In the bizarre versatility of this extraordinary movement, which was sweeping along with it the bulk of the womanhood of its day, it was not only the members of the non-militant societies who continued to hold their many little festivals for fund-raising and reunion. The W.S.P.U., with its militants tortured in prison, outdid the rest in its gaiety. A pageant of the Suffragette as the May Queen, led by flower-roped children,

---

[1] A Bill to confer the Parliamentary franchise on women Municipal voters (about 1,000,000 women). Lord Haldane supported, but said no Government would make itself responsible for such a measure. Lord Crewe, well known as an anti-Suffragist and a member of the Government, spoke and voted against it. It was defeated by 104 votes to 60.

was sent through the London streets to advertise its organ. A water carnival was announced for the Serpentine. Women paraded with decorated sunshades. Others appeared in dominoes, each carrying a letter of the word "Suffragette" on her chest. One girl in Japanese dress turned up in a rickshaw drawn by a girl companion in knee-breeches. The Office of Works, shocked by the prospect of such merry advertising by persons who had banded themselves together for the commission of serious crime, had prohibited the Serpentine to all comers that day, the boats being lashed together in midwater to prevent their use. Nothing daunted, the Suffragettes flung off their wraps, revealing themselves in bathing costumes, swam out to the craft and cut them free. The police sprang into boats and followed them, captured the offending navigators, brought them to the bank, and took them dripping in their bathing dress to the police station, refusing to permit them to take the cloaks stretched out to them by their friends.

Changes the Gladstonian era would have deemed remarkable were passing through Parliament with scant public notice; by the inconclusive manner of their enactment, even evoking contempt. The Lords had been shorn of their veto, but the powers of delay awarded them, and the talk of presently reforming the Upper House dwarfed the importance of the advance. To those who were fighting for the sex which was wholly outside the Constitution; to those whose hopes were set on the creation of a new social order, the abolition of the Lords' veto, the Trade Union Act, which reversed the Osborne Judgement, the disestablishment of the Welsh Church seemed trivial. To the Irish, only the abolition of the Lords' veto was of moment, and that solely because it might open the door to Home Rule. To the Suffragettes the Irish conflict remained a perpetual incitement to intensified militancy. Comparison of their punishments, and the immunity of the Ulster rebels, had become the favourite slogans of their fight. The signing by Lord Roberts, and others exalted in Army, Church and State, of the Ulster Covenant, with its pledge to obstruct British troops in any attempt to coerce Ulster into obedience to the Home Rule Act; the resignation of General Gough and other officers at the Curragh; the Government's parleying with them, which lead to the cry of " the people against the army "; the resignation of Colonel Seeley, and the assumption of his position by the Prime Minister; the landing of fifty thousand rifles from Germany at Larne, and their distribution throughout Protestant Ulster; the repeated concessions by the Liberal Government to Ulster militants—all brought new recruits and supporters to the W.S.P.U. and were a spur and a stimulus to feminine militancy. " Will you not make some concession to these brave, determined women also? " demanded Pratt, the Liberal M.P. for Linlithgow. Outhwaite, the single taxer, Wedgwood, and, as always, Keir Hardie, urged the same point. D. M. Mason, the Liberal Member for Coventry, had given so strong a support to the Suffragettes, both in Parliament and out, that his election committee had given him notice that it would seek another Liberal candidate to replace him at the next election. The *Ulster Covenanter*, with its pictures of armed volunteers at rifle practice, raised the constant question : " Why does the Government only persecute *The Suffragette*? " J. A. Hobson,[1] the Liberal philosopher, wrote :

> " Can it be wondered that the Suffragettes are asking how much further the Government invites them to advance along the road of crime before capitulating to the only sort of argument it seems to understand? "

High hopes had been raised by the promise of Votes for Women under the Ulster provisional Government; hopes fantastic indeed, for all are invited to participate when danger threatens. They were dashed to the ground when concession after concession had narrowed the Ulster struggle to one merely of boundaries. On March 6th a deputation of Ulster women, led by Dorothy Evans, the W.S.P.U. organizer in Belfast, came to London to see Sir Edward Carson. They sat on his doorstep from Friday to Monday waiting to be received. As he was not a Cabinet Minister, the police made no attempt to arrest them. Eventually they were invited within, their host remarking that, as a fighting man himself, he was not offended by their persistence. He plainly stated, however, that as his colleagues were not united on the subject of Votes for Women, he would not raise dissension amongst them by introducing it. Thus the much applauded promise of Votes for Ulster Women was withdrawn.

As always, the W.S.P.U. reply was militancy. There had been no trace of it by Suffragettes in Ulster until this point. Now bombs exploded, buildings burst into flames, even the hospitals awaiting the use of the Ulster Volunteers when the threatened Civil War should break out, were set on fire. Under an Act passed in the early days of Irish militancy, and not applying to England, Sir Hugh McCalmont was awarded £11,000 from the Belfast local authorities for the destruction of his house, " Abbeylands," by Suffragettes, and the executors of Bishop Henry obtained £20,000 for the burning of " Orlands." The county of Antrim

---

[1] *Traffic in Treason*, by J. A. Hobson. (T. Fisher Unwin.)

was compelled to pay £92,000 damages to various claimants whose property had been destroyed—a threepenny rate in the £ on the county rates. In churches, theatres, picture houses and restaurants the Suffragette voice was heard. The Ulster patriots, to whom so many compliments had previously been paid, responded in kind: women were roughly handled when poster parading, and Dorothy Evans had occasion to bring an action for assault and false imprisonment against a gallant captain. After an attempt had been made to burn Lisburn Castle, Dorothy Evans and Maud Muir were arrested for being in possession of explosives. When brought into Court, on April 8th, they struggled repeatedly to leave it, and kept up a constant flow of speech-making, asking continually why Captain Craig, Sir Edward Carson and their friends were not arrested, since, most obviously, they were guilty of the same offence. Refusal to be tried and continual interruption of the Court proceedings was now the policy of the W.S.P.U. Dorothy Evans, a sturdy, handsome young woman, educated at the North London Collegiate School, had been physical culture mistress at a Yorkshire girls' school before her first arrest as a militant in 1909. Since that year she had been a W.S.P.U. organizer. Physically most vigorous, and a practised speaker, she was eminently capable of making the policy of Court obstruction as effective as it could be. She acted with great bravery. Though twice knocked senseless by the gaolers, she rallied to the struggle as soon as she regained consciousness. The proceedings were suspended for an hour and finally adjourned. Bail being refused to them, the defendants hunger struck. After three days in prison, bail was offered them. They now rejected it, and continued their strike. Next day they were liberated without conditions. On April 20th the case came up again, but the defendants had failed to appear. They were re-arrested next day. The trial was resumed. They repeated the same obstruction. To minimize the disturbance, Dorothy Evans was removed whilst Maud Muir was dealt with. The latter was committed for trial, and offered release on bail in the meantime, but she refused to enter into recognizances, and was therefore returned to prison, still hunger striking. Dorothy Evans was also offered bail and refused it, continuing her strike. Brought into Court three days later, though weak from fasting, she still obstructed proceedings, and was removed to a cell, where she was held by four constables, whilst the depositions were read in the corridor outside. She was committed for trial, still refusing to accept bail. Three days later both prisoners were released. On June 2nd, Maud Muir was arrested, with another woman, on a new charge of arson, and released after five days' hunger strike. On June 4th Dorothy Evans and a companion penetrated to the dining-room of Sir Edward Carson, and spoke with him till they were ejected. Carson, arch-rebel as he was, nevertheless was accorded police protection from the Suffragettes during his visit to Ulster. On July 21st Dorothy Evans was re-arrested at the Lord Mayor's house, where she had called demanding shelter from arrest. Brought to trial next day, her speech-making was so persistent that Justice Dodd adjourned the case to the next Assizes, in 1915. She was taken back to prison, again hunger struck, and was released after a further three days.

Meanwhile, on April 4th, the Ulster Unionist Militants organized a demonstration with processions to Hyde Park, to rally English support for the coming Civil War, the preparations for which did not slacken in spite of repeated concessions by the Government, who were actually providing police protection for this Ulster effort, the Office of Works giving its official sanction to the platforms in Hyde Park. Indeed a truly curious state of affairs!

Such a challenge to the Suffragettes (still, Sunday by Sunday, battling to regain the old meeting place, which the Government had forbidden them) could scarcely be allowed to pass. The W.S.P.U. immediately demanded the raising of the ban against its meetings, but met the old refusal. A procession to the park was accordingly announced, and members of the local W.S.P.U.'s marched in with sticks decorated in the purple, white and green, escorting Mrs. Drummond in a dog-cart. Lively scenes ensued. The police led the vehicle out of the park. Flora Drummond descended and was hoisted to speak on the shoulders of her supporters, but was immediately arrested. Women rushed for the Ulster platforms and were repelled by the police. Ulster speakers strove for a hearing against Suffragettes bobbing up to make unauthorized speeches and police rushes to suppress them.

When Mrs. Drummond was tried for obstruction next day, she announced her intention of doing " all the talking," called Musket, the prosecuting solicitor, " Jack-in-the-Box," and asked the Magistrate if he had been to see " Bluebeard " at the Home Office. The case was twice adjourned, in the hope that she would see fit to be quiet, and was at last heard in her absence, a copy of the evidence being supplied to her. Finally, after she had torn off a policeman's whistle, and thrown it at the Magistrate, he closed the proceedings with: " Forty shillings or one month." The fine was paid.

CHAPTER VII

DEPUTATION TO THE KING—PRISON OFFICIALS CHARGED WITH
DRUGGING SUFFRAGETTES

BEFORE May was out I was again in prison, Mrs. Pankhurst had been arrested on a deputation to the King, Annie Kenney had been arrested at Lambeth Palace, whilst Lincoln's Inn House had been seized by the police.

The deputation to the King on May 21st was the last great militant raid of the W.S.P.U. From January it had been advertised with appeals to women all over the country to join it. Women, it was said, had a greater right to have audience of the King than men, as women had no part or lot in Parliamentary Government. Moreover, in Christabel's flamboyant terms: "Ministers have degraded themselves by their cruelty and treachery. The W.S.P.U. desires to have no further interviews with them." Mrs. Pankhurst wrote to the King:

" It would not only be repugnant to our womanly sense of dignity, but it would be absurd and futile for us to interview the very men against whom we bring the accusations of betraying the Women's Cause and torturing us who fight for that Cause."

On being informed that the Home Secretary had advised against the reception of the deputation, Mrs. Pankhurst replied to the King, stigmatizing the advice as "unconstitutional and disloyal." She informed him that, in spite of the refusal, the deputation would wait upon him at Buckingham Palace on May 21st.

Enormous crowds of the sympathetic, the curious, and the hostile, assembled to see the fray. A large number of women had volunteered for the struggle. Thousands of police were mustered to repel them, and even soldiers were stationed in the vicinity of the Palace. The procession formed up in Grosvenor Square, and marched to the Wellington Arch up Constitution Hill, where the main contest took place. The gates of the Arch were closed, and police on horse and foot massed before it. The women, just as they had done again and again in Parliament Square, advanced continually against the police cordon, and were continually flung back. The old order had been given to drive them away, with as few arrests as possible; and the violence meted out to them was said to be even greater than that on " Black

551

Friday." Probably it was true, for a small number of women retaliated as they had never done in the early days. One struck about her with a horse-whip, some brandished Indian clubs, and threw red and green powder. For the few who used any force other than the persistent pressure of their bodies, the many received drastic punishment. Gladys Schutze, an author and wife of Dr. Harry Schutze at the Lister Institute, signed a statement that she was "a completely passive resister, standing by the railings." A mounted policeman struck her on the head with his truncheon, and deliberately backed his horse against her, as a result of which she received a kick in the abdomen which rendered her unfit for her professional work for some time. She heard a constable advising another to take a woman by the breasts. Mrs. Metge of Lisburn made a sworn statement that a woman under arrest and held by two constables was savagely ill-treated by one of them. Mrs. Metge protested and he replied: "There won't be much of her left when I have done with her." Mrs. Drake of the East London Federation wrote of the scenes:

"The police charged the people outside Wellington Gate. Those who had come for sport went back, but our women were splendid! The police got hold of them in dozens, and threw them back amongst the crowd. On the women came again, and each time they came back the police took greater liberties with them—twisting their arms, punching them and tearing their hair."

Miss Billinghurst, a cripple with paralysed legs who worked a tricycle with her arms, pushed her machine amongst the horsemen, indomitable in perseverance. Wrote Mrs. Drake:

"I was beside her. They threw us back, but we returned. Two policemen picked up the tricycle with Miss Billinghurst in it, turned it over, and dropped her on to the ground. The excitement gave me strength—I picked her up bodily, and lifted her back. We straightened the machine as best we could, rested a little to take breath, and struggled on again. The police would not take us—only knock us about. Then in the enormous crowd I got sent flying one way, she another. I tried to find her. It seemed as though the earth had swallowed her. . . ."

Jennie Petersen from Denmark went to see:

"A frightful struggle started. A young woman fell on her knees—her hair had been torn down—she seemed to have fainted. The mounted police rode amongst the women, not caring whether they trampled them down or not. A man said: 'Poor women; they are being roughly handled!' Another said: 'I think the reason is that all these people do not understand.' But the women who are struggling in England to-day have understood. They have seen that

something must be done to alter the bad English social conditions.
. . . As the police dragged the women past, the crowd shouted what
they thought: ' Brave women! ' Only a few young men, with tall
silk hats on their heads, said: ' It serves them right.' "

The people might not enter by the Wellington Arch, but the
other gates were open to them, and in they streamed. Mrs.
Moore, and some others from Bow, went in by the Admiralty
Arch, and soon found themselves in a crowd of youths, who held
up their walking-sticks to which they had tied comic effigies of
the Suffragettes. Each time the sticks went up they raised loud
roars. These were redoubled when some thirty women, hatless
and dishevelled, were hauled past by the police, and an old
woman was carried out on a stretcher. Mrs. Parsons of Canning
Town made her way to the Victoria Memorial. She saw the
Palace windows crowded with people watching the scene and
detectives on the roof. Every now and then a woman would
rush out from the dense throng of spectators into the space kept
clear before the Palace. The police would catch her and fling
her into the crowd. Then the straw-hatted young men in the
crowd would turn on her and beat her, tearing her clothes and
pulling her hair and shouting: " You ought to be burnt! " At
last the mounted police came up at a gallop and drove the crowd
away. Mrs. Parsons was driven in the press down Bird Cage
Walk. She saw a young woman in the midst of a jeering mob
facing her tormentors with back to the wall. A sentry struck
her in the face with his fist. It was a day of woman bating
indeed! "What we have to fear is the toffs in silk hats, not the
poor people," said a man from the East End.

Mrs. Pankhurst had marched with the procession from a
house where she had been waiting in Grosvenor Place. When
the Wellington Gates were opened to admit police reinforcements,
she and a crowd of others slipped through. She had made her
way to the very gates of the Palace before she was seized by a
huge police Inspector, who carried her to a taxi. Detectives
immediately sped off with her to Holloway, where she entered
upon her eighth hunger and thirst strike, and was released after
five days.

Sixty-six women and two men appeared at Bow Street next
morning, the majority refusing their names and being designated
by numbers. In the old days, when they were orderly and obedient,
women had been refused admission to the trials. To-day the
prisoners and their friends who crowded the Court made
pandemonium of the proceedings. Shouts drowned the voice of
the Magistrate. Folded copies of *The Suffragette* were hurled at
him. Only when a bag of flour had been flung was the Court

cleared after a violent struggle.   Eight arrests were made outside.
The sentences, perhaps at the King's request, were in the main
trivial, as compared with those imposed in the early days.   The
majority of the women were ordered to be bound over, and on
refusal, instead of getting six weeks or two months' imprisonment
as of old, they were simply discharged.   A woman who had
assaulted a policeman with an Indian club and covered his clothes
with red powder was sent to prison for ten days.   The accused
in most cases refused to walk into Court, and when dragged into
the dock struggled and shouted until removed.   Those charged
with serious damage were committed for trial at the Sessions.
When their cases came on, many of them, having hunger struck
and been forcibly fed in the meantime, were in a pitiable
condition, and had to be carried into Court, two of them being
laid on benches apparently unconscious.

Whilst the women had been battling outside Buckingham
Palace the previous day, May Spencer had damaged Clausen's
" Primavera " at the Royal Academy.   Whilst the cases were
being heard at Bow Street, five pictures were slashed at the
National Gallery, and a mummy case broken at the British
Museum; Lavery's portrait of the King in the Royal Scottish
Academy was damaged.   The King and Queen, attending
a matinée at His Majesty's Theatre, witnessed extraordinary
scenes.   A woman chained to her seat in the stalls shouted:
" You Russian Tsar! "   Another climbed over the footlights on
to the stage and began a speech; leaflets were thrown, shouts and
violent ejections punctuated the performance: " Stop forcible
feeding! "   " Release Mrs. Pankhurst! "   " Give women the
vote! "   " The Royal name and office " being, according to
Christabel, " dishonoured," the King was henceforth to receive
the same treatment as a Cabinet Minister.   Women spoke outside
the Palace and chained themselves to the railings.   At a Court
function afterwards, Mary Blomfield dropped on her knees before
the King and cried: " For God's sake, Your Majesty, put a stop
to forcible feeding! "   She was hurried, as the *Daily Mirror* put
it, from " the Presence," which, so the public was relieved to
learn, had remained serene.   Lady Blomfield intimated to the
Press her repudiation of what her daughter had done.   Lady
Blomfield had been enthusiastic for militancy of the most extreme
kind, so long as it was committed by other people's daughters.
She had come to me at a Kensington W.S.P.U. " At Home,"
shortly after my release in 1913, expressing her delight that
'Abdu'l Bahá, of whom she was proud to call herself a follower,
had spoken with sympathy of the Suffragettes; he had suffered
forty years' imprisonment, she told me ecstatically, for preaching

the unity of religions and the brotherhood of man. Under his teaching she had lost all regard for the pomps and vanities of earthly existence.

On the day after the deputation to the King, polling took place in the Ipswich by-election. The contest had been warmly fought. Lloyd George had spoken there, saying that Mrs. Pankhurst and Bonar Law were " the two anarchist leaders in this country," each in their own way pursuing a lawless policy. Carson also had visited the town, hurling defiance at the Government and preaching Civil War. A " Mouse," Arabella Scott (Catherine Reid), whose licence expired on polling day, appeared challenging the Government to arrest her in the midst of the electors. She spoke at meetings indoors and out, met Sir Edward Carson at the station, and hoisted a placard: " Shall I, Arabella Scott, be arrested, whilst you, Carson, are free? " She leapt on the step of the Liberal candidate's motor. " Who are you? " he asked her. She answered: " I am a victim of the ' Cat and Mouse ' Act. I want to know if I am to be arrested during this election! " The sequel is unpleasant; she was not arrested then, but some weeks later, and once she was in prison again, she was forcibly fed, though this had not been done during her previous incarcerations under the same sentence. When McKenna was asked the reason for the change, he replied that she had broken the terms of her licence on the last occasion.

On the morning of the deputation to the King the police had raided a flat in Lauderdale Mansions, and arrested there the wife of Leonard Hall (our old friend from the early I.L.P. days in Manchester, who had gone to prison in the Boggart Hole Clough free speech struggle), also their daughters, Nellie and Emmeline, and two other women. Emmeline, named after Mrs. Pankhurst, had been the little baby who was " on the way " when Mrs. Hall had been left destitute by her husband's imprisonment. Nellie Hall was now a W.S.P.U. organizer. Her mother and sister had come up to London for the deputation to the King. The police found at the flat twenty-two pieces of tube containing gunpowder, with fuses attached, a large number of hammers, and seventy-two black calico bags, with strings to tie round the waist, some of them filled with flints. A basket of flints covered with lettuce leaves, ammunition for the window-smashing to take place later in the day, was brought to the door as the police arrived. The women were at first charged with being " loose, idle and disorderly persons," but afterwards were prosecuted for being in possession of explosives for unlawful purposes, and for conspiring with others to commit malicious damage. Lincoln's Inn House was raided two days later, the police remaining in possession. Grace Roe, a young Irishwoman, now called the general secretary of the W.S.P.U., was arrested on the premises and charged with conspiring with the Halls. Roe had not previously been imprisoned, and was unknown to the police, her arrest being due to her name occurring in certain documents found at Lauderdale Mansions. Mrs. Hall hunger struck with the rest and became very ill. The charge against her was eventually dropped, whilst her young daughter Emmeline and the two other women arrested with them were discharged. Nellie Hall and Grace Roe were alone convicted. Both at the Police Court hearings, and during the subsequent trial, they followed out, as fully as they could, the instruction to refuse to be tried. Nellie Hall hurled one of her shoes at the Magistrate, Grace Roe a bundle of pamphlets at the Judge. They struggled and refused to walk, flung themselves to the ground, fought to get out of the dock, and shouted at the top of their voices as continuously as they could. They were refused bail, and were forcibly fed for many weeks before they came to be tried.

Undoubtedly the new policy of obstruction assisted the Press in maligning the militants as half-demented rowdies. It strengthened the hand of McKenna in his determination to track down the few women who committed the serious acts of extreme militancy, and to incapacitate them for further destruction. The *Daily Express* uttered and helped to form the most hostile view in reporting doings of the accused:

" It flung itself backwards and forwards, and punctuated its struggles by repeating the cry: ' I will not be tried! ' "

Yet others were not deceived. R. D. Muir, K.C., the senior prosecuting council for the Treasury, in addressing a literary gathering on " The Criminal and the Police," observed that he had known Mrs. Pankhurst and other gifted women, and insisted it was " impossible to go on punishing them for breaches of the law when they were prepared to die for their opinions." It seemed to him that the only way out was to give women the vote.[1]

To make matters worse, Grace Roe was caught in an attempt to get a drug smuggled into the prison to her. As a prisoner awaiting trial she had been permitted access to the W.S.P.U. solicitors: Hatchett Jones, Bisgood and Marshall. Grace Roe had arranged that a letter should be conveyed to her by the solicitor's clerk, containing a powerful emetic (apomorphine hydrochloride), which would procure her speedy release by causing her to vomit the food administered in forcible feeding. The

[1] *Newspaper World*, 30th May, 1914.

drug was discovered, and action taken against the clerk, who was let off with a fine of £10 and costs, on an undertaking being given that his firm would not again act for the W.S.P.U.

Each time they were brought into Court the two young women were in a more pitiable condition. Nellie Hall, who was only twenty-one, appeared six times, being tried on the two charges, Grace Roe five times. "Do you know what it is for young women to be tortured? They are slowly murdering us!" their cries resounded. They complained repeatedly of being drugged. Leonard Hall was in despair about his daughter. She wrote him the sort of brave, affectionately patronizing little letter which young people write to their parents in such hard cases :

"I have known all the time that you were suffering intensely because I was here, but I hoped that knowing how I felt about it you would be a little consoled. . . .
"No free spirit has ever been wrecked by a mean-spirited oppression yet. And mine will not be either. . . .
"I am thankful beyond measure that from my parents I inherit a love of liberty and the spirit to fight for it. When the call came to *you*, you answered it; you did not fail, and in your heart, dear, you would not like me to. The public will ever be non-understanding, unimaginative and unsympathetic, as you say, until by our determination and enthusiasm we create a new spirit."

As a child she had suffered for the rebellion of her father; she had grown up with the mould of that suffering upon her body and its influence upon her mind. Perhaps it was to please him that in her separate trial at the Old Bailey, on June 26th, she abandoned obstructionist tactics. When asked if she objected to any of the jurors she said : "I object to all these jurors. It is an unlawful trial without a woman on the jury." She said she had only been at the flat in Lauderdale Mansions one night and had never done more than break a window, but she made no attempt to secure acquittal on that ground, and added : "I feel the profoundest admiration and respect for those women who hear the call of conscience and answer in the only way open to them."

She protested that she was too ill to follow the evidence, and not fit to plead, and read her speech in a low voice from a seat near the jury box. Dr. Haden Guest[1] asked to be allowed to make a statement about her health. The Judge was understood to refuse. Leonard Hall stood up in his old imperious way : "I am her father; the doctor has a very serious report to make."

[1] From Manchester. Afterwards a Labour M.P.

The Judge ordered his removal; he went out protesting: "This is a great shame both on the Court and the Government."[1]

When brought into Court to be tried together on the conspiracy charge, Nellie Hall and Grace Roe again obstructed the proceedings and were removed to the cells, the trial proceeding without them. Nellie Hall's request that a solicitor might visit her in prison to aid her in preparing her defence had been refused; the fact was communicated to Justice Avory, but the only concession made to her was a few moments' consultation whilst the case was proceeding; and this rather with the object of persuading her to be quiet than for the purposes of defence. The sentences were less severe than had been expected, and considerably lighter than those in the two previous conspiracy trials, though the exhibits in this case were more formidable than before. The jury had recommended Nellie Hall to mercy, on the ground that she was "only a paid agent of those who ought to have been in the dock beside her." The Judge applied the recommendation to both prisoners. Perhaps he was moved by their cries of suffering, though he had warned the jury to disregard them. His sentence was a further three months' imprisonment. They had already been forcibly fed seven weeks pending the trial.

The discovery of Grace Roe's attempt to smuggle a drug into prison was highly unfortunate for the hunger strikers. The cry was raised that their sufferings were largely caused by their own acts. As though Fate had determined to play a malignant prank, there occurred at that juncture the suicide of an unfortunate girl, Joan Lavender Baillie Guthrie, who called herself Laura Grey. She had been reared in a sheltered middle-class home, and the Press declared that she had been a Suffragette. This was true; she had been arrested on "Black Friday," November, 1910, and twice arrested in November, 1911, receiving six months' imprisonment for window smashing. She had hunger struck and been forcibly fed. Indeed, to Antonia Moser, whose advice she had asked in 1912, she had mentioned the bad effects of forcible feeding as one of the causes which had led her to resort to drugs.[2]

[1] The protest resulted in Parliamentary questions by Josiah Wedgwood and others, and a promise by the Home Secretary that bail should not be opposed by the prosecution in these cases if the defendants would undertake not to commit further offences during the trial; yet the refusal of bail and forcible feeding of prisoners awaiting trial continued nevertheless.

[2] About 1911 there was unrest amongst some of the young Suffragettes, stirred by the realization of poverty and social problems, economic and sexual. Unsatisfied by the reply that Votes for Women would cure all these difficulties, some of them joined the "Fabian Nursery," which for a time bulked large as a daring and drastic-thinking body in the eyes of some sections of ardent youth. Some interested themselves in the "New Age" and the "Free Woman," some few kicked over the traces of conventional usage, and where they stood alone without the backing of friends and influence,

In the circumstances of to-day, with their wider opportunities for women, this girl would probably have been trained for a profession which would have absorbed her energies and supplied the scope and interests she required.

The suicide of Laura Grey had been a nine days' sensation for the public. The drug-taking of Grace Roe was of more serious moment; it gravely discounted the statements of hunger strikers in the minds of many who were disposed to condemn forcible feeding. The Home Secretary was not slow to take advantage of it. When Frances Gordon (Frances Graves) was released from Perth prison in a deplorable condition and making serious accusations concerning her treatment, he retorted in the House of Commons that the medical officers of the prison were convinced she had undergone " a course of systematic drugging " before admission. The passing of a drug to Grace Roe was seized upon by McKenna as an important piece of evidence to aid him in rebutting the charge which the W.S.P.U. was making that the hunger strikers had been drugged by the prison officials; indeed when the lawyer's clerk was tried for conveying the drug, the prosecutor stated that the Holloway medical officers were in Court prepared to declare on oath that they had never administered any hypnotic drug to the Suffragettes.

The W.S.P.U. charge of drugging had originated when Phyllis Brady (Olive Beamish) was released on February 11th— Dr. Flora Murray, who treated her, was of opinion that she had been given " large doses of bromide " whilst in prison. On March 19th, in reply to a Parliamentary question, McKenna declared that neither bromide nor any other hypnotic drug had

---

found society coldly unready for their conceptions of freedom. A few, and one of these was Laura Grey, took to investigating the conditions of the submerged poor, for this purpose sleeping in common lodgings and on the Embankment. Christabel, when consulted, as she was, by some of them, severely condemned every other course save concentration upon the winning of the vote. Laura Grey drifted away from the Union. She was deserted by a man who had obtained an influence over her; eventually followed her tragic end. A little poem she wrote for *Votes for Women* leaves a pathetic memory:

" *To D.R.*

(" In the exercise yard, March, 1912)

" Beyond the bars I see her move,
　A mystery of blue and green,
As though across the prison yard
　The Spirit of the Spring had been;
And when she lifts her hands to press
　The happy sunshine from her hair,
From the grey ground the pigeons rise
　And rustle upwards through the air,
As though her two hands held a key
To set imprisoned spirits free."

been administered. Dr. Murray had consulted Dr. Frank Moxon, and with him continued to observe all the " Mice " who had been forcibly fed. On March 25th Phyllis Brady was released from a further thirty days' forcible feeding. She excreted bromine on the day of release, but not afterwards, as proved by the analysis of a well-known pathological laboratory. Mary Richardson, when released after forcible feeding, excreted bromine for five days. The same thing was discovered in the case of Kitty Marion and others. Dr. Moxon, in the *Suffragette*, averred that " chemical restraint," to reduce the patient's power of resistance in cases of epilepsy and acute mania, had long been applied in lunatic asylums. The result was great muscular weakness, depression of the nervous system and the vital centres of respiration and circulation, and mental deterioration, in many cases leading to permanent mental breakdown.

When Grace Roe's attempt to drug herself was discovered, a Government statement was issued to the Press, repeating the denials that sedative, or hypnotic drugs of any kind, had been administered to the prisoners, and announcing that it would be shown that drugs were being conveyed to prisoners, " in order that they might be made violently sick after being forcibly fed." Frank Moxon and Mansell Moullin replied that drugs producing sickness can in no way be confounded with drugs such as the bromides, which in fact counteract vomiting. The effect of emetics is temporary; " in no way could they lead to the same disastrous results to mind and body as the bromides, or other sedative or hypnotic drugs." Christabel Pankhurst in the *Suffragette* defended Grace Roe :

" It is in order to save herself from the appalling fate, which the Government, by drugging her, are preparing for her, that a suffragist prisoner has resorted to the expedient of taking another, and a different drug, which would quickly free her, either by killing her, or by forcing the Government to unlock the prison door and let her go."

Libel actions were presently commenced on behalf of the medical officers of Holloway prison against Dr. Moxon, Mrs. Pankhurst and other W.S.P.U. officials in respect of the allegations of drugging.

Looking back on the drugging charge it remains, as it always was, a mystery to me. The evidence of the pathological laboratory appears irrefutable proof that drugs were administered. That sleeping draughts were given to prisoners in Holloway I had been long aware, having had one thrust on me during my first imprisonment. It was done in the prison way : two wardresses rushing in—seizing one's shoulders; thrusting the spoon into one's mouth—administering the dose with a cheery word, but by force nevertheless—in my case mainly by surprise. When Dr. Murray first stated that bromide had been given, I was inclined to think it simply an over-liberal dosing of prisoners who complained of sleeplessness. When, however, bromine continued to be excreted after the authorities had denied the administration of sedatives of any sort, the case assumed a graver aspect. The charge of self-drugging by the prisoners is inadmissible; the symptoms were found in prisoners unknown to each other, and confined in different prisons, and the symptoms of drugging in each case disappeared after release. Moreover the authorities had the prisoners in their power for long periods; if the prisoners had been drugging themselves, the fact, and the drugs in their possession, should surely have been discovered by the prison officials. Those who knew the prisoners dismissed as impossible the notion that they would take drugs the effect of which would lead to their lengthened imprisonment, apart from other serious consequences. Phyllis Brady was well known to me. She was obliged to undergo an operation for appendicitis after her last hunger strike. She was afterwards one of our East End organizers, and later built up, by steady perseverance, a successful city typewriting business employing several workers.

Annie Kenney had not been imprisoned since October 13th. On the morning after the deputation to the King she betook herself to Lambeth Palace "to stay with the Archbishop of Canterbury." Her intention was announced by a W.S.P.U. communication to the Press, her objects being stated as : firstly, to take sanctuary and remain safe from arrest; secondly, to urge that the Church should protest against the coercion of militant women, whilst militant men, like Sir Edward Carson and Lord Lansdown, were not attacked; and thirdly, to demand that the Church should take action to secure the immediate enactment of Votes for Women. Annie Kenney tackled the escapade with her usual aplomb, from the height of her belief in the impeccable W.S.P.U. She motored to the Palace and interviewed the Archbishop, but about six o'clock in the evening the police appeared and removed her to Holloway. The W.S.P.U. issued a statement that the Archbishop had shown " culpable weakness by delivering her to the police. The W.S.P.U. holds the Archbishop responsible for anything that may happen to her in prison." After six days of hunger strike Annie Kenney returned to the Palace attended by a doctor and two nurses. The Archbishop refused to receive her; the gates were barred. She lay down on the stones outside, but was removed on a hand ambulance to Kennington Lane police station, and from thence, on refusing to leave, to Lambeth Infirmary. On arrival there she at once decided to leave for "Mouse Castle" with her doctor and nurses, and next morning she motored with them to Fulham Palace to interview the Bishop of London. The Bishop was out, but she waited in the car with her attendants till his return at five-thirty in the evening. He went to her at once, and asked her to come into the garden for tea. She said she would prefer the house, perhaps suspecting re-capture by detectives. The Bishop took her into the hall, considering it safest, no doubt, to keep her near the door, but such nervousness regarding her intentions as he may have experienced was apparently disarmed, for on leaving shortly afterwards, he invited her to rest there for a time. She availed herself of the invitation, remaining till late in the evening.

Meanwhile Mrs. Drummond and Mrs. Dacre Fox had been summoned to appear at Bow Street on May 14th, for using inciting language. Instead of going to the Court, Mrs. Drummond proceeded to the house of Sir Edward Carson, Mrs. Dacre Fox to that of Lord Lansdowne, who had praised the "extraordinary efficiency" of the gun running at Larne. In each case shelter was claimed with a "fellow militant" who enjoyed immunity from prosecution. Warrants having been issued for their arrest, both women were seized and sentenced to a month's imprisonment, in default of finding sureties. After a hunger and thirst strike, Mrs. Drummond was released on May 21st, but when asked where the wardresses were to take her, she refused to give any address. She was therefore sent off to Highgate Workhouse Infirmary, where the wardresses handed in a note from the governor. The Poor Law authorities decided they had no power to detain her, and the wardresses having returned to the prison, she took a taxi, collected a couple of nurses retained for attendance on W.S.P.U. "Mice," and went off to the residence of the Home Secretary, where she lay on the pavement outside. The police removed her on an ambulance to Rochester Row police station, where she spent a night in the cells. She was charged with obstruction, but pleurisy having supervened, she agreed to go home, and the charge was withdrawn. She was re-arrested on June 3rd, and released on June 9th. Mrs. Dacre Fox had been released on May 19th. On July 5th she appeared in Westminster Abbey, and interrupted a sermon of the Bishop of London. She was taken out by the vergers, and re-arrested at the door. After a second release she was again re-arrested outside Buckingham Palace.

CHAPTER VIII

IT was often difficult for me to believe the Government really desired to re-arrest me. I had spoken in Victoria Park in April unmolested; I had travelled to Budapest and returned in safety. Again we were organizing a " Women's May Day " in Victoria Park on the last Sunday in May, three days after the deputation to the King. The procession was to halt for me at the door of the Women's Hall; I was to march in the centre of twenty women, chained to me and to each other; a spectacular guard, rather than a sure one. I was safer in a dense, closely-packed crowd, with a substantial number of men, better able than women to resist the sheer weight of the police. Our stalwarts were carrying banners, attending to the carts of children, the maypoles, one of which was erected on each of the nine platforms, the literature, and so on. We could not seriously contemplate an attack. The detectives were not in sight, yet presently big men, dressed as costers, but of remarkably different build, began to appear from the side roads, pushing their way towards me. I knew them for detectives; there were fifty of them, it was said. At every step they were gaining their object, now insidiously, now roughly penetrating the crowd, drawing always more closely towards the chain-guard.

As we neared the park gates the police cleared a space amongst the waiting throng, as though to let the procession through, then made a fierce onslaught on the people, the coster-detectives laying about them with their sticks. Finally they dragged me and the chain-guard within the boating enclosure and locked its gates behind them. The Inspector demanded the keys of the locks which held our chains together, whilst his subordinates tore at my neck where they expected to find the keys hidden. Finally they smashed the padlocks with their truncheons. We received many a blow during the process, and any woman who attempted to hinder the work had her face pinched, her hair pulled, arms twisted and thumbs bent back, whilst her tormentors gave vent to most lurid epithets. The police were enraged; if the people showed turbulence in a strike they were accustomed to quell them with a good bludgeoning, but these crowds had been disciplined with the truncheon again and again, and still they reappeared. Outside the enclosure the people were charged by the horses and beaten with truncheons. Many were injured; a child had her knee broken. Sections of the crowd retaliated, calling for the gates to be opened, and presently broke down some of the railings, whereat the people poured into the park and the meeting was held.

As soon as the locks had been smashed I was flung on to the floor of a taxi-cab, with a good deal of swearing, pinching, and arm twisting; then four of the big men jumped in and occupied the seats, cursing the East End and its people. I was silent, and presently one of them insisted I should have a place on the seat. They began to question me: Why should I come to live amongst these "roughs" in the East End? I answered by reminding them that they had canvassed all the people in Ford Road, trying to get a room from which they could watch for me, and had offered "a small fortune" for it; yet at every house in the street they had been refused. "It's all in the game," one of my captors muttered shamefacedly. "You'll never get the vote," another jeered; but the best of them answered: "Oh, yes, they'll get it." I asked how it was that on the eve of the Poplar election and other occasions they had made no fight to take me; they answered: "The crowd was too strong!" When the more aggressive of them jumped out of the cab at the prison gates, one of the others said: "The best part of it all is the way the people fight for you and are willing to make sacrifices for the cause."

On May 30th I was free again with new resolutions for the struggle. The popular Suffrage movement, with the East End as its most active centre, must make itself felt by the Cabinet. The objection of Asquith and others that the demand was not democratic, and the movement not of the masses, but of the classes, must be swept away. A deputation to the Prime Minister must be elected, not by the Federation, or any group of Suffragists, but by great open rally meetings in the East End of London. These same open meetings should decide the terms of the demand. Asquith would probably refuse to receive the deputation. We should take no denial, but go in procession to interview him nevertheless. I should accompany the deputation; my licence having expired, I should be re-arrested of course. Then I should not only repeat the usual hunger and thirst strike in prison, but continue it after release until the deputation should be received. Asquith might maintain his refusal to the bitter end; he had always been stubborn. In that case I must leave the others to carry on the fight. I did not want to die and leave all that we hoped to do—yet I was willing to die if it might help to ensure the victory.

My immediate colleagues and our East End people generally

received the project with great enthusiasm, hopeful that the latter part of my scheme would not be put to the test. As soon as I was liberated the rally meetings were put in hand. In each case they were thronged. In each case the following suggestions, all or any of which were open to amendment, were laid before them:

" I. To demand *Votes for Women*, leaving it to the Government to draft the actual Bill embodying this reform, and reserving to ourselves the right to criticize its terms.

" II. To demand *Votes for Women on the terms at present exercised by men*, with a promise that women are to have an equal share in the Adult Suffrage Reform Bill, which the Government say they intend to introduce.

" III. To demand *a vote for every woman over twenty-one years of age.*"

I was anxious for the people to speak their own mind, and in formulating the demands I urged them to choose which they preferred, reminding them that on the floor of the House of Commons all three proposals might come to much the same thing; the Anti-Suffragists would fight to give women as few votes as possible, whilst we, with what support we could muster inside, and what pressure we could make without, would fight to get as broad a franchise as we could. Without exception, each of the rally meetings unanimously selected the third demand: " *A vote for every woman over twenty-one.*" It was an answer to the contention (still made by Suffrage societies) that there was no demand in the country for adult suffrage and an evidence supporting my long-held opinion that the limited demand had divided and discouraged the popular movement. The people, as all the greatest reformers have known, do not see matters as they appear to the politicians, but in broader and larger outlines.

I now wrote to the Prime Minister explaining the character of the deputation and requesting him to receive it on the evening of June 10th, or at some other early date. He refused. I replied in plain terms:

" . . . you have on many occasions stated that you are unaware of any widespread popular demand for Votes for Women. . . .

" Do you realize that since I was arrested for a speech to the people who had come in procession from East London to Trafalgar Square, in which I asked them to go to your house in Downing Street to hoot you for your refusal to give votes to women, I have spoken at dozens of immense public meetings when liable to re-arrest by the police; and in each case the general public, who have come quite freely and without tickets or payment, into the largest halls of those districts, have rallied round me, to a man and to a woman, to protect me from the police, although they have incurred many hard blows and risked imprisonment in doing so? . . . A large proportion of the women of East London are living under terrible conditions. . . . The women are impatient to take a constitutional part in moulding the conditions under which they have to live. . . .

" . . . I cannot think that if you realized the strength and earnestness of the movement here . . . it would fail to make an impression on you. I regard this deputation as of such importance that I have determined, should you refuse to receive the deputation and I be snatched away from the people, as I probably shall be, and taken back to Holloway, my ' Cat and Mouse ' licence having expired, I will not merely hunger strike in Holloway, as I have done eight times under this present sentence, but when I am released, I shall continue my hunger strike at the door of the Strangers' Entrance to the House of Commons, and shall not take either food or water until you agree to receive this deputation. I know very well from what has happened in the past that I am risking my life in coming to this conclusion, because, so far, you have almost invariably refused the appeals which Suffragists have made to you. At the same time I feel it my duty to take this course, and I shall not give way, although it may end in my death."

Again he refused. I wrote to Keir Hardie, Will Thorne and the Bishops of London and Kensington, urging them to march with our procession, as their presence would be a protection to the people. Keir Hardie was obliged to be away from London; I had hoped it would be otherwise. The others failed to reply. At the last of the rally meetings, when Asquith's second refusal to me was made known, the women broke forth in weeping. A nurse who had written asking if she might accompany me on the march appeared at the door of the hall. The women suspected she was a spy; I was obliged to send the stewards to protect her from injury.

Faithful Nevinson, the Rev. Wills and Evelyn Sharp were the only well-known friends who came to march with us from Bow. Lansbury and Scurr chose the more peaceful path, and were marching with the Poplar contingent. The whole district was aroused; the roadway thronged. Wills asked to be allowed to say a prayer from the window. We knew he was probably jeopardizing his livelihood, and respected his courage. I looked out on the throng, believing I might be seeing these crowds who had fought with me for the last time, their work-worn forms, their anxious, loving faces impressing themselves deeply upon my mind. I repeated my intention, striving to cheer and hearten them, beseeching them to keep up the fight should the issue prove fatal to me. They were earnest and silent, the men with bared heads, and the women with streaming tears. I was taken out on a long carrying chair, with poles for the bearers, on the shoulders of four of the men. The women wailed and stretched out their hands.

All happened as I expected: in Grove Road the detectives were gathering thickly to the left of us; our ranks were reduced by the narrowing of the road, and by a stationary taxi-cab to the right of us—placed there with intent. The plain clothes men swept inward with a quick, concerted movement; an Inspector wheeled round his horse, and seized me by the wrists: " You are arrested, Miss Pankhurst! " The bearers were hurled aside. Nevinson clung to the carrying chair and was thrown to the ground. I was in the taxi with the detectives on my way to Holloway.

The processionists re-formed and pressed on, though harassed by the mounted police, the horses curveting amongst their ranks. Again and again they were scattered, but always they re-formed. Nevinson and the others from the West End commented on the unanimity of the cheers and the welcome received on the way. To our people it was a commonplace. In the Jewish quarter, the Mile End Road and Whitechapel, there was the characteristic demand for literature—people rushing eagerly into the roadway to get it—always surprising to propagandists accustomed to the slow toil of selling propaganda papers elsewhere. There was less readiness for a fight with the stick and the fist in these teeming hordes gathered from all the nationalities oppressed, or once oppressed, in Europe, than one found in the typical Cockney crowd, but more of desire for information, a more general diffusion of sympathy with all movements of liberation. Everywhere people were breaking into the ranks to catch the arm of some passing marcher and ask the news. At Gardner's Corner the Poplar contingent joined the procession. Marching past the Old Bailey, Nevinson, towards the rear, could see the dense crowd filling the roadway reaching down Ludgate Hill across the Circus, and surging half-way up the incline of Fleet Street. At the Gaiety Theatre in the Strand a cordon of police halted the throng. The ranks, if such they could be termed—the swarm rather— were broken, as we had given warning they must be, within a mile of Parliament. The people proceeded in their own fashion to Parliament Square. The House was strongly guarded by an army of police. The elected deputation, nine women and three men, were refused admission, but Lansbury was allowed to pass in as an ex-Member. He brought out Sir William Byles to escort the others inside. Finally they were interviewed by Illingworth, the Chief Liberal Whip, who told them Asquith was away, and promised to convey their message. Unwilling to leave without protest, the women of the deputation made speeches to the vast crowds on the forbidden ground of Parliament Square, but there were no arrests. Authority was conciliatory towards the people in their multitudes.

Next day, June 11th, the hunger strike was debated in the Commons. Lord Robert Cecil protested against forcible feeding, and urged his old scheme of deporting the militants. He asked whether the French Government could be induced to take action against Christabel. McKenna, defending his administration, declared he had to deal with " a phenomenon absolutely without precedent in our history." He was advised to let the hunger strikers die. The advice was given by those who believed the women would surrender their strike if told they would on no consideration be released.

" We have to face the fact, however, that they would die . . . in many cases they have got in their refusals of food and water beyond the point where they could help themselves. . . . There are those who . . . think that after one or two deaths in prison, militancy would cease. . . . So far from putting an end to militancy, I believe it would be the greatest incentive to militancy which could ever happen. For every woman who died there would be scores who would come forward for the honour, as they would deem it, of the crown of martyrdom. . . . They have a courage, part of their fanaticism, which undoubtedly stands at nothing. . . . They would seek death; and I am sure that however strong public opinion outside might be to-day in favour of letting them die, when there were twenty, thirty, forty or more deaths in prison, you would have a violent reaction of public opinion. . . . We should have woman after woman, whose only offence may have been obstructing the police, breaking a window, or even burning down an empty house, dying because she was obstinate. I do not believe that is a policy which, on consideration, will ever recommend itself to the British people, and I am bound to say for myself that I could never take a hand in carrying that policy out."

As to deportation; if the Suffragettes were sent to a distant island, it must either be treated as a prison, in which case they would hunger strike as before, or the wealthy supporters of the militant movement would very quickly charter a yacht and bring the prisoners away. As to putting the prisoners into lunatic asylums, he made the startling admission :

" I have on many occasions . . . had the prisoners examined by doctors, but in no case have they been willing to certify them as lunatics."

As to giving them the franchise, that was not his province as Home Secretary. He did not think the suggestion could be seriously treated as a remedy for the existing state of lawlessness. It was said the women were not punished for their offences.

" There never was a greater delusion. . . . Owing to their misconduct they are punished far more heavily than if they served their sentences."

The Home Secretary's remedy was " patient and determined action." The number of women committing crimes was comparatively small, though the number of their supporters was very large. He did not believe a single one of these crimes was committed by a person who was not paid. (A " Mouse" retaliated by sending a donation of £500 to the W.S.P.U. funds.) He intended to proceed against the W.S.P.U. subscribers by civil action; the insurance companies would certainly follow suit. If that were done the day of militancy would soon be over. He would also consider criminal proceedings against the subscribers; no pains would be spared. If the actions were successful it would destroy the revenue of the W.S.P.U. and " the last will be seen of the power of Mrs. Pankhurst and her friends." The result was more money for the W.S.P.U. £15,350 was presently raised at a meeting in the Holland Park Rink. The debate revealed the Government still determined to end the militant movement by coercion—not by satisfaction of its demand. Whilst McKenna was speaking a loud report was heard : a bomb had exploded in Westminster Abbey, damaging the Coronation chair and stone and the wall of Edward the Confessor's chapel.

After their night march to Westminster and failure to find the Prime Minister there the women of our East End deputation had met at once and dispatched a letter to Asquith, demanding to be received. He replied, through his secretary, that he had already twice written to the secretary of the Federation giving a refusal; he did not think there was " any reason why the East London Federation should receive exceptional treatment." Remote indeed was any sign of relenting. Melvina Walker was summoned for her speech at the Limehouse Town Hall rally meeting, and sent to prison for a month. The branches of the Federation were hard at work, striving to get the deputation received : lobbying at the House, writing to Members of Parliament, holding meetings and poster parades, distributing bills. The prison was picketed night and day. Married women rose earlier and worked later, young factory girls gave up their leisure to take their share of the toil. Mrs. Mansell Moullin organized a meeting of the Cymric Suffrage Union at the Caxton Hall, where some of our East End women, with Lansbury, Nevinson and Evelyn Sharp, voiced our demand. The United Suffragists lent their aid. Norah Smyth, who believed that Asquith would remain obdurate till my death, wrote pleading with Mrs. Pankhurst to join the W.S.P.U. effort to ours. She replied that our action was not in conformity with W.S.P.U. policy; as to me, she said: " Tell her I advise her when she comes out of prison to go home and let her friends take care of her, as Annie Kenney and Mrs. Drummond have done." Norah Smyth was shocked by the reply. She knew me well enough to understand that I should not withdraw. Moreover she considered it would be humiliating to me and to the Federation to give way. " It is like Asquith saying the women could walk out of prison if they would give an undertaking! " she protested when she afterwards showed me the letter. " You ought not to have written at all," I told her. " Did you not understand in Paris that no family or other considerations are permitted to intervene? " But this was later.

In prison the days crawled by, weary and painful from illness, yet otherwise calm. For the first time I made no fight to hasten release—the longer they kept me, the better for my purpose. I made no effort to write. My thoughts were occupied with the struggle before me. I wondered how long it would last. I had never believed myself so near the limit of my endurance as the doctors, in prison and out, had assured me to be the case. I suspected one could last much longer without food and water than was generally supposed by those who had dealt with the hunger strikers. I anticipated that the end would be very painful and protracted. I conceived a possibility, not, I hoped, a probability, that at a certain stage I might lose command of myself, lose perhaps my memory of present events, and fall into a state of semi-consciousness when nourishment could be pressed upon me. If that were to happen, with returning strength I should have to begin all the weary struggle over again. I hoped this might not be, that my mind would remain alert until the last. Yet I was resolved for all contingencies.

Release came on June 18th. The wardresses took me, as usual, in a taxi to Old Ford Road. A crowd had collected, for the pickets had telephoned I was coming. Norah Smyth had a motor at the door, waiting to take me to Westminster. Mrs. Payne helping me, I washed my face, changed the dress I had worn night and day in the prison, and came out immediately to take my seat in the car. The women were weeping. In a bodily sense I was weak, for this last hunger and thirst strike had followed only ten days after the preceding one, but I was cool and collected; only when I attempted to stand or sit upright I felt faint. I told Norah Smyth to call to the women to be of good cheer, and to drive with speed to the House of Commons. My mind was concentrated on the object, emotionless and unfearing, like one who is running a race.

The long summer evening was fading as we reached the House. A little crowd of our women were waiting for us there. We drew up near Richard Cœur de Lion's statue. Keir Hardie and Josiah Wedgwood came out to the car, both very gentle and kind. Keir Hardie said it would be best for me to go with them to wait in St. Stephen's Hall whilst they made efforts to communicate with Asquith. I smiled at his thoughtfulness: " I would, but they will not let me in," I told him. He went to arrange it, but came back saying that I was still black-listed.[1] I must do, he told me, as Members of Parliament do when compelled to withdraw from the Chamber; I must write a letter to Mr. Speaker apologizing for having " broken the rules of the House." It was simply a matter of form, he urged. To please him I consented. He returned with the news I expected: Mr. Speaker maintained his prohibition. " I must go to the steps; there is nothing else for it," I told him. He begged me to wait in the car a little while longer, and hurried away to get speech with Asquith. My companions, too, begged me to wait his return. I waited; the time seemed endless.

I called to my friends to help me, over-riding kind efforts to delay and obstruct me. Norah Smyth and the others supported me. They swerved from the Stranger's Entrance, unable, I saw, to face the policemen standing on the steps. Their instinct might be right—I should be moved immediately from that spot. I indicated the little square door to the left, nearer to Cromwell's statue, and there they laid me. A police inspector came forward to tell me I could not stay there. I replied I must wait there till the Prime Minister would consent to receive the deputation. There was some altercation. Policemen were bending to seize me, when Lansbury and Nevinson came running out to say that Asquith had agreed to receive us. I thought they might be mistaken, or saying it just to induce me to go away; to save me from being taken to prison. Then I saw Keir Hardie beside me. He told me, in his quiet way, that Asquith would receive six of our women on Saturday morning. I knew it was true; he would not lie. People began to cheer. Everyone was laughing and talking around me. Keir Hardie and Nevinson, Norah Smyth and Mrs. Watkins, dozens of people were helping me back to the car, amid waving of hands and handkerchiefs, congratulations and delight. " We are winning! At last we are winning! " Everyone felt this an omen of the turning of the tide. As many women as possible crowded on to the car. Back we went racing to the East End. Then: " Do you not think we could stop for a drink of water now? " I asked them. They laughed again.

[1] For throwing a stone at the picture of Speaker Finch being held in the chair.

We pulled up at a " Cabin " Restaurant; a jug of hot water was brought to the car. The news had flown round. "Happy to bring it! Of course no charge!"

Outside 400 Old Ford Road the crowd of women had been fretting and crying throughout the evening. The telephone rang. Mrs. Payne rushed out, her dear face beaming, to give them the news. They responded with laughing and cheering. The road was thronged when I reached it. What cheers! What laughter, and what excitement! Mrs. Payne hugged me; we kissed each other and laughed. What talk and excitement! We could not sleep.

Next day I prepared a statement to be read by Mrs. Julia Scurr. She was to lead the deputation. I did not care to go. Let these working mothers speak for themselves; it was for this I had struggled. The statement would give them their cue and break the ice for them. I had put into it what I knew to be near their hearts. They were photographed at our door before starting. Stout old Mrs. Savoy; the brush-maker, jolly and brave in spite of her dropsy and her palpitations—an example, indeed, to the *malades imaginaires.* " The best woman in Old Ford," George Lansbury called her. In spite of her poverty, she was bringing up two orphan boys, and was ever ready to share her last crust, or perform any service for a neighbour, from bringing her baby into the world to scrubbing out her room, or minding her children at need. She had called herself " Mrs. Hughes " for the day, because her husband, an elderly eccentric, almost past work, objected to having his " name in the papers." Motherly, anxious Mrs. Payne. Mrs. Bird, the wife of a transport worker, keeping a home for him and their six children on his wage of 25s. a week. Mrs. Parsons, a frail little woman, who, having a delicate father, had worked to help her mother to support her little brothers since she was twelve years of age; and now with a husband earning a small wage, was caring for her two little girls and an orphaned niece. Mrs. Watkins. Mrs. Scurr, who till the first advent of the Suffragettes in 1905-6, had been a " quiet housewife," but aroused by them to a sense of public duty, as she often told me, was now a vigilant Poor Law Guardian. They had been selected by the mass meetings as women known and respected in the districts where they lived.

They brought before the Prime Minister, in simple, moving phrases, the toilsome life of poor women. The Alien Immigration Board had but recently refused to permit a Russian girl to come into this country, because her prospective employer offered her a weekly wage of only 13s. 6d.; the Board declared she could not live in London under 17s. 6d. Yet none of the Trade Boards set up to alleviate the conditions of women wage earners had fixed a higher minimum wage than 13s. 6d. for a full week's work, and in most of the industries concerned there was much short time. Mrs. Savoy herself, who had worked forty-three years as a brush-maker, was only paid 1¼d. for a brush which took her nearly two hours to make. The Prime Minister and his companions started, as though it had been a bomb, when she put the brush, with its two hundred holes, on the table. "I do all the work; I keep my home; I ought to have a vote for it!" As a girl Mrs. Parsons had earned less than 1s. a day by packing cigarettes. Mrs. Bird, with her six children, declared herself better off than thousands of other wives, for thousands of husbands earned only 18s. a week, and many had larger families than hers. "The husband scarcely knows how the money is spent," one of them urged. "A man brings his money home and lays it on the table, and then he is able to go out. There are all the expenses of rent, clubs and everything, and then clothes wear out; and you have to find clothes for the children, and the things that wear out in the home: it all has to come out of the weekly money; you do not get any extra." "You can tell we do not get a living, but an existence." They spoke of the housing conditions, so hideous in their district; the yards "only fit for a dirt pail." "We have to leave our children to the mercy of the street." It was but a little while after the deputation that the child of one of our active members was run over and killed by a motor-'bus. "In a strike it is the mother who has to do the ferreting." "Our husbands die on the average at an earlier age than the men of other classes; modern industrialism kills them off rapidly by accident and overwork. . . . The Poor Law has treated us mercilessly. It is hated by every poor woman. In many cases out-relief is altogether denied to the widow and the deserted wife; only the Workhouse is offered, which means separation from the children. Where out-relief is given, it is surrounded by humiliating conditions. . . . The women local government voters number only one-sixth of the electorate. The Boards of Guardians are obliged to administer the rules of the Local Government Board, which is controlled by Parliament." Mrs. Payne disclosed her great sorrow: "I have had to work at the side of my husband making shoes, and to look after my daughter and do everything for her. From the time she was born until she died she never combed her own hair; she was mentally deficient and lived to be twenty-seven. . . . Once when my girl was taken bad she went into the Poplar Workhouse. My husband thought he was compelled to let her go. When I got there next morning they had put her in a padded room. I asked the doctor why she was there. He told me I had no voice, I was not to ask the why or the wherefore—only the father had that right." Mrs. Parsons had a conscientious objection to vaccination, but when she applied to make her declaration she was turned away—their father alone was the parent of her children. "We know that every year large numbers of poor women are sent to prison for contempt of Court because they are unable to pay their rates. Some of these are quite old women who have worked hard all their lives and never before have come into conflict with the law."

The high rate of sickness amongst married women wage-earners, revealed to Government officials by the working of the Insurance Acts, Unemployment, the law in relation to Separation Orders and Affiliation Orders; by daily contact with hard, familiar cases, they knew the bitterness of them all. The sorrowful plight of the unmarried mother, the painful questions of prostitution and the White Slave Traffic were no remote romance; they knew the victims. Mrs. Watkins told a common story: "A girl friend of mine at the factory . . . the manager. . . . She had to go to the Workhouse to have a baby. When she came out she had no home and no mother to go to. I took her in. She shared my bed and my room. Money was very short, and rather than take the food out of my children's mouths she went away. I did not see her till three days after, when she was drawn out of the River Lea with her child."

Always they returned to their demand for a place in the constitution.

" We know there are some who belittle representative Government and declare the vote useless, but we cannot think that you, sir, as Prime Minister of this country, will assent to that view.

" . . . Our demand is for the form of franchise for women you have repeatedly said you could best understand, and with which you would be most in sympathy. It is the form of franchise which you have declared your intention of establishing for men in the near future. It is the one for which your Party is supposed to stand—a vote for every woman over twenty-one.

" The great public demonstrations which elected us to speak to you to-day unanimously decided that we should lay before you the demand for an immediate Government measure for a vote for every woman over twenty-one. This demand is supported by an enormous volume of working-class opinion throughout the country, especially in our own district. . . . Organized Labour has long made this demand, and for many years past the Trade Union Congress and later the Labour Party annual conferences have declared for it."

Each woman repeated and emphasized the demand in her own fashion, and each one added a plea that Mrs. Walker and I should be unconditionally released.[1] They urged that I had already served sixty-five days of my sentence without food or water.

Asquith's reply revealed an unmistakable softening in his long hostility; almost he seemed to declare himself a convert:

" . . . I tell you quite frankly that I have listened with the greatest interest to the statement read by Mrs. Scurr, and to . . . the special, individual experience of the various members of the deputation, by which the statement has been reinforced. I think it is a very moderate and well-reasoned presentation of your case and I will give it, you may be quite sure, very careful and mature consideration.

" I am not going to enter into anything of argument, or to deal, so far as I can avoid it, with any controversial topic; but I think I am right in saying that the substance of the case you have to-day presented to me comes to this : that the economic conditions under which women labour in a community like, for instance, the East End of London, are such that either in the way of legislation, or perhaps in the way of administration, we cannot get substantial and intelligent reform unless women themselves have a voice in choosing representatives for Parliament. I think that is your case.

" I think that fairly states the substance of it, and you have each of you given me special illustrations, drawn from your own experience, or from the experience of your leaders, to show that this is not a mere rhetorical statement, but does correspond to the actual facts of East End life. As I say, I am not going to argue, because I will take all these things into careful consideration."

Then followed a plea that the Liberal Government had done something to improve the lot of women wage-earners, by passing the Trade Boards Act, and that he had himself always been a strong advocate of women factory inspectors. He continued:

" On one point I am glad to say I am in complete agreement with you . . . if you are going to give the franchise to women, you must give it to them on the same terms that you do to men. That is, make it a democratic measure. It is no good tinkering with a thing of this kind. If the discrimination of sex is not sufficient to justify the giving of the vote to the one sex and the withholding of it from another, it follows, *a fortiori*, it seems to me, that discrimination of sex does not justify, and cannot warrant giving the woman a restricted form of franchise while you give the man an unrestricted form.

" On that point I am entirely with you. If the change has to come, we must face it boldly, and make it thoroughgoing and democratic in its basis."

[1] This was their own decision. I had at one moment thought of including in the object of my hunger strike at the House of Commons a demand for my unconditional release—as a protest against the " Cat and Mouse " Act. I discarded, however, that point, as too narrow and personal. I did not mention it in my correspondence with the Prime Minister.

As to the plea for the prisoners, he would confer with the Home Secretary: " I am sure there is not the faintest disposition in any quarter to be vindictive."

" I will give this memorial you have presented me, and the arguments with which you have supported it, the most careful consideration."

He essayed, by the way, though not very strongly, to draw from the women a repudiation of the more violent militancy, but they stoutly refused it. Mrs. Scurr said: " While our organization has not at present committed arson, we do not want to criticize the other organizations; we know that in the past men have used all sorts of methods."

Following as it did on his capitulation in receiving the deputation, the answer, though without any promise of action, seemed to pave the way for a change of front on the part of the Prime Minister and his Government. There was general rejoicing. Hosts of letters came to me expressing this hopeful view. The East London Federation was " at home " to its friends on July 8th. They came crowding in to congratulate us, from far and near. Nevinson wrote:

" . . . delighted to come . . . delighted to see you again. You have accomplished the greatest piece of work achieved for many years."

Mrs. Cavendish Bentinck was enthusiastic:

" I never wrote to congratulate you on your victory, because it was such an immense triumph that it seemed quite superfluous to do so.

" You know quite well that every Suffragist was full of joy— and pride in you. I only trust that you are getting over it gradually —that those savage idiots will now leave you in peace."

The Press was of the same mind. The *Labour Leader*:

" . . . beneath the Prime Minister's words there seemed to be a recognition that Women's Suffrage cannot long be delayed."

The Nation:

" . . . a new departure and a new chapter of hope in the history of the question. . . . After the instructive history of this Parliament no man who cares for his own repute as a sincere and clear-thinking politician will play with proposals for a private Members' Bill, or waste his energy on face-saving efforts by unofficial groups of Members. The thing can only be done by a Government which knows its own mind from the first. Those Ministers who believe in Women's Suffrage are clearly bound to put it in their electoral programme, and to declare for a Government measure. . . . The next Liberal Cabinet is bound to be a Suffragist Cabinet. There may,

of course, be a Tory Cabinet which will aim at a narrow Bill. . . .
Liberalism can only adopt this reform with full convictions and
enthusiasm in a democratic shape."

Even the W.S.P.U. observed an advance. Wrote Christabel
in *The Suffragette*:

" He in effect admitted the justice of the case of Votes for Women.
. . . Once upon a time Mr. Asquith stood at the point of ' Never '
as regards Votes for Women. Now he has reached the stage of ' If.' "

She added, of course: " Beware of politicians when they say
' If ': but indeed we all knew we must ' go on pestering.' "

The United Suffragists invited the East London Federation to
a joint Trafalgar Square demonstration to demand an autumn
session to be devoted to a Government measure for Women's
Suffrage. We agreed to join, though the resolution was not
entirely satisfactory to us, for it avoided specifying any terms for
the measure. Indeed we were still alone in our determination
to press for womanhood suffrage, and in our realization that only
this demand would consolidate the working class movements in
a firm pressure for legislation. All through the speeches,
reported the *Manchester Guardian*, ran the thought of the
concession obtained from Mr. Asquith—" one of the greatest
steps forward the movement had ever made, said Miss Nina
Boyle."

CHAPTER IX

CERTAINLY there was an atmosphere of tremendous hope,
though on the other side of the shield was the growing
harshness towards the militants in prison, the diabolical
extension of forcible feeding plus the " Cat and Mouse " Act,
first to women accused of arson, then to those convicted of lesser
offences, window breaking, incitement, and so on, and even to
untried prisoners. By the end of July seven women[1] had been
incarcerated continuously under forcible feeding for upwards of
eight weeks, one of them, Gertrude Ansell, for thirteen weeks.
Several, with long sentences before them, were at the beginning
of the torture. Rachel Peace, with fifteen months to serve, had
hunger struck repeatedly, but again and again had broken down
from fear that forcible feeding would destroy her reason.

The administration of the " Cat and Mouse " Act was
growing more ruthless in every respect. In the first place
McKenna had told the House of Commons that the Act gave no
power to force admission to private houses for the purpose of
making re-arrests, but now detectives were actually demanding
entry to houses where they merely suspected that " Mice " might
be concealed. On June 18th five suspected houses were raided;
one " Mouse," Arabella Scott, being re-captured. Detectives also
forced their way into 2 Campden Hill Square to procure the
examination of Freda Graham by a doctor they brought with
them. Having been committed for trial for damaging pictures
at the National Gallery, she had practised a concealed hunger
and thirst strike, remaining fifteen days without food and water,

Name	No. of weeks forcibly fed	Sentence	Alleged offence
[1] Gertrude Ansell	13	6 months	Injuring picture at Royal Academy.
Hilda Burkitt	12	2 years	Arson.
Florence Tunks	12	9 months	Arson.
Nellie Hall	10	3 months	Being in possession of explosives.
Grace Roe	9	3 months	Conspiracy to commit damage.
Phyllis North	8	3 months	Window smashing.
Mary Spencer	10	6 months	Damaging picture at Royal Academy.

578

and before release had cut off her hair in delirium. She was so gravely enfeebled that for three weeks no statement could be obtained from her. Six weeks had now passed, but the police doctor declared her too ill for removal. Hunger strikers were now held for longer terms than had hitherto obtained: Kitty Marion had been forcibly fed from early January till April 16th and had lost three stone in weight. The knowledge that a long term of forcible feeding would purchase but a brief period of release created in some prisoners a disposition to more serious acts of destruction. The career as a " Mouse " of Mary Richardson was remarkable:

July 8th, 1913. Sentenced to three months' hard labour for assaulting the police when I was arrested outside the Bromley Public Hall. Released in four days.

July 18th. Sentenced to one month's hard labour for breaking a window at the Home Office, and flung an inkpot through the window of the police station " to demonstrate the absurdity " of the " Cat and Mouse " Act. Released five days later.

July 28th (afternoon). Arrested and released on bail for obstructing the police when Annie Kenney was arrested at the London Pavilion.

July 28th (evening). Arrested for breaking windows at Holloway Gaol. Sentenced next day to two months' imprisonment. Released August 3rd.

August 8th. Arrested for breaking windows at Colonial Office. Committed for trial. Released August 12th.

October 4th. Arrested for arson, Hampton. Remanded and forcibly fed. Released, October 24th, suffering from appendicitis.

March 10th, 1914. Slashed the Rokeby Venus in the National Gallery. Sentenced to six months' imprisonment. Her medical adviser stated the appendicitis quiescent but not cured. Forcibly fed. Released April 6th with appendicitis. Operation postponed on account of complication making operation precarious.

May 20th. Re-arrested. Forcibly fed. Released with appendicitis May 25th.

June 6th. Re-arrested. Forcibly fed. Released July 28th with acute appendicitis after several attacks. Operation July 30th, appendix much inflamed and diseased, with other signs of recurring and acute inflammation. According to Dr. Flora Murray's report her mouth was scarred and painful from the finger-nails of prison officials. There were cuts, scratches and bruises on her body, one large bruise being in the region of the appendix where pain and tenderness were greatest.

After the vote had been won Mary Richardson became a Labour candidate for Parliament, though she was dropped when the seat became a promising one. She at one time desired to

enter a religious sisterhood.   She came to me once with a scheme
for establishing a Communist nunnery of social and religious
service.

All the hunger strikers committed in Scotland were now
taken to Perth prison for forcible feeding, because, according to
the Secretary of State for Scotland, McKinnon Wood:

" We have there medical officers who are accustomed to perform
the operation in the criminal lunatic department there."

It was one of these medical officers from Perth who had
gone up to the Calton Gaol, Edinburgh, to feed Ethel Moorhead
in 1913, and had accidentally poured food into her lungs, causing
pneumonia.   She complained on release that her left ear had
been burnt with hot wires during the feeding, apparently either
to lessen her resistance, or to deter her from the struggle.   Two
prisoners confined in Perth prison now made serious allegations
against their treatment.   Frances Gordon (Graves) was serving
a year's imprisonment for housebreaking with intent to commit
arson.   She declared that she had been forcibly fed by tube from
June 24th.   From June 29th, till her release on July 3rd,
injections (which she had not been allowed to see) had also been
made into the bowel three times a day.   These made her drowsy
and were never retained.   Dr. Mabel Jones, M.D. (Lond.), who
attended her on release, reported that: Her appearance was
appalling—like a famine victim—her joints were stiff and
swollen from poisoning, and she had lost control over the bowel.
Questioned in the Commons on July 16th, the Scottish Secretary
replied that there had been no bowel feeding, but " the patient's
condition required the administration of enemata."

A still more startling case was that of Janet Arthur (Miss
Parker, a niece of Lord Kitchener), an untried prisoner, accused
of attempting to blow up the birthplace of Robert Burns, and on
July 8th committed to Ayr prison " pending inquiry."   She
alleged, in a signed statement, that on the sixth day of her
hunger and thirst strike she was taken to Perth.   She was there
fed by tube with unnecessary violence, a wardress slapping her
face in the doctor's presence.   After the feeding she was held
down for two hours; first by the assistant doctor, who kept his
hands over her mouth and " tightened his grip " when she
showed signs of vomiting, then by a wardress.   On the third
day she lost consciousness after the morning feeding, and instead
of being subjected to the nasal tube again at midday, she alleged
that three wardresses attempted, with great cruelty, to feed her
by the rectum.   The process was repeated next day.   Her
account is of a painful nature, and is best given in her own words:

" Thursday, 16th July. . . . the three wardresses appeared again. One of them said that if I did not resist she would send the others away and do what she had come to do as gently and decently as possible. I consented. This was another attempt to feed me by the rectum, and was done in a cruel way, causing me great pain.

" She returned some time later and said she had ' something else ' to do. I took it to be another attempt to feed me in the same way, but it proved to be a grosser and more indecent outrage, which could have been done for no other purpose than to torture. It was followed by soreness which lasted for several days.

" I was released on that afternoon. . . .

" While lying in the cell I could not help wondering how the doctors and wardresses could ever become so cruel. It suggests a long course of deliberate cruelty practised in convict prison life. . . ."[1]

It should be observed that the special charges in these three cases all related to prison officials from Perth, where there was the criminal lunatic asylum. No similar statement was made concerning any other gaol.

That old gentleman, the Prime Minister, whose obstinacy had barred the enfranchisement of women for so long, might, with cautious deliberation, be preparing to change his mind; but a day was a year to the hunger strikers in prison.

I resolved to see other Members of the Government. Lloyd George, Grey, Simon, all the reputed Suffragist Ministers perhaps, and some of the Antis. Certainly McKenna: I wanted to beard the author of the " Cat and Mouse " Act. He had hitherto declared himself an opponent. Yet in his references to the hunger strikers a tinge of admiration had betrayed itself. I would probe him for myself.

I broached the subject of an interview with Lloyd George to Lansbury. He took up the idea with enthusiasm and at once agreed to arrange it. There was then much Press gossip, not unmixed with sneers, about the breakfast-table conferences which Lloyd George was holding with the leaders of various factions; Ramsay Macdonald, as Chairman of the Labour Party, was suspected of electoral bargaining over the tea-cups. Lloyd George was cordiality itself: Lansbury and I were invited to breakfast, Lloyd George would guarantee my immunity from re-arrest. Lansbury could not accept the invitation: had not the *Herald* condemned the breakfast parties? He replied we would come later.

It was a folly, typical of my habitual economies in respect of my own needs, and the financial pressure always attendant on our

[1] This statement was not published till August 7th, when this country was already at war. It appeared only in *Votes for Women*, being too late for the last issue of *The Suffragette*.

activities with so poor a membership, not to have procured a taxi. The early start, the long 'bus journey had reduced me, in my weakness, to a condition of acute fatigue. Lloyd George sat with his back to the window. The light hurt my eyes when I looked at his face. At once I felt that the interview would not be a success; I was too tired to get behind his defences. He was far too nimble in mind for Lansbury, who, in any case, was only the usher on this occasion. Lloyd George took the lead, and kept it throughout the interview. He assumed that a General Election would have intervened before the next session of Parliament, and declared that he would refuse to join the new Liberal Cabinet, except on condition that a Reform Bill should be introduced, in which (to meet the Speaker's ruling) a clause giving votes to women on broad, general lines should be left to a free vote of the House of Commons. He would sponsor this amendment and start campaigning for it immediately, and to indicate his intentions he would introduce a private Members' Bill on the same lines. He would " stake " his " political reputation " on the passage of votes for women on broad lines in the next session of Parliament, and resign if it were defeated. He would give us written guarantees of this, which it would be " political dishonour " for him to repudiate, but in the meantime militancy must be suspended; that was imperative, for otherwise it would be impossible for him to swing the Liberal Party machine into line behind him.[1] At present there was a resentment amongst the Liberal officials which it would be necessary to assuage.

If the promised guarantees were really of a binding character, Lloyd George's offer was important, and might mean, not only a struggle for Women's Suffrage, but a contest for power between himself and his political rivals in the Liberal Party. If Asquith should choose to turn Suffragist, and come forward with a Government measure, the personal comedy would be interesting, and the advantage would be ours. Did Lloyd George mean business? I was anxious to see the written guarantees, and wondering whether their publication would precipitate the conversion of the Prime Minister. As soon as I got outside I realized that I ought to have asked Lloyd George to draft the guarantees, then and there. I ought to have discovered also

---

[1] George Lansbury (*My Life*, by George Lansbury, p. 126. (Constable.)) has given a different version of the interview : " We got on very well with Lloyd George, who informed us that Sir Edward Grey, Sir John Simon and himself were willing to give a public pledge that they would decline to enter any Government after the next General Election which did not make Women's Suffrage the first plank in its legislative programme." I adhere to my own version of the interview. My letter to Mr. Lloyd George at the time indicates that he was not prepared to go so far as Mr. Lansbury says. Moreover, Lloyd George did not pledge Simon and Grey.

whether he was willing to have them published.   Instead of that, whilst my mind was probing the question as to the Minister's actual intentions and whether he could be brought to go further, I made a false step by expressing what was a second thought in my mind, and by expressing it baldly: " I do not know whether Christabel would consent to a truce to militancy for anything short of a Government measure."   He had been waiting perhaps an expression of gratitude for an offer he regarded as a great one. At any rate he stiffened perceptibly.   " I shall be quite prepared to debate it with Miss Christabel," he answered tartly, in a tone which seemed to imply: " I shall do nothing of the kind! " Yet we parted under the understanding that I should communicate his proposals to all concerned.

I intended to proceed with the other interviews I had projected.   Then to see him again.   Material might, I hoped, be obtained for a further approach to the Prime Minister.   It might be that the pro-Suffrage Ministers could be induced to make a concerted move.   Lloyd George had made an offer. Others might have something better to propose.   I did not intend to disclose the negotiations to anyone till I had seen the other Ministers.   George Lansbury, however, jubilant at Lloyd George's offer, at once communicated it to H. D. Harben, who rushed off immediately to give the news to Christabel in Paris. Whether, at second hand, she got an accurate version of the interview I never knew.   Certainly she spurned the offer, announcing that the W.S.P.U. would fight to the bitter end and never again suspend militancy till a Government measure were secured.   I was sorry that the situation had been thus complicated. I wished I might have been permitted to continue my explorations unhindered, and that I might have been left to convey the result of the interview in my own way.   I wrote to Christabel that I knew she had been told I had seen Lloyd George; that I intended to interview also other Members of the Government, and when I had done so I would go over to Paris to see her.   I said I thought there might be a good many attempts at negotiation before success was assured.   The reply was a telegram from Christabel to Norah Smyth :

" Tell your friend not to come."

In a couple of issues of the *Suffragette* Christabel's leading articles, in type of unusually large size, were devoted to the repudiation of negotiations :

" The W.S.P.U. desires to receive no private communications from the Government, or any of its members."[1]

[1] July 17th.

"Militancy will continue unless and until the Lords carry a Votes for Women Bill, and that Bill, receiving the Royal assent, becomes an Act of Parliament.

"The Government are spreading about a piece of clap-trap invented for the deluding of women who want votes. It is that 'there must come a negotiations stage.' Not at all, says the W.S.P.U. The militant women say to the Government: 'When you give us votes, we will give you peace.'

"No militant will believe a single word that the Government may say. No militant will trust in a single promise that the Government may make. Then down with negotiations!"[1]

It was curious, with all this outcry against negotiation, that in the July 17th issue of the *Suffragette* appeared a statement that a W.S.P.U. deputation had interviewed Sir Edward Grey. He had given the usual reply that as the Cabinet was divided no Government action could be taken.

In the meantime, two days after the East End deputation to the Prime Minister, Mrs. Scurr had written to him on our behalf asking the result of his promised consideration. Before an answer was received Colonel Wedgwood had put a question in the Commons as to my release from the operations of the "Cat and Mouse" Act, and had received the old reply that I could have my freedom if I would give an undertaking to refrain from law-breaking and incitement. This by no means disturbed me, for were I released under that sentence, I knew that to carry on the agitation I should only have to get myself imprisoned on another charge. On July 1st the Prime Minister replied to Mrs. Scurr's letter in evasive terms, referring her to the last interview he had had with Mrs. Fawcett and the N.U.W.S.S. on the franchise question, and to the reply to Colonel Wedgwood's question in respect of Mrs. Walker and myself. I was undismayed by this apparent hardening of the Prime Minister's attitude; he had admitted the justice, both of our claim to the vote and the terms of our demand. I believed his mind was moving towards the adoption of women's enfranchisement as a Government measure, but I anticipated he would take time to arrive at that point. Remission of my sentence had been refused, but I went about freely as though it had been granted. I drove in a great procession to Canning Town. There was no attempt at arrest. I was determined to proceed with the negotiations I had projected, but I judged it wisest to wait a while for the effect of Christabel's utterances to subside, and at the moment to turn my attention to the Labour Party, in order to bring to bear another type of pressure on the Government. I wrote to Lloyd George, further

[1] July 24th.

discussing the points he had raised in our interview and urging him to act without waiting a cessation of militancy :

" 21st *July*, 1913.

" DEAR MR. LLOYD GEORGE,—When Mr. Lansbury and I saw you a short time ago we agreed to communicate with you again.

" The proposal that the Women's Suffrage clauses in a Government Reform Bill should be left to the decision of a free vote of the House seems open to the objections which attended the amendment plan in the case of the Bill of 1913 prior to the Speaker's ruling.

" I need not remind you of the general feeling amongst Suffragists that it is difficult, if not absolutely impossible, to get important measures through without the Government Whips, and of the persistent rumours that if the amendment were carried the Government would be endangered and the Prime Minister would resign.

" I should not perhaps realize this point so clearly, but for the fact that I was in the Grand Committee Room of Westminster Hall with a deputation of fifty working women just before the Speaker gave his ruling, and before that ruling was given Member after Member came to us, saying that though he was a Suffragist, he was going to vote against the women's amendments, in order to save the Prime Minister from embarrassment, and to prevent trouble in the Cabinet. I remember especially Sir William Byles saying that he was going to vote against Votes for Women ' for the sake of women.'

" I know you feel, as you said, that ' there are other causes,' and it is perhaps a big thing for a public man who holds high office in the State to go even so far as to say that he will refuse to join a Cabinet which will not leave the question of women's enfranchisement to a free vote of the House; but in taking such a step, is it not necessary to ensure that it shall be big enough both to achieve success in Parliament and to win the general confidence of the women in the country?

" I am sure you must comprehend the anxiety of women to see something tangible in this Parliament and their impatience and fear of delay after so many years of struggle and disappointment.

" If you were to say that you would not remain in the Cabinet to lend your aid in carrying the Franchise Bill should the women's clause be voted out of it, it would seem to balance the fear of other resignations or rumoured resignations. But if you were to take that course, would it not come to the same thing, only that it would be simpler and more easily understood in the country, to say that you would not join a Cabinet unless it would make itself responsible for the women's clauses as well as for the rest of the Franchise Bill?

" Of course you must work out your plans in your own way, but would it not be possible to take up this question and push it through as you have done others?

" Surely the question of admitting the women of our country to equal citizenship ought to make a statesman feel that he could do as much for it and stake as much on it as Gladstone did to secure better land laws for the Irish. I know that there are always difficulties where great and far-reaching changes are concerned, and that in this case there is bitterness and old-standing prejudice to be reckoned with; but, after all, it is the women they see every day, and amongst whom are their own mothers, sisters, wives, with whom men have to deal, not the people of another race. Gladstone had to contend with the strong insular prejudices of the English when he took up the cause of Ireland, just as those who made the Boer War had those prejudices as assets on their side.

" There is the question of militancy. The feeling amongst militant women is very deep and earnest. They absolutely believe that only militancy can win the vote and that it is their duty to continue militancy till victory is assured.

" I can see no possibility of a cessation of militancy until some very definite guarantee of action has been given. The probability is that the more extreme militants would not consent to accept any guarantee until some steps had actually been taken and all the more moderate militants and 'Constitutional' Suffragists had been convinced.

" In the case of the Conciliation Bill the W.S.P.U. was late in accepting the Bill and declaring a truce to facilitate its passage. I personally always disliked the Conciliation Bill and thought the truce in its favour ill-timed; but I mention this matter to show that though at first they refused to countenance the Bill, on the ground that it gave to women less than even technical equality with men, the most militant section agreed to make peace as soon as they were convinced of the good faith of the Conciliation Committee.

" Indeed that is the main point; the women must be convinced of the good faith and determination to see the matter through of those who make suggestions. They are difficult to convince. You may say they are unnecessarily suspicious, but you know that this has been a long struggle and the leaders feel very keenly that their leadership is a trust in which they must not fail. Militancy is taken up by women only after much trial and disappointment; but with women, as with men, it is not a weapon easily laid down. The situation in Ulster and the militant preparations there are much dwelt on by the militant women, but they would gladly make peace—who can doubt it?—if they could but feel it to be the right thing to do.

" I know that you must be much occupied with the Irish situation just now, but that will be settled soon, no doubt, and the women's question affects a greater number of human beings, and, as I think you will agree, is a deeper issue.

" I wonder whether you can realize the tremendous rejoicing there would be amongst women if a forward step towards Votes for Women, in which they could feel a genuine confidence, were taken from within the Cabinet, and the enormous enthusiasm with which it would be backed. What a splendid rally there would be if a Franchise Bill for Manhood and Womanhood Suffrage were carried this Parliament!

" If the Lords threw it out it would not matter at all—it would only be a temporary delay which would but make the enthusiasm greater and it would be the best possible rallying cry for the General Election.

"That opens up a wonderful prospect, and the present is so dark and thorny in some respects, surely something can be done!

"Faithfully yours,

"E. SYLVIA PANKHURST."

To this letter I received no answer. I was not surprised; I knew that negotiations in that quarter could proceed no further for the moment.

I next had a long conference with Keir Hardie. Norah Smyth and I went for a week-end to Penshurst. Keir Hardie followed for our discussion. We had taken rooms under an assumed name. Keir Hardie telegraphed the time of his arrival to "Pankhurst." The innkeeper was distressed and begged us to remove our E.L.F.S. badges; the Suffragettes had burnt some banners in Penshurst Place, and Lord de L'Isle would be angry, she said, if any of them were given shelter at his doors. Keir Hardie arrived in due course. He was still somewhat under the influence of the old argument of the "Manhood Suffrage danger." I converted him, however, to my view. The result was an article in the *Labour Leader*, of July 2nd, entitled: "Our Election Cry." He urged therein that Adult Manhood and Womanhood Suffrage should be the Labour Party's main plank at the coming General Election. The Labour Bill for that purpose, already introduced, but never given a place for debate, should be "forced upon the attention of the Government in Parliament and in the constituencies." He proposed a special conference of the Party, and asked for an expression of opinion from the movement. On June 29th I went with our women who had interviewed the Prime Minister to meet a committee of the Labour Party at the House of Commons. Our policy was cordially received.

The situation was developing as I desired; I was convinced that we were nearing the end. Yet still the struggle might be protracted. The women under forcible feeding were slowly being done to death; those faithful zealots who did the will of their leaders; unknown women, for whom the public would not bestir itself as it does for the very few who capture its imagination.

"The Suffragettes can go on for ever. . . . It is not they, but the onlookers, who are most concerned for the end of the struggle.

"The militants will rejoice when victory comes . . . and yet, mixed with their joy, will be regret that the most glorious chapter in women's history is closed and the militant fight over—over, while so many have not yet known the exaltation, the rapture of battle . . ."

So wrote Christabel in Paris. There were many who felt so. To some of us it was only our great impatience for the end which kept us going—a temperamental diversity. As a hunger striker, enduring recurrent periods of acute physical suffering, never well in health, never resting, always straining and working to the point of exhaustion, I was yet in spirit raised above the battle. I felt no touch of the small frictions and irritations apt to intrude on ordinary life. Viewing the great movement, working and planning for it, I could say, and still can say it, those were tremendous days! Yet I was acutely conscious that for the women constrained under the misery of forcible feeding, a bestial squalor for all concerned, the joy and the splendour of the struggle was attenuated to so fine a point, that it might well become imperceptible. For them there was urgency, great and pressing. I grieved that the flame of youthful valour should be expended between the fight against the stomach tube in the narrow cell, and the stealthy destruction of the incendiary. Comradeship in sacrifice is a thing of power, able to lift its members to the high peaks of transcendent being. They knew it in the West End, where women forsook the social round to stand in the gutter selling papers. We in the East End knew it, where life was sterner, and women whose health was sapped by privation and toil, yet gave their time and their pennies, wore out their poor shoes on long marches, and received, without complaining, the heavy blows of the police. The fire of divine impatience was the life and the essence of that comradeship.

I wanted a " charge of the light brigade " to hasten the pace of advancing victory—an appeal to the public conscience, in which there should be no violence—only sacrifice. There had been hunger strikes for the status of political offenders, and to secure release from prison. I had hunger struck that Asquith should receive the East End women; it would be more logical to hunger strike for the vote itself. I believed, with McKenna, that if one woman would lead, fifty would follow. I determined to put my faith to the test, waiting only what should appeal to me as the appropriate moment, knowing that presently such a moment would arise.

Fires and explosions, arrests and re-arrests followed in swift succession. Wholesale newsagents were informed by the police that to circulate the *Suffragette* might render them liable to incitement; proprietors of halls were given a similar warning. The police occupying Lincoln's Inn House, the W.S.P.U. had opened headquarters in Tothill Street. These being seized by the police on June 9th, a move had been made to 2 Campden Hill Square, which was seized in its turn on June 12th. The police having now vacated Lincoln's Inn House, Mrs. Pankhurst wrote to *The Times* announcing her intention to resume work there on July 9th and challenging the Government to re-arrest and forcibly feed her. She was re-arrested at the door. " They must do us violence, or do us justice," was an old saying of hers. Now she insisted : " They must give us the vote, or they must give us death." On July 15th preparations were made to carry her to a meeting in the Holland Park Rink. Doctors and clergy were at the door to accompany her. The police commandeered the ambulance, and took her back to Holloway for the tenth time under her sentence of three years' penal servitude. She had served forty-two days since her sentence on April 3rd, 1913. Since the attempt to smuggle a drug into the prison, she had been forcibly stripped and searched each time she was brought in, an indignity which wounded her more than physical suffering.

Events were moving fast. The Buckingham Palace Conference to avert civil war in Ireland met on July 20th. The points at issue had been narrowed to the inclusion or exclusion under the Irish Parliament of the counties of Fermanagh and Tyrone, which between them had a population of 61,836, just about equal to the number of women who had marched in the Suffrage procession to the Albert Hall, on June 18th, 1910. Whilst the conference was sitting, our women from the East End were outside selling the *Dreadnought* with posters : " The King must call a conference on Votes for Women." They were driven away by the police, but continually returned. Mrs. Pankhurst had written to the King, protesting that since he had taken the initiative in calling a conference of militant men, it could no longer be urged that he was precluded from receiving the Suffragettes. Lady Barclay, wife of the well-known authority on international law, was arrested at the gates of the Palace, attempting to deliver the letter. She was afterwards discharged. On July 25th a deputation of Kentish men was at Downing Street, vainly attempting to see the Prime Minister, with a demand for the enactment of Votes for Women before the life of that Parliament must expire in the forthcoming winter.

Next day, disregarding the " Cat and Mouse " Act, I was at a picnic of our members in Epping Forest, and the same evening speaking at Helions Bumpstead to the Essex agricultural labourers on strike.[1] That same week-end came the tragic firing by young soldiers upon a crowd at Bachelor's Walk, Dublin. Men and a woman had been killed, children and adults injured.

[1] The organizer, now a well-known Labour leader entertaining no such desperate ideas, asked me if I could send some Suffragettes down to set fire to the hayricks, to terrorize the farmers, who would think it had been done by the labourers. I answered that our organization did not commit arson.

Horrified by the news, I decided to go to Dublin to investigate the affair, intending to remain in Ireland for a fortnight's rest before beginning the next fight.

As I made my preparations to leave, the war was approaching. Hostilities between Austria and Serbia had already begun. The Press was suggesting that we might be on the brink of a European conflict in which Great Britain might be involved. *The Times* was declaring our readiness to fight. To me the tragedy was unthinkable. My mind shrank from the possibility, as in childhood we thrust away the thought of death in our own homes. Yet when I spoke to a gathering of our members before leaving for the night boat, I said, in the flash of a sudden apprehension : " If war comes I shall return at once."

The next days I was in and out of the homes of suffering and bereavement—a little boy of ten shot in the back; a schoolgirl with ankle shattered; a good father lost to his home. . . . The town was seething with anger. At the inquest the military were censured. Resolutions of censure were tabled for the City Council. They were never debated—War had been declared.

. . . .

Soldiers were marching to battle through the European cities I had seen that Easter, our own men leaving home to fight. Progress was stayed, the hopes of humanitarians and reformers overthrown.

That night I returned to England with the first batch of soldiers from Ireland. Crowds wrestled at the entrance to the boat station; men, drunk and sober, shouting and fighting, women with sobs and pleading, striving in frantic grief to bar the doorway and thrust them back. The quays around Dublin were teeming with people cheering and waving; the men on board were cheering and waving too. All through the voyage they sang and laughed and shouted. So this was war.

CHAPTER X

THE EUROPEAN WAR AND THE AMNESTY

THE French Government had immediately released all its political prisoners. In this country frantic private efforts were being made to secure the release of the Suffragette militants. On August 7th McKenna told the House of Commons that he would liberate only those prisoners who would "undertake not to commit further crimes and outrages." Three days later he announced the reversal of his decision : all the Suffragettes would be released. He politely added : "This course has been taken without solicitation on their part, and without requiring any undertaking from them." The amnesty covered also the many prisoners of the industrial disputes.

There was some quibbling about the remanded Suffragette prisoners, who were held some days longer than their companions. Dorothy Evans and three others, released without being apprised of the amnesty, immediately broke windows and were taken back to gaol, but mutual explanations secured their release. Mrs. Crow, by a detective's mistake, was re-arrested on August 27th. Mrs. Drummond and sixteen other "Mice" at once rushed to the Home Office to complain to McKenna; they were thrown out and taken to Cannon Row police station, but presently discharged.

With this final release the Militant Suffragette Movement was virtually at an end. We in the East End continued our work till the vote was won, but militancy was no more. The *Suffragette* of August 7th, 1914, contained an appeal from Christabel :

"Women of the W.S.P.U., we must protect our Union through everything . . . for the sake of the human race . . . women must be free."

Next week the *Suffragette* failed to appear. Mrs. Pankhurst issued a statement through the Press that militancy would be rendered "less effective" by contrast with the greater violence of the war, that work for the vote on the lines of peaceful argument being, "as we know, futile," the Union would suspend activities. Money and energy would thus be saved, and "an opportunity" given to "recuperate after the tremendous strain and suffering of the past two years."

In the East End, war hardships arose immediately. The women in trouble came at once to the Women's Hall and asked for "Sylvia." I was deeply impressed by their faith in the Federation and in me. They had fought with us and made sacrifices: I would strive to mitigate for them the burden of war. Our staff and members rose bravely to the occasion, the poor gallantly helping the poor. The Federation acted as a Trade Union, or a family solicitor on behalf of the people in need, approaching Government Departments, Magistrates and local authorities, as the case might require, and meanwhile, if other assistance were lacking, supplying the immediate sustenance required.

Prices rose in the first week to famine height; factories were shut down in panic; men and women thrown out of employment. Reservists were called up. Separation allowances were slow in coming, and when they came how meagre! Despairing mothers came to us with their wasted infants. I appealed through the Press for money to buy milk, but the babies were ill from waiting; doctors, nurses and invalid requirements were added, of necessity. Soon we had five Mother and Infant Welfare Centres in East End districts, and a toy and garment factory for unemployed women and girls. Before August, 1914, was out we had opened our Cost Price Restaurants, where twopenny meals to adults and penny meals to children were served to all comers, with free meal tickets for the destitute. The Gunmakers' Arms, a disused public-house, we turned into a clinic, day nursery and Montessori school; the last under the direction of Muriel Matters, the heroine of the grille, just returned from studying in Barcelona under Montessori.

We were at work before the Prince of Wales's Fund and Queen Mary Work Rooms. We regarded our relief work as a lever for securing similar institutions from public funds, and were amongst the first to organize such work. We agitated by meetings, processions and deputations to Government departments to protect the people from exploitation by profiteers, to secure that wages should rise with the cost of living, to gain for the women soon flocking from all quarters into what had hitherto been masculine occupations, a rate of pay equal to that of men. We set up a League of Rights for Soldiers' and Sailors' Wives and Relatives to strive for better naval and military pensions and allowances. We opposed attempts to revive the Contagious Diseases Regulations, against which Josephine Butler fought her historic fight. We toiled for the preservation of Civil Liberties, always so gravely attacked in war time. Votes for Women we never permitted to fall into the background. We worked continuously for peace, in face of the bitterest opposition from old enemies, and sometimes, unhappily, from old friends. To us came many tried militant stalwarts of the W.S.P.U. We were giving the lead to a substantial share of the Labour, Socialist and Suffrage organizations. " We are always two years ahead of the others," Norah Smyth used to say. Much of this activity hung on me. I had often a stiff fight to keep going with the broken health left to me from the hunger strike.

.   .   .   .

The War had rent the women's movement in twain. The old non-militant N.U.W.S.S. suffered the most profound fissure in its history. Its majority, under Mrs. Fawcett, immediately dropped all Suffrage work, though recalled to it before the close of the War by the raising of the franchise issue from unexpected quarters. In the meantime the National Union turned itself into a " Women's Active Service Corps," to assist, it declared, in " sustaining the vital energies of the nation " and in winning the War. The seceders took the initiative in forming the British section of the Women's International League, which arose from the women's conference called by Dr. Aletta Jacobs at the Hague. Suffragists, militant and non-militant, Quakers and Socialists, formed the membership of this body. I was elected to its first executive at its inaugural conference. We formed an East London branch of the League because of its international affiliations; though our own policy covered all the points in its programme, and our conclusions on Adult Suffrage and every other question were more advanced.

The United Suffragists concentrated on Suffrage work in a quiet way, and on the production of *Votes for Women*, at this juncture presented to them by its founders, the Pethick Lawrences. The U.S. undertook no war relief work, but they gave their support to an active relief agency, the Women's Emergency Corps, as did many other Suffragists and Suffrage organizations. The Women's Freedom League continued Suffrage work and supported an effort to secure the establishment of women police.

The W.S.P.U. reappeared after a brief interval which seemed an age in those rapidly moving days. It had now entirely departed from the Suffrage movement. Giving its energies wholly to the prosecution of the War, it rushed to a furious extreme, its Chauvinism unexampled amongst all the other women's societies.

On September 8th, 1914, Christabel re-appeared at the London Opera House, after her long exile, to utter a declaration, not on women's enfranchisement, but on " The

German Peril." Mrs. Pankhurst toured the country, making recruiting speeches. Her supporters handed the white feather to every young man they encountered wearing civilian dress, and bobbed up at Hyde Park meetings with placards: " Intern Them All." The *Suffragette* appeared again on April 16th, 1915, as a war paper, and on October 15th changed its name to *Britannia*.[1] There week by week Christabel demanded the military conscription of men, and the industrial conscription of women, " national service " as it was termed. In flamboyant terms she called also for the internment of all people of enemy race, men and women, young and old, found on these shores, and for a more complete and ruthless enforcement of the blockade of enemy and neutral nations. She insisted that this must be " a war of attrition." In her ferocious zeal for relentless prosecution of the War, she demanded the resignation of Sir Edward Grey, Lord Robert Cecil, General Sir William Robertson and Sir Eyre Crowe, whom she considered too mild and dilatory in method. So furious was her attack that, in its over-fervent support of the National War policy, *Britannia* was many times raided by the police, and experienced greater difficulty in appearing than had befallen the *Suffragette*. Indeed it was compelled at last to set up its own printing press. A gentler impulse was embodied in an early proposal of Mrs. Pankhurst to set up Women's Social and Political Union Homes for illegitimate girl " war babies," but only five children were adopted. Sterner interests prevailed. Lloyd George, whom Christabel had regarded as the most bitter and dangerous enemy of women, was now the one politician in whom she and Mrs. Pankhurst placed confidence.

When the first Russian Revolution took place and Kerensky rose to power, Mrs. Pankhurst—like many others—journeyed to Russia, in the vain effort to prevent that vast country with its starving multitudes from retiring from the War. Her circuit was like that of Hervé, the French " anti-patriot," as for many years he had called himself, and of whom she had been an ardent admirer in her youth. Christabel received the commendation of many war enthusiasts. Lord Northcliffe observed that she ought to be in the Cabinet. Lord Astor told me, when I happened to be seated beside him at dinner, that he had received two letters from her; he had sent one of them to the War Office, the other to the Minister of Blockade. Undoubtedly he was much impressed by their contents.

When first I read in the Press that Mrs. Pankhurst and Christabel were returning to England for a recruiting campaign

[1] *Britannia* announced the transformation of the W.S.P.U. to the *Women's Party*, November 2nd, 1917.

I wept. To me this seemed a tragic betrayal of the great movement to bring the mother-half of the race into the councils of the nations. "Women would stand for peace!" How often, how often had they and all of us averred it!

My own activities were no more to their taste than theirs to mine, and I was publicly repudiated by Mrs. Pankhurst,[1] through the medium of the Press. Adela in Australia was working with Vida Goldstein in the Women's Party there much as I was doing here. She took a prominent part in opposing Conscription and in securing its defeat when submitted to Referendum. She, too, was publicly repudiated by Mrs. Pankhurst. Families which remain on unruffled terms, though their members are in opposing political parties, take their politics less keenly to heart than we Pankhursts. Yet often in those days I woke in the night, hearing the words of the father who had guided our early thoughts: "My children are the four pillars of my house!"

It was at a great joint meeting we had organized in Trafalgar Square on Sunday, September 26th, 1915, that the newsboys began crying: "Death of Keir Hardie!" The news stared at me from the posters in their hands. Shocked and trembling, I turned to W. C. Anderson, M.P., of the I.L.P., who stood beside me: "Is it true?" "It must be," he answered gently, and turned with practical mind to draft a resolution. "I will move it," he said; "he was our man." I knew that Keir Hardie had been failing since the early days of the War. The great slaughter, the rending of the bonds of international fraternity, on which he had built his hopes, had broken him. Quite early he had had a stroke in the House of Commons after some conflict with the jingoes. When he left London for the last time he had told me quietly that his active life was ended, and that this was forever farewell, for he would never return. In his careful way he arranged for the disposal of his books and furniture and gave up his rooms, foreseeing his end, and fronting it without flinching or regret.

I spent the day which followed his death writing an article about him for the *Dreadnought* and refusing to see anyone; my sole respite for mourning and tribute to this great friend; then I was back in the surge of work, with the charge on my conscience to be doubly steadfast and true.

---

[1] *Britannia*, April 28th, 1916, published the following paragraph:

"A MESSAGE FROM MRS. PANKHURST.

"Hearing of a demonstration recently held in Trafalgar Square, Mrs. Pankhurst, who is at present in America, sent the following cable: 'Strongly repudiate and condemn Sylvia's foolish and unpatriotic conduct. Regret I cannot prevent use of name. Make this public.'"

[This was a demonstration for Adult Suffrage and against Conscription.]

CHAPTER XI

AS the War dragged on, involving the entire population in its sacrifices, and as the imminence of Conscription became apparent, it seemed to me that the claim of the whole people to enfranchisement could be urged with overwhelming logic. With the East End as our base we had worked without ceasing to advance the idea of Womanhood Suffrage. In view of the dislike to the term " Adult Suffrage," and the fear and suspicion it had so long aroused in the Suffrage movement, we raised a new slogan: " Human Suffrage." We urged the enfranchisement of both sexes, on the New Zealand model, with continuous registration and re-distribution of seats on the basis of population every five years. Later we advocated also the " Initiative, Referendum and Recall " on the United States plan, which I still believe would enhance popular interest in politics and give the people at large a greater share in the control of public affairs. To popularize Universal Suffrage we canvassed the views of prominent publicists. We propagated the idea systematically amongst the Labour organizations; a continuous stream of resolutions from which reached the Government as a result of our efforts. No organization in London held so many meetings on any question, indoors or out, as we. Whilst many organizations abandoned all open-air meetings, ours were continuous. Again and again we took the lead in calling such Suffrage and Labour organizations as were prepared to co-operate to joint demonstrations in Trafalgar Square, in Hyde Park and in theatres and large halls. Whatever additional subjects such gatherings might strive to promote, " Human Suffrage " took always a prominent place. We formed an Adult Suffrage Joint Committee, to which more than seventy London Labour organizations were soon affiliated. We lobbied the House of Commons persistently. Week by week Mrs. Drake, our Poplar secretary, was at St. Stephen's, and our members were urged to meet her there and get coached in the Parliamentary ropes.

In March, 1915, a Board of Trade circular was issued appealing to women to register at the Labour Exchanges for war service. Our East London Federation, which presently became the Workers' Suffrage Federation, immediately wrote to Runciman, the President of the Board of Trade, as well as to Asquith and Lloyd George, demanding equal pay for women with men, and proper conditions and safeguards for women's labour. We also issued an appeal through the Press for a joint conference of women's organizations to protect women's interests. I rushed about interviewing Labour officials: Mary MacArthur, J. S. Middleton and others, and induced them to take the initiative in arranging for a preliminary conference on the position of women in war work on March 22nd at the Trade Union Congress offices. The outcome was a larger conference at the Caxton Hall on April 16th called by the Labour War Emergency Committee.

In the meantime Lloyd George had entered into the Treasury Agreement with the Trade Union officials in regard to the replacing of skilled men by semi-skilled men and women. I managed, by correspondence, to draw from him a pledge (not always kept) that women should get the same piece-work rates as the men they replaced; but no pledge as to time rates was ever obtained and no guarantee to put women on piece rates when they had been trained. On April 13th Runciman called a conference of the women's organizations at the Board of Trade to encourage the registration of women war workers. Mrs. Drake and I, on behalf of our Federation, were the first to speak. We urged for women the vote and equal pay with men. Most of the other Suffrage societies took the same line, but the National Union of Women's Suffrage Societies and the Women's Liberal and Conservative Organizations promised unconditional co-operation with the Government. The W.S.P.U. was not represented.

When the National Register for war work was organized, our Federation advised women to refuse registration as a protest against war and the conscription which we believed the National Register designed to facilitate; or if they felt unable to adopt so strong a line, at least to impose the condition of receiving equal pay with men for any work undertaken. We called a conference of Suffrage and Labour organizations to adopt this policy and to support it by large demonstrations. The Munitions Act was passed during that summer; we opposed it for its failure to safeguard equal pay, as well as on other grounds.

At this juncture the W.S.P.U. came forward demanding compulsory national service for women, and organized a monster procession with this object, which was reviewed and addressed by Lloyd George and Mrs. Pankhurst, with mutual laudation. He paid the huge bill for the demonstration from Government funds; but not, perhaps, the whole bill, for the W.S.P.U., by this time called the Women's Party, and Mrs. Pankhurst herself were in serious financial embarrassments when their war work came to an end.

I demanded from Lloyd George a hearing for our programme of Votes for Women and the safeguarding of women's labour. A big procession marched up from the East End, brought together virtually without expenditure. Lloyd George had promised to receive us, but sent Dr. Addison as a substitute. By resorting to the old methods I might have compelled an interview, but my time was too much occupied with the needs of our poor people to justify running the risk of imprisonment then—at least I thought so.

One morning I woke up with the idea : " I will call on Lord Northcliffe." I detested his politics and his influence; he had been an Anti-Suffragist and had disparaged the Suffragettes, yet I recognized his power.

Though I arrived unannounced, he received me without delay. I was surprised to hear him talking precisely like a leading article from one of his own papers, with pompous deliberation : " The British people are a slow people; but they are a very wise people—and that is why they are going to have Conscription." He was cordial enough, but heavy and stiff; there was nothing unaffected or impulsive about him. I outlined my thesis that the old electoral limitations must be superseded; the nation, men and women alike, having become, perforce, a unit of service and sacrifice, the hour had struck for large, generous action in relation to the franchise. He listened patiently, with some appearance of cautious assent, and an occasional keen glare at me as though some remark of mine had gone home. He promised consideration, with the august airs of a super-Premier.

Our efforts to drag the franchise to the fore were presently reinforced from an unexpected quarter. The extreme jingoes, with Northcliffe's support, began demanding the enfranchisement of the men at the front. It was part of the movement, nourished by Northcliffe, to drive Asquith from office. Ballot boxes were taken to the front that the soldiers of the British Dominions might vote. As the law stood, the soldiers of the Mother Country would have no share in the decision should an election take place here. Munitioners in large numbers had been drafted from their homes to other areas; they also would be disfranchised. Faced by a storm, largely fictitious as regards sincerity, which blew up on this point, the Government proposed legislation to evade the dilemma, by postponing the General Election for eight months. On November 4th, 1915, Lord Willoughby de Broke attempted to force the matter to a head by introducing a Service Franchise Bill. Lord Lansdowne induced him to withdraw it, by a promise that the Government would deal with the soldiers' claim. It was rumoured that a Franchise Bill was to be introduced. We wrote to Asquith, to Lansdowne and to the Press, declaring that if the franchise issue were to be raised the Women's Suffrage movement must be reckoned with. We reminded Asquith of his promise to us in July, 1914, that he would give sympathetic consideration to our demands. Every other Suffrage society which had remained alive to the Suffrage cause wrote in similar terms, and we co-operated with them in a joint letter. Asquith replied that no change in the franchise would be made by the proposed Bill.

My next move was an effort to unite the Suffrage societies in the demand for Adult Suffrage. We invited them to an informal meeting in the little room behind the International Suffrage shop kept by Miss Thring in Adam Street. They came in good number, almost all the societies still active for Suffrage being represented. The large idea gripped them; all was enthusiasm. A formal conference in Essex Hall in January, 1916, was resolved on. We parted in high hope; but when the delegates returned to their executives and officials the ancient formula resumed its domination; the old guard would not permit its old policy to be dislodged, would not budge from refusal to advocate a widening of the franchise. The January conference was acrimonious. Our Federation was bitterly attacked, our East End women howled down by the well-to-do members of other organizations. All the societies, even the W.S.P.U., had sent delegates, but it was impossible to unite even a small group of them for our demand. We still stood alone for Adult Suffrage. The United Suffragists were moving in our direction, but would not yet take the plunge.

On the executive of the Women's International League I was working to commit the league to my policy. On February 3rd, 1916, its Council adopted a resolution declaring that the franchise should be based neither on sex nor on property. The heterogeneous composition of the committee: Suffragists, Quakers, Socialists and Pacifists, had made it comparatively easy to secure this pious expression of view. Practical adoption of Adult Suffrage was another matter; the majority of the officials had spent their political life under Mrs. Fawcett in the N.U.W.S.S. They had been brought to a formal approval of the complete demand, but remained willing to accept, and to expect, the narrowest measure of Women's Suffrage. This willingness, extending to every Suffrage society, with the sole exception of our own W.S.F., was, in my view, the great weakness of our situation. I was convinced that no franchise measure could now be passed without the inclusion of women, and that war changes had made a Franchise Act for men inevitable. I believed the form of Suffrage we should get for women largely depended on the Suffrage movement itself.

In April the Liberal and Unionist War Committees demanded a vote for every soldier in the trenches, and *The Times* threatened to force a General Election. The thought came to me: " Call another Suffrage conference." Norah Smyth, our financial secretary, funked the expense. I made the proposal to the executive of the Women's International League. After all, I thought, by working from another angle new influences might be brought into play. The conference met at the Fabian rooms in June. After two days' discussion some of the organizations withdrew, whilst those which found themselves able to work together for a wider demand formed a small provisional committee. A further meeting in the Central Hall, Westminster, was called on September 2nd, 1916, when a National Council for Adult Suffrage was set up. The active officials were Miss Katharine Marshall, Mrs. Swanwick and Miss K. D. Courtney, all of whom were members of the Women's International League and seceders from the National Union of Suffrage Societies. They were determined to run the new organization in their own way and to do all the wire-pulling, at which they were adept. In spite of their secession from her on her War policy, they were still obsessed by the methods and ideals they had acquired under Mrs. Fawcett.

Meanwhile a new factor had arisen: Asquith had come forward definitely as a convert to Women's Suffrage. Speaking in Parliament on August 14th, 1916, he said:

" The moment you begin a general enfranchisement on these lines of State Service you are brought face to face with another most formidable proposition. What are you going to do with the women? I have received a great many representations from those who are authorized to speak for them, and I am bound to say that they have presented to me not only a reasonable, but I think, from their point of view, an unanswerable case. They say . . . If we are going to bring in a new class of electors, on whatever ground of State Service, they point out—and we cannot possibly deny their claim—that during this War the women of this country have rendered as effective service in the prosecution of the War as any other class of the community . . . what is more—and this is a point which makes a special appeal to me—they say when the War comes to an end . . . when the process of industrial reconstruction has to be set on foot, have not the women a special claim to be heard on the many questions which will arise directly affecting their interest, and possibly meaning for them large displacement of labour? I say quite frankly that I cannot deny that claim."

Since our deputation of 1914 I had regarded him as a convert, whether of expediency or conviction mattered not, though I like to believe that conviction had at least some part in the change. This last utterance was a clear declaration on which to build. I wrote on behalf of our Federation, congratulating him, and urging him to implement his statement in legislation.

Still stranger indeed than the change in Asquith was that in Mrs. Pankhurst and Christabel. Asquith had not long made his statement when Commander Bellairs rose up to say that he had been called out and authorized by Mrs. Pankhurst on behalf of the Women's Social and Political Union to repudiate the statement of the Prime Minister and to say that they would " not allow themselves to be used to prevent soldiers and sailors from being given the vote." Mrs. Pankhurst and Christabel were now in fact demanding, not votes for women—but votes for the men in the fighting forces. At a meeting held with this object in the Queen's Hall, on October 1st, Mrs. Pankhurst complained that Asquith, having previously attempted " to use the men to dish the women," was now " using the women to dish the men."

" The men had proved their claim to the vote by making it possible to keep a country in which to vote. Could any woman face the possibility of the affairs of the country being settled by Conscientious Objectors, passive resisters and shirkers? . . . In the name of the women she declared that they were ready to make every sacrifice, in order that the sacrifices already made should not be made in vain."

Christabel's organ, *Britannia*, stated that the question of women's enfranchisement would " arise again in practical shape after the victory of the Allies."[1]

An effort to stave off the inevitable Franchise Extension Act was made in the Special Register Bill, which passed its Second Reading on August 16th, 1916, and which Asquith himself admitted to be " a lopsided temporary makeshift." On November 1st he stated that he was prepared to give the House an opportunity to decide, either by Bill or Resolution, whether a Special Franchise should be created for soldiers and sailors as such. We wrote again and repeatedly to remind him of his many promises. We recalled to him the fiasco of the last Reform Bill with its promised " opportunity " for a Women's Amendment, urging him on this occasion to include women in the original Bill.

Asquith's tenure of office was daily growing more precarious. The factions which were presently to place Lloyd George in his political shoes were employing votes for the men in the trenches

[1] *Britannia*, November 26th, 1915.

as a rallying cry. The establishment of a Parliamentary Conference, representative of all Parties, and presided over by the
Speaker to report on Electoral Reform, was resorted to by
Asquith's Government as an expedient for avoiding disruptive
controversy. The Speaker's Conference held its first meeting on
October 12th. Our Federation at once presented to it a memorial
advocating the New Zealand system of franchise and registration,
and pointing out that during the War four Canadian Provinces
had granted complete Womanhood Suffrage. The other
women's societies, and even the Antis sent in their manifestoes.
We of the W.S.F. redoubled our efforts, holding great meetings
in the Euston Theatre, the Glasgow City Hall and other
prominent centres, enlisting prominent speakers from the
Suffrage, Labour, Socialist and Co-operative movements. Every
week-end at least I was in the provinces, addressing crowded
audiences in the largest halls.

Mrs. Fawcett has recorded the interesting fact that in
December, 1916, Lord Northcliffe wrote to Lady Betty Balfour:
" There is absolutely no movement for Women's Suffrage anywhere." This was no doubt a convenient manner of stating that
there was no agitation amongst the women whose political
attitude on other matters met with his approval. This letter
being sent to Mrs. Fawcett, she replied indignantly that the
abandonment of Suffrage work by her organization, in what they
regarded as the national interest, was not appreciated. Northcliffe, having received her letter, wrote to her on Christmas Day,
1916, advising either a great meeting or a united deputation of
Suffragists, and adding: " Lady Betty has asked me to speak to
the Prime Minister and I will do so to-morrow." The Prime
Minister by this time was Lloyd George, whom Northcliffe had
placed where he was. Mrs. Fawcett replied, characteristically,
that she preferred a deputation to a public meeting, in order not
to weaken the impression on the public mind of her Union's
" whole-hearted love of country and reverence for its aims."
Two days later Northcliffe wrote that he had talked with Lloyd
George, who was " very keen on the subject, and very practical
too."

Nevertheless the Press up to the third week in January, 1917,
was unanimous in asserting that the Speaker's Conference would
ignore the subject of " Votes for Women." Then it was
announced that " some sort " of women's franchise would be
recommended. In the same month votes were accorded to
women by the Legislature of the Canadian State of Manitoba.
The women congregated in the visitors' galleries broke forth in
song: " O Canada! " and " For they are jolly good fellows! "

The Legislators responded. This was heartening news to us. Surely our victory also must be at hand!

At last the terms of the Speaker's Conference Report were announced: "Votes for Women over thirty or thirty-five years of age who were local government electors or wives of local government electors (i.e., owners and tenant householders and the wives of both), and University graduates over thirty or thirty-five years of age." The Report was widely condemned. Mrs. Pethick Lawrence wrote in the *Daily News*:

" By what grotesque working of the political mind has the conclusion been reached that the welfare of the community can only be safeguarded by the exclusion of women from the human commonwealth until they have attained the age of thirty or thirty-five years? "

The Nation declared:

" You cannot have a property basis for the women's vote and a flesh-and-blood basis for the men's. You cannot maintain so wide an age-space between the man and the woman voter as twenty-one and thirty-five."

Yet in spite of such criticism from many sources, the only robust determination to struggle for Adult Suffrage was to be found in the Workers' Suffrage Federation. We embodied our complaints in a letter to the Prime Minister, pointing out that the 1911 census had shown that of the women workers whose claims it was proposed to safeguard by enfranchisement, 2,699,369 were under thirty-five and only 793,036 women between thirty-five and sixty-five. We further urged that the pauper disqualification which it was proposed to continue would debar large numbers of working-class widows from enfranchisement, and also numbers of men and women disabled and unemployed by the War.

" The other Suffrage societies, even though some of them criticized the Speaker's Conference recommendations, were prepared to accept them with little demur. The National Union of Women's Suffrage Societies led the way in acceptance. It now held its first public meeting on Women's Suffrage since the declaration of the War, to request legislation on the lines of the Speaker's Conference Report. It also summoned a conference, whereat a large number of Women's Suffrage and Labour organizations were induced to welcome the recommendation to admit women to the franchise which the Speaker's Conference had made, without expressing an opinion as to the terms. This resolution was afterwards quoted as an acceptance of the terms of the report by all the societies concerned.

The officials of the National Council for Adult Suffrage, who had come over from the N.U.W.S.S., were in the Lobby of the

House of Commons, asking Members of Parliament what sort of Suffrage they should ask for, and whether they should accede to the age limit of thirty or thirty-five. When I saw this attitude dominating the Council, of which I had been the author, I set to work to secure the formation of a representative Labour Council for Adult Suffrage. Fred Bramley became a member of the provisional committee of this organization. In a stormy interview, the officials of the National Council endeavoured to draw him away from us, but he stood firm, though he accepted co-option also to the National Council.

On my nomination George Lansbury had also been co-opted to the National Council. When the executive decided to recommend acceptance of the Speaker's Conference terms to the Council, which was to meet next day, I went to George Lansbury to apprise him of the fact. After a lengthy executive meeting, which had lasted from morning to evening, I reached his house in Bow about 10 p.m. His family, who practised the admirable maxim " Early to bed and early to rise," had retired for the night. He received me in his dressing-gown. Exhausted by hunger and fatigue, I begged him for a piece of bread before explaining my errand, and he gave me a dry chunk from the loaf. When I told him of the executive proposals, he said: " They cannot do it whilst I am there, because I shall not accept it." He was emphatic, and pooh-poohed my perturbation. The Council was meeting at the Central Hall, Westminster, at ten o'clock next morning; the delegates from the London affiliated societies being summoned.

I arrived a little late; the delegate of the British Socialist Party was on his feet, opposing the executive resolution to accept a limited franchise, and claiming that it was the business of the Adult Suffrage Council to work unswervingly for the object for which it had so recently been formed. To my astonishment George Lansbury immediately rose in opposition to the delegate of the B.S.P., and supported acceptance of the Speaker's Conference proposals as emphatically as he had denounced them the previous night. At a larger conference, to which delegates were summoned from affiliated organizations in the Provinces a little later, the acceptance of the limiting proposals was again debated. Olive Schreiner and Fred Bramley were the only well-known people who supported our Federation in the claim that we must not thus surrender in advance the Adult Suffrage pass.

The Labour Council for Adult Suffrage continued its work; our effort was merely a gallant forlorn hope. When the National Council, for which I had taken the initiative, and to which I had urged the affiliation of Labour organizations, deserted Adult

Suffrage, I knew that we were out-generalled. I had given the officials of the National Council the lead; if the vote were to come now there would be no time to recapture it. The one slender hope was a firm stand by organized Labour in support of Adult Suffrage; but the Parliamentary Labour Party at once deserted that old standard. It recommended acceptance of the Speaker's Conference Report and called a representative conference, in order to commit the Labour movement to this course. Those who throughout the long pre-war Suffragette struggle had prevented Labour Party action for the limited Bill, on the plea of loyalty to Adult Suffrage, now abandoned Adult Suffrage without even a formal protest. J. R. Clynes cited the resolution of the conference convened by the N.U.W.S.S., whereat they had been manœuvred into accepting the official resolution, as proof that the women's organizations approved the limited franchise. In vain did delegates of the Women's Co-operative Guild, the Women's Labour League and the Fabian women protest that they had never accepted the terms of the Report. Dragooned by official assertions that unless the Speaker's Conference proposals were accepted without amendment all franchise reform would be lost, the conference defeated the Adult Suffrage amendment, of which I was one of the movers, by 2,000,000 votes to 88,000. An amendment by the Miners' Federation to accept the Report, provided women were given the vote on the same terms as men, was also rejected, but by a narrower vote—931,000 votes to 562,000.

Historically it was odd that it should be Asquith who moved in Parliament the Resolution asking Lloyd George's Government for legislation on the lines of the Speaker's Conference Report. Some of his friends would say of him, he observed, that, like Stesichorus, his eyes

" which for years in this matter had been clouded by fallacies and sealed by illusions, at last had been opened to the truth."

Politicians, however, are always pliable. His conversion was no surprise to me. We desired him to go further; but it was in vain that we wrote to him recalling his words to our deputations of 1914:

" I have always said that if you are going to give the franchise to women you must give it to them on the same terms as you do to men. . . . Discrimination of sex does not justify, and cannot warrant giving the women a restricted form of franchise while you give the men an unrestricted form."

In any case he was now no longer responsible for legislation : Lloyd George, his successor, was deaf to our arguments. He promised at an early date to hear what we had to urge, but when on March 29th, 1917, he received a deputation of Suffragists, he excluded our Federation, because he knew we should press for Adult Suffrage. Moreover he was aware that we should never enter his political orbit: we were irrevocably opposed to his Government, we were striving against his war policy, and our hopes were set on the creation of another social order. To the societies he had called to meet him, he said of the Speaker's Conference solution: " Stand by this proposal and say it will satisfy you." He urged, in his persuasive fashion, that no broader measure had a chance; not even the Labour Party would support it, for the men of the working class feared a preponderance of women's votes. This, he asserted, was the view put to him by the Labour Party deputation which had waited on him a few days before. Strangely enough his assertion was not repudiated by those concerned. The old N.U.W.S.S. and the W.S.P.U. were both present. Mrs. Pankhurst asked the Prime Minister to give such a measure as he felt " just and practicable " and could be passed with as little discussion and debate as possible. It would be " a wonderful thing," she said, if Votes for Women came in war time. If it did, women would work with greater energy, enthusiasm and patriotism for the security of their native land. " It is men themselves who have raised the Women's Suffrage issue at that time, but having raised it they could not fail to settle it without inflicting grave insult and injury before the eyes of the whole world." That was the W.S.P.U. standpoint as expressed in *Britannia*.

Though the W.S.F. had been excluded, Mrs. Drake was present, uninvited, to utter our point of view. Many of the delegates congratulated her on her demand for equal Suffrage, but none of them had the courage to support her uncompromising stand. A crowd of young munitioners, brought up to give spectacular interest to the deputation, heard with surprise her intimation that the great majority of them would not participate in the expected franchise, which they had been told was to be granted largely on their account.

When the Government Bill embodying the terms of the Speaker's Conference Report was before the House, it was made clear that though, in view of the Speaker's ruling on the last occasion, the women's franchise had been made part of the Bill, the Government would take no responsibility for the women's vote; if the women's clauses were defeated, the Government would proceed with the rest of the Bill. On the other hand, if the amendment to enfranchise women at twenty-one years were carried, the Government would abandon the entire measure.

Thus masculine timidity entrenched itself against the dangers of majority rule!

Introduced on May 15th, the Bill reached Committee in June. On June 19th Sir Frederick Banbury's motion to leave out the women's franchise was defeated by 385 votes to 55. Mr. Peto's amendment to lower the age limit for women to twenty-one was yet more heavily beaten by the votes of 291 cautious males to 25 who were prepared to take the risk of a preponderance of women in the electorate. The proposal to grant the Parliamentary franchise[1] to women over thirty years of age who were occupiers, or wives of occupiers, of land or premises of not less than £5 annual value, and to women over thirty who held University degrees was accepted by 214 votes to 17. The local government franchise clauses proposed to give women the vote on the same terms as men: a six months' ownership or tenant basis, and in addition to enfranchise the wives of all male electors. The timid Mrs. Fawcett, with her mid-nineteenth century outlook, had feared this proposal as far too broad. It was accepted nevertheless without a division. The Bill as a whole passed Third Reading on December 7th, 1917. With so smooth a passage through the Commons, acceptance by the Lords was a foregone conclusion; the opposition of anti-Suffrage Peers dwindled like mist before the sun.

The limited Suffrage, absurd as it was, gave votes to approximately six times the number of women whose enfranchisement had been attempted under the pre-War Conciliation Bills, for which so much hard effort and painful sacrifice had been given, and to which the opposition was so stubborn and so ruthless. Even those of us who had striven to the last for the full solution knew that now the breach in the sex barrier had been made, the fight for womanhood suffrage had been won.

Undoubtedly the large part taken by women during the War in all branches of social service had proved a tremendous argument for their enfranchisement. Yet the memory of the old militancy, and the certainty of its recurrence if the claims of women were set aside, was a much stronger factor in overcoming the reluctance of those who would again have postponed the settlement. The shock to the foundations of existing social institutions already reverberating from Russia across Europe, made many old opponents desire to enlist the new enthusiasm of women voters to stabilize the Parliamentary machine. Above

---

[1] The Parliamentary suffrage for men was now based on six months' residence in a constituency, or six months' occupation of land or premises of not less than £10 annual value, and on the holding of a University degree. Plural votes were restricted to two.

all, the changed attitude of the large public of all classes towards the position of women, which had grown up in the great militant struggle, made impossible a further postponement of our enfranchisement.

The pageantry and rejoicing, the flaming ardour, which in pre-war days would have greeted the victory, were absent when it came. The sorrows of the world conflict precluded jubilations, alike to those who believed it a war of freedom against oppression, and to those who deplored it as a tragic blot on the escutcheon of all the combatant nations. The groups which held to the Suffrage cause through the dark days of war, and struggled for it doggedly to the end, had clung to it as one of the influences which might aid in the building of a kinder future.

The Suffrage movement, which lived through the vast holocaust of peaceful life, was a more intelligent and informed movement than that which, gallant as it was, had fought the desperate, pre-war fight. Gone was the mirage of a society regenerated by enfranchised womanhood as by a magic wand. Men and women had been drawn closer together by the suffering and sacrifice of the War. Awed and humbled by the great catastrophe, and by the huge economic problems it had thrown into naked prominence, the women of the Suffrage movement had learnt that social regeneration is a long and mighty work. The profound divergences of opinion on war and peace had been shown to know no sex.

The Act of 1928, which swept away the absurd restrictions of 1917, came virtually without effort. It was quietly received. Women had already taken a wide and important part in Parliamentary politics, and both men and women had completely assimilated the view that all women were potential voters. Thus the extension was regarded as a matter of course. The old prediction that the classes of women first enfranchised would oppose the extension of the vote to new classes proved utterly false; every women's organization, every section which had joined in the original movement advocated the further extension.

As though Fate had detained her till the completion of the edifice, Emmeline Pankhurst, who had accomplished so much in making the disfranchised state of women a burning sore in the body politic, passed away when the final Act became law.

That the women who went forward to seats in Parliament and to Government office were not they who had taken a foremost part in the long struggle was of no moment; the fight of the pioneers had been waged for generations yet unborn. The militant movement had effected far more than the winning of the political franchise for this country: it had stimulated the women's emancipation movement in all countries, even in the Far East, where subjection had been greatest.

It had acted as a leaven from which public spirit, self-confidence and initiative had spread amongst the women of its time and had accelerated the building of a new, a higher and freer status for the womanhood of all races. The young women of to-day scarcely realize the great changes which have already taken place.

The professional women were the first and the most obvious gainers from the struggle. Their status and number between 1900 and 1914 had greatly risen. When the War came they were ready to seize the opportunity of service and advancement its necessities offered them. The maternity and infant clinics and widows' pensions, the demand for which was nourished in the Suffrage struggle, are of its fruits; they are the first, halting steps towards the development of a new Social Order for Motherhood.

Great is the work which remains to be accomplished!

THE END

INDEX

Abbott, Mary, 43
'Abdu'l Bahá, 554
Aberdeen Free Press, 275
Aberdeen, Lord, 406, 407
Abolition of House of Lords, 97
Academia delle Belle Arti, 162
Accrington Times, 14
Actresses' Franchise League, 395
Acts of Parliament:
  Bill of Rights, 1689, 307
  C.D. (Contagious Diseases), 31
  Corrupt Practices, 60
  Education, 1870, 14, 15, 24, 47
  34 Edward III, 458, 459, 472, 473, 489, 491
  Guardianship of Infants, 1886, 31
  Local Government, 1894, 116, 117, 118
  Married Women's Property, 1870, 1882, 31, 48
  Master and Servants, 20
  Municipal Corporations, 1835, 46
  Municipal Corporations, 1869, 46
  National Insurance, 353, 354
  Newspaper Libel and Registration, 79
  Parliament, 356, 357
  Public Meetings, 329
  Reform Act, 1832, 30
  Reform Act, 1867, 37
  Reform Act, 1884, 69
  Reform Act, 1918, 607
  Reform Act, 1928, 608, 609
  Romilly's, Lord (13, 14 Vict., chapter 21), 38
  Tumultuous Petitions (13 Charles II, chapter 5), 277, 309
Adams, Mrs. Bridges, 158
Addams, Jane, of Hull House, 349, 493
Addison, Dr. Christopher, M.P., 598
Adler, Victor, of Austria, 389
Adult Suffrage, 203, 205, 357, 372, 575, 388, 587, 596; Dr. Pankhurst on, 60, 71; Sir Charles Dilke's Bill, 205; controversy, 242, 302-304, 353, 436, 512; conferences on, 599, 600, 604; abandoned, 605; National Council for, 600, 603
Adult Suffrage Joint Committee, 596
Adult Suffrage League, 245
Age of Consent, Bishop of London's Bill, 546
Agg-Gardner, J. T., M.P., 376

Agnosticism, 18, 19, 73-77, 78, 108-110
Agricultural worker, 22
Albert Hall, 283; Anti-Suffragists in, 371; Campbell-Bannerman's meeting in, 192-193; I.L.P. in, 371; Larkin release meeting in, 502, 503, 504; Lloyd George in, 295-298; Asquith in, 330; W.S.P.U. meetings in, 223, 279, 283, 339 and note, 353, 361, 371, 376, 413, 414; N.U.W.S.S. in, 529
Alfieri, Bernard, Press photographer, 198
Alford, Dean, 34
Allan, Grant, 90
Allen, Mary, 311
Alverstone, Lord (Lord Chief Justice), 319, 326 and note
American prisons, 348, 349
American State legislatures, 347, 348
American Suffragists, first procession, 382
American sympathy with Suffragettes, 347, 355, 382, 493
American Universities, 348, 382
Amnesty, 591
Ancient constitutional rights of women, 42, 43, 44, 45
Ancient Order of Hibernians, 404, 464
Ancoats Brotherhood, 125
Ancoats University Settlement, 187
Anderson, Garrett. *See* Garrett Anderson
——, W. C., M.P., 595
Anglo-Russian Secret Convention, 24, 26
Anglo-Turkish Secret Convention, 24, 26
Anker, Ella, of Norway, 353
Anmer, King's Horse, 498
Ann Arbor, Michigan, U.S.A., 382
Annexations, 25
" Annie, Miss," 84
A Nö (The Woman), Hungarian Suffrage paper, 537
Ansell, Gertrude, 578
Anstey, Chisholm, 42
Anthony, Susan B., 347
Anti-Corn Law League, 53
Anti-German War Propaganda, 367-368
" Anti-Guzzling League," 205
Anti-Suffragists, 338, 339, 361, 362, 371
Arbeiter Zeitung (Vienna), 540
Arson, first arrest for, 362
" Arthur, Janet " (Miss Parker), 580

One Hand Tied Behind Us

JILL LIDDINGTON AND JILL NORRIS

The north of England was the cradle of the suffrage movement: here women worked long hours in factories and mills, struggled against poverty and hardship at home, and, at the turn of the century, fought not only for the vote but for a wide range of women's rights. These radical suffragists, amongst them remarkable women like Selina Cooper and Ada Nield Chew, called for equal pay, birth control and child allowances. They took their message to women at the factory gate and the cottage door, to the Co-operative Guilds and trade union branches.

One Hand Tied Behind Us, using much unpublished material and interviews with the last surviving descendants of these suffragists, creates a vivid and moving portrait of strong women who, over seventy years ago, envisaged freedoms for which we are still fighting today.

'A brilliant and original contribution to the history of female suffrage' – *The Times*

Round About A Pound A Week

MAUD PEMBER REEVES

How does a working man's wife bring up a family on twenty shillings a week?

From 1909 to 1913, undaunted by the proposition that a 'bi-weekly visit to Lambeth is like a plunge into Hades', the Fabian Women's Group recorded the daily budgets of thirty families in Lambeth living on about a pound a week. In 1913 they published this record in *Round About A Pound A Week*, a rare and vivid portrait of the daily life of working people.

We learn about family life, births, marriages and deaths; of grinding work carried out on a diet of little more than bread, jam and margarine. We learn how they coped with damp, vermin and bedbugs – how they slept: four to a bed, in banana crates – how they washed, cooked, cleaned, scrimped for furniture and clothes, saved for the all too frequent burials . . .

With a vivid and compassionate eye *Round About A Pound A Week* captures, as no camera could, the everyday life of seventy years ago. Historically unique, and more, a moving and evocative human document.

'Highly readable' – Naomi Mitchison, *Books & Bookmen*

'Well-written, informative, humorous and compassionate – essential reading both for historians and for all socialists and feminists interested in working class life' – Caroline Rowan, *Comment*

The Cause

RAY STRACHEY

'The history of the Women's Movement is the whole history of the nineteenth century. Nothing which occurred in those years could be irrelevant to the great social change which was going on.'
Ray Strachey

In this famous work, Ray Strachey (1887-1940) records in rich detail women's struggles for personal, legal, political and social liberties from the late eighteenth century until after the First World War. It is a balanced and immensely readable record both of human character and collective determination – from the awakenings of individual women, through the growth of Radicalism and philanthropy to the decade after the vote was won.

Considered one of the great historians of the women's movement, Ray Strachey draws remarkable portraits of the personalities involved – Harriet Taylor, John Stuart Mill, Elizabeth Garrett Anderson, Millicent Fawcett, Josephine Butler – and many, many others. *The Cause* also includes Florence Nightingale's *Cassandra*, her famous and impassioned autobiographical comment on women's position. Today, for a new generation wondering how the struggle began, Ray Strachey's panoramic book provides a unique account of a great cause – the emancipation of women.

Ray Strachey (1887-1940) was the daughter of Mary Pearsall Smith (Mrs Bernard Berenson) and married Oliver Strachey, brother of Lytton. Her daughter, Barbara Strachey, writer and former BBC producer, provides a new preface to this edition.

Prisons & Prisoners

CONSTANCE LYTTON

In 1909 a working-class woman called Jane Warton was arrested during a suffragette protest in Liverpool and sentenced to fourteen days' imprisonment. After four days on hunger-strike, she was forcibly fed for the first time. But still she managed to call a message of support to her suffrage sisters. Seven more forcible feedings followed. The prisoner was, in fact, not Jane Warton but Lady Constance Lytton (1869-1923). Twice that year she was arrested and spent weeks in Holloway and in Newcastle prisons. She had been on hunger-strike in Newcastle but was released without being forcibly fed because of a heart condition discovered by the prison doctor. Lady Constance was convinced that she had been given preferential treatment because of her rank, and it was this that made her pose later as Jane. *Prisons and Prisoners* is a stirring account of Constance Lytton's involvement with the suffragette movement and her experiences in prison. Seriously ill when released from Liverpool's Walton Gaol, she suffered a severe heart attack in 1912. Partially paralysed, she was forced to write with her left hand, 'slowly and laboriously'; the book appeared in 1914. Constance Lytton never recovered her health and died in 1923.